Grace Livingston Hill is one of the most popular authors of all time because of her unique style of combining elements of the Christian faith with tasteful and exciting romance.

Find out why generations of readers of all ages have been entertained and inspired by the fiction of Grace Livingston Hill.

Grace Livingston Hill ... fiction that fills the heart as well as the spirit!

GRACE LIVINGSTON HILL

Marcia Schuyler
Phoebe Deane

Two complete and unabridged novels in one volume

Barbour Books
164 Mill Street
Westwood, New Jersey 07675

Marcia Schuyler

Chapter 1

The sun was already up and the grass blades were twinkling with sparkles of dew, as Marcia stepped from the kitchen door.

She wore a chocolate calico with little sprigs of red and white scattered over it, her hair was in smooth brown braids down her back, and there was a flush on her round cheeks that might have been but the reflection of the rosy light in the East. Her face was as untroubled as the Summer morning, in its freshness, and her eyes as dreamy as the soft clouds that hovered upon the horizon uncertain where they were to be sent for the day.

Marcia walked lightly through the grass, and the way behind her sparkled again like that of the girl in the fairy tale who left jewels wherever she passed.

A rail fence stopped her, which she mounted as though it had been a steed to carry her onward, and sat a moment looking at the beauty of the morning, her eyes taking on that far-away look that annoyed her stepmother when she wanted her to hurry with the dishes, or finish a long seam before it was time to get supper.

She loitered but a moment, for her mind was full of business, and she wished to accomplish much before the day was done. Swinging easily down to the other side of the fence she moved on through the meadow, over another fence, and another meadow, skirting the edge of a cool little strip of woods which lured her with its green mysterious shadows, its whispering leaves, and twittering birds. One wistful glance she gave into the sweet silence, seeing a clump of maiden-hair ferns rippling their feathery locks in the breeze. Then resolutely turning away she sped on to the slope of Blackberry Hill.

It was not a long climb to where the blackberries grew, and she was soon at work, the great luscious berries dropping into her pail almost with a touch. But while she worked the vision of the hills, the sheep meadow below, the river winding between the neighboring farms, melted away, and she did not even see the ripe fruit before her, because she was planning the new frock she was to buy with these berries she had come to pick.

Pink and white it was to be; she had seen it in the store the last time she went for sugar and spice. There were dainty sprigs of pink over the white ground, and every berry that dropped into her bright pail was no longer a berry but a sprig of pink chintz. While she worked she went over her plans for the day.

There had been busy times at the old house during the past weeks. Kate, her elder sister, was to be married. It was only a few days now to the wedding.

There had been a whole year of preparation: spinning and weaving and fine sewing. The smooth white linen lay ready, packed between rose leaves and lavender. There had been yards and yards of tatting and embroidery made by the two girls for the trousseau, and the village dressmaker had spent days at the house, cutting, fitting, shirring, till now there was a goodly array of gorgeous apparel piled high upon bed, and chairs, and hanging in the closets of the great spare bedroom. The outfit was as fine as that made for Patience Hartrandt six months before, and Mr. Hartrandt had given his one daughter all she had asked for in the way of a "setting out." Kate had seen to it that her things were as fine as Patience's — but — they were all for Kate!

Of course, that was right! Kate was to be married, not Marcia, and everything must make way for that. Marcia was scarcely more than a child as yet, barely seventeen. No one thought of anything new for her just then, and she did not expect it. But into her heart there had stolen a longing for a new frock herself amid all this finery for Kate. She had her best one of course. That was good, and pretty, and quite nice enough to wear to the wedding, and her stepmother had taken much relief in the thought that Marcia would need nothing during the rush of getting Kate ready.

But there were people coming to the house every day, especially in the afternoons, friends of Kate, and of her stepmother, to be shown Kate's wardrobe, and to talk things over curiously. Marcia could not wear her best dress all the time. And *he* was coming! That was the way Marcia always denominated the prospective bridegroom in her mind.

His name was David Spafford, and Kate often called him Dave, but Marcia, even to herself, could never bring herself to breathe the name so familiarly. She held him in great awe. He was so fine and strong and good, with a face like a young saint in some old picture, she thought. She often wondered how her wild, sparkling sister Kate dared to be so familiar with him. She had ventured the thought once when she watched Kate dressing to go out with some young people and preening herself like a bird of Paradise before the glass. It all came over her, the vanity and frivolousness of the life that Kate loved, and she spoke out with conviction:

"Kate, you'll have to be very different when you're married." Kate had faced about amusedly and asked why.

"Because *he* is so good," Marcia had replied, unable to explain further.

"Oh, is that all?" said the daring sister, wheeling back to the glass. "Don't you worry; I'll soon take that out of him."

But Kate's indifference had never lessened her young sister's awe of her prospective brother-in-law. She had listened to his conversations with her father during the brief visits he had made, and she had watched his face at church while he and Kate sang together as the minister lined it out: "Rock of Ages cleft for me, Let me hide myself in Thee," a new song which had just been written. And she had mused upon the charmed life Kate would lead. It was wonderful to be a woman and be loved as Kate was loved, thought Marcia.

So in all the hurry no one seemed to think much about Marcia, and she was not satisfied with her brown delaine afternoon dress. Truth to tell, it needed letting down, and there was no more left to let down. It made her feel like last year to go about in it with her slender ankles so plainly revealed. So she set her heart upon the new chintz.

Now, with Marcia, to decide was to do. She did not speak to her stepmother about it, for she knew it would be useless; neither did she think it worth while to go to her father, for she knew that both his wife and Kate would find it out and charge her with useless expense just now when there were so many other uses for money, and they were anxious to have it all flow their way. She had an independent spirit, so she took the time that belonged to herself, and went to the blackberry patch which belonged to everybody.

Marcia's fingers were nimble and accustomed, and the sun was not very high in the heavens when she had finished her task and turned happily toward the village. The pails would not hold another berry.

Her cheeks were glowing with the sun and exercise, and little wisps of wavy curls had escaped about her brow, damp with perspiration. Her eyes were shining with her purpose, half fulfilled, as she hastened down the hill.

Crossing a field she met Hanford Weston with a rake over his shoulder and a wide-brimmed straw hat like a small shed over him. He was on his way to the South meadow. He blushed and greeted her as she passed shyly by. When she had passed he paused and looked admiringly after her. They had been in the same classes at school all winter, the girl at the head, the boy at the foot. But Hanford Weston's father owned the largest farm in all the country round about, and he felt that did not so much matter. He would rather see Marcia at the head anyway, though there never had been the slightest danger that he would take her place. He felt a sudden desire now to follow her. It would be a pleasure to carry those pails that she bore as if they were mere featherweights.

He watched her long, elastic step for a moment, considered the sun in the sky, and his father's command about the South meadow, and then strode after her.

It did not take long to reach her side, swiftly as she had gone.

As well as he could, with the sudden hotness in his face and the tremor in his throat, he made out to ask if he might carry her burden for her. Marcia stopped annoyed. She had forgotten all about him, though he was an attractive fellow, sometimes called by the girls "handsome Hanford."

She had been planning exactly how that pink sprigged chintz was to be made, and which parts she would cut first in order to save time and material. She did not wish to be interrupted. The importance of the matter was too great to be marred by the appearance of just a schoolmate whom she might meet every day, and whom she could so easily "spell down." She summoned her thoughts from the details of mutton-leg sleeves and looked the boy over, to his great confusion. She did not want him along, and she was considering how best to get rid of him.

"Weren't you going somewhere else?" she asked sweetly. "Wasn't there a rake over your shoulder? What have you done with it?"

The culprit blushed deeper.

"Where were you going?" she demanded.

"To the South meadow," he stammered out.

"Oh, well, then you must go back. I shall do quite well, thank you. Your father will not be pleased to have you neglect your work for me, though I'm much obliged I'm sure."

Was there some foreshadowing of her womanhood in the decided way she spoke, and the quaint, prim set of her head as she bowed him good morning and went on her way once more? The boy did not understand. He only felt abashed, and half angry that she had ordered him back to work; and, too, in a tone that forbade him to take her memory with him as he went. Nevertheless her image lingered by the way, and haunted the South meadow all day long as he worked.

Marcia, unconscious of the admiration she had stirred in the boyish heart, went her way on fleet feet, her spirit one with the sunny morning, her body light with anticipation, for a new frock of her own choice was yet an event in her life.

She had thought many times, as she spent long hours putting delicate stitches into her sister's wedding garments, how it would seem if they were being made for her. She had whiled away many a dreary seam by thinking out, in a sort of dream-story, how she would put on this or that at will if it were her own, and go here or there, and have people love and admire her as they did Kate. It would never come true, of course. She never expected to be admired and loved like Kate. Kate was beautiful, bright and gay. Everybody loved her, no matter how she treated them. It was a matter of course for Kate to have everything she wanted. Marcia felt that she never could attain to such heights. In the first place she considered her own sweet serious face with its pure brown eyes as exceedingly plain. She could not catch the lights that played at hide and seek in her eyes when she talked with animation. Indeed few saw her at her best, because she seldom talked freely. It was only with certain people that she could forget herself.

She did not envy Kate. She was proud of her sister, and loved her, though there was an element of anxiety in the love. But she never thought of her many faults. She felt that they were excusable because Kate was Kate. It was as if you should find fault with a wild rose because it carried a thorn. Kate was set about with many a thorn, but amid them all she bloomed, her fragrant pink self, as apparently unconscious of the many pricks she gave, and unconcerned, as the flower itself.

So Marcia never thought to be jealous that Kate had so many lovely things, and was going out into the world to do just as she pleased, and lead a charmed life with a man who was greater in the eyes of this girl than any prince that ever walked in fairy tale. But she saw no harm in playing a delightful little dream-game of "pretend" now and then, and letting her imagination make herself the beautiful, admired, elder sister instead of the plain younger one.

But this morning on her way to the village store with her berries she thought no more of her sister's things, for her mind was upon her own little frock which she would purchase with the price of the berries, and then go home and make.

A whole long day she had to herself, for Kate and her stepmother were gone up to the neighboring town on the packet to make a few last purchases.

She had told no one of her plans, and was awake betimes in the morning to see the travellers off, eager to have them gone that she might begin to carry out her plan.

Just at the edge of the village Marcia put down the pails of berries by a large flat stone and sat down for a moment to tidy herself. The lacing of one shoe had come untied, and her hair was rumpled by exercise. But she could not sit long to rest, and taking up her burdens was soon upon the way again.

Mary Ann Fothergill stepped from her own gate lingering till Marcia should come up, and the two girls walked along side by side. Mary Ann had stiff, straight, light hair, and high cheek bones. Her eyes were light and her eyelashes almost white. They did not show up well beneath her checked sunbonnet. Her complexion was dull and tanned. She was a contrast to Marcia with her clear red and white skin. She was tall and awkward and wore a linsey-woolsey frock as though it were a meal sack temporarily appropriated. She had the air of always trying to hide her feet and hands. Mary Ann had some find qualities, but beauty was not one of them. Beside her Marcia's delicate features showed clear-cut like a cameo, and her every movement spoke of patrician blood.

Mary Ann regarded Marcia's smooth brown braids enviously. Her own sparse hair barely reached to her shoulders, and straggled about her neck helplessly and hopelessly, in spite of her constant efforts.

"It must be lots of fun at your house these days," said Mary Ann wistfully. "Are you most ready for the wedding?"

Marcia nodded. Her eyes were bright. She could see the sign of the village store just ahead and knew the bolts of new chintz were displaying their charms in the window.

"My, but your cheeks do look pretty," admired Mary Ann impulsively. "Say, how many of each has your sister got?"

"Two dozens," said Marcia conscious of a little swelling of pride in her breast. It was not every girl that had such a setting out as her sister.

"My!" sighed Mary Ann. "And outside things, too. I 'spose she's got one of every color. What are her frocks? Tell me about them. I've been up to Dutchess county and just got back last night, but Ma wrote Aunt Tilly that Mis' Hotchkiss said her frocks was the prettiest Miss Hancock's ever sewed on."

"We think they are pretty," admitted Marcia modestly. "There's a sprigged chin —" here she caught herself, remembering and laughed. "I mean muslin-de-laine, and a blue delaine, and a blue silk —"

"My! silk!" breathed Mary Ann in an ecstasy of wonder. "And what's she going to be married in?"

"White," answered Marcia, "white satin. And the veil was mother's — our own mother's, you know."

Marcia spoke it reverently, her eyes shining with something far away that made Mary Ann think she looked like an angel.

"Oh, my! Don't you just envy her?"

"No," said Marcia slowly; "I think not. At least — I hope not. It wouldn't be right, you know. And then she's my sister and I love her dearly, and it's nearly as nice to have one's sister have nice things and a good time as to have them one's self."

"You're good," said Mary Ann decidedly as if that were a foregone conclusion. "But I should envy her, I just should. Mis' Hotchkiss told Ma there wa'nt many lots in life so all honey-and-dew-prepared like your sister's. All the money she wanted to spend on clo'es, and a nice set out, and a man as handsome as you'll find anywhere, and he's well off too, ain't he? Ma said she heard he kept a horse and lived right in the village too, not as how he needed to keep one to get anywhere, either. That's what I call luxury — a horse to ride around with. And then Mr. What's-his-name? I can't remember. Oh, yes, Spafford. He's good, and everybody says he won't make a bit of fuss if Kate does go around and have a good time. He'll just let her do as she pleases. Only old Grandma Doolittle says she doesn't believe it. She thinks every man, no matter how good he is, wants to manage his wife, just for the name of it. She says your sister'll have to change her ways or else there'll be trouble. But that's Grandma! Everybody knows her. She croaks! Ma says Kate's got her nest feathered well if ever a girl had. My! I only wish I had the same chance!"

Marcia held her head a trifle high when Mary Ann touched upon her sister's personal character, but they were nearing the store, and everybody knew Mary Ann was blunt. Poor Mary Ann! She meant no harm. She was but repeating the village gossip. Besides, Marcia must give her mind to sprigged chintz. There was no time for discussions if she would accomplish her purpose before the folks came home that night.

"Mary Ann," she said in her sweet, prim way that always made the other girl stand a little in awe of her, "you mustn't listen to gossip. It isn't worth while. I'm sure my sister Kate will be very happy. I'm going in the store now, are you?" And the conversation was suddenly concluded.

Mary Ann followed meekly watching with wonder and envy as Marcia made her bargain with the kindly merchant, and selected her chintz. What a delicious swish the scissors made as they went through the width of cloth, and how delightfully the paper crackled as the bundle was being wrapped! Mary Ann did not know whether Kate or Marcia was more to be envied.

"Did you say you were going to make it up yourself?" asked Mary Ann.

Marcia nodded.

"Oh, my! Ain't you afraid? I would be. It's the prettiest I ever saw. Don't you go and cut both sleeves for one arm. That's what I did the only time Ma ever let me try." And Mary Ann touched the package under Marcia's arm with wistful fingers.

They had reached the turn of the road and Mary Ann hoped that Marcia would ask her out to "help," but Marcia had no such purpose.

"Well, good-bye! Will you wear it next Sunday?" she asked.

"Perhaps," answered Marcia breathlessly, and sped on her homeward way, her cheeks bright with excitement.

In her own room she spread the chintz out upon the bed and with trembling fingers set about her task. The bright shears clipped the edge and tore off the lengths exultantly as if in league with the girl. The bees hummed outside in the clover, and now and again buzzed between the muslin curtains of the open window, looked in and grumbled out again. The birds sang across the meadows and the sun mounted to the zenith and began its downward march, but still the busy fingers worked on. Well for Marcia's scheme that the fashion of the day was simple, wherein were few puckers and plaits and tucks, and little trimming required, else her task would have been impossible.

Her heart beat high as she tried it on at last, the new chintz that she had made. She went into the spare room and stood before the long mirror in its wide gilt frame that rested on two gilt knobs standing out from the wall like giant rosettes. She had dared to make the skirt a little longer than that of her best frock. It was almost as long as Kate's, and for a moment she lingered, sweeping backward and forward before the glass and admiring herself in the long graceful folds. She caught up her braids in the fashion that Kate wore her hair and smiled at the reflection of herself in the mirror. How funny it seemed to think she would soon be a woman like Kate. When Kate was gone they would begin to call her "Miss" sometimes. Somehow she did not care to look ahead. The present seemed enough. She had so wrapped her thoughts in her sister's new life that her own seemed flat and stale in comparison.

The sound of a distant hay wagon on the road reminded her that the sun was near to setting. The family carryall would soon be coming up the lane from the evening packet. She must hurry and take off her frock and be dressed before they arrived.

Marcia was so tired that night after supper that she was glad to slip away to bed, without waiting to hear Kate's voluble account of her day in town, the beauties she had seen and the friends she had met.

She lay down and dreamed of the morrow, and of the next day, and the next. In strange bewilderment she awoke in the night and found the moonlight streaming full into her face. Then she laughed and rubbed her eyes and tried to go to sleep again; but she could not, for she had dreamed that she was a bride herself, and the words of Mary Ann kept going over and over in her mind. "Oh, don't you envy her?" *Did* she envy her sister? But that was wicked. It troubled her to think of it, and she tried to banish the dream, but it would come again and again with a strange sweet pleasure.

She lay wondering if such a time of joy would ever come to her as had come to Kate, and whether the spare bed would ever be piled high with clothes and fittings for her new life. What a wonderful thing it was anyway to be a woman and be loved!

Then her dreams blended again with the soft perfume of the honeysuckle at the window, and the hooting of a young owl.

The moon dropped lower, the bright stars paled, dawn stole up through the edges of the woods far away and awakened a day that was to bring a strange transformation over Marcia's life.

Chapter 2

As a natural consequence of her hard work and her midnight awakening, Marcia overslept the next morning. Her stepmother called her sharply and she dressed in haste, not even taking time to glance toward the new folds of her chintz that drew thoughts closetward. She dared not say anything about it yet. There was much to be done, and not even Kate had time for an idle word with her. Marcia was called upon to run errands, to do odds and ends of things, to fill in vacant places, to sew on lost buttons, to do everything for which nobody else had time. The household had suddenly become aware that there was now but one more intervening day between them and the wedding.

It was not until late in the afternoon that Marcia ventured to put on her frock. Even then she felt shy about appearing in it.

Madam Schuyler was busy in the parlor with callers, and Kate was locked in her own room whither she had gone to rest. There was no one to notice if Marcia should "dress up," and it was not unlikely that she might escape much notice even at the supper table, as everybody was so absorbed in other things.

She lingered before her own little glass looking wistfully at herself. She was pleased with the frock she had made and liked her appearance in it, but yet there was something disappointing about it. It had none of the style of her sister's garments, newly come from the hand of the village mantua-maker. It was girlish, and showed her slip of a form prettily in the fashion of the day, but she felt too young. She wanted to look older. She searched her drawer and found a bit of black velvet which she pinned about her throat with a pin containing the miniature of her mother, then with a second thought she drew the long braids up in loops and fastened them about her head in older fashion. It suited her well, and the change it made astonished her. She decided to wear them so and see if others would notice. Surely, some day she would be a young woman, and perhaps then she would be allowed to have a will of her own occasionally.

She drew a quick breath as she descended the stairs and found her stepmother and the visitor just coming into the hall from the parlor.

They both involuntarily ceased their talk and looked at her in surprise. Over Madam Schuyler's face there came a look as if she had received a revelation. Marcia was no longer a child, but had suddenly blossomed into young womanhood. It was not the time she would have chosen for such an event. There was enough going on, and Marcia was still in school. She had no desire to steer another young soul through the various dangers and follies that beset a pretty girl from the time she puts up her hair until she is safely married to the right man — or the wrong one. She had just begun to look forward with relief to having Kate well settled in life. Kate had been a hard one to manage. She had too much will of her own and a pretty way of always having it. She had no deep sense of reverence for old, staid manners and customs. Many a long lecture had Madam Schuyler delivered to Kate upon her unseemly ways. It did not please her to think of having to go through it all so soon again, therefore upon her usually complacent brow there came a look of dismay.

"Why!" exclaimed the visitor, "is this the bride? How tall she looks! No! Bless me! it isn't, is it? Yes, — Well! I'll declare. It's just Marsh! What have you got on, child? How old you look!"

Marcia flushed. It was not pleasant to have her young womanhood questioned, and in a tone so familiar and patronizing. She disliked the name of "Marsh" exceedingly, especially upon the lips of this woman, a sort of second cousin of her stepmother's. She would rather have chosen the new frock to pass under inspection of her stepmother without witnesses, but it was too late to turn back now. She must face it.

Though Madam Schuyler's equilibrium was a trifle disturbed, she was not one to show it before a visitor. Instantly she recovered her balance, and perhaps Marcia's ordeal was less trying than if there had been no third person present.

"That looks very well, child!" she said critically with a shade of complacence in her voice. It is true that Marcia had gone beyond orders in purchasing and making garments unknown to her, yet the neatness and fit could but reflect well upon her training. It did no harm for cousin Maria to see what a child of her training could do. It was, on the whole, a very creditable piece of work, and Madam Schuyler grew more reconciled to it as Marcia came down toward them.

"Make it herself?" asked cousin Maria. "Why, Marsh, you did real well. My Matilda does all her own clothes now. It's time you were learning. It's a trifle longish to what you've been wearing them, isn't it? But you'll grow into it, I dare say. Got your hair a new way too. I thought you were Kate when you first started down stairs. You'll make a good-looking young lady when you grow up; only don't be in too much hurry. Take your girlhood while you've got it, is what I always tell Matilda."

Matilda was well on to thirty and showed no signs of taking anything else.

Madam Schuyler smoothed an imaginary pucker across the shoulders and again pronounced the work good.

"I picked berries and got the cloth," confessed Marcia.

Madam Schuyler smiled benevolently and patted Marcia's cheek.

"You needn't have done that, child. Why didn't you come to me for money? You needed something new, and that is a very good purchase, a little light, perhaps, but very pretty. We've been so busy with Kate's things you have been neglected."

Marcia smiled with pleasure and passed into the dining room wondering what power the visitor had over her stepmother to make her pass over this digression from her rules so sweetly, — nay, even with praise.

At supper they all rallied Marcia upon her changed appearance. Her father jokingly said that when the bridegroom arrived he would hardly know which sister to choose, and he looked from one comely daughter to the other with fatherly pride. He praised Marcia for doing the work so neatly, and inwardly admired the courage and independence that prompted her to get the money by her own unaided efforts rather than to ask for it, and later, as he passed through the room where she was helping to remove the dishes from the table, he paused and handed her a crisp five-dollar note. It had occurred to him that one daughter was getting all the good things and the other was having nothing. There was a pleasant tenderness in his eyes, a recognition of her rights as a young woman, that made Marcia's heart exceedingly light. There was something strange about the influence this little new frock seemed to have upon people.

Even Kate had taken a new tone with her. Much of the time at supper she had sat staring at her sister. Marcia wondered about it as she walked down toward the gate after her work was done. Kate had never seemed so quiet. Was she just beginning to realize that she was leaving home forever, and was she thinking how the home would be after she had left it? How she, Marcia, would take the place of elder sister, with only little Harriet and the boys, their stepsister and brothers, left? Was Kate sad over the thought of going so far away from them, or was she feeling suddenly the responsibility of the new position she was to occupy and the duties that would be hers? No, that could not be it, for surely that would bring a softening of expression, a sweetness of anticipation, and Kate's expression had been wondering, perplexed, almost troubled. If she had not been her own sister Marcia would have added, "hard," but she stopped short at that.

It was a lovely evening. The twilight was not yet over as she stepped from the low piazza that ran the length of the house bearing another above it on great white pillars. A drapery of wisteria in full bloom festooned across one end and half over the front. Marcia stepped back across the stone flagging and driveway to look up the purple clusters of graceful fairy-like shape that embowered the house, and thought how beautiful it would look when the wedding guests should arrive the day after the morrow. Then she turned into the gravel path, box-bordered, that led to the gate. Here and there on either side luxuriant blooms of dahlias, peonies and roses leaned over into the night and peered at her. The yard had never looked so pretty. The flowers truly had done their best for the occasion, and they seemed to be asking some word of commendation from her.

They nodded their dewy heads sleepily as she went on.

To-morrow the children would be coming back from Aunt Eliza's, where they had been sent safely out of the way for a few days, and the last things would arrive, — and *he* would come. Not later than three in the afternoon he ought to arrive, Kate had said, though there was a possibility that he might come in the morning, but Kate was not counting upon it. He was to drive from his home to Schenectady and, leaving his own horse there to rest, come on by coach. Then he and Kate would go back in fine style to Schenectady in a coach and pair, with a colored coachman, and at Schenectady take their own horse and drive on to their home, a long beautiful ride, so thought Marcia half enviously. How beautiful it would be! What endless delightful talks they might have about the birds and things they saw in passing only Kate did not love to talk about such things. But then she would be with David, and he talked beautifully about nature or anything else. Kate would learn to love it if she loved him. Did Kate love David? Of course she must or why should she marry him? Marcia resented the thought that Kate might have other objects in view, such as Mary Ann Fothergill had suggested for instance. Of course Kate would never marry any man unless she loved him. That would be a dreadful thing to do. Love was the greatest thing in the world. Marcia looked up to the stars, her young soul thrilling with awe and reverence for the great mysteries of life. She wondered again if life would open sometime for her in some such great way, and if she would ever know better than now what it meant. Would some one come and love her? Some one whom she could love in return with all the fervor of her nature?

She had dreamed such dreams before many times, as girls will, while lovers and future are all in one dreamy, sweet blending of rosy tints and joyous mystery, but never had they come to her with such vividness as that night. Perhaps it was because the household had recognized the woman in her for the first time that evening. Perhaps because the vision she had seen reflected in her mirror before she left her room that afternoon had opened the door of the future a little wider than it had ever opened before.

She stood by the gate where the syringa and lilac bushes leaned over and arched the way, and the honeysuckle climbed about the fence in a wild pretty way of its own and flung sweetness on the air in vivid, erratic whiffs.

The sidewalk outside was brick, and whenever she heard footsteps coming she stepped back into the shadow of the syringa and was hidden from view. She was in no mood to talk with anyone.

She could look out into the dusty road and see dimly the horses and carryalls as they passed, and recognize an occasional laughing voice of some village maiden out with her best young man for a ride. Others strolled along the sidewalk, and fragments of talk floated back. Almost every one had a word to say about the wedding as they neared the gate, and if Marcia had been in another mood it would have been interesting and gratifying to her pride. Every one had a good word for Kate, though many disapproved of her in a general way for principle's sake.

Hanford Weston passed, with long, slouching gait, hands in his trousers pockets, and a frightened, hasty, sideways glance toward the lights of the house beyond. He would have gone in boldly to call if he had dared, and told Marcia that he had done her bidding and now wanted a reward, but John Middleton had joined him at the corner and he dared not make the attempt. John would have done it in a minute if he had wished. He was brazen by nature but Hanford knew that he would as readily laugh at another for doing it. Hanford shrank from a laugh more than from the cannon's mouth, so he slouched on, not knowing that his goddess held her breath behind a lilac bush not three feet away, her heart beating in annoyed taps to be again interrupted by him in her pleasant thoughts.

Merry, laughing voices mingling with many footsteps came sounding down the street and paused beside the gate. Marcia knew the voices and again slid behind the shrubbery that bordered all the way to the house, and not even a gleam of her light frock was visible. They trooped in, three or four girl friends of Kate's and a couple of young men.

Marcia watched them pass up the box-bordered path from her shadowy retreat, and thought how they would miss Kate, and wondered if the young men who had been coming there so constantly to see her had no pangs of heart that their friend and leader was about to leave them. Then she smiled at herself in the dark. She seemed to be doing the retrospect for Kate, taking leave of all the old friends, home, and life, in Kate's place. It was not her life anyway, and why should she bother herself and sigh and feel this sadness creeping over her for some one else? Was it that she was going to lose her sister? No, for Kate had never been much of a companion to her. She had always put her down as a little girl and made distinct and clear the difference in their ages. Marcia had been the little maid to fetch and carry, the errand girl, and unselfish, devoted slave in Kate's life. There had been nothing protective and elder-sisterly in her manner toward Marcia. At times Marcia had felt this keenly, but no expression of this lack had ever crossed her lips, and afterwards her devotion to her sister had been the greater, to in a measure compensate for this reproachful thought.

But Marcia could not shake the sadness off. She stole in further among the trees to think about it till the callers should go away. She felt no desire to meet any of them.

She began again to wonder how she would feel if day after to-morrow were her wedding day, and she were going away from home and friends and all the scenes with which she had been familiar since babyhood. Would she mind very much leaving them all? Father? Yes, father had been good to her, and loved her and was proud of her in a way. But one does not lose one's father no matter how far one goes. A father is a father always; and Mr. Schuyler was not a demonstrative man. Marcia felt that her father would not miss her deeply, and she was not sure she would miss him so very much. She had read to him a great deal and talked politics with him whenever he had no one better by, but aside from that her life had been lived much apart from him. Yet stepmother? Yes, she would miss her as one misses a perfect mentor and guide. She had been used to looking to her for direction. She was thoroughly conscious that she had a will of her own and would like a chance to exercise it, still, she knew that in many cases without her stepmother she would be like a rudderless ship, a guideless traveller. And she loved her stepmother too, as a young girl can love a good woman who has been her guide and helper, even though there never has been great tenderness between them. Yes, she would miss her stepmother, but she would not feel so very sad over it. Harriet and the little brothers? Oh, yes she would miss them, they were dear little things and devoted to her.

Then there were the neighbors, and the schoolmates, and the people of the village. She would miss the minister, — the dear old minister and his wife. Many a time she had gone with her arms full of flowers to the parsonage down the street, and spent the afternoon with the minister's wife. Her smooth white hair under its muslin cap, and her soft wrinkled cheek were very dear to the young girl. She had talked to this friend more freely about her innermost thoughts than she had ever spoken to any living being. Oh, she would miss the minister's wife very much if she were to go away.

The names of her schoolmates came to her. Harriet Woodgate, Eliza Buchanan, Margaret Fletcher, three girls who were her intimates. She would miss them, of course, but how much? She could scarcely tell. Margaret Fletcher more than the other two. Mary Ann Fothergill? She almost laughed at the thought of anybody missing Mary Ann. John Middleton? Hanford Weston? There was not a boy in the school she would miss for an instant, she told herself with conviction. Not one of them realized her ideal. There was much pairing off of boy and girl in school, but Marcia, like the heroine of "Comin' thro' the Rye," was good friends with all the boys and intimate with none. They all counted it an honor to wait upon her, and she cared not a farthing for any. She felt herself too young, of course, to think of such things, but when she dreamed her day dreams the lover and prince who figured in them bore no familiar form or feature. He was a prince and these were only schoolboys.

The merry chatter of the young people in the house floated through the open windows, and Marcia could hear her sister's voice above them all. Chameleon-like she was all gaiety and laughter now, since her gravity at supper.

They were coming out the front door and down the walk. Kate was with them. Marcia could catch glimpses of the girls' white frocks as they came nearer. She saw that her sister was walking with Captain Leavenworth. He was a handsome young man who made a fine appearance in his uniform. He and Kate had been intimate for two years, and it might have been more than friendship had not Kate's father interfered between them. He did not think so well of the handsome young captain as did either his daughter Kate or the

United States Navy who had given him his position. Squire Schuyler required deep integrity and strength of moral character in the man who aspired to be his son-in-law. The captain did not number much of either among his virtues.

There had been a short, sharp contest which had ended in the departure of young Leavenworth from the town some three years before, and the temporary plunging of Kate Schuyler into a season of tears and pouting. But it had not been long before her gay laughter was ringing again, and her father thought she had forgotten. About that time David Spafford had appeared and promptly fallen in love with the beautiful girl, and the Schuyler mind was relieved. So it came about that, upon the reappearance of the handsome young captain wearing the insignia of his first honors, the Squire received him graciously. He even felt that he might be more lenient about his moral character, and told himself that perhaps he was not so bad after all, he must have something in him or the United States government would not have seen fit to honor him. It was easier to think so, now Kate was safe.

Marcia watched her sister and the captain go laughing down to the gate, and out into the street. She wondered that Kate could care to go out to-night when it was to be almost her last evening at home; wondered, too, that Kate would walk with Captain Leavenworth when she belonged to David now. She might have managed it to go with one of the girls. But that was Kate's way. Kate's ways were not Marcia's ways.

Marcia wondered if she would miss Kate, and was obliged to acknowledge to herself that in many ways her sister's absence would be a relief to her. While she recognized the power of her sister's beauty and will over her, she felt oppressed sometimes by the strain she was under to please, and wearied of the constant, half-fretful, half playful faultfinding.

The gay footsteps and voices died away down the village street, and Marcia ventured forth from her retreat. The moon was just rising and came up a glorious burnished disk, silhouetting her face as she took a moment listening to the stirring of a bird among the branches. It was her will to-night to be alone and let her fancies wander where they would. The beauty and the mystery of a wedding was upon her, touching all her deeper feelings, and she wished to dream it out and wonder over it. Again it came to her what if the day after the morrow were her wedding day and she stood alone thinking about it. She would not have gone off down the street with a lot of giggling girls nor walked with another young man. She would have stood here, or down by the gate — and she moved on toward her favorite arch of lilac and syringa — yes, down by the gate in the darkness looking out and thinking how it would be when he should come. She felt sure if it had been herself who expected David she would have begun to watch for him a week before the time he had set for coming, heralding it again and again to her heart in joyous thrills of happiness, for who knew but he might come sooner and surprise her? She would have rejoiced that to-night she was alone, and would have excused herself from everything else to come down there in the stillness and watch for him, and think how it would be when he would really get there. She would hear his step echoing down the street and would recognize it as his. She would lean far over the gate to listen and watch, and it would come nearer and nearer, and her heart would beat faster and faster, and her breath come quicker, until he was at last by her side, his beautiful surprise for her in his eyes. But now, if David should really try to surprise Kate by coming that way to-night he would not find her waiting nor thinking of him at all, but off with Captain Leavenworth.

With a passing pity for David she went back to her own dream. With one elbow on the gate and her cheek in her hand she thought it all over. The delayed evening coach rumbled up to the tavern not far away and halted. Real footsteps came up the street, but Marcia did not notice them only as they made more vivid her thoughts.

Her dream went on and the steps drew nearer until suddenly they halted and some one appeared out of the shadow. Her heart stood still, for form and face in the darkness seemed unreal, and the dreams had been most vivid. Then with tender masterfulness two strong arms were flung about her and her face was drawn close to his across the vine-twined gate until her lips touched his. One long clinging kiss of tenderness he gave her and held her head close against his breast for just a moment while he murmured: "My darling! My precious, precious Kate, I have you at last!"

The spell was broken! Marcia's dream was shattered.

Her mind awoke. With a scream she sprang from him, horror and a wild but holy joy mingling with her perplexity. She put her hand upon her heart, marvelling over the sweetness that lingered upon her lips, trying to recover her senses as she faced the eager lover who opened the little gate and came quickly toward her, as yet unaware that it was not Kate to whom he had been talking.

Chapter 3

Marcia stood quivering, trembling. She comprehended all in an instant. David Spafford had come a day earlier than he had been expected, to surprise Kate, and Kate was off having a good time with some one else. He had mistaken her for Kate. Her long dress and her put-up hair had deceived him in the moonlight. She tried to summon some womanly courage, and in her earnestness to make things right she forgot her natural timidity.

"It is not Kate," she said gently; "it is only Marcia. Kate did not know you were coming to-night. She did not expect you till to-morrow. She had to go out,—that is—she has gone with—" the truthful, youthful, troubled sister paused. To her mind it was a calamity that Kate was not present to meet her lover. She should at least have been in the house ready for a surprise like this. Would David not feel the omission keenly? She must keep it from him if she could about Captain Leavenworth. There was no reason why he should feel badly about it, of course, and yet it might annoy him. But he stepped back laughing at his mistake.

"Why! Marcia, is it you, child? How you have grown! I never should have known you!" said the young man pleasantly. He had always a grave tenderness for this little sister of his love. "Of course your sister did not know I was coming," he went on, "and doubtless she has many things to attend to. I did not expect her to be out here watching for me, though for a moment I did think she was at the gate. You say she is gone out? Then we will go up to the house and I will be there to surprise her when she comes."

Marcia turned with relief. He had not asked where Kate was gone, nor with whom.

The Squire and Madam Schuyler greeted the arrival with elaborate welcome. The Squire like Marcia seemed much annoyed that Kate had gone out. He kept fuming back and forth from the window to the door and asking: "What did she go out for to-night? She ought to have stayed at home!"

But Madam Schuyler wore ample satisfaction upon her smooth brow. The bridegroom had arrived. There could be no further hitch in the ceremonies. He had arrived a day before the time, it is true; but he had not found *her* unprepared. So far as she was concerned, with a few extra touches the wedding might proceed at once. She was always ready for everything in time. No one could find a screw loose in the machinery of her household.

She bustled about, giving orders and laying a bountiful supper before the young man, while the Squire sat and talked with him and Marcia hovered watchfully, waiting upon the table, noticing with admiring eyes the beautiful wave of his abundant hair, tossed back from his forehead. She took a kind of pride of possession in his handsome face, — the far removed possession of a sister-in-law. There was his sunny smile, that seemed as though it could bring joy out of the gloom of a bleak December day, and there were the two dimples — not real dimples, of course men never had dimples — but hints, suggestions of dimples, that caught themselves when he smiled, here and there like hidden mischief well kept under control, but still merrily ready to come to the surface. His hands were white and firm, the fingers long and shapely, the hands of a brain worker. The vision of Hanford Weston's hands, red and bony, came up to her in contrast. She had not known that she looked at them that day when he had stood awkwardly asking if he might walk with her. Poor Hanford! He would ill compare with this cultured scholarly man who was his senior by ten years, though it is possible that with the ten years added he would have been quite worthy of the admiration of any of the village girls.

The fruit cake and raspberry preserves and doughnuts and all the various viands that Madam Schuyler had ordered set out for the delectation of her guest had been partaken of, and David and the Squire sat talking of the news of the day, touching on politics, with a bit of laughter from the Squire at the man who thought he had invented a machine to draw carriages by steam in place of horses.

"There's a good deal in it, I believe," said the younger man. "His theory is all right if he can get some one to help him carry it out."

"Well maybe, maybe," said the Squire shaking his head dubiously, "but it seems to me a very fanciful scheme. Horses are good enough for me. I shouldn't like to trust myself to an unknown quantity like steam, but time will tell."

"Yes, and the world is progressing. Something of the sort is sure to come. It has come in England. It would make a vast change in our country, binding city to city and practically eradicating space."

"Visionary schemes, David, visionary schemes, that's what I call them. You and I'll never see them in our day, I'm sure of that. Remember this is a new country and must go slow." The Squire was half laughing, half in earnest.

Amid the talk Marcia had quietly slipped out. It had occurred to her that perhaps the captain might return with her sister.

She must watch for Kate and warn her. Like a shadow in the moonlight she stepped softly down the gravel path once more and waited at the gate. Did not that sacred kiss placed upon her lips all by mistake bind her to this solemn duty? Had it not been given to her to see as in a revelation, by that kiss, the love of one man for one woman, deep and tender and true?

In the fragrant darkness her soul stood still and wondered over Love, the marvellous. With an insight such as few have who have not tasted years of wedded joy, Marcia comprehended the possibility and joy of sacrifice that made even sad things bright because of Love. She saw like a flash how Kate could give up her gay life, her home, her friends, everything that life had heretofore held dear for her, that she might be by the side of the man who loved her so. But with this knowledge of David's love for Kate came a troubled doubt. Did Kate love David that way? If Kate had been the one who received that kiss would she have returned it with the same tenderness and warmth with which it was given? Marcia dared not try to answer this. It was Kate's question, not hers, and she must never let it enter her mind again. Of course she must love him that way or she would never marry him.

The night crept slowly for the anxious little watcher at the gate. Had she been sure where to look for her sister, and not afraid of the tongues of a few interested neighbors who had watched everything at the house for days that no item about the wedding should escape them, she would have started on a search at once. She knew if she just ran into old Miss Pemberton's, whose house stood out upon the street with two straight-backed little, high, white seats each side of the stoop, a most delightful post of observation, she could discover at once in which direction Kate had gone, and perhaps a good deal more of hints and suggestions besides. But Marcia had no mind to make gossip. She must wait as patiently as she could for Kate. Moreover Kate might be walking even now in some secluded, rose-lined lane arm in arm with the captain, saying a pleasant farewell. It was Kate's way and no one might gainsay her.

Marcia's dreams came back once more, the thoughts that had been hers as she stood there an hour before. She thought how the kiss had fitted into the dream. Then all at once conscience told her it was Kate's lover, not her own, whose arms had encircled her. And now there was a strange unwillingness to go back to the dreams at all, a lingering longing for the joys into whose glory she had been for a moment permitted to look. She drew back from all thoughts and tried to close the door upon them. They seemed too sacred to enter. Her maidenhood was but just begun and she had much yet to learn of life. She was glad, glad for Kate that such wonderfulness was coming to her. Kate would be sweeter, softer in her ways now. She could not help it with a love like that enfolding her life.

At last there were footsteps! Hark! Two people — only two! Just what Marcia had expected. The other girls and boys had dropped into other streets or gone home. Kate and her former lover were coming home alone. And, furthermore, Kate would not be glad to see her sister at the gate. This last thought came with sudden conviction, but Marcia did not falter.

"Kate, David has come!" Marcia said it in low, almost accusing tones, at least so it sounded to Kate, before the two had hardly reached the gate. They had been loitering along talking in low tones, and the young captain's head was bent over his companion in an earnest, pleading attitude. Marcia could not bear to look, and did not wish to see more, so she had spoken.

Kate, startled, sprang away from her companion, a white angry look in her face.

"How you scared me, Marsh!" she exclaimed pettishly. "What if he has come? That's nothing. I guess he can wait a few minutes. He had no business to come to-night anyway. He knew we wouldn't be ready for him till to-morrow."

Kate was recovering her self-possession in proportion as she realized the situation. That she was vexed over her bridegroom's arrival neither of the two witnesses could doubt. It stung her sister with a deep pity for David. He was not getting as much in Kate as he was giving. But there was no time for such thoughts, besides Marcia was trembling from head to foot, partly with her own daring, partly with wrath at her sister's words.

"For shame, Kate!" she cried. "How can you talk so, even in fun! David came to surprise you, and I think he had a right to expect to find you here so near to the time of your marriage."

There was a flash in the young eyes as she said it, and a delicate lifting of her chin with the conviction of the truth she was speaking, that gave her a new dignity even in the moonlight. Captain Leavenworth looked at her in lazy admiration and said:

"Why, Marsh, you're developing into quite a spitfire. What have you got on to-night that makes you look so tall and handsome? Why didn't you stay in and talk to your fine gentleman? I'm sure he would have been just as well satisfied with you as your sister."

Marcia gave one withering glance at the young man and then turned her back full upon him. He was not worth noticing. Besides he was to be pitied, for he evidently cared still for Kate.

But Kate was fairly white with anger. Perhaps her own accusing conscience helped it on. Her voice was imperious and cold. She drew herself up haughtily and pointed toward the house.

"Marcia Schuyler," she said coldly, facing her sister, "go into the house and attend to your own affairs. You'll find that you'll get into serious trouble if you attempt to meddle with mine. You're nothing but a child yet and ought to be punished for your impudence. Go! I tell you!" she stamped her foot, "I will come in when I get ready."

Marcia went. Not proudly as she might have gone the moment before, but covered with confusion and shame, her head drooping like some crushed lily on a bleeding stalk. Through her soul rushed indignation, mighty and forceful; indignation and shame, for her sister, for David, for herself. She did not stop to analyze her various feelings, nor did she stop to speak further with those in the house. She fled to her own room, and burying her face in the pillow she wept until she fell asleep.

The moon-shadows grew longer about the arbored gateway where the two she had left stood talking in low tones, looking furtively now and then toward the house, and withdrawing into the covert of the bushes by the walk. But Kate dared not linger long. She could see her father's profile by the candle light in the dining room. She did not wish to receive further rebuke, and so in a very few minutes the two parted and Kate ran up the box-edged path, beginning to hum a sweet old love song in a gay light voice, as she tripped by the dining-room windows, and thus announced her arrival. She guessed that Marcia would have gone straight to her room and told nothing. Kate intended to be fully surprised. She paused in the hall to hang up the light shawl she had worn, calling good-night to her stepmother and saying she was very tired and was going straight to bed to be ready for to-morrow. Then she ran lightly across the hall to the stairs.

She knew they would call her back, and that they would all come into the hall with David to see the effect of his surprise upon her. She had planned to a nicety just which stair she could reach before they got there, and where she would pause and turn and poise, and what pose she would take with her round white arm stretched to the handrail, the sleeve turned carelessly back. She had ready her countenances, a sleepy indifference, then a pleased surprise, and a climax of delight. She carried it all out, this little bit of impromptu acting, as well as though she had rehearsed it for a month.

They called her, and she turned deliberately, one dainty, slippered foot, with its crossed black ribbons about the slender ankle, just leaving the stair below, and showing the arch of the aristocratic instep. Her gown was blue and she held it back enough for the stiff white frill of her petticoat to peep below. Well she read the admiration in the eyes below her. Admiration was Kate's life: she thrived upon it. She could not do without it.

David stood still, his love in his eyes, looking upon the vision of his bride, and his heart swelled within him that so great a treasure should be his. Then straightway they all forgot to question where she had been or to rebuke her that she had been at all. She had known they would. She ever possessed the power to make others forget her wrong doings when it was worth her while to try.

The next morning things were astir even earlier than usual. There was the sound of the beating of eggs, the stirring of cakes, the clatter of pots and pans from the wide, stoneflagged kitchen.

Marcia, fresh as a flower from its morning dew in spite of her cry the night before, had arisen to new opportunities for service. She was glad with the joyous forgetfulness of youth when she looked at David's happy face, and she thought no more of Kate's treatment of herself.

David followed Kate with a true lover's eyes and was never for more than a few moments out of her sight, though it seemed to Marcia that Kate did not try very hard to stay with him. When afternoon came she dismissed him for what she called her "beauty nap." Marcia was passing through the hall at the time and she caught the tender look upon his face as he touched her brow with reverent fingers and told her she had no need for that. Her eyes met Kate's as they were going up the stairs, and in spite of what Kate had said the night before

Marcia could not refrain from saying: "Oh, Kate! how could you when he loves you so? You know you never take a nap in the daytime!"

"You silly girl!" said Kate pleasantly enough, "don't you know the less a man sees of one the more he thinks of her?" With this remark she closed and fastened her door after her.

Marcia pondered these words of wisdom for some time, wondering whether Kate had really done it for that reason, or whether she did not care for the company of her lover. And why should it be so that a man loved you less because he saw you more? In her straightforward code the more you loved persons the more you desired to be in their company.

Kate had issued from her "beauty nap" with a feverish restlessness in her eyes, an averted face, and ink upon one finger. At supper she scarcely spoke, and when she did she laughed excitedly over little things. Her lover watched her with eyes of pride and ever increasing wonder over her beauty, and Marcia, seeing the light in his face, watched for its answer in her sister's, and finding it not was troubled.

She watched them from her bedroom window as they walked down the path where she had gone the evening before, decorously side by side, Kate holding her light muslin frock back from the dew on the hedges. She wondered if it was because Kate had more respect for David than for Captain Leavenworth that she never seemed to treat him with as much familiarity. She did not take possession of him in the same sweet imperious way.

Marcia had not lighted her candle. The moon gave light enough and she was very weary, so she undressed in the dim chamber and pondered upon the ways of the great world. Out there in the moonlight were those two who to-morrow would be one, and here was she, alone. The world seemed all circling about that white chamber of hers, and echoing with her own consciousness of self, and a loneliness she had never felt before. She wondered what it might be. Was it all sadness at parting with Kate, or was it the sadness over inevitable partings of all human relationships, and the aloneness of every living spirit?

She stood for a moment, white-robed, beside her window, looking up into the full round moon, and wondering if God knew the ache of loneliness in His little human creatures' souls that He had made, and whether He had ready something wherewith to satisfy. Then her meek soul bowed before the faith that was in her and she knelt for her shy but reverent evening prayer.

She heard the two lovers come in early and go upstairs, and she heard her father fastening up the doors and windows for the night. Then stillness gradually settled down and she fell asleep. Later, in her dreams, there echoed the sound of hastening hoofs far down the deserted street and over the old covered bridge, but she took no note of any sound, and the weary household slept on.

Chapter 4

The wedding was set for ten o'clock in the morning, after which there was to be a wedding breakfast and the married couple were to start immediately for their new home.

David had driven the day before with his own horse and chaise to a town some twenty miles away, and there left his horse at a tavern to rest for the return trip, for Kate would have it that they must leave the house in high style. So the finest equipage the town afforded had been secured to bear them on the first stage of their journey, with a portly negro driver and everything according to the custom of the greatest of the land. Nothing that Kate desired about the arrangements had been left undone.

The household was fully astir by half past four, for the family breakfast was to be at six promptly, that all might be cleared away and in readiness for the early arrival of the various aunts and uncles and cousins and friends who would "drive over" from the country round about. It would have been something Madam Schuyler would never have been able to get over if aught had been awry when a single uncle or aunt appeared upon the scene, or if there seemed to be the least evidence of fluster and nervousness.

The rosy sunlight in the East was mixing the morning with fresher air, and new odors for the new day that was dawning, when Marcia awoke. The sharp click of spoons and dishes, the voices of the maids, the sizzle, sputter, odor of frying ham and eggs, mingled with the early chorus of the birds, and calling to life of all living creatures, like an intrusion upon nature. It seemed not right to steal the morning's "quiet hour" thus rudely. The thought flitted through the girl's mind, and in an instant more the whole panorama of the day's excitement was before her, and she sprang from her bed. As if it had been her own wedding day instead of her sister's, she performed her dainty toilet, for though there was need for haste, she knew she would have no further time beyond a moment to slip on her best gown and smooth her hair.

Marcia hurried downstairs just as the bell rang for breakfast, and David, coming down smiling behind her, patted her cheek and greeted her with, "Well, little sister, you look as

rested as if you had not done a thing all day yesterday."

She smiled shyly back at him, and her heart filled with pleasure over his new name for her. It sounded pleasantly from his happy lips. She was conscious of a gladness that he was to be so nearly related to her. She fancied how it would seem to say to Mary Ann: "My brother-in-law says so and so." It would be grand to call such a man "brother."

They were all seated at the table but Kate, and Squire Schuyler waited with pleasantly frowning brows to ask the blessing on the morning food. Kate was often late. She was the only member of the family who dared to be late to breakfast, and being the bride and the centre of the occasion more leniency was granted her this morning than ever before. Madam Schuyler waited until every one at the table was served to ham and eggs, coffee and bread-and-butter, and steaming griddle cakes, before she said, looking anxiously at the tall clock: "Marcia, perhaps you better go up and see if your sister needs any help. She ought to be down by now. Uncle Joab and Aunt Polly will be sure to be here by eight. She must have overslept, but we made so much noise she is surely awake by this time."

Marcia left her half-eaten breakfast and went slowly upstairs. She knew her sister would not welcome her, for she had often been sent on like errands before, and the brunt of Kate's anger had fallen upon the hapless messenger, wearing itself out there so that she might descend all smiles to greet father and mother and smooth off the situation in a most harmonious manner.

Marcia paused before the door to listen. Perhaps Kate was nearly ready and her distasteful errand need not be performed. But though she held her breath to listen, no sound came from the closed door. Very softly she tried to lift the latch and peep in. Kate must still be asleep. It was not the first time Marcia had found that to be the case when sent to bring her sister.

But the latch would not lift. The catch was firmly down from the inside. Marcia applied her eye to the keyhole, but could get no vision save a dim outline of the window on the other side of the room. She tapped gently once or twice and waited again, then called softly: "Kate, Kate! Wake up. Breakfast is ready and everybody is eating. Aunt Polly and Uncle Joab will soon be here."

She repeated her tapping and calling, growing louder as she received no answer. Kate would often keep still to tease her thus. Surely though she would not do so upon her wedding morning!

She called and called and shook the door, not daring, however, to make much of an uproar lest David should hear. She could not bear he should know the shortcomings of his bride.

But at last she grew alarmed. Perhaps Kate was ill. At any rate, whatever it was, it was time she was up. She worked for some minutes trying to loosen the catch that held the latch, but all to no purpose. She was forced to go downstairs and whisper to her stepmother the state of the case.

Madam Schuyler, excusing herself from the table, went upstairs, purposeful decision in every line of her substantial body, determination in every sound of her footfall. Bride though she be, Kate would have meted out to her just dues this time. Company and a lover and the nearness of the wedding hour were things not to be trifled with even by a charming Kate.

But Madam Schuyler returned in a short space of time, puffing and panting, somewhat short of breath, and color in her face. She looked troubled, and she interrupted the Squire without waiting for him to finish his sentence to David.

"I cannot understand what is the matter with Kate," she said, looking at her husband. "She does not seem to be awake, and I cannot get her door open. She sleeps soundly, and I suppose the unusual excitement has made her very tired. But I should think she ought to hear my voice. Perhaps you better see if you can open the door."

There was studied calm in her voice, but her face belied her words. She was anxious lest Kate was playing one of her pranks. She knew Kate's careless, fun-loving ways. It was more to her that all things should move decently and in order than that Kate should even be perfectly well. But Marcia's white face behind her stepmother's ample shoulder showed a dread of something worse than a mere indisposition. David Spafford took alarm at once. He put down the silver syrup jug from which he had been pouring golden maple syrup on his cakes, and pushed his chair back with a click.

"Perhaps she has fainted!" he said, and Marcia saw how deeply he was concerned. Father and lover both started up the stairs, the father angry, the lover alarmed. The Squire grumbled all the way up that Kate should sleep so late, but David said nothing. He waited anxiously behind while the Squire worked with the door. Madam Schuyler and Marcia had followed them, and halting curiously just behind came the two maids. They all loved Miss Kate and were deeply interested in the day's doings. They did not want anything to interfere with the well-planned pageant.

The Squire fumbled nervously with the latch, all the time calling upon his daughter to open the door; then wrathfully placed his solid shoulder and knee in just the right place, and with a groan and wrench the latch gave way, and the solid oak door swung open, precipitating the anxious group somewhat suddenly into the room.

Almost immediately they all became aware that there was no one there. David had stood with averted eyes at first, but that second sense which makes us aware without sight when others are near or absent, brought with it an unnamed anxiety. He looked wildly about.

The bed had not been slept in; that they all saw at once. The room was in confusion, but perhaps not more than might have been expected when the occupant was about to leave on the morrow. There were pieces of paper and string upon the floor and one or two garments lying about as if carelessly cast off in a hurry. David recognized the purple muslin frock Kate had worn the night before, and put out his hand to touch it as it lay across the foot of the bed, vainly reaching after her who was not there.

They stood in silence, father, mother, sister, and lover, and took in every detail of the deserted room, then looked blankly into one another's white faces, and in the eyes of each a terrible question began to dawn. Where was she?

Madam Schuyler recovered her senses first. With her sharp, practical system she endeavored to find out the exact situation. "Who saw her last? Has she been downstairs this morning?" she looked straight at Marcia this time, but the girl shook her head.

"I went to bed last night before they came in," she said, looking questioningly at David, but a sudden remembrance and fear seized her heart. She turned away to the window to face it where they could not look at her.

"We came in early," said David, trying to keep the anxiety out of his voice, as he remembered his well-beloved's good-night. Surely, surely, nothing very dreadful could have happened just over night, and in her father's own house. He looked about again to see the natural, every-day, little things that would help him drive away the thoughts of possible tragedy.

"Kate was tired. She said she was going to get up very early this morning and wash her face in the dew on the grass." He braved a smile and looked about on the troubled group. "She must be out somewhere upon the place," he continued, gathering courage with the thought; "she told me it was an old superstition. She has maybe wandered further than she intended, and perhaps got into some trouble. I'd better go and search for her. Is there any place near here where she would be likely to be?" He turned to Marcia for help.

"But Kate would never delay so long I'm sure," said the stepmother severely. "She's not such a fool as to go traipsing through the wet grass before daylight for any nonsense. If it were Marcia now, you might expect anything, but Kate would be satisfied with the dew on the grass by the kitchen pump. I know Kate."

Marcia's face crimsoned at her stepmother's words, but she turned her troubled eyes to David and tried to answer him.

"There are plenty of places, but Kate has never cared to go to them. I could go out and look everywhere." She started to go down, but as she passed the wide mahogany bureau she saw a bit of folded paper lying under the corner of the pincushion. With a smothered exclamation she went over and picked it up. It was addressed to David in Kate's handwriting, fine and even like copperplate. Without a word Marcia handed it to him and then stood back where the wide draperies of the window would shadow her.

Madam Schuyler, with sudden keen prescience, took alarm. Noticing the two maids standing wide-mouthed in the hallway, she summoned her most commandatory tone, stepped into the hall, half closing the door behind her, and cowed the two handmaidens under her glance.

"It is all right!" she said calmly. "Miss Kate has left a note, and will return soon. Go down and keep her breakfast warm, and not a word to a soul! Dolly,

Debby, do you understand! Not a word of this! Now hurry and do all that I told you before breakfast."

They went with downcast eyes and disappointed droops to their mouths, but she knew that not a word would pass their lips. They know that if they disobeyed that command they need never hope for favor more from madam. Madam's word was law. She would be obeyed. Therefore with remarkable discretion they masked their wondering looks and did as they were bidden. So while the family stood in solemn conclave in Kate's room the preparations for the wedding moved steadily forward below stairs, and only two solemn maids, of all the helpers that morning, knew that a tragedy was hovering in the air and might burst about them.

David had grasped for the letter eagerly, and fumbled it open with trembling hand, but as he read, the smile of expectation froze upon his lips and his face grew ashen. He tottered and grasped for the mantel shelf to steady himself as he read further, but he did not seem to take in the meaning of what he read. The others waited breathless, a reasonable length of time, Madam Schuyler impatiently patient. She felt that long delay would be perilous to her arrangements. She ought to know the whole truth at once and be put in command of the situation. Marcia with sorrowful face and drooping eyelashes stood quiet behind the curtain, while over and over the echo of a horse's hoofs in a silent street and over a bridge sounded in her brain. She did not need to be told, she knew intuitively what had happened, and she dared not to look at David.

"Well, what has she done with herself?" said the Squire impatiently. He had not finished his plate of cakes, and now that there was word he wanted to know at once and go back to his breakfast. The sight of his daughter's handwriting relieved and reassured him. Some crazy thing she had done of course, but then Kate had always done queer things, and probably would to the end of time. She was a hussy to frighten them so, and he meant to tell her so when she returned, if it was her wedding day. But then, Kate would be Kate, and his breakfast was getting cold. He had the horses to look after and orders to give the hands before the early guests arrived.

But David did not answer, and the sight of him was alarming. He stood as one stricken dumb all in a moment. He raised his eyes to the Squire's—pleading, pitiful. His face had grown strained and haggard.

"Speak out, man, doesn't the letter tell?" said the Squire imperiously. "Where is the girl?"

And this time David managed to say brokenly: "She's gone!" and then his head dropped forward on his cold hand that rested on the mantel. Great beads of perspiration stood out upon his white forehead, and the letter fluttered gaily, coquettishly to the floor, a reminder of the uncertain ways of its writer.

The Squire reached for it impatiently, and wiping his spectacles laboriously put them on and drew near to the window to read, his heavy brows lowering in a frown. But his wife did not need to read the letter, for she, like Marcia, had divined its purport, and already her able faculties were marshalled to face the predicament.

The Squire with deepening frown was studying his elder daughter's letter, scarce able to believe the evidence of his senses that a girl of his could be so heartless.

Dear David, — the letter ran, — written as though in a hurry, done at the last moment, — which indeed it was: —

I want you to forgive me for what I am doing. I know you will feel bad about it, but really I never was the right one for you. I'm sure you thought me all too good, and I never could have stayed in a strait-jacket, it would have killed me. I shall always consider you the best man in the world, and I like you better than anyone else except Captain Leavenworth. I can't help it, you know, that I care more for him than anyone else, though I've tried. So I am going away to-night and when you read this we shall have been married. You are so very good that I know you will forgive me, and be glad I am happy. Don't think hardly of me for I always did care a great deal for you.

> *Your loving*
> *Kate*

It was characteristic of Kate that she demanded the love and loyalty of her betrayed lover to the bitter end, false and heartless though she had been. The coquette in her played with him even now in the midst of the bitter pain she must have known she was inflicting. No word of contrition spoke she, but took her deed as one of her prerogatives, just as she had always taken everything she chose. She did not even spare him the loving salutation that had been her custom in her letters to him, but wrote herself down as she would have done the day before when all was fair and dear between them. She did not hint at any better day for David, or give him permission to forget her, but held him for all time as her own, as she had known she would by those words of hers, "I like you better than anyone else except! — " Ah! That fatal "except!" Could any knife cut deeper and more ways? They sank into the young man's heart as he stood there those first few minutes and faced his trouble, his head bowed upon the mantel-piece.

Meantime Madam Schuyler's keen vision had spied another folded paper beside the pincushion. Smaller it was than the other, and evidently intended to be placed further out of sight. It was addressed to Kate's father, and her stepmother opened it and read with hard pressure of her thin lips, slanted down at the corners, and a steely look in her eyes. Was it possible that the girl, even in the midst of her treachery, had enjoyed with a sort of malicious glee the thought of her stepmother reading that note and facing the horror of a wedding party with no bride? Knowing her stepmother's vast resources did she not think that at last she had brought her to a situation to which she was unequal? There had always been this unseen, unspoken struggle for supremacy between them; though it had been a friendly one, a sort of testing on the girl's part of the powers and expedients of the woman, with a kind of vast admiration, mingled with amusement, but no fear for the stepmother who had been uniformly kind and loving toward her, and for whom she cared, perhaps as much as she could have cared for her own mother. The other note read:

Dear Father: — I am going away to-night to marry Captain Leavenworth. You wouldn't let me have him in the right way, so I had to take this. I tried very hard to forget him and get interested in David, but it was no use. You couldn't stop it. So now I hope you will see it the way we do and forgive us. We are going to Washington and you can write us there and say you forgive us, and then we will come home. I know you will forgive us, Daddy dear. You know you always loved your little Kate and you couldn't really want me to be unhappy. Please send my trunks to Washington. I've tacked the card with the address on the envelope.

Your loving girl,
Kate

There was a terrible stillness in the room, broken only by the crackling of the paper as the notes were turned in the hands of their readers. Marcia felt as if centuries were passing. David's soul was pierced by one awful thought. He had no room for others. She was gone! Life was a blank for him! stretching out into interminable years. Of her treachery and false-heartedness in doing what she had done in the way she had done it, he had no time to take account. That would come later. Now he was trying to understand this one awful fact.

Madam Schuyler handed the second note to her husband, and with set lips quickly skimmed through the other one. As she read, indignation rose in her, and a great desire to outwit everybody. If it had been possible to bring the erring girl back and make her face her disgraced wedding alone, Madam Schuyler would have been glad to do it. She knew that upon her would likely rest the re-arrangements, and her ready brain was already taking account of her servants and the number of messages that would have to be sent out to stop the guests from arriving. She waited impatiently for her husband to finish reading that she might consult with him as to the best message to send, but she was scarcely prepared for the burst of anger that came with the finish of the letters. The old man crushed his daughter's note in his hand and flung it from him. He had great respect and love for David, and the sight of him broken in grief, the deed of his daughter, roused in him mighty indignation. His voice shook, but there was a deep note of command in it that made Madam Schuyler step aside and wait. The Squire had arisen to the situation, and she recognized her lord and master.

"She must be brought back at once at all costs!" he exclaimed. "That rascal shall not outwit us. Fool that I was to trust him in the house! Tell the men to saddle the horses. They cannot have gone far yet, and there are not so many roads to Washington. We may yet overtake them, and married or unmarried the hussy shall be here for her wedding!"

But David raised his head from the mantel-shelf and steadied his voice:

"No, no, you must not do that — father —" the appellative came from his lips almost tenderly, as if he had long considered the use of it with pleasure, and now he spoke it as a tender bond meant to comfort.

The older man started and his face softened. A flash of understanding and love passed between the two men.

"Remember, she has said she loves some one else. She could never be mine now."

There was a terrible sadness in the words as David spoke them, and his voice broke. Madam Schuyler turned away and took out her handkerchief, an article of apparel for which she seldom had use except as it belonged to every well ordered toilet.

The father stood looking hopelessly at David and taking in the thought. Then he too bowed his head and groaned.

"And my daughter, *my little Kate,* has done it!" Marcia covered her face with the curtains and her tears fell fast.

David went and stood beside the Squire and touched his arm.

"Don't!" he said pleadingly. "You could not help it. It was not your fault. Do not take it so to heart!"

"But it is my disgrace. I have brought up a child who could do it. I cannot escape from that. It is the most dishonorable thing a woman can do. And look how she has done it, brought shame upon us all! Here we have a wedding on our hands, and little or no time to do anything! I have lived in honor all my life, and now to be disgraced by my own daughter!"

Marcia shuddered at her father's agony. She could not bear it longer. With a soft cry she went to him, and nestled her head against his breast unnoticed.

"Father, father, don't!" she cried.

But her father went on without seeming to see her.

"To be disgraced and deserted and dishonored by my own child! Something must be done. Send the servants! Let the wedding be stopped!"

He looked at Madam and she started toward the door to carry out his bidding, but he recalled her immediately.

"No, stay!" he cried. "It is too late to stop them all. Let them come. Let them be told! Let the disgrace rest upon the one to whom it belongs!"

Madam stopped in consternation! A wedding without a bride! Yet she knew it was a serious thing to try to dispute with her husband in that mood. She paused to consider.

"Oh, father!" exclaimed Marcia, "we couldn't! Think of David."

Her words seemed to touch the right chord, for he turned toward the young man, intense, tender pity in his face.

"Yes, David! We are forgetting David! We must do all we can to make it easier for you. You will be wanting to get away from us as quickly as possible. How can we manage it for you? And where will you go? You will not want to go home just yet?"

He paused, a new agony of the knowledge of David's part coming to him.

"No, I cannot go home," said David hopelessly, a look of keen pain darting across his face, "for the house will be all ready for her, and the table set. The friends will be coming in, and we are invited to dinner and tea everywhere. They will all be coming to the house, my friends, to welcome us. No, I cannot go home." Then he passed his hand over his forehead blindly, and added, in a stupefied tone, "and yet I must — sometime — I must — go — home!"

Chapter 5

The room was very still as he spoke. Madam Schuyler forgot the coming guests and the preparations, in consternation over the thought of David and his sorrow. Marcia sobbed softly upon her father's breast, and her father involuntarily placed his arm about her as he stood in painful thought.

"It is terrible!" he murmured, "terrible! How could she bear to inflict such sorrow! She might have saved us the scorn of all our friends. David, you must not go back alone. It must not be. You must not bear that. There are lovely girls in plenty elsewhere. Find another one and marry her. Take your bride home with you, and no one in your home need be the wiser. Don't sorrow for that cruel girl of mine. Give her not the satisfaction of feeling that your life is broken. Take another. Any girl might be proud to go with you for the asking. Had I a dozen other daughters you should have your pick of them, and one should go with you, if you would condescend to choose another from the home where you have been so treacherously dealt with. But I have only this one girl. She is but a child as yet and cannot compare with what you thought you had. I blame you not if you do not wish to wed another Schuyler, but if you will she is yours. And she is a good girl, David, though she is but a child. Speak up, child, and say if you will make amends for the wrong your sister has done!"

The room was so still one could almost hear the heartbeats. David raised his head once more and was looking at Marcia. Sad and searching was his gaze, as if he fain would find the features of Kate in her face, yet it seemed to Marcia, as she raised wide tear-filled eyes from her father's breast where her head still lay, that he saw her not. He was looking beyond her and facing the home-going alone, and the empty life that would follow.

Her thoughts the last few days had matured her fully. She understood and pitied, and her woman-nature longed to give comfort, yet she shrunk from going unasked. It was all terrible, this sudden situation thrust upon her, yet she felt a willing sacrifice if she but felt sure it was his wish.

But David did not seem to know that he must speak. He waited, looking earnestly at her, through her, beyond her, to see if Heaven would grant this small relief to his sufferings. At last Marcia summoned her voice:

"If David wishes I will go."

She spoke the words solemnly, her eyes lifted slightly above him as if she were speaking to Another One higher than he. It was like an answer to a call from God. It had come to Marcia this way. It seemed to leave her no room for drawing back, if indeed she had wished to do so. Other considerations were not present. There was just one great desire in her heart to make amends in some measure for the wrong that had been done. She felt almost responsible for it, a family responsibility. She seemed to feel the shame and pain as her father was feeling it. She would step into the empty place that Kate had left and fill it as far as she could. Her only fear was that she was not acceptable, not worthy to fill so high a place. She trembled over it, yet she could not hold back from the high calling. It was so she stood in a kind of sorrowful exaltation waiting for David. Her eyes lowered again, looking at him through the lashes and pleading for recognition. She did not feel that she was pleading for anything for herself, only for the chance to help him.

Her voice had broken the spell. David looked down upon her kindly, a pleasant light of gratitude flashing through the sternness and sorrow in his face. Here was comradeship in trouble, and his voice recognized it as he said:

"Child, you are good to me, and I thank you. I will try to make you happy if you will go with me, and I am sure your going will be a comfort in many ways, but I would not have you go unwillingly."

There was a dull ache in Marcia's heart, its cause she could not understand, but she was conscious of a gladness that she was not counted unworthy to be accepted, young though she was, and child though he called her. His tone had been kindness itself, the gentle kindness that had won her childish sisterly love when he first began to visit her sister. She had that answer to remember for many a long day, and to live upon, when questionings and loneliness came upon her. But she raised her face to her father now, and said: "I will go, father!"

The Squire stooped and kissed his little girl for the last time. Perhaps he realized that from this time forth she would be a little girl no longer, and that he would never look into those child-eyes of hers again, unclouded with the sorrows of life, and filled only with the wonder-pictures of a rosy future. She seemed to him and to herself to be renouncing her own life forever, and to be taking up one of sacrificial penitence for her sister's wrong doing.

The father then took Marcia's hand and placed it in David's, and the betrothal was complete.

Madam Schuyler, whose reign for the time being was set aside, stood silent, half disapproving, yet not interfering. Her conscience told her that this wholesale disposal of Marcia was against nature. The new arrangement was a relief to her in many ways, and would make the solution of the day a less trying one for every one. But she was a woman and knew a woman's heart. Marcia was not having her chance in life as her sister had, as every woman had a right to have. Then her face hardened. How had Kate used her chances? Perhaps it was better for Marcia to be well placed in life before she grew headstrong enough to make a fool of herself as Kate had done. David would be good to her, that was certain. One could not look at the strong, pleasant lines of his well cut mouth and chin and not be sure of that. Perhaps it was all for the best. At least it was not her doing. And it was only the night before that she had been looking at Marcia and worrying because she was growing into a woman so fast. Now she would be relieved of that care, and could take her ease and enjoy life until her own children were grown up. But the voice of her husband aroused her to the present.

"Let the wedding go on as planned, Sarah, and no one need know until the ceremony is over except the minister. I myself will go and tell the minister. There will need to be but a change of names."

"But," said the Madam, with housewifely alarm, as the suddenness of the whole thing flashed over her, "Marcia is not ready. She has no suitable clothes for her wedding."

"Not ready! No clothes!" said the Squire, now thoroughly irritated over this trivial objection, as a fly will sometimes ruffle the temper of a man who has kept calm under fire of an enemy. "And where are all the clothes that have been making these weeks and months past? What more preparation does she need? Did the hussy take her wedding things with her? What's in the trunk?"

"But those are Kate's things, father," said Marcia in gentle explanation. "Kate would be very angry if I took her things. They were made for her, you know."

"And what if they were made for her?" answered the father, very angry now at Kate. "You are near of a size. What will do for one is good enough for the other, and Kate may be angry and get over it, for not one rag of it will she get, nor a penny of my money will ever go to her again. She is no daughter of mine from henceforth. That rascal has beaten me and stolen my daughter, but he gets a dowerless lass. Not a penny will ever go from the Schuyler estate into his pocket, and no trunk will ever travel from here to Washington for that heartless girl. I forbid it. Let her feel some of the sorrow she has inflicted upon others more innocent. I forbid it, do you hear?" He brought his fist down upon the mahogany bureau until the prisms on a candle-stand in front of the mirror jangled discordantly.

"Oh, father!" gasped Marcia, and turned with terror to her stepmother. But David stood with his back toward the rest looking out the window. He had forgotten them all.

Madam Schuyler was now in command again. For once the Squire had anticipated his wife, and the next move had been planned without her help, but it was as she would have it. Her face had lost its consternation and beamed with satisfaction beneath its mask of grave perplexity. She could not help it that she was glad to have the terrible ordeal of a wedding without a bride changed to something less formidable.

At least the country round about could not pity, for who was to say but that David was as well suited with one sister as with the other? And Marcia was a good girl; doubtless she would grow into a good wife. Far more suitable for so good and steady a man as David than pretty, imperious Kate.

Madam Schuyler took her place of command once more and began to issue her orders.

"Come, then, Marcia, we have no time to waste. It is all right, as your father has said. Kate's things will fit you nicely and you must go at once and put everything in readiness. You will want all your time to dress, and pack a few things, and get calm. Go to your room right away and pick up anything you want to take with you, and I'll go down and see that Phoebe takes your place and then come back."

David and Squire went out like two men who had suddenly grown old, and had not the strength to walk rapidly. No one thought any more of breakfast. It was half past seven by the old tall clock that stood upon the stair-landing. It would not be long before Aunt Polly and Uncle Joab would be driving up to the door.

Straight ahead went the preparations, just as if nothing had happened, and if Mistress Kate Leavenworth could have looked into her old room an hour after the discovery of her flight she would have been astonished beyond measure.

Up in her own room stood poor bewildered Marcia. She looked about upon her little white bed, and thought she would never likely sleep in it again. She looked out of the small-paned window with its view of distant hill and river, and thought she was bidding it good-bye forever. She went toward her closet and put out her hand to choose what she would take with her, and her heart sank. There hung the faded old ginghams short and scant, and scorned but yesterday, yet her heart wildly clung to them. Almost would she have put one on and gone back to her happy care-free school life. The thought of the new life frightened her. She must give up her girlhood all at once. She might not keep a vestige of it, for that would betray David. She must be Kate from morning to evening. Like a sword thrust came the remembrance that she had envied Kate, and God had given her the punishment of being Kate in very truth. Only there was this great difference. She was not the chosen one, and Kate had been. She must bear about forever in her heart the thought of Kate's sin.

The voice of her stepmother drew nearer and warned her that her time alone was almost over, and out on the lawn she could hear the voices of Uncle Joab and Aunt Polly who had just arrived.

She dropped on her knees for one brief moment and let her young soul pour itself out in one great cry of distress to God, a cry without words borne only on the breath of a sob. Then she arose, hastily dashed cold water in her face, and dried away the traces of tears. There was no time to think. With hurried hand she began to gather a few trifles together from closet and drawer.

One last lingering look she took about her room as she left it, her arms filled with the things she had hastily culled from among her own. Then she shut the door quickly and went down the hall to her sister's room to enter upon her new life. She was literally putting off herself and putting on a new being as far as it was possible to do so outwardly.

There on the bed lay the bridal outfit. Madam Schuyler had just brought it from the spare room that there might be no more going back and forth through the halls to excite suspicion. She was determined that there should be no excitement or demonstration or opportunity for gossip among the guests at least until the ceremony was over. She had satisfied herself that not a soul outside the family save the two maids suspected that aught was the matter, and she felt sure of their silence.

Kate had taken very little with her, evidently fearing to excite suspicion, and having no doubt that her father would relent and send all her trousseau as she had requested in her letter. For once Mistress Kate had forgotten her fineries and made good her escape with but two frocks and a few other necessaries in a small hand-bag.

Madam Schuyler was relieved to the point of genuine cheerfulness, over this, despite the cloud of tragedy that hung over the day. She began to talk to Marcia as if she had been Kate, as she smoothed down this and that article and laid them back into the trunk, telling how the blue gown would be the best for church and the green silk for going out to very fine places, to tea drinkings and the like, and how she must always be sure to wear the cream undersleeves with the Irish point lace with her silk gown as they set it off to perfection. She recalled, too, how little experience Marcia had in the ways of the world, and all the while the girl was being dressed in the dainty bridal garments she gave her careful instructions in the art of being a success in society, until Marcia felt that the green fields and the fences and trees to climb and the excursions after blackberries, and all the joyful merry-makings of the boys and girls were receding far from her. She could even welcome Hanford Weston as a playfellow in her near future, if thereby a little fresh air and freedom of her girlhood might be left. Nevertheless there gradually came over her an elation of excitement. The feel of the dainty garments, the delicate embroidery, the excitement lest the white slippers would not fit her, the difficulty in making her hair stay up in just Kate's style—for her stepmother insisted that she must dress it exactly like Kate's and make herself look as nearly as possible as Kate would have looked,— all drove sadness from her mind and she began to take a little delight in the pretty clothes, the great occasion, and her own importance. The vision in the looking glass, too, told her that her own face was winsome, and the new array not unbecoming. Something of this she had seen the night before when she put on the new chintz; now the change was complete, as she stood in the white satin and lace with a string of seed pearls that had been her mother's tied about her soft white throat. She thought about the tradition of the pearls that Kate's girlfriends had laughingly reminded her of a few days before when they were looking at the bridal garments. They had said that each pearl a bride wore meant a tear she would shed. She wondered if Kate had escaped the tears with the pearls, and left them for her.

She was ready at last, even to the veil that had been her mother's and her mother's before her. It fell in its rich folds, yellowed by age, from her head to her feet, with its creamy frost-work of rarest handiwork, transforming the girl into a woman and a bride.

Madam Schuyler arranged and rearranged the folds, and finally stood back to look with half-closed eyes at the effect, deciding that very few would notice that the bride was other than they had expected until the ceremony was over and the veil thrown back. The sisters had never looked alike, yet there was a general family resemblance that was now accentuated by the dress; perhaps only those nearest would notice that it was Marcia instead of Kate. At least the guests would have the good grace to keep their wondering to themselves until the ceremony was over.

Then Marcia was left to herself with trembling hands and wildly throbbing heart. What would Mary Ann think! What would all the girls and boys think? Some of them would be there, and others would be standing along the shady streets to watch the progress of the carriage as it drove away. And they would see her going away instead of Kate. Perhaps they would think it was all a great joke and that she had going to be married all the time and not Kate. But no; the truth would soon come out. People would not be astonished at anything Kate did. They would only say it was just what they had all along expected from her, and pity her father, and pity her perhaps. But they would look at her and admire her and for once she would be the centre of attraction. The pink of pride swelled up into her cheeks, and then realizing what she was thinking she crushed the feeling down. How could she think of such things when Kate had done such a dreadful thing, and David was suffering so terribly? Here was she actually enjoying, and delighting in the thought of being in Kate's place. Oh, she was wicked, wicked! She must not be happy for a moment in what was Kate's shame and David's sorrow. Of her future with David she did not now think. It was of the pageant of the day that her thoughts were full. If the days and weeks and months that were to follow came into her mind at all between the other things it was always that she was to care for David and to help him, and that she would have to grow up quickly; and remember all the hard housewifely things her stepmother had taught her; and try to order his house well. But that troubled her not at all at present. She was more concerned with the ceremony, and the many eyes that would be turned upon her. It was a relief when a tap came on the door and the dear old minister entered.

Chapter 6

He stood a moment by the door looking at her, half startled. Then he came over beside her, put his hands upon her shoulders, looking down into her upturned, veiled face.

"My child!" he said tenderly, "my little Marcia, is this you? I did not know you in all this beautiful dress. You look as your own mother looked when she was married. I remember perfectly as it were but yesterday, her face as she stood by your father's side. I was but a young man then, you know, and it was my first wedding in my new church, so you see I could not forget it. Your mother was a beautiful woman, Marcia, and you are like her both in face and life."

The tears came into Marcia's eyes and her lips trembled.

"Are you sure, child," went on the gentle voice of the old man, "that you understand what a solemn thing you are doing? It is not a light thing to give yourself in marriage to any man. You are so young yet! Are you doing this thing quite willingly, little girl? Are you sure? Your father is a good man, and a dear old friend of mine, but I know what has happened has been a terrible blow to him, and a great humiliation. It has perhaps unnerved his judgment for the time. No one should have brought pressure to bear upon a child like you to make you marry against your will. Are you sure it is all right, dear?"

"Oh, yes, sir!" Marcia raised her tear-filled eyes. "I am doing it quite of myself. No one has made me. I am glad I might. It was so dreadful for David!"

"But child, do you love him?" the old minister said, searching her face closely.

Marcia's eyes shone out radiant and childlike through her tears.

"Oh, yes, sir! I love him of course. No one could help loving David."

There was a tap at the door and the Squire entered. With a sigh the minister turned away, but there was trouble in his heart. The love of the girl had been all too frankly confessed. It was not as he would have had things for a daughter of his, but it could not be helped of course, and he had no right to interfere. He would like to speak to David, but David had not come out of his room yet. When he did there was but a moment for them alone and all he had opportunity to say was:

"Mr. Spafford, you will be good to the little girl, and remember she is but a child. She has been dear to us all."

David looked at him wonderingly, earnestly, in reply:

"I will do all in my power to make her happy," he said.

The hour had come, and all things, just as Madam Schuyler had planned, were ready. The minister took his place, and the impatient bridesmaids were in a flutter, wondering why Kate did not call them in to see her. Slowly, with measured step, as if she had practiced many times, Marcia, the maiden, walked down the hall on her father's arm. He was bowed with his trouble and his face bore marks of the sudden calamity that had befallen his house, but the watching guests thought it was for sorrow at giving up his lovely Kate, and they said to one another, "How much he loved her!"

The girl's face drooped with gentle gravity. She scarcely felt the presence of the guests she had so much dreaded, for to her the ceremony was holy. She was giving herself as a sacrifice for the sin of her sister. She was too young and inexperienced to know all that would be thought and said as soon as the company understood. She also felt secure behind that film of lace. It seemed impossible that they could know her, so softly and so mistily it shut her in from the world. It was like a kind of moving house about her, a protection from all eyes. So sheltered she might go through the ceremony with composure. As yet she had not begun to dread the afterward. The hall was wide through which she passed, and the day was bright, but the windows were so shadowed by the waiting bridesmaids that the light did not fall in full glare upon her, and it was not strange they did not know her at once. She heard their smothered exclamations of wonder and admiration, and one, Kate's dearest friend, whispered softly behind her: "Oh, Kate, why did you keep us waiting, you sly girl! How lovely you are! You look like an angel straight from heaven."

There were other whispered words which Marcia heard sadly. They gave her no pleasure. The words were for Kate, not her. What would they say when they knew all?

There was David in the distance waiting for her. How fine he looked in his wedding clothes! How proud Kate might have been of him! How pitiful was his white face! He had summoned courage and put on a mask of happiness for the eyes of those who saw him, but it could not deceive the heart of Marcia. Surely not since the days when Jacob served seven years for Rachel and then lifted the bridal veil to look upon the face of her sister Leah, walked there sadder bridegroom on this earth than David Spafford walked that day.

Down the stairs and through the wide hall they came, Marcia not daring to look up, yet seeing familiar glimpses as she passed. That green plaid silk lap at one side of the parlor door, in which lay two nervous little hands and a neatly folded pocket handkerchief, belonged to Sabrina Bates, she knew; and the round lace collar a little farther on, fastened by the brooch with a colored daguerreotype encircled by a braid of faded brown hair under glass, must be about the neck of Aunt Polly. There was not another brooch like that in New York state, Marcia felt sure. Beyond were Uncle Joab's small meek Sunday boots, toeing in, and next were little feet covered by white stockings and slippers fastened with crossed black ribbons, some child's, not Harriet — Marcia dared not raise her eyes to identify them now. She must fix her mind upon the great things before her. She wondered at herself for noticing such trivial things when she was walking up to the presence of the great God, and there before her stood the minister with his open book!

Now, at last, with most of the audience behind her, shut in by the film of lace, she could raise her eyes to the minister's familiar face, take David's arm without letting her hand tremble much, and listen to the solemn words read out to her. For her alone they seemed to be read. David's heart she knew was crushed, and it was only a form for him. She must take double vows upon her for the sake of the wrong done to him. So she listened:

"Dearly beloved, we are gathered together" — how the words thrilled her! — "in the sight of God and in the presence of this company to join together this man and woman in the bonds of holy matrimony;" — a deathly stillness rested upon the room and the painful throbbing of her heart was all the little bride could hear. She was glad she might look straight into the dear face of the old minister. Had her mother felt this way when she was being married? Did her stepmother understand it? Yes, she must, in part at least, for she had bent and kissed her most tenderly upon the brow just before leaving her, a most sentimental thing for her to do. It touched Marcia deeply, though she was fond of her stepmother at all times.

She waited breathless with drooped eyes while the minister demanded, "If any man can show just cause why they may not be lawfully joined together, let him now declare it, or else hereafter hold his peace." What if some one should recognize her and, thinking she had usurped Kate's place, speak out and stop the marriage! How would David feel? And she? She would sink to the floor. Oh, did any of them know? How she wished she dared raise her eyes to look about and see. But she must not. She must listen. She must shake off these worldly thoughts. She was not hearing for idle thinking. It was a solemn, holy vow she was taking upon herself for life. She brought herself sharply back to the ceremony. It was to David the minister was talking now:

"Wilt thou love her, comfort her, honor and keep her, in sickness and in health, and forsaking all other, keep thee only unto her, so long as ye both shall live?"

It was hard to make David promise that when his heart belonged to Kate. She wondered that his voice could be so steady when it said, "I will," and the white glove of Kate's which was just a trifle too large for her, trembled on David's arm as the minister next turned to her:

"Wilt thou, Marcia" — Ah! It was out now! and the sharp rustle of silk and stiff linen showed that all the company were aware at last of who was the bride; but the minister went steadily on. He cared not what the listening assembly thought. He was talking earnestly to his little friend, Marcia, — "have this man to be thy wedded husband, to live together after God's ordinance in the holy estate of matrimony? Wilt thou obey him, and serve him, love, honor, and keep him, in sickness and in health"—the words of the pledge went on. It was not hard. The girl felt she could do all that. She was relieved to find it no more terrible, and to know that she was no longer acting a lie. They all knew who she was now. She held up her flower-like head and answered in a clear voice, that made her few schoolmates gasp in admiration:

"I will!"

And the dear old minister's wife, sitting sweet and dove-like in her soft grey poplin, fine white kerchief, and cap of book muslin, smiled to herself at the music in Marcia's voice and nodded approval. She felt that all was well with her little friend.

They waited, those astonished people, till the ceremony was concluded and the prayer over, and then they broke forth. There had been lifted brows and looks passing from one to another, of question, of disclaiming any knowledge in the matter, and just as soon as the minister turned and took the bride's hand to congratulate her the heads bent together behind fans and the soft buzz of whispers began.

What does it mean? Where is Kate? She isn't in the room! Did he change his mind at the last minute? How old is Marcia? Mercy me! Nothing but a child! Are you sure? Why, my Mary Ann is older than that by three months, and she's no more able to become mistress of a home than a nine-days-old kitten. Are you sure that's Marcia? Didn't the minister make a mistake in the name? It looked to me like Kate. Look again. She's put her veil back. No, it can't be! Yes, it is! No, it looks like Kate! Her hair's done the same, but, no, Kate never had such a sweet innocent look like that. Why, when she was a child her face always had a sharpness to it. Look at Marcia's eyes, poor lamb! I don't see how her father could bear it, and she so young. But Kate! Where can she be? What has happened? You don't say! Yes, I did see that captain about again last week or so. Do you believe it? Surely she never would. Who told you? Was he sure? But Maria and Janet are bridesmaids and they didn't see signs of anything. They were over here yesterday. Yes, Kate showed them everything and planned how they would all walk in. No, she didn't do anything queer, for Janet would have mentioned it. Janet always sees everything. Well, they say he's a good man and Marcia'll be well provided for. Madam Schuyler'll be relieved about that. Marcia can't ever lead her the dance Kate has among the young men. How white he looks! Do you suppose he loves her? What on earth can it all mean? Do you s'pose Kate feels bad? Where is she anyway? Wouldn't she come down? Well, if 'twas his choosing it serves her right. She's too much of a flirt for a good man and maybe he found her out. She's probably got just what she deserves, and I think Marcia'll make a good little wife. She always was a quiet, grown-up child and Madam Schuyler trained her well! But what will Kate do now? Hush! They are coming this way. How do you suppose we can find out? Go ask Cousin Janet, perhaps they've told her, or Aunt Polly. Surely she knows.

But Aunt Polly sat with pursed lips of disapproval. She had not been told, and it was her prerogative to know everything. She always made a point of being on hand early at all funerals and weddings, especially in the family circle, and learning the utmost details, which she dispensed at her discretion to late comers in fine sepulchral whispers.

Now she sat silent, disgraced, unable to explain a thing. It was unhandsome of Sarah Schuyler, she felt, though no more than she might have expected of her, she told herself. She had never liked her. Well, wait until her opportunity came. If they did not wish her to say the truth she must say something. She could at least tell what she thought. And what more natural than to let it be known that Sarah Schuyler had always held a dislike for Marcia, and to suggest that it was likely she was glad to get her off her hands. Aunt Polly meant to find a trail somewhere, no matter how many times they threw her off the scent.

Meantime for Marcia the sun seemed to have shined out once more with something of its old brightness. The terrible deed of self-renunciation was over, and familiar faces actually were smiling upon her and wishing her joy. She felt the flutter of her heart in her throat beneath the string of pearls, and wondered if after all she might hope for a little happiness of her own. She could climb no more fences nor wade in gurgling brooks, but might there not be other happy things as good? A little touch of the pride of life had settled upon her. The relatives were coming with pleasant words and kisses. The blushes upon her cheeks were growing deeper. She almost forgot David in the pretty excitement. A few of her girl friends ventured shyly near, as one might look at a mate suddenly and unexpectedly translated into eternal bliss. They put out cold fingers in salute with distant, stiff phrases belonging to a grown-up world. Not one of them save Mary Ann dared recognize their former bond of playmates. Mary Ann leaned down and whispered with a giggle: "Say, you didn't need to envy Kate, did you? My! Ain't you in clover! Say, Marsh," wistfully, "do invite me fer a visit sometime, won't you?"

Now Mary Ann was not quite on a par with the Schuylers socially, and had it not been for a distant mutual relative she would not have been asked to the wedding. Marcia never liked her very much, but now, with the uncertain, dim future it seemed pleasant and home-like to think of a visit from Mary Ann and she nodded and said childishly: "Sometime, Mary Ann, if I can."

Mary Ann squeezed her hand, kissed her, blushed and giggled herself out of the way of the next comer.

They went out to the dining room and sat around the long table. It was Marcia's timid hand that cut the bridecake, and all the room full watched her. Seeing the pretty color come and go in her excited cheeks, they wondered that they had never noticed before how beautiful Marcia was growing. A handsome couple they would make! And they looked from Marcia to David and back again, wondering and trying to fathom the mystery.

It was gradually stealing about the company, the truth about Kate and Captain Leavenworth. The minister had told it in his sad and gentle way. Just the facts. No gossip. Naturally every one was bristling with questions, but not much could be got from the minister.

"I really do not know," he would say in his courteous, old-worldly way, and few dared ask further. Perhaps the minister, wise by reason of much experience, had taken care to ask as few questions as possible himself, and not to know too much before undertaking this task for his old friend the Squire.

And so Kate's marriage went into the annals of the village, at least so far as that morning was concerned, quietly, and with little exclamation before the family. The Squire and his wife controlled their faces wonderfully. There was an austerity about the Squire as he talked with his friends that was new to his pleasant face, but Madam conversed with her usual placid self-poise, and never gave cause for conjecture as to her true feelings.

There were some who dared to offer their surprised condolences. To such the stepmother replied that of course the outcome of events had been a sore trial to the Squire, and all of them, but they were delighted at the happy arrangement that had been made. She glanced contentedly toward the child-bride.

It was a revelation to the whole village that Marcia had grown up and was so handsome.

Dismay filled the breasts of the village gossips. They had been defrauded. Here was a fine scandal which they had failed to discover in time and spread abroad in its due course.

Everybody was shy of speaking to the bride. She sat in her lovely finery like some wild rose caught as a sacrifice. Yet every one admitted that she might have done far worse. David was a good man, with prospects far beyond most young men of his time. Moreover he was known to have a brilliant mind, and the career he had chosen, that of journalism, in which he was already making his mark, was one that promised to be lucrative as well as influential.

It was all very hurried at the last, Madam Schuyler and Dolly the maid helped her off with the satin and lace finery, and she was soon out of her bridal attire and struggling with the intricacies of Kate's travelling costume.

Marcia was not Marcia any longer, but Mrs. David Spafford. She had been made to feel the new name almost at once, and it gave her a sense of masquerading pleasant enough for the time being, but with a dim foreboding of nameless dread and emptiness for the future, like all masquerading which must end sometime. And when the mask is taken off how sad if one is not to find one's real self again: or worse still if one may never remove the mask, but must grow to it and be it from the soul.

All this Marcia felt but dimly of course, for she was young and light hearted naturally, and the excitement and pretty things about her could not but be pleasant.

To have Kate's friends stand about her, half shyly trying to joke with her as they might have done with Kate, to feel their admiring glances, and half envious references to her handsome husband, almost intoxicated her for the moment. Her cheeks grew rosier as she tied on Kate's pretty poke bonnet whose nodding blue flowers had been brought over from Paris by a friend of Kate's. It seemed a shame that Kate should not have her things after all. The pleasure died out of Marcia's eyes as she carefully looped the soft blue ribbons under her round chin and drew on Kate's long gloves. There was no denying the fact that Kate's outfit was becoming to Marcia, for she had that complexion that looks well with any color under the sun, though in blue she was not at her best.

When Marcia was ready she stood back from the little looking-glass, with a frightened, half-childish gaze about the room.

Now that the last minute was come, there was no one to understand Marcia's feelings nor help her. Even the girls were merely standing there waiting to say the last formal farewell that they might be free to burst into an astonished chatter of exclamations over Kate's romantic disappearance. They were Kate's friends, not Marcia's, and they were bidding Kate's clothes good-bye for want of the original bride. Marcia's friends were too young and too shy to do more than stand back in awe and gaze at their mate so suddenly promoted to a life which but yesterday had seemed years away for any of them.

So Marcia walked alone down hall — yet, no, not all the way alone. A little wrinkled hand was laid upon her gloved one, and a little old lady, her true friend, the minister's wife, walked down the stairs with the bride arm in arm. Marcia's heart fluttered back to warmth again and was glad for her friend, yet all she had said was: "My dear!" but there was that in her touch and the tone of her gentle voice that comforted Marcia.

She stood at the edge of the steps, with her white hair shining in the morning, her kind-faced husband just behind her during all the farewell, and Marcia felt happier because of her motherly presence.

The guests were all out on the piazza in the gorgeousness of the summer morning. David stood on the flagging below the step beside the open coach door, a carriage lap-robe over his arm and his hat on, ready. He was talking with the Squire. Every one was looking at them, and they were entirely conscious of the fact. They laughed and talked with studied pleasantness, though there seemed to be an undertone of sadness that the most obtuse guest could not fail to detect.

Harriet, as a small flower-girl, stood upon the broad low step ready to fling posies before the bride as she stepped into the coach.

The little boys, to whom a wedding merely meant a delightful increase in opportunities, stood behind a pillar munching cake, more of which protruded from their bulging pockets.

Marcia, with a lump in her throat that threatened tears, slipped behind the people, caught the two little step-brothers in her arms and smothered them with kisses, amid their loud protestations and the laughter of those who stood about. But the little skirmish had served to hide the tears, and the bride came back most decorously to where her stepmother stood awaiting her with a smile of complacent — almost completed — duty upon her face.

She wore the sense of having carried off a trying situation in a most creditable manner, and she knew she had won the respect and awe of every matron present thereby. That was a great deal to Madam Schuyler.

The stepmother's arms were around her and Marcia remembered how kindly they had felt when they first clasped her little body years ago, and she had been kissed, and told to be a good little girl. She had always liked her stepmother. And now, as she came to say good-bye to the only mother she had ever known, who had been a true mother to her in many ways, her young heart almost gave way, and she longed to hide in that ample bosom and stay under the wing on one who had so ably led her thus far along the path of life.

Perhaps Madam Schuyler felt the clinging of the girl's arms about her, and perchance her heart rebuked her that she had let so young and inexperienced a girl go out to the cares of life all of a sudden in this way. At least she stooped and kissed Marcia again and whispered: "You have been a good girl, Marcia."

Afterwards, Marcia cherished that sentence among memory's dearest treasures. It seemed as though it meant that she had fulfilled her stepmother's first command, given on the night when her father brought home their new mother.

Then the flowers were thrown upon the pavement, to make it bright for the bride. She was handed into the coach behind the white-haired negro coachman, and by his side Kate's fine new hair trunk. Ah! That was a bitter touch! Kate's trunk! Kate's things! Kate's husband! If it had only been her own little moth-eaten trunk that had belonged to her mother, and filled with her own things — and if he had only been her own husband! Yet she wanted no other than David — only if he could have been her David.

Then Madam Schuyler, her heart still troubled about Marcia, stepped down and whispered:

"David, you will remember she is young. You will deal gently with her?"

Gravely David bent his head and answered:

"I will remember. She shall not be troubled. I will care for her as I would care for my own sister." And Madam Schuyler turned away half satisfied. After all, was that what woman wanted? Would she have been satisfied to have been cared for as a sister?

Then gravely, with his eyes half unseeing her, the father kissed his daughter good-bye, David got into the coach, the door was slammed shut, and the white horses arched their necks and stepped away, amid a shower of rice and slippers.

Chapter 7

For some distance the way was lined with people they knew, servants and negroes, standing about the driveway and outside the fence, people of the village grouped along the sidewalk, everybody out upon their doorsteps to watch the coach go by, and to all the face of the bride was a puzzle and a surprise. They half expected to see another coach coming with the other bride behind.

Marcia nodded brightly to those she knew, and threw flowers from the great nosegay that had been put upon her lap by Harriet. she felt for a few minutes like a girl in a fairy tale riding in this fine coach in grand attire. She stole a look at David. He certainly looked like a prince, but gravity was already settling about his mouth. Would he always look so now, she wondered, would he never laugh and joke again as he used to do? Could she manage to make him happy sometimes for a little while and help him to forget?

Down through the village they passed, in front of the store and post-office where Marcia had bought her frock but three days before, and they turned up the road she had come with Mary Ann. How long ago that seemed! How light her heart was then, and how young! All life was before her with its delightful possibilities. Now it seemed to have closed for her and she was some one else. A great ache came upon her heart. For a moment she longed to jump down and run away from the coach and David and the new clothes that were not hers. Away from the new life that had been planned for some one else which she must live now. She must always be a woman, never a girl any more.

Out past Granny McVane's they drove, the old lady sitting upon her front porch knitting endless stockings. She stared mildly, unrecognizingly at Marcia and paused in her rocking to crane her neck after the coach.

The tall corn rustled and waved green arms to them as they passed, and the cows looked up munching from the pasture in mild surprise at the turnout. The little coach dog stepped aside from the road to give them a bark as he passed, and then pattered and pattered his tiny feet to catch up. The old school house came in sight with its worn playground and dejected summer air, and Marcia's eyes searched out the window where she used to sit to eat her lunch in winters, and the tree under which she used to sit in summers, and the path by which she and Mary Ann used to wander down to the brook, or go in search of butternuts, even the old door knob that her hand would probably never grasp again. She searched them all out and bade them good-bye with her eyes. Then once she turned a little to see if she could catch a glimpse of the old blackboard through the window where she and Susanna Brown and Miller Thompson used to do arithmetic examples. The dust of the coach, or the bees in the sunshine, or something in her eyes blurred her vision. She could only see a long slant ray of a sunbeam crossing the wall where she knew it must be. Then the road wound around through a maple grove and the school was lost to view.

They passed the South meadow belonging to the Westons, and Hanford was plowing. Marcia could see him stop to wipe the perspiration from his brow, and her heart warmed even to his boy admirer now that she was going from him forever.

Hanford had caught sight of the coach and he turned to watch it thinking to see Kate sitting in the bride's place. He wondered if the bride would notice him, and turned a deeper red under his heavy coat of tan.

And the bride did notice him. She smiled the sweetest smile the boy had ever seen upon her face, the smile he had dreamed of as he thought of her, at night standing under the stars all alone by his father's gatepost whittling the cross bar of the gate. For a moment he forgot that it was the bridal party passing, forgot the stern-faced bridegroom and saw only Marcia—his girl love. His heart stood still, and a bright light of response filled his eyes. He took off his wide straw hat and bowed her reverence. He would have called to her, and tried three times, but his dry throat gave forth no utterance, and when he looked again the coach was passed and only the flutter of a white handkerchief came back to him and told him the beginning of the truth.

Then the poor boy's face grew white, yes, white and stricken under the tan, and he tottered to the roadside and sat down with his face in his hands to try and comprehend what it might mean, while the old horse dragged the plow whither he would in search of a bite of tender grass.

What could it mean? And why did Marcia occupy that place beside the stranger, obviously the bridegroom? Was she going on a visit? He had heard of no such plan. Where was her sister? Would there be another coach presently, and was this man then not the bridegroom but merely a friend of the family? Of course, that must be it. He got up and staggered to the fence to look down the road, but no one came by save the jogging old gray and carryall, with Aunt Polly grim and offended and Uncle Joab meek and depressed beside her. Could he have missed the bridal carriage when he was at the other end of the lot? Could they have gone another way? He had a half a mind to call to Uncle Joab to enquire only he was a timid boy and shrank back until it was too late.

But why had Marcia as she rode away wafted that strange farewell that had in it the familiarity of the final? And why did he feel so strange and weak in his knees?

Marcia was to help his mother next week at the quilting bee. She had not gone away to stay, of course. He got up and tried to whistle and turn the furrows evenly as before, but his heart was heavy, and, try as he would, he could not understand the feeling that kept telling him Marcia was gone out of his life forever.

At last his day's work was done and he could hasten to the house. Without waiting for his supper, he "slicked up," as he called it, and went at once to the village, where he learned the bitter truth.

It was Mary Ann who told him.

Mary Ann, the plain, the awkward, who secretly admired Hanford Weston as she might have admired an angel, and who as little expected him to speak to her as if he had been one. Mary Ann stood by her front gate in the dusk of the summer evening, the halo of her unusual wedding finery upon her, for she had taken advantage of being dressed up to make two or three visits since the wedding, and so prolong the holiday. The light of the sunset softened her plain features, and gave her a gentler look than was her wont. Was it that, and an air of lonesomeness akin to his own, that made Hanford stop and speak to her?

And then she told him. She could not keep it in long. It was the wonder of her life, and it filled her so that her thought had no room for anything else. To think of Marcia taken in a day, gone from their midst forever, gone to be a grown-up woman in a new world! It was as strange as sudden death, and almost as terrible and beautiful.

There were tears in her eyes, and in the eyes of the boy as they spoke about the one who was gone, and the kind dusk hid the sight so that neither knew, but each felt a subtle sympathy with the other, and before Hanford started upon his desolate way home under the burden of his first sorrow he took Mary Ann's slim bony hand in his and said quite stiffly: "Well, good-night, Miss Mary Ann. I'm glad you told me," and Mary Ann responded, with a deep blush under her freckles in the dark, "Good-night, Mr. Weston, and — call again!"

Something of the sympathy lingered with the boy as he went on his way and he was not without a certain sort of comfort, while Mary Ann climbed to her little chamber in the loft with a new wonder to dream over.

Meanwhile the coach drove on, and Marcia passed from her childhood's home into the great world of men and women, changes, heartbreakings, sorrows and joys.

David spoke to her kindly now and then; asked if she was comfortable; if she would prefer to change seats with him; if the cushions were right; and if she had forgotten anything. He seemed nervous, and anxious to have this part of the journey over and asked the coachman frequent questions about the horses and the speed they could make. Marcia thought she understood that he was longing to get away from the painful reminder of what he had expected to be a joyful trip, and her young heart pitied him, while yet it felt an undertone of hurt for herself. She found so much unadulterated joy in this charming ride with the beautiful horses, in this luxurious coach, that she could not bear to have it spoiled by the thought that only David's sadness and pain had made it possible for her.

Constantly as the scene changed, and new sights came upon her view, she
had to restrain herself from crying out with happiness over the beauty and calling
David's attention. Once she did point out a bird just leaving a stalk of goldenrod,
its light touch making the spray to bow and bend. David had looked with
unseeing eyes, and smiled with uncomprehending assent. Marcia felt she might
as well have been talking to herself. He was not even the old friend and brother
he used to be. She drew a gentle little sigh and wished this might have been only
a happy ride with the ending at home, and a longer girlhood uncrossed by this
wall of trouble that Kate had put up in a night for them all.

The coach came at last to the town where they were to stop for dinner and
a change of horses.

Marcia looked about with interest at the houses, streets, and people. There
were two girls of about her own age with long hair braided down their backs.
They were walking with arms about each other as she and Mary Ann had often
done. She wondered if any such sudden changes might be coming to them as
had come into her life. They turned and looked at her curiously, enviously it
seemed, as the coach drew up to the tavern and she was helped out with
ceremony. Doubtless they thought of her as she had thought of Kate but last
week.

She was shown into the dim parlor of the tavern and seated in a stiff
hair-cloth chair. It was all new and strange and delightful.

Before a high gilt mirror set on great glass knobs like rosettes, she smoothed
her wind-blown hair, and looked back at the reflection of her strange self with
startled eyes. Even her face seemed changed. She knew the bonnet and
arrangement of hair were becoming, but she felt unacquainted with them, and
wished for her own modest braids and plain bonnet. Even a sunbonnet would
have been welcome and have made her feel more like herself.

David did not see how pretty she looked when he came to take her to the
dining room ten minutes later. His eyes were looking into the hard future, and
he was steeling himself against the glances of others. He must be the model
bridegroom in the sight of all who knew him. His pride bore him out in this. He
had acquaintances all along the way home.

They were expecting the bridal party, for David had arranged that a fine
dinner should be ready for his bride. Fine it was, with the best cooking and table
service the mistress of the tavern could command, and with many a little touch
new and strange to Marcia, and therefore interesting. It was all a lovely play till
she looked at David.

David ate but little, and Marcia felt she must hurry through the meal for his
sake. Then when the carryall was ready he put her in and they drove away.

Marcia's keen intuition told her how many little things had been thought of
and planned for, for the comfort of the one who was to have taken this journey
with David. Gradually the thought of how terrible it was for him, and how

dreadful of Kate to have brought this sorrow upon him, overcame all other thoughts.

Sitting thus quietly, with her hands folded tight in the faded bunch of roses little Harriet had given her at parting, the last remaining of the flowers she had carried with her, Marcia let the tears come. Silently they flowed in gentle rain, and had not David been borne down with the thought of his own sorrow he must have noticed long before he did the sadness of the sweet young face beside him. But she turned away from him as much as possible that he might not see, and so they must have driven for half an hour through a dim sweet wood before he happened to catch a sight of the tear-wet face, and knew suddenly that there were other troubles in the world beside his own.

"Why, child, what is the matter?" he said, turning to her with grave concern. "Are you so tired? I'm afraid I have been very dull company," with a sigh. "You must forgive me–child, to-day."

"Oh, David, don't," said Marcia putting her face down into her hands and crying now regardless of the roses. "I do not want you to think of me. It is dreadful, dreadful for you. I am so sorry for you. I wish I could do something."

"Dear child!" he said, putting his hand upon hers. "Bless you for that. But do not let your heart be troubled about me. Try to forget me and be happy. It is not for you to bear, this trouble."

"But I must bear it," said Marcia, sitting up and trying to stop crying. "She was my sister and she did an awful thing. I cannot forget it. How could she, how *could* she do it? How could she leave a man like you that –" Marcia stopped, her brown eyes flashing fiercely as she thought of Captain Leavenworth's hateful look at her that night in the moonlight. She shuddered and hid her face in her hands once more and cried with all the fervor of her young and undisciplined soul.

David did not know what to do with a young woman in tears. Had it been Kate his alarm would have vied with a delicious sense of his own power to comfort, but even the thought of comforting anyone but Kate was now a bitter thing. Was it always going to be? Would he always have to start and shrink with sudden remembrance of his pain at every turn of his way? He drew a deep sigh and looked helplessly at his companion. Then he did a hard thing. He tried to justify Kate, just as he had been trying all the morning to justify her to himself. The odd thing about it all was that the very deepest sting of his sorrow was that Kate could have done this thing! His peerless Kate!

"She cared for him," he breathed the words as if they hurt him.

"She should have told you so before then. She should not have let you think she cared for you – *ever!*" said Marcia fiercely. Strangely enough the plain truth was bitter to the man to hear, although he had been feeling it in his soul ever since they had discovered the flight of the bride.

"Perhaps there was too much pressure brought to bear upon her," he said lamely. "Looking back I can see times when she did not second me with regard to hurrying the marriage, so warmly as I could have wished. I laid it to her shyness. Yet she seemed happy when we met. Did you — did she — have you any idea she had been planning this for long, or was it sudden?"

The words were out now, the thing he longed to know. It had been writing its fiery way through his soul. Had she meant to torture him this way all along, or was it the yielding to a sudden impulse that perhaps she had already repented? He looked at Marcia with piteous, almost pleading eyes, and her tortured young soul would have given anything to have been able to tell him what he wanted to know. Yet she could not help him. She knew no more than he. She steadied her own nerves and tried to tell all she knew or surmised, tried her best to reveal Kate in her true character before him. Not that she wished to speak ill of her sister, only that she would be true and give this lover a chance to escape some of the pain if possible, by seeing the real Kate as she was at home without varnish or furbelows. Yet she reflected that those who knew Kate's shallowness well, still loved her in spite of it, and always bowed to her wishes.

Gradually their talk subsided into deep silence once more, broken only by the jog-trot of the horse or the stray note of some bird.

The road wound into the woods with its fragrant scents of hemlock, spruce and wintergreen, and out into a broad, hot, sunny way.

The bees hummed in the flowers, and the grasshoppers sang hotly along the side of the dusty road. Over the whole earth there seemed to be the sound of a soft simmering, as if nature were boiling down her sweets, the better to keep them during the winter.

The strain of the day's excitement and hurry and the weariness of sorrow were beginning to tell upon the two travellers. The road was heavy with dust and the horse plodded monotonously through it. With the drone of the insects and the glare of the afternoon sun, it was not strange that little by little a great drowsiness came over Marcia and her head began to droop like a poor wilted flower until she was fast asleep.

David noticed that she slept, and drew her head against his shoulder that she might rest more comfortably. Then he settled back to his own pain, a deeper pang coming as he thought how different it would have been if the head resting against his shoulder had been golden instead of brown. Then soon he too fell asleep, and the old horse, going slow, and yet more slowly, finding no urging voice behind her and seeing no need to hurry herself, came at last on the way to the shade of an apple tree, and halted, finding it a pleasant place to remain and think until the heat of the afternoon was passed. Awhile she ate the tender grass that grew beneath the generous shade, and nipped daintily at an apple or two that hung within tempting reach. Then she too drooped her white lashes, and nodded and drooped, and took an afternoon nap.

A farmer, trundling by in his empty hay wagon, found them so, looked curiously at them, then drew up his team and came and prodded David in the chest with his long hickory stick.

"Wake up, there, stranger, and move on," he called, as he jumped back into his wagon and took up the reins. "We don't want no tipsy folks around these parts," and with a loud clatter he rode on.

David, whose strong temperance principles had made him somewhat marked in his own neighborhood, roused and flushed over the insinuation, and started up the lazy horse, which flung out guiltily upon the way as if to make up for lost time. The driver, however, was soon lost in his own troubles, which returned upon him with redoubled sharpness as new sorrow always does after brief sleep.

But Marcia slept on.

Chapter 8

Owing to the horse's nap by the roadside, it was quite late in the evening when they reached the town and David saw the lights of his own neighborhood gleaming in the distance. He was glad it was late, for now there would be no one to meet them that night. His friends would think, perhaps, that they had changed their plans and stopped over night on the way, or met with some detention.

Marcia still slept.

David as he drew near the house began to feel that perhaps he had made a mistake in carrying out his marriage just as if nothing had happened and everything was all right. It would be too great a strain upon him to live there in that house without Kate, and come home every night just as he had planned it, and not to find her there to greet him as he had hoped. Oh, if he might turn even now and flee from it, out into the wilderness somewhere and hide himself from human kind, where no one would know, and no one ever ask him about his wife!

He groaned in spirit as the horse drew up to the door, and the heavy head of the sweet girl who was his wife reminded him that he could not go away, but must stay and face the responsibilities of life which he had taken upon himself, and bear the pain that was his. It was not the fault of the girl he had married. She sorrowed for him truly, and he felt deeply grateful for the great thing she had done to save his pride.

He leaned over and touched her shoulder gently to rouse her, but her sleep was deep and healthy, the sleep of exhausted youth. She did not rouse nor even open her eyes, but murmured half audibly, "David has come, Kate, hurry!"

Half guessing what had passed the night he arrived, David stooped and tenderly gathered her up in his arms. He felt a bond of kindliness far deeper than brotherly love. It was a bond of common suffering, and by her own choice she had made herself his comrade in his trouble. He would at least save her what suffering he could.

She did not waken as he carried her into the house, nor when he took her upstairs and laid her gently upon the white bed that had been prepared for the bridal chamber.

The moonlight stole in at the small-paned windows and fell across the floor, showing every object in the room plainly. David lighted a candle and set it upon the high mahogany chest of drawers. The light flickered and played over the sweet face and Marcia slept on.

David went downstairs and put up the horse, and then returned, but Marcia had not stirred. He stood a moment looking at her helplessly. It did not seem right to leave her this way, and yet it was a pity to disturb her sleep, she seemed so weary. It had been a long ride and the day had been filled with unwonted excitement. He felt it himself, and what must it be for her? She was a woman.

David had the old-fashioned gallant idea of a woman.

Clumsily he untied the gay blue ribbons and pulled the jaunty poke bonnet out of her way. The luxuriant hair, unused to the confinement of combs, fell rich about her sleep-flushed face. Contentedly she nestled down, the bonnet out of her way, her red lips parted the least bit with a half-smile, the black lashes lying upon her rosy cheek, one childish hand upon which gleamed the new wedding ring — that was not hers, — lying relaxed and appealing upon her breast, rising and falling with her breath. A lovely bride!

David, stern, true, pained and appreciative, suddenly awakened to what a dreadful thing he had done.

Here was this lovely woman, her womanhood not yet unfolded from the bud, but lovely in promise even as her sister had been in truth, her charms, her dreams, her woman's ways, her love, her very life, taken by him as ruthlessly and as thoughtlessly as though she had been but a wax doll, and put into a home where she could not possibly be what she ought to be, because the place belonged to another. Thrown away upon a man without a heart! That was what she was! A sacrifice to his pride! There was no other way to put it.

It fairly frightened him to think of the promises he had made. "Love, honor, cherish," yes, all those he had promised, and in a way he could perform, but not in the sense that the wedding ceremony had meant, not in the way in which he would have performed them had the bride been Kate, the choice of his love. Oh, why, why had this awful thing come upon him!

And now his conscience told him he had done wrong to take this girl away from the possibilities of joy in the life that might have been hers, and sacrifice her for the sake of saving his own sufferings, and to keep his friends from knowing that the girl he was to marry had jilted him.

As he stood before the lovely, defenseless girl her very beauty and innocence arraigned him. He felt that God would hold him accountable for the act he had so thoughtlessly committed that day, and a burden of responsibility settled upon his weight of sorrow that made him groan aloud. For a moment his soul cried out against it in rebellion. Why could he not have loved this sweet self-sacrificing girl instead of her fickle sister? Why? Why? She might perhaps have loved him in return, but now nothing could ever be! Earth was filled with a black sorrow, and life henceforth meant renunciation and one long struggle to hide his trouble from the world.

But the girl he had selfishly drawn into the darkness of his sorrow with him, she must not be made to suffer more than he could help. He must try to make her happy, and keep her as much as possible from knowing what she had missed by coming with him! His lips in stern resolve, and a purpose, half prayer, went up on record before God, that he would save her as much as he knew how.

Lying helpless so, she appealed to him. Asking nothing she yet demanded all from him in the name of true chivalry. How readily she had given up all for him! How sweetly she had said she would fill the place left vacant by her sister, just to save him pain and humiliation!

A desire to stoop and kiss the fair face came to him, not for affection's sake, but reverently, as if to render to her before God some fitting sign that he knew and understood her act of self sacrifice, and would not presume upon it.

Slowly, as though he were performing a religious ceremony, a sacred duty laid upon him on high, David stooped over her, bringing his face to the gentle sleeping one. Her sweet breath fanned his cheek like the imperceptible fragrance of a bud not fully opened yet to give forth its sweetness to the world. His soul, awake and keen through the thoughts that had just come to him, gave homage to her sweetness, sadly, wistfully, half wishing his spirit free to gather this sweetness for his own.

And so he brought his lips to hers, and kissed her, his bride, yet not his bride. Kissed her for the second time. That thought came to him with the touch of the warm lips and startled him. Had there been something significant in the fact that he had met Marcia first and kissed her instead of Kate by mistake?

It seemed as though the sleeping lips clung to his lingeringly, and half responded to the kiss, as Marcia in her dreams lived over and over again the kiss she had received by her father's gate in the moonlight. Only the dream lover was her own and not another's. David, as he lifted up his head and looked at her gravely, saw a half smile illuminating her lips as if the sleeping soul within had felt the touch and answered to the call.

With a deep sigh he turned away, blew out the candle, and left her with the moonbeams in her chamber. He walked sadly to a rear room of the house and lay down upon the bed, his whole soul crying out in agony at his miserable state.

Kate, the careless one, who had made all this heart-break and misery, had quarreled with her husband already because he did not further some expensive whim of hers. She had told him she was sorry she had not stayed where she was and carried on her marriage with David as she had planned to do. Now she sat sulkily in her room alone, too angry to sleep; while her husband smoked sullenly in the barroom below, and drank frequent glasses of brandy to fortify himself against Kate's moods.

Kate was considering whether or not she had been a fool in marrying the captain instead of David, though she called herself by a much milder word than that. The romance was already worn away. She wished for her trunk and her pretty furbelows. Her father's word of reconciliation would doubtless come in a few days, also the trunks.

After all there was intense satisfaction to Kate in having broken all bounds and done as she pleased. Of course it would have been a bit more comfortable if David had not been so absurdly in earnest, and believed in her so thoroughly. But it was nice to have someone believe in you no matter what you did, and David would always do that. It began to look doubtful if the captain ever would. But David would never marry, she was sure, and perhaps, by and by, when everything had been forgotten and forgiven, she might establish a pleasant relationship with him again. It would be charming to coquet with him. He made love so earnestly, and his great eyes were so handsome when he looked at one with his whole soul in them. Yes, she certainly must keep in with him, for it would be good to have a friend like that when her husband was off at sea with his ship. Now that she was a married woman she would be free of all such childish trammels as being guarded at home and never going anywhere alone. She could go to New York, and she would let David know where she was and he would come up on business and perhaps take her to the theatre. To be sure, she had heard David express views against theatre-going, and she knew he was as much of a church man, almost, as her father, but she was sure she could coax him to do anything for her, and she had always wanted to go to the theatre. His scruples might be strong, but she knew his love for her, and thought it was stronger. She had read in his eyes that it would never fail her. Yes, she thought, she would begin at once to make a friend of David. She would write him a letter asking forgiveness, and she would keep him under her influence. There was no telling what would happen with her husband off at sea so much. It was well to be foresighted, besides, it would be wholesome for the captain to know she had another friend. He might be less stubborn. What a nuisance the marriage vows had to be taken for life! It would be much nicer if they could be put off as easily as they were put on. Rather hard on some women, perhaps, but she could keep any man as long as she chose, and then—she snapped her pretty thumb and finger in the air to express her utter disdain for the man she chose to cast off.

It seemed that Kate, in running away from her father's house and her betrothed bridegroom, and in breaking the laws of respectable society, had with that act given over all attempt at any principle.

So she set herself down to write her letter, with a pout here and a dimple there, and as much pretty gentleness as if she had been talking with her own bewitching face and eyes quite near to his. She knew she could bewitch him if she chose, and she was in the mood just now to choose very much, for she was deeply angry with her husband.

She had ever been utterly heartless when she pleased, knowing that it needed but her returning smile, sweet as a May morning, to bring her much abused subjects fondly to her feet once more. It did not strike her that this time she had sinned not only against her friends, but against heaven, and God-given love, and that a time of reckoning must come to her, — had come, indeed.

She had never believed they would be angry with her, her father least of all. She had no thought they would do anything desperate. She had expected the wedding would be put off indefinitely, that the servants would be sent out hither and yon in hot haste to unbid the guests, upon some pretext of accident or illness, and that it would be left to rest until the village had ceased to wonder and her real marriage with Captain Leavenworth could be announced.

She had counted upon David to stand up for her. She had not understood how her father's righteous soul would be stirred to the depths of shame and utter disgrace over her wanton action. Not that she would have been in the least deterred from doing as she pleased had she understood, only that she counted upon too great power with all of them.

When the letter was written it sounded quite pathetic and penitent, putting all the blame of her action upon her husband, and making herself out a poor, helpless, sweet thing, bewildered by so much love put upon her, and suggesting, just in hint, that perhaps after all she had made a mistake not to have kept David's love instead of a wilder, fiercer one. She ended by begging David to be her friend forever, and leaving an impression with him, though it was slight, that already shadows had crossed her path that made her feel his friendship might be needed some day.

It was a letter calculated to drive such a lover as David had been, half mad with anguish, even without the fact of his hasty marriage added to the situation.

And in due time, by coach, the letter came to David.

Chapter 9

The morning sunbeams fell across the floor when Marcia awoke suddenly to a sense of her new surroundings. For a moment she could not think where she was or how she came there. She looked about the unfamiliar walls, covered with paper decorated in landscapes — a hill in the distance with a tall castle among the trees, a blue lake in the foreground and two maidens sitting pensively upon a green bank with their arms about one another. Marcia liked it. She felt there was a story in it. She would like to imagine about the lives of those two girls when she had more time.

There were no pictures in the room to mar those upon the paper, but the walls did not look bare. Everything was new and stiff and needed a woman's hand to bring the little homey touches, but the newness was a delight to the girl. It was as good as the time when she was a little girl and played house with Mary Ann down on the old flat stone in the pasture, with acorns for cups and saucers, and bits of broken china carefully treasured upon the mossy shelves in among the roots of the old elm tree that arched over the stone.

She was stiff from the long ride, but her sleep had wonderfully refreshed her, and now she was ready to go to work. She wondered as she rose how she got upon that bed, how the blue bonnet got untied and laid upon the chair beside her. Surely she could not have done it herself and have no memory of it. Had she walked upstairs by herself, or did some one carry her? Did David perhaps? Good kind David! A bird hopped upon the window seat and trilled a song, perked his head knowingly at her and flitted away. Marcia went to the window to look after him, and was held by the new sights that met her gaze. She could catch glimpses of houses through bowers of vines, and smoke rising from chimneys. She wondered who lived near, and if there were girls who would prove pleasant companions. Then she suddenly remembered that she was a girl no longer and must associate with married women hereafter.

But suddenly the clock on the church steeple across the way warned her that it was late, and with a sense of deserving reprimand she hurried downstairs.

The fire was already lighted and David had brought in fresh water. So much his intuition had told him was necessary. He had been brought up by three maiden aunts who thought that a man in the kitchen was out of his sphere, so the kitchen was an unknown quantity to him.

Marcia entered the room as if she were not quite certain of her welcome. She was coming into a kingdom she only half understood.

"Good morning," she said shyly, and a lovely color stole into her cheeks. Once more David's conscience smote him as her waking beauty intensified the impression made the night before.

"Good morning," he said gravely, studying her face as he might have studied some poor waif whom he had unknowingly run over in the night and picked up to resuscitate. "Are you rested? You were very tired last night."

"What a baby I was!" said Marcia deprecatingly, with a soft little gurgle of a laugh like a merry brook. David was amazed to find she had two dimples located about where Kate's were, only deeper, and more gentle in their expression.

"Did I sleep all the afternoon after we left the canal? And did you have hard work to get me into the house and upstairs?"

"You slept most soundly," said David, smiling in spite of his heavy heart. "It seemed a pity to waken you, so I did the next best thing and put you to bed as well as I knew how."

"It was very good of you," said Marcia, coming over to him with her hands clasped earnestly, "and I don't know how to thank you."

There was something quaint and old-fashioned in her way of speaking, and it struck David pitifully that she should be thanking her husband, the man who had pledged himself to care for her all his life. It seemed that everywhere he turned his conscience would continually be reproaching him.

It was a dainty breakfast to which they presently sat down. There was plenty of bread and fresh butter just from the hands of the best butter-maker in the county; the eggs had been laid the day before and the bacon was browned just right. Marcia well knew how to make coffee, there was cream rich and yellow as ever came from the cows at home and there was blackberries as large and fine every bit as those Marcia picked but a few days before for the purchase of her pink sprigged chintz.

David watched her deft movements and all at once keen smiting conscience came to remind him that Marcia was defrauded of all the loving interchange of mirth that would have been if Kate had been here. Also, keener still the thought that Kate had not wanted it: that she had preferred the love of another man to his, and that these joys had not been held in dear anticipation with her as they had with him. He had been a fool. All these months of waiting for his marriage he had thought that he and Kate held feelings in common, joys and hopes and tender thoughts of one another; and, behold, he was having these feelings all to himself, fool and blind that he was! A bitter sigh came to his lips, and Marcia, eager in the excitement of getting her first breakfast upon her own responsibility, heard and forgot to smile over the completed work. She could hardly eat what she had prepared, her heart felt David's sadness so keenly.

Shyly she poured the amber coffee and passed it to David. She was pleased that he drank it eagerly and passed his cup back for more. He ate but little, but seemed to approve of all she had done.

After breakfast David went down to the office. He had told Marcia that he would step over and tell his aunts of their arrival, and they would probably come over in the course of the day to greet her. He would be back to dinner at twelve. He suggested that she spend her time in resting, as she must be weary yet. Then hesitating, he went out and closed the door behind him. He waited again on the door stone outside and opened the door to ask:

"You won't be lonesome, will you, child?" He had the feeling of troubled responsibility upon him.

"Oh, no!" said Marcia brightly, smiling back. She thought it so kind of him to take the trouble to think of her. She was quite anticipating a trip of investigation over her new domain, and the pleasure of feeling that she was mistress and might do as she pleased. Yet she stood by the window after he was gone and watched his easy strides down the street with a feeling of mingled pride and disappointment. It was a very nice play she was going through, and David was handsome, and her young heart swelled with pride to belong to him, but after all there was something left out. A great lack, a great unknown longing unsatisfied. What was it? What made it? Was it David's sorrow?

She turned with a sigh as he disappeared around a curve in the sidewalk and was lost to view. Then casting aside the troubles which were trying to settle upon her, she gave herself up to a morning of pure delight.

She flew about the kitchen putting things to rights, washing the delicate sprigged china with its lavender sprays and buff bands, and putting it tenderly upon the shelves behind the glass doors; shoving the table back against the wall demurely with dropped leaves. It did not take long.

There was no need to worry about the dinner. There was a leg of lamb beautifully cooked, half a dozen pies, their flaky crusts bearing witness to the culinary skill of the aunts, a fruit cake, a pound cake, a jar of delectable cookies and another of fat sugary doughnuts, three loaves of bread, and a sheet of puffy rusks with their shining tops dusted with sugar. Besides the preserve closet was rich in all kinds of preserves, jellies and pickles. No, it would not take long to get dinner.

It was into the great parlor that Marcia peeped first. It had been toward that room that her hopes and fears had turned while she washed the dishes.

The Schuylers were one of the few families in those days that possessed a musical instrument, and it had been the delight of Marcia's heart. She seemed to have a natural talent for music, and many an hour she spent at the old spinet drawing tender tones from the yellowed keys. The spinet had been in the family for years and very proud had the Schuyler girls been of it. Kate could rattle off gay waltzes and merry, rollicking tunes that fairly made the feet of the sedate village maidens flutter in time to their melody, but Marcia's music had always been more tender and spiritual. Dear old hymns, she loved, and some of the old classics. "Stupid old things without any tune," Kate called them. But Marcia persevered in playing them until she could bring out the beautiful passages in a way that at least satisfied herself. Her one great desire had been to take lessons of a real musician and be able to play the wonderful things that the old masters had composed. It is true that very few of these had come her way. One somewhat mutilated copy of Handel's "Creation," a copy of Haydn's "Messiah," and a few fragments of an old book of Bach's Fugues and Preludes. Many of these she could not play at all, but others she had managed to pick out. A visit from a cousin who lived in Boston and told of the concerts given there by the Handel and Haydn Society had served to strengthen her deeper interest in music. The one question that had been going over in her mind ever since she awoke had been whether there was a musical instrument in the house. She felt that if there was not she would miss the old spinet in her father's house more than any other thing about her childhood's home.

So with fear and trepidation she entered the darkened room, where the careful aunts had drawn the thick green shades. The furniture stood about in shadowed corners, and every footfall seemed a fearsome thing.

Marcia's bright eyes hurried furtively about, noting the great glass knobs that held the lace curtains with heavy silk cords, the round mahogany table, with its china vase of "everlastings," the high, stiff-backed chairs all decked in elaborate antimacassars of intricate pattern. Then, in the furthest corner, shrouded in dark coverings she found what she was searching for. With a cry she sprang to it, touched its polished wood with gentle fingers, and lovingly felt for the keyboard. It was closed. Marcia pushed up the shade to see better, and opened the instrument cautiously.

It was a pianoforte of the latest pattern, and with exclamations of delight she sat down and began to strike chords, softly at first, as if half afraid, then more boldly. The tone was sweeter than the old spinet, or the harpsichord owned by Squire Hartrandt. Marcia marvelled at the volume of sound. It filled the room and seemed to echo through the empty halls.

She played soft little airs from memory, and her soul was filled with joy. Now she knew she would never be lonely in the new life, for she would always have this wonderful instrument to flee to when she felt homesick.

Across the hall were two rooms, the front one furnished as aa library. Here were rows of books behind glass doors. Marcia looked at them with awe. Might she read them all? She resolved to cultivate her mind that she might be a fit companion for David. She knew he was wise beyond his years for she had heard her father say so. She went nearer and scanned the titles, and at once there looked out to her from the rows of bindings a few familiar faces of books she had read and re-read. *Thaddeus of Warsaw, The Scottish Chiefs, Mysteries of*

Udolpho, Romance of the Forest, Baker's *Livy,* Rollin's *History, Pilgrim's Progress,* and a whole row of Sir Walter Scott's novels. She caught her breath with delight. What a pleasure was opening before her! All of Scott! And she had read but one!

It was with difficulty she tore herself away from the tempting shelves and went on to the rest of the house.

Back of David's library was a sunny sitting room, or breakfast room, — or "dining room" as it would be called at the present time. In Marcia's time the family ate most of their meals in one end of the large bright kitchen, that end furnished with a comfortable lounge, a few bookshelves, a thick ingrain carpet, and a blooming geranium in the wide window seat. But there was always the other room for company, for "high days and holidays."

Out of this morning room the pantry opened with its spicy odors of preserves and fruit cake.

Marcia looked about her well pleased. The house itself was a part of David's inheritance, his mother's family homestead. Things were all on a grand scale for a bride. Most brides began in a very simple way and climbed up year by year. How Kate would have liked it all! David must have had in mind her fastidious tastes, and spent a great deal of money in trying to please her. The piano must have been very expensive. Once more Marcia felt how David had loved Kate and a pang went through her as she wondered however he was to live without her. Her young soul had not yet awakened to the question of how *she* was to live with *him,* while his heart went continually mourning for one who was lost to him forever.

The rooms upstairs were all pleasant, spacious, and comfortably furnished. There was no suggestion of bareness or anything left unfinished. Much of the furniture was old, having belonged to David's mother, and was in a state of fine preservation, a possession of which to be justly proud.

There were four rooms besides the one in which Marcia had slept: a front and back on the opposite side of the hall, a room just back of her own, and one at the end of the hall over the large kitchen.

She entered them all and looked about. The three beside her own in the front part of the house were all large and airy, furnished with high four-posted bedsteads, and pretty chintz hangings. Each was immaculate in its appointments. Cautiously she lifted the latch of the back room. David had not slept in any of the others, for the bedcoverings and pillows were plump and undisturbed. Ah! It was here in the back room that he had carried his heavy heart, as far away from the rest of the house as possible!

The bed was rumpled as if some one had thrown himself heavily down without stopping to undress. There was water in the washbowl and a towel lay carelessly across a chair as if it had been hastily used. There was a newspaper on the bureau and a handkerchief on the floor. Marcia looked sadly about at the signs of occupancy, her eyes dwelling upon each detail. It was here that David had suffered, and her loving heart longed to help him in his suffering.

But there was nothing in the room to keep her, and remembering the fire she had left upon the hearth, which must be almost spent and need replenishing by this time, she turned to go downstairs.

Just at the door something caught her eye under the edge of the chintz valence round the bed. It was but the very tip of the corner of an old daguerreotype, but for some reason Marcia was moved to stoop and draw it from its concealment. Then she saw it was her sister's saucy, pretty face that laughed back at her in defiance from the picture.

As if she had touched something red hot Marcia dropped it, and pushed it with her foot far back under the bed. Then shutting the door quickly she went downstairs. Was it always to be thus? Would Kate ever blight all her joy from this time forth?

Chapter 10

Marcia's cheeks were flushed when David came home to dinner, for at the last she had to hurry.

As he stood in the doorway of the wide kitchen and caught the odor of the steaming platter of green corn she was putting on the table, David suddenly realized that he had scarcely eaten anything for breakfast.

Also, he felt a certain comfort from the sweet steady look of wistful sympathy in Marcia's eyes. Did he fancy it, or was there a new look upon her face, a more reserved bearing, less childish, more touched by sad knowledge of life and its bitterness? It was mere fancy of course, something he had just not noticed. He had seen so little of her before.

In the heart of the maiden there stirred a something which she did not quite understand, something brought to life by the sight of her sister's daguerreotype lying at the edge of the valence, where it must have fallen from David's pocket without his knowledge as he lay asleep. It had seemed to put into tangible form the solid wall of fact that hung between her and any hope of future happiness as a wife, and for the first time she too began to realize what she had sacrificed in thus impetuously throwing her young life into the breach that it might be healed. But she was not sorry, — not yet, anyway, — only frightened, and filled with dreary forebodings.

The meal was a pleasant one, though constrained. David roused himself to be cheerful for Marcia's sake, as he would have done for any stranger, and the girl, suddenly grown sensitive, felt it, and appreciated it, yet did not understand why it made her unhappy.

She was anxious to please him, and kept asking if the potatoes were seasoned right and if his corn were tender, and if he wouldn't have another cup of coffee. Her cheeks were quite red with the effort at matronly dignity when David was finally through his dinner and gone back to the office, and two big tears came and sat in her eyes for a moment, but were persuaded with a determined effort to sink back again into the unfathomable wells that lie in the depths of a woman's eyes. She longed to get out of doors and run wild and free in the old South pasture for relief. She did not know how different it all was from the first dinner of the ordinary young married couple; so stiff and formal, with no gentle touches, no words of love, no glances that told more than words. And yet, child as she was, she felt it, a lack somewhere, she knew not what.

But training is a great thing. Marcia had been trained to be on the alert for the next duty and to do it before she gave herself time for any of her own thoughts. The dinner table was awaiting her attention, and there was company coming.

She glanced at the tall clock in the hall and found she had scarcely an hour before she might expect David's aunts, for David had brought her word that they would come and spend the afternoon and stay for tea.

She shrank from the ordeal and wished David had seen fit to stay and introduce her. It would have been a relief to have had him for a shelter. Somehow she knew that he would have stayed if it had been Kate, and the thought pained her, with a quick sharpness like the sting of an insect. She wondered if she were growing selfish, that it should hurt to find herself of so little account. And, yet, it was to be expected, and she must stop thinking about it. Of course, Kate was the one he had chosen and Kate would always be the only one to him.

It did not take her long to reduce the dinner table to order and put all things in readiness for tea time; and in doing her work Marcia's thoughts flew to pleasanter themes. She wondered what Dolly and Debby, the servants at home, would say if they could see her pretty china and the nice kitchen. They had always been fond of her, and naturally her new honors made her wish to have her old friends see her. What would Mary Ann say? What fun it would be to have Mary Ann there sometime. It would be almost like the days when they had played house under the old elm on the big flat stone, only this would be a real house with real sprigged china instead of bits of broken things. Then she fell into a song, one they sang in school,

> "Sister, thou wast mild and lovely,
> Gentle as the summer breeze,
> Pleasant as the air of evening
> When it floats among the trees."

But the first words set her to thinking of her own sister, and how little the song applied to her, and she thought with a sigh how much better it would have been, how much less bitter, if Kate had been that way and had lain down to die and they could have laid her away in the little hilly graveyard under the weeping willows, and felt about her as they did about the girl for whom that song was written.

The work was done, and Marcia arrayed in one of the simplest of Kate's afternoon frocks, when the brass knocker sounded through the house, startling her with its unfamiliar sound.

Breathlessly she hurried downstairs. The crucial moment had come when she must stand to meet her new relatives alone. With her hand trembling she opened the door, but there was only one person standing on the stoop, a girl of about her own age, perhaps a few months younger. Her hair was red, her face was freckled, and her blue eyes under the red lashes danced with repressed mischief. Her dress was plain and she wore a calico sunbonnet of chocolate color.

"Let me in quick before Grandma sees me," she demanded unceremoniously, entering at once before there was opportunity for invitation. "Grandma thinks I've gone to the store, so she won't expect me for a little while. I was jest crazy to see how you looked. I've ben watchin' out o' the window all the morning, but I couldn't ketch a glimpse of you. When David came out this morning I thought you'd sure be at the kitchen door to kiss him good-bye, but you wasn't, and I watched every chance I could get, but I couldn't see you till you ran out in the garden fer corn. Then I saw you good, fer I was out hangin' up the dish towels. You didn't have a sunbonnet on, so I could see real well. And when I saw how young you was I made up my mind I'd get acquainted in spite of Grandma. You don't mind my comin' over this way without bein' dressed up, do you? There wouldn't be any way to get here without Grandma seeing me, you know, if I'd put on my Sunday clo'es."

"I'm glad you came!" said Marcia impulsively, feeling a rush of something like tears in her throat at the relief of delay from the aunts. "Come in and sit down. Who are you, and why wouldn't your Grandmother like you to come?"

The strange girl laughed a mirthless laugh.

"Me? Oh, I'm Mirandy. Nobody ever calls me anything but Mirandy. My pa left ma when I was a baby an' never come back, an' ma died, and I live with Grandma Heath. An' Grandma's mad 'cause David didn't marry Hannah Heath. She wanted him to an' she did everything she could to make him pay 'tention to Hannah, give her fine silk frocks, two of 'em, and a real pink parasol, but David he never seemed to know the parasol was pink at all, fer he'd never offer to hold it over Hannah even when Grandma made him walk with her home from church ahead of us. So when it came out that David was really going to marry, and wouldn't take Hannah, Grandma got as mad as mad could be and said we never any of us should step over his door sill. But I've stepped, I have, and Grandma can't help herself."

"And who is Hannah Heath?" questioned the dazed young bride. It appeared there was more than a sister to be taken into account.

"Hannah? Oh, Hannah is my cousin, Uncle Jim's oldest daughter, and she's getting on toward thirty somewhere. She has whitey-yellow hair and light blue eyes and is tall and real pretty. She held her head high fer a good many years waitin' fer David, and I guess she feels she made a mistake now. I noticed she bowed real sweet to Hermon Worcester last Sunday and let him hold her parasol all the way to Grandma's gate. Hannah was mad as hops when she heard that you had gold hair and blue eyes, for it did seem hard to be beaten by a girl of the same kind? but you haven't, have you? Your hair is almost black and your eyes are brownie-brown. You're years younger than Hannah, too. My! Won't she be astonished when she sees you! But I don't understand how it got around about your having gold hair. It was a man that stopped at your father's house once told it — "

"It was my sister!" said Marcia, and then blushed crimson to think how near she had come to revealing the truth which must not be known.

"Your sister? Have you got a sister with gold hair?"

"Yes, he must have seen her," said Marcia confusedly. She was not used to evasion.

"How funny!" said Miranda. "Well, I'm glad he did, for it made Hannah so jealous it was funny. But I guess she'll get a set-back when she sees how young you are. You're not as pretty as I thought you would be, but I believe I like you better."

Miranda's frank speech reminded Marcia of Mary Ann and made her feel quite at home with her curious visitor. She did not mind being told she was not up to the mark of beauty. From her point of view she was not nearly so pretty as Kate, and her only fear was that her lack of beauty might reveal the secret and bring confusion to David. But she need not have feared: no one watching the two girls, as they sat in the large sunny room and faced each other, but would have smiled to think the homely crude girl could suggest that the other calm, cool bud of womanhood was not as near perfection of beauty as a bud could expect to come. There was always something childlike about Marcia's face, especially her profile, something deep and other-world-like in her eyes, that gave her an appearance so distinguished from other girls that the word "pretty" did not apply, and surface observers might have passed her by when searching for prettiness, but not so those who saw soul beauties.

But Miranda's time was limited, and she wanted to make as much of it as possible.

"Say, I heard you making music this morning. Won't you do it for me? I'd just love to hear you."

Marcia's face lit up with responsive enthusiasm, and she led the way to the darkened parlor and folded back the covers of the precious piano. She played some tender little airs she loved as she would have played them for Mary Ann, and the two young things stood there together, children in thought and feeling, half a generation apart in position, and neither recognized the difference.

"My land!" said the visitor, " 'f I could play like that I wouldn't care ef I had freckles and no father and red hair," and looking up Marcia saw tears in the light blue eyes, and knew she had a kindred feeling in her heart for Miranda.

They had been talking a minute or two when the knocker suddenly sounded through the long hall again making both girls start. Miranda boldly tiptoed over to the front window and peeped between the green slats of the Venetian blind to see who was at the door, while Marcia started guiltily and quickly closed the instrument.

"It's David's aunts," announced Miranda in a stage whisper hurriedly. "I might 'a' known they would come this afternoon. Well, I had first try at you anyway, and I like you real well. May I come again and hear you play? You go quick to the door, and I'll slip into the kitchen till they get in, and then I'll go out the kitchen door and round the house out the little gate so Grandma won't see me. I must hurry for I ought to have been back ten minutes ago."

"But you haven't been to the store," said Marcia in a dismayed whispered.

"Oh, well, that don't matter! I'll tell her they didn't have what she sent me for. Good-bye. You better hurry." So saying, she disappeared into the kitchen; and Marcia, startled by such easy morality, stood dazed until the knocker sounded forth again, this time a little more peremptorily, as the elder aunt took her turn at it.

And so at last Marcia was face to face with the Misses Spafford.

They came in, each with her knitting in a black silk bag on her slim arm, and greeted the flushed, perturbed Marcia with gentle, righteous, rigid inspection. She felt with the first glance that she was being tried in the fire, and that it was to be no easy ordeal through which she was to pass. They had come determined to sift her to the depths and know at once the worst of what their beloved nephew had brought upon himself. If they found aught wrong with her they meant to be kindly and loving with her, but they meant to take it out of her. This had been the unspoken understanding between them as they wended their dignified, determined way to David's house that afternoon, and this was what Marcia faced as she opened the door for them.

She gasped a little, as any girl overwhelmed thus might have done. She did not tilt her chin in defiance as Kate would have done. The thought of David came to support her, and she grasped for her own little part and tried to play it creditably. She did not know whether the aunts knew of her true identity or not, but she was not left long in doubt.

"My dear, we have long desired to know you, of whom we have heard so much," recited Miss Amelia, with slightly agitated mein, as she bestowed a cool kiss of duty upon Marcia's warm cheek. It chilled the girl, like the breath of a funeral flower.

"Yes, it is indeed a pleasure to us to at last look upon our dear nephew's wife," said Miss Hortense quite precisely, and laid the sister kiss upon the other cheek. In spite of her there flitted through Marcia's brain the verse, "Whosoever shall smite thee on thy right cheek, turn to him the other also." Then she was shocked at her own irreverence and tried to put away a hysterical desire to laugh.

The aunts, too, were somewhat taken aback. They had not looked for so girlish a wife. She was not at all what they had pictured. David had tried to describe Kate to them once, and this young, sweet, disarming thing did not in the least fit their preconceived ideas of her. What should they do? How could they carry on a campaign planned against a certain kind of enemy, when lo, as they came upon the field of action the supposed enemy had taken another and more bewildering form than the one for whom they prepared. They were for the moment silent, gathering their thoughts, and trying to fit their intended tactics to the present situation.

During this operation, Marcia helped them to remove their bonnets and silk capes and to lay them neatly on the parlor sofa. She gave them chairs, suggested palm-leaf fans, and looked about, for the moment forgetting that this was not her old home plentifully supplied with those gracious breeze wafters.

They watched her graceful movements, those two angular old ladies, and marvelled over her roundness and suppleness. They saw with appalled hearts what a power youth and beauty might have over a man. Perhaps she might be even worse than they had feared, though if you could have heard them talk about their nephew's coming bride to their neighbors for months beforehand, you would have supposed they knew her to be a model in every required direction. But their stately pride required that of them, an outward loyalty at least. Now that loyalty was to be tried, and Marcia had two old, narrow and well-fortified hearts to conquer ere her way would be entirely smooth.

Well might Madam Schuyler have been proud of her pupil as alone and unaided she faced the trying situation and mastered it in a sweet and unassuming way.

They began their inquisition at once, so soon as they were seated, and the preliminary sentences uttered. The gleaming knitting needles seemed to Marcia like so many swarming, vindictive bees, menacing her peace of mind.

"You look young, child, to have the care of so large a house as this," said Aunt Amelia, looking at Marcia over her spectacles as if she were expected to take the first bite out of her. "It's a great responsibility!" she shut her thin lips tightly and shook her head, as if she had said: "It's a great *impossibility.*"

"Have you ever had the care of a house?" asked Miss Hortense, going in a little deeper. "David likes everything nice, you know, he has always been used to it."

There was something in the tone, and in the set of the bow on Aunt Hortense's purple trimmed cap that roused the spirit in Marcia.

"I think I rather enjoy housework," she responded coolly. This unexpected statement somewhat mollified the aunts. They had heard to the contrary from some one who had lived in the same town with the Schuylers. Kate's reputation was widely known, as that of a spoiled beauty, who did not care to work, and would do whatever she pleased. The aunts had entertained many forebodings from the few stray hints an old neighbor of Kate's had dared utter in their hearing.

The talk drifted at once to household matters, as though that were the first division of the examination the young bride was expected to undergo. Marcia took early opportunity to further mollify her visitors by her warmest praise of the good things with which the pantry and store-closet had been filled. The expression that came upon the two old faces was that of receiving but what is due. If the praise had not been forthcoming they would have marked it down against her, but it counted for very little with them, warm as it was.

"Can you make good bread?"

The question was flung out by Aunt Hortense like a challenge, and the very set of her nostrils gave Marcia warning. But it was in a relieved voice that ended almost in a ripple of a laugh that she answered quite assuredly: "Oh, yes, indeed. I can make beautiful bread. I just love to make it, too!"

"But how do you make it?" quickly questioned Aunt Amelia, like a repeating rifle. If the first shot had not struck home, the second was likely to. "Do you use hop yeast? Potatoes? I thought so. Don't know how to make salt-rising, do you? It's just what might have been expected."

"David has always been used to salt-rising bread," said Aunt Hortense with a grim set of her lips as though she were delivering a judgement. "He was raised on it."

"If David does not like my bread," said Marcia with a rising color and a nervous little laugh, "then I shall try to make some that he does like."

There was an assurance about the "if" that did not please the oracle.

"David was raised on salt-rising bread," said Aunt Hortense again as if that settled it. "We can send you down a loaf or two every time we bake until you learn how."

"I'm sure it's very kind of you," said Marcia, not at all pleased, "but I do not think that will be necessary. David has always seemed to like our bread when he visited at home. Indeed he often praised it."

"David would not be impolite," said Aunt Amelia, after a suitable pause in which Marcia felt disapprobation in the air. "It would be best for us to send it. David's health might suffer if he was not suitably nourished."

Marcia's cheeks grew redder. Bread had been one of her stepmother's strong points, well infused into her young pupil. Madam Schuyler had never been able to say enough to sufficiently express her scorn of people who made salt-rising bread.

"My stepmother made beautiful bread," she said quite childishly; "she did not think salt-rising bread was so healthy as that made from hop yeast. She disliked the odor in the house from salt-rising bread."

Now indeed the aunts exchanged glances of "On to the combat." Four red spots flamed giddily out in their four sallow cheeks, and eight shining knitting needles suddenly became idle. The moment was too momentous to work. It was as they feared, even the worst. For, be it known, salt-rising bread was one of their tender points, and for it they would fight to the bitter end. They looked at her with four cold, forbidding, steely, spectacled eyes, and Marcia felt that their looks said volumes: "And she so young too! To be so out of the way!" was what they might have expressed to one another. Marcia felt she had been unwise in uttering her honest, indignant sentiments concerning salt-rising bread.

The pause was long and impressive, and the bride felt like a naughty little four-year-old.

At last Aunt Hortense took up her knitting again with the air that all was over and an unrevokable verdict was passed upon the culprit.

"People have never seemed to stay away from our house on that account," she said dryly. "I'm sure I hope it will not be so disagreeable that it will affect your coming to see us sometimes with David."

There was an iciness in her manner that seemed to suggest a long line of offended family portraits of ancestors frowning down upon her.

Marcia's cheeks flamed crimson and her heart fairly stopped beating.

"I beg your pardon," she said quickly, "I did not mean to say anything disagreeable. I am sure I shall be glad to come as often as you will let me." As she said it Marcia wondered if that were quite true. Would she ever be glad to go to the home of those two severe-looking aunts? There were three of them. Perhaps the other one would be even more withered and severe than these two. A slight shudder passed over Marcia, and a sudden realization of a side of married life that had never come into her thoughts before. For a moment she longed with all the intensity of a child for her father's house and the shelter of his loving protection, amply supported by her stepmother's capable, self-sufficient, comforting countenance. Her heart sank with the fear that she would never be able to do justice to the position of David's wife, and David would be disappointed in her and sorry he had accepted her sacrifice. She roused herself to do better, and bit her tongue to remind it that it must make no more blunders. She praised the garden, the house and the furnishings, in voluble, eager, girlish language until the thin lines of lips relaxed and the drawn muscles of the aunt's cheeks took on a less severe aspect. They liked to be appreciated, and they certainly had taken a great deal of pains with the house — for David's sake — not for hers. They did not care to have her deluded by the idea that they had done it for her sake. David was to them a young god, and with this one supreme idea of his supremacy they wished to impress his young wife. It was a foregone conclusion in their minds that no mere pretty young girl was capable of appreciating David, as could they, who had watched him from babyhood, and pampered and petted and been severe with him by turns, until if he had not had the temper of an angel he would surely have been spoiled.

"We did our best to make the house just as David would have wished it," said Aunt Amelia at last, a self-satisfied shadow of what answered for a smile with her, passing over her face for a moment.

"We did not at all approve of this big house, nor indeed of David's setting up in a separate establishment for himself," said Aunt Hortense, taking up her knitting again. "We thought it utterly unnecessary and uneconomical, when he might have brought his wife home to us, but he seemed to think you would want a house to yourself, so we did the best we could."

There was a martyr-like air in Aunt Hortense's words that made Marcia feel herself the criminal, albeit she knew she was suffering vicariously. But in her heart she felt a sudden thankfulness that she was spared the trial of living daily under the scrutiny of these two, and she blest David for his thoughtfulness, even though it had not been meant for her. She went into pleased ecstasies once more over the house, and its furnishings, and ended by her pleasure over the piano.

There was a grim stillness when she touched upon that subject. The aunts did not approve of that musical instrument, that was plain. Marcia wondered if they always paused so long before speaking when they disapproved, in order to show their displeasure. In fact, did they always disapprove of everything?

"You will want to be very careful of it," said Aunt Amelia, looking at the disputed article over her glasses, "it cost a good deal of money. It was the most foolish thing I ever knew David to do, buying that."

"Yes," said Aunt Hortense, "you will not want to use it much, it might get scratched. It has a fine polish. I'd keep it closed up only when I had company. You ought to be very proud to have a husband who could buy a thing like that. There's not many has them. When I was a girl my grandfather had a spinet, the only one for miles around, and it was taken great care of. The case hadn't a scratch on it."

Marcia had started toward the piano intending to open it and play for her new relatives, but she halted midway in the room and came back to her seat after that speech, feeling that she must just sit and hold her hands until it was time to get supper, while these dreadful aunts picked her to pieces, body, soul and spirit.

It was with great relief that at last she heard David's step and knew she might leave the room and put the tea things upon the table.

Chapter 11

They got through the supper without any trouble, and the aunts went home in the early twilight, each with her bonnet strings tied precisely, her lace mitts drawn smoothly over her bony hands, and her little knitting bag over her right arm. They walked decorously up the shaded, elm-domed street, each mindful of her aristocratic instep, and trying to walk erect as in the days when they were gazed upon with admiration, knowing that still an air of former greatness hovered about them wherever they went.

They had brightened considerably at the supper table, under the genial influence of David's presence. They came as near to worshiping David as one can possibly come to worshiping a human being. David, desirous above all things of blinding their keen, sure-to-say-"I-told-you-so" old eyes, roused to be his former gay self with them, and pleased them so that they did not notice how little lover-like reference he made to his bride, who was decidedly in the background for the time, the aunts, perhaps purposely, desiring to show her a wife's true place, — at least the true place of a wife of a David.

They had allowed her to bring them her things and help them on with capes and bonnets, and, when they were ready to leave, Aunt Amelia put out a lifeless hand, that felt in its silk mitt like a dead fish in a net, and said to Marcia:

"Our sister Clarinda is desirous of seeing David's wife. She wished us most particularly to give you her love and say to you that she wishes you to come to her at the earliest possible moment. You know she is lame and cannot easily get about."

"Young folks should always be ready to wait upon their elders," said Aunt Hortense, grimly. "Come as soon as you can, — that is, if you think you can stand the smell of salt-rising."

Marcia's face flushed painfully, and she glanced quickly at David to see if he had noticed what his aunt had said, but David was already anticipating the moment when he would be free to lay aside his mask and bury his face in his hands and his thoughts in sadness.

Marcia's heart sank as she went about clearing off the supper things. Was life always to be thus? Would she be forever under the espionage of those two grim specters of women, who seemed, to her girlish imagination, to have nothing about them warm or loving or woman-like?

She seemed to herself to be standing outside a married life and looking on at it as one might gaze on a panorama. It was all new and painful, and she was one of the central figures expected to act on through all the pictures, taking another's place, yet doing it as if it were her own. She glanced over at David's pale grave face, set in its sadness, and a sharp pain went through her heart. Would he ever get over it? Would life never be more cheerful than it now was?

He spoke to her occasionally, in a pleasant abstracted way, as to one who understood him and was kind not to trouble his sadness, and he lighted a candle for her when the work was done and said he hoped she would rest well, that she must still be weary from the long journey. And so she went up to her room again.

She did not go to bed at once, but sat down by the window looking out on the moonlit street. There had been some sort of a meeting at the church across the way, and the people were filing out and taking their various ways home, calling pleasant good nights, and speaking cheerily of the morrow. The moon, though beginning to wane, was bright and cast sharp shadows. Marcia longed to get out into the night. If she could have got downstairs without being heard she would have slipped out into the garden. But downstairs she could hear David pacing back and forth like some hurt, caged thing. Steadily, dully, he walked from the front hall back into the kitchen and back again. There was no possibility of escaping his notice. Marcia felt as if she might breathe freer in the open air, so she leaned far out of her window and looked up and down the street, and thought. Finally, — her heart swelled to bursting, as young hearts with their first little troubles will do, — she leaned down her dark head upon the window seat and wept and wept, alone.

It was the next morning at breakfast that David told her of the festivities that were planned in honor of their home coming. He spoke as if they were a great trial through which they both must pass in order to have any peace, and expressed his gratitude once more that she had been willing to come here with him and pass through it. Marcia had the impression, after he was done speaking and had gone away to the office, that he felt she had come merely for these few days of ceremony and after they were passed she was dismissed, her duty done, and she might go home. A great lump arose in her throat and she suddenly wished very much that it were so. For if it were, how much, how very much she would enjoy queening it for a few days — except for David's sadness. But already, there had begun to be an element to her in that sadness which in spite of herself she resented. It was a heavy burden which she began dimly to see would be harder and harder to bear as the days went by. She had not yet begun to think of the time before her in years.

They were to go to the aunts' to tea that evening, and after tea a company of David's old friends — or rather the old friends of David's aunts — were coming to meet them. This the aunts had planned: but it seemed they had not counted her worthy to be told of the plans, and had only divulged them to David. Marcia had not thought that a little thing could annoy her so much, but she found it vexed her more and more as she thought upon it going about her work.

There was not so much to be done in the house that morning after the breakfast things were cleared away. Dinners and suppers would not be much of a problem for some days to come, for the house was well stocked with good things.

The beds done and the rooms left in dainty order with the sweet summer breeze blowing the green tassels on the window shades, Marcia went softly down like some half guilty creature to the piano. She opened it and was forthwith lost in delight of the sounds her own fingers brought forth.

She had been playing perhaps half an hour when she became conscious of another presence in the room. She looked up with a start, feeling that some one had been there for some time, she could not tell just how long. Peering into the shadowy room lighted only from the window behind her, she made out a head looking in at the door, the face almost hidden by a capacious sunbonnet. She was not long in recognizing her visitor of the day before. It was like a sudden dropping from a lofty mountain height down into a valley of annoyance to hear Miranda's sharp metallic voice:

"Morning!" she curtsied, coming in as soon as she perceived she was seen. "At it again? I ben listening sometime. It's as pretty as Silas Drew's harmonicker when he comes home evenings behind the cows."

Marcia drew her hands sharply from the keys as if she had been struck. Somehow Miranda and music were inharmonious. She scarcely knew what to say. She felt as if her morning were spoiled. But Miranda was too full of her own errand to notice the clouded face and cool welcome. "Say, you can't guess how I got over here. I'll tell you. You're going over to the Spafford house to-night, ain't you? and there's going to be a lot of folks there. Of course we all know all about it. It's been planned for months. And my cousin Hannah Heath has an invite. You can't think how fond Miss Amelia and Miss Hortense are of her. They tried their level best to make David pay attention to her, but it didn't work. Well, she was talking about what she'd wear. She's had three frocks made last week, all frilled and fancy. You see she don't want to let folks think she is down in the mouth the least bit about David. She'll likely make up to you, to your face, a whole lot, and pretend she's the best friend you've got in the world. But I've just got this to say, don't you be too sure of her friendship. She's smooth as butter, but she can give you a slap in the face if you don't serve her purpose. I don't mind telling you for she's given me many a one," and the pale eyes snapped in unison with the color of her hair. "Well, you see I heard her talking to Grandma, and she said she'd give anything to know what you were going to wear to-night."

"How curious!" said Marcia surprised. "I'm sure I do not see why she should care!" There was the coolness born of utter indifference in her reply that filled the younger girl with admiration. Perhaps too there was the least mite of haughtiness in her manner, born of the knowledge that she belonged to an old and honored family, and that she had in her possession a trunk full of clothes that could vie with any that Hannah Hearth could display. Miranda wished silently that she could convey that cool manner and that wide-eyed indifference to the sight of her cousin Hannah.

"H'm!" giggled Miranda. "Well, she does! If you were going to wear blue you'd see she'd put on her green. She's got one that'll kill any blue that's in the same room with it, no matter if it's on the other side. It's just sick'ning to see them together. And she looks real well in it too. So when she said she wanted to know so bad, Grandma said she'd send me over to know if you'd accept a jar of her fresh pickle-lily, and mebbe I could find out about your clothes. The pickle-lily's on the kitchen table. I left it when I came through. It's good, but there ain't any love in it." And Miranda laughed a hard mirthless laugh, and then settled down to her subject again.

"Now, you needn't be a mite afraid to tell me about it. I won't tell it straight, you know. I'd just like to see what you are going to wear so I could keep her out of her tricks for once. Is your frock blue?"

Now it is true that the trunk upstairs contained a goodly amount of the color blue, for Kate Schuyler had been her bonniest in blue, and the particular frock which had been made with reference to this first very significant gathering was blue. Marcia had accepted the fact as unalterable. The garment was made for a purpose, and its mission must be fulfilled however much she might wish to wear something else, but suddenly as Miranda spoke there came over her mind the thought of rebellion. Why should she be bound down to do as Kate would do in her place? If she had accepted the sacrifice of living Kate's life for her, she might at least have the privilege of living it in the pleasantest possible way, and surely the matter of the dress was one she might be allowed to settle for herself if she was old enough at all to be trusted away from home. Among the pretty things Kate had made was a sweet rose-pink silk tissue. Madam Schuyler had frowned upon it as frivolous, and besides she did not think it becoming to Kate. She had a fixed theory that people with blue eyes and gold hair should never wear pink or red, but Kate as usual had her own way, and with her wild rose complexion had succeeded in looking like the wild rose itself in spite of blue eyes and golden hair. Marcia knew in her heart, in fact she had known from the minute the lovely pink thing had come into the house, that it was the very thing to set her off. Her dark eyes and hair made a charming contrast with the rose, and her complexion was even fresher than Kate's. Her heart grew suddenly eager to don this dainty, frilly thing and outshine Hannah Heath beyond any chance of further trying. There were other frocks, too, in the trunk. Why should she be confined to the stately blue one that had been marked out for this occasion? Marcia, with sudden inspiration, answered calmly, just as though all these tumultuous possibilities of clothes had not been whirling through her brain in that half second's hesitation: "I have not quite decided what I shall wear. It is not an important matter, I'm sure. Let us go and see the piccalilli. I'm very obliged to your grandmother, I'm sure. It was very kind of her."

Somewhat awed, Miranda followed her hostess into the kitchen. She could not reconcile this girl's face with the stately little airs that she wore, but she liked her and forthwith she told her so.

"I like you," she said fervently. "You remind me of one of Grandma's sturtions, bright and independent and lively, with a spice and a color to 'em, and Hannah makes you think of one of them tall spikes of gladiolus all fixed up without any smell."

Marcia tried to smile over the doubtful compliment. Somehow there was something about Miranda that reminded her of Mary Ann. Poor Mary Ann! *Dear* Mary Ann! For suddenly she realized that everything that reminded her of the precious life of her childhood, left behind forever, was dear. If she could see Mary Ann at this moment she would throw her arms about her neck and call her "Dear Mary Ann," and say, "I love you," to her. Perhaps this feeling made her more gentle with the annoying Miranda than she might have been.

When Miranda was gone the precious play hour was gone too. Marcia had only time to steal hurriedly into the parlor, close the instrument, and then fly about getting her dinner ready. But as she worked she had other thoughts to occupy her mind. She was becoming adjusted to her new environment and she found many unexpected things to make it hard. Here, for instance, was Hannah Heath. Why did there have to a Hannah Heath? And what was Hannah Heath to her? Kate might feel jealous, indeed, but not she, not the unloved, unreal, wife of David. She would rather pity Hannah that David had not loved her instead of Kate, or pity David that he had not. But somehow she did not, somehow she could not. Somehow Hannah Heath had become a living, breathing enemy to be met and conquered. Marcia felt her fighting blood rising, felt the Schuyler in her coming to the front. However little there was in her wifehood, its name at least was hers. The tale that Miranda had told was enough, if it were true, to put any woman, however young she might be, into battle array. Marcia was puzzling her mind over the question that has been more or less of a weary burden to every woman since the fatal day that Eve made her great mistake.

David was silent and abstracted at the dinner table, and Marcia absorbed in her own problems did not feel cut by it. She was trying to determine whether to blossom out in pink, or to be crushed and set aside into insignificance in blue, or to choose a happy medium and wear neither. She ventured a timid little question before David went away again: Did he, would he, — that is, was there any thing, — any word he would like to say to her? Would she have to do anything to-night?

David looked at her in surprise. Why, no! He knew of nothing. Just go and speak pleasantly to every one. He was sure she knew what to do. He had always thought her very well behaved. She had manners like any woman. She need not feel shy. No one knew of her peculiar position, and he felt reasonably sure that the story would not soon get around. Her position would be thoroughly established before it did, at least. She need not feel uncomfortable. He looked down at her thinking he had said all that could be expected of him, but somehow he felt the trouble in the girl's eyes and asked her gently if there was anything more.

"No," she said slowly, "unless, perhaps — I don't suppose you know what it would be proper for me to wear."

"Oh, that does not matter in the least," he replied promptly. "Anything. You always look nice. Why, I'll tell you, wear the frock you had on the night I came." Then he suddenly remembered the reason why that was a pleasant memory to him, and that it was not for her sake at all, but for the sake of one who was lost to him forever. His face contracted with sudden pain, and Marcia, cut to the heart, read the meaning, and felt sick and sore too.

"Oh, I could not wear that," she said sadly, "it is only chintz. It would not be nice enough, but thank you. I shall be all right. Don't trouble about me," and she forced a weak smile to light him from the house, and shut from his pained eyes the knowledge of how he had hurt her, for with those words of his had come the vision of herself that happy night as she stood at the gate in the stillness and moonlight looking from the portal of her maidenhood into the vista of her womanhood, which had seemed then so far away and bright, and was now upon her in sad reality. Oh, if she could but have caught that sentence of his about her little chintz frock to her heart with the joy of possession, and known that he said it because he too had a happy memory about her in it, as she had always felt the coming, misty, dream-expected lover would do!

She spread the available frocks out upon the bed after the other things were put neatly away in closet and drawer, and sat down to decide the matter. David's suggestion while impossible had given her an idea, and she proceeded to carry it out. There was a soft sheer white muslin, whereon Kate had expended her daintiest embroidering, edged with the finest of little lace frills. It was quaint and simple and girlish, the sweetest, most simple affair in all of Kate's elaborate wardrobe, and yet, perhaps, from an artistic point of view, the most elegant. Marcia soon made up her mind.

She dressed herself early, for David had said he would be home by four o'clock and they would start as soon after as he could get ready. His aunts wished to show her the old garden before dark.

When she came to the arrangement of her hair she paused. Somehow her soul rebelled at the style of Kate. It did not suit her face. It did not accord with her feeling. It made her seem unlike herself, or unlike the self she would ever wish to be. It suited Kate well, but not her. With sudden determination she pulled it all down again from the top of her head and loosened its rich waves about her face, then loosely twisted it behind, low on her neck, falling over her delicate ears, until her head looked like that of an old Greek statue. It was not fashion, it was pure instinct the child was following out, and there was enough conformity to one of the fashionable modes of the day to keep her from looking odd. It was lovely. Marcia could not help seeing herself that it was much more becoming than the way she had arranged it for her marriage, though then she had had the wedding veil to soften the tightly drawn outlines of her head. She put on the sheer white embroidered frock then, and as a last touch pinned the bit of black velvet about her throat with a single pearl that had been her mother's. It was the bit of black velvet she had worn the night David came. It gave her pleasure to think that in so far she was conforming to his suggestion.

She had just completed her toilet when she heard David's step coming up the walk.

David, coming in out of the sunshine and beholding this beautiful girl in the coolness and shadow of the hall awaiting him shyly, almost started back as he rubbed his eyes and looked at her again. She was beautiful. He had to admit it to himself, even in the midst of his sadness, and he smiled at her, and felt another pang of condemnation that he had taken this beauty from some other man's lot perhaps, and appropriated it to shield himself from the world's exclamation about his own lonely life.

"You have done it admirably. I do not see that there is anything left to be desired," he said in his pleasant voice that used to make her girl-heart flutter with pride that her new brother-to-be was pleased with her. It fluttered now, but there was a wider sweep to its wings, and a longer flight ahead of the thought.

Quite demurely the young wife accepted her compliment, and then she meekly folded her little white muslin cape with its dainty frills about her pretty shoulders, drew on the new lace mitts, and tied beneath her chin the white strings of a shirred gauze bonnet with tiny rosebuds nestling in the ruching of tulle about the face.

Once more the bride walked down the world the observed of all observers, the gazed at of the town, only this time it was brick pavement not oaken stairs she trod, and most of the eyes that looked upon her were sheltered behind green jalousies. None the less, however, she was conscious of them as she made her way to the house of solemn feasting with David by her side. Her eyes rested upon the ground, or glanced quietly at things in the distance, when they were not lifted for a moment in wifely humility to her husband's face at some word of his. Just as she imagined a hundred times in her girlish thoughts that her sister Kate would do, so did she, and after what seemed to her an interminable walk, though in reality it was but four village blocks, they arrived at the house of Spafford.

Chapter 12

"This is your Aunt Clarinda!"

There was a challenge in the severely spoken pronoun Aunt Hortense used. It seemed to Marcia that she wished to remind her that all her old life and relations were passed away, and she had nothing now but David's, especially David's relatives. She shrank from lifting her eyes, expecting to find the third aunt, who was older, as much sourer and sharper in proportion to the other two, but she controlled herself and lifted her flower face to meet a gentle, meek old face set in soft white frills of a cap, with white ribbons flying, and though the old lady leaned upon a crutch she managed to give the impression that she had fairly flown in her gladness to welcome her new niece. There was the lighting of a repressed nature let free in her kind old face as she looked with true pleasure upon the lovely young one, and Marcia felt herself folded in truly loving arms in an embrace which her own passionate, much repressed, loving nature returned with heartiness. At last she had found a friend!

She felt it every time she spoke, more and more. They walked out into the garden almost immediately, and Aunt Clarinda insisted upon hobbling along by Marcia's side, though her sisters both protested that it would be too hard for her that warm afternoon. Every time Marcia spoke she felt the kind old eyes upon her, and she knew that at least one of the aunts was satisfied with her as a wife for David, for her eyes would travel from David to Marcia and back again to David, and when they met Marcia's there was not a shade of disparagement in them.

It was rather a tiresome walk through a tiresome old garden, laid out in the ways of the past generation, and bordered with much funereal box. The sisters, Amelia and Hortense, took the new member of the family, conscientiously, through every path, and faithfully told her how each spot was associated with some happening in the family history. Occasionally there was a solemn pause for the purpose of properly impressing the new member of the house, and Amelia wiped her eyes with her carefully folded handkerchief. Marcia felt extremely like laughing. She was sure that if Kate had been obliged to pass through this ordeal she would have giggled out at once and said some shockingly funny thing that would have horrified the aunts beyond forgiveness. The thought of this nerved her to keep a sober face. She wondered what David thought of it all, but when she looked at him she wondered no longer, for David stood as one waiting for a certain ceremony to be over, a ceremony which he knew to be inevitable, but which was wholly and familiarly uninteresting. He did not even see how it must strike the girl who was going through it all for him, for David's thoughts were out on the flood-tide of sorrow, drifting against the rocks of the might-have-been.

They went in to tea presently, just when the garden was growing loveliest with a tinge of the setting sun, and Marcia longed to run up and down the little paths like a child and call to them all to catch if they could. The house was dark and stately and gloomy.

"You are coming up to my room for a few minutes after supper," whispered Aunt Clarinda encouragingly as they passed into the dark hall. The supper table was alight with a fine old silver candelabra whose wavering lights cast a solemn, grotesque shadow on the different faces.

Beside her plate the young bride saw an ostentatious plate of puffy soda biscuits, and involuntarily her eyes searched the table for the bread plate.

Aunt Clarinda almost immediately pounced upon the bread plate and passed it with a smile to Marcia, and as Marcia with an answering smile took a generous smile she heard the other two aunts exclaim in chorus: "Oh, don't pass her the bread, Clarinda; take it away sister, quick! She does not like salt-rising! It is unpleasant to her!"

Then with blazing cheeks the girl protested that she wished to keep the bread, that they were mistaken, she had not said it was obnoxious to her, but had merely given them her stepmother's opinion when they asked. They must excuse her for her seeming rudeness, for she had not intended to hurt them. She presumed salt-rising bread was very nice; it looked beautiful. This was a long speech for shy Marcia to make before so many strangers, but David's wondering, troubled eyes were upon her, questioning what it all might mean, and she felt she could do anything to save David from more suffering or annoyance of any kind.

David said little. He seemed to perceive that there had been an unpleasant prelude to this, and perhaps knew from former experience that the best thing to do was to change the subject. He launched into a detailed account of their wedding journey. Marcia on her part was grateful to him, for when she took the first brave bite into the very puffy, very white slice of bread she had taken, she perceived that it was much worse than that which had been baked for their home-coming, and not only justified all her stepmother's execrations, but in addition it was sour. For an instant, perceiving down the horoscope of time whole calendars full of such suppers with the aunts, and this bread, her soul shuddered and shrank. Could she ever learn to like it? Impossible! Could she ever tolerate it? Could she? She doubted. Then she swallowed bravely and perceived that the impossible had been accomplished once. It could be again, but she must go slowly else she might have to eat two slices instead of one. David was kind. He had roused himself to help his helper. Perhaps something in her girlish beauty and helplessness, helpless here for his sake, appealed to him. At least his eyes sought hers often with a tender interest to see if she were comfortable, and once, when Aunt Amelia asked if they stopped nowhere for rest on their journey, his eyes sought Marcia's with a twinkling reminder of their roadside nap, and he answered, "Once, Aunt Amelia. No, it was not a regular inn. It was quieter than that. Not many people stopping there."

Marcia's merry laugh almost bubbled forth, but she suppressed it just in time, horrified to think what Aunt Hortense would say, but somehow after David had said that her heart felt a trifle lighter and she took a big bite from the salt-rising and smiled as she swallowed it. There were worse things in the world, after all, than salt-rising, and, when one could smother it in Aunt Amelia's peach preserves, it was quite bearable.

Aunt Clarinda slipped her off to her own room after supper, and left the other two sisters with their beloved idol, David. In their stately parlor lighted with many candles in honor of the occasion, they sat and talked in low tones with him, their voices suggesting condolence with his misfortune of having married out of the family, and disapproval with the married state in general. Poor souls! How their hard, loving hearts would have been wrung could they but have known the true state of the case! And, strange anomaly, how much deeper would have been their antagonism toward poor, self-sacrificing, loving Marcia! Just because she had dared to think herself fit for David, belonging as she did to her renegade sister Kate. But they did not know, and for this fact David was profoundly thankful. Those were not the days of rapid transit, of telegraph and telephone, nor even much letter writing, else the story would probably have reached the aunts even before the bride and bridegroom arrived at home. As it was, David had some hope of keeping the tragedy of his life from the ears of his aunts forever. Patiently he answered their questions concerning the wedding, questions that were intended to bring out facts showing whether David had received his due amount of respect, and whether the family he had so greatly honored felt the burden of that honor sufficiently.

Upstairs in a quaint old-fashioned room Aunt Clarinda was taking Marcia's face in her two wrinkled hands and looking lovingly into her eyes; then she kissed her on each rosy cheek and said:

"Dear child! You look just as I did when I was young. You wouldn't think it from me now, would you? But it's true. I might not have grown to be such a dried-up old thing if I had somebody like David. I'm so glad you've got David. He'll take good care of you. He's a dear boy. He's always been good to me. But you mustn't let the others crush the roses out of your cheeks. They crushed mine out. They wouldn't let me have my life the way I wanted it, and the pink in my cheeks all went back into my heart and burst it a good many years ago. But they can't spoil your life, for you've got David and that's worth every-thing."

Then she kissed her on the lips and cheeks and eyes and let her go. But that one moment had given Marcia a glimpse into another life-story and put her in touch forever with Aunt Clarinda, setting athrob the chord of loving sympathy.

When they came into the parlor the other two aunts looked up with a quick, suspicious glance from one to the other and then fastened disapproving eyes upon Marcia. They rather resented it that she was so pretty. Hannah had been their favorite, and Hannah was beautiful in their eyes. They wanted no other to outshine her. Albeit they would be proud enough before their neighbors to have it said that their nephew's wife was beautiful.

After a chilling pause in which David was wondering anew at Marcia's beauty, Aunt Hortense asked, as though it were an omission from the former examination, "Did you ever make a shirt?"

"Oh, plenty of them!" said Marcia, with a merry laugh, so relieved that she fairly bubbled. "I think I could make a shirt with my eyes shut."

Aunt Clarinda beamed on her with delight. A shirt was something she had never succeeded in making quite right. It was one of the things that her sisters had against her that she could not make good shirts. Any one who could not make a good shirt was deficient. Clarinda was deficient. She could not make a shirt. Meekly she had tried year after year. Humbly had she ripped out gusset and seam and band, having put them on upside down or inside out. Never could she learn the ins and outs of a shirt. But her old heart trembled with delight that the new girl, who was going to take the place in her heart of her old dead self and live out all the beautiful things which had been lost to her, had mastered this one great accomplishment in which she had failed so supremely.

But Aunt Hortense was not pleased. True, it was one of the seven virtues in her mind which a young wife should possess, and she had carefully instructed Hannah Heath for a number of years back, while Hannah bungled out a couple for her father occasionally, but Aunt Hortense had been sure that if Hannah ever became David's wife she might still have the honor of making most of David's shirts. That had been her happy task ever since David had worn a shirt, and she hoped to hold the position of shirt-maker to David until she left this mortal clay. Therefore Aunt Hortense was not pleased, even though David's wife was not lacking, and, too, even though she foreheard herself telling her neighbors next day how many shirts David's wife had made.

"Well, David will not need any for some time," she said grimly. "I made him a dozen before he was married."

Marcia reflected that it seemed to be impossible to make any headway into the good graces of either Aunt Hortense or Aunt Amelia. Aunt Amelia then took her turn at a question.

"Hortense," said she, and there was an ominous inflection in the word as if the question were portentous, "have you asked our new niece by what name she desires us to call her?"

"I have not," said Miss Hortense solemnly, "but I intend to do so immediately," and then both pairs of steely eyes were leveled at the girl. Marcia suddenly was face to face with a question she had not considered, and David started upright from his position on the hair-cloth sofa. But if a thunderbolt had fallen from heaven and rendered him utterly unconscious David would not have been more helpless than he was for the time being. Marcia saw the mingled pain and perplexity in David's face, and her own courage gathered itself to brave it out in some way. The color flew to her cheeks, and rose slowly in David's, through heavy veins that swelled in his neck till he could feel their pulsation against his stock, but his smooth shaven lips were white. He felt that a moment had come which he could not bear to face.

Then with a hesitation that was but pardonable, and with a shy sweet look, Marcia answered; and though her voice trembled just the least bit, her true, dear eyes looked into the battalion of steel ones bravely.

"I would like you to call me Marcia, if you please."

"Marcia!" Miss Hortense snipped the word out as if with scissors of surprise.

But there was a distinct relaxation about Miss Amelia's mouth. She heaved a relieved sigh. Marcia was so much better than Kate, so much more classical, so much more to be compared with Hannah, for instance.

"Well, I'm glad!" she allowed herself to remark. "David has been calling you Kate till it made me sick, such a frivolous name and no sense in it either. Marcia sounds quite sensible. I suppose Katherine is your middle name. Do you spell it with a K or a C?"

But the knocker sounded on the street door and Marcia was spared the torture of a reply. She dared not look at David's face, for she knew there must be pain and mortification mingling there, and she hoped that the trying subject would not come up again for discussion.

The guests began to arrive. Old Mrs. Heath and her daughter-in-law and grand-daughter came first.

Hannah's features were handsome and she knew exactly how to manage her shapely hands with their long white fingers. The soft delicate undersleeves fell away from arms white and well moulded, and she carried her height gracefully. Her hair was elaborately stowed upon the top of her head in many puffs, ending in little ringlets carelessly and coquettishly straying over temple, or ears, or gracefully curved neck. She wore a frock of green, and its color sent a pang through the bride's heart to realize that perhaps it had been worn with an unkindly purpose. Nevertheless Hannah Heath was beautiful and fascinated Marcia. She resolved to try to think the best of her, and to make her a friend if possible. Why, after all, should she be to blame for wanting David? Was he not a man to be admired and desired? It was unwomanly, of course, that she had let it be known, but perhaps her relatives were more to blame than herself. At least Marcia made up her mind to try to like her.

Hannah's frock was of silk, not a common material in those days, soft and shimmery and green enough to take away the heart from anything blue that was ever made, but Hannah was stately and her skin was white as the lily she resembled, in her bright leaf green.

Hannah chose to be effusive and condescending to the bride, giving the impression that she and David had been like brother and sister all their lives and that she might have been his choice if she had chosen, but as she had not chosen, she was glad that David had found some one wherewith to console himself. She did not say this in so many words, but Marcia found that impression left after the evening was over.

With sweet dignity Marcia received her introductions, given in Miss Amelia's most commanding tone, "Our niece, Marcia!"

"Marshy, Marshy!" the bride heard old Mrs. Heath murmur to Miss Spafford. "Why, I thought 'twas to be Kate!"

"Her name is Marcia," said Miss Amelia in a most satisfied tone; "you must have misunderstood."

Marcia caught a look in Miss Heath's eyes, alert, keen, questioning, which flashed all over her like something searching and bright but not friendly.

She felt a painful shyness stealing over her and wished that David were by her side. She looked across the room at him. His face had recovered its usual calmness, though he looked pale. He was talking on his favorite theme with old Mr. Heath: the newly invented steam engine and its possibilities. He had forgotten everything else for the time, and his face lighted with animation as he tried to answer William Heath's arguments against it.

"Have you read what the Boston *Courier* said, David? 'Long in June it was I think," Marcia heard Mr. Heath ask. Indeed his voice was so large that it filled the room, and for the moment Marcia had been left to herself while some new people were being ushered in. "It says, David, that the project of a railroad from Bawston to Albany is impracticable as everybody knows who knows the simplest rule of arithmetic, and the expense would be little less than the market value of the whole territory of Massachusetts; and which, if practicable, every person of common sense knows would be as useless as a railroad from Bawston to the moon. There, David, what do ye think o' that?" and William Heath slapped David on the knee with his broad, fat fist and laughed heartily, as though he had him in a tight corner.

Marcia would have given a good deal to slip in beside David on the sofa and listen to the discussion. She wanted with all her heart to know how he would answer this man who could be so insufferably wise, but there was other work for her, and her attention was brought back to her own uncomfortable part by Hannah Heath's voice:

"Come right ovah heah, Mistah Skinnah, if you want to meet the bride. You must speak verra nice to me or I sha'n't introduce you at all."

A tall lanky man with stiff sandy hair and a rubicund complexion was making his way around the room. He had a small mouth puckered a little as if he might be going to whistle, and his chin had the look of having been pushed back out of the way, a stiff fuzz of sandy whiskers made a hedge down either cheek, and but for that he was clean shaven. The skin over his high cheek bones was stretched smooth and tight as if it were a trifle too close a fit for the genial cushion beneath. He did not look brilliant, and he certainly was not handsome, but there was an inoffensive desire to please about him. He was introduced as Mr. Lemuel Skinner. He bowed low over Marcia's hand, said a few embarrassed, stiff sentences and turned to Hannah Heath with relief. It was evident that Hannah was in his eyes a great and shining light, to which he fluttered as naturally as does the moth to the candle. But Hannah did not scruple to singe his wings whenever she chose. Perhaps she knew, no matter how badly he was burned he would only flutter back again whenever she scintillated. She had turned her back upon him now, and left him to Marcia's tender mercies. Hannah was engaged in talking to a younger man. "Harry Temple, from New York," Lemuel explained to Marcia.

The young man, Harry Temple, had large lazy eyes and heavy dark hair. There was a discontented look in his face, and a looseness about the set of his lips that Marcia did not like, although she had to admit that he was handsome. Something about him reminded her of Captain Leavenworth, and she instinctively shrank from him. But Harry Temple had no mind to talk to any one but Marcia that evening, and he presently so managed it that he and she were ensconced in a corner of the room away from others. Marcia felt perturbed. She did not feel flattered by the man's attentions, and she wanted to be at the other end of the room listening to the conversation.

She listened as intently as she might between sentences, and her keen ears could catch a word or two of what David was saying. After all, it was not so much the new railroad project that she cared about, though that was strange and interesting enough, but she wanted to watch and listen to David.

Harry Temple said a great many pretty things to Marcia. She did not half hear some of them at first, but after a time she began to realize that she must have made a good impression, and the pretty flush in her cheeks grew deeper. She did little talking. Mr. Temple did it all. He told her of New York. He asked if she were not dreadfully bored with this little town and its doings, and bewailed her lot when he learned that she had not had much experience there. Then he asked if she had ever been to New York and began to tell of some of its attractions. Among other things he mentioned some concerts, and immediately Marcia was all attention. Her dark eyes glowed and her speaking face gave eager response to his words. Seeing he had interested her at last, he kept on, for he was possessor of a glib tongue, and what he did not know he could fabricate without the slightest compunction. He had been about the world and gathered up superficial knowledge enough to help him do this admirably, therefore he was able to use a few musical terms, and to bring before Marcia's vivid imagination the scene of the performance of Handel's great "Creation" given in Boston, and of certain musical events that were to be attempted soon in New York. He admitted that he could play a little upon the harpsichord, and, when he learned that Marcia could play also and that she was the possessor of a piano, one of the latest improved makes, he managed to invite himself to play upon it. Marcia found to her dismay that she actually seemed to have invited him to come some afternoon when her husband was away. She had only said politely that she would like to hear him play sometime, and expressed her great delight in music, and he had done the rest, but in her inexperience somehow it had happened and she did not know what to do.

It troubled her a good deal, and she turned again toward the other end of the room, where the attention of most of the company was riveted upon the group who were discussing the railroad, its pros and cons. David was the center of that group.

"Let us go over and hear what they are saying," she said, turning to her companion eagerly.

"Oh, it is all stupid politics and arguments about that ridiculous fairy-tale of a railroad scheme. You would not enjoy it," answered the young man disappointedly. He saw in Marcia a beautiful young soul, the only one who had really attracted him since he had left New York, and he wished to become intimate enough with her to enjoy himself.

It mattered not to him that she was married to another man. He felt secure in his own attractions. He had ever been able to while away the time with whom he chose, why should a simple village maiden resist him? And this was an unusual one, the contour of her head was like a Greek statue.

Nevertheless he was obliged to stroll after her. Once she had spoken. She had suddenly become aware that they had been in their corner together a long time, and that Aunt Amelia's cold eyes were fastened upon her in disapproval.

"The farmers would be ruined, man alive!" Mr. Heath was saying. "Why, all the horses would have to be killed, because they would be wholly useless if this new fandango came in, and then where would be a market for the wheat and oats?"

"Yes, an' I've heard some say the hens wouldn't lay, on account of the noise," ventured Lemuel Skinner in his high voice. "And think of the fires from the sparks of the engine. I tell you it would be dangerous." He looked over at Hannah triumphantly, but Hannah was endeavoring to signal Harry Temple to her side and did not see nor hear.

"I tell you," put in Mr. Heath's heavy voice again, "I tell you, Dave, it can't be done. It's impractical. Why, no car could advance against the wind."

"They told Columbus he couldn't sail around the earth, but he did it!"

There was sudden stillness in the room, for it was Marcia's clear, grave voice that had answered Mr. Heath's excited tones, and she had not known she was going to speak aloud. It came before she realized it. She had been used to speak her mind sometimes with her father, but seldom when there were others by, and now she was covered with confusion to think what she had done. The aunts, Amelia and Hortense, were shocked. It was so unladylike. A woman should not speak on such subjects. She should be silent and leave such topics to her husband.

"Deah me, she's strong minded, isn't she?" giggled Hannah Heath to Lemuel, who had taken the signals to himself and come to her side.

"Quite so, quite so!" murmured Lemuel, his lips looking puffier and more cherry-fied than ever and his chin flattened itself back till he looked like a frustrated old hen who did not understand the perplexities of life and was clucking to find out, after having been startled half out of its senses.

But Marcia was not wholly without consolation, for David had flashed a look of approval at her and had made room for her to sit down by his side on the sofa. It was almost like belonging to him for a minute or two. Marcia felt her heart glow with something new and pleasant.

Mr. William Heath drew his heavy grey brows together and looked at her grimly over his spectacles, poking his bristly under-lip out in astonishment, bewildered that he should have been answered by a gentle, pretty woman, all frills and sparkle like his own daughter. He had been wont to look upon a woman as something like a kitten, — that is, a young woman, — and suddenly the kitten had lifted a velvet paw and struck him squarely in the face. He had felt there were claws in the blow, too, for there had been a truth behind her words that set the room a mocking him.

"Well, Dave, you've got your wife well trained already!" he laughed, concluding it was best to put a smiling front upon the defeat. "She knows just when to come in and help when your side's getting weak!"

They served cake and raspberry vinegar then, and a little while after everybody went home. It was later than the hours usually kept in the village, and the lights in most of the houses were out, or burning dimly in upper stories. The voices of the guests sounded subdued in the misty waning moonlight air. Marcia could hear Hannah Heath's voice ahead giggling affectedly to Harry Temple and Lemuel Skinner, as they walked one on either side of her, while her father and mother and grandmother came more slowly.

David drew Marcia's hand within his arm and walked with her quietly down the street, making their steps hushed instinctively that they might so seem more removed from the others. They were both tired with the unusual excitement and the strain they had been through, and each was glad of the silence of the other.

But when they reached their own doorstep David said: "You spoke well, child. You must have thought about these things."

Marcia felt a sob rising in a tide of joy into her throat. Then he was not angry with her, and he did not disapprove as the two aunts had done. Aunt Clarinda had kissed her good-night and murmured, "You are a bright little girl, Marcia, and you will make a good wife for David. You will come soon to see me, won't you?" and that made her glad, but these words of David's were so good and so unexpected that Marcia could hardly hide her happy tears.

"I was afraid I had been forward," murmured Marcia in the shadow of the front stoop.

"Not at all, child, I like to hear a woman speak her mind, — that is, allowing she has any mind to speak. That can't be said of all women. There's Hannah Heath, for instance. I don't believe she would know a railroad project from an essay on ancient art."

After that the house seemed a pleasant place aglow as they entered it, and Marcia went up to her rest with a lighter heart.

But the child knew not that she had made a great impression that night upon all who saw her as being beautiful and wise.

The aunts would not express it even to each other — for they felt in duty bound to discountenance her boldness in speaking out before the men and making herself so prominent, joining in their discussions, — but each in spite of her convictions felt a deep satisfaction that their neighbors had seen what a beautiful and bright wife David had selected. They even felt triumphant over their favorite Hannah, and thought secretly that Marcia compared well with her in every way, but they would not have told this even to themselves, no, not for worlds.

So the kindly gossipy town slept, and the young bride became a part of its daily life.

Chapter 13

Life began to take on a more familiar and interesting aspect to Marcia after that. She had her daily round of pleasant household duties and she enjoyed them.

There were many other gatherings in honor of the bride and groom, tea-drinkings and evening calls, and a few called in to a neighbor's house to meet them. It was very pleasant to Marcia as she became better acquainted with the people and grew to like some of them, only there was the constant drawback of feeling that it was all a pain and weariness to David.

But Marcia was young, and it was only natural that she should enjoy her sudden promotion to the privileges of a matron, and the marked attention that was paid her. It was a mercy that her head was not turned, living as she did to herself, and with no one in whom she could confide. For David had shrunk within himself to such an extent that she did not like to trouble him with anything.

It was only two days after the evening at the old Spafford house that David came home to tea with ashen face, haggard eyes and white lips. He scarcely tasted his supper and said he would go and lie down, that his head ached. Marcia heard him sigh deeply as he went upstairs. It was that afternoon that the post had brought him Kate's letter.

Sadly Marcia put away the tea things, for she could not eat anything either, though it was an unusually inviting meal she had prepared. Slowly she went up to her room and sat looking out into the quiet, darkening summer night, wondering what additional sorrow had come to David.

David's face looked like death the next morning when he came down. He drank a cup of coffee feverishly, then took his hat as if he would go to the office, but paused at the door and came back saying he wold not go if Marcia would not mind taking a message for him. His head felt badly. She need only tell the man to go on with things as they had planned and say he was detained. Marcia was ready at once to do his bidding with quiet sympathy in her manner.

She delivered her message with the frank straightforward look of a school girl, mingled with a touch of matronly dignity she was trying to assume, which added to her charm; and she smiled her open smile of comradeship, such as she would have dispensed about the old red school house at home, upon boys and girls alike, leaving the clerk and type-setters in a most subjected state, and ready to do anything in the service of their master's wife. It is to be feared that they almost envied David. They watched her as she moved gracefully down the street, and their eyes had a reverent look as they turned away from the window to their work, as though they had been looking upon something sacred.

Harry Temple watched her come out of the office.

She impressed him again as something fresh and different from the common run of maidens in the village. He lazily stepped from the store where he had been lounging and walked down the street to intercept her as she crossed and turned the corner.

"Good morning, Mrs. Spafford," he said, with a courtly grace that was certainly captivating, "are you going to your home? Then our ways lie together. May I walk beside you?"

Marcia smiled and tried to seem gracious, though she would rather have been alone just then, for she wanted to enjoy the day and not be bothered with talking.

Harry Temple mentioned having a letter from a friend in Boston who had lately heard a great chorus rendered. He could not be quite sure of the name of the composer because he had read the letter hurriedly and his friend was a blind-writer, but that made no difference to Harry. He could fill in facts enough about the grandeur of the music from his own imagination to make up for the lack of a little matter like the name of a composer. He was keen enough to see that Marcia was more interested in music than in anything he said, therefore he racked his brains for all the music talk he had ever heard, and made up what he did not know, which was not hard to do, for Marcia was very ignorant on the subject.

At the door they paused. Marcia was eager to get in. She began to wonder how David felt, and she longed to do something for him. Harry Temple looked at her admiringly, noted the dainty set of chin, the clear curve of cheek, the lovely sweep of eyelashes, and resolved to get better acquainted with this woman, so young and lovely.

"I have not forgotten my promise to play for you," he said lightly, watching to see if the flush of rose would steal into her cheek, and that deep light into her expressive eyes. "How about this afternoon? Shall you be at home and disengaged?"

But welcome did not flash into Marcia's face as he had hoped. Instead a troubled look came into her eyes.

"I am afraid it will not be possible this afternoon," said Marcia, the trouble in her eyes creeping into her voice. "That is—I expect to be at home, but—I am not sure of being disengaged."

"Ah! I see!" he raised his eyebrows archly, looking her meanwhile straight in the eyes; "some one else more fortunate than I. Some one else coming?"

Although Marcia did not in the least understand his insinuation, the color flowed into her cheeks in a hurry now, for she instinctively felt that there was something unpleasant in his tone, something below her standard of morals or culture, she did not quite know what. But she felt she must protect herself at any cost. She drew up a little mantle of dignity.

"Oh, no," she said quickly, "I'm not expecting any one at all, but Mr. Spafford had a severe headache this morning, and I am not sure but the sound of the piano would make it worse. I think it would be better for you to come another time, although he may be better by that time."

"Oh, I see! Your husband's at home!" said the young man with relief. His manner implied that he had a perfect understanding of something that Marcia did not mean nor comprehend.

"I understand perfectly," he said, with another meaning smile as though he and she had a secret together; "I'll come some other time," and he took himself very quickly away, much to Marcia's relief. But the trouble did not go out of her eyes as she saw him turn the corner. Instead she went in and stood at the dining room window a long time looking out on the Heaths' hollyhocks beaming in the sun behind the picket fence, and wondered what he could have meant, and why he smiled in that hateful way. She decided she did not like him, and she hoped he would never come. She did not think she would care to hear him play. There was something about him that reminded her of Captain Leavenworth, and now that she saw it in him she would dislike to have him about.

With a sigh she turned to the getting of a dinner which she feared would not be eaten. Nevertheless, she put more dainty thought in it than usual, and when it was done and steaming upon the table she went gently up and tapped on David's door. A voice hoarse with emotion and weariness answered. Marcia scarcely heard the first time.

"Dinner is ready. Isn't your head any better,—David?" There was caressing in his name. It wrung David's heart. Oh, if it were Kate, his Kate, his little bride that were calling him, how his heart would leap with joy! How his headache would disappear and he would be with her in an instant.

For Kate's letter had had its desired effect. All her wrong doings, her crowning outrage of his noble intentions, had been forgotten in the one little plaintive appeal she had managed to breathe in a minor wail throughout that treacherous letter, treacherous alike to her husband and to her lover. Just as Kate had always been able to do with every one about her, she had blinded him to her faults, and managed to put herself in the light of an abused, troubled maiden, who was in a predicament through no fault of her own, and sat in sorrow and a baby-innocence that was bewilderingly sweet.

There had been times when David's anger had been hot enough to waft away this filmy mist of fancies that Kate had woven about herself and let him see the true Kate as she really was. At such times David would confess that she must be wholly heartless. That bright as she was it was impossible for her to have been so easily persuaded into running away with a man she did not love. He had never found it so easy to persuade her against her will. Did she love him? Had she truly loved him, and was she suffering now? His very soul writhed in agony to think of his bride the wife of another against her will. If he might but go and rescue her. If he might but kill that other man! Then his soul would be confronted with the thought of murder. Never before had he felt hate, such hate, for a human being. Then again his heart would soften toward him as he felt how the other must have loved her, Kate, his little wild rose! and there was a fellow feeling between them too, for had she not let him see that she did not half care aright for that other one? Then his mind would stop in a whirl of mingled feeling and he would pause, and pray for steadiness to think and know what was right.

Around and around through this maze of arguing he had gone through the long hours of the morning, always coming sharp against the thought that there was nothing he could possibly do in the matter but bear it, and that Kate, after all, the Kate he loved with his whole soul, had done it and must therefore be to blame. Then he would read her letter over, burning every word of it upon his brain, until the piteous minor appeal would torture him once more and he would begin again to try to get hold of some thread of thought that would unravel this snarl and bring peace.

Like a sound from another world came Marcia's sweet voice, its very sweetness reminding him of that other lost voice, whose tantalizing music floated about his imagination like a string of phantom silver bells that all but sounded and then vanished into silence.

And while all this was going on, this spiritual torture, his living, suffering, physical self was able to summon its thoughts, to answer gently that he did not want any diner; that his head was no better; that he thanked her for her thought of him; and that he would take the tea she offered if it was not too much trouble.

Gladly, with hurried breath and fingers that almost trembled, Marcia hastened to the kitchen once more and prepared a dainty tray, not even glancing at the dinner table all so fine and ready for its guest, and back again she went to his door, an eager light in her eyes, as if she had obtained audience to a king.

He opened the door this time and took the tray from her with a smile. It was a smile of ashen hue, and fell like a pall upon Marcia's soul. It was as if she had been permitted for a moment to gaze upon a martyred soul upon the rack. Marcia fled from it and went to her own room, where she flung herself on her knees beside her bed and buried her face in the pillows. There she knelt, unmindful of the dinner waiting downstairs, unmindful of the bright day that was droning on its hours. Whether she prayed she knew not, whether she was weeping she could not have told. Her heart was crying out in one great longing to have this cloud of sorrow that had settled upon David lifted.

She might have knelt there until night had there not come the sound of a knock upon the front door. It startled her to her feet in an instant, and she hastily smoothed her rumpled hair, dashed some water on her eyes, and ran down.

It was the clerk from the office with a letter for her. The post chaise had brought it that afternoon, and he had thought perhaps she would like to have it at once as it was postmarked from her home. Would she tell Mr. Spafford when he returned—he seemed to take it for granted that David was out of town for the day—that everything had been going on all right at the office during his absence and the paper was ready to send to press.

He took his departure with a series of bows and smiles, and Marcia flew up to her room to read her letter. It was in the round unformed hand of Mary Ann. Marcia tore it open eagerly. Never had Mary Ann's hand-writing looked so pleasant as at that moment. A letter in those days was a rarity at all times, and this one to Marcia in her distress of mind seemed little short of a miracle. It began in Mary Ann's abrupt way, and opened up to her the world of home since she had left it. But a few short days had passed, scarcely yet numbering into weeks, since she left, yet it seemed half a life-time to the girl promoted so suddenly into womanhood without the accompanying joy of love and close companionship that usually makes desolation impossible.

Dear Marsh,—the letter ran:

—I expect you think queer of me to write you so soon. I ain't much on writing you know, but something happened right after you leaving and has kept right on happening that made me feel I kinder like to tell you. Don't you mind the mistakes I make. I'm thankful to goodness you ain't the school teacher or I'd never write 'slong s' I'm living, but ennyhow I'm going to tell you all about it. The night you went away I was standing down by the gate under the old elm. I had on my best things yet from the wedding, and I hated to go in and have the day over and have to begin putting on my old calico tomorrow morn-ing again, and washing dishes just the same. Seemed as if I couldn't bear to have the world just the same now you was gone away. Well, I heard someone coming down the street, and who do you think it was? Why, Hanford Weston. He came right up to the gate and stopped. I don't know's he ever spoke two words to me in my life except that time he stopped the big boys from snow-balling me and told me to run along quick and git in the school house while he fit 'em. Well, he stopped and spoke, and he looked so sad, seemed like I knew just what he was feeling sad about, and I told him all about you getting married instead of your sister. He looked at me like he couldn't move for a while and his face was as white as that marble man in the cemetery over Squire Hancock's grave. He grabbed the gate real hard and I thought he was going to fall. He couldn't even move his lips for a while. I felt just awful sorry for him. Something came in my throat like a big stone and my eyes got all blurred with the moonlight. He looked real handsome. I just couldn't help thinking you ought to see him. By and by he got his voice back again, and we talked a lot about you. He told me how he used to watch you when you was a little girl wearing pantalettes. You used to sit in the church pew across from his father's and he could just see your big eyes over

the top of the door. He says he always thought to himself he would marry you when he grew up. Then when you began to go to school and was so bright he tried hard to study and keep up just to have you think him good enough for you. He owned up he was a bad speller and he'd tried his level best to do better but it didn't seem to come natural, and he thought maybe if he was a good farmer you wouldn't mind about the spelling. He hired out to his father for the summer and he was trying with all his might to get to be the kind of man t'would suit you, and then when he was plowing and planning all what kind of a house with big columns to the front he would build, here comes the coach driving by and you in it! He said he thought the sky and fields was all mixed up and his heart was going out of him. He couldn't work any more and he started out after supper to see what it all meant.

That wasn't just the exact way he told it, Marsh, it was more like poetry, the kind in our reader about Lord Ullin's daughter— you know. We used to recite it on examination exhibition. I didn't know Hanford could talk like that. His words were pretty, kind of sorrowful you know. And it all come over me that you ought to know about it. You're married of course, and can't help it now, but 'taint every girl that has a boy care for her like that from the time she's a baby with a red hood on, and you ought to know 'bout it, fer it wasn't Hanford's fault he didn't have time to tell you. He's just been living fer you fer a number of years, and its kind of hard on him. 'Course you may not care, being you're married and have a fine house and lots of clo'es of your own and a good time, but it does seem hard for him. It seems as if somebody ought to comfort him. I'd like to try if you don't mind. He does seem to like to talk about you to me, and I feel so sorry for him I guess I could comfort him a little, for it seems as if it would be the nicest thing in the world to have some one like you that way for years, just as they do in books, only every time I think about being a comfort to him I think he belongs to you and it ain't right. So Marsh, you just speak out and say if your willing I should try to comfort him a little, and make up to him fer what he lost in you, being as you're married and fixed so nice yourself. Of course, I know I ain't pretty like you, nor can't hold my head proud and step high as you always did, even when you was little, but I can feel, and perhaps that's something. Anyhow Hanford's been down three times to talk about you to me, and if you don't mind I'm going to let him come some more. But if you mind the leastest little bit I want you should say so, for things are mixed in this world and I don't want to get to trmpl any other person's feelings, much less you who have always been my best friend and always will be as long as I live I guess. 'Member how we used to play house on the old flat stone in the orchard, and you give me all the prettiest pieces of china with sprigs on 'em? I ain't forgot that, and never will. I shall always say you made the prettiest bride I ever saw, no matter how many more I see, and I hope you won't forget me. It's lonesome here without you. If it wasn't for comforting Hanford I shouldn't care much for anything. I can't think of you a grown up woman. Do you feel any different? I spose you wouldn't climb a fence nor run through the pasture lot for anything now. Have you got a lot of new *friends? I wish I could see you. And now Marsh, I want you to write right off and tell me what to do about comforting Hanford, and if you've any message to send him I think it would be real nice. I hope you've got a good husband and are happy. From your devoted and loving school mate,*

Mary Ann Fothergill.

Marcia laid down the letter and buried her face in her hands. To her too had come a thrust which must search her life and change it. So while David wrestled with his sorrow Marcia entered upon the knowledge of her own heart.

There was something in the revelation by Mary Ann of Hanford Weston's feelings toward her that touched her immeasurably. Had it all happened before she left him, had Hanford come to her and told her of his love, she would have turned from him in dismay, almost disgust, and have told him that they were both but children, how could they talk of love. She could never have loved him. She would have felt it instantly, and her mocking laugh might have done a good deal toward saving him from sorrow. But now, with miles between them, with the wall of the solemn marriage vows to separate them forever, with her own youth locked up as she supposed until the day of eternity should perhaps set it free, with no hope of any bright dream of life such as girls have, could she turn from even a school boy's love without a passing tenderness, such as she would never have felt if she had not come away from it all? Told in Mary Ann's blunt way, with her crude attempts at pathos, it reached her as it could not otherwise. With her own new view of life she could sympathize better with another's disappointments. Perhaps her own loneliness gave her pity for another. Whatever it was, Marcia's heart suddenly turned toward Hanford Weston with a great throb of gratitude. She felt that she had been loved, even though it had been impossible for that love to be returned, and that whatever happened she would not go unloved down to the end of her days. Suddenly, out of the midst of the perplexity of her thoughts, there formed a distinct knowledge of what was lacking in her life, a lack she had never felt before, and probably would not have felt now had she not thus suddenly stepped into a place much beyond her years. It seemed to the girl as she sat in the great chintz chair and read and re-read that letter, as if she lived years that afternoon, and all her life was to be changed henceforth. It was not that she was sorry that she could not go back, and live out her girlhood and have it crowned with Hanford Weston's love. Not at all. She knew, as well now as she ever had known, that he could never be anything to her, but she knew also, or thought she knew, that he could have given her some-thing, in his clumsy way, that now she could never have from any man, seeing she was David's and David could not love her that way, of course.

Having come to this conclusion, she arose and wrote a letter giving and bequeathing to Mary Ann Fothergill all right, title, and claim to the affections of Hanford Weston, past, present, and future — sending him a message calculated to smooth his ruffled feelings, with her pretty thanks for his youthful adoration; comfort his sorrow with the thought that it must have been a hallucination, that some day he would find his true ideal which he had only thought he had found in her; and send him on his way rejoicing with her blessings and good wishes for a happy life. As for Mary Ann, for once she received her meed of Marcia's love, for homesick Marcia felt more tenderness for her than she had ever been able to feel before; and Marcia's loving messages set Mary Ann in a flutter of delight, as she laid her plans for comforting Hanford Weston.

Chapter 14

David slowly recovered his poise. Faced by that terrible, impenetrable wall of impossibility he stood helpless, his misery eating upon his soul, but there still remained the fact that there was nothing, absolutely nothing, which he could possibly do. At times the truth rose to the surface, the wretched truth, that Kate was at fault, that having done the deed she should abide by it, and not try to keep a hold upon him, but it was not often he was able to think in this way. Most of the time he mourned over and for the lovely girl he had lost.

As for Marcia, she came and went unobtrusively, making quiet comfort for David which he scarcely noticed. At times he roused himself to be polite to her, and made a labored effort to do something to amuse her, just as if she had been visiting him as a favor and he felt in duty bound to make the time pass pleasantly, but she troubled him so little with herself, that nearly always he forgot her. Whenever there was any public function to which they were bidden he always told her apologetically, as though it must be as much of a bore to her as to him, and he regretted that it was necessary to go in order to carry out their mutual agreement. Marcia, hailing with delight every chance to go out in search of something which would keep her from thinking the new thoughts which had come to her, demurely covered her pleasure and dressed herself dutifully in the robes made for her sister, hating them secretly the while, and was always ready when he came for her. David had nothing to complain of in his wife, so far as outward duty was concerned, but he was too busy with his own heart's bitterness to even recognize it.

One afternoon, of a day when David had gone out of town not expecting to return until late in the evening, there came a knock at the door.

There was something womanish in the knock, Marcia thought, as she hastened to answer it, and she wondered, hurriedly smoothing her shining hair, if it could be the aunts come to make their fortnightly-afternoon penance visit. She gave a hasty glance into the parlor hoping all was right, and was relieved to make sure she had closed the piano. The aunts would consider it a great breach of housewifely decorum to allow a moment's dust to settle upon its sacred keys.

But it was not the aunts who stood upon the stoop, smiling and bowing with a handsome assurance of his own welcome. It was Harry Temple.

Marcia was not glad to see him. A sudden feeling of unreasoning alarm took possession of her.

"You're all alone this time, sweet lady, aren't you?" he asked with easy nonchalance, as he lounged into the hall without waiting her bidding.

"Sir!" said Marcia, half frightened, half wondering.

But he smiled reassuringly down upon her and took the door knob in his own hands to close the door.

"Your good man is out this time, isn't he?" he smiled again most delightfully. His face was very handsome when he smiled. He knew this fact well.

Marcia did not smile. Why did he speak as if he knew where David was, and seemed to be pleased that he was away?

"My husband is not in at present," she said guardedly, her innocent eyes searching his face, "did you wish to see him?"

She was beautiful as she stood there in the wide hall, with only the light from the high transom over the door, shedding an afternoon glow through its pleated Swiss oval. She looked more sweet and little-girlish than ever, and he felt a strong desire to take her in his arms and tell her so, only he feared, from something he saw in those wide, sweet eyes, that she might take alarm and run away too soon, so he only smiled and said that his business with her husband could wait until another time, and meantime he had called to fulfil his promise to play for her.

She took him into the darkened parlor, gave him the stiffest and stateliest hair-cloth chair; but he walked straight over to the instrument, and with not at all the reverence she liked to treat it, flung back the coverings, threw the lid open, and sat down.

He had white fingers, and he ran them over the keys with an air of being at home among them, light little airs dripping from his touch like dew from a glistening grass blade. Marcia felt there were butterflies in the air, and buzzing bees, and fairy flowers dancing on the slightest of stems, with a sky so blue it seemed to be filled with the sound of lily bells. The music he played was of the nature of what would be styled to-day "popular," for this man was master of nothing but having a good time. Quick music with a jingle he played, that to the puritanic-bred girl suggested nothing but a heart bubbling over with gladness, but he meant it should make her heart flutter and her foot beat time to the tripping measure. In his world feet were attuned to gay music. But Marcia stood with quiet dignity a little away from the instrument, her lips parted, her eyes bright with the pleasure of the melody, her hands clasped, and her breath coming quickly. She was all absorbed with the music. All unknowingly Marcia had placed herself where the light from the window fell full across her face, and every flitting expression as she followed the undulant sounds was visible. The young man gazed, almost as much pleased with the lovely face as Marcia was with the music.

At last he drew a chair quite near his own seat.

"Come and sit down," he said, "and I will sing to you. You did not know I could sing, too, did you? Oh, I can. But you must sit down for I couldn't sing right when you are standing."

He ended with his fascinating smile, and Marcia shyly sat down, though she drew the chair a bit back from where he had placed it and sat up quite straight and stiff with her shoulders erect and her head up. She had forgotten her distrust of the man in what seemed to her his wonderful music. It was all new and strange to her, and she could not know how little there really was to it. She had decided as he played that she liked the kind best that made her think of the birds and the sunny sky, rather than the wild whirly kind that seemed all a mad scramble.

She meant to ask him to play over again what he played at the beginning, but he struck into a Scotch love ballad. The melody intoxicated her fancy, and her face shone with pleasure. She had not noticed the words particularly, save that they were of love, and she thought with pain of David and Kate, and how the pleading tenderness might have been his heart calling to hers not to forget his love for her. But Harry Temple mistook her expression for one of interest in himself. With his eyes still upon hers, as a cat might mesmerize a bird, he changed into a minor wail of heart-broken love, whose sadness brought great tears to Marcia's eyes, and deep color to her already burning cheeks, while the music throbbed out her own half-realized loneliness and sorrow. It was as if the sounds painted for her a picture of what she had missed out of love, and set her sorrow flowing tangibly.

The last note died away in an impressive diminuendo, and the young man turned toward her. His eyes were languishing, his voice gentle, persuasive, as though it had but been the song come a little nearer.

"And that is the way I feel toward you, dear," he said, and reached out his white hands to where hers lay forgotten in her lap.

But his hands had scarcely touched hers, before Marcia sprang back, in her haste knocking over the chair.

Erect, her hands snatched behind her, frightened, alert, she stood a moment bewildered, all her fears to the front.

Ah! but he was used to shy maidens. He was not to be baffled thus. A little coaxing, a little gentle persuasion, a little boldness—that was all he needed. He had conquered hearts before, why should he not this unsophisticated one?

"Don't be afraid, dear; there is no one about. And surely there is no harm in telling you I love you, and letting you comfort my poor broken heart to think that I have found you too late—"

He had arisen and with a passionate gesture put his arms about Marcia and before she could know what was coming had pressed a kiss upon her lips.

But she was aroused now. Every angry force within her was fully awake. Every sense of right and justice inherited and taught came flocking forward. Horror unspeakable filled her, and wrath, that such a dreadful thing should come to her. There was no time to think. She brought her two strong supple hands up and beat him in the face, mouth, cheeks, and eyes, with all her might, until he turned blinded; and then she struggled away crying, "You are a wicked man!" and fled from the room.

Out through the hall she sped to the kitchen, and flinging wide the door before her, the nearest one at hand, she fairly flew down the garden walk, past the nodding dahlias, past the basking pumpkins, past the whispering corn, down through the berry bushes, at the lower end of the lot, and behind the currant bushes. She crouched a moment looking back to see if she were pursued. Then imagining she heard a noise from the open door, she scrambled over the low back fence, the high comb with which her hair was fastened falling out unheeded behind her, and all her dark waves of hair coming about her shoulders in wild disarray.

She was in a field of wheat now, and the tall shocks were like waves all about her, thick and close, kissing her as she passed with their bended stalks. Ahead of her it looked like an endless sea to cross before she could reach another fence, and a bare field, and then another fence and the woods. She knew not that in her wake she left a tracks clear as if she had set up signals all along the way. She felt that the kind wheat would flow back like real waves and hide the way she had passed over. She only sped on, to the woods. In all the wide world there seemed no refuge but the woods. The woods were home to her. She loved the tall shadows, the whispering music in the upper branches, the quiet places underneath, the hushed silence like a city of refuge with cool wings whereunder to hide. And to it, as her only friend, she was hastening. She went to the woods as she would have flown to the minister's wife at home, if she only had been near, and buried her face in her lap and sobbed out her horror and shame. Breathless she sped, without looking once behind her, now over the next fence and still another. They were nothing to her. She forgot that she was wearing Kate's special sprigged muslin, and that it might tear on the rough fences. She forgot that she was a matron and must not run wild through strange fields. She forgot that some one might be watching her. She forgot everything save that she must get away and hide her poor shamed face.

At last she reached the shelter of the woods, and, with one wild furtive look behind her to assure herself that she was not pursued, she flung herself into the lap of mother earth, and buried her face in the soft moss at the foot of a tree. There she sobbed out her horror and sorrow and loneliness, sobbed until it seemed to her that her heart had gone out with great shudders. Sobbed and sobbed and sobbed! For a time she could not even think clearly. Her brain was confused with the magnitude of what had come to her. She tried to go over the whole happening that afternoon and see if she might have prevented anything. She blamed herself most unmercifully for listening to the foolish music and, too, after her own suspicions had been aroused, though how could she dream any man in his senses would do a thing like that! Not even Captain Leavenworth would stoop to that, she thought. Poor child! She knew so little of the world, and her world had been kept so sweet and pure and free from contamination. She turned cold at the thought of her father's anger if he should hear about this strange young man. She felt sure he would blame her for allowing it. He had tried to teach his girls that they must exercise judgment and discretion, and surely, surely, she must have failed in both or this would not have happened. Oh, why had not the aunts come that afternoon! Why had they not arrived before this man came! And yet, oh, horror! if they had come after he was there! How disgusting he seemed to her with his smirky smile, and slim white fingers! How utterly unfit beside David did he seem to breathe the same air even. David, her David—no, Kate's David! Oh, pity! What a pain the world was!

There was nowhere to turn that she might find a trace of comfort. For what would David say, and how could she ever tell him? Would he find it out if she did not? What would he think of her? Would he blame her? Oh, the agony of it all! What would the aunts think of her! Ah! that was worse than all, for even now she could see the tilt of Aunt Hortense's head, and the purse of Aunt Amelia's lips. How dreadful if they should have to know of it. They would not believe her, unless perhaps Aunt Clarinda might. She did not look wise, but she seemed kind and loving. If it had not been for the other two she might have fled to Aunt Clarinda. Oh, if she might but flee home to her father's house! How could she ever play on that dreadful piano again? She would always see that hateful, smiling face sitting there and think how he had looked at her. Then she shuddered and sobbed harder than ever. And mother earth, true to all her children, received the poor child with open arms. There she lay upon the resinous pine needles, at the foot of the tall trees, and the trees looked down tenderly upon her and consulted in whispers with their heads bent together. The winds blew sweetness from the buckwheat fields in the valley about her, murmuring delicious music in the air above her, and even the birds hushed their loud voices and peeped curiously at the tired, sorrowful creature of another kind that had come among them.

Marcia's overwrought nerves were having their revenge. Tears had their way until she was worn out, and then the angel of sleep came down upon her. There upon the pine-needle bed, with tear-wet cheeks she lay, and slept like a tired child come home to its mother from the tumult of the world.

Harry Temple, recovering from his rebuff, and left alone in the parlor, looked about him with surprise. Never before in all his short and brilliant career as a heart breaker had he met with the like, and this from a mere child! He could not believe his senses! She must have been in play. He would sit still and presently she would come back with eyes full of mischief and beg his pardon. But even as he sat down to wait her coming, something told him he was mistaken and that she would not come. There had been something beside mischief in the smart raps whose tingle even now his cheeks and lips felt. The house, too, had grown strangely hushed as though no one else besides himself were in it. She must have gone out. Perhaps she had been really frightened and would tell somebody! How awkward if she should presently return with one of those grim aunts, or that solemn puritan-like husband of hers. Perhaps he had better decamp while the coast was still clear. She did not seem to be returning and there was no telling what the little fool might do.

With a deliberation which suddenly became feverish in his haste to be away, he compelled himself to walk slowly, nonchalantly out through the hall. Still as a thief he opened and closed the front door and got himself down the front steps, but not so still but that a quick ear caught the sound of the latch as if flew back into place, and the scrape of a boot on the path; and not so invisibly nor so quickly but that a pair of keen eyes saw him.

When Harry Temple had made his way toward the Spafford house that afternoon, with his dauntless front and conceited smile, Miranda had been sent out to pick raspberries along the fence that separated the Heath garden from the Spafford garden.

Harry Temple was too new in the town not to excite comment among the young girls wherever he might go, and Miranda was always having her eye out for anything new. Not for herself! Bless you! No! Miranda never expected anything from a young man for herself, but she was keenly interested in what befell other girls.

So Miranda, crouched behind the berry bushes, watched Harry Temple saunter down the street and saw with surprise that he stopped at the house of her new admiration. Now, although Marcia was a married woman, Miranda felt pleased that she should have the attention of others, and a feeling of pride in her idol, and of triumph over her cousin Hannah that he had not stopped to see her, swelled in her brown calico breast.

She managed to bring her picking as near to the region of the Spafford parlor windows as possible, and much did her ravished ear delight itself in the music that tinkled through the green shaded window, for Miranda had tastes that were greatly appealed to by the gay dance music. She fancied that her idol was the player. But then she heard a man's voice, and her picking stopped short insomuch that her grandmother's strident tones mingled with the liquid tenor or Mr. Temple, calling to Miranda to "be spry there or the sun'll catch you 'fore you get a quart." All at once the music ceased, and then in a minute or two Miranda hear the Spafford kitchen door thrown violently open and saw Marcia rush forth.

She gazed in astonishment, too surprised to call out to her, or to remember to keep on picking for a moment. She watched her as she fairly flew down between the rows of currant bushes, saw the comb fly from her hair, saw the glow of excitement on her cheek, and the fire in her eye, saw her mount the first fence. Then suddenly a feeling of protection arose within her, and, with a hasty glance toward her grandmother's window to satisfy herself that no one else saw the flying figure, she fell to picking with all her might, but what went into her pail, whether raspberries or green leaves or briars, she did not know. Her eyes were on the flying figure through the wheat, and she progressed in her picking very fast toward the lower end of the lot where nothing but runty old sour berries ever grew, if any at all. Once hidden behind the tall corn that grew between her and her grandmother's vigilant gaze, she hastened to the end of the lot and watched Marcia; watched her as she climbed the fences, held her breath at the daring leaps from the top rails, expecting to see the delicate muslin catch on the rough fence and send the flying figure to the ground senseless perhaps. It was like a theatre to Miranda, this watching the beautiful girl in her flight, the long dark hair in the wind, the graceful untrammeled bounds. Miranda watched with unveiled admiration until the dark of the green-blue wood had swallowed her up, then slowly her eyes traveled back over the path which Marcia had taken, back through the meadow and the wheat, to the kitchen door left standing wide. Slowly, painfully, Miranda set herself to understand it. Something had happened! That was flight with fear behind it, fear that left everything else forgotten. What had happened?

Miranda was wiser in her generation than Marcia. She began to put two and two together. Her brows darkened, and a look of cunning came into her honest blue eyes. Stealthily she crept with cat-like quickness along the fence near to the front, and there she stood like a red-haired Nemesis in a sunbonnet, with irate red face, confronting the unsuspecting man as he sauntered forth from the unwelcoming roof where he had whiled away a mistaken hour.

"What you ben sayin' to her?"

It was as if a serpent had stung him, so unexpected, so direct. He jumped aside and turned deadly pale. She knew her chance arrow had struck the truth. But he recovered himself almost immediately when he saw what a harmless looking creature had attacked him.

"Why, my dear girl," he said patronizingly, "you quite startled me! I'm sure you must have made some mistake!"

"I ain't your girl, thank goodness!" snapped Miranda, "and I guess by your looks there ain't anybody 'dear' to you but yourself. But I ain't made a mistake. It's you I was asking. *What you bin in there for?*" There was a blaze of defiance in Miranda's eyes, and her stubby forefinger pointed at him like a shotgun. Before her the bold black eyes quailed for an instant. The young man's hand sought his pocket, brought a piece of money and extended it.

"Look here my friend," he said trying another line, "you take this and say nothing more about it. That's a good girl. No harm's been done."

Miranda looked him in the face with noble scorn, and with a sudden motion of her brown hand sent the coin flying on the stone pavement.

"I tell you I'm not your friend, and I don't want your money. I wouldn't trust its goodness any more than your face. As fer keepin' still I'll do as I see fit about it. I intend to know what this means, and if you've made her any trouble you'd better leave this town, for I'll make it too unpleasant fer you to stay here!"

With a stealthy glance about him, cautious, concerned, the young man suddenly hurried down the street. He wanted no more parley with this loud-voiced avenging maiden. His fear came back upon him in double force, and he was seen to glance at his watch and quicken his pace almost to a run as though a forgotten engagement had suddenly come to mind. Miranda, scowling, stood and watched him disappear around the corner, than she turned back and began to pick raspberries with a diligence that would have astonished her grandmother had she not been for the last hour engaged with a calling neighbor in the room at the other side of the house, where they were overhauling the character of a fellow church member.

Miranda picked on, and thought on, and could not make up her mind what she ought to do. From time to time she glanced anxiously toward the woods, and then at the lowering sun in the West, and half meditated going after Marcia, but a wholesome fear of her grandmother held her hesitating.

At length she heard a firm step coming down the street. Could it be? Yes, it was David Spafford. How was it he happened to come so soon? Miranda had heard in a round-about-way, as neighbors hear and know these things, that David had taken the stage that morning, presumably on business to New York, and was hardly expected to return for several days. She had wondered if Marcia would stay all night alone in the house or if she would go to the aunts. But now here was David!

Miranda looked again over the wheat, half expecting to see the flying figure returning in haste, but the parted wheat waved on and sang its song of the harvest, unmindful and alone, with only a fluttering butterfly to give life to the landscape. A little rusty-throated cricket piped a doleful sentence now and then between the silences.

David Spafford let himself in at his own door, and went in search of Marcia.

He wanted to find Marcia for a purpose. The business which had taken him away in the morning, and which he had hardly expected to accomplish before late that night, had been partly transacted at a little tavern where the coach horses had been changed that morning, and where he had met most unexpectedly the two men whom he had been going to see, who were coming straight to his town. So he turned him back with them and came home, and they were at this minute attending to some other business in the town, while he had come home to announce to Marcia that they would take supper with him and perhaps spend the night.

Marcia was nowhere to be found. He went upstairs and timidly knocked at her door, but no answer came. Then he thought she might be asleep and knocked louder, but only the humming-bird in the honeysuckle outside her window sent back a little humming answer through the latch-hole. Finally he ventured to open the door and peep in, but he saw that quiet loneliness reigned there.

He went downstairs again and searched in the pantry and kitchen and then stood still. The back door was stretched open as though it had been thrown back in haste. He followed its suggestion and went out, looking down the little brick path that led to the garden. Ah! what was that? Something gleamed in the sun with a spot of blue behind it. The bit of blue ribbon she had down at her throat, with a tiny gold brooch unclasped sticking in.

Miranda caught sight of him coming, and crouched behind the currants.

David came on searching the path every side. A bit of branch had been torn from a succulent, tender plant that leaned over the path and was lying in the way. It seemed another blaze along the trail. Further down where the bushes almost met a single fragment of a thread waved on a thorn as though it had snatched for more in the passing and had caught only this. David hardly knew whether he was following these little things or not, but at any rate they were apparently not leading him anywhere for he stopped abruptly in front of the fence and looked both ways behind the bushes that grew along in front of it. Then he turned to go back again. Miranda held her breath. Something touched David's foot in turning, and, looking down, he saw Marcia's large shell comb lying there in the grass. Curiously he picked it up and examined it. It was like finding fragments of a wreck along the sand.

All at once Miranda arose from her hiding place and confronted him timidly. She was not the same Miranda who came down upon Harry Temple, however.

"She ain't in the house," she said hoarsely. "She's gone over there!"

David Spafford turned surprised.

"Is that you, Miranda? Oh, thank you! Where do you say she has gone? Where?"

"Through there, don't you see?" and again the stubby forefinger pointed to the rift in the wheat.

David gazed stupidly at the path in the wheat, but gradually it began to dawn upon him that there was a distinct line through it where some one must have gone.

"Yes, I see," he said thinking aloud, "but why should she have gone there? There is nothing over there."

"She went on further, she went to the woods," said Miranda, looking fearfully around lest even now her grandmother might be upon her, "and she was scared, I guess. She looked it. He hair all come tumblin' down when she clum the fence, an' she just went flyin' over like some bird, didn't care a feather if she did fall, an' she never once looked behind her till she come to the woods."

David's bewilderment was growing uncomfortable. There was a shade of alarm in his face and of the embarrassment one feels when a neighbor divulges news about a member of one's own household.

"Why, surely, Miranda, you must be mistaken. Maybe it was some one else you saw. I do not think Mrs. Spafford would be likely to run over there that way, and what in the world would she have to be frightened at?"

"No, I ain't mistaken," said Miranda half sullenly, nettled at his unbelief. "It was her all right. She came flyin' out the kitchen door when I was picking raspberries, and down that path to the fence, and never stopped fer fence ner wheat, ner medder lot, but went into them woods there, right up to the left of them tall pines, and she, — she looked plum scared to death 's if a whole circus menagerie was after her, lions and 'nelefunts an' all. An' I guess she had plenty to be scared at ef I ain't mistaken. That dandy Temple feller went there to call on her, an' I heard him tinklin' that music box, and it's my opinion he needs a wallupin'! You better go after her! It's gettin' late and you'll have hard times finding her in the dark. Just you foller her path in the wheat, and then make fer them pines. I'd a gone after her myself only grandma'd make sech a fuss, and hev to know it all. You needn't be afraid o' me. I'll keep still."

By this time David was thoroughly alive to the situation and much alarmed. He mounted the fence with alacrity, gave one glance with "thank you" at Miranda, and disappeared through the wheat. Miranda watched him till she was sure he was making for the right spot, then with a sigh of relief she hastened into the house with her now brimming pail of berries.

Chapter 15

As David made his way with rapid strides through the rippling wheat, he experienced a series of sensations. For the first time since his wedding day he was aroused to entirely forget himself and his pain. What did it mean? Marcia frightened! What at? Harry Temple at their house! What did he know of Harry Temple? Nothing beyond the mere fact that Hannah Heath had introduced him and that he was doing business in the town. But why had Mr. Temple visited the house? He could have no possible business with himself, David was sure; moreover he now remembered having seen the young man standing near the stable that morning when he took his seat in the coach, and knew that he must have heard his remark that he would not return till the late coach that night, or possibly not till the next day. He remembered as he said it that he had unconsciously studied Mr. Temple's face and noted its weak points. Did the young man have a purpose in coming to the house during his absence? A great anger rose within him at the thought.

There was one strange thing about David's thoughts. For the first time he looked at himself in the light of Marcia's natural protector — her husband. He suddenly saw a duty from himself to her, aside from the mere feeding and clothing her. He felt a personal responsibility, and an actual interest in her. Out of the whole world, now, he was the only one she could look to for help.

It gave him a feeling of possession that was new, and almost seemed pleasant. He forgot entirely the errand that had made him come to search for Marcia in the first place, and the two men who were probably at that moment preparing to go to his house according to their invitation. He forgot everything but Marcia, and strode into the purply-blue shadows of the wood and stopped to listen.

The hush there seemed intense. There were no echoes lingering of flying feet down that pine-padded pathway of the aisle of the woods. It was long since he had had time to wander in the woods, and he wondered at their silence. So much whispering above, the sky so far away, the breeze so quiet, the bird notes so subdued, it seemed almost uncanny. He had not remembered that is was thus in the woods. It struck him in passing that here would be a good place to bring his pain some day when he had time to face it again, and wished to be alone with it.

He took his hat in his hand and stepped firmly into the vast solemnity as if he had entered a great church when the service was going on, on an errand of life and death that gave excuse for profaning the holy silence. He went a few paces and stopped again, listening. Was that a long-drawn sighing breath he heard, or only the wind soughing through the waving tassels overhead? He summoned his voice to call. It seemed a great effort, and sounded weak and feeble under the grandeur of the vaulted green dome. "Marcia!" he called, —and "Marcia!" realizing as he did so that it was the first time he had called her by her name, or sought after her in any way. He had always said "you" to her, or "child," or spoken of her in company as "Mrs. Spafford," a strange and far-off mythical person whose very intangibility had separated her from himself immeasurably.

He went further into the forest, called again, and yet again, and stood to listen. All was still about him, but in the far distance he heard the faint report of a gun. With a new thought of danger coming to mind he hurried further into the shadows. The gun sounded again more clearly. He shuddered involuntarily and looked about in all directions, hoping to see the gleam of her gown. It was not likely there were any wild beasts about these parts, so near the town and yet, they had been seen occasionally, —a stray fox, or even a bear, —and the sun was certainly very low. He glanced back, and the low line of the horizon gleamed the gold of the intensified shining that is the sun's farewell for the night. The gun again! Stray shots had been known to kill people wandering in the forest. He was growing nervous as a woman now, and went this way and that calling, but still no answer came. He began to think he was not near the clump of pines of which Miranda spoke, and went a little to the right and then turned to look back to where he had entered the wood, and there, almost at his feet, she lay!

She slept as soundly as if she had been lying on a couch of velvet, one round white arm under her cheek. Her face was flushed with weeping, and her lashes still wet. Her tender sensitive mouth still quivered slightly as she gave a long-drawn breath with a catch in it that seemed like a sob, and all her lovely dark hair floated about her as if it were spread upon a wave that upheld her. She was beautiful indeed as she lay there sleeping, and the man, thus suddenly come upon her, anxious and troubled and every nerve quivering, stopped, awed with the beauty of her as if she had been some heavenly being suddenly confronting him. He stepped softly to her side and bending down observed her, first anxiously, to make sure she was alive and safe, then searchingly, as though he would know every detail of the picture before him because it was his, and he not only had a right but a duty to possess it, and to care for it.

She might have been a statue or a painting as he looked upon her and noted the lovely curve of her flushed cheek, but when his eyes reached the firm brown hand and the slender finger on which gleamed the wedding ring that was not really hers, something pathetic in the tear-wet lashes, and the whole sorrowful, beautiful figure touched him with a great tenderness, and he stooped down gently and put his arm about her.

"Marcia,—child!" he said in a low, almost crooning voice, as one might wake a baby from its sleep, "Marcia, open your eyes, child, and tell me if you are all right."

At first she only stirred uneasily and slept on, the sleep of utter exhaustion; but he raised her, and, sitting down beside her, put her head on his shoulder, speaking gently. Then Marcia opened her eyes bewildered, and with a start, sprang back and looked at David, as though she would be sure it was he and not that other dreadful man from whom she had fled.

"Why, child! What's the matter?" said David, brushing her hair back from her face. Bewildered still, Marcia scarcely knew him, his voice was so strangely sweet and sympathetic. The tears were coming back, but she could not stop them. She made one effort to control herself and speak, but her lips quivered a moment, and then the flood-gates opened again, and she covered her face with her hands and shook with sobs. How could she tell David what a dreadful thing had happened, now, when he was kinder to her than he had ever thought of being before! He would grow grave and stern when she had told him, and she could not bear that. He would likely blame her too, and how could she endure more?

But he drew her to him again and laid her head against his coat, trying to smooth her hair with unaccustomed passes of his hand. By and by the tears subsided and she could control herself again. She hushed her sobs and drew back a little from the comforting rough coat where she had lain.

"Indeed, indeed, I could not help it, David,"—she faltered, trying to smile like a bit of rainbow through the rain.

"I know you couldn't, child." His answer was wonderfully kind and his eyes smiled at her as they had never done before. Her heart gave a leap of astonishment and fluttered with gladness over it. It was so good to have David care. She had not known how much she wanted him to speak to her as if he saw her and thought a little about her.

"And now what was it? Remember I do not know. Tell me quick, for it is growing late and damp, and you will take cold out here in the woods with that thin frock on. You are chilly already."

"I better go at once," she said reservedly, willing to put off telling him as long as possible, peradventure to avoid it altogether.

"No, child," he said firmly drawing her back again beside him, "you must rest a minute yet before taking that long walk. You are weary and excited, and besides it will do you good to tell me. What made you run off up here? Are you homesick?"

He scanned her face anxiously. He began to fear with sudden compunction that the sacrifice he had accepted so easily had been too much for the victim, and it suddenly began to be a great comfort to him to have Marcia with him, to help him hide his sorrow from the world. He did not know before that he cared.

"I was frightened," she said with drooping lashes. She was trying to keep her lips and fingers from trembling, for she feared greatly to tell him all. But though the woods were growing dusky he saw the fluttering little fingers and gathered them firmly in his own.

"Now, child," he said in that tone that even his aunts obeyed, "tell me all. What frightened you, and why did you come up here away from everybody instead of calling for help?"

Brought to bay she lifted her beautiful eyes to his face and told him briefly the story, beginning with the night when she had first met Harry Temple. She said as little about music as possible, because she feared that the mention of the piano might be painful to David, but made the whole matter quite plain in a few words, so that David could readily fill in between the lines.

"Scoundrel!" he murmured clenching his fists, " he ought to be strung up!" Then quite gently again, "Poor child! How frightened you must have been! You did right to run away, but it was a dangerous thing to run out here! Why, he might have followed you!"

"Oh!" said Marcia, turning pale, "I never thought of that. I only wanted to get away from everybody. It seemed so dreadful I did not want anybody to know. I did not want you to know. I wanted to run away and hide, and never come back!" She covered her face with her hands and shuddered. David thought the tears were coming back again.

"Child, child!" he said gently, "you must not talk that way. What would I do if you did that?" and he laid his hand softly upon the bowed head.

It was the first time anything like a personal talk had passed between them, and Marcia felt a thrill of delight at his words. It was like heavenly comfort to her wounded spirit.

She stole a shy look at him under her lashes, and wished she dared say something, but no words came. They sat for a moment in silence, each feeling a sort of comforting sense of the other's presence, and each clasping the hand of the other with clinging pressure, yet neither fully aware of the fact.

The last rays of the sun which had been lying for a while at their feet upon the pine needles suddenly slipped away unperceived, and behold! the world was in gloom, and the place where the two sat was almost utterly dark. David became aware of it first, and with sudden remembrance of his expected guests he started in dismay.

"Child!" said he, — but he did not let go of her hand, nor forget to put tenderness in his voice, "the sun has gone down, and here have I been forgetting what I came to tell you in the astonishment over what you had to tell me. We must hurry and get back. We have guests to-night to supper, two gentlemen, very distinguished in their lines of work. We have business together, and I must make haste. I doubt not they are at the house already, and what they think of me I cannot tell; let us hurry as fast as possible."

"Oh, David!" she said in dismay. "And you had to come out here after me, and have stayed so long! What a foolish girl I have been and what a mess I have made! They will perhaps be angry and go away, and I will be to blame. I am afraid you can never forgive me."

"Don't worry, child," he said pleasantly. "It couldn't be helped you know, and is in no wise your fault. I am only sorry that these two gentlemen will delay me in the pleasure of hunting up that scoundrel of a Temple and suggesting that he leave town by the early morning stage. I should like to give him what Miranda suggested, a good 'wallupin,' but perhaps that would be undignified."

He laughed as he said it, a hearty laugh with a ring to it like his old self. Marcia felt happy at the sound. How wonderful it would be if he would be like that to her all the time! Her heart swelled with the great thought of it.

He helped her to her feet and taking her hand led her out to the open field where they could walk faster. As he walked he told her about Miranda waiting for him behind the currant bushes. They laughed together and made the way seem short.

It was quite dark now, with the faded moon trembling feebly in the West as though it meant to retire early, and wished they would hurry home while she held her light for them. David had drawn Marcia's arm within his, and then, noticing that her dress was thin, he pulled off his coat and put it firmly about her despite her protest that she did not need it, and so, warmed, comforted, and cheered Marcia's feet hurried back over the path she had taken in such sorrow and fright a few hours before.

When they could see the lights of the village twinkling close below them David began to tell her about the two men who were to be their guests, if they were still waiting, and so interesting was his brief story of each that Marcia hardly knew they were home before David was helping her over their own back fence.

"Oh, David! There seems to be a light in the kitchen! Do you suppose they have gone in and are getting their own supper? What shall I do with my hair? I cannot go in with it this way. How did that light get there?"

"Here!" said David, fumbling in his pocket, "will this help you?" and he brought out the shell comb he had picked up in the garden.

By the light of the feeble old moon David watched her coil her long wavy hair and stood to pass his criticism upon the effect before they should go in. They were just back of the tall sunflowers, and talked in whispers. It was all so cheery, and comradely, and merry, that Marcia hated to go in and have it over, for she could not feel that this sweet evening hour could last. Then they took hands and swiftly, cautiously, stole up to the kitchen window and looked in. The door stood open as both had left it that afternoon, and there seemed to be nobody in the kitchen. A candle was burning on the high little shelf over the table, and the tea kettle was singing on the crane above the hearth, but the room was without occupant. Cautiously, looking questioningly at each other, they stole into the kitchen, each dreading lest the aunts had come by chance and discovered their lapse. There was a light in the front part of the house and they could hear voices, two men were earnestly discussing politics. They listened longer, but no other presence was revealed.

David in pantomime outlined the course of action, and Marcia, understanding perfectly flew up the back stairs as noiselessly as a mouse, to make her toilet after her nap in the woods, while David with much show and to-do of opening and shutting the wide-open kitchen door walked obviously into the kitchen and hurried to greet his guests wondering, — not suspecting the least, — what good angel had been there to let them in.

Good fortune had favored Miranda. The neighbor had staid longer than usual, perhaps in hopes of an invitation to stay to tea and share in the gingerbread she could smell being taken from the oven by Hannah, who occasionally varied her occupations by a turn at the culinary art. Hannah could make delicious gingerbread. Her grandmother had taught her when she was but a child.

Miranda stole into the kitchen when Hannah's back was turned and picked over the berries so fast that when Hannah came into the pantry to set her gingerbread to cool Miranda had nearly all her berries in a big yellow bowl ready to wash, and Hannah might conjecture if she pleased that Miranda had been some time picking them over. It is not stated how thoroughly those berries were picked over. But Miranda cared little for that. Her mind was upon other things. The pantry window overlooked the hills and the woods. She could see if David and Marcia were coming back soon. She wanted to watch her play till the close, and had no fancy for having the curtain fall in the middle of the most exciting act, the rescue of the princess. But the talk in the sitting room went on and on. By and by Hannah Heath washed her hands, untied her apron, and taking her sunbonnet slipped over to Ann Bertram's for a pattern of her new sleeve. Miranda took the opportunity to be off again.

Swiftly down behind the currants she ran, and standing on the fence between the corn she looked off across the wheat, but no sign of anybody yet coming out of the woods was granted her. She stood so a long time. It was growing dusk. She wondered if Harry Temple had shut the front door when he went out. But David went in that way, and he would have closed it, of course. Still, he went away in a hurry, maybe it would be as well to go and look. She did not wish to be caught by her grandmother, so she stole along like a cat close to the dark berry bushes, and the gathering dusk hid her well. She thought she could see from the front of the fence whether the door looked as if it were closed. But there were people coming up the street. She would wait until they had passed before she looked over the fence.

They were two men coming, slowly, and in earnest conversation upon some deeply interesting theme. Each carried a heavy carpet-bag, and they walked wearily, as if their business were nearly over for the day and they were coming to a place of rest.

"This must be the house, I think," said one. "He said it was exactly opposite the Seceder church. That's the church, I believe. I was here once before."

"There doesn't seem to be a light in the house," said the other, looking up to the windows over the street. "Are you sure? Brother Spafford said he was coming directly home to let his wife know of our arrival."

"A little strange there's no light yet, for it is quite dark now, but I'm sure this must be the house. Maybe they are all in the kitchen and not expecting us quite so soon. Let's try anyhow," said the other, setting down his carpet-bag on the stoop and lifting the big brass knocker.

Miranda stood still debating but a moment. The situation was made plain to her in an instant. Not for nothing had she stood at Grandma Heath's elbow for years watching the movements of her neighbors and interpreting exactly what they meant. Miranda's wits were sharpened for situations of all kinds. Miranda was ready and loyal to those she adored. Without further ado she hastened to a sheltered spot she knew and climbed the picket fence which separated the Heath garden from the Spafford side yard. Before the brass knocker had sounded through the empty house the second time Miranda had crossed the side porch, thrown her sunbonnet upon a chair in the dark kitchen, and was hastening with noisy encouraging steps to the front door.

She flung it wide open, saying in a breezy voice, "Just wait till I get a light, won't you, the wind blew the candle out."

There wasn't a particle of wind about that soft September night, but that made little difference to Miranda. She was part of a play and she was acting her best. If her impromptu part was a little irregular, it was at least well meant, boldly and bravely presented.

Miranda found a candle on the shelf and, stooping to the smoldering fire upon the hearth, blew and coaxed it into flame enough to light it.

"This is Mr. Spafford's home, is it not?" questioned the old gentleman whom Miranda had heard speak first on the sidewalk.

"Oh, yes, indeed," said the girl glibly. "Jest come in and set down. Here, let me take your hats. Jest put your bags right there on the floor."

"You are—Are you—Mrs. Spafford?" hesitated the courtly old gentleman.

"Oh, landy sakes, no, I ain't her," laughed Miranda well pleased. "Mis' Spafford had jest stepped out a bit when her husband come home, an' he's gone after her. You see she didn't expect her husband home till late to-night. But you set down. They'll be home real soon now. They'd oughter ben here before this. I 'spose she'd gone on further'n she thought she'd go when she stepped out."

"It's all right," said the other gentleman, "no harm done, I'm sure. I hope we shan't inconvenience Mrs. Spafford any coming so unexpectedly."

"No, indeedy!" said quick-witted Miranda. "You can't ketch Mis' Spafford unprepared if you come in the middle o' the night. She's allus ready fer comp'ny." Miranda's eyes shone. She felt she was getting on finely doing the honors.

"Well, that's very nice. I'm sure it makes one feel at home. I wonder now if she would mind if we were to go right up to our room and wash our hands. I feel so travel stained. I'd like to be more presentable before we meet her," said the first gentleman, who looked very weary.

But Miranda was not dashed.

"Why, that's all right. 'Course you ken go right up. Jest you set in the keepin' room a minnit while I run up'n be sure the water pitcher's filled. I ain't quire sure 'bout it. I won't be long."

Miranda seated them in the parlor with great gusto and hastened up the back stairs to investigate. She was not at all sure which room would be called the guest room and whether the two strangers would have a room apiece or occupy the same together. At least it would be safe to show them one till the mistress of the house returned. She peeped into Marcia's room, and knew it instinctively before she caught sight of a cameo brooch on the pin cushion, and a rose colored ribbon neatly folded lying on the foot of the bed where it had been forgotten. That question settled, she thought any other room would do, and chose the large front room across the hall with its high four-poster and the little ball fringe on the valance and canopy. Having lighted the candle which stood in a tall glass candlestick on the high chest of drawers, she hurried down to bid her guests come up.

Then she hastened back into the kitchen and went to work with swift skillful fingers. Her breath came quickly and her cheeks grew red with the excitement of it all. It was like playing fairy. She would get supper for them and have everything all ready when the mistress came, so that there would be no bad breaks. She raked the fire and filled the tea kettle, swinging it from the crane. Then she searched where she thought such things should be and found a table cloth and set the table. Her hands trembled as she put out the sprigged china that was kept in the corner cupboard. Perhaps this was wrong, and she would be blamed for it, but at least it was what she would have done, she thought, if she were mistress of this house and had two nice gentlemen come to stay to tea. It was not often that Grandmother Heath allowed her to handle her sprigged china, to be sure, so Miranda felt the joy and daring of it all the more. Once a delicate cup slipped and rolled over on the table and almost reached the edge. A little more and it would have rolled off to the floor and been shivered into a dozen fragments, but Miranda spread her apron in front and caught it fairly as it started and then hugged it in fear and delight for a moment as she might have done a baby that had been in danger. It was a great pleasure to her to set that table. In the first place she was not doing it to order but because she wanted to please and surprise some one whom she adored, and in the second place it was an adventure. Miranda had longed for an adventure all her life and now she thought it had come to her.

When the table was set it looked very pretty. She slipped into the pantry and searched out the stores. It was not hard to find all that was needed; cold ham, cheese, pickles, seed cakes, gingerbread, fruit cake, preserves and jelly, bread and raised biscuit, then she went down cellar and found the milk and cream and butter. She had just finished the table and set out the tea pot and caddy of tea when she heard the two gentlemen coming down the stairs. They went into the parlor and sat down, remarking that their friend had a pleasant home, and then Miranda heard them plunge into a political discussion again and she felt that they were safe for a while. She stole out into the dewy dark to see if there were yet signs of the home-comers. A screech owl hooted across the night. She stood a while by the back fence looking out across the dark sea of whispering wheat. By and by she thought she heard subdued voices above the soft swish of the parting wheat, and by the light of the stars she saw them coming. Quick as a wink she slid over the fence into the Heath back-yard and crouched in her old place behind the currant bushes. So she saw them come up together, saw David help Marcia over the fence and watched them till they had passed up the walk to the light of the kitchen door. Then swiftly she turned and glided to her own home, well knowing the reckoning that would be in store for her for this daring bit of recreation. There was about her, however, an air of triumphant joy as she entered.

"Where have you ben to, Miranda Griscom, and what on airth you ben up to now?" was the greeting she received as she lifted the latch of the old green kitchen door of her grandmother's house.

Miranda knew that the worst was to come now, for her grandmother never mentioned the name of Griscom unless she meant business. It was a hated name to her because of the man who had broken the heart of her daughter. Grandma Heath always felt that Miranda was an out and out Griscom with not a streak of Heath about her. The Griscoms all had red hair. But Miranda lifted her chin high and felt like a princess in disguise.

"Ben huntin' hen's eggs down in the grass," she said, taking the first excuse that came into her head. "Is it time to get supper?"

"Hen's eggs? This time o' night an' dark as pitch. Miranda Griscom, you ken go up to your room an' not come down tell I call you!"

It was a dire punishment, or would have been if Miranda had not had her head full of other things, for the neighbor had been asked to tea and there would have been much to hear at the table. Besides, it was apparent that her disgrace was to be made public. However, Miranda did not care. She hastened to her little attic window, which looked down, as good fortune would have it, upon the dining-room windows of the Spafford house. With joy Miranda observed that no one had thought to draw down the shades and she might sit and watch the supper served over the way, — the supper she had prepared, — and might think how delectable the doughnuts were, and let her mouth water over the currant jelly and the quince preserves and pretend she was a guest, and forget the supper downstairs she was missing.

Chapter 16

David made what apology he could for his absence on the arrival of his guests, and pondered in his heart who it could have been that they referred to as "the maid," until he suddenly remembered Miranda, and inwardly blessed her for her kindliness. It was more than he would have expected from any member of the Heath household. Miranda's honest face among the currant bushes when she had said, "You needn't be afraid of me, I'll keep still," came to mind. Miranda had evidently scented out the true state of the case and filled in the breach, taking care not to divulge a word. He blest her kindly heart and resolved to show his gratitude to her in some way. Could poor Miranda, sitting supperless in the dark, have but known his thought, her lonely heart would have fluttered happily. But she did not, and virtue had to bring its own reward in a sense of duty done. Then, too, there was a spice of adventure to Miranda's monotonous life in what she had done, and she was not altogether sad as she sat and let her imagination revel in what the Spaffords had said and thought, when they found the house lighted and supper ready. It was better than playing house down behind the barn when she was a little girl.

Marcia was the most astonished when she slipped down from her hurried toilet and found the table decked out in all the house afforded, fairly groaning under its weight of pickles, preserves, doughnuts, and pie. In fact, everything that Miranda had found she had put upon that table, and it is safe to say that the result was not quite as it would have been had the preparation of the supper been left to Marcia.

She stood before it and looked, and could not keep from laughing softly to herself at the array of little dishes of things. Marcia thought at first that one of the aunts must be here, in the parlor, probably entertaining the guests, and that the supper was a reproof to her for being away when she should have been at home attending to her duties, but still she was puzzled. It scarcely seemed like the aunts to set a table in such a peculiar manner. The best china was set out, it is true, but so many little bits of things were in separate dishes. There was half a mould of currant jelly in a large china plate, there was a fresh mould of quince jelly quivering on a common dish. All over the table in every available inch there was something. It would not do to call the guests out to a table like that. What would David say? And yet, if one of the aunts had set it and was going to stay to tea, would she be hurt? She tiptoed to the door and listened, but heard no sound save of men's voices. if an aunt had been here she was surely gone now and would be none the wiser if a few dishes were removed.

With swift fingers Marcia weeded out the things, and set straight those that were to remain, and then made the tea. She was so quick about it David had scarcely time to begin to worry because supper was not announced before she stood in the parlor door, shy and sweet, with a brilliant color in her cheeks. His little comrade, David felt her to be, and again it struck him that she was beautiful as he arose to introduce her to the guests. He saw their open admiration as they greeted her, and he found himself wondering what they would have thought of Kate, wild-rose Kate with her graceful witching ways. A tinge of sadness came into his face, but something suggested to him the thought that Marcia was even more beautiful than Kate, more like a half-blown bud of a thing. He wondered that he had never noticed before how her eyes shone. He gave her a pleasant smile as they passed into the hall, which set the color flaming in her cheeks again. David seemed different somehow, and that lonely, set-apart feeling that she had had ever since she came here to live was gone. David was there and he understood, at least a little bit, and they had something — just something, even though it was but a few minutes in a lonely woods and some gentle words of his, — to call their very own together. At least that experience did not belong to Kate, never had been hers, and could not have been borrowed from her. Marcia sighed a happy sigh as she took her seat at the table.

The talk ran upon Andrew Jackson, and some utterances of his in his last message to Congress. The elder of the two gentlemen expressed grave fears that a mistake had been made in policy and that the country would suffer.

Governor Clinton was mentioned and his policy discussed. But all this talk was familiar to Marcia. Her father had been interested in public affairs always, and she had been brought up to listen to discussions deep and long, and to think about such things for herself. When she was quite a little girl her father had made her read the paper aloud to him, from one end to the other, as he lay back in his big chair with his eyes closed and his shaggy brows drawn thoughtfully into a frown. Sometimes as he read he would burst forth with a tirade against this or that man or set of men who were in opposition to his own pronounced views, and he would pour out a lengthy reply to little Marcia as she sat patient, waiting for a chance to go on with her reading. As she grew older she became proud of the distinction of being her father's *confidant* politically, and she was able to talk on such matters as intelligently and as well if not better than most of the men who came to the house. It was a position which no one disputed with her. Kate had been much too full of her own plans and Madam Schuyler too busy with household affairs to bother with politics and newspapers, so Marcia had always been the one called upon to read when her father's eyes were tired. As a consequence she was far beyond other girls of her age in knowledge on public affairs. Well she knew what Andrew Jackson thought about the tariff, and about the system of canals, and about improvements in general. She knew which men in Congress were opposed to and which in favor of certain bills. All through the struggle for improvements in New York state she had been an eager observer. The minutest detail of the Erie Canal project had interested her, and she was never without her own little private opinion in the matter, which, however, seldom found voice except in her eager eyes, whose listening lights would have been an inspiration to the most eloquent speaker.

Therefore, Marcia as she sat behind her sprigged china teacups and demurely poured tea, was taking in all that had been said, and she drew her breath quickly in a way she had when she was deeply excited, as at last the conversation neared the one great subject of interest which to her seemed of most importance in the country at the present day, the project of a railroad run by steam.

Nothing was too great for Marcia to believe. Her father had been inclined to be conservative in great improvements. He had favored the Erie Canal, though had feared it would be impossible to carry so great a project through, and Marcia in her girlish mind had rejoiced with a joy that to her was unspeakable when it had been completed and news had come that many packets were travelling day and night upon the wonderful new water way. There had been a kind of triumph in her heart to think that men who could study out these big schemes and plan it all, had been able against so great odds to carry out their project and prove to all unbelievers that it was not only possible but practicable.

Marcia's brain was throbbing with the desire for progress. If she were a man with money and influence she felt she would so much like to go out into the world and make stupid people do the things for the country that ought to be done. Progress had been the keynote of her upbringing, and she was teeming with energy which she had no hope could ever be used to help along that for which she felt her ambitions rising. She wanted to see the world alive, and busy, the great cities connected with one another. She longed to have free access to cities, to great libraries, to pictures, to wonderful music. She longed to meet great men and women, the men and women who were making the history of the world, writing, speaking, and doing things that were moulding public opinion. Reforms of all sorts were what helped along and made possible her desires. Why did not the people want a steam railroad? Why were they so ready to say it could never succeed, that it would be an impossibility; that the roads could not be made strong enough to bear so great weights and so constant wear and tear? Why did they interpose objections to every suggestion made by inventors and thinking men? Why did even her dear father who was so far in advance of his times in many ways, why did even he too shake his head and say that he feared it would never be in this country, at least not in his day, that it was impracticable?

The talk was very interesting to Marcia. She ate bits of her biscuit without knowing, and she left her tea untasted till it was cold. The younger of the two guests was talking. His name was Jervis. Marcia thought she had heard the name somewhere, but had not yet placed him in her mind.

"Yes," said he, with an eager look on his face, "it is coming, it is coming sooner than they think. Oliver Evans said, you know, that good roads were all we could expect one generation to do. The next must make canals, the next might build a railroad which should run by horse power, and perhaps the next would run a railroad by steam. But we shall not have to wait so long. We shall have steam moving railway carriages before another year."

"What!" said David, "you don't mean it! Have you really any foundation for such a statement?" He leaned forward, his eyes shining and his whole attitude one of deep interest. Marcia watched him, and a great pride began to glow within her that she belonged to him. She looked at the other men. Their eyes were fixed upon David with a heightening pleasure and pride.

The older man watched the little tableau a moment and then he explained: "The Mohawk and Hudson Company have just made an engagement with Mr. Jervis as chief engineer of their road. He expects to run that road by steam!"

He finished his fruit cake and preserves under the spell of astonishment he had cast upon his host and hostess.

David and Marcia turned simultaneously toward Mr. Jervis for a confirmation of this statement. Mr. Jervis smiled in affirmation.

"But will it not be like all the rest, no funds?" asked David a trifle sadly. "It may be years even yet before it is really started."

But Mr. Jervis' face was reassuring.

"The contract is let for the grading. In fact work has already begun. I expect to begin laying the track by next Spring, perhaps sooner. As soon as the track is laid we shall show them."

David's eyes shone and he reached out and grasped the hand of the man who had the will and apparently the means of accomplishing this great thing for the country.

"It will make a wonderful change in the whole land," said David musingly. He had forgotten to eat. His face was aglow and a side of his nature which Marcia did not know was uppermost. Marcia saw the man, the thinker, the writer, the former of public opinion, the idealist. Heretofore David had been to her in the light of her sister's lover, a young man of promise, but that was all. Now she saw something more earnest, and at once it was revealed to her what a man he was, a man like her father. David's eyes were suddenly drawn to meet hers. He looked on Marcia and seemed to be sharing his thought with her, and smiled a smile of comradeship. He felt all at once that she could and would understand his feelings about this great new enterprise, and would be glad too. It pleased him to feel this. It took a little of his loneliness away. Kate would never have been interested in these things. He had never expected such sympathy from her. She had been something beautiful and apart from his world, and as such he had adored her. But it was pleasant to have some one who could understand and feel as he did. Just then he was not thinking of his lost Kate.

So he smiled and Marcia felt the glow of warmth from his look and returned it, and the two visitors knew that they were among friends who understood and sympathized.

"Yes, it will make a change," said the older man. "I hope I may live to see at least a part of it."

"If you succeed there will be many others to follow. The land will soon be a network of railroads," went on David, still musing.

"We shall succeed!" said Mr. Jervis, closing his lips firmly in a way that made one sure he knew whereof he spoke.

"And now tell me about it," said David, with his most engaging smile, as a child will ask to have a story. David could be most fascinating when he felt he was in a sympathetic company. At other times he was wont to be grave, almost to severity. But those who knew him best and had seen him thus melted into childlike enthusiasm, felt his lovableness as the others never dreamed.

The table talk launched into a description of the proposed road, the road bed, the manner of laying the rails, their thickness and width, and the way of bolting them down to the heavy timbers that lay underneath. It was all intensely fascinating to Marcia. Mr. Jervis took knives and forks to illustrate and then showed by plates and spoons how they were fastened down.

David asked a question now and then, took out his note book and wrote down some things. The two guests were eager and plain in their answers. They wanted David to write it up. They wanted the information to be accurate and full.

"The other day I saw a question in a Baltimore paper, sent in by a subscriber, 'What is a railroad?'" said the old gentleman, "and the editor's reply was, 'Can any of our readers answer this question and tell us what is a railroad?'"

There was a hearty laugh over the unenlightened unbelievers who seemed to be only too willing to remain in ignorance of the march of improvement.

David finally laid down his note book, feeling that he had gained all the information he needed at present. "I have much faith in you and your skill, but I do not quite see how you are going to overcome all the obstacles. How, for instance, are you going to overcome the inequalities in the road? Our country is not a flat even one like those abroad where the railroad has been tried. There are sharp grades, and many curves will be necessary," said he.

Mr. Jervis had shoved his chair back from the table, but now he drew it up again sharply and began to move the dishes back from his place, a look of eagerness gleaming in his face.

Once again the dishes and cups were brought into requisition as the engineer showed a crude model, in china and cutlery, of an engine he proposed to have constructed, illustrating his own idea about a truck for the forward wheels which should move separately from the back wheels and enable the engine to conform to curves more readily.

Marcia sat with glowing cheeks watching the outline of history that was to be, not knowing that the little model before her, made from her own teacups and saucers, was to be the model for all the coming engines of the many railroads of the future.

Finally the chairs were pushed back, and yet the talk went on. Marcia slipped silently about conveying the dishes away. And still the guests sat talking. She could hear all they said even when she was in the kitchen washing the china, for she did it very softly and never a clink hid a word. They talked of Governor Clinton again and of his attitude toward the railroad. They spoke of Thurlow Weed and a number of others whose names were familiar to Marcia in the papers she had read to her father. They told how lately on the Baltimore and Ohio railroad Peter Cooper had experimented with a little locomotive, and had beaten a gray horse attached to another car.

Marcia smiled brightly as she listened, and laid the delicate china teapot down with care lest she should lose a word. But ever with her interest in the march of civilization, there were other thoughts mingling. Thoughts of David and of how he would be connected with it all. He would write it up and be identified with it. He was brave enough to face any new movement.

David's paper was a temperance paper. There were not many temperance papers in those days. David was brave. He had already faced a number of unpleasant circumstances in consequence. He was not afraid of sneers or sarcasms, nor of being called a fanatic. He had taken such a stand that even those who were opposed had to respect him. Marcia felt the joy of a great pride in David to-night.

She sang a happy little song at the bottom of her heart as she worked. The new railroad was an assured thing, and David was her comrade, that was the song, and the refrain was, "David, David, David!"

Later, after the guests had talked themselves out and taken their candles to their rooms, David with another comrade's smile, and a look in his eyes that saw visions of the country's future, and for this one night at least promised not to dream of the past, bade her good night.

She went up to her white chamber and lay down upon the pillow, whose case was fragrant of lavender blossoms, dreaming with a smile of to-morrow. She thought she was riding in a strange new railroad train with David's arm about her and Harry Temple running along at his very best pace to try to catch them, but he could not.

Miranda, at her supperless window, watched the evening hours and thought many thoughts. She wondered why they stayed in the dining room so late, and why they did not go into the parlor and make Marcia play the "music box" as she called it; and why there was a light so long in that back chamber over the kitchen. Could it be they had put one of the guests there? Surely not. Perhaps that was David's study. Perhaps he was writing. Ah! She had guessed aright. David was sitting up to write while the inspiration was upon him.

But Miranda slept and ceased to wonder long before David's light was extinguished, and when he finally lay down it was with a body healthily weary, and a mind for the time free from any intruding thought of himself and his troubles.

He had written a most captivating article that would appear in his paper in a few days, and which must convince many doubters that a railroad was at last an established fact among them.

There were one or two points which he must ask the skilled engineer in the morning, but as he reviewed what he had written he felt a sense of deep satisfaction, and a true delight in his work. His soul thrilled with the power of his gift. He loved it, exulted in it. It was pleasant to feel that delight in his work once more. He had thought since his marriage that it was gone forever, but perhaps by and by it would return to console him, and he would be able to do greater things in the world because of his suffering.

Just as he dropped to sleep there came a thought of Marcia, pleasantly, as one remembers a flower. He felt that there was a comfort about Marcia, a something helpful in her smile. There was more to her than he had supposed. She was not merely a child. How her face had glowed as the men talked of the projected railroad, and almost she seemed to understand as they described the proposed engine with its movable trucks. She would be a companion who would be interested in his pursuits. He had hoped to teach Kate to understand his life work and perhaps help him some, but Kate was by nature a butterfly, a bird of gay colors, always on the wing. He would not have wanted her to be troubled with deep thoughts. Marcia seemed to enjoy such things. What if he should take pains to teach her, read with her, help cultivate her mind? It would at least be an occupation for leisure hours, something to interest him and keep away the awful pall of sadness.

How sweet she had looked as she lay asleep in the woods with the tears on her cheek like the dew-drops upon a rose petal! She was a dear little girl and he must take care of her and protect her. That scoundrel Temple! What were such men made for? He must settle him to-morrow.

And so he fell asleep.

Chapter 17

Harry Temple sat in his office the next morning with his feet upon the table and his wooden armed chair titled back against the wall.

He had letters to write, a number of them, that should go out with the afternoon coach, to reach the night packet. There were at least three men he ought to go and see at once if he would do the best for his employers, and the office he sat in was by no means in the best of order. But his feet were elevated comfortably on the table and he was deep in the pages of a story of the French Court, its loves and hates and intrigues.

It was therefore with annoyance that he looked up at the opening of the office door.

But the frown changed to apprehension, as he saw who was his visitor. He brought the chair legs suddenly to the floor and his own legs followed them swiftly. David Spafford was not a man before whom another would sit with his feet on a table, even to transact business.

There was a look of startled enquiry on Harry Temple's face. For an instant his self-complacency was shaken. He hesitated, wondering what tack to take. Perhaps after all his alarm was unnecessary. Marcia likely had been too frightened to tell of what had occurred. He noticed the broad shoulder, the lean, active body, the keen eye, and the grave poise of his visitor, and thought he would hardly care to fight a duel with that man. It was natural for him to think at once of a duel on account of the French court life from which his mind had just emerged. A flash of wonder passed through his mind whether it would be swords or pistols, and then he set himself to face the other man.

David Spafford stood for a full minute and looked into the face of the man he had come to shame. He looked at him with a calm eye and brow, but with a growing contempt that did not need words to express it. Harry Temple felt the color rise in his cheek, and his soul quaked for an instant. Then his habitual conceit arose and he tried to parry with his eye that keen piercing gaze of the other. It must have lasted a full minute, though it seemed to Mr. Temple it was five at least. He made an attempt to offer his visitor a chair, but it was not noticed. David Spafford looked his man through and through, and knew him for exactly what he was. At last he spoke, quietly, in a tone that was too courteous to be contemptuous, but it humiliated the listener more even than contempt:

"It would be well for you to leave town at once."

That was all. The listener felt that it was a command. His wrath arose hotly, and beat itself against the calm exterior of his visitor's gaze in a look that was brazen enough to have faced a whole town of accusers. Harry Temple could look innocent and handsome when he chose.

"I do not understand you, sir!" he said. "That is a most extraordinary statement!"

"It would be well for you to leave town at once."

This time the command was imperative. Harry's eyes blazed.

"Why?" He asked it with that impertinent tilt to his chin which usually angered his opponent in any argument. Once he could break that steady, iron, self-control he felt he would have the best of things. He could easily persuade David Spafford that everything was all right if he could get him off his guard and make him angry. An angry man could do little but bluster.

"You understand very well," replied David, his voice still, steady and his gaze not swerving.

"Indeed! Well, this is most extraordinary," said Harry, losing control of himself again. "Of what do you accuse me, may I enquire?"

"Of nothing that your own heart does not accuse you," said David. And somehow there was more than human indignation in the gaze now: there was pity, a sense of shame for another soul who could lower himself to do unseemly things. Before that look the blood crept into Harry's cheek again. An uncomfortable sensation entirely new was stealing over him. A sense of sin—no, not that exactly,—a sense that he had made a mistake, perhaps. He never was very hard upon himself even when the evidence was clear against him. It angered him to feel humiliated. What a fuss to make about a little thing! What a tiresome old cad to care about a little flirtation with his wife! He wished he had let the pretty baby alone entirely. She was of no finer stuff than many another who had accepted his advances with pleasure. He stiffened his neck and replied with much haughtiness:

"My heart accuses me of nothing, sir. I assure you I consider your words an insult! I demand satisfaction for your insulting language, sir!" Harry Temple had never fought a duel, and had never been present when others fought, but that was the language in which a challenge was usually delivered in French novels.

"It is not a matter for discussion!" said David Spafford, utterly ignoring the other's blustering words. "I am fully informed as to all that occurred yesterday afternoon, and I tell you once more, it would be well for you to leave town at once. I have nothing further to say."

David turned and walked toward the door, and Harry stood, ignored, angry, crestfallen, and watched him until he reached the door.

"You would better ask your informant further of her part in the matter!" he hissed, suddenly, an open sneer in his voice and a covert implication of deep meaning.

David turned, his face flashing with righteous indignation. The man who was withered by the scorn of that glance wished heartily that he had not uttered the false sentence. He felt the smallness of his own soul, during the instant of silence in which his visitor stood looking at him.

Then David spoke deliberately:

"I knew you were a knave," said he, "but I did not suppose you were also a coward. A man who is not a coward will not try to put the blame upon a woman, especially upon an innocent one. You, sir, will leave town this evening. Any business further than you can settle between this and that I will see properly attended to. I warn you, sir, it will be unwise for you to remain longer than till the evening coach."

Perfectly courteous were David's tones, keen command was in his eye and determination in every line of his face. Harry could not recover himself to reply, could not master his frenzy of anger and humiliation to face the righteous look of his accuser. Before he realized it, David was gone.

He stood by the window and watched him go down the street with rapid, firm tread and upright bearing. Every line in that erect form spoke of determination. The conviction grew within him that the last words of his visitor were true, and that it would be wise for him to leave town. He rebelled at the idea. He did not wish to leave, for business matters were in such shape, or rather in such chaos, that it would be extremely awkward for him to meet his employers and explain his desertion at that time. Moreover there were several homes in the town open to him whenever he chose, where were many attractions. It was a lazy pleasant life he had been leading here, fully trusted, and wholly disloyal to the trust, troubled by no uneasy overseers, not even his own conscience, dined and smiled upon with lovely languishing eyes. He did not care to go, even though he had decried the town as dull and monotonous.

But, on the other hand, things had occurred — not the unfortunate little mistake of yesterday, of course, but others, more serious things — that he would hardly care to have brought to the light of day, especially through the keen sarcastic columns of David Spafford's paper. He had seen other sinners brought to a bloodless retribution in those columns by dauntless weapons of sarcasm and wit which in David Spafford's hands could be made to do valiant work. He did not care to be humiliated in that way. He could not brazen it out. He was convinced that the man meant what he said, and from what he knew of his influence he felt that he would leave no stone unturned till he had made the place too hot to hold him. Only Harry Temple himself knew how easy that would be to do, for no one else knew how many "mistakes" Harry had made, and he, unfortunately for himself, did not know how many of them were not known, by any who could harm him.

He stood a long time clinking some sixpences and shillings together in his pocket, and scowling down the street after David had disappeared from sight.

"Blame that little pink-cheeked, baby-eyed fool!" he said at last, turning on his heel with a sigh. "I might have known she was too goody-goody. Such people ought to die young before they grow up to make fools of other people. Bah! Think of a wife like that with no spirit of her own. A baby! Merely a baby!

Nevertheless, in his secret heart, he knew he honored Marcia and felt a true shame that she had looked into his tarnished soul.

Then he looked round about upon his papers that represented a whole week's hard work and maybe more before they were cleared away, and reflected how much easier after all it would be to get up a good excuse and go away, leaving all this to some poor drudge who should be sent here in his place. He looked around again and his eyes lighted upon his book. He remembered the exciting crisis in which he had left the heroine and down he sat to his story again. At least there was nothing demanding attention this moment. He need not decide what he would do. If he went there were few preparations to make. He would toss some things into his carpet-bag and pretend to have been summoned to see a sick and dying relative, a long-lost brother something. It would be easy to invent one when the time came. Then he could leave directions for the rest of his things to be packed if he did not return, and get rid of the trouble of it all. As for the letters, if he was going what use to bother with them? Let them wait till his successor should come. It mattered little to him whether his employers suffered for his negligence or not so long as he finished his story. Besides, it would not do to let that cad think he had frightened him. He would pretend he was not going, at least during his hours of grace. So he picked up his book and went on reading.

At noon he sauntered back to his boarding house as usual for his dinner, having professed an unusually busy morning to those who came in to the office on business and made appointments with them for the next day. This had brought him much satisfaction as the morning wore away and he was left free to his book, and so before dinner he had come to within a very few pages of the end.

After a leisurely dinner he sauntered back to the office again, rejoicing in the fact that circumstances had so arranged themselves that he had passed David Spafford in front of the newspaper office and given him a most elaborate and friendly bow in the presence of four to five bystanders. David's look in return had meant volumes, and decided Harry Temple to do as he had been ordered, not, of course, because he had been ordered to do so, but because it would be an easier thing to do. In fact he made up his mind that he was weary of this part of the country. He went back to his book.

About the middle of the afternoon he finished the last pages. He rose up with alacrity then and began to think what he should do. He glanced around the room, sought out a few papers, took some daguerreotypes of girls from a drawer of his desk, gave a farewell glance around the dismal little room that had seen so much shirking for the past few months, and then went out and locked the door.

He paused at the corner. Which way should he go? He did not care to go back to the office, for his book was done, and he scarcely needed to go to his room at his boarding place yet either, for the afternoon was but half over and he wished his departure to appear to be entirely unpremeditated. A daring thought came into his head. He would walk past David Spafford's house. He would let Marcia see him if possible. He would show them that he was not afraid in the least. He even meditated going in and explaining to Marcia that she had made a great mistake, that he had been merely admiring her, and that there was no harm in anything he had said or done yesterday, that he was exceedingly grieved and mortified that she should have mistaken his meaning for an insult, and so on and so on. He knew well how to make such honeyed talk when he chose, but the audacity of the thing was a trifle too much for even his bold nature, so he satisfied himself by strolling in a leisurely manner by the house.

When he was directly opposite to it he raised his eyes casually and bowed and smiled with his most graceful air. True, he did not see any one, for Marcia had caught sight of him as she was coming out upon the stoop and had fled into her own room with the door buttoned, she was watching unseen from behind the folds of her curtain, but he made the bow as complete as though a whole family had been greeting him from the windows. Marcia, poor child, thought he must see her, and she felt frozen to the spot, and stared wildly through the little fold of her curtain with trembling hands and weak knees till he was passed. Well pleased at himself the young man walked on, knowing that at least three prominent citizens had seen him bow and smile, and that they would be witnesses, against anything David might say to the contrary, that he was on friendly terms with Mrs. Spafford.

Hannah Heath was sitting on the front stoop with her knitting. She often sat there dressed daintily of an afternoon. Her hands were white and looked well against the blue yarn she was knitting. Besides there was something domestic and sentimental in a stocking. It gave a cozy, homey, air to a woman, Hanna considered. So she sat and knitted and smiled at whomsoever passed by, luring many in to sit and talk with her, so that the stockings never grew rapidly, but always kept at about the same stage. If it had been Miranda, Grandmother Heath would have made some sharp remarks about the length of time it took to finish that blue stocking, but as it was Hannah it was all right.

Hannah sat upon the stoop and knitted as Harry Temple came by. Now, Hannah was not so great a favorite with Harry as Harry was with Hannah. She was of the kind who was conquered too easily, and he did not consider it worth his while to waste time upon her simperings usually. But this afternoon was different. He had nowhere to go for a little while, and Hannah's appearance on the stoop was opportune and gave him an idea. He would lounge there with her. Perchance fortune would favor him again and David Spafford would pass by and see him. There would be one more opportunity to stare insolently at him and defy him, before he bent his neck to obey. David had given him the day in which to do what he would, and he would make no move until the time was over and the coach he had named departed, but he knew that then he would bring down retribution. In just what form that retribution would come he was not quite certain, but he knew it would be severe.

So when Hannah smiled upon him, Harry Temple stepped daintily across the mud in the road, and came and sat down beside her. He toyed with her knitting, caught one of her plump white hands, the one on the side away from the street, and held it, while Hannah pretended not to notice, and dropped her long eyelashes in a telling way. Hannah knew how. She had been at it a good many years.

So he sat, toward five o'clock, when David came by, and bowed gravely to Hannah, but seemed not to see Harry. Harry let his eyes follow the tall figure in an insolent stare.

"What a dough-faced cad that man is!" he said lazily, "no wonder his little pink-cheeked wife seeks other society. Handsome baby, though, isn't she?"

Hannah pricked up her ears. Her loss of David was too recent not to cause her extreme jealousy of his pretty young wife. Already she fairly hated her. Her upbringing in the atmosphere of Grandmother Heath's sarcastic, ill-natured gossip had prepared her to be quick to see meaning in any insinuation.

She looked at him keenly, archly for a moment, then replied with dropping gaze and coquettish manner:

"You should not blame any one for enjoying your company."

Hannah stole sly glances to see how he took this, but Harry was an old hand and proof against such scrutiny. He only shrugged his shoulder carelessly, as though he dropped all blame like a garment that he had no need for.

"And what's the matter with David?" asked Hannah, watching David as he mounted his own steps, and thinking how often she had watched that tall form go down the street, and thought of him as destined to belong to her. The mortification that he had chosen some one else was not yet forgotten. It amounted almost to a desire for revenge.

Harry lingered longer than he intended. Hannah begged him to remain to supper, but he declined, and when she pressed him to do so he looked troubled and said he was expecting a letter and must hurry back to see if it came in the afternoon coach. He told her that a dear friend, a beloved cousin, was lying very ill, and he might be summoned at any moment to his bedside, and Hannah said some comforting little things in a caressing voice, and hoped he would find the letter saying the cousin was better. The he hurried away.

It was easy at his boarding house to say he had been called away, and he rushed up to his room and threw some necessaries into his carpet-bag, scattering things around the room and helping out the impression that he was called away in a great hurry. When he was ready he looked at this watch. It was growing late. The evening coach left in half an hour. He knew its route well. It started at the village inn, and went down the old turnpike, stopping here and there to pick up passengers. There was always a convocation when it started. Perhaps David Spafford would be there and witness his obedience to the command given him. He set his lips and made up his mind to escape that at least. He would cheat his adversary of that satisfaction.

It would involve a sacrifice. He would have to go without his supper, and he could smell the frying bacon coming up the stairs. But it would help the illusion and he could perhaps get something on the way when the coach stopped to change horses.

He rushed downstairs and told his landlady that he must start at once, as he must see a man before the coach went, and she, poor lady, had no chance to suggest that he leave her a little deposit on the sum of his board which he already owed her. There was perhaps some method in his hurry for that reason also. It always bothered him to pay his bills, he had so many other ways of spending his money.

So he hurried away and caught a ride in a farm wagon toward the Cross Roads. When it turned off he walked a little way until another wagon came along; finally crossed several fields at a breathless pace and caught the coach just as it was leaving the Cross Roads, which was the last stopping place anywhere near the village. He climbed up beside the driver, still in a breathless condition, and detailed to him how he had received word, just before the coach started, by a messenger who came across-country on horseback, that his cousin was dying.

After he had answered the driver's minutest questions, he sat back and reflected upon his course with satisfaction. He was off, and he had not been seen nor questioned by a single citizen, and by to-morrow night his story as he had told it to the driver would be fully known and circulated through the place he had just left. The stage driver was one of the best means of advertisement. It was well to give him full particulars.

The driver after he had satisfied his curiosity about he young man by his side, and his reasons for leaving town so hastily, began to wax eloquent upon the one theme which now occupied his spare moments and his fluent tongue, the subject of a projected railroad. Whether some of the sentiments he uttered were his own, or whether he had but borrowed from others, they were at least uttered with force and apparent conviction, and many a traveller sat and listened as they were detailed and viewed the subject from the standpoint of the loud-mouthed coachman.

A little later Tony Weller, called by some one "the best beloved of all coachmen," uttered much the same sentiments in the following words:

"I consider that the railroad is unconstitutional and an invader o' privileges. As to the comfort, as an old coachman I may say it, — vere's the comfort o' sittin' in a harm-chair a lookin' at brick walls, and heaps o' mud, never comin' to a public 'ouse, never seein' a glass o' ale, never goin' through a pike, never meetin' a change o' no kind (hosses or otherwise), but always comin' to a place, ven you comes to vun at all, the werry picter o' the last.

"As to the honor an' dignity o' travellin' vere can that be without a coachman, and vat's the rail, to sich coachmen as is sometimes forced to go by it, but an outrage and an hinsult? As to the ingen, a nasty, wheezin', gapsin', puffin', bustin' monster always out o' breath, with a shiny green and gold back like an onpleasant beetle; as to the ingen as is always a pourin' out red 'ot coals at night an' black smoke in the day, the sensiblest thing it does, in my opinion, is ven there's somethin' in the vay, it sets up that 'ere frightful scream vich seems to say, 'Now 'ere's two 'undred an' forty passengers in the werry greatest extremity o' danger, an' 'ere's their two 'undred an' forty screams in vun!'"

But such sentiments as these troubled Harry Temple not one whit. He cared not whether the present century had a railroad or whether it travelled by foot. He would not lift a white finger to help it along or hinder. As the talk went on he was considering how and where he might get his supper.

Chapter 18

The weather turned suddenly cold and raw that Fall, and almost in one day, the trees that had been green, or yellowing in the sunshine, put on their autumn garments of defeat, flaunted them for a brief hour, and dropped them early in despair. The pleasant woods, to which Marcia had fled in her dismay, became a mass of finely penciled branches against a wintry sky, save for the one group of tall pines that hung out heavy above the rest, and seemed to defy even snowy blasts.

Marcia could see those pines from her kitchen window, and sometimes as she worked, if her heart was heavy, she would look out and away to them, and think of the day she laid her head down beneath them to sob out her trouble, and awoke to find comfort. Somehow the memory of that little talk that she and David had then grew into vast proportions in her mind, and she loved to cherish it.

There had come letters from home. Her stepmother had written, a stiff, not unloving letter, full of injunctions to be sure to remember this, and not do that, and on no account to let any relative or neighbor persuade her out of the ways in which she had been brought up. She was attempting to do as many mothers do, when they see the faults in the child they have brought up, try to bring them up over again. At some of the sentences a wild homesickness took possession of her. Some little homely phrase about one of the servants, or the mention of a pet hen or cow, would bring the longing tears to her eyes, and she would feel that she must throw away this new life and run back to the old one.

School was begun at home. Mary Ann and Hanford would be taking the long walk back and forth together twice a day to the old school-house. She half envied them their happy, care-free life. She liked to think of the shy courting that she had often seen between scholars in the upper classes. Her imagination pleased itself sometimes when she was going to sleep, trying to picture out the school goings and home comings, and their sober talk. Not that she ever looked back to Hanford Weston with regret, not she. She knew always that he was not for her, and perhaps, even so early as that in her new life, if the choice had been given her whether she would go back to her girlhood again and be as she was before Kate had run away, or whether she would choose to stay here in the new life with David, it is likely she would have chosen to stay.

There were occasional letters from Squire Schulyer. He wrote of politics, and sent many messages to his son-in-law which Marcia handed over to David at the tea table to read, and which always seemed to soften David and bring a sweet sadness into his eyes. He loved and respected his father-in-law. It was as if he were bound to him by the love of some one who had died. Marcia thought of that every time she handed David a letter, and sat and watched him read it.

Sometimes little Harriet or the boys printed out a few words about the family cat, or the neighbors' children, and Marcia laughed and cried over the poor little attempts at letters and longed to have the eager childish faces of the writers to kiss.

But in all of them there was never a mention of the bright, beautiful, selfish girl around whom the old home life used to centre and who seemed now, judging from the home letters, to be worse than dead to them all. But since the afternoon upon the hill a new and pleasant intercourse had sprung up between David and Marcia. True it was confined mainly to discussions of the new railroad, the possibilities of its success, and the construction of engines, tracks, etc. David was constantly writing up the subject for his paper, and he fell into the habit of reading his articles aloud to Marcia when they were finished. She would listen with breathless admiration, sometimes combating a point ably, with the old vim she had used in her discussion over the newspaper with her father, but mainly agreeing with every word he wrote, and always eager to understand it down the to minutest detail.

He always seemed pleased at her praise, and wrote on while she put away the tea-things with a contented expression as though he had passed a high critic, and need not fear any other. Once he looked up with a quizzical expression and made a jocose remark about "our article," taking her into a sort of partnership with him in it, which set her heart to beating happily, until it seemed as if she were really in some part at least growing into his life.

But after all their companionship was a shy, distant one, more like that of a brother and sister who had been separated all their lives and were just beginning to get acquainted, and ever there was a settled sadness about the lines of David's mouth and eyes. They sat around one table now, the evenings when they were at home, for there were still occasional tea-drinkings at their friends' houses; and there was one night a week held religiously for a formal supper with the aunts, which David kindly acquiesced in—more for the sake of his Aunt Clarinda than the others,—whenever he was not detained by actual business. Then, too, there was the weekly prayer meeting held at "early candle light" in the dim old shadowed church. They always walked down the twilighted streets together, and it seemed to Marcia there was a sweet solemnity about that walk. They never said much to each other on the way. David seemed preoccupied with holy thoughts, and Marcia walked softly beside him as if he had been the minister, looking at him proudly and reverently now and then. David was often called upon to pray in meeting and Marcia loved to listen to his words. He seemed to be more intimate with God than the others, who were mostly old men and prayed with long, rolling, solemn sentences that put the whole community down into the dust and ashes before their Creator.

Marcia rather enjoyed the hour spent in the somberness of the church, with the flickering candle-light making grotesque forms of shadows on the wall and among the tall pews. The old minister reminded her of the one she had left at home, though he was more learned and scholarly, and when he had read the Scripture passages he would take his spectacles off and lay them across the great Bible where the candle-light played at glances with the steel bows, and say: "Let us pray!" Then would come that soft stir and hush as the people took the attitude of prayer. Marcia sometimes joined in the prayer in her heart, uttering shy little petitions that were vague and indefinite, and had to do mostly with the days when she was troubled and homesick, and felt that David belonged wholly to Kate. Always her clear voice joined in the slow hymns that quavered out now and again, lined out to the worshippers.

Marcia and David went out from that meeting down the street to their home with the hush upon them that must have been upon the Israelites of old after they had been to the solemn congregation.

But once David had come in earlier than usual and had caught Marcia reading the Scottish Chiefs, and while she started guiltily to be found thus employed he smiled indulgently. After supper he said: "Get your book, child, and sit down. I have some writing to do, and after it is done I will read it to you." So after that, more and more often, it was a book that Marcia held in her hands in the long evenings when they sat together, instead of some useful employment, and so her education progressed. Thus she read Epictetus, Rasselas, *The Deserted Village, The Vicar of Walkfield, Paradise Lost, the Mysteries of the Human Heart,* Marshall's *Life of Columbus, The Spy, The Pioneers,* and *The Last of the Mohicans.*

She had been asked to sing in the village choir. David sang a sweet high tenor there, and Marcia's voice was clear and strong as a blackbird's, with the plaintive sweetness of the wood-robin's.

Hannah Heath was in the choir also, and jealously watched her every move, but of this Marcia was unaware until informed of it by Miranda. With her inherited sweetness of nature she scarcely credited it, until one Sunday, a few weeks after the departure of Harry Temple, Hannah leaned forward from her seat among the altos and whispered quite distinctly, so that those around could hear — it was just before the service — "I've just had a letter from your friend Mr. Temple. I thought you might like to know that his cousin got well and he has gone back to New York. He won't be returning here this year. On some accounts he thought it was better not."

It was all said pointedly, with double emphasis upon the "your friend," and "some accounts." Marcia felt her cheeks glow, much to her vexation, and tried to control her whisper to seem kindly as she answered indifferently enough.

"Oh, indeed! But you must have made a mistake. Mr. Temple is a very slight acquaintance of mine. I have met him only a few times, and I know nothing about his cousin. I was not aware even that he had gone away."

Hannah raised her speaking eyebrows and replied, quite loud now, for the choir leader had stood up already with his tuning-fork in hand, and one could hear it faintly twang:

"Indeed!" — using Marcia's own word — and quite coldly, "I should have thought differently from what Harry himself told me," and there was that in her tone which deepened the color in Marcia's cheeks and caused it to stay there during the entire morning service as she sat puzzling over what Hannah could have meant. It rankled in her mind during the whole day. She longed to ask David about it, but could not get up the courage.

She could not bear to revive the memory of what seemed to be her shame. It was at the minister's donation party that Hannah planted another thorn in her heart, — Hannah, in a green plaid silk with delicate undersleeves of lace, and a tiny black velvet jacket.

She selected a time when Lemuel was near, and when Aunt Amelia and Aunt Hortense, who believed that all the young men in town were hovering about David's wife, sat one on either side of Marcia, as if to guard her for their beloved nephew — who was discussing politics with Mr. Heath — and who never seemed to notice, so blind he was in his trust of her.

"I've had another letter from New York, from your friend Mr. Temple," she said it with the slightest possible glance over her shoulder to get the effect of her words upon the faithful Lemuel, "and he tells me he has met a sister of yours. By the way, she told him that David used to be very fond of her before she was married. I suppose she'll be coming to visit you now she's so near as New York."

Two pairs of suspicious steely eyes flew like stinging insects to gaze upon her, one on either side, and Marcia's heart stood still for just one instant, but she felt that here was her trying time, and if she would help David and do the work for which she had become his wife, she must protect him now from any suspicions or disagreeable tongues. By very force of will she controlled the trembling of her lips.

"My sister will not likely visit us this winter, I think," she replied as coolly as if she had had a letter to that effect that morning, and then she deliberately looked at Lemuel Skinner and asked if he had heard of the offer of prizes of four thousand dollars in cash that the Baltimore and Ohio railroad had just made for the most approved engine delivered for trial before June first, 1831, not to exceed three and a half tons in weight and capable of drawing, day by day, fifteen tons inclusive of weight of wagons, fifteen miles per hours. Lemuel looked at her blankly and said he had not heard of it. He was engaged in thinking over what Hannah had said about a letter from Harry Temple. He cared nothing about railroads.

"The second prize is thirty-five hundred dollars," stated Marcia eagerly, as though it were of the utmost importance to her.

"Are you thinking of trying for one of the prizes?" sneered Hannah, piercing her with her eyes, and now indeed the ready color flowed into Marcia's face. Her ruse had been detected.

"If I were a man and understood machinery I believe I would. What a grand thing it would be to be able to invent a thing like an engine that would be of so much use to the world," she answered bravely.

"They are most dangerous machines," said Aunt Amelia disapprovingly. "No right-minded Christian who wishes to live out the life his Creator has given him would ever ride behind one. I have heard that boilers always explode."

"They are most unnecessary!" said Aunt Hortense severely, as if that settled the question for all time and all railroad corporations.

But Marcia was glad for once of their disapproval and entered most heartily into a discussion of the pros and cons of engines and steam, quoting largely from David's last article for the paper on the subject, until Hannah and Lemuel moved slowly away. The discussion served to keep the aunts from inquiring further that evening about the sister in New York.

Marcia begged them to go with her into the kitchen and see the store of good things that had been brought to the minister's house by his loving parishioners. Bags of flour and meal, pumpkins, corn in the ear, eggs, and nice little pats of butter. A great wooden tub of doughnuts, baskets of apples and quinces, pounds of sugar and tea, barrels of potatoes, whole hams, a side of pork, a quarter of beef, hanks of yarn, and strings of onions. It was a goodly array. Marcia felt that the minister must be beloved by his people. She watched him and his wife as they greeted their prople, and wished she knew them better, and might come and see them sometimes, and perhaps eventually feel as much at home with them as with her own dear minister.

She avoided Hannah during the remainder of the evening. When the evening was over and she went upstairs to get her wraps from the high four-poster bedstead, she had almost forgotten Hannah and her ill-natured, prying remarks. But Hannah had not forgotten her. She came forth from behind the bed curtains where she had been searching for a lost glove, and remarked that she should think Marcia would be lonely this first winter away from home and want her sister with her for a while.

But the presence of Hannah always seemed a mental stimulus to the spirit of Marcia.

"Oh, I'm not in the least lonely," she laughed merrily. "I have a great many interesting things to do, and I love music and books."

"Oh, yes, I forgot you are very fond of music. Harry Temple told me about it," said Hannah. Again there was that disagreeable hint of something more behind her words, that aggravated Marcia almost beyond control. For an instant a cutting reply was upon her lips and her eyes flashed fire; then it came to her how futile it would be, and she caught the words in time and walked swiftly down the stairs. David watching her come down saw the admiring glances of all who stood in the hall below, and took her under his protection with a measure of pride in her youth and beauty that he did not himself at all realize. All the way home he talked with her about the new theory of railroad construction, quite contented in her companionship, while she, poor child, much perturbed in spirit, wondered how he would feel if he knew what Hannah had said.

David fell into a deep study with a book and his papers about him, after they had reached home. Marcia went up to her quiet, lonely chamber, put her face in the pillow and thought and wept and prayed. When at last she lay down to rest she did not know anything she could do but just to go on living day by day and helping David all she could. At most there was nothing to fear for herself, save a kind of shame that she had not been the first sister chosen, and she found to her surprise that that was growing to be deeper than she had supposed.

She wished as she fell asleep that her girl-dreams might have been left to develop and bloom like other girls', and that she might have had a real lover, — like David in every way, yet of course not David because he was Kate's. But a real lover who would meet her as David had done that night when he thought she was Kate, and speak to her tenderly.

One afternoon David, being wearied with an unusual round of taxing cares, came home to rest and study up some question in his library.

Finding the front door fastened, and remembering that he had left his key in his other pocket, he came around to the back door, and much preoccupied with thought went through the kitchen and nearly to the hall before the unusual sounds of melody penetrated to his ears. He stopped for an instant amazed, forgetting the piano, then comprehending he wondered who was playing. Perhaps some visitor was in the parlor. He would listen and find out. He was weary and dusty with the soil of the office upon his hands and clothes. He did not care to meet a visitor, so under cover of the music he slipped into the door of his library across the hall from the parlor and dropped into his great arm-chair.

Softly and tenderly stole the music through the open door, all about him, like the gentle dropping of some tender psalms or comforting chapter in the Bible to an aching heart. It touched his brow like a soft soothing hand, and seemed to know and recognize all the agonies his heart had been passing through, and all the weariness his body felt.

He put his head back and let it float over him and rest him. Tinkling brooks and gently zephyrs, waving of forest trees, and twitterings of birds, calm lazy clouds floating by, a sweetness in the atmosphere, bells far away, lowing herds, music of the angels high in heaven, the soothing strain from each extracted and brought to heal his broken heart. It fell like dew upon his spirit. Then, like a fresh breeze with zest and life borne on, came a new strain, grand and fine and high, calling him to better things. He did not know it was a strain of Handel's music grown immortal, but his spirit recognized the higher call, commanding him to follow, and straightway he felt strengthened to go onward in the course he had been pursuing. Old troubles seemed to grow less, anguish fell away from him. He took new lease of life. Nothing seemed impossible.

Then she played by ear one or two of the old tunes they sang in church, touching the notes tenderly and almost making them speak the words. It seemed a benediction. Suddenly the playing ceased and Marcia remembered it was nearly supper time.

He met her in the doorway with a new look in his eyes, a look of high purpose and exultation. He smiled upon her and said: "That was good, child. I did not know you could do it. You must give it to us often." Marcia felt a glow of pleasure in his kindliness, albeit she felt that the look in his eyes set him apart and above her, and made her feel the child she was. She hurried out to get the supper between pleasure and nameless unrest. She was glad of this much, but she wanted more, a something to meet her soul and satisfy.

Chapter 19

The world had not gone well with Mistress Kate Leavenworth, and she was ill-pleased. She had not succeeded in turning her father's heart toward herself as she had confidently expected to do when she ran away with her sea captain. She had written a gay letter home, taking for granted, in a pretty way, the forgiveness she did not think it necessary to ask, but there had come in return a brief harsh statement from her father that she was no longer his daughter and must cease from further communication with the family in any way; that she should never enter his house again and not a penny of his money should ever pass to her. He also informed her plainly that the trousseau made for her had been given to her sister who was now the wife of the man she had not seen fit to marry.

Over this letter Mistress Kate at first stormed, then wept, and finally sat down to frame epistle after epistle in petulant, penitent language. These epistles following each other by daily mail coaches still brought nothing further from her irate parent, and my lady was at least forced to face the fact that she must bear the penalty of her own misdeeds; a lesson she should have learned much earlier in life.

The young captain, who had always made it appear that he had plenty of money, had spent his salary, and most of his mother's fortune, which had been left in his keeping as administrator of his father's estate; so he had really very little to offer the spoiled and petted beauty, who simply would not settle down to the inevitable and accept the fact she had brought upon herself and others. Day after day she fretted and blamed her husband until he heartily wished her back from whence he had taken her; wished her back with her straitlaced lover from whom he had stolen her; wished her anywhere save where she was. Her brightness and beauty seemed all gone: she was a sulky child insisting upon the moon or nothing. She wanted to go to New York and be established in a fine house with plenty of servants and a carriage and horses, and the young captain had not the wherewithal to furnish these accessories to an elegant and luxurious life.

He had loved her so far as his shallow nature could love, and perhaps she had returned it in the beginning. He wanted to spend his furlough in quite places where he might have a honeymoon of his ideal, bantering Kate's sparkling sentences, looking into her beautiful eyes, touching her rosy lips with his own as often as he chose. But Mistress Kate had lost her sparkle. She would not be kissed until she had gained her point, her lovely eyes were full of disfiguring tears and angry flashes, and her speech scintillated with cutting sarcasms, which

were none the less hard to bear that they pressed home some disagreeable truths
to the easy, careless spendthrift. The rose had lost its dew and was making its
thorns felt.

And so they quarreled though their honeymoon, and Captain Leavenworth
was not sorry when a hasty and unexpected end came to his furlough and he was
ordered off with his ship for an indefinite length of time.

Even then Kate thought to get her will before he left, and held on her sullen
ways and her angry, blameful talk until the last minute, so that he hurried away
without even one good-bye kiss, and with her angry sentences sounding in his
ears.

True, he repented somewhat on board the ship and sent her back more
money than she could reasonably have expected under the circumstances, but
he sent it without one word of gentleness, and Kate's heart was hard toward her
husband.

Then with bitterness and anguish, — that was new and fairly astonishing that
it had come to her who had always had her way, — she sat down to think of the
man she had jilted. He would have been kind to her. He would have given her
all she asked and more. He would even have moved his business to New York
to please her, she felt sure. Why had she been so foolish! And then, like many
another sinner who is made at least to see the error of his ways, she cast hard
thoughts at a Fate which had allowed her to make so great a mistake, and pitied
her poor little self out of all recognition of the character she had formed.

But she took her money and went to New York, for she felt that there only
could she be at all happy, and have some little taste of the delights of true living.

She took up her abode with an ancient relative of her own mother's, who
lived in a quiet respectable part of the city, and who was glad to piece out her
small annuity with the modest sum that Kate agreed to pay for her board.

It was not long before Mistress Kate, with her beautiful face, and the pretty
clothes which she took care to provide at once for herself, spending lavishly out
of the diminishing sum her husband had sent her, and thinking not of the
morrow, nor the day when the board bills would due, became well know. The
musty little parlor of the ancient relative was daily filled with visitors, and every
evening Kate held court, with the old aunt nodding in her chair by the fireside.

Neither did the poor old lady have a very easy time of it, in spite of the
promise of weekly pay. Kate laughed at the old furniture and the old ways. She
demanded new things, and got them, too, until the old lady saw little hope of
any help from the board money when Kate was constantly saying: "I saw this in
a shop down town, auntie, and as I knew you needed it I just bought it. My board
this week will just pay for it." As always, Kate ruled. The little parlor took on
an air of brightness, and Kate became popular. A few women of fashion took
her up, and Kate launched herself upon a gay life, her one object to have as good
a time as possible, regardless of what her husband or anyone else might think.

When Kate had been in New York about two months it happened one day that she went out to a drive with one of hew new acquaintançes, a young married woman of about her own age, who had been given all in a worldly way that had been denied to Kate.

They made some calls in Brooklyn, and returned on the ferry-boat, carriage and all, just as the sun was setting.

The view was marvelous. The water a flood of pink and green and gold; the sails of the vessels along the shore lit up resplendently; the buildings of the city beyond sent back occasional flashes of reflected light from window glass or church spire. It was a picture worth looking upon, and Kate's companion was absorbed in it.

Not so Kate. She loved display above all thing. She sat up stately, aware that she looked well in her new frock with the fine lace collar she had extravagantly purchased the day before, and her leghorn bonnet with its real ostrich feather, which was becoming in the extreme. She enjoyed sitting back of the colored coachman, her elegant friend by her side, and being admired by the two ladies and the little girl who sat in the ladies' cabin and occasionally peeped curiously at her from the window. She drew herself up haughtily and let her soul "delight itself in fatness" — borrowed fatness, perhaps, but still, the long desired. She told herself she had a right to it, for was she not a Schulyer? That name was respected everywhere.

She bore a grudge at a man and woman who stood by the railing absorbed in watching the sunset haze that lay over the river showing the white sails in gleams like flashes of white birds here and there.

A young man well set up, and fashionably attired, sauntered up to the carriage. He spoke to Kate's friend, and was introduced. Kate felt in her heart it was because of her presence there he came. His bold black eyes told her as much and she was flattered.

They fell to talking.

"You say you spent the summer near Albany, Mr. Temple," said Kate presently, "I wonder if you happen to know of any of my friends. Did you meet a Mr. Spafford? David Spafford?"

"Of course I did, knew him well," said the young man with guarded tone. But a quick flash of dislike, and perhaps fear had crossed his face at the name. Kate was keen. She analyzed that look. She parted her charming red lips and showed her sharplittle teeth like the treacherous pearls in a white kitten's pink mouth.

"He was once a lover of mine," said Kate carelessly, wrinkling her piquant little nose as if the idea were comical, and laughing out a sweet ripple of mirth that would have cut David to the heart.

"Indeed!" said the ever ready Harry, "and I do not wonder. Is not every one that at once they see you Madam Leavenworth? How kind of your husband to stay at sea for so long a time and give us other poor fellows a chance to say pleasant things."

Then Kate pouted her pretty lips in a way she had and tapped the delighted Harry with her carriage parasol cross the fingers of his hand that had taken familiar hold of the carriage beside her arm.

"Oh, you naughty man!" she exclaimed prettily. "How dare you! Yes, David Spafford and I were quite good friends. I almost gave in at one time and became Mrs. Spafford, but he was too good for me!"

She uttered this truth in a mocking tone, and Harry saw her lead and hastened to follow. Here was a possible chance for revenge. He was ready for any. He studied the lady before him keenly. Of what did that face remind him? Had he ever seen her before? "I should judge him a little straitlaced for your merry ways," he responded gallantly, "but he's like all the rest, fickle, you know. He's married. Have you heard?"

Kate's face darkened with something hard and cruel, but her voice was soft as a cat's purr: "Yes," she sighed, "I know. He married my sister. Poor child! I am sorry for her. I think he did it out of revenge, and she was too young to know her own mind. But they, poor things, will have to bear the consequences of what they have done. Isn't it a pity that that has to be, Mr. Temple? It is dreadful to have the innocent suffer. I have been greatly anxious about my sister." She lifted her large eyes swimming in tears, and he did not perceive the insincerity in her purring voice just then. He was thanking his lucky stars that he had been saved from any remarks about young Mrs. Spafford, whom her sister seemed to love so deeply. It had been on the tip of his tongue to suggest that she might be able to lead her husband a gay little dance if she chose. How lucky he had not spoken! He tried to say some pleasant comforting nothings, and found it delightful to see her face clear into smiles and her blue eyes look into his so confidingly. By the time the boat touched the New York side the two felt well acquainted, and Harry Temple had promised to call soon, which promise he lost no time in keeping.

Kate's heart had grown bitter against the young sister who had dared to take her place, and against the lover who had so easily solaced himself. She could not understand it.

She resolved to learn all that Mr. Temple knew about David, and to find out if possible whether he were happy. It was Kate's nature not to be able to give up anything even though she did not want it. She desired the life-long devotion of every man who came near her, and have it she would or punish him.

Harry Temple, meanwhile, was reflecting upon his chance meeting that afternoon and wondering if in some way he might not yet have revenge upon the man who had humbled him. Possibly this woman could help him.

After some thought he sat down and penned a letter to Hannah Heath, beginning it here and there with devoted sentences which caused that young woman's eyes to sparkle and a smile of anticipation to wreathe her lips. When she heard of the handsome sister in New York, and of her former relations with David Spafford, her eyes narrowed speculatively, and her fair brow drew into puzzled frowns. Harry Temple had drawn a word picture of Mrs. Leavenworth. Harry should have been a novelist. If he had not been too lazy he would have been a success. Gold hair! Ah! Hannah had heard of gold hair before, and in connection with David's promised wife. Here was a mystery and Hannah resolved to look into it. It would at least be interesting to note the effect of her knowledge upon the young bride next door. She would try it.

Meantime, the acquaintance of Harry Temple and Kate Leavenworth had progressed rapidly. The second sight of the lady proved more interesting than the first, for now her beautiful gold hair added to the charm of her handsome face. Harry ever delighted in beauty of whatever type, and a blonde was more fascinating to him than a brunette. Kate had dressed herself bewitchingly, and her manner was charming. She knew how to assume pretty child-like airs, but she was not afraid to look him boldly in the eyes, and the light in her own seemed to challenge him. Here was a delightful new study. A woman fresh from the country, having all the charm of innocence, almost as child-like as her sister, yet with none of her prudishness. Kate's eyes held latent wickedness in them, or he was much mistaken. She did not droop her lids and blush when he looked boldly and admiringly into her face, but stared him back, smilingly, merrily, daringly, as though she would go quite as far as he would. Moreover with her he was sure he need feel none of the compunctions he might have felt with her younger sister who was so obviously innocent, for whether Kate's boldness was from lack of knowledge, or from lack of innocence, she was quite able to protect herself, that was plain.

So Harry settled into his chair with a smile of pleasant anticipation upon his face. He not only had the prospect before him of a possible ally in revenge against David Spafford, but he had the promise of a most unusually delightful flirtation with a woman who was worthy of his best efforts in that line.

Almost at once it began, with pleasant banter, adorned with personal compliments.

"Lovelier than I thought, my lady," said Harry, bowing low over the hand she gave him, in a courtly manner he had acquired, perhaps from the old-world novels he had read, and he brushed her pink finger tips with his lips in a way that signified he was her abject slave.

Kate blushed and smiled, greatly pleased, for though she had held her own little court in the village where she was brought up, and queened it over the young men who had flocked about her willingly, she had not been used to the fulsome flattery that breathed from Harry Temple in every word and glance.

He looked at her keenly as he stood back a moment, to see if she were in any wise offended with his salutation, and saw as he expected that she was pleased and flattered. Her cheeks had grown rosier, and her eyes sparkled with pleasure as she responded with a pretty, gracious speech.

Then they sat down and faced one another. A good woman would have called his look impudent—insulting. Kate returned it with a look that did not shrink, nor waver, but fearlessly, recklessly accepted the challenge. Playing with fire, were these two, and with no care for the fearful results which might follow. Both knew it was dangerous, and liked it the better for that. There was a long silence. The game was opening on a wider scale than either had every played before.

"Do you believe in affinities?" asked the devil, through the man's voice.

The woman colored and showed she understood his deeper meaning. Her eyes drooped for just the shade of an instant, and then she looked up and faced him saucily, provokingly:

"Why?"

He admired her with his gaze, and waited, lazily watching the color play in her cheeks.

"Do you need to ask why?" he said at last, looking at her significantly. "I knew that you were my affinity the moment I laid my eyes upon you, and I hoped you felt the same. But perhaps I was mistaken." He searched her face.

She kept her eyes upon his, returning their full gaze, as if to hold it from going too deep into her soul.

"I did not say you were mistaken, did I?" said the rosy lips coquettishly, and Kate drooped her long lashes till they fell in becoming sweeps over her burning cheeks.

Something in the curve of cheek and chin, and sweep of dark lash over velvet skin, reminded him of her sister. It was so she had sat, though utterly unconscious, while he had been singing, when there had come over him that overwhelming desire to kiss her. If he should kiss this fair lady would she slap him in the face and run into the garden? He thought not. Still, she was brought up by the same father and mother in all likelihood, and it was well to go slow. He reached forward, drawing his chair a little nearer to her, and then boldly took one of her small unresisting hands, gently, that he might not frighten her, and smoothed it thoughtfully between his own. He held it in a close grasp and looked into her face gain, she meanwhile watching her hand amusedly, as though it were something apart from herself, a sort of distant possession, for which she was in no wise responsible.

"I feel that you belong to me," he said boldly looking into her eyes with a languishing gaze. "I have known it from the first moment."

Kate let her hand lie in his as if she liked it, but she said:

"And what makes you think that, most audacious sir? Did you not know that I am married?" Then she swept her gaze up provokingly at him again and smiled, showing her dainty, treacherous, little teeth. She was so bewitchingly pretty and tempting then that he had mind to kiss her on the spot, but a thought came to him that he would rather lead her further first. He was succeeding well. She had no mind to be afraid. She did her part admirably.

"That makes no difference," said he smiling. "That another man has secured you first, and has the right to provide for you, and be near you, is my misfortune of course, but it makes no difference, you are mine! By all the power of love you are mine. Can any other man keep my soul from yours, can he keep my eyes from looking into yours, or my thoughts from hovering over you, or —" he hesitated and looked at her keenly, while she furtively watched him, holding her breath and half inviting him — "or my lips from drinking life from yours?" He stooped quickly and pressed his lips upon hers.

Kate gave a quick little gasp like a sob and drew back. The aunt nodding over her Bible in the next room had not heard, — she was very deaf, — but for an instant the young woman felt that all the shades of her worthy patriarchal ancestors were hurrying around and away from her in horror. She had come of too good Puritan stock not to know that she was treading in the path of unrighteousness. Nevertheless it was a broad path, and easy. It tempted her. It was exciting. It lured her with promise of satisfying some of her untamed longings and impulses.

She did not look offended. She only drew back to get breath and consider. The wild beating of her heart, the tumult of her cheeks and eyes were all a part of a new emotion. Her vanity was excited, and she thrilled with a wild pleasure. As a duck will take to swimming so she took to the new game, with wonderful facility.

"But I didn't say you might," she cried with a bewildering smile.

"I beg your pardon, fair lady, may I have another?"

His bold, bad face was near her own, so that she did not see the evil triumph that lurked there. She had come to the turning of another way in her life, and just here she might have drawn back if she would. Half she knew this, yet she toyed with the opportunity, and it was gone. The new way seemed so alluring.

"You will first have to prove your right!" she said decidedly, with that pretty commanding air that had conquered so many times.

And in like manner on they went through the evening, frittering the time away at playing with edged tools.

A friendship so begun — if so unworthy an intimacy may be called by that sweet name — boded no good to either of the two, and that evening marked a decided turn for the worse in Kate Leavenworth's career.

Chapter 20

David had found it necessary to take a journey which might keep him away for several weeks.

He told Marcia in the evening when he came home from the office. He told her as he would have told his clerk. It meant nothing to him but an annoyance that he had to start out in the early winter, leave his business in other's hands for an indefinite period, and go among strangers. He did not see the whitening of Marcia's lips, nor the quick little movement of her hand to her heart. Even Marcia herself did not realize all that it meant to her. She felt as if a sudden shock had almost knocked her off her feet. This quiet life in the big house, with only David at intervals to watch and speak to occasionally, and no one to open her true heart to, had been lonely; and many a time when she was alone at night she had wept bitter tears upon her pillow,—why she did not quite know. But now when she knew that it was to cease, and David was going away from her for a long time, perhaps weeks, her heart suddenly tightened and she knew how sweet it had been growing. Almost the tears came to her eyes, but she made a quick errand to the hearth for the teapot, busying herself there till they were under control again. When she returned to her place at the table she was able to ask David some commonplace question about the journey which kept her true feeling quite hidden from him

He was to start the next evening if possible. It appeared that there was something important about railroading coming up in Congress. It was necessary that he should be present to hear the debate, and also that he should see and interview influential men. It meant much to the success of the great new enterprises that were just in their infancy that he should go and find out all about them and write them up as only he whose heart was in it could do. He was pleased to have been selected for this; he was lifted for the time above himself and his life troubles, and given to feel that he had a work in the world that was worth while, a high calling, a chance to give a push to the unrolling of the secret possibilities of the universe, and help them on their way.

Marcia understood it all, and was proud and glad for him, but her own heart which beat in such perfect sympathy with the work felt lonely and left out. If only she could have helped too!

There was no time for David to take Marcia to her home to stay during his absence. He spoke of it regretfully just as he was about to leave, and asked if she would like him to get some one to escort her by coach to her father's house until he could come for her; but she held back the tears by main force and shook her head. She had canvassed that question in the still hours of the night. She had met in imagination the home village with its kindly and unkindly curiosity, she had seen their hands lifted in suspicion; heard their covert whispers as to why her husband did not come with her; why he had left her so soon after the honeymoon; why—a hundred things. She had even thought of Aunt Polly and her acrid tongue and made up her mind that whatever happened she did not want to go home to stay.

The only other alternative was to go to the aunts. David expected it, and the aunts spoke of it as if nothing else were possible. Marcia would have preferred to remain alone in her own house, with her beloved piano, but David would not consent, and the aunts were scandalized at the suggestion. So to the aunts went Marcia, and they took her in with a hope in their hearts that she might get the same good from the visit that the sluggard in the Bible is bidden to find.

"We must do our duty by her for David's sake," said Aunt Hortense, with pursed lips and capable, folded hands that seemed fairly to ache to get at the work of reconstructing the new niece.

"Yes, it is our opportunity," said Aunt Amelia with a snap as though she thoroughly enjoyed the prospect. "Poor David!" and so they sat and laid out their plans for their sweet young victim, who all unknowingly was coming to one of those tests in her life whereby we are tried for greater things and made perfect in patience and sweetness.

It began with the first breakfast—the night before she had been company, at supper—but when the morning came they felt she must be counted one of the family. They examined her thoroughly on what she had been taught with regard to housekeeping. They made her tell her recipes for pickling and preserving. They put her through a catechism of culinary lore, and always after her most animated account of the careful way in which she had been trained in this or that housewifely art she looked up with wistful eyes that longed to please, only to be met by the hard set lips and steely glances of the two mentors who regretted that she should not been taught their way which was so much better.

Aunt Hortense even went so far once as to suggest that Marcia write to her stepmother and tell her how much better it was to salt the water in which potatoes were to be boiled before putting them in, and was much offended by the clear girlish laugh that bubbled up involuntarily at the thought of teaching her stepmother anything about cooking.

"Excuse me," she said, instantly sobering as she saw the grim look of the aunt, and felt frightened at what she had done. "I did not mean to laugh, indeed I did not; but it seemed so funny to think of my telling mother how to do anything."

"People are never too old to learn," remarked Aunt Hortense with offended mien, "and one ought never to be too proud when there is a better way."

"But mother thinks there is no better way I am sure. She says that it makes potatoes soggy to boil them in salt. All that grows below the ground should be salted after it is cooked and all that grows above the ground should be cooked in salted water, is her rule."

"I am surprised that your stepmother should uphold any such superstitious ideas," said Aunt Amelia with a self-satisfied expression.

"One should never be too proud to learn something better," Aunt Hortense said grimly, and Marcia retreated in dire consternation at the thought of what might follow if these three notable housekeeping gentlewomen should come together. Somehow she felt a wicked little triumph in the thought that it would be hard to down her stepmother.

Marcia was given a few light duties ostensibly to "make her feel at home," but in reality, she knew, because the aunts felt she needed their instruction. She was asked if she would like to wash the china and glass; and regularly after each meal a small wooden tub and a mop were brought in with hot water and soap, and she was expected to handle the costly heirlooms under the careful scrutiny of their worshipping owners, who evidently watched each process with strained nerves lest any bit of treasured pottery should be cracked or broken. It was a trying ordeal.

The girl would have been no girl if she had not chafed under this treatment. To hold her temper steady and sweet under it was almost more than she could bear.

There were long afternoons when it was decreed that they should knit.

Marcia had been used to take long walks at home, over the smooth crust of the snow, going to her beloved woods, where she delighted to wander among the bare and creaking trees; fancying them whispering sadly to one another of the summer that was gone and the leaves they had borne now dead. But it would be a dreadful thing in the aunts' opinion for a woman, and especially a young one, to take a long walk in the woods alone, in winter too, and with no object whatever in view but a walk! What a waste of time!

There were two places of refuge for Marcia during the weeks that followed. There was home. How sweet that word sounded to her! How she longed to go back there, with David coming home to his quiet meals three times a day, and with her own time to herself to do as she pleased. With housewifely zeal that was commendable in the eyes of the aunts, Marcia insisted upon going down to her own house every morning to see that all was right, guiltily knowing that in her heart she meant to hurry to her beloved books and piano. To be sure it was cold and cheerless in the empty house. She dared not make up fires and leave them, and she dared not stay too long lest the aunts would feel hurt at her absence, but she longed with an inexpressible longing to be back there by herself, away from that terrible supervision and able to live her own glad little life and think her own thoughts untrammeled by primness.

Sometimes she would curl up in David's big arm-chair and have a good cry, after which she would take a book and read until the creeping chills down her spine warned her she must stop. Even then she would run up and down the hall or take a broom and sweep vigorously to warm herself and then go to the cold keys and play a sad little tune. All her tunes seemed sad like a wail while David was gone.

The other place of refuge was Aunt Clarinda's room. Thither she would betake herself after supper, to the delight of the old lady. Then the other two occupants of the house were left to themselves and might unbend from their rigid surveillance for a little while. Marcia often wondered if they ever did unbend.

There was a large padded rocking chair in Aunt Clarinda's room and Marcia would laughingly take the little old lady in her arms and place her comfortably in it, after a pleasant struggle on Miss Clarinda's part to put her guest into it. They had this same little play every evening, and it seemed to please the old lady mightily. Then when she was conquered she always sat meekly laughing, a fine pink color in her soft peachy cheek, the candle light from the high shelf making flickering sparkles in her old eyes that always seemed young; and she would say: "That's just as David used to do."

Then Marcia drew up the little mahogany stool covered with the worsted dog which Aunt Clarinda had worked when she was ten years old, and snuggling down at the old lady's feet exclaimed delightedly: "Tell me about it!" and they settled down to solid comfort.

There came a letter from David after he had been gone a little over a week. Marcia had not expected to hear from him. He had said nothing about writing, and their relations were scarcely such as to make it necessary. Letters were an expensive luxury in those days. But when the letter was handed to her, Marcia's heart went pounding against her breast, the color flew into her cheeks, and she sped away home on feet swift as the wings of a bird. The postmaster's daughter looked after her, and remarked to her father: "My, but don't she think a lot of him!"

Straight to the cold, lonely house she flew, and sitting down in his big chair read it.

It was a pleasant letter, beginning formally: *My dear Marcia,* and asking after her health. It brought back a little of the unacquaintedness she had felt when he was at home, and which had been swept away in part by her knowledge of his childhood. But it went on quite happily telling all about his journey and describing minutely the places he had passed through and the people he had met on the way; detailing every little incident as only a born writer and observer could do, until she felt as if he were talking to her. He told her of the men whom he had met who were interested in the new project. He told of new plans and described minutely his visit to the foundry at West Point and the machinery he had seen. Marcia read it all breathlessly, in search of something, she knew not what, that was not there. When she had finished and found it not, there was a sense of aloofness, a sad little disappointment which welled up in her throat. She sat back to think about it. He was having a good time, and he was not lonely. He had no longing to be back in the house and everything running as before he had gone. He was out in the big glorious world having to do with progress, and coming in contact with men who were making history. Of course he did not dream how lonely she was here, and how she longed, if for nothing else, just to be back here alone and do as she pleased, and not to be watched over. If only she might steal Aunt Clarinda and bring her back to live here with her while David was away! But that was not to be thought of, of course. By and by she mustered courage to be glad of her letter, and to read it over once more.

That night she read the letter to Aunt Clarinda and together they discussed the great inventions, and the changes that were coming to pass in the land. Aunt Clarinda was just a little beyond her depth in such a conversation, but Marcia did most of the talking, and the dear old lady made an excellent listener, with a pat here, and a "Dearie me! Now you don't say so!" there, and a "Bless the boy! What great things he does expect. And I hope he won't be disappointed."

That letter lasted them for many a day until another came, this time from Washington, with many descriptions of public men and public doings, and a word picture of the place which made it appear much like any other place after all if it was the capitol of the country. And once there was a sentence which Marcia treasured. It was, *I wish you could be here and see everything. You would enjoy it I know.*

There came another letter later beginning, *My dear little girl.* There was nothing else in it to make Marcia's heart throb, it was all about his work, but Marcia carried it many days in her bosom. It gave her a thrill of delight to think of those words at the beginning. Of course it meant no more than that he thought of her as a girl, his little sister that was to have been, but there was a kind of ownership in the words that was sweet to Marcia's lonely heart. It had come to her that she was always looking for something that would make her feel that she belonged to David.

Chapter 21

When David had been in New York about three weeks, he happened one day to pass the house where Kate Leavenworth was living.

Kate was standing listlessly by the window looking into the street. She was cross and felt a great depression settling over her. The flirtation with Harry Temple had begun to pall upon her. She wanted new worlds to conquer. She was restless and feverish. There was not excitement enough in the life she was living. She would like to meet more people, senators and statesmen — and to have plenty of money to dress as became her beauty, and be admired publicly. She half wished for the return of her husband, and meditated making up with him for the sake of going to Washington to have a good time in society there. What was the use of running away with a naval officer if one could not have the benefit of it? She had been a fool. Here she was almost to the last penny, and so many things she wanted. No word had come from her husband since he sent her the money at sailing. She felt a bitter resentment toward him for urging her to marry him. If she had only gone on and married David she would be living a life of ease now — plenty of money — nothing to do but what she pleased and no anxiety whatever, for David would have done just what she wanted.

Then suddenly she looked up and David passed before her!

He was walking with a tall splendid-looking man, with whom he was engaged in most earnest conversation, and his look was grave and deeply absorbed. He did not know of Kate's presence in New York, and passed the house in utter unconsciousness of the eyes watching him.

Kate's lips grew white, and her limbs seemed suddenly weak, but she strained her face against the window to watch the retreating figure of the man who had almost been her husband. How well she knew the familiar outline. How fine and handsome he appeared now! Why had she not thought so before? Were her eyes blind, or had she been under some strange enchantment? Why had she not known that her happiness lay in the way that had been marked out for her? Well, at least she knew it now.

She sat all day by that window and watched. She professed to have no appetite when pressed to come to the table, though she permitted herself to languidly consume the bountiful tray of good things that was brought her, but her eyes were on the street. She was watching to see if David would pass that way again. But though she watched until the sun went down and dusk sifted through the streets, she saw no sign nor heard the sound of his footsteps. Then she hastened up to her room, which faced upon the street also, and there, wrapped in blankets she sat in the cold frosty air, waiting and listening. And while she watched she was thinking bitter feverish thoughts. She heard Harry Temple knock and knew that he was told that she was not feeling well and had retired early. She watched him pause on the stoop thoughtfully as if considering what to do with the time thus unexpectedly thrown upon his hands, then saw him saunter up the street unconcernedly, and she wondered idly where he would go, and what he would do.

It grew late, even for New York. One by one the lights in the houses along the street went out, and all was quiet. She drew back from the window at last, weary with excitement and thinking, and lay down on the bed, but she could not sleep. The window was open and her ears were on the alert, and by and by there came the distant echo of feet ringing on the pavement. Some one was coming. She sprang up. She felt sure he was coming. Yes, there were two men. They were coming back together. She could hear their voices. She fancied she heard David's long before it was possible to distinguish any words. She leaned far out of her upper window till she could discern dim forms under the starlight, and then just as they were under the window she distinctly heard David say:

"There is no doubt but we shall win. The right is on our side, and it is the march of progress. Some of the best men in Congress are with us, and now that we are to have your influence, I do not feel afraid of the issue."

They had passed by rapidly, like men who had been on a long day's jaunt of some kind and were hastening home to rest. There was little in the sentence that Kate could understand. She had no more idea whether the subject of their discourse was railroads or the last hay crop. The sentence meant to her but one thing. It showed that David companioned with the great men of the land, and his position would have given her a standing that would have been above the one she now occupied. Tears of defeat ran down her cheeks. She had made a bad mistake and she saw no way to rectify it. If her husband should die,—and it might be, for the sea was often treacherous—of course there were all sorts of possibilities,—but even then there was Marcia! She set her sharp little teeth into her red lips till the blood came. She could not get over her anger at Marcia. It would not have been so bad if David had remained her lone lorn lover, ready to fly to her if others failed. Her self-love was wounded sorely, and she, poor silly soul, mistook it for love of David. She began to fancy that after all she had loved him, and that Fate had somehow played her a mad trick and tied her to a husband she had not wanted.

Then out of the watchings of the day and the fancies of the night, there grew a thought—and the thought widened into a plan. She thought of her intimacy with Harry and her new found power. Might she perhaps exercise it over others as well as Harry Temple? Might she possibly lead back this man who had once been her lover, to bow at her feet again and worship her? If that might be she could bear all the rest. She began to long with intense craving to see David grovel at her feet, to hear him plead for a kiss from her, and tell her once more how beautiful she was, and how she fulfilled all his soul's ideals. She sat by the open window yet with the icy air of the night blowing upon her, but her cheeks burned red in the darkness, and her eyes glowed like coals of fire from the tawny framing of her fallen hair. The blankets slipped away from her throat and still she heeded not the cold, but sat with hot clenched hands planning with the devil's own strategy her shameless scheme.

By and by she lighted a candle and drew her writing materials toward her to write, but it was long she sat and thought before she finally wrote the hastily scrawled note, signed and sealed it, and blowing out her candle lay down to sleep.

The letter was addressed to David, and it ran thus:

Dear David:
I have just heard that you are in New York. I am in great distress and do not know where to turn for help. For the sake of what we have been to each other in the past will you come to me?

Hastily, your loving Kate.

She did not know where David was but she felt reasonably sure she could find out his address in the morning. There was a small boy living next door who was capable of ferreting out almost anything for money. Kate had employed him more than once as an amateur detective in cases of minor importance. So, with a bit of silver and her letter she made her way to his familiar haunts and explained most carefully that the letter was to be delivered to no one but the man to whom it was addressed, naming several stopping places where he might be likely to be found, and hinting that there was more silver to be forthcoming when he should bring her an answer to the note. With a minute description of David the keen-eyed urchin set out, while Kate betook herself to her room to dress for David's coming. She felt sure he would be found, and confident that he would come at once.

The icy wind of the night before blowing on her exposed throat and chest had given her a severe cold, but she paid no heed to that. Her eyes and cheeks were shining with fever. She knew she was entering upon a dangerous and unholy way. The excitement of it stimulated her. She felt she did not care for anything, right or wrong, sin or sorrow, only to win. She wanted to see David at her feet again. It was the only thing that would satisfy this insatiable longing in her, this wounded pride of self.

When she was dressed she stood before the mirror and surveyed herself. She knew she was beautiful, and she defied the glass to tell her anything else. She raised her chin in haughty challenge to the unseen David to resist her charms. She would bring him low before her. She would make him forget Marcia, and his home and his staid Puritan notions, and all else he held dear but herself. He should bend and kiss her hand as Harry had done, only more warmly, for instinctively she felt that his had been the purer life and therefore his surrender would mean more. He should do whatever she chose. And her eyes glowed with an unhallowed light.

She had chosen to array herself regally, in velvet, but in black, without a touch of color or of white. From her rich frock her slender throat rose daintily, like a stem upon which nodded the tempting flower of her face. No enameled complexion could have been more striking in its vivid reds and whites, and her mass of gold hair made her seem more lovely than she really was, for in her face was love of self, alluring, but heartless and cruel.

The boy found David, as Kate had thought he would, in one of the quieter hostelries where men of letter were to stop when in New York, and David read the letter and came at once. She had known that he would do that, too. His heart beat wildly, to the exclusion of all other thoughts save that she was in trouble, his love, his dear one. He forgot Marcia, and the young naval officer, and everything but her trouble, and before he had reached her house the sorrow had grown in his imagination into some great danger to protect her from which he was hastening.

She received him alone in the room where Harry Temple had first called, and a moment later Harry himself came to knock and enquire for the health of Mistress Leavenworth, and was told she was very much engaged at present with a gentleman and could not see any one, whereupon Harry scowled, and set himself at a suitable distance from the house to watch who should come out.

David's face was white as death as he entered, his eyes shining like dark jewels blazing at her as if he would absorb the vision for the lonely future. She stood and posed,—not by any means the picture of broken sorrow he had expected to find her from her note,—and let the sense of her beauty reach him. There she stood with the look on her face he had pictured to himself many a time when he had thought of her as his wife. It was a look of love unutterable, bewildering, alluring, compelling. It was so he had thought she would meet him when he came home to her from his daily business cares. And now she was there, looking that way, and he stood here, so near her, and yet a great gulf fixed! It was heaven and hell met together, and he had no power to change either.

He did not come over to her and bow low to kiss the white hand as Harry had done,—as she had thought she could compel him to do. He only stood and looked at her with the pain of an anguish beyond her comprehension, until the look would have burned through to her heart—if she had had a heart.

"You are in trouble," he spoke hoarsely, as if murmuring an excuse for having come.

She melted at once into the loveliest sorrow, her mobile features taking on a wan cast only enlivened by the glow of her cheeks.

"Sit down," she said, "you were so good to come to me, and so soon—" and her voice was like lily-bells in a quite church-yard among the head-stones. She placed him a chair.

"Yes, I am in trouble. But that is a slight thing compared to my unhappiness. I think I am the most miserable creature that breathes upon this earth."

And with that she dropped into a low chair and hid her glowing face in a dainty, lace bordered kerchief that suppressed a well-timed sob.

Kate had wisely calculated how she could reach David's heart. If she had looked up then and seen his white, drawn look, and the tense grasp of his hands that only the greatest self-control kept quiet on his knee, perhaps even her mercilessness would have been softened. But she did not look, and she felt her part was well taken. She sobbed quietly, and waited, and his hoarse voice asked once more, as gently as a woman's though his pain:

"Will you tell me what it is and how I can help you?" He longed to take her in his arms like a little child and comfort her, but he might not. She was another's. And perhaps that other had been cruel to her! His clenched fists showed how terrible was the thought. But still the bowed figure in its piteous black sobbed and did not reply anything except, "Oh, I am so unhappy! I cannot bear it any longer."

"Is—your—your—husband unkind to you?" The words tore themselves from his tense lips as though they were beyond his control.

"Oh, no—not exactly unkind—that is—he was not very nice before he went away," wailed out a sad voice from behind the linen cambric and lace, "and he went away without a kind word, and left me hardly any money—and he hasn't sent me any word since—and fa-father won't have anything to do with me any more—but—but—it's not that I mind, David. I don't think about those things at all. I'm so unhappy about you. I feel you do not forgive me, and I cannot stand it any longer. I have made a fearful mistake, and you are angry with me—I think about it at night"—the voice was growing lower now, and the sentences broken by sobs that told better than words what distress the sufferer would convey.

"I have been so wicked—and you were so good and kind—and now you will never forgive me—I think it will kill me to keep on thinking about it—" her voice trailed off in tears again.

David white with anguish sprang to his feet.

"Oh, Kate," he cried, "my darling! Don't talk that way. You know I forgive you. Look up and tell me you know I forgive you."

Almost she smiled her triumph beneath her sobs in the little lace border, but she looked up with real tears on her face. Even her tears obeyed her will. She was a good actress, also she knew her power over David.

"Oh, David," she cried, standing up and clasping her hands beseechingly, "can it be true? Do you really forgive me? Tell me again."

She came and stood temptingly near to the stern, suffering man wild with the tumult that raged within him. Her golden head was near his shoulder where it had rested more than once in time gone by. He looked down at her from his suffering height his arms folded tightly and said, as though taking oath before a court of justice:

"I do."

She looked up with her pleading blue eyes, like two jewels of light now, questioning whether she might yet go one step further. Her breath came quick and soft, he fancied it touched his cheek, though she was not tall enough for that. She lifted her tear-wet face like a flower after a storm, and pleaded with her eyes once more, saying in a whisper very soft and sweet:

"If you really forgive me, then kiss me, just once, so I may remember it always."

It was more than he could bear. He caught her to himself and pressed his lips upon hers in one frenzied kiss of torture. It was as if wrung from him against his will. Then suddenly it came upon him what he had done, as he held her in his arms, and he put her from him gently, as a mother might put away the precious child she was sacrificing tenderly, agonizingly, but finally. He put her from him thus and stood a moment looking at her, while she almost sparkled her pleasure at him through the tears. She felt that she had won.

But gradually the silence grew ominous. She perceived he was not smiling. His mien was like one who looks into an open grave, and gazes for the last time at all that remains of one who is dear. He did not seem like one who had yielded a moral point and was ready now to serve her as she would. She grew uneasy under his gaze. She moved forward and put out her hands inviting, yielding, as only such a woman could do, and the spell which bound him seemed to be broken. He fumbled for a moment in his waistcoat pocket and brought out a large roll of bills which he laid upon the table, and taking up his hat turned toward the door. A cold wave of weakness seemed to pass over her, stung here and there by mortal pride that was in fear of being wounded beyond recovery.

"Where are you going?" she asked weakly, and her voice sounded to her from miles away, and strange.

He turned and looked at her again and she knew the look meant farewell. He did not speak. Her whole being rose for one more mighty effort.

"You are not going to leave me — now?" There was angelic sweetness in the voice, pleading, reproachful, piteous.

"I must!" he said, and his voice sounded harsh. "I have just done that for which, were I your husband, I would feel like killing any other man. I must protect you against yourself, — against myself. You must be kept pure before God if it kills us both. I would gladly die if that could help you, but I am not even free to do that, for I belong to another."

Then he turned and was gone.

Kate's hands fell to her sides, and seemed stiff and lifeless. The bright color faded from her cheeks, and a cold frenzy of horror took possession of her. "Pure before God!" She shuddered at the name, and crimson shame rolled over forehead and cheek. She sank in a little heap on the floor with her face buried in the chair beside which she had been standing, and the waters of humiliation rolled wave on wave above her. She had failed, and for one brief moment she was seeing her own sinful heart as it was.

But the devil was there also. He whispered to her now the last sentence that David had spoken: "I belong to another!"

Up to that moment Marcia had been a very negative factor in the affair to Kate's mind. She had been annoyed and angry at her as one whose ignorance and impertinence had brought her into an affair where she did not belong, but now she suddenly faced the fact that Marcia must be reckoned with. Marcia the child, who had for years been her slave and done her bidding, had arisen in her way, and she hated her with a sudden vindictive hate that would have killed without flinching if the opportunity had presented at that moment. Kate had no idea how utterly uncontrolled was her whole nature. She was at the mercy of any passing passion. Hate and revenge took possession of her now. With flashing eyes she rose to her feet, brushing her tumbled hair back and wiping away angry tears. She was too much agitated to notice that some one had knocked at the front door and been admitted, and when Harry Temple walked into the room he found her standing so with hands clenched together, and tears flowing down her cheeks unchecked.

Now a woman in tears, when the tears were not caused by his own actions, was Harry's opportunity. He had ways of comforting which were as unscrupulous as they generally proved effective, and so with affectionate tenderness he took Kate's hand and held it impressively, calling her "dear." He spoke soothing words, smoothed her hair, and kissed her flushed cheeks and eyes. It was all very pleasant to Kate's hurt pride. She let Harry comfort her, and pet her a while, and at last he said:

"Now tell me all about it, dear. I saw Lord Spafford trail dejectedly away from here looking like death, and I come here and find my lady in a fine fury. What has happened? If I mistake not the insufferable cad has got badly hurt, but it seems to have ruffled the lady also."

This helped. It was something to feel that David was suffering. She wanted him to suffer. He had brought shame and humiliation upon her. She never realized that the thing that shamed her was that he thought her better than she was.

"He is offensively good. I *hate* him!" she remarked as a kitten might who had got hurt at playing with a mouse in a trap.

The man's face grew bland with satisfaction.

"Not so good, my lady, but that he has been making love to you, if I mistake not, and he with a wife at home." The words were said quietly, but there was more of a question in them than the tone conveyed. The man wished to have evidence against his enemy.

Kate colored uneasily and drooped her lashes.

Harry studied her face keenly, and then went on cautiously:

"If his wife were not your sister I should say that one might punish him well through her."

Kate cast him a hard, scrutinizing look.

"You have some score against him yourself," she said with conviction.

"Perhaps I have, my lady. Perhaps I too hate him. He is offensively good, you know."

There was silence in the room for a full minute while the devil worked in both hearts.

"What did you mean by saying one might punish him through his wife? He does not love his wife."

"Are you sure?"

"Quite sure."

"Perhaps he loves some one else, my lady."

"He does." She said it proudly.

"Perhaps he loves you, my lady." He said it softly like the suggestion from another world. The lady was silent, but he needed no other answer.

"Then indeed, the way would be even clearer, — were not his wife your sister."

Kate looked at him, a half knowledge of his meaning beginning to dawn in her eyes.

"How?" she asked laconically.

"In case his wife should leave him do you think my lord would hold his head so high?"

Kate still looked puzzled.

"If some one else should win her affection, and should persuade her to leave a husband who did not love her, and who was bestowing his heart" — he hesitated an instant and his eye travelled significantly to the roll of bills still lying where David had left them — "and his gifts," he hazarded, "upon another woman — "

Kate grasped the thought at once and an evil glint of eagerness showed in her eyes. She could see what an advantage it would be to herself to have Marcia removed from the situation. It would break one more cord of honor that bound David to a code which was hateful to her now, because its existence shamed her. Nevertheless, unscrupulous as she was she could not see how this was a possibility.

"But she is offensively good too," she said as if answering her own thoughts.

"All goodness has its weak spot," sneered the man. "If I mistake not you have found my lord's. It is possible I might find his wife's."

The two pairs of eyes met then, filled with evil light. It was as if for an instant they were permitted to look into the pit, and see the possibilities of wickedness, and exult in it. The lurid glare of their thoughts played in their faces. All the passion of hate and revenge rushed upon Kate in a frenzy. With all her heart she wished this might be. She looked her co-operation in the plan even before her hard voice answered:

"You need not stop because she is my sister."

He felt he had her permission, and he permitted himself a glance of admiration for the depths to which she could go without being daunted. Here was evil courage worthy of his teaching. She seemed to him beautiful enough and daring enough for Satan himself to admire.

"And may I have the pleasure of knowing that I would by so doing serve my lady in some wise?"

She drooped her shameless eyes and murmured guardedly, "Perhaps." Then she swept him a coquettish glance that meant they understood one another.

"Then I shall feel well rewarded," he said gallantly, and bowing with more than his ordinary flattery of look bade her good day and went out.

Chapter 22

David stumbled blindly out the door and down the street. His one thought was to get to his room at the tavern and shut the door. He had an important appointment that morning, but it passed completely from his mind. He met one or two men whom he knew, but he did not see them, and passed them swiftly without a glance of recognition. They said one to another, "How absorbed he is in the great themes of the world!" but David passed on in his pain and misery and humiliation and never knew they were near him.

He went to the room that had been his since he had reached New York, and fastening the door against all intrusion fell upon his knees beside the bed, and let the floodtide of his sorrow roll over him. Not even when Kate had played him false on his wedding morning had he felt the pain that now cut into his very soul. For now there was mingled with it the agony of consciousness of sin. He had sinned against heaven, against honor and love, and all that was pure and good. He was just like any bad man. He had yielded to sudden temptation and taken another man's wife in his arms and kissed her! That the woman had been his by first right, and that he loved her: that she had invited the kiss, indeed pleaded for it, his sensitive conscience told him in no wise lessened the offense. He had also caused her whom he loved to sin. He was a man and knew the world. He should have shielded her against herself. And yet as he went over and over the whole painful scene through which he had just passed his soul cried out in agony and he felt his weakness more and more. He had failed, failed most miserably. Acted like any coward!

The humiliation of it was unspeakable. Could any sorrow be like unto his? Like a knife flashing through the gloom of his own shame would come the echo of her words as she pleaded with him to kiss her. It was a kiss of forgiveness she had wanted, and she had put her heart into her eyes and begged as for her very life. How could he have refused? Then he would parley with himself for a long time trying to prove to himself that the kiss and the embrace were justified, that he had done no wrong in God's sight. And ever after this round of confused arguing he would end with the terrible conviction that he had sinned.

Sometimes Marcia's sweet face and troubled eyes would appear to him as he wrestled all alone, and seemed to be longing to help him, and again would come the piercing thought that he had harmed this gentle girl also. He had tangled her into his own spoiled web of life, and been disloyal to her. She was pure and true and good. She had given up everything to help him and he had utterly forgotten her. He had promised to love, cherish, and protect her! That was another sin. He could not love and cherish her when his whole heart was another's. Then he thought of Kate's husband, that treacherous man who had stolen his bride and now gone away and left her sorrowing—left her without money, penniless in a strange city. Why had he not been more calm and questioned her before he came away? Perhaps she was in great need. It comforted him to think he had left her all the money he had with him. There was enough to keep her from want for a while. And yet, perhaps he had been wrong to give it to her. He had no right to give it!

He groaned aloud at the thought of his helplessness to help her helplessness. Was there not some way he could find out and help her without doing wrong?

Over and over he went through the whole dreadful day, until his brain was weary and his heart failed him. The heavens seemed brass and no answer came to his cry,—the appeal of a broken soul. It seemed that he could not get up from his knees, could not go out into the world again and face life. He had been tried and had failed, and yet though he knew his sin he felt an intolerable longing to commit it over again. He was frightened at his own weakness, and with renewed vigor he began to pray for help. It was like the prayer of Jacob of old, the crying out of a soul that would not be denied. All day long the struggle continued, and far into the night. At last a great peace began to settle upon David's soul. Things that had been confused by his passionate longings grew clear as day. Self dropped away, and sin, conquered, slunk out of sight. Right and Wrong were once more clearly defined in his mind. However wrong it might or might not be he was here in this situation. He had married Marcia and promised to be true to her. He was doubly cut off from Kate by her own act and by his. That was his punishment,—and hers. He must not seek to lessen it even for her, for it was God-sent. Henceforth his path and hers must be apart. If she were to be helped in any way from whatsoever trouble was hers, it was not permitted him to be the instrument. He had shown his unfitness for it in his interview that morning, even if in the eyes of the world it could have been at all. It was his duty to cut himself off from her forever. He must not even think of her any more. He must be as true and good to Marcia as was possible. He must do no more wrong. He must grow strong and suffer.

The peace that came with conviction brought sleep to his weary mind and body.

When he awoke it was almost noon. He remembered the missed appointment of the day before, and the journey to Washington which he had planned for that day. With a start of horror he looked at his watch and found he had but a few hours in which to try to make up for the remissness of yesterday before the evening coach left for Philadelphia. It was as if some guardian angel had met his first waking thoughts with business that could not be delayed and so kept him from going over the painful events of the day before. He arose and hastened out into the world once more.

Late in the afternoon he found the man he was to have met the day before, and succeeded in convincing him that he ought to help the new enterprise. He was standing on the corner saying the last words as the two separated, when Kate drove by in a friend's carriage, surrounded by parcels. She had been on a shopping tour spending the money that David had given her, for silks and laces and jewelry, and now she was returning in high glee with her booty. The carriage passed quite near to David who stood with his back to the street, and she could see his animated face as he smiled at the other man, a fine looking man who looked as if he might be some one of note. The momentary glance did not show the haggard look of David's face nor the lines under his eyes, and Kate was angered to see him so unconcerned and forgetful of his pain of yesterday. Her face darkened with spite, and she resolved to make him suffer yet, and to the utmost, for the sin of forgetting her.

But David was in the way of duty, and he did not see her, for his guardian angel was hovering close at hand.

As the Fall wore on and the winter set in Harry's letters became less frequent and less intimate. Hannah was troubled, and after consultation with her grandmother, to which Miranda listened at the latch hole, duly reporting quotations to her adored Mrs. Spafford, Hannah decided upon an immediate trip to the metropolis.

"Hannah's gone to New York to find out what's become of that nimshi Harry Temple. She thought she had him fast, an' she's been holdin' him over poor Lemuel Skinner's head like thet there sword hangin' by a 'air I heard the minister tell about last Sunday, till Lemuel, he don't know but every minute's gone'll be his last. You mark my words, she'll hev to take poor Lem after all, an' be glad she's got him, too, — and she's none too good for him neither. He's ben faithful to her ever since she wore pantalets, an' she's ben keepin' him off'n on an' hopin' an' tryin' fer somebody bigger. It would jes' serve her right ef she'd get that fool of a Harry Temple, but she won't. He's too sharp for that ef he *is* a fool. He don't want to tie himself up to no woman's aprun strings. He rather dandle about after 'em all an' say pretty things, an' keep his earnin's fer himself."

Hannah reached New York the week after David left for Washington. She wrote beforehand to Harry to let him know she was coming, and made plain that she expected his attentions exclusively while there, and he smiled blandly as he read the letter and read her intentions between the lines. He told Kate a good deal about her that evening when he went to call, told her how he had heard she was an old flame of David's, and Kate's jealousy was immediately aroused. She wished to meet Hannah Heath. There was a sort of triumph in the thought that she had scorned and flung aside the man whom this woman had "set her cap" for, even though another woman was now in the place that neither had. Hannah went to visit a cousin in New York who lived in a quiet part of the city and did not go out much, but for reasons best known to themselves, both Kate Leavenworth and Harry Temple elected to see a good deal of her while she was in the city. Harry was pleasant and attentive, but not more to one woman than to the other. Hannah, watching him jealously, decided that at least Kate was not her rival in his affections, and so Hannah and Kate became quite friendly. Kate had a way of making much of her women friends when she chose, and she happened to choose in this case, for it occurred to her it would be well to have a friend in the town where lived her sister and her former lover. There might be reasons why, sometime. She opened her heart of hearts to Hannah, and Hannah, quite discreetly, and without wasting much of her scanty store of love, entered, and the friendship was sealed. They had not known each other many days before Kate had confided to Hannah the story of her own marriage and her sister's, embellished of course as she chose. Hannah, astonished, puzzled, wondering, curious, at the tragedy that had been enacted at her very home door, became more friendly than ever and hated more cordially than ever the young and innocent wife who had stepped into the vacant place and so made her own hopes and ambitions impossible. She felt that she would like to put down the pert young thing for daring to be there, and to be pretty, and now she felt she had the secret which would help her to do so.

As the visit went on and it became apparent to Hannah Heath that she was not the one woman in all the world to Harry Temple, she hinted to Kate that it was likely she would be married soon. She even went so far as to say that she had come away from home to decide the matter, and that she had but to say the word and the ceremony would come off. Kate questioned eagerly, and seeing her opportunity asked if she might come to the wedding. Hannah, flattered, and seeing a grand opportunity for a wholesale triumph and revenge, assented with pleasure. Afterward as Hannah had hoped and intended, Kate carried the news of the impending decision and probable wedding to the ears of Harry Temple.

But Hannah's hint had no further effect upon the redoubtable Harry. Two days later he appeared, smiling, congratulatory, deploring the fact that she would be lost in a certain sense to his friendship, although he hoped always to be looked upon as a little more than a friend.

Hannah covered her mortification under a calm and condescending exterior. She blushed appropriately, said some sentimental things about hoping their friendship would not be affected by the change, told him how much she had enjoyed their correspondence, but gave him to understand that it had been mere friendship of course from her point of view, and Harry indulgently allowed her to think that he had hoped for more and was grieved but consolable over the outcome.

They waxed a trifle sentimental at the parting, but when Harry was gone, Hannah wrote a most touching letter to Lemuel Skinner which raised him to

the seventh heaven of delight, causing him to feel that he was treading upon air
as he walked the prosaic streets of his native town where he had been going
about during Hannah's absence like a lost spirit without a guiding star.

Dear Lemuel: she wrote: —
I am coming home. I wonder if you will be glad? (Artful Hannah, as if she
did not know!)
*It is very delightful in New York and I have been having a gay time since I came,
and everybody has been most pleasant, but —*
*"Mid pleasures and palaces though we may roam, Still, be it ever so humble,
there's no place like home. A charm from the skies seems to hallow it there, which,
go through the world, you'll not meet elsewhere. Home, home, sweet home! There's
no place like home."*
*That is a new song, Lemuel, that everybody here is singing. It is written by a
young American named John Howard Payne who is in London now acting in a
great playhouse. Everybody is wild over this song. I'll sing it for you when I come
home.*
*I shall be at home in time for singing school next week, Lemuel. I wonder if
you'll come to see me at once and welcome me. You cannot think how glad I shall
be to get home again. It seems as though I had been gone a year at least. Hoping
to see you soon, I remain*

> *Always your sincere friend,*
> *Hannah Heath.*

And thus did Hannah make smooth her path before her, and very soon after
inditing this epistle she bade good-bye to New York and took her way home
resolved to waste no further time in chasing will-o-the-wisps.

When Lemuel received that letter he took a good look at himself in the
glass. More than seven years had he served for Hannah, and little hope had he
had of a final reward. He was older by ten years than she, and already his face
began to show it. He examined himself critically, and was pleased to find with
that light of hope in his eyes he was not so bad looking as he feared. He betook
himself to the village tailor forthwith and ordered a new suit of clothes, though
his Sunday best was by no means shiny yet. He realized that he if did not win
now he never would, and he resolved to do his best.

On the way home, during all the joltings of the coach over rough roads
Hannah Heath was planning two campaigns, one of love with Lemuel, and one
of hate with Marcia Spafford. She was possessed of knowledge which she felt
would help her in the latter, and often she smiled vindictively as she laid her
neat plans for the destruction of the bride's complacency.

That night the fire in the Heath parlor burned high and glowed, and the
candles in their silver holders flickered across fair Hannah's face as she dimpled

and smiled and coquetted with poor Lemuel. But Lemuel needed no pity. He was not afraid of Hannah. Not for nothing had he served his seven years, and he understood every fancy and foible of her shallow nature. He knew his time had come at last, and he was getting what he had wanted long, for Lemuel had admired and loved Hannah in spite of the dance she had led him, and in spite of the other lovers she had allowed to come between them.

Hannah had not been at home many days before she called upon Marcia.

Marcia had just seated herself at the piano when Hannah appeared to her from the hall, coming in unannounced through the kitchen door according to old neighborly fashion.

Marcia was vexed. She arose from the instrument and led the way to the little morning room which was sunny and cozy, and bare of music or books. She did not like to visit with Hannah in the parlor. Somehow her presence reminded her of the evil face of Harry Temple as he had stooped to kiss her.

"You know how to play, too, don't you?" said Hannah as they sat down. "Your sister plays beautifully. Do you know the new song, 'Home, Sweet Home?' She plays it with so much feeling and sings it so that one would think her heart was breaking for her home. You must have been a united family." Hannah said it with sharp scrutiny in voice and eyes.

"Sit down, Miss Heath," said Marcia coolly, lowering the yellow shades that her visitor's eyes might not be troubled by a broad sunbeam. "Did you have a pleasant time in New York?"

Hannah could not be sure whether or not the question was an evasion. The utterly child-like manner of Marcia disarmed suspicion.

"Oh, delightful, of course. Could any one have anything else in New York?" Hannah laughed disagreeably. She realized the limitations of life in a town.

"I suppose," said Marcia, her eyes shining with the thought, "that you saw all the wonderful things of the city. I should enjoy being in New York a little while. I have heard of so many new things. Were there any ships in the harbor? I have always wanted to go over a great ship. Did you have opportunity of seeing one?"

"Oh, dear me. No!" said Hannah. "I shouldn't have cared in the least for that. I'm sure I don't know whether there were any ships in or not. I suppose there were. I saw a lot of sails on the water, but I did not ask about them. I'm not interested in dirty boats. I liked visiting the shops best. Your sister took me about everywhere. She is a most charming creature. You must miss her greatly. You were a sly little think to cut her out."

Marcia's face flamed crimson with anger and amazement. Hannah's dart had hit the mark, and she was watching keenly to see her victim quiver.

"I do not understand you," said Marcia with girlish dignity.

"Oh, now don't pretend to misunderstand. I've heard all about it from headquarters," she said it archly, laughing. "But then I don't blame you. David was worth it." Hannah ended with a sigh. If she had ever cared for any one besides herself that one was David Spafford.

"I do not understand you," said Marcia again, drawing herself up with all the Schuyler haughtiness she could master, till she quite resembled her father.

"Now, Mrs. Spafford," said the visitor, looking straight into her face and watching every expression as a cat would watch a mouse, "you don't mean to tell me your sister was not at one time very intimate with your husband."

"Mr. Spafford has been intimate in our family for a number of years," said Marcia proudly, her fighting fire up, "but as for my having 'cut my sister out' as you call it, you certainly have been misinformed. Excuse me, I think I will close the kitchen door. It seems to blow in here and make a draft."

Marcia left the room with her head up and her fine color well under control, and when she came back her head was still up and a distant expression was in her face. Somehow Hannah felt she had not gained much after all. But Marcia, after Hannah's departure, went up to her cold room and wept bitter tears on her pillow alone.

After that first visit Hannah never found the kitchen door unlocked when she came to make a morning call, but she improved every little opportunity to torment her gentle victim. She had had a letter from Kate and had Marcia heard? How often did Kate write her? Did Marcia know how fond Harry Temple was of Kate? And where was Kate's husband? Would he likely be ordered home soon? These little annoyances were almost unbearable sometimes and Marcia had much ado to keep her sweetness of outward demeanor.

People looked upon Lemuel with new respect. He had finally won where they had considered him a fool for years for hanging on. The added respect brought added self-respect. He took on new manliness. Grandmother Heath felt that he really was not so bad after all, and perhaps Hannah might as well have taken him at first. Altogether the Heath family were well pleased, and preparations began at once for a wedding in the near future.

And still David lingered, held here and there by a call from first one man and then another, and by important doings in Congress. He seemed to be rarely fitted for the work.

Once he was called back to New York for a day or two, and Harry Temple happened to see him as he arrived. That night he wrote to Hannah a friendly letter — Harry was by no means through with Hannah yet — and casually remarked that he saw David Spafford was in New York again. He supposed now that Mrs. Leavenworth's evenings would be fully occupied and society would see little of her while he remained.

The day after Hannah received that letter was Sunday.

The weeks had gone by rapidly since David left his home, and now the Spring was coming on. The grass was already green as summer and the willow tree by the graveyard gate was tender and green like a spring-plume. All the foliage was out and fluttering its new leaves in the sunshine as Marcia passed from the old stone church with the two aunts and opened her little green sunshade. Her motion made David's last letter rustle in her bosom. It thrilled her with pleasure that not even the presence of Hannah Heath behind her could cloud.

However prim and fault-finding the two aunts might be in the seclusion of their own home, in public no two could have appeared more adoring than Amelia and Hortense Spafford. They hovered near Marcia and delighted to show how very close and intimate was the relationship between themselves and their new and beautiful niece, of whom in their secret hearts they were prouder than they would have cared to tell. In their best black silks and their fine lace shawls they walked beside her and talked almost eagerly, if those two stately beings could have anything to do with a quality so frivolous as eagerness. They wished it understood that David's wife was worthy of appreciation and they were more conscious than she of the many glances of admiration in her direction.

Hannah Heath encountered some of those admiring glances and saw jealously for whom they were meant. She hastened to lean forward and greet Marcia, her spiteful tongue all ready for a stab.

"Good morning, Mrs. Spafford. Is that husband of yours not home yet? Really! Why, he's quite deserted you. I call that hard for the first year, and your honeymoon scarcely over yet."

"He's been called back to New York again," said Marcia annoyed over the spiteful little sentences. "He says he may be at home soon, but he cannot be sure. His business is rather uncertain."

"New York!" said Hannah, and her voice was annoyingly loud. "What! Not again! There must be some great attraction there," and then with a meaning glance, "I suppose your sister is still there!"

Marcia felt her face crimsoning, and the tears starting from angry eyes. She felt a sudden impulse to slap Hannah. What if she should! What would the aunts say? The thought of the tumult she might make roused her sense of humor and a laugh bubbled up instead of the tears, and Hannah, watching, cat-like, could only see eyes dancing with fun though the cheeks were charmingly red. By Hannah's expression Marcia knew she was baffled, but Marcia could not get away from the disagreeable suggestion that had been made.

Yes, David was in New York, and Kate was there. Not for an instant did she doubt her husband's nobleness. She knew David would be good and true. She knew little of the world's wickedness, and never thought of any blame, as other women might, in such a suggestion. But a great jealousy sprang into being that she never dreamed existed. Kate was there, and he would perhaps see her, and all his old love and disappointment would be brought to mind again. Had she, Marcia, been hoping he would forget it? Had she been claiming something of him in her heart for herself? She could not tell. She did not know what all this tumult of feeling meant. She longed to get away and think it over, but the solemn Sunday must be observed. She must fold away her church things, put on another frock and come down to the oppressive Sunday dinner, hear Deacon Brown's rheumatism discussed, or listen to a long comparison of the morning's sermon with one preached twenty years ago by the minister, now long dead, upon the same text. It was all very hard to keep her mind upon, with these other thoughts rushing pell-mell through her brain; and when Aunt Amelia asked her to pass the butter, she handed the sugar bowl instead. Miss Amelia looked as shocked as if she had broken the great-grandmother's china teapot.

Aunt Clarinda claimed her after dinner and carried her off to her room to talk about David, so that Marcia had no chance to think even then. Miss Clarinda looked into the sweet shadowed eyes and wondered why the girl looked so sad. She thought it was because David stayed away so long, and so she kept her with her all the rest of the day.

When Marcia went to her room that night she threw herself on her knees beside the bed and tried to pray. She felt more lonely and heartsick than she ever felt before in her life. She did not know what the great hunger in her heart meant. It was terrible to think David had loved Kate. Kate never loved him in return in the right way. Marcia felt very sure of that. She wished she might have had the chance in Kate's place, and then all of a sudden the revelation came to her. She loved David herself with a great overwhelming love. Not just a love that could come and keep house for him and save him from the criticisms and comments of others; but with a love that demanded to be loved in return; a love that was mindful of every dear lineament of his countenance. The knowledge thrilled through her with a great sweetness. She did not seem to care for anything else just now, only to know that she loved David. David could never love her of course, not in that way, but she would love him. She would try to shut out the thought of Kate from him forever.

And so, dreaming, hovering on the edge of all that was bitter and all that was sweet, she fell asleep with David's letter clasped close over her heart.

Chapter 23

Marcia had gone down to her own house the next morning very early. She had hoped for a letter but none had come. Her soul was in torment between her attempt to keep out of her mind the hateful things Hannah Heath had said, and reproaching herself for what seemed to her unseemly feeling toward David, who loved another and could never love her. It was not a part of her life-dream to love one who belonged to another. Yet her heart was his and she was beginning to know that everything belonging to him was dear to her. She went and sat in his place at the table, she touched with tenderness the books upon his desk that he had used before he went away, she went up to his room and laid her lips for one precious daring instant upon his pillow, and then drew back with wildly beating heart ashamed of her emotion. She knelt beside his bed and prayed: "Oh, God, I love him, I love him! I cannot help it!" as if she would apologize for herself, and then she hugged the thought of her love to herself, feeling its sweet pain drift through her like some delicious agony. Her love had come through sorrow to her, and was not as she would have had it could she have chosen. It brought no ray of happy hope for the future, save just the happiness of loving in secret, and of doing for the object she loved, with no thought of a returned affection.

Then she went slowly down the stairs, trying to think how it would seem when David came back. He had been so long gone that it seemed as if perhaps he might never return. She felt that it had been no part of the spirit of her contract with David that she should render to him this wild sweet love that he had expected Kate to give. He had not wanted it. He had only wanted a wife in name.

Then the color would sweep over her face in a crimson drift and leave it painfully white, and she would glide to the piano like a ghost of her former self and play some sad sweet strain and sometimes sing.

She had no heart for her dear old woods in these days. She had tried it one day in Spring; slipped over the back fence and away through the ploughed field where the sea of silver oats had surged, and up into the hillside and the woods; but she was so reminded of David that it only brought heart aches and tears. She wondered if it was because she was getting old that the hillside did not seem so joyous now, and she did not care to look up into the sky just for the pure joy of sky and air and clouds, nor to listen to the branches whisper to the robins nesting. She stooped and picked a great handful of Spring beauties, but they did not seem to give her pleasure, and by and by she dropped them from listless fingers and walked sedately down to the house once more.

On this morning she did not even care to play. She went into the parlor and touched a few notes, but her heart was heavy and sad. Life was growing too complex.

Last week there had come a letter from Harry Temple. It had startled her when it arrived. She feared it was some ill-news about David, coming as it did from New York and being written in a strange hand.

It had been a plea for forgiveness, representing that the writer had experienced nothing but deep repentance and sorrow since the time he had seen her last. He set forth his case in a masterly way, with little touching facts of his childhood, and lonely upbringing, with no mother to guide. He told her that her noble action toward him had but made him revere her the more, and that, in short, she had made a new creature of him by refusing to return his kiss that day, and leaving him alone with so severe a rebuke. He felt that if all women were so good and true men would be a different race, and now he looked up to an angel, and he felt he could never be happy again on this earth until he had her written word of forgiveness. With that he felt he could live a new life, and she must rest assured that he would never offer other than reverence to any woman again. He further added that his action had not intended any insult to her, that he was merely expressing his natural admiration for a spirit so good and true, and that his soul was innocent of any intention of evil. With sophistry in the use of which he was an adept, he closed his epistle, fully clearing himself, and assuring her that he could have made her understand it that day if she had not left so suddenly, and he had not been almost immediately called away to the dying bed of his dear cousin. This contradictory letter had troubled Marcia greatly. She was keen enough to see that his logic was at fault, and that the two pages of his letter did not hang together, but one thing was plain, that he wished her forgiveness. The Bible said that one must forgive, and surely it was right to let him know that she did, though when she thought of the fright he had given her it was hard to do. Still, it was right, and if he was so unhappy, perhaps she had better let him know. She would rather have waited until David returned to consult him in the matter, but the letter seemed so insistent that she had finally written a stiff little note, in formal language, *Mrs. Spafford sends herewith her full and free forgiveness to Mr. Harry Temple, and promises to think no more of the matter.*

She would have liked to consult some one. She almost thought of taking Aunt Clarinda into her confidence, but decided that she might not understand. So she finally sent off the brief missive, and let her troubled thoughts wander after it more than once.

She was standing by the window looking out into the yard perplexing herself over this again when there came a loud knocking at the front door. She started, half frightened, for the knock sounded through the empty house so insistently. It seemed like trouble coming. She felt nervous as she went down the hall.

It was only a little urchin, barefoot, and tow-headed. He had ridden an old mare to the door, and left her nosing at the dusty grass. He brought her a letter. Again her heart fluttered excitedly. Who could be writing to her? It was not David. Why did the handwriting look familiar? It could not be from any one at home. Father? Mother? No, it was no one she knew. She tore it open, and the boy jumped on his horse and was off down the street before she realized that he was gone.

DEAR MADAM: the letter read, *I bring you news of your husband, and having met with with an accident I am unable to come further. You will find me at the Green Tavern two miles out on the corduroy road. As the business is private, please come alone.*

A Messenger

Marcia trembled so that she sat down on the stairs. A sudden weakness went over her like a wave, and the hall grew dark around her as though she were going to faint. But she did not. She was strong and well and had never fainted in her life. She rallied in a moment and tried to think. Something had happened to David. Something dreadful, perhaps, and she must go at once and find out. Still it must be something mysterious, for the man had said it was private. Of course that meant David would not want it known. David had intended that the man would come to her and tell her by herself. She must go. There was nothing else to be done. She must go at once and get rid of this awful suspense. It was a good day for the message to have come, for she had brought her lunch expecting to do some Spring cleaning. David had been expected home soon, and she liked to make a bustle of preparation as if he might come in any day, for it kept up her good cheer.

Having resolved to go she got up at once, closed the doors and windows, put on her bonnet and went out down the street toward the old corduroy road. It frightened her to think what might be at the end of her journey. Possibly David himself, hurt or dying, and he had sent for her in this way that she might break the news gently to his aunts. As she walked along she conjured various forms of trouble that might have come to him. Now and then she would try to take a cheerful view, saying to herself that David might have needed more important papers, papers which he would not like everyone to know about, and had sent by special messenger to her to get them. Then her face would brighten and her step grow more brisk. But always would come the dull thud of possibility of something more serious. Her heart beat so fast sometimes that she was forced to lessen her speed to get her breath, for though she was going through town, and must necessarily walk somewhat soberly lest she call attention to herself, she found that her nerves and imagination were fairly running ahead, and waiting impatiently for her feet to catch up at every turning place.

At last she came to the corduroy road—a long stretch of winding way overlaid with logs which made an unpleasant path. Most of the way was swampy, and bordered in some places by thick, dark woods. Marcia sped on from log to log, with a nervous feeling that she must step on each one or her errand would not be successful. She was not afraid of the loneliness, only of what might be coming at the end of her journey.

But suddenly, in the densest part of the wood, she became conscious of footsteps echoing hers, and a chill laid hold upon her. She turned her head and there, wildly gesticulating and running after her, was Miranda!

Annoyed, and impatient to be on her way, and wondering what to do with Miranda, or what she could possibly want, Marcia stopped to wait for her.

"I thought—as you was goin' 'long my way"— puffed Miranda, "I'd jes' step along beside you. You don't mind, do you?"

Marcia looked troubled. If she should say she did then Miranda would think it queer and perhaps suspect something.

She tried to smile and ask how far Miranda was going.

"Oh, I'm goin' to hunt fer wild strawberries," said the girl nonchalantly clattering a big tin pail.

"Isn't it early yet for strawberries?" questioned Marcia.

"Well, mebbe, an' then ag'in mebbe 'tain't. I know a place I'm goin' to look anyway. Are you goin' 's fur 's the Green Tavern?"

Miranda's bright eyes looked her through and through, and Marcia's truthful ones could not evade. Suddenly as she looked into the girl's homely face, filled with a kind of blind adoration, her heart yearned for counsel in this trying situation. She was reminded of Miranda's helpfulness the time she ran away to the woods, and the care with which she had guarded the whole matter so that no one ever heard of it. An impulse came to her to confide in Miranda. She was a girl of sharp common sense, and would perhaps be able to help with her advice. At least she could get comfort from merely telling her trouble and anxiety.

"Miranda," she said, "can you keep a secret?"

The girl nodded.

"Well, I'm going to tell you something, just because I am so troubled and I feel as if it would do me good to tell it." She smiled and Miranda answered the smile with much satisfaction and no surprise. Miranda had come for this, though she did not expect her way to be so easy.

"I'll be mum as an oyster," said Miranda. "You jest tell me anything you please. You needn't be afraid Hannah Heath'll know a grain about it. She 'n' I are two people. I know when to shut up."

"Well, Miranda, I'm in great perplexity and anxiety. I've just had a note from a messenger my husband has sent asking me to come out to that Green Tavern you were talking about. He was sent to me with some message and has had an accident so he couldn't come. It kind of frightened me to think what might be the matter. I'm glad you are going this way because it keeps me from thinking about it. Are we nearly there? I never went out this road so far before."

"It ain't fur," said Miranda as if that were a minor matter. "I'll go right along in with you, then you needn't feel lonely. I guess likely it's business. Don't you worry." The tone was reassuring, but Marcia's face looked troubled.

"No, I guess that won't do, Miranda, for the note says it is a private matter and I must come alone. You know Mr. Spafford has matters to write about that are very important, railroads, and such things, and sometimes he doesn't care to have any one get hold of his ideas before they appear in the paper. His enemies might use them to stop the plans of the great improvements he is writing about."

"Let me see that note!" demanded Miranda. "Got it with you?" Marcia hesitated. Perhaps she ought not to show it, and yet there was nothing in the note but what she had already told the girl, and she felt sure she would not breathe a word to a living soul after her promise. She handed Miranda the letter, and they stopped a moment while she slowly spelled it out. Miranda was no scholar. Marcia watched her face eagerly, as if to gather a ray of hope from it, but she was puzzled by Miranda's look. A kind of satisfaction had overspread her homely countenance.

"Should you think from that that David was hurt — or ill — or — or — killed or anything?" She asked the question as if Miranda were a wizard, and hung anxiously upon her answer.

"Naw, I don't reckon so!" said Miranda. "Don't you worry. David's all right somehow. I'll take care o' you. You go 'long up and see what's the business, an' I'll wait here out o' sight o' the tavern. Likely's not he might take a notion not to tell you ef he see me come along with you. You jest go ahead, and I'll be on hand when you get through. If you need me fer anything you jest holler out 'Randy!' good and loud an' I'll hear you. Guess I'll set on this log. The tavern's jest round that bend in the road. Naw, you needn't thank me. This is a real pretty mornin' to set an' rest. Good-bye."

Marcia hurried on, glancing back happily at her protector in a calico sunbonnet seated stolidly on a log with her tin pail beside her.

Poor stupid Miranda! Of course she could not understand what a comfort it was to have confided her trouble. Marcia went up to the tavern with almost a smile on her face, though her heart began to beat wildly as a slatternly girl led her into a big room at the right of the hall.

As Marcia disappeared behind the bend in the road, Miranda stealthily stole along the edge of the woods, till she stood hidden behind a clump of alders where she could peer out and watch Marcia until she reached the tavern and passed safely by the row of lounging, smoking men, and on into the doorway. Then Miranda waited just an instant to look in all directions, and sped across the road, mounting the fence and on through two meadows, and the barnyard to the kitchen door of the tavern.

"Mornin'! Mis' Green," she said to the slovenly looking woman who sat by the table peeling potatoes. "Mind givin' me a drink o' water? I'm terrible thirsty, and seemed like I couldn't find the spring. Didn't thare used to be a spring 'tween here'n town?"

"Goodness sakes! Randy! Where'd you come from? Water! Jes' help yourself. There's the bucket jes' from the spring five minutes since, an' there's the gourd hanging up on the wall. I can't get up, I'm that busy. Twelve to dinner to-day, an' only me to do the cookin'. 'Melia she's got to be upstairs helpin' at the bar."

"Who all you got here?" questioned Miranda as she took a draught from the old gourd.

"Well, got a gentleman from New York fur one. He's real pretty. Quite a beau. His clo'es are that nice you'd think he was goin' to court. He's that particular 'bout his eatin' I feel flustered. Nothin' would do but he hed to hev a downstairs room. He said he didn't like goin' upstairs. He don't look sickly, neither."

"Mebbe he's had a accident an' lamed himself," suggested Miranda cunningly. "Heard o' any accidents? How'd he come? Coach or horseback?"

"Coach," said Mrs. Green. "Why do you ask? Got any friends in New York?"

"Not many," responded Miranda importantly, "but my cousin Hannah Heath has. You know she's ben up there fer a spell visitin' an' they say there was lots of gentlemen in love with her. There's one in particular used to come round a good deal. It might be him come round to see ef it's true Hannah's goin' to get married to Lem Skinner. Know what this fellow's name is?"

"You don't say! Well now it might be. No, I don't rightly remember his name. Seems though it was something like Church er Chapel. 'Melia could tell ye, but she's busy."

"Where's he at? Mebbe I could get a glimpse o' him. I'd jest like to know ef he was coming to bother our Hannah."

"Well, now. Mebbe you could get a sight of him. There's a cupboard between his room an' the room back. It has a door both sides. Mebbe ef you was to slip in there you might see him through the latch hole. I ain't usin' that back room fer anythin' but a store-room this Spring, so look out you don't stumble over nothin' when you go in fer it's dark as a pocket. You go right 'long in, I reckon you'll find the way. Yes, it's on the right hand side o' the hall. I've got to set here an' finish these potatoes er dinner'll be late. I'd like to know real well ef he's one o' Hannah Heath's beaux."

Miranda needed no second bidding. She slipped through the hall and store room, and in a moment stood before the door of the closet. Softly she opened it, and stepped in, lifting her feet cautiously, for the closet floor seemed full of old boots and shoes.

It was dark in there, very dark, and only one slat of light stabbed the blackness coming through the irregular shape of the latch hole. She could hear voices in low tones speaking on the other side of the door. Gradually her eyes grew accustomed to the light and one by one objects came out of the shadows and looked at her. A white pitcher with a broken nose, a row of bottles, a bunch of seed corn with the husks braided together and hung on a nail, an old coat on another nail.

Down on her knees beside the crack of light went Miranda. First her eye and then her ear were applied to the small aperture. She could see nothing but a table directly in front of the door about a foot away on which were quills, paper, and a large horn inkstand filled with ink. Some one evidently had been writing, for a page was half done, and the pen was laid down beside a word.

The limits of the latch hole made it impossible for Miranda to make out any more. She applied her ear and could hear a man's voice talking in low insinuating tones, but she could make little of what was said. It drove her fairly frantic to think that she was losing time. Miranda had no mind to be balked in her purpose. She meant to find out who was in that room and what was going on. She felt a righteous interest in it.

Her eyes could see quite plainly now in the dark closet. There was a big button on the door. She no sooner discovered it than she put up her hand and tried to turn it. It was tight and made a slight squeak in turning. She stopped but the noise seemed to have no effect upon the evenly modulated tones inside. Cautiously she moved the button again, holding the latch firmly in her other hand lest the door should suddenly fly open. It was an exciting moment when at last the button was turned entirely away from the door frame and the lifted latch swung free in Miranda's hand. The door opened outward. If it were allowed to go it would probably strike against the table. Miranda only allowed it to open a crack. She could hear words now, and the voice reminded her of something unpleasant. The least little bit more she dared open the door, and she could see, as she had expected, Marcia's bonnet and shoulder cape as she sat at the other side of the room. This then was the room of the messenger who had sent for Mrs. Spafford so peremptorily. The next thing was to discover the identity of the messenger. Miranda had suspicions.

The night before she had seen a man lurking near the Spafford house when she went out in the garden to feed the chickens. She had watched him from behind the lilac bush, and when he had finally gone away she had followed him some distance until he turned into the old corduroy road and was lost in the gathering dusk. The man she had seen before, and had reason to suspect. It was not for nothing that she had braved her grandmother and gone hunting wild strawberries out of season.

With the caution of a creature of the forest Miranda opened the door an inch further, and applied her eye to the latch hole again. The man's head was in full range of her eye then, and her suspicion proved true.

When Marcia entered the big room and the heavy oak door closed behind her her heart seemed almost choking her, but she tried with all her might to be calm. She was to know the worst now.

On the other side of the room in a large arm-chair, with his feet extended on another and covered by a travelling shawl, reclined a man. Marcia went toward him eagerly, and then stopped:

"Mr. Temple!" There was horror, fear, reproach in the way she spoke it.

"I know you are astonished, Mrs. Spafford, that the messenger should be one so unworthy, and let me say at the beginning that I am more thankful than I can express that your letter of forgiveness reached me before I was obliged to start on my sorrowful commission. I beg you will sit down and be as comfortable as you can while I explain further. Pardon my not rising. I have met with a bad sprain caused by falling from my horse on the way, and was barely able to reach this stopping place. My ankle is swollen so badly that I cannot step upon my foot."

Marcia, with white face, moved to the chair he indicated near him, and sat down. The one thought his speech had conveyed to her had come through those words "my sorrowful commission." She felt the need of sitting down, for her limbs would no longer bear her up, and she felt she must immediately know what was the matter.

"Mrs. Spafford, may I ask you once more to speak your forgiveness? Before I begin to tell you what I have come for, I long to hear you say the words 'I forgive you.' Will you give me your hand and say them?"

"Mr. Temple, I beg you will tell me what is the matter. Do not think any further about that other matter. I meant what I said in the note. Tell me quick! Is my husband—has anything happened to Mr. Spafford? Is he ill? Is he hurt?"

"My poor child! How can I bear to tell you? It seems terrible to put your love and trust upon another human being and then suddenly find—But wait. Let me tell the story in my own way. No, your husband is not hurt, physically. Illness, and death even, are not the worst things that can happen to a mortal soul. It seems to me cruel, as I see you sit there so young and tender and beautiful, that I should have to hurt you by what I have to say. I come from the purest of motives to tell you a sad truth about one who should be nearest and dearest to you of all the earth. I beg you will look upon me kindly and believe that it hurts me to have to tell you these things. Before I begin I pray you will tell me that you forgive me for all I have to say. Put you hand in mine and say so."

Marcia had listened to this torrent of words unable to stop them, a choking sensation in her throat, fear gripping her heart. Some terrible thing had happened. Her senses refused to name the possibility. Would he never tell? What ailed the man that he wanted her hand in forgiveness? Of course she forgave him. She could not speak, and he kept urging.

"I cannot talk until I have your hand as a pledge that you will forgive me and think not unkindly of me for what I am about to tell you."

He must have seen how powerfully he wrought upon her, for he continued until wild with frantic fear she stumbled toward him and laid her hand in his. He grasped it and thanked her profusely. He looked at the little cold hand in his own, and his lying tongue went on:

"Mrs. Spafford, you are good and true. You have saved me from a life of uselessness, and your example and high noble character have given me new inspiration. It seems a poor gratitude that would turn and stab you to the heart. Ah! I cannot do it, and yet I must."

This was torture indeed! Marcia drew her hand sharply away and held it to her heart. She felt her brain reeling with the strain. Harry Temple saw he must go on at once or he would lose what he had gained. He had meant to keep that little hand and touch it gently with a comforting pressure as his story went on, but it would not do to frighten her or she might take sudden alarm.

"Sit down," he begged, reaching out and drawing a chair near to his own, but she stepped back and dropped into the one which she had first taken.

"You know your husband has been in New York?" he began. She nodded. She could not speak.

"Did you never suspect why he is there and why he stays so long?" A cold vise gripped Marcia's heart, but though she turned white she said nothing, only looked steadily into the false eyes that glowed and burned at her like two hateful coals of fire that would scorch her soul and David's to a horrid death.

"Poor child, you cannot answer. You have trusted perfectly. You thought he was there on business connected with his writing, but did it never occur to you what a very long time he has been away and that—that there might be some other reason also which he has not told? But you must know it now, my child. I am sorry to say it, but he has been keeping it from you, and those who love you think you ought to know. Let me explain. Very soon after he reached New York he met a lady whom he used to know and admire. She is a very beautiful woman, and though she is married is still much sought after. Your husband, like the rest of her admirers, soon lost his heart completely, and his head. Strange that he could so easily forget the pearl of women he had left behind! He went to see her. He showed his affection for her in every possible way. He gave her large sums of money. In fact, to make a long story short, he is lingering in New York just to be near her. I hesitate to speak the whole truth, but he has surely done that which you cannot forgive. You with your lofty ideas—Mrs. Spafford—he has cut himself off from any right to your respect or love.

"And now I am here to-day to offer to do all in my power to help you. From what I know of your husband's movements, he is likely to return to you soon. You cannot meet him knowing that the lips that will salute you have been pressed upon the lips of another woman, and that woman *your own sister*, dear Mrs. Spafford!

"Ah! Now you understand, poor child. Your lips quiver! You have reason to understand. I know, I know you cannot think what to do. Let me think for you." His eyes were glowing and his face animated. He was using all his persuasive power, and her gaze was fixed upon him as though he had mesmerized her. She could not resist the flood-tide of his eloquence. She could only look on and seem to be gradually turning to stone—frozen with horror.

He felt he had almost won, and with demoniacal skill he phrased his sentences.

"I am here for that purpose. I am here to help you and for no other reason. In the stable are horses harnessed and a comfortable carriage. My advice to you is to fly from here as fast as these fleet horses can carry you. Where you go is for you to say. I should advise going to your father's house. That I am sure is what will please him best. He is your natural refuge at such a time as this. If, however, you shrink from appearing before the eyes of the village gossips in your native town, I will take you to the home of a dear old friend of mine, hidden among the quiet hills, where you will be cared for most royally and tenderly for my sake, and where you can work out your life problem in the way that seems best to you. It is there that I am planning to take you to-night. We can easily reach there before evening if we start at once."

Marcia started to her feet in horror.

"What do you mean?" she stammered in a choking voice. "I could never go anywhere with you Mr. Temple. You are a bad man! You have been telling me lies! I do not believe one word of what you have said. My husband is noble and good. If he did any of those things you say he did he had a reason for it. I shall never distrust him."

Marcia's head was up grandly now and her voice had come back. She looked the man in the eye until he quailed, but still he sought to hold his power over her.

"You poor child!" and his voice was gentleness and forbearance itself. "I do not wonder in your first horror and surprise that you feel as you do. I anticipated this. Sit down and calm yourself and let me tell you more about it. I can prove everything that I have said. I have letters here—" and he swept his hand toward a pile of letters lying on the table; Miranda in the closet marked well the position of those letters. "All that I have said is only too true, I am sorry to say, and you must listen to me—"

Marcia interrupted him, her eyes blazing, her face excited. "Mr. Temple, I shall not listen to another word you say. You are a wicked man and I was wrong to come here at all. You deceived me or I should not have come. I must go home at once." With that she started toward the door.

Harry Temple flung aside the shawl that covered his sometime sprained ankle and arose quickly, placing himself before her, forgetful of his invalid role:

"Not so fast, my pretty lady," he said, grasping her wrists fiercely in both his hands. "You need not think to escape so easily. You shall not leave this room except in my company. Do you not know that you are in my power? You have spent nearly an hour alone in my bedchamber, and what will your precious husband have to do with you after this is known?"

Chapter 24

Miranda's time had come. She had seen it coming and was prepared.

With a movement like a flash she pushed open the closet door, seized the pot of ink from the table, and before the two excited occupants of the room had time to even hear her or realize that she was near, she hurled the ink pot full into the insolent face of Harry Temple. The inkstand itself was a light affair of horn and inflicted only a slight wound, but the ink came into his eyes in a deluge blinding him completely, as Miranda had meant it should do. She had seen no other weapon of defense at hand.

Harry Temple dropped Marcia's wrists and groaned in pain, staggering back against the wall and sinking to the floor. But Miranda would not stay to see the effect of her punishment. She seized the frightened Marcia, dragged her toward the cupboard door, sweeping as she passed the pile of letters, finished and unfinished, into her apron, and closed the cupboard doors carefully behind her. Then she guided Marcia through the dark mazes of the store room to the hall, and pushing her toward the front door, whispered: "Go quick 'fore he gets his eyes open. I've got to go this way. Run down the road fast as you can an' I'll be at the meetin' place first. Hurry, quick!"

Marcia went with feet that shook so that every step seemed like to slip, but with beating heart she finally traversed the length of the piazza with a show of dignity, passed the loungers, and was out in the road. Then indeed she took courage and fairly flew.

Miranda, breathless, but triumphant, went back into the kitchen: "I guess 'tain't him after all," she said to the interested woman who was putting on the potatoes to boil. "He's real interested to look at though. I'd like to stop and watch him longer but I must be goin'. I come out to hunt fer" — Miranda hesitated for a suitable object before this country-bred woman who well knew that strawberries were not ripe yet — "wintergreens fer Grandma," she added cheerfully, not quite sure whether they grew around these parts, "and I must be in a hurry. Good-bye! Thank you fer the drink."

Miranda whizzed out of the door breezily, calling a good morning to one of the hostlers as she passed the barnyard, and was off through the meadows and over the fence like a bird, the package of letters rustling loud in her bosom where she had tucked them before she entered the kitchen.

Neither of the two girls spoke for some minutes after they met, but continued their rapid gait, until the end of the corduroy road was in sight and they felt comparatively safe.

"Wal, that feller certainly ought to be strung up an' walluped, now, fer sure," remarked Miranda, "an' I'd like to help at the wallupin'."

Marcia's overstrung nerves suddenly dissolved into hysterical laughter. The contrast from the tragic to the ridiculous was too much for her. She laughed until the tears rolled down her cheeks, and then she cried in earnest. Miranda stopped and put her arms about her as gently as a mother might have done, and smoothed her hair back from the hot cheek, speaking tenderly:

"There now, you poor pretty little flower. Jest you cry 's hard 's you want to. I know how good it makes you feel to cry. I've done it many a time up garret where nobody couldn't hear me. That old Satan, he won't trouble you fer a good long spell again. When he gets his evil eyes open, if he ever does, he'll be glad to get out o' these parts or I miss my guess. Now don't you worry no more. He can't hurt you one mite. An' don't think a thing about what he said. He's a great big liar, that's what he is."

"Miranda, you saved me. Yes, you did. I never can thank you enough. If you hadn't come and helped me something awful might have happened!" Marcia shuddered and began to sob convulsively again.

"Nonsense!" said Miranda, pleased. "I didn't do a thing worth mentioning. Now you jest wipe your eyes and chirk up. We've got to go through town an' you don't want folks to wonder what's up."

Miranda led Marcia up to the spring whose location had been known to her all the time of course, and Marcia bathed her eyes and was soon looking more like herself, though there was a nervous tremor to her lips now and then. But her companion talked gaily, and tried to keep her mind from going over the events of the morning.

When they reached the village Miranda suggested they go home by the back street, slipping through a field of spring wheat and climbing the garden fence. She had a mind to keep out of her grandmother's sight for a while longer.

"I might's well be hung for a sheep 's a lamb," she remarked as she slid in at Marcia's kitchen door in the shadow of the morning-glory vines. "I'm goin' to stay here a spell an' get you some dinner while you go upstairs an' lie down. You don't need to go back to your aunt's till near night, an' you can wait till dusk an' I'll go with you. Then you needn't be out alone at all. I know how you feel, but I don't believe you need worry. He'll be done with you now forever, er I'll miss my guess. Now you go lie down till I make a cup o' tea."

Marcia was glad to be alone, and soon fell asleep, worn out with the excitement, her brain too weary to go over the awful occurrences of the morning. That would come later. Now her body demanded rest.

Miranda, coming upstairs with the tea, tiptoed in and looked at her,—one round arm thrown over her head, and her smooth peachy cheek resting against it. Miranda, homely, and with no hope of ever attaining any of the beautiful things of life, loved unselfishly this girl who had what she had not, and longed with all her heart to comfort and protect the sweet young thing who seemed so ill-prepared to protect herself. She stooped over the sleeper for one yearning moment, and touched her hair lightly with her lips. She felt a great desire to kiss the soft round cheek, but was afraid of wakening her. Then she took the cup of tea and tiptoed out again, her eyes shining with satisfaction. She had a self-imposed task before her, and was well pleased that Marcia slept, for it gave her plenty of opportunity to carry out her plans.

She went quickly to David's library, opened drawers and doors in the desk until she found writing materials, and sat down to work. She had a letter to write, and a letter, to Miranda, was the achievement of a lifetime. She did not much expect to ever have to write another. She plunged into her subject at once.

Dear Mr. David: (she was afraid that sounded a little stiff, but she felt it was almost too familiar to say "David" as he was always called.)

I ain't much on letters, but this one has got to be writ. Something happened and somebody's got to tell you about it. I'm most sure she wont, and nobody else knows cept me.

Last night 'bout dark I went out to feed the chickens, an' I see that nimshi Harry Temple skulkin round your house. It was all dark there, an he walked in the side gate and tried to peek in the winders, only the shades was down an he couldn't see a thing. I thought he was up to some mischief so I followed him down the old corduroy road. It was dark by then an I come home, but I was on the watchout this morning, and after Mis' Spafford come down to the house I heard a horse gallopin by an I looked out an saw a boy get off an take a letter to the door an ride away, an pretty soon all in a hurry your wife come out tyin her bonnet and hurrin along lookin scared. I grabbed my sunbonnet an clipped after her, but she went so fast I didn't get up to her till she got on the old corduroy road. She was awful scared lookin an she didn't want me much I see, but pretty soon she up an told me she had a note sayin there was a messenger with news from you out to the old Green Tavern. He had an accident an couldn't come no further. He wanted her to come alone cause the business was private, so I stayed down by the turn of the road till she got in an then I went cross lots an round to the kitchen an called on Mis' Green a spell. She was tellin me about her boarders an I told her I thought mebbe one of em was a friend o' Hannah Heath's so she said I might peek through the key hole of the cubberd an see. She was busy so I went alone.

Well sir, I jest wish you'd been there. That lying nimshi was jest goin' on the sweetest, as respectful an nice a thankin your wife fer comin, an excusin himself fer sendin fer her, and sayin he couldn't bear to tell her what he'd come fer, an pretty soon when she was scared 's death he up an told her a awful fib bout you an a woman called Kate, whoever she is, an he jest poured the words out fast so she couldn't speak, an he said things about you he shouldn't uv, an you could see he was makin it up as he went along, an he said he had proof. So he pointed at a pile of letters on the table an I eyed em good through the hole in the door. Pretty soon he ups and perposes that he carry her off in a carriage he has all ready, and takes her to a friend of his, so she won't be here when you come home, cause you're so bad, and she gets up looking like she wanted to scream only she didn't dare, and she says he don't tell the truth, it wasn't so any of it, and if it was it was all right anyway, that you had some reason, an she wouldn't go a step with him anywhere. An then he forgets all about the lame ankle he had kept covered up on a chair pertendin it was hurt fallin off his horse when the coach brought him all the way fer I asked Mis' Green — and he ketches her by the wrists, and he says she can't go without him, and she needn't be in such a hurry fer you wouldn't have no more to do with her anyway after her being shut up there with him so long, an then she looked jest like she was going to faint, an I bust out through the door an ketched up the ink pot, it want heavy enough to kill him, an I slung it at him, an the ink went square in his eyes, an we slipped through the closet an got away quick fore anybody knew a thing.

I brought all the letters along so here they be. I havn't read a one, cause I thought mebbe you'd ruther not. She aint seen em neither. She dont know I've got em. I hid em in my dress. She's all wore out with cryin and hurryin, and being scared, so she's upstairs now asleep, an she dont know I'm writing. I'm goin to send this off fore she knows, fer I think she wouldn't tell you fear of worryin you. I'll look after her es well's I can till you get back, but I think that feller ought to be strung up. But you'll know what to do, so no more at present from your obedient servent ,

Miranda Griscom.

Having at last succeeded on sealing her packet to her satisfaction and the diminishing of the stick of sealing wax she had found in the drawer, Miranda slid out the front door, and by a detour went to David Spafford's office.

"Good afternoon, Mr. Clark," she said to the clerk importantly. "Grandma sends her respects and wants to know if you'd be so kind as to back this letter fer her to Mr. David Spafford. She's writin' to him on business an' she don't rightly know his street an' number in New York."

Mr. Clark willingly wrote the address, and Miranda took it to the post office, and sped back to Marcia, happy in the accomplishment of her purpose.

In the same mail bag that brought Miranda's package came a letter from Aunt Clarinda. David's face lit up with a pleased smile. Her letters were so infrequent that they were a rare pleasure. He put aside the thick package written in this clerk's hand. It was doubtless some business papers and could wait.

Aunt Clarinda wrote in a fine old script that in spite of her eighty years was clear and legible. She told about the beauty of the weather, and how Amelia and Hortense were almost done with the house cleaning, and how Marcia had been going to their house every day putting it in order. Then she added a paragraph which David, knowing the old lady well, understood to be the *raison d'etre* of the whole letter:

I think your wife misses you very much, Davie, she looks sort of peeked and sad. It is hard on her being separated from you so long this first year. Men don't think of those things, but it is lonely for a young thing like her here with three old women, and you know Hortense and Amelia never try to make it lively for anybody. I have been watching her, and I think if I were you I would let the business finish itself up as soon as possible and hurry back to put a bit of cheer into that child. She's whiter than she ought to be.

David read it over three times in astonishment with growing, mingled feelings which he could not quite analyze.

Poor Aunt Clarinda! Of course she did not understand the situation, and equally of course she was mistaken. Marcia was not sighing for him, though it might be dull for her at the old house. He ought to have thought of that; and a great burden suddenly settled down upon him. He was not doing right by Marcia. It could not be himself of course that Marcia was missing, if indeed Aunt Clarinda was right and she was worried about anything. Perhaps something has occurred to trouble her. Could that snake of a Temple have turned up again? No, he felt reasonably sure he would have heard of that, besides he saw him not long ago on the street at a distance. Could it be some boy-lover at home whose memory came to trouble her? Or had she discovered what a sacrifice she had made of her young life? Whatever it was, it was careless and cruel of him to have left her alone with his aunts all this time. He was a selfish man, he told himself, to have accepted her quiet little sacrifice of all for him. He read the letter over again, and suddenly there came to him a wish that Marcia *was* missing him. It seemed a pleasant thought to have her care. He had been trying to train himself to the fact that no one would ever care for him again, but now it seemed dear and desirable that his sweet young companion should like to have him back. He had vision of home as it had been, so pleasant and restful, always the food that he liked, always the thought for his wishes, and he felt condemned. He had not noticed or cared. Had she thought him ungrateful?

He read the letter over again, noting every mention of his wife in the account of the daily living at home. He was searching for some clue that would give him more information about her. And when he reached the last paragraph about missing him, a little tingle of pleasure shot through him at the thought. He did not understand it. After all she was his, and if it was possible he must help to make up to her for what she had lost in giving herself to him. If the thought of doing so brought a sense of satisfaction to him that was unexpected, he was not to blame in any wise.

Since his interview with Kate, and the terrible night of agony through which he had passed, David had plunged into his business with all his might. Whenever a thought of Kate came he banished it if possible, and if it would not go he got out his writing materials and went to work at an article, to absorb his mind. He had several times arisen in the night to write because he could not sleep, and must think.

When he was obliged to be in New York he had steadily kept away from the house where Kate lived, and never walked through the streets without occupying his mind as fully as possible so that he should not chance to see her. In this way his sorrow was growing old without having been worn out, and he was really regaining a large amount of the former happiness and interest in life. Not so often now did the vision of Kate come to trouble him. He thought she was still his one ideal of womanly beauty and grace and perfection of course, and always would be, but she was not for him to think upon any more. A strong true man he was growing, out of his sorrow. And now when the thought of Marcia came to him with a certain sweetness he could be glad that it was so, and not resent it. Of course no one could ever take the place of Kate, that was impossible.

So reflecting, with a pleasant smile upon his face, he opened Miranda's epistle.

Puzzled and surprised he began to read the strange chirography, and as he read his face darkened and he drew his brows in a heavy frown. "The scoundrel!" he muttered as he turned the sheet. Then as he went on his look grew anxious. He scanned the page quickly as if he would gather the meaning from the crooked ill-spelled words without taking them one by one. But he had to go slowly, for Miranda had not written with as much plainness as haste. He fairly held his breath when he thought of the gentle girl in the hands of the unscrupulous man of the world. A terrible fear gripped his heart. Marcia, little Marcia, so sweet and pure and good. A vision of her face as she lay asleep in the woods came between him and the paper. Why had he left her unprotected all these months? Fool that he was! She was worth more than all the railroads put together. As if his own life was in the balance, he read on, growing sick with horror. Poor child! What had she thought? And how had his own sin and weakness been found out, or was it merely Harry Temple's wicked heart that had evolved these stories? The letter smote him with terrible accusation, and all at once it was fearful to him to think that Marcia had heard such things about him. When he came to her trust in him he groaned aloud and buried his face in the letter, and then raised it quickly to read to the end.

When he had finished he rose with sudden determination to pack his carpet-bag and go home at once. Marcia needed him, and he felt a strong desire to be near her, to see her and know she was safe. It was overwhelming. He had not known he could ever feel strongly again. He must confess his own weakness of course, and he would. She should know all and know that she might trust him after all.

But the motion of rising had sent the other papers to the floor, and in falling the bundle of letters that Miranda had enclosed, scattered about him. He stooped to pick them up and saw his own name written in Kate's handwriting. Old association held him, and wondering, fearful, not wholly glad to see it, he picked up the letter. It was an epistle of Kate's, written in intimate style to Harry Temple and speaking of himself in terms of the utmost contempt. She even stooped to detail to Harry an account of her own triumph on that miserable morning when he had taken her in his arms and kissed her. There were expressions in the letter that showed her own wicked heart, as nothing else could ever have done, to David. As he read, his soul growing sick within him, — read one letter after another, and saw how she had plotted with this bad man to wreck the life of her young sister for her own triumph and revenge, — the beautiful woman whom he had loved, and whom he had thought beautiful within as well as without, crumbled into dust before him. When he looked up at last with white face and firmly set lips, he found that his soul was free forever from the fetters that had bound him to her.

He went to the fireplace and laid the pile of letters among the embers, blowing them into a blaze, and watched them until they were eaten up by the fire and nothing remained but dead grey ashes. The thought came to him that that was like his old love. It was burnt out. There had not been the right kind of fuel to feed it. Kate was worthless, but his own self was alive, and please God he would yet see better days. He would go home at once to the child wife who needed him, and whom now he might love as she should be loved. The thought became wondrously sweet to him as he rapidly threw the things into his travelling bag and went about arrangements for his trip home. He determined that if he ever came to New York again Marcia should come with him.

Chapter 25

Marcia hurried down to her own house early one morning. The phantoms of her experiences in the old Green Tavern were pursuing her.

Once there she could do nothing but go over and over the dreadful things that Harry Temple had said. In vain did she try to work. She went into the library and took up a book, but her mind would wander to David.

She sat down at the piano and played a few tender chords and sang an Old Italian song which somebody had left at their house several years before:

> Dearest, believe,
> When e'er we part:
> Lonely I grieve,
> In my sad heart: —

With a sob her head dropped upon her hands in one sad little crash of wailing tones, while the sound died away in reverberation after reverberation of the strings till Marcia felt as if a sea of sound were about her in soft ebbing, flowing waves.

The sound covered the lifting of the side door latch and quiet step of a foot. Marcia was absorbed in her own thoughts. Her smothered sobs were mingling with the dying sounds of the music, still audible to her fine ear.

David had come by instinct to his own home first. He felt that Marcia would be there, and now that he was come and the morning sun flooded everything and made home look so good he felt that he must find her first of all before his relationship with home had been re-established. He passed through kitchen, dining room and hall, and by the closed parlor door. He never thought of her being in there with the door closed. He glanced into the library and saw the book lying in his chair as she had left it, and it gave a touch of her presence which pleased him. He went softly toward the stairs thinking to find her. He had stopped at a shop the last thing and bought a beautiful creamy shawl of China crepe heavily embroidered, and finished with long silken fringe. He had taken it from his carpet-bag and was carrying it in its rice paper wrapping lest it should be crushed. He was pleased a child at the present he had brought her, and felt strangely shy about giving it to her.

Just then there came a sound from the parlor, sweet and tender and plaintive. Marcia had conquered her sobs and was singing again with her whole soul, singing as she were singing to David. The words drew him strangely, wonderingly toward the parlor door, yet so softly that he heard every syllable.

Dearest, believe,
When e'er we part
Lonely I grieve
In my sad heart:
Thy faithful slave,
Languishing sighs,
Haste then and save—

Here the words trailed away again into a half sob, and the melody continued in broken, halting chords that flickered out and faded into the shadows of the room.

David's heart was pierced with a belief that Aunt Clarinda was right and something was the matter with Marcia. A great trouble and tenderness, and almost jealousy, leaped up in his heart which were incomprehensible to him. Who was Marcia singing this song for? That it was a true cry from a lonely soul he could but believe. Was she feeling her prison-bars here in the lonely old house with only a forlorn man whose life and love had been thrown away upon another? Poor child! Poor child! If he might but save her from suffering, cover her with his own tenderness and make her content with that. Would it be possible if he devoted himself to it to make her forget the one for whom she was sighing; to bring peace and a certain sort of sweet forgetfulness and interest in other things into her life? He wanted to make a new life for her, his little girl whom he had so unthinkingly torn from the home nest and her future, and compelled to take up his barren way with him. He would make it up to her if such a thing were possible. Then he opened the door.

In the soft green light of the noonday coming through the shades Marcia's color did not show as it flew into her cheeks. Her hands grew weak and dropped upon the keys with a soft little tinkle of surprise and joy. She sprang up and came a step toward him, then clasped her hands against her breast and stopped shyly. David coming into the room, questioning, wondering, anxious, stopped midway too, and for an instant they looked upon one another. David saw a new look in the girl's face. She seemed older, much older than when he had left her. The sweet round cheeks were thinner, her mouth drooped sadly, pathetically. For an instant he longed to take her in his arms and kiss her. The longing startled him. So many months he had thought of only Kate in that way, and then had tried to teach himself never to think of Kate or any woman as one to be caressed by him, that it shocked him. He felt that he had been disloyal to himself, to honor,—to Kate—no—not to Kate, he had no call to be loyal to her. She had not been loyal to him ever. Perhaps rather he would have put it loyalty to Love for Love's sake, love that is worthy to be crowned by a woman's love.

With all these mingling feelings David was embarrassed. He came toward her slowly, trying to be natural, trying to get back his former way with her. He put out his hand stiffly to shake hands as he had done when he left, and timidly she put hers into it, yet as their fingers closed there leaped from one to the other a thrill of sweetness, that neither guessed the other knew and each put by in memory for closer inspection as to what it could mean. Their hands clung together longer than either had meant, and there was something pleasant to each in the fact that they were together again. David thought it was just because it was home, rest, and peace, and a relief from his anxiety about Marcia now that he saw she was all right. Marcia knew it was better to have David standing there with his strong fingers about her trembling ones, than to have anything else in the world. But she would not have told him so.

"That was a sweet song you were singing," said David. "I hope you were singing it for me, and that it was true! I am glad I am come home, and you must sing it again for me soon."

It was not in the least what he intended to say, and the words tumbled themselves out so tumultuously that he was almost ashamed and wondered if Marcia would think he had lost his mind in New York. Marcia, dear child, treasured them every word and hugged them to heart, and carried them in her prayers.

They went out together and got dinner as if they had been two children, with a wild excited kind of glee; and they tried to get back their natural ways of doing and saying things, but they could not.

Instead they were forever blundering and halting in what they said; coming face to face and almost running over one another as they tried to help each other; laughing and blushing and blundering again.

When they each tried to reach for the tea kettle to fill the coffee pot and their fingers touched, each drew back and pretended not to notice, but yet had felt the contact sweet.

They were lingering over the dinner when Hannah Heath came to the door. David had been telling of some of his adventures in detail and was enjoying the play of expression on Marcia's face as she listened eagerly to every word. They had pushed their chairs back a little and were sitting there talking, — or rather David was talking, Marcia listening. Hannah stood for one jealous instant and saw it all. This was what she had dreamed for her own long years back, she and David. She had questioned much just what feeling there might be between him and Marcia, and now more than ever she desired to bring him face to face with Kate and read for herself what the truth had been. She hated Marcia for that look of intense delight and sympathy upon her face; hated her that she had the right to sit there and hear what David had to say—some stupid stuff about railroads. She did not see that she herself would have made an ill companion for a man like David.

As yet neither Marcia nor David had touched upon the subjects which had troubled them. They did not realize it, but were so suddenly happy in each other's company they had forgotten for the moment. The pleasant converse was broken up at once. Marcia's face hardened into something like alarm as saw who stood in the doorway.

"Why, David, have you got home at last?" said Hannah. "I did not know it." That was an untruth. She had watched him from behind Grandmother Heath's rose bush. "Where did you come from last? New York? Oh, then you saw Mrs. Leavenworth. How is she? I fell in love with her when I was there."

Now David had never fully taken in Kate's married name. He knew it of course, but in his present state of happiness at getting home, and his absorption in the work he had been doing, the name "Mrs. Leavenworth" conveyed nothing whatever to David's mind. He looked blankly at Hannah and replied indifferently enough with a cool air. "No, Miss Hannah, I had no time for social life. I was busy every minute I was away."

David never expected Hannah to say anything worth listening to, and he was so full of his subject that he had not noticed that she made no reply.

Hannah watched him curiously as he talked, his remarks after all were directed more to Marcia than to her, and when he paused she said with a contemptuous sneer in her voice, "I never could understand, David, how you who seem to have so much sense in other things will take up with such fanciful, impractical dreams as this railroad. Lemuel says it'll never run."

Hannah quoted her lover with a proud bridling of her head as if the matter were settled once and for all. It was the first time she allowed the world to see that she acknowledged her relation to Lemuel. She was not averse to having David understand that she felt there were other men in the world besides himself. But David turned merry eyes on her.

"Lemuel says?" he repeated, and he made a sudden movement with his arm which sent a knife and spoon from the table in a clatter upon the floor.

"And how much does Lemuel know about the matter?"

"Lemuel has good practical common sense," said Hannah, vexed, "and he knows what is possible and what is not. He does not need to travel all over the country on wild goose chase to learn that."

Now that she had accepted him Hannah did not intend to allow Lemuel to be discounted.

"He has not long to wait to be convinced," said David thoughtfully and unaware of her tart tone. "Before the year is out it will be a settled fact that every one can see."

"Well, it's beyond comprehension that you care, anyway," said Hannah contemptuously. "Did you really spend all your time in New York on such things? It seems incredible. There certainly must have been other attractions?"

There was insinuation in Hannah's voice though it was smooth as butter, but David had had long years of experience in hearing Hannah Heath's sharp tongue. He minded it no more than he would have minded the buzzing of a fly. Marcia's color rose, however. She made a hasty errand to the pantry to put away the bread, and her eyes flashed at Hannah through the close drawn pantry door. But Hannah did not give up so easily.

"It is strange you did not stay with Mrs. Leavenworth," she said. "She told me you were one of her dearest friends, and you used to be quite fond of one another."

Then it suddenly dawned upon David who Mrs. Leavenworth was, and a sternness overspread his face.

"Mrs. Leavenworth, did you way? Ah! I did not understand. I saw her but once and that for only a few minutes soon after I first arrived. I did not see her again." His voice was cool and steady. Marcia coming from the pantry with set face, ready for defence if there was any she could give, marvelled at his coolness. Her heart was gripped with fear, and yet leaping with joy at David's words. He had not seen Kate but once. He had known she was there and yet had kept away. Hannah's insinuations were false. Mr. Temple's words were untrue. She had known it all the time, yet what sorrow they had given her!

"By the way, Marcia," said David, turning toward her with a smile that seemed to erase the sternness in his voice but a moment before. "Did you not write me some news? Miss Hannah, you are to be congratulated I believe. Lemuel is a good man. I wish you much happiness."

And thus did David, with a pleasant speech, turn aside Hannah Heath's dart. Yet while she went from the house with a smile and a sound of pleasant wishes in her ears, she carried with her a bitter heart and a revengeful one.

David was suddenly brought face to face with the thing he had to tell Marcia. He sat watching her as she went back and forth from pantry to kitchen, and at last he came and stood beside her and took her hands in his looking down earnestly into her face. It seemed terrible to him to tell this thing to the innocent girl, no, just when he was growing anxious to win her confidence, but it must be told, and better now than later lest he might be tempted not to tell it at all.

"Marcia!" He said the name tenderly, with an inflection he had never used before. It was not lover-like, nor passionate, but it reached her heart and drew her eyes to his and the color to cheeks. She thought how different his clasp was from Harry Temple's hateful touch. She looked up at him trustingly, and waited.

"You heard what I said to Hannah Heath just now, about—your—" He paused, dissatisfied— "about Mrs. Leavenworth"— it was as if he would set the subject of his words far from them. Marcia's heart beat wildly, remembering all that she had been told, yet she looked bravely, trustingly into his eyes.

"It was true what I told her. I met Mrs. Leavenworth but once while I was away. It was in her own home and she sent for me saying she was in trouble.

She told me that she was in terrible anxiety lest I would not forgive her. She begged me to say that I forgave her, and when I told her I did she asked me to kiss her once to prove it. I was utterly overcome and did so, but the moment my lips touched hers I knew that I was doing wrong and I put her from me. She begged me to remain, and I now know that she was utterly false from the first. It was but a part she was playing when she touched my heart until I yielded and sinned. I have only learned that recently, within a few days, and from words written by her own hand to another. I will tell you about it all sometime. But I want to confess to you this wrong I have done, and to let you know that I went away from her that day and have never seen her since. She had said she was without money, and I left her all I had with me. I feel that all this was a sin against you. I would like you to forgive me if you can, I want you to know that this other woman who was the cause of our coming together, is no longer anything to me. Even if she and I were both free as we were when we first met, we could never be anything but strangers. Can you forgive me now, Marcia, and can you ever trust me after what I told you?"

Marcia looked into his eyes, and loved him but the more for his confession. She felt she could forgive him anything, and her whole soul in her countenance answered with her voice, as she said: "I can." It made David think of their wedding day, and suddenly it came over him with a thrill that this sweet womanly woman belonged to him. He marvelled at her sweet forgiveness. The joy of it surprised him beyond measure.

"You have had some sad experiences yourself. Will you tell me now all about it?" He asked the question wistfully still holding her hands in a firm close grasp, and she let them lie nestling these feeling safe as birds in the nest.

"Why, how did you know?" questioned Marcia, her whole face flooded with rosy light for joy at his kind ways and relief that she did not have to open the story.

"Oh, a little bird, or a guardian angel whispered the tale," he said pleasantly. "Come into the room where we can be sure no Hannah Heaths will trouble us," and he drew her into the library and seated her beside him on the sofa.

"But, indeed, Marcia," and his face sobered, "it is no light matter to me, what has happened to you. I have been in an agony all the way home lest I might not find you safe and well after having escaped so terrible a danger."

He drew the whole story from her bit by bit, tenderly questioning her, his face blazing with righteous wrath, and darkening with his wider knowledge as she told on to the end, and showed him plainly the black heart of the villain who had dared so diabolical a conspiracy; and the inhumanity of the woman who had helped in the intrigue against her own sister, — nay even instigated it. His feeling were too deep for utterance. He was shaken to the depths. His new comprehension of Kate's character was confirmed at the worst. Marcia could only guess his deep feelings from his shaken countenance and the earnest way in which he folded his hands over hers and said in low tones filled with emotion: "We should be deeply thankful to God for saving you, and I must be very careful of you after this. That villain shall be searched out and punished if it takes a lifetime, and Miranda, — what shall we do for Miranda? Perhaps we can induce her grandmother to let us have her sometime to help take care of us. We seem to be unable to get on without her. We'll see what we can do sometime in return for the great service she has rendered."

But the old clock striking in the hall suddenly reminded David that he should go at once to the office, so he hurried away and Marcia set about her work with energy, a happy song of praise in her heart.

There was much to be done. David had said he would scarcely have time to go over to his aunts that night, so she had decided to invite them to tea. She would far rather have had David to herself this first evening, but it would please them to come, especially Aunt Clarinda. There was not much time to prepare supper to be sure, but she would stir up a gingerbread, make some puffy cream biscuits, and there was lovely white honey and fresh eggs and peach preserves.

So she ran to Deacon Appleby's to get some cream for her biscuits, and to ask Tommy Appleby to harness David's horse and drive over for Aunt Clarinda. Then she hurried down to the aunts to give her invitation.

Aunt Clarinda sat down in her calico-covered rocking chair, wiped her dear old eyes and her glasses, and said, over and over again: "Dear child! Bless her! Bless her!"

It was a happy gathering that evening. David was as pleased as they could have desired, and looked about upon the group in the dining-room with genuine boyish pleasure. It did his heart good to see Aunt Clarinda there. It had never occurred to him before that she could come. He turned to Marcia with a light in his eyes that fully repaid her for the little trouble she had had in carrying out her plan. He began to feel that home meant something even though he had lost the home of his long dreams and ideals.

He talked a great deal about his trip, and in between the sentences, he caught himself watching Marcia, noting the curve of her round chin, the dimple on her left cheek when she smiled, the way her hair waved off from her forehead, the pink curves of her well-shaped ears. He found a distinct pleasure in noting these things and he wondered at himself. It was as if he had suddenly been placed before some great painting and become possessed of the knowledge wherewith to appreciate art to its fullest. It was as if he had heard a marvellous piece of music and had the eyes and ears of his understanding opened to take in the gracious melodies and majestic harmonies.

Aunt Clarinda watched his eyes, and Aunt Clarinda was satisfied. Aunt Hortense watched his eyes, jealously and sighed. Aunt Amelia watched his eyes and set her lips and feared to herself. "He will spoil her if he does like that. She will think she can walk right over him." But Aunt Clarinda knew better. She recognized the eternal right of love.

They took the three old ladies home in the rising of an early moon, Marcia walking demurely on the sidewalk with Aunt Amelia, while David drove the chaise with Aunt Clarinda and Aunt Hortense.

As he gently lifted Aunt Clarinda down and helped her to her room David felt her old hands tremble and press his arm, and when he had reached her door he stooped and kissed her.

"Davie," she said in the voice that used to comfort his little childish troubles, or tell him of some nice surprise she had for him, "Davie, she's a dear child! She's just as good as gold. She's the princess I used to put in all your fairy-tales. David, she's just the right one for you!" and David answered earnestly, solemnly, as if he were discovering a truth which surprised him but yet was not unwelcome. "I believe she is, Aunt Clarinda."

They drove to the barn and Marcia sat in the chaise in the sweet hay-scented darkness while David put up the horse by the cobwebby light of the lantern; then they walked quietly back to the house. David had drawn Marcia's hand through his arm and it rested softly on his coat sleeve. She was silently happy, she knew not why, afraid to think of it lest to-morrow would show her there was nothing out of the ordinary monotony to be happy about.

David was silent, wondering at himself. What was this that had come to him? A new pleasure in life. A little trembling rill of joy bubbling up in his heart; a rift in the dark clouds of fate; a show of sunshine where he had expected never to see the light again. Why was it so pleasant to have that little hand resting upon his arm? Was it really pleasant or was it only a part of the restfulness of getting home again away from strange faces and uncomfortable beds, and poor tables?

They let themselves into the house as if they were walking into a new world together and both were glad to be there again. When she got up to her room Marcia went and stood before the glass and looked at herself by the flickering flame of the candle. Her eyes were bright and her cheeks burned red in the centre like two soft deep roses. She felt she hardly knew herself. She tried to be critical. Was this person she was examining a pretty person? Would she be called so in comparison with Kate and Hannah Heath? Would a man, — would David, — if his heart were not filled, — think so? She decided not. She felt she was too immature. There was too much shyness in her glance, too much babyishness about her mouth. No, David could never have thought her beautiful, even if he had seen her before he knew Kate. But perhaps, if Kate had been married first and away and then he had come to their home, perhaps if he knew no one else well enough to love, — could he have cared for her?

Oh, it was a dreadful, beautiful thought. It thrilled through and through her till she hid her face from her own gaze. She suddenly kissed the hand that had rested on his sleeve, and then reproached herself for it. She loved him, but was it right to do so?

As for David, he was sitting on the side of his bed with his chin in his hands examining himself.

He had supposed that with the reading of those letters which had come to him but two short days before all possibility of love and happiness had died, but lo! he found himself thrilling with pleasure over the look in a girl's soft eyes, and the touch of her hand. And that girl was his wife. It was enough to keep him awake to try to understand himself.

Chapter 26

Hannah Heath's wedding day dawned bright enough for a less calculating bride.

David did not get home until half past three. He had been obliged to drive out to the starting place of the new railroad, near Albany, where it was important that he get a few points correctly. On the morrow was to be the initial trip, by the Mohawk and Hudson Railroad, of the first train drawn by a steam engine in the state of New York.

His article about it, bargained for by a New York paper, must be on its way by special post as soon after the starting of the train as possible. He must have all items accurate; technicalities of preparation; description of engine and coaches; details of arrangements, etc.; before he added the final paragraphs describing the actual start of the train. His article was practically done now, save for these few items. He had started early that morning on his long drive, and, being detained longer than he had expected, arrived at home with barely time to put himself into wedding garments, and hasten in at the last moment with Marcia who stood quietly waiting for him in the front hall. They were the last guests to arrive. It was time for the ceremony, but the bride, true to her nature to the last, still kept Lemuel waiting; and Lemuel, true to the end, stood smiling and patient awaiting her pleasure.

David and Marcia entered the wide parlor and shook hands here and there with those assembled, though for the most part a hushed air pervaded the room, as it always does when something is about to happen.

Soon after their arrival some one in purple silk came down the stairs and seated herself in a vacant chair close to where the bride was to stand. She had gold hair and eyes like forget-me-nots. She was directly opposite to David and Marcia. David was engrossed in a whispered conversation with Mr. Brentwood about the events of the morrow, and did not notice her entrance, though she paused in the doorway and searched him directly from amongst the company before she took her seat. Marcia, who was talking with Rose Brentwood, caught the vision of purple and gold and turned to face for one brief instant the scornful, half-merry glance of her sister. The blood in her face fled back to her heart and left it white.

Then Marcia summoned all her courage and braced herself to face what was to come. She forced herself to smile in answer to Rose Brentwood's question. But all the while she was trying to understand what it was in her sister's look that had hurt her so. It was not the anger, — for that she was prepared. It was not the scorn, for she had often faced that. Was it the almost merriment?

Yes, there was the sting. She had felt it so keenly when as a little girl Kate had taken to making fun of some whim of hers. She could not see why Kate should find cause for fun just now. It was as if she by her look ignored Marcia's relation to David in scornful laugh and appropriated him herself. Marcia's inmost soul rebelled. The color came back as if by force of her will. She would show Kate, — or she would show David at least, — that she could bear all things for him. She would play well her part of wife this day. The happy two months that had passed since David came back from New York had made her almost feel as if she was really his and he hers. For this hour she would forget that it was otherwise. She would look at him and speak to him as if he had been her husband for years, as if there were the truest understanding between them, — as indeed, of a certain wistful, pleasant sort there was. She would not let the dreadful thought of Kate cloud her face for others to see. Bravely she faced the company, but her heart under Kate's blue frock sent up a swift and pleading prayer demanding of a higher Power something she knew she had not in herself, and must therefore find in Him who had created her. It was the most trustful, and needy prayer that Marcia ever uttered and yet there were no words, not even the closing of an eyelid. Only her heart took the attitude of prayer.

The door upstairs opened in a business-like way, and Hannah's composed voice was heard giving a direction. Hannah's silken tread began to be audible. Miranda told Marcia afterward that she kept her standing at the window for an hour beforehand to see when David arrived, and when they started over to the house. Hannah kept herself posted on what was going on in the room below as well as if she were down there. She knew where David and Marcia stood, and told Kate exactly where to go. It was like Hannah that in the moment of her sacrifice of the long cherished hopes of her life she should have planned a dramatic revenge to help carry her through.

The bride's rustle became at last so audible that even David and Mr. Brentwood heard and turned from their absorbing conversation to the business in hand.

Hannah was in the doorway when David looked up, very cold and beautiful in her bridal array despite the years she had waited, and almost at once David saw the vision in purple and gold like a saucy pansy, standing near her.

Kate's eyes were fixed upon him with their most bewitching, dancing smile of recognition, like a naughty little child who had been in hiding for a time and now peeps out laughing over the discomfiture of its elders. So Kate encountered the steadfast gaze of David's astonished eyes.

But there was no light of love in those eyes as she had expected to see. Instead there grew in his face such a blaze of righteous indignation as the lord of the wedding feast might have turned upon the person who came in without a wedding garment. In spite of herself Kate was disconcerted. She was astonished. She felt that David was challenging her presence there. It seemed to her he was looking through her, searching her, judging her, sentencing her, and casting her out, and presently his eyes wandered beyond her through the open hall door and out into God's green world; and when they came back and next rested upon her his look had frozen into the glance of a stranger.

Angry, ashamed, baffled, she bit her lips in vexation, but tried to keep the merry smile. In her heart she hated him, and vowed to make him bow before her smiles once more.

David did not see the bride at all to notice her, but the bride, unlike the one of the psalmist's vision whose eyes were upon "her dear bridegroom's face," was looking straight across the room with evident intent to observe David.

The ceremony proceeded, and Hannah went through her part correctly and calmly, aware that she was giving herself to Lemuel Skinner irrevocably, yet perfectly aware also of the discomfiture of the sweet-faced girl-wife who sat across the room bravely watching the ceremony with white cheeks and eyes that shone like righteous lights.

Marcia did not look at David. She was with him in heart, suffering with him, feeling for him, quivering in every nerve for what he might be enduring. She had no need to look. Her part was to ignore, and help to cover.

They went through it all well. Not once did Aunt Amelia or Aunt Hortense notice anything strange in the demeanor of their nephew or his wife. Aunt Clarinda was not there. She was not fond of Hannah.

As soon as the service was over and the relatives had broken the solemn hush by kissing the bride, David turned and spoke to Rose Brentwood, making some smiling remark about the occasion. Rose Brentwood was looking her very prettiest in a rose-sprigged delaine and her wavy dark hair in a beaded net tied round with a rose-colored lute-string ribbon.

Kate flushed angrily at this. If it had been Marcia to whom he had spoken she would have judged he did it out of pique, but a pretty stranger coming upon the scene at this critical moment was trying. And then, too, David's manner was so indifferent, so utterly natural. He did not seem in the least troubled by the sight of herself.

David and Marcia did not go up to speak to the bride at once. David stepped back into the deep window seat to talk with Mr. Brentwood, and seemed to be in no hurry to follow the procession who were filing past the calm bride to congratulate her. Marcia remained quietly talking to Rose Brentwood. At last David turned toward his wife with a smile as though he had known she was there all the time, and had felt her sympathy. Her heart leaped up with new strength at that look, and her husband's firm touch as he drew her hand within his arm to lead her over to the bride gave her courage. She felt that she could face the battle, and with a bright smile that lit up her whole lovely face she marched bravely to the front to do or to die.

"I had about given up expecting any congratulations from you," said Hannah sharply as they came near. It was quite evident she had been watching for them.

"I wish you much joy, Mrs. Skinner," said David mechanically, scarcely feeling that she would have it for he knew her unhappy, dissatisfied nature.

"Yes," said Marcia, "I wish you may be happy,—as happy as I am!"

It was an impetuous, childish thing to say, and Marcia scarcely realized what words she meant to speak until they were out, and then she blushed rosy red. Was she happy? Why was she happy? Yes, even in the present trying circumstances she suddenly felt a great deep happiness bubbling up in her heart. Was it David's look and his strong arm under her hand?

Hannah darted a look at her. She was stung by the words. But did the girl-bride before her mean to flaunt her own triumphs in her face? Did she fully understand? Or was she trying to act a part and make them believe she was happy? Hannah was baffled once more as she had been before with Marcia.

Kate turned upon Marcia for one piercing instant again, that look of understanding, mocking merriment, which cut through the soul of her sister.

But did Marcia imagine it, or was it true that at her words to Hannah, David's arm had pressed hers closer as they stood there in the crowd? The thought thrilled through her and gave her greater strength.

Hannah turned toward Kate.

"David," she said, as she had always called him, and it is possible that she enjoyed the triumph of this touch of intimacy before her guest, "you knew my friend Mrs. Leavenworth!"

David bowed gravely, but did not attempt to put out his hand to take the one which Kate offered in greeting. Instead he laid it over Marcia's little trembling one on his arm as if to steady it.

"We have met before," said David briefly in an impenetrable tone, and turning passed out of the room to make way for the Brentwoods who were behind him.

Hannah scarcely treated the Brentwoods with decency, so vexed was she with the way things were turning out. To think that David should so completely baffle her. She turned an annoyed look at Kate, who flashed her blue eyes contemptuously as if to blame Hannah.

Soon the whole little gathering were in the dining-room and wide hall being served with Grandmother Heath's fried chicken and currant jelly, delicate soda biscuits, and fruit cake baked months before and left to ripen.

The ordeal through which they were passing made David and Marcia feel, as they sat down, that they would not be able to swallow a mouthful, but strangely enough they found themselves eating with relish, each to encourage the other perhaps, but almost enjoying it, and feeling that they had not yet met more than they would be able to withstand.

Kate was seated on the other side of the dining-room, by Hannah, and she watched the two incessantly with that half merry contemptuous look, toying with her own with food, and apparently waiting for their acting to cease and David to put on his true character. She never doubted for an instant that they were acting.

The wedding supper was over at last. The guests crowded out to the front stoop to bid good-bye to the happy bride-groom and cross-looking bride, who seemed as if she left the gala scene reluctantly.

Marcia, for the instant, was separated from David, who stepped down upon the grass and stood to one side to let the bridal party pass. The minister was at the other side. Marcia had slipped into the shelter of Aunt Amelia's black silk presence and wished she might run out the back door and away home.

Suddenly a shimmer of gold with the sunlight through it caught her gaze, and a glimpse of sheeny purple. There, close behind David, standing upon the top step, quite unseen by him, stood her sister Kate.

Marcia's heart gave a quick thump and seemed to stop, then went painfully laboring on. She stood quite still watching for the moment to come when David would turn around and see Kate that she might look into his face and read there what was written.

Hannah had been put carefully into the carriage by the adoring Lemuel, with many a pat, and shaking of cushions, and adjustment of curtains to suit her whim. It pleased Hannah, now in her last lingering moment of freedom, to be exacting and show others what a slave her husband was.

They all stood for an instant looking after the carriage, but Marcia watched David. Then, just as the carriage wound around the curve in the road and was lost from view, she saw him turn, and at once knew she must not see his face as he looked at Kate. Closing her eyes like a flash she turned and fled upstairs to get her shawl and bonnet. There she took refuge behind the great white curtains, and hid her face for several minutes, praying wildly, she hardly knew what, thankful she had been kept from the sight which yet she had longed to behold.

As David turned to go up the steps and search for Marcia he was confronted by Kate's beautiful, smiling face, radiant as it used to be when it had first charmed him. He exulted, as he looked into it, that it did not any longer charm.

"David, you don't seem a bit glad to see me," blamed Kate sweetly in her pretty, childish tones, looking into his face with those blue eyes so like to liquid skies. Almost there was a hint of tears in them. He had been wont to kiss them when she looked like that. Now he felt only disgust as some of the flippant sentences in her letters to Harry Temple came to his mind.

His face was stern and unrecognizing.

"David, you are angry with me yet! You said you would forgive!" The gentle reproach minimized the crime, and enlarged the punishment. It was Kate's way.

The pretty pout on the rosy lips was the same as it used to be when she chided him for some trifling forgetfulness of her wishes.

The other guests had all gone into the house now. David made no response, but nothing daunted, Kate spoke again.

"I have something very important to consult you about. I came here on purpose. Can you give me some time tomorrow morning?"

She wrinkled her pretty face into a thousand dimples and looked her most bewitching like a naughty child who knew she was loved in spite of anything, and coquettishly putting her head on one side, added, in the tone she used of old to cajole him:

"You know you never could refuse me anything, David."

David did not smile. He did not answer the look. With a voice that recognized her only as a stranger he said gravely: "I have an important engagement to-morrow morning."

"But you will put off the engagement." She said it confidently.

"It is impossible!" said David decidedly. "I am starting quite early to drive over to Albany. I am under obligation to be present at the starting of the new steam railroad."

"Oh, how nice!" said Kate, clapping her hands childishly, "I have wanted to be there, and now you will take me. Then I — we — can talk on the way. How like old times that will be!" She flashed him a smile of molten sunshine, alluring and transforming.

"That, too, is impossible, Mrs. Leavenworth. My wife accompanies me!" he answered her promptly and clearly and with a curt bow left her and went into the house.

Kate Leavenworth was angry, and for Kate to be angry, meant to visit it upon some one, the offender if possible, if not the nearest to the offender. She had failed utterly in her attempt to win back the friendship of her former lover. She had hoped to enjoy his attention to a certain extent and bathe her sad heart in the wistful glances of the man she had jilted; and incidentally perhaps be invited to spend a little time in his house, by which she would contrive to have a good many of her own ways. A rich brother-in-law who adored one was not a bad thing to have, especially when his wife was one's own little sister whom one had always dominated. She was tired of New York and at this season of the year the country was much preferable. She could thus contrive to hoard her small income, and save for the next winter, as well as secure a possible entrance finally into her father's good graces again through the forgiveness of David and Marcia. But she had failed. Could it be that he cared for Marcia! That child! Scout the idea! She would discover at once.

Hurriedly she searched through the rooms downstairs and then went stealthily upstairs. Instinctively she went to the room where Marcia had hidden herself.

Marcia, with that strong upward breath of prayer had grown steady again. She was standing with her back to the door looking out of the window toward her own home when Kate entered the room. Without turning about she felt Kate's presence and knew that it was she. The moment had come. She turned around, her face calm and sweet, with two red spots upon her cheeks, and her bonnet,—Kate's bonnet and shawl, Kate's fine lace shawl sent from Paris— grasped in her hands.

They faced each other, the sisters, and much was understood between them in a flash without a word spoken, Marcia suddenly saw herself standing there in Kate's rightful place, Kate's things in her hands, Kate's garments upon her body, Kate's husband held by her. It was as if Kate charged her with all these things, as she looked her through and over, from her slipper tips to the ruffle around the neck. And oh, the scorn that flamed from Kate's eyes playing over her, and scorching her cheeks into crimson, and burning her lips dry and stiff! And yet when Kate's eyes reached her face and charged her with the supreme offense of taking David from her, Marcia's eyes looked bravely back, and were not burned by the fire, and she felt that her soul was not even scorched by it. Something about the thought of David like an angelic presence seemed to save her.

The silence between them was so intense that nothing else could be heard by the two. The voices below were drowned by it, the footstep on the stair was as if it were not.

At last Kate spoke, angered still more by her sister's soft eyes which gazed steadily back and did not droop before her own flashing onslaught. Her voice was cold and cruel. There was nothing sisterly in it, nothing to remind either that the other had ever been beloved.

"Fool!" hissed Kate. "Silly fool! Did you think you could steal a husband as you stole your clothes? Did you suppose marrying David would make him yours, as putting on my clothes seemed to make them yours? Well I can tell you he will never be a husband to you. He doesn't love you and he never can. He will always love me. He's as much mine as if I had married him, in spite of all your attempts to take him. Oh, you needn't put up your baby mouth and pucker it as if you were going to cry. Cry away. It won't do any good. You can't make a man yours, any more than you can make somebody's clothes yours. They don't fit you any more than he does. You look horrid in blue, and you know it, in spite of all your prinking around and pretending. I'd be ashamed to be tricked out that way and know that every dud I had was made for somebody else. As for going around and pretending you have a husband—it's a lie. You know he's nothing to you. You know he never told you he cared for you. I tell you he's mine, and he always will be."

"Kate, you're married!" cried Marcia in shocked tones. "How can you talk like that?"

"Married! Nonsense! What difference does that make? It's hearts that count, not marriages. Has your marriage made you a wife? Answer me that! Has it? Does David love you? Does he ever kiss you? Yet he came to see me in New York this winter, and took me in his arms and kissed me. He gave me money too. See this brooch?"—she exhibited a jeweled pin—"that was bought with his money. You see he loves me still. I could bring him to my feet with a word to-day. He would kiss me if I asked him. He is weak as water in my hands."

Marcia's cheeks burned with shame and anger. Almost she felt at the limit of her strength. For the first time in her life she felt like striking,—striking her own sister. Horrified over her feelings, and the rage which was tearing her soul, she looked up, and there stood David in the doorway, like some tall avenging angel!

Kate had her back that way and did not see at once, but Marcia's eyes rested on him hungrily, pleadingly, and his answered hers. From her sudden calmness Kate saw there was some one near, and turning, looked at David. But he did not glance her way. How much or how little he had heard of Kate's tirade, which in her passion had been keyed in a high voice, he never let them know and neither dared to ask him, lest perhaps he had not heard anything. There was a light of steel in his eyes toward everything but Marcia, and his tone had in it kindness and a recognition of mutual understanding as he said:

"If you are ready we had better go now, dear, had we not?"

Oh how gladly Marcia followed her husband down the stairs and out the door! She scarcely knew how she went through the formalities of getting away. It seemed as she looked back upon them that David had sheltered her from it all, and said everything needful for her, and all she had done was to smile an assent. He talked calmly to her all the way home; told her Mr. Brentwood's opinion about the change in the commerce of the country the new railroad was going to make; told her though he must have known she could not listen. Perhaps both were conscious of the bedroom window over the way and a pair of blue eyes that might be watching them as they passed into the house. David took hold of her arm and helped her up the steps of their own home as if she had been some great lady. Marcia wondered if Kate saw that. In her heart she blessed David for this outward sign of their relationship. It gave her shame a little cover at least. She glanced up toward the next house as she passed in and felt sure she saw a glimmer of purple move away from the window. Then David shut the door behind them and led her gently in.

Chapter 27

He made her go into the parlor and sit down and she was all unnerved by his gentle ways. The tears would come in spite of her. He took his own fine wedding handkerchief and wiped them softly off her hot cheeks. He untied the bonnet that was not hers, and flung it far into a corner in the room. Marcia thought he put force into the fling. Then he unfolded the shawl from her shoulders and threw that into another corner. Kate's beautiful thread lace shawl. Marcia felt a hysterical desire to laugh, but David's voice was steady and quiet when he spoke as one might speak to a little child in trouble.

"There now, dear," he said. He had never called her dear before. "There, that was an ordeal, and I'm glad it's over. It will never trouble us that way again. Let us put it aside and never think about it any more. We have our own lives to live. I want you to go with me to-morrow morning to see the train start if you feel able. We must start early and you must take a good rest. Would you like to go?"

Marcia's face like a radiant rainbow answered for her as she smiled behind her tears, and all the while he talked David's hand, as tender as a woman's, was passing back and forth on Marcia's hot forehead and smoothing the hair. He talked on quietly to soothe her, and give her a chance to regain her composure, speaking of a few necessary arrangements for the morning's ride. Then he said, still in his quiet voice: "Now dear, I want you to go to bed, for we must start rather early, but first do you think you could sing me that little song you were singing the day I came home? Don't if you feel too tired, you know."

Then Marcia, an eager light in her eyes, sprang up and went to the piano, and began to play softly and sing the tender words she had sung once before when he was listening and she knew it not.

> Dearest, believe,
> Whene'r we part,
> Lonely I grieve,
> In my sad heart: —

Kate, standing within the chintz curtains across the yard shedding angry tears upon her purple silk, heard presently the sweet tones of the piano, which might have been hers; heard her sister's voice singing, and began to understand that she must bear the punishment of her own rash deeds.

The room had grown from a purple dusk into quiet darkness while Marcia was singing, for the sun was almost down when they walked home. When the song was finished David stood half wistfully looking at Marcia for a moment. Her eyes shone to his through the dusk like two bright stars. He hesitated as though he wanted to say something more, and then thought better of it. At last he stooped and lifted her hand from the keys and led her toward the door.

"You must go to sleep at once," he said gently. "You'll need all the rest you can get." He lighted a candle for her and said good-night with this eyes as well as his lips. Marcia felt that she was moving up the stairs under a spell of some gentle loving power that surrounded her and would always guard her.

And it was about this time that Miranda, having been sent over to take a forgotten piece of bride's cake to Marcia, and having heard the piano, and stolen discreetly to the parlor window for a moment, returned and detailed for the delectation of that most unhappy guest Mrs. Leavenworth why she could not get in and would have to take it over in the morning:

"The window was open in the parlor and they were in there, them two, but they was so plum took up with their two selves, as they always are, that there wasn't no use knockin' fer they'd never hev heard."

Miranda enjoyed making those remarks to the guest. Some keen instinct always told her where best to strike her blows.

When Marcia had reached the top stair she looked down and there was David smiling up to her.

"Marcia," said he in a tone that seemed half ashamed and half amused, "have you, any — that is — things — that you had before — all your own I mean?" With quick intuition Marcia understood and her own sweet shame about her clothes that were not her own came back upon her with double force. She suddenly saw herself again standing before the censure of her sister. She wondered if David had heard. If not, how then did he know? Oh, the shame of it!

"Yes," said she, trying to think. "Some old things, and one frock."

"Wear it then to-morrow, dear," said David, in a compelling voice and with the sweet smile that took the hurt out of his most severe words.

Marcia smiled. "It is very plain," she said, "only chintz, pink and white. I made it myself."

"Charming!" said David. "Wear it, dear. Marcia, one thing more. Don't wear any more things that don't belong to you. Not a dud. Promise me? Can you get along without it?"

"Why, I guess so," said Marcia laughing joyfully. "I'll try to manage. But I haven't any bonnet. Nothing but a pink sunbonnet."

"All right, wear that," said David.

"It will look a little queer, won't it?" said Marcia doubtfully, and yet as if the idea expressed a certain freedom which was grateful to her.

"Never mind," said David. "Wear it. Don't wear any more of those other things. Pack them all and send them where they belong, just as quick as we get home."

There was something masterful and delightful in David's voice, and Marcia with a happy laugh took her candle and got up saying, with a ring of joy in her voice: "All right!" She went to her room with David's second good-night ringing in her ears and her heart so light she wanted to sing.

Not at once did Marcia go to her bed. She set her candle upon the bureau and began to search wildly in a little old haircloth trunk, her own special old trunk that had contained her treasures and which had been sent her after she left home. She had scarcely looked into it since she came to the new home. It seemed as if her girlhood were shut up in it. Now she pulled it out from the closet.

What a flood of memories rushed over her as she opened it! There were relics of her school days, and of her little childhood. But she had no time for them now. She was in search of something. She touched them tenderly, but laid them all out one after another upon the floor until down in the lower corner she found a roll of soft white cloth. It contained a number of white garments, half a dozen perhaps in all, finished, and several others cut out barely begun. They were her own work, every stitch, the first begun when she was quite a little girl, and her stepmother started to teach her to sew. What pride she had taken in them! How pleased she had been when allowed to put real tucks in some of them! She had thought as she sewed upon them at different times that they were to be a part of her own wedding trousseau. And then her wedding had come upon her unawares, with the trousseau ready-made, and everything belonged to some one else. She had folded her own poor little garments away and thought never to take them out again, for they seemed to belong to her dead self.

But now that dead self had suddenly come to life again. These hated things that she had worn for a year that were not hers were to be put away, and, pretty as they were, many of them, she regretted not a thread of them.

She laid the white garments out upon a chair and decided that she would put on what she needed of them on the morrow, even though they were rumpled with long lying away. She even searched out an old pair of her own stockings and laid them on a chair with the other things. They were neatly darned as all things had always been under her stepmother's supervision. Further search brought a pair of partly worn prunella slippers to light, with narrow ankle ribbons.

Then Marcia took down the pink sprigged chintz that she had made a year ago and laid it near the other things, with a bit of black velvet and the quaint old brooch. She felt a little dubious about appearing on such a great occasion, almost in Albany, in a chintz dress and with no wrap. Stay! There was the white crepe shawl, all her own, that David had brought her. She had not felt like wearing it to Hannah Heath's wedding, it seemed too precious to take near an unloving person like Hannah. Before that she had never felt an occasion great enough. Now she drew it forth breathlessly. A white crepe shawl and a pink calico sunbonnet! Marcia laughed softly. But then, what matter! David had said wear it.

All things were ready for the morrow now. There were even her white lace mitts that Aunt Polly in an unusual fit of benevolence had given her.

Then, as if to make the change complete, she searched out an old night robe, plain but smooth and clean and arrayed herself in it, and so, thankful, happy, she lay down as she had been bidden and fell asleep.

David in the room below pondered, strange to say, the subject of dress. There was some pride beneath it all, of course; there always is behind the great problem of dress. It was the rejected bonnet lying in the corner with its blue ribbons limp and its blue flowers crushed that made that subject paramount among so many others he might have chosen for his night's meditation.

He was going over to close the parlor window, when he saw the thing lying innocent and discarded in the corner. Though it bore an injured look, it yet held enough of its original aristocratic style to cause him to stop and think.

It was all well enough to suggest that Marcia wear a pink sunbonnet. It sounded deliciously picturesque. She looked lovely in pink and a sunbonnet was pretty and sensible on any one; but the morrow was a great day. David would be seen of many and his wife would come under strict scrutiny. Moreover it was possible that Kate might be upon the scene to jeer at her sister in a sunbonnet. In fact, when he considered it he would not like to take his wife to Albany in a sunbonnet. It behoved him to consider. The outrageous words which he had heard Mistress Leavenworth speak to his wife still burned in his brain like needles of torture: revelation of the true character of the woman he had once longed to call his own.

But that bonnet! He stood and examined it. What was a bonnet like? The proper kind of a bonnet for a woman in his wife's position to wear. He had never noticed a woman's bonnet before except as he had absent-mindedly observed them in front of him in meeting. Now he brought his mind to bear upon that bonnet. It seemed to be made up of three component parts — a foundation; a girdle apparently to bind together and tie on the head; and a decoration. Straw, silk and some kind of unreal flowers. Was that all? He stooped down and picked the thing up with the tips of his fingers, held it at arms length as though it were contaminating, and examined the inside. Ah! There was another element in its construction, a sort of frill of something thin, — hardly lace, — more like the foam of a cloud. He touched the tulle clumsily with his thumb and finger and then he dropped the bonnet back into the corner again. He thought he understood well enough to know one again. He stood pondering a moment, and looked at his watch.

Yes, it was still early enough to try at least, though of course the shop would be closed. But the village milliner lived behind her little store. It would be easy enough to rouse her, and he had known her all his life. He took his hat as eagerly as he had done when a boy Aunt Clarinda had given him a penny to buy a top and permission to go to the corner and buy it before Aunt Amelia woke up from her nap. He went quietly out of the door, fastening it behind him and walked rapidly down the street.

Yes, the milliner's shop was closed, but a light in the side windows shining through the veiling hop-vines guided him, and he was presently tapping at Miss Mitchell's side door. She opened the door cautiously and peeped over her glasses at him, and then a bright smile overspread her face. Who in the whole village did not welcome David whenever he chanced to come? Miss Mitchell was resting from her labors and reading the village paper. She had finished the column of gossip and was quite ready for a visitor.

"Come right in, David," she said heartily, for she had known him all the years, "it does a body good to see you though your visits are as few and far between as angels' visits. I'm right glad to see you! Sit down." But David was too eager about his business.

"I haven't any time to sit down to-night, Miss Susan," he said eagerly, "I've come to buy a bonnet. Have you got one? I hope it isn't too late because I want it very early in the morning."

"A bonnet! Bless me! For yourself?" said Miss Mitchell from mere force of commercial habit. But neither of them saw the joke, so intent upon business were they. "For my wife, Miss Mitchell. You see she is going with me over to Albany to-morrow morning and we start quite early. We are going to see the new railroad train start, you know, and she seems to think she hasn't a bonnet that's suitable."

"Going to see a steam engine start, are you! Well, take care, David, you don't get too near. They do say they're terrible dangerous things, and fer my part I can't see what good they'll be, fer nobody'll ever be willin' to ride behind 'em, but I'd like to see it start well enough. And that sweet little wife of yours thinks she ain't got a good enough bonnet. Land sakes! What is the matter with her Dunstable straw, and what's become of that one trimmed with blue lutestrings, and where's the shirred silk one she wore last Sunday? They're every one fine bonnets and ought to last her a good many years yet if she cares fer 'em. The mice haven't got into the house and et them, hev they?"

"No, Miss Susan, those bonnets are all whole yet I believe, but they don't seem to be just the suitable thing. In fact, I don't think they're over-becoming to her, do you? You see they're mostly blue—"

"That's so!" said Miss Mitchell. "I think myself she'd look better in pink. How'd you like white? I've got a pretty thing that I made fer Hannah Heath an' when it was done Hannah thought it was too plain and wouldn't have it. I sent for the flowers to New York and they cost a high price. Wait! I will show it to you."

She took a candle and he followed her to the dark front room ghostly with bonnets in various stages of perfection.

It was a pretty thing. Its foundation was of fine Milan braid, creamy white and smooth and even. He knew at a glance it belonged to the higher order of things, and was superior to most of the bonnets produced in the village.

It was trimmed with plain white taffeta ribbon, soft and silky. That was all on the outside. Around the face was a soft ruching of tulle, and clambering among it a vine of delicate green leaves that looked as if they were just plucked from a wild rose bank. David was delighted. Somehow the bonnet looked like Marcia. He paid the price at once, declining to look at anything else. It was enough that he liked it and that Hannah Heath had not. He had never admired Hannah's taste. He carried it home in triumph, letting himself softly into the house, lighted three candles, took the bonnet out and hung it upon a chair. Then he walked around it surveying it critically, first from this side, then from that. It pleased him exceedingly. He half wished Marcia would hear him and come down. He wanted to see it on her, but concluded that he was growing boyish and had better get himself under control.

The bonnet approved, he walked back and forth through the kitchen and dining-room thinking. He compelled himself to go over the events of the afternoon and analyze most carefully his own innermost feelings. In fact, after doing that he began further back and tried to find out how he felt toward Marcia. What was this something that had been growing in him unaware through the months; that had made his homecoming so sweet, and had brightened every succeeding day; and had made this meeting with Kate a mere common-place? What was this precious thing that nestled in his heart? Might he, had he a right to call it love? Surely! Now all at once his pulses thrilled with gladness. He loved her! It was good to love her! She was the most precious being on earth to him. What was Kate in comparison with her? Kate who had shown herself cold and cruel and unloving in every way?

His anger flamed anew as he thought of those cutting sentences he had overheard, taunting her own sister about the clothes she wore. Boasting that he still belonged to her! She, a married woman! A woman who had of her own free will left him at the last moment and gone away with another! His whole nature recoiled against her. She had sinned against her womanhood, and might no longer demand from man the homage that a true woman had a right to claim.

Poor little bruised flower! His heart went out to Marcia. He could not bear to think of her having to stand and listen to that heartless tirade. And he had been the cause of all this. He had allowed her to take a position which threw her open to Kate's vile taunts.

Up and down he paced till the torrent of his anger spent itself, and he was able to think more calmly. Then he went back in his thoughts to the time when he had first met Kate and she had bewitched him. He could see now the heartlessness of her. He had met her first at the house of a friend where he was visiting, partly on pleasure, partly on business. She had devoted herself to him during the time of her stay in a most charming way, though now he recalled that she had also been equally devoted to the son of the house whom he was visiting. When she went home she had asked him to come and call, for her home was but seven miles away. He had been so charmed with her that he had accepted the invitation, and, rashly he now saw, had engaged himself to her, after having known her in all face to face but a few days. To be sure he had known of her father for years, and he took a good deal for granted on account of her fine family. They had corresponded after their engagement which had lasted for nearly a year, and in that time David had seen her but twice, for a day or two at a time, and each time he had thought her grown more lovely. Her letters had been marvels of modesty, and shy admiration. It was easy for Kate to maintain her character upon paper, though she had had little trouble in making people love her under any circumstances. Now as he looked back he could recall many instances when she had shown a cruel, heartless nature.

Then, all at once, with a throb of joy, it came to him to be thankful to God for the experience through which he had passed. After all it had not been taken from him to love with a love enduring, for though Kate had been snatched from him just at the moment of his possession, Marcia had been given to him. Fool that he was! He had been blind to his own salvation. Suppose he had been allowed to go on and marry Kate! Suppose he had had her character revealed to him suddenly as those letters of hers to Harry Temple had revealed it — as it surely would have been revealed in time, for such things cannot be hid, — and she had been his *wife!* He shuddered. How he would have loathed her! How he loathed her now!

Strangely enough the realization of that fact gave him joy. He sprang up and waved his hands about in silent delight. He felt as if he must shout for gladness. Then he gravely knelt beside his chair and uttered an audible thanksgiving for his escape and the joy he had been given. Nothing else seemed fitting expression of his feelings.

There was one other question to consider — Marcia's feelings. She had always been kind and gentle and loving to him, just as a sister might have been. She was exceedingly young yet. Did she know, could she understand what it meant to be loved the way he was sure he could love a woman? And would she ever be able to love him in that way? She was so silent and shy he hardly knew whether she cared for him or not. But there was one thought that gave him unbounded joy and that was that she was his wife. At least no one else could take her from him. He had felt condemned that he had married her when his heart was heavy lest she would lose the joy of life, but all that was changed now. Unless she loved some one else surely such love as his could compel hers and finally make her as happy as a woman could be made.

A twinge of misgiving crossed his mind as he admitted the possibility that Marcia might love some one else. True, he knew of no one, and she was so young it was scarcely likely she had left any one back in her girlhood to whom her heart had turned when she was out of his sight. Still there were instances of strong union of hearts of those who had loved from early childhood. It might be that Marcia's sometime-sadness was over a companion of her girlhood.

A great longing took possession of him to rush up and waken her and find out if she could ever care for him. He scarcely knew himself. This was not his dignified contained self that he had lived with for twenty-seven years.

It was very late before he finally went upstairs. He walked softly lest he disturb Marcia. He paused before her door listening to see if she was asleep, but there was only the sound of the katydids in the branches outside her window, and the distant tree-toads singing a fugue in an orchard not far away. He tiptoed to his room but he did not light his candle, therefore there was no light in the back room of the Spafford house that night for any watching eyes to ponder over. He threw himself on the bed. He was weary in body yet his soul seemed buoyant as a bird in the morning air. The moon was casting long bars of silver across the rag carpet and white counterpane. It was almost full moon. Yes, to-morrow it would be entirely full. It was full moon the night he had met Marcia down by the gate, and kissed her. It was the first time he had thought of that kiss with anything but pain. It used to hurt him that he had made the mistake and taken her for Kate. It had seemed like an ill-omen of what was to come. But now, it thrilled him with a great new joy. After all he had given the kiss to the right one. It was Marcia to whom his soul bowed in the homage that a man may give to a woman. Did his good angel guide him to her that night? And how was it he had not seen the sweetness of Marcia sooner? How had he lived with her nearly a year, and watched her dainty ways, and loving ministry and not known that his heart was hers? How was it he had grieved so long over Kate, and now since he had seen her once more, not a regret was in his heart that she was not his; but a beautiful revelation of his own love to Marcia had been wrought in him? How came it?

And the importunate little songsters in the night answered him a thousand times: "Kate-did-it! Kate-she-did-it! Yes she did! I say she did. Kate did it!"

Had angel voices reached him through his dreams, and suddenly given him the revelation which the little insects had voiced in their ridiculous colloquy? It was Kate herself who had shown him how he loved Marcia.

Chapter 28

Slowly the moon rode over the house, and down toward its way in the West, and after its vanishing chariot the night stretched wistful arms. Softly the grey in the East tinged into violet and glowed into rose and gold. The birds woke up and told one another that the first of August was come and life was good.

The breath that came in the early dawn savored of new-mown hay, and the bird songs thrilled Marcia as if it were the day of her dreams.

She forgot all her troubles; forgot even her wayward sister next door; and rose with the song of the birds in her heart. This was to be a great day. No matter what happened she had now this day to date from. David had asked her to go somewhere just because he wanted her to. She knew it from the look in his eyes when he told her, and she knew it because he might have asked a dozen men to go with him. There was no reason why he need have taken her to-day, for it was distinctly an affair for men, this great wonder of machinery. It was a privilege for a woman to go. She felt it. She understood the honor.

With fingers trembling from joy she dressed. Not the sight of her pink calico sunbonnet lying on the chair, nor the thought of wearing it upon so grand an occasion, could spoil the pleasure of the day. Among so large a company her bonnet would hardly be noticed. If David was satisfied why what difference did it make? She was glad it would be early when they drove by the aunts, else they might be scandalized. But never mind! Trill! She hummed a merry little tune which melted into the melody of the song she had sung last night.

Then she smiled at herself in the glass. She was fastening the brooch in the bit of velvet round her neck, and she thought of the day a year ago when she had fastened that brooch. She had wondered then how she would feel if the next day was to be her own wedding day. Now as she smiled back at herself in the glass all at once she thought it seemed as if this was her wedding day. Somehow last night had seemed to realize her dreams. A wonderful joy had descended upon her heart. Maybe she was foolish, but was she not going to ride with David? She did not long for the green fields and a chance to run wild through the wood now. This was better than those childish pleasures. This was real happiness. And to think it should have come through David!

She hurried with the arrangement of her hair until her fingers trembled with excitement. She wanted to get downstairs and see if it were all really true or if she were dreaming it. Would David look at her as he had done last night? Would he speak that precious word "dear" to her again to-day? Would he take her by the hand and lead her sometimes, or was that a special gentleness because he knew she had suffered from her sister's words? She clasped her hands with a quick, convulsive gesture over her heart and looking back to the sweet face in the glass, said softly, "Oh, I love him, love him! And it cannot be wrong for Kate is married."

But though she was up early David had been down before her. The fire was ready lighted and kettle singing over it on the crane. He had even pulled out the table and put up the leaf, and made some attempt to put the dishes upon it for breakfast. He was sitting by the hearth impatient for her coming, with a bandbox by his side.

It was like another sunrise to watch their eyes light up as they saw one another. Their glances rushed together as though they had been a long time withholden from each other, and a rosy glow came over Marcia's face that made her long to hide it for a moment from view. Then she knew in her heart that her dream was not all a dream. David was the same. It had lasted, whatever this wonderful thing was that bound them together. She stood still in her happy bewilderment, looking at him, and he enjoying the radiant morning vision of her, stood too.

David found that longing to take her in his arms overcoming him again. He had made strict account with himself and was resolved to be careful and not frighten her. He must be sure it would not be unpleasant to her before he let her know his great deep love. He must be careful. He must not take advantage of the fact that she was his and could not run away from him. If she dreaded his attentions, neither could she any more say no.

And so their two looks met, and longed to come closer, but were held back, and a lovely shyness crept over Marcia's sweet face. Then David bethought himself of his bandbox.

He took up the box and untied it with unaccustomed fingers, fumbling among the tissue paper for the handle end of the thing. Where did they take hold of bonnets anyway? He had no trouble with it the night before, but then he was not thinking about it. Now he was half afraid she might not like it. He remembered that Hannah Heath had pronounced against it. It suddenly seemed impossible that he should have bought a bonnet that a pretty woman had said was not right. There must be something wrong with it after all.

Marcia stood wondering.

"I thought maybe this would do instead of the sunbonnet," he said at last, getting out the bonnet by one string and holding it dangling before him.

Marcia caught it with deft careful hands and an exclamation of delight. He watched her anxiously. It had all the requisite number of materials, — one, two, three, four, — like the despised bonnet he threw on the floor — straw, silk, lace and flowers. Would she like it? Her face showed that she did. Her cheeks flushed with pleasure, and her eyes danced with joy. Marcia's face always showed it when she liked anything. There was nothing half-way about her.

"Oh, it is beautiful!" she said delightedly. "It is so sweet and white and cool with that green vine. Oh, I am glad, glad, glad! I shall never wear that old blue bonnet again." She went over to the glass and put it on. The soft ruching settled about her brown hair, and made a lovely setting for her face. The green vine twined and peeped in and out under the round brim and the ribbon sat in a prim bow beneath her pretty chin.

She gave one comprehensive glance at herself in the glass and then turned to David. In that glance was revealed to her just how much she had dreaded wearing her pink sunbonnet, and just how relieved she was to have a substitute.

Her look was shy and sweet as she said with eyes that dared and then drooped timidly:

"You — are — very — good to me."

Almost he forgot his vow of carefulness at that, but remembered when he got half across the room toward her, and answered earnestly:

"Dear, *you* have been very good to *me.*"

Marcia's eyes suddenly sobered and half the glow faded from her face. Was it then only gratitude? She took off the bonnet and touched the bows with wistful tenderness as she laid it by till after breakfast. He watched her and misinterpreted the look. Was she then disappointed in the bonnet? Was it not right after all? Had Hannah known better than he? He hesitated and then asked her:

"Is there — Is it — That is — perhaps you would rather take it back and choose another. You know how to choose one better than I. There were others I think. In fact, I forgot to look at any but this because I liked it, but I'm only a man — " he finished helplessly.

"No! No! No!" said Marcia, her eyes sparkling emphatically again. "There couldn't be a better one. This is just exactly what I like. I do not want anything else. And I — like it all the better because you selected it," she added daringly, suddenly lifting her face to his with a spice of her own childish freedom.

His eyes admired her.

"She told me Hannah Heath thought it too plain," he added honestly.

"Then I'm sure I like it all the better for that," said Marcia so emphatically that they both laughed.

It all at once became necessary to hurry, for the old clock in the hall clanged out the hour and David became aware that haste was imperative.

Early as Marcia had come down, David had been up long before her, his heart too light to sleep. In a dream, or perchance on the borders of the morning, an idea had come to him. He told Marcia that he must go out now to see about the horse, but he also made a hurried visit to the home of his office clerk and another to the aunts, and when he returned with the horse he had left things in such train that if he did not return that evening he would not be greatly missed. But he said nothing to Marcia about it. He laughed to himself as he thought of the sleepy look on his clerk's face, and the offended dignity expressed in the ruffle of Aunt Hortense's night cap all awry as she had peered over the balusters to receive his unprecedentedly early visit. The aunts were early risers. They prided themselves upon it. It hurt their dignity and their pride to have anything short of sudden serious illness, or death, or a fire cause others to arise before them. Therefore they did not receive the message that David was meditating another trip away from the village for a few days with good grace. Aunt Hortense asked Aunt Amelia if she had ever feared that Marcia would have a bad effect upon David by making him frivolous. Perhaps he would lose interest in his business with all his careering around the country. Aunt Amelia agreed that Marcia must be to blame in some way, and then discovering they had a whole hour before their usual rising time, the two good ladies settled themselves with indignant composure to their interrupted repose.

Breakfast was ready when David returned. Marcia supposed he had only been to harness the horse. She glanced out happily through the window to where the horse stood tied to the post in front of the house. She felt like waving her hand to him, and he turned and seemed to see her; rolling the whites of his eyes around, and tossing his head as if in greeting.

Marcia would scarcely have eaten anything in her excitement if David had not urged her to do so. She hurried with her clearing away, and then flew upstairs to arrange her bonnet before the glass and don the lovely folds of the creamy crepe shawl, folding it demurely around her shoulders and knotting it in front. She put on her mitts, took her handkerchief folded primly, and came down ready.

But David no longer seemed in such haste. He made a great fuss fastening up everything. She wondered at his unusual care, for she thought everything quite safe for the day.

She raised one shade toward the Heath house. It was the first time she had permitted herself this morning to think of Kate. Was she there yet? Probably, for no coach had left since last night, and unless she had gone by private conveyance there would have been no way to go. She looked up to the front corner guest room where the windows were open and the white muslin curtains swayed in the morning breeze. No one seemed to be moving about in the room. Perhaps Kate was not awake. Just then she caught the flutter of a blue muslin down on the front stoop. Kate was up, early as it was, and was coming out. A sudden misgiving seized Marcia's heart, as when a little child, she had seen her sister coming to eat up the piece of cake or sweetmeat that had been given to her. Many a time had that happened. Now, she felt that in some mysterious way Kate would contrive to take from her her new-found joy.

She could not resist her, — David could not resist her, — no one could ever resist Kate. Her face turned white and her hand began to tremble so that she dropped the curtain she had been holding up.

Just then came David's clear voice, louder than would have been necessary, and pitched as if he were calling to some one upstairs, though he knew she was just inside the parlor where she had gone to make sure of the window fastening.

"Come, dear! Aren't you ready? It is more than time we started."

There was a glad ring in David's voice that somehow belied the somewhat exacting words he had spoken, and Marcia's heart leaped up to meet him.

"Yes, I'm all ready, dear!" she called back with a hysterical little laugh. Of course Kate could not hear so far, but it gave her satisfaction to say it. The final word was unpremeditated. It bubbled up out of the depths of her heart and made the red rush back into her cheeks when she realized what she had said. It was the first time she had ever used a term of endearment toward David. She wondered if he noticed it and if he would think her very—bold,—queer,—immodest, to use it. She looked shyly up at him, enquiring with her eyes, as she came out to him on the front stoop, and he looked down with such a smile she felt as if it were a caress. And yet neither was quite conscious of this little real by-play they were enacting for benefit of the audience of one in blue muslin over the way. How much she heard, or how little they could not tell, but it gave satisfaction to go through with it inasmuch as it was real, and not acting at all.

David fastened the door and then helped Marcia into the carriage. They were both laughing happily like two children starting upon a picnic. Marcia was serenely conscious of her new bonnet, and it was pleasant to have David tuck the linen lap robe over chintz frock so carefully. She was certain Kate could not identify it now at that distance, thanks to the lap robe and her crepe shawl. At least Kate could not see any of her own trousseau on her sister now.

Kate was sitting on the little white seat in the shelter of the honeysuckle vine facing them on the stoop of the Heath house. It was impossible for them to know whether she was watching them or not. They did not look up to see. She was talking with Mr. Heath who, in his milking garb, was putting to rights some shrubs and plants near the walk that had been trampled upon during the wedding festivities. But Kate must have seen a good deal that went on.

David took up the reins, settled himself with a smile at Marcia, touched the horse with the tip of the whip, which caused him to spring forward in astonishment—that from David! No horse in town would have expected it of him. They had known him from babyhood, most of them, and he was gentleness itself. It must have been a mistake. But the impression lasted long enough to carry them a rod or two past the Heath house at swift pace, with only time for a lifting of David's hat, prolonged politely,—which might or might not have included Kate, and they were out upon their way together.

Marcia could scarcely believe her senses that she was really here beside David, riding with him swiftly through the village and leaving Kate behind. She felt a passing pity for Kate. Then she looked shyly up at David. Would his gaiety pass when they were away, and would he grow grave and sad again as soon as he was out of Kate's sight? She had learned enough of David's principles to know that he would not think it right to let his thoughts stray to Kate now, but did his heart still turn that way in spite of him?

Through the town they sped, glad with every roll of wheels that took them further away from Kate. Each was conscious, as they rolled along, of that day one year ago when they rode together thus, out through the fields into the country. It was a day much as that other one, just as bright, just as warm, yet oh, so much more radiant to both! Then they were sad and fearful of the future. All their life seemed in the past. Now the darkness had been led through, and they had reached the brightness again. In fact, all the future stretched out before them that fair morning and looked bright as the day.

They were conscious of the blueness of the sky, of the soft clouds that hovered in haziness on the rim of the horizon, as holding off far enough to spoil no moment of that perfect day. They were conscious of the waving grains and of the perfume of the buckwheat drifting like snow in the fields beyond the wheat; conscious of the meadow-lark and the wood-robin's note; of the whir of a locust; and the thud of a frog in the cool green of a pool deep with brown shadows; conscious of the circling of mated butterflies in the simmering gold air; of the wild roses lifting fair pink petals from the brambly banks beside the road; conscious of the whispering pine needles in a wood they passed; the fluttering chatter of leaves and silver flash of the lining of poplar leaves, where tall trees stood like sentinels, apart and sad; conscious of a little brook that tinkled under a log bridge they crossed, then hurried on its way unmindful of their happy crossing; conscious of the dusty daisy beside the road, closing with a bumbling bee who wanted honey below the market price; conscious of all these things; but most conscious of each other, close, side by side.

It was all so dear, that ride, and over so soon. Marcia was just trying to get used to looking up into the dazzling light of David's eyes. She had to droop her own almost immediately for the truth she read in his was overpowering. Could it be? A fluttering thought came timidly to her heart and would not be denied.

"Can it be, can it be that he cares for me? He loves me. He loves me!" It sang its way in with thrill after thrill of joy and more David's eyes told the story which his lips dared not risk yet. But eyes and hearts are not held by the conventions that bind lips. They rushed into their inheritance of each other and had that day ahead, a day so rare and sweet that it would do to set among the jewels of fair days for all time and for any one.

All too soon they began to turn into roads where were other vehicles, many of them, and all going in the same direction. Men and women in gala day attire all laughing and talking expectantly and looking at one another as the carriages passed with a degree of familiar curiosity which betokens a common errand. Family coaches, farm wagons, with kitchen chairs for accommodation of the family; old one-horse chaises, carryalls, and even a stage coach or two wheeled into the old turnpike. David and Marcia settled into subdued quiet, their joy not expressing itself in the ripples of laughter that had rung out earlier in the morning when they were alone. They sought each other's eyes often and often, and in one of these excursions that David's eyes made to Marcia's face he noticed how extremely becoming the new bonnet was. After thinking it over he decided to risk letting her know. He was not shy about it now.

"Do you know, dear," he said, — there had been a good many "dear's" slipping back and forth all unannounced during that ride, and not openly acknowledged either. "Do you know how becoming your new bonnet is to you? You look prettier than I ever saw you look but once before." He kept his eyes upon her face and watched the sweet color steal up to her drooping eyelashes.

"When was that?" she asked coyly, to hide her embarrassment, and sweeping him one laughing glance.

"Why, that night, dear, at the gate, in the moonlight. Don't you remember?"

"Oh-h-h-h!" Marcia caught her breath and a thrill of joy passed through her that made her close her eyes lest the glad tears should come. Then the little bird in her heart set up the song in earnest to the tune of Wonder: "He loves me, He loves me, He loves me!"

He leaned a little closer to her.

"If there were not so many people looking I think I should have to kiss you now."

"Oh-h-h-h!" said Marcia drawing in her breath and looking around frightened on the number of people that were driving all about them, for they were come almost to the railroad now, and could see the black smoke of the engine a little beyond as it stood puffing and snorting upon its track like some sulky animal that had been caught and chained and harnessed and was longing to leap forward and upset its load.

But though Marcia looked about in her happy fright, and sat a trifle straighter in the chaise, she did not move her hand away that lay next to David's, underneath the linen lap robe, and he put his own hand over it and covered it close in his firm hold. Marcia trembled and was so happy she was almost faint with joy. She wondered if she were very foolish indeed to feel so, and if all love had this terrible element of solemn joy in it that made it seem too great to be real.

They had to stop a number of times to speak to people. Everybody knew David, it appeared. This man and that had a word to speak with him, some bit of news that he must not omit to notice in his article, some new development about the attitude of a man of influence that was important; the change of two or three of those who were to go in the coaches on this trial trip.

To all of them David introduced his wife, with a ring of pride in his voice as he said the words "My wife," and all of them stopped whatever business they had in hand and stepped back to bow most deferentially to the beautiful woman who sat smiling by his side. They wondered why they had not heard of her before, and they looked curiously, enviously at David, and back in admiration at Marcia. It was quite a little court she held sitting there in the chaise by David's side.

Men who have since won a mention in the pages of history were there that day, and nearly all of them had a word for David Spafford and his lovely wife. Many of them stood for some time and talked with her. Mr. Thurlow Weed was the last one to leave them before the train was actually ready for starting, and he laid an urging hand upon David's arm as he went. "Then you think you cannot go with us? Better come. Mrs. Spafford will let you I am sure. You're not afraid are you, Mrs. Spafford? I am sure you are a brave woman. Better come, Spafford."

But David laughingly thanked him again as he had thanked others, and said that he would not be able to go, as he and his wife had other plans, and he must go on to Albany as soon as the train had started.

Marcia looked up at him half worshipfully as he said this, wondering what it was, instinctively knowing that it was for her sake he was giving up this honor which they all wished to put upon him. It would naturally have been an interesting thing to him to have taken this first ride behind the new engine "Dewitt Clinton."

Then, suddenly, like a chill wind from a thunder cloud that has stolen up unannounced and clutched the little wild flowers before they have time to bind up their windy locks and duck their heads under cover, there happened a thing that clutched Marcia's heart and froze all the joy in her veins.

Chapter 29

A coach was approaching filled with people, some of them Marcia knew; they were friends and neighbors from their own village, and behind it plodding along came a horse with a strangely familiar gait drawing four people. The driver was old Mr. Heath looking unbelievingly at the scene before him. He did not believe that an engine would be able to haul a train any appreciable distance whatever, and he believed that he had come out here to witness this entire company of fanatics circumvented by the ill-natured iron steed who stood on the track ahead surrounded by gaping boys and a flock of quacking ganders, living symbol of the people who had come to see the thing start; so thought Mr. Heath. He told himself he was as much of a goose as any of them to have let this chit of a woman fool him into coming off out here when he ought to have been in the hay field to-day.

By his side in all the glory of shimmering blue with a wide white lace bertha and a bonnet with a steeple crown wreathed about heavily with roses sat Kate, a blue silk parasol shading her eyes from the sun, those eyes that looked to conquer, and seemed to pierce beyond and through her sister and ignore her. Old Mrs. Heath and Miranda were along, but they did not count, except to themselves. Miranda was all eyes, under an ugly bonnet. She desired above all things to see that wonderful engine in which David was so interested.

Marcia shrunk and seemed to wither where she sat. All her bright bloom faded in an instant and a kind of frenzy seized her. She had a wild desire to get down out of the carriage and run with all her might away from this hateful scene. The sky seemed to have suddenly clouded over and the hum and buzz of voices about seemed a babel that would never cease.

David felt the arm beside his cringe, and shrink back, and looking down saw the look upon her sweet frightened face; following her glance his own face hardened into what might have been termed righteous wrath. But not a word did he say, and neither did he apparently notice the oncoming carriage. He busied himself at once talking with a man who happened to pass the carriage, and when Mr. Heath drove by to get a better view of the engine he was so absorbed in his conversation that he did not notice them, which seemed but natural.

But Kate was not to be thus easily foiled. She had much at stake and she must win if possible. She worked it about that Squire Heath should drive around to the end of the line of coaches, quite out of sight of the engine and where there was little chance of seeing the train and its passengers, — the only thing Squire Heath cared about. But there was an excellent view of David's carriage and

Kate would be within hailing distance if it should transpire that she had no further opportunity of speaking with David. It seemed strange to Squire Heath, as he sat there behind the last coach patiently, that he had done what she asked. She did not look like a woman who was timid about horses, yet she had professed a terrible fear that the screech of the engine would frighten the staid old Heath horse. Miranda, at that, had insisted upon changing seats, thereby getting herself nearer the horse, and the scene of action. Miranda did not like to miss seeing the engine start.

At last word to start was given. A man ran along by the train and mounted into his high seat with his horn in his hand ready to blow. The fireman ceased his raking of the glowing fire and every traveller sprang into his seat and looked toward the crowd of spectators importantly. This was a great moment for all interested. The little ones whose fathers were in the train began to call good-bye and wave their hands, and one old lady whose only son was going as one of the train assistants began to sob aloud.

A horse in the crowd began to act badly. Every snort of the engine as the steam was let off made him start and rear. He was directly behind Marcia, and she turned her head and looked straight into his fiery frightened eyes, red with fear and frenzy, and felt his hot breath upon her cheek. A man was trying most ineffectually to hold him, but it seemed as if in another minute he would come plunging into the seat with them. Marcia uttered a frightened cry and clutched at David's arm. He turned, and seeing instantly what was the matter, placed his arm protectingly about her and at once guided his own horse out of the crowd, and around nearer to the engine. Somehow that protecting arm gave Marcia a steadiness once more and she was able to watch the wonderful wheels begin to turn and the whole train slowly move and start on its way. Her lips parted, her breath came quick, and for the instant she forgot her trouble. David's arm was still about her, and there was a reassuring pressure in it. He seemed to have forgotten that the crowd might see him—if the crowd had not been too busy watching something more wonderful. It is probable that only one person in that whole company saw David sitting with his arm about his wife—for he soon remembered and put it quietly on the back of the seat, where it would call no one's attention—and that person was Kate. She had not come to this hot dusty place to watch an engine creak along a track, she had come to watch David, and she was vexed and angry at what she saw. Here was Marcia flaunting her power over David directly in her face. Spiteful thing! She would pay her back yet and let her know that she could not touch the things that she, Kate, had put her own sign and seal upon. For this reason it was that at the last minute Kate allowed poor Squire Heath to drive around near the front of the train, saying that as David Spafford seemed to find it safe she supposed she ought not to hold them back for her fears. It needed but the word to send the vexed and curious Squire around through the crowd to a spot directly behind David's carriage, and there

Miranda could see quite well, and Kate could sit and watch David and frame her plans for immediate action so soon as the curtain should fall upon this ridiculous engine play over which everybody was wild.

And so, amid shouts and cheers, and squawking of the geese that attempted to precede the engine like a white frightened body-guard down the track; amid the waving of handkerchiefs, the shouts of excited little boys, and the neighing of frightened horses, the first steam engine that ever drew a train in New York state started upon its initial trip.

Then there came a great hush upon the spectators assembled. The wheels were rolling, the carriages were moving, the train was actually going by them, and what had been so long talked about was an assured fact. They were seeing it with their own eyes, and might be witnesses of it to all their acquaintances. It was true. They dared not speak nor breathe lest something should happen and the great miracle should stop. They hushed simultaneously as though at the passing of some great soul. They watched in silence until the train went on between the meadows, grew smaller in the distance, slitted into the shadow of the wood, flashed out into the sunlight beyond again, and then was lost behind a hill. A low murmur growing rapidly into a shout of cheer arose as the crowd turned and faced one another and the fact of what they had seen.

"By gum! She kin do it!" ejaculated Squire Heath, who had watched the melting of his skeptical opinions in speechless amazement.

The words were the first intimation the Spaffords had of the proximity of Kate. They made David smile, but Marcia turned white with sudden fear again. Not for nothing had she lived with her sister so many years. She knew that cruel nature and dreaded it.

David looked at Marcia for sympathy in his smile at the old Squire, but when he saw her face he turned frowning toward those behind him.

Kate saw her opportunity. She learned forward with honeyed smile, and wily as the serpent addressed her words to Marcia, loud and clear enough for all those about them to hear.

"Oh, Mrs. Spafford! I am going to ask a great favor of you. I am sure you will grant it when you know I have so little time. I am extremely anxious to get a word of advice from your husband upon business matters that are very pressing. Would you kindly change places with me during the ride home, and give me a chance to talk with him about it? I would not ask it but that I must leave for New York on the evening coach and shall have no other opportunity to see him."

Kate's smile was roses and cream touched with frosty sunshine, and to onlookers nothing could have been sweeter. But her eyes were coldly cruel as sharpened steel, and they said to her sister as plainly as words could have spoken: "Do you obey my wish, my lady, or I will freeze the heart out of you."

Marcia turned white and sick. She felt as if her lips had suddenly stiffened and refused to obey her when they ought to have smiled. What would all these people think of her, and how was she behaving? For David's sake she ought to do something, say something, look something, but what—what should she do?

While she was thinking this, with the freezing in her heart creeping up into her throat, the great tears beating at the portals of her eyes, and time standing suddenly still waiting for her leaden tongue to speak, David answered:

All gracefully 'twas done, with not much as a second's hesitation,—though it had seemed so long to Marcia, —nor the shadow of a sign that he was angry:

"Mrs. Leavenworth," he said in his masterful voice, "I am sure my wife would not wish to seem ungracious, or unwilling to comply with your request, but as it happens it is impossible. We are not returning home for several days. My wife has some shopping to do in Albany, and in fact we are expecting to take a little trip. A sort of second honeymoon, you know," —he added, smiling toward Mrs. Heath and Miranda; "it is the first time I have had leisure to plan for it since we were married. I am sorry I have to hurry away, but I am sure that my friend Squire Heath can give as much help in a business way as I could, and furthermore, Squire Schuyler is now in New York for a few days as I learned in a letter from him which arrived last evening. I am sure he can give you more and better advice than any I could give. I wish you good morning. Good morning, Mrs. Heath. Good morning, Miss Miranda!"

Lifting his hat David drove away from them and straight over to the little wayside hostelry where he was to finish his article to send by the messenger who was even then ready mounted for the purpose.

"My! Don't he think a lot of her though!" said Miranda, rolling the words as a sweet morsel under her tongue. "It must be nice to have a man so fond of you." This was one of the occasions when Miranda wished she had eyes in the back of her head. She was sharp and she had seen a thing or two, also she had heard scraps of her cousin Hannah's talk. But she sat demurely in the recesses of her deep, ugly bonnet and tried to imagine how the guest behind her looked.

All trembling sat Marcia in the rusty parlor of the little hostelry, while David at the table wrote with hurried hand, glancing up at her to now and then, and passing over the sheets as he finished them for her criticism. She thought she had seen the Heath wagon drive away in the home direction, but she was not sure. She half expected to see the door open and Kate walk in. Her heart was thumping so she could scarcely sit still and the brightness of the world outside seemed to make her dizzy. She was glad to have the sheets to look over, for it took her thoughts away from herself and her nameless fears. She was not quite sure what it was she feared, only that in some way Kate would have power over David to take him away from her. As he wrote she studied the dear lines of his face and knew, as well as human heart may ever know, how dear another soul had grown to hers.

David had not much to write and it was soon signed, approved, and sealed. He sent his messenger on the way and then coming back closed the door and went and stood before Marcia.

As though she felt some critical moment had come she arose, trembling, and looked into his eyes questioningly.

"Marcia," he said, and his tone was grave and earnest, putting her upon an equality with him, not as if she were a child any more. "Marcia, I have come to ask your forgiveness for the terrible thing I did to you in allowing you, who scarcely knew what you were doing then, to give your life away to a man who loved another woman."

Marcia's heart stood still with horror. It had come then, the dreadful thing she had feared. The blow was going to fall. He did not love her! What a fool she had been!

But the steady voice went on, though the blood in her neck and temples throbbed in such loud waves that she could scarcely hear the words to understand them.

"It was a crime, Marcia, and I have come to realize it more and more during all the days of this year that you have so uncomplainingly spent yourself for me. I know now, as I did not think in my careless, selfish sorrow, that I was as cruel to you, with your sweet young life, as your sister was cruel to me. You might already have given your heart to some one else; I never stopped to inquire. You might have had plans and hopes for your own future; I never even thought of it. I was a brute. Can you forgive me? Sometimes the thought of the responsibility I took upon myself has been so terrible to me that I felt I could not stand it. You did not realize what it was then that you were giving, perhaps, but somehow I think you have begun to realize now. Will you forgive me?" He stopped and looked at her anxiously. She was drooped and white as if a blast has suddenly struck her and faded her sweet bloom. Her throat was hot and dry and she had to try three times before she could frame the words, "Yes, I forgive."

There was no hope, no joy in the words, and sudden fear descended upon David's heart. Had he then done more damage than he knew? Was the child's heart broken by him, and did she just realize it? What could he do? Must he conceal his love from her? Perhaps this was no time to tell it. But he must. He could not bear the burden of having done her harm and not also tell her how he loved her. He would be very careful, very considerate, he would not press his love as a claim, but he must tell her.

"And Marcia, I must tell you the rest," he went on, his own words seeming to stay upon his lips, and then tumble over one another; "I have learned to love you as I never loved your sister. I love you more and better that I ever could have loved her. I can see how God has led me away from her and brought me to you. I can look back to that night when I came to her and found you there waiting for me, and kissed you, — darling. Do you remember?" He took her cold little trembling hands and held them firmly as he talked, his whole soul in his face, as if his life depended upon the next few moments. "I was troubled at the time, dear, for having kissed you, and given you the greeting that I thought belonged to her. I have rebuked myself for thinking since how lovely you looked as you stood there in the moonlight. But afterward I knew that it was you after all that my love belonged to, and to you rightfully the kiss should have gone. I am glad it was so, glad that God overruled my foolish choosing. Lately I have been looking back to that night I met you at the gate, and feeling jealous that that meeting was not all ours; that it should be shadowed for us by the heart-lessness of another. It gives me much joy now to think how I took you in my arms and kissed you. I cannot bear to think it was mistake. Yet glad as I am that God sent you down to that gate to meet me, and much as I love you, I would rather have died than feel that I have brought sorrow into your life, and bound you to one whom you cannot love. Marcia, tell me truly, never mind my feelings, tell me! Can you ever love me?"

Then did Marcia lift her flowerlike face, all bright with tears of joy and a flood of rosy smiles, the light of seven stars in her eyes. But she could not speak, she could only look, and after a little whisper, "Oh, David, I think I have always loved you! I think I was waiting for you that night, though I did not know it. And look!" — with sudden thought —

She drew from the folds of her dress a little old-fashioned locket hung by a chain about her neck out of sight. She opened it and showed him a soft gold curl which she touched gently with her lips, as though it were something very sacred.

"What is it, darling?" asked David perplexed, half happy, half afraid as he took the locket and touched the curl more thrilled with the thought that she had carried it next her heart than with the sight of it.

"It is yours," she said, disappointed that he did not understand. "Aunt Clarinda gave it to me while you were away. I've worn it ever since. And she gave me other things, and told me all about you. I know it all, about the tops and marbles, and the spelling book, and I've cried with you over your punish-ments, and — I — love it all!"

He had fastened the door before he began to talk, but he caught her in his arms now, regardless of the fact that the shades were not drawn down, and that they swayed in the summer breeze.

"Oh, my darling! My wife!" he cried, and kissed her lips for the third time.

The world was changed then for those two. They belonged to each other they believed, as no two that ever walked through Eden had ever belonged. When they thought of the precious bond that bound them together their hearts throbbed with a happiness that well-nigh overwhelmed them.

A dinner of stewed chickens and little white soda biscuits was served them, fit for a wedding breakfast, for the barmaid whispered to the cook that she was sure there was a bride and groom in the parlor they looked so happy and seemed to forget anybody else was by. But it might have been ham and eggs for all they knew what it was they ate, these two who were so happy they could but look into each other's eyes.

When the dinner was over and they started on their way again, with Albany shimmering in the hot sun in the distance, and David's arm sliding from the top of the seat to circle Marcia's waist, David whispered:

"This is our real wedding journey, dearest, and this is our bridal day. We'll go to Albany and buy you a trousseau, and then we will go wherever you wish. I can stay a whole week if you wish. Would you like to go home for a visit?"

Marcia, with shining eyes and glowing cheeks, looked her love into his face and answered: "Yes, now I would like to go home, — just for a few days — and then back to our home."

And David looking into her eyes understood why she had not wanted to go before. She was taking her husband, her husband, not Kate's, with her now, and might be proud of his love. She could go among her old comrades and be happy, for he loved her. He looked a moment, comprehended, sympathized, and then pressing her hand close — for he might not kiss her, as there was a load of hay coming their way — he said: "Darling!" But their eyes said more.

Phoebe Deane

Chapter 1

The night was hot and dark, for the moon rose late. The perfume of the petunia bed hung heavy in the air, and the katydids and crickets kept up a continual symphony in the orchard close to the house. Its music floated in at the open window, and called to the girl allluringly, as she sat in the darkened upper room patiently rocking Emmeline's baby to sleep in the little wooden cradle.

She had washed the supper dishes. The tea towels hung smoothly on the little line in the wood-shed, the milk pans stood in a shining row ready for the early milking, and the kitchen, swept and garnished and dark, had settled into its nightly repose. The day had been long and full of hard work, but now as soon as the baby slept Phoebe would be free for a while before bedtime.

Unconsciously her foot tapped faster on the rocker in her impatience to be out, and the baby stirred and opened his round eyes at her, murmuring sleepily: "Pee-bee, up-e-knee! Pee-bee, up-e-knee!" Which being interpreted was a demand to be taken up on Phoebe's knee. But Phoebe, knowing from experience that she would be tied for the evening if she acceded to this request, toned her rocking into a sleepy motion, and the long lashes suddenly dropped again upon the fat little cheeks. At last the baby was asleep.

With careful touch Phoebe slowed the rocking until the motion was scarcely perceptible, waiting a minute in hushed attention to hear the soft regular breathing after the cradle had stopped. Then she rose noiselessly from her chair, and posed on tiptoe over the cradle to listen once more and be sure, before she stole softly from the room.

As she reached the door the baby heaved a long, deep sigh, doubtless of satisfaction with its toys in dreamland, and Phoebe paused, her heart standing still for an instant lest, after all, that naughty baby would waken and demand to be taken up. How many times had she just reached the door, on other hot summer nights, and been greeted by a loud cry which served to bring Emmeline to the foot of the stairs, with: "I declare, Phoebe Deane! I should think if you would half try you could keep that poor child from crying all night!" and Phoebe would be in for an hour or two of singing, and rocking and amusing the fretful baby.

But the baby slept on, and Phoebe stepped cautiously over the creaking boards in the floor, and down the stairs lightly, scarcely daring yet to breathe. Like a fairy she slipped past the sitting-room door, scarcely daring to glance in lest she would be seen, yet carrying with her the perfect mental picture of the room and its occupants as she glided out into the night.

Albert, her half-brother, was in the sitting-room. She could see his outline through the window: Albert, with his long, thin, kindly-careless face bent over the village paper he had brought home just before supper. Emmeline sat over by the table close to the candle, with her sharp features intent upon the hole in Johnny's stocking. She had been threading her needle as Phoebe passed the door, and the fretful lines between her eyes were intensified by the effort to get the thread into the eye of the needle.

Hiram Green was in the sitting-room also. He was the neighbor whose farm adjoined Albert Deane's on the side next the village. He was sitting opposite the hall door, his lank form in a splint-bottomed chair tilted back against the wall. His slouch hat was drawn down over his eyes and his hands were in his pockets. He often sat so with Albert in the evening. Sometimes Emmeline called Phoebe in and gave her some darning or mending, and then Phoebe had to listen to Hiram Green's dull talk, to escape which she had fallen into the habit of slipping out into the orchard after her work was done. But it was not always that she could elude the vigilance of Emmeline, who seemed to be determined that Phoebe should not have a moment to herself, day or night.

Phoebe wore a thin white frock—that was one of Emmeline's grievances, those thin white frocks that Phoebe would insist on wearing afternoons, so uneconomical and foolish; besides, they would wear out sometime. Emmeline felt that Phoebe should keep her mother's frocks till she married, and so save Albert having to spend so much on her setting out. Emmeline had a very poor opinion of Phoebe's dead mother; her frocks had been too fine and too daintily trimmed to belong to a sensible woman, Emmeline thought.

Phoebe flashed across the path of light that fell from the door and into the orchard like some winged creature. She loved the night with its sounds and its scents and its darkness—darkness like velvet, with depths for hiding and a glimpse of the vaulted sky set with far-away stars. Soon the summer would be gone, the branches would be bare against the stark whiteness of the snow, and all her solitude and dreaming would be over until the spring again. She cherished every moment of the summer as if it were worth rich gold. She loved to sit on the fence that separated the orchard from the meadow, and wonder what the rusty-throated crickets were saying as they chirped or moaned. She liked to listen to the argument about Katy, and wonder over and over again what it was that Katy-did and why she did it, and whether she really did it at all as the little green creatures in the branches declared, for all the world the way people were picked to pieces at the sewing bees. That was just the way they used to talk about young Mrs. Spafford. Nobody was safe from gossip—for they said Mrs. Spafford belonged to the old Schuyler family. When she came a bride to the town, how cruel tongues were, and how babbling and irresponsible, like the katydids!

The girl seated herself in her usual place, leaning against the high crotch of the two upright rails which supported that section of fence. It was cool and delicious here, with the orchard for screening and the wide pasture meadow for scenery. The sky was powdered with stars, the fragrant breath of the pasture fanned her cheek, the tree-toads joined in the nightly concert, with a deep frog-bass keeping time. A stray night-owl with a piccolo note, the far-away bleat of a sheep, and the deep sweet moo-oo of a cow thrilled along her sensitive soul as some great orchestra might have done. Then, suddenly, there came a discordant crackle of the apple branches and Hiram Green stepped heavily out from the shadows and stood beside her.

Phoebe had never liked Hiram Green since the day she had seen him shove his wife out of his way and say to her roughly, "Aw, shut up, can't you? Women are forever talking about what they don't understand!" She had watched the faint color flicker into the white-cheeked wife's face and then flicker out whitely again as she tried to laugh his roughness off before Phoebe, but the girl had never forgotten it. She had been but a little girl, then, very shy and quiet, almost a stranger in the town, for her mother had just died and she had come to live with the half-brother who had been married so long that he was almost a stranger to her. Hiram Green had not noticed the young girl then, and had treated his wife as if no one were present. But Phoebe had remembered. She had grown to know and love the sad wife, to watch her gentle, patient ways with her boisterous boys, and her blowsy little girl who looked like Hiram and had none of her mother's delicacy; and her heart used to fill with indignation over the rude ways of the coarse man with his wife.

Hiram Green's wife had been dead a year. Phoebe had been with her for a week before she died, and watched the stolid husband with never a shadow of anxiety in his eyes while he told the neighbors that "Annie would be all right in a few days. It was her own fault, anyway, that she got down sick. She *would* drive over to see her mother when she wasn't able." He neglected to state that she had been making preserves and jelly for his special benefit, and had prepared dinner for twelve men who were harvesting for a week. He did not state that she only went to see her mother once in six months, and it was her only holiday.

Phoebe had listened, and inwardly fumed over the blindness and hardness of his nature. When Annie died he blamed her as he had always done, and hinted that he guessed now she was sorry she hadn't listened to him and been content at home. As if any kind of heaven wouldn't be better than Hiram Green's house to his poor disappointed wife.

But Phoebe had stood beside the dying woman as her life flickered out and heard her say: "I ain't sorry to go, Phoebe, for I'm tired. I'm that tired that I'd rather rest through eternity than do anything else. I don't think Hiram'll miss me much, and the children ain't like me. They never took after me, only the baby that died. They didn't care when I went away to mother's. I don't think anybody in the world'll miss me, unless it's mother, and she has the other girls, and never saw me much anyway now. Maybe the baby that died'll want me."

And so the weary eyes had closed, and Phoebe had been glad to fold the thin, work-worn hand across her breast and feel that she was at rest. The only expression of regret that Hiram gave was, "It's going to be mighty unhandy, her dying just now. Harvesting ain't over yet, and the meadow lot ought to be cut before it rains or the hull thing'll be lost." Then Phoebe felt a fierce delight in the fact that everything had to stop for Annie. Whether Hiram would or no, for very decency's sake, the work must stop and the forms of respect must be gone through with even though his heart was not in it. The rain came, too, to do Annie honor, and before the meadow lot was cut.

The funeral over, the farm work had gone on with doubled vigor, and Phobe overheard Hiram tell Albert that "burying Annie had been mighty expensive 'count o' that thunder-storm coming so soon, it spoiled the whole south meadow; and it was just like Annie to upset everything. If she had only been a little more careful and not gone off to her mother's on pleasure, she might have kept up a little longer till harvest was over."

Phoebe had been coming into the sitting-room with her sewing when Hiram said that — it was a fall evening, not six weeks after Annie had been laid to rest — and she looked indignantly at her brother to see if he would not give Hiram a rebuke; but he only leaned back against the wall and said, "Such things were to be expected in the natural course of life," he supposed. Phoebe turned her chair so that she would not have to look at Hiram. She despised him. She wished she knew how to show him what a despicable creature he was, but as she was only a young girl she could do nothing but turn her back. Perhaps Phoebe never realized how effective that method might be. At least she never knew that all that evening Hiram Green watched the back of her shining head, its waves of bright hair bound about with a ribbon, and conforming to the beautiful shape of her head with exquisite grace. He studied the shapely shoulders and graceful movements of the indignant girl as she patiently mended Johnny's stockings, let down the hem of Alma's linsey-woolsey, and set a patch on the seat of Bertie's trousers, with her slender capable fingers. He remembered that Annie had been "pretty" when he married her, and it gratified him to feel that he had given her this tribute in his thoughts. He felt himself to be a truly sorrowful widower. At the same time he could see the good points in the girl Phoebe, even though she sat with her indignant shoulders toward him. In fact, the very sauciness of those shoulders, as the winter went by, attracted him more and more. Annie had never dared be saucy nor indifferent. Annie had loved him from the first and had unfortunately let him know it too soon and too often. It was a new experience to have someone indifferent to him. He rather liked it, knowing as he did that he had always had his own way when he got ready for it.

As the winter went by Hiram had more and more spent his evenings with the Deanes and Phoebe had more and more spent her evenings with Johnny, or the cradle, or in her own room — anything as an excuse to get away from the constant unwelcome companionship. Then Emmeline had objected to the extravagance of an extra candle; and moreover, Phoebe's room was cold. It was not that there was not plenty of wood stored in the Deane wood-house, or that there was a need for rigid economy, but Emmeline was "thrifty," and could see no sense in a girl wasting a candle when one light would do for all, so the days went by for Phoebe full of hard work, and constant companionship, and the evenings also with no leisure, and no seclusion. Phoebe had longed and longed for the spring to come, when she might get out into the night alone, and take long deep breaths that were all her own, for it seemed as if even her breathing were ordered and supervised.

But through it all, strange to say, it had never once entered Phoebe's head that Hiram was turning his thoughts toward her, and so, when he came and stood there beside her in the darkness he startled her merely because he was something she disliked, and she shrank from him as one would shrink from a snake in the grass.

Then Hiram came closer to her and her heart gave one warding thud of alarm as she shrank away from him.

"Phoebe," he said, boldly, putting out his hand to where he supposed her hands would be in the darkness — though he did not find hers, "ain't it about time you and I was comin' to an understandin'?"

Phoebe slid off the fence and backed away in the darkness. She knew the location of every apple-tree and could have led him a chase through their labyrinths if she had chosen. Her heart froze within her for fear of what might be coming, and she felt she must not run away, but stay and face it whatever it was.

"Whatever do you mean?" asked Phoebe, her voice full of antagonism.

"Mean?" said Hiram, sidling after her. "I mean it's time we set up a partnership. I've waited long enough. I need somebody to look after the children. You suit me pretty well, and I guess you'd be well enough fixed with me."

Hiram's air of assurance made Phoebe's heart chill with fear. For a moment she was speechless with horror and indignation.

Taking her silence as a favorable indication, Hiram drew near her and once more tried to find her hands in the darkness.

"I've always liked you, Phoebe," he said, insinuatingly. "Don't you like me?"

"No, No, No!" almost screamed Phoebe, snatching her hands away. "Don't ever dare to think of such a thing again!"

Then she turned and vanished in the dark like a wraith of mist, leaving the crestfallen Hiram alone, feeling very foolish and not a little astonished. He had not expected his suit to be met quite in this way.

"Phoebe, is that you?" called Emmeline's metallic voice, as she lifted her sharp eyes to peer into the darkness of the entry. "Albert, I wonder if Hiram went the wrong way and missed her?"

But Phoebe, keen of instinct, light of foot, drifted like a breath past the door, and was up in her room before Emmeline decided whether she had heard anything or not, and Albert went on reading his paper.

Phoebe sat alone in her little kitchen chamber, with the button on the door fastened, and faced the situation, looking out into the night. She kept very still that Emmeline might not know she was there. She almost held her breath for a time, for it seemed as if Hiram had so much assurance that he almost had the power to draw her from her room against her will. Her indignation and fear were beyond all possible need of the occasion. Yet every time she thought of the hateful sound of his voice as he made his cold-blooded proposition, the fierce anger boiled within her, so that she wished over and over again that she might have another opportunity to answer him and make her refusal more emphatic. Yet, when she thought of it, what could she say more than "No"? Great waves of hate surged through her soul for the man who had treated one woman so that she was glad to die, and now wanted to take her life and crush it out. With the intensity of a very young girl she took up the cause of the dead Annie, and felt like fighting for her memory.

By and by she heard Albert and Emmeline shutting up the house for the night. Hiram did not come back as she feared he might.

He half started to come, then thought better of it, and felt his way through the orchard to the other fence and climbed lumberingly over it into the road. His self-love had been wounded and he did not care to appear before his neighbors to-night. Moreover, he felt a little dazed and wanted to think things over and adjust himself to Phoebe's point of view. He felt a half resentment toward the Deanes for Phoebe's action, as if the rebuff she had given him had been their fault somehow. They should have prepared her better. They understood the situation fully. There had often been an interchange of remarks between them on the subject and Albert had responded by a nod and wink. It was tacitly understood that it would be a good thing to have the farms join, and keep them "all in the family." Emmeline, too, had often given some practical hints about Phoebe's capabilities as a housewife and mother to his wild little children. It was Emmeline who had given the hint tonight as to Phoebe's hiding-place. He began to feel as if Emmeline had somehow tricked him. He resolved to stay away from the Deanes for a long time — perhaps a week, or at any rate two or three days — certainly one day, at least. Then he began to wonder if perhaps after all Phoebe was not just flirting with him. Surely she could not refuse him in earnest. His farm was as pretty as any in the county, and every one knew he had money in the bank. Surely, Phoebe was only being coy for a time. After all, perhaps, it was natural for a girl to be a little shy. It was a way they had, and if it pleased them to hold off a little, why it showed they would be all the more sensible afterward. Now Annie had always been a great one for sweet speeches. "Soft-soap" he designated it after their marriage. Perhaps he ought to have made a little more palaver about it to Phoebe, and not have frightened her. But pooh! It was a good sign. A bad beginning made a good ending generally. Maybe it was a good thing that Phoebe wasn't just ready to fall into his arms, the minute he asked her, then she wouldn't be always bothering around, clinging to him and sobbing in that maddening way that Annie had.

By the time he had reached home he had reasoned himself into complaisance again, and was pretty well satisfied with himself. As he closed the kitchen door he reflected that perhaps he might fix things up a bit in the house in view of a new mistress. That would probably please Phoebe, and he certainly did need a wife. Then Hiram went to bed and slept soundly.

Emmeline came to Phoebe's door before she went to bed, calling softly, "Phoebe, are you in there?" and tapping on the door two or three times. When no answer came from the breathless girl in the dark behind the buttoned door, Emmeline lifted the latch and tried to open the door, but when she found it resisted her, she turned away and said to Albert in a fretful tone:

"I s'pose she's sound asleep, but I don't see what call she has to fasten her door every night. It looks so unsociable, as if she was afraid we weren't to be trusted. I wonder you don't speak to her about it."

But Albert only yawned good-naturedly, and said: "I don't see how it hurts you any."

"It hurts my self-respect," said Emmeline in an injured tone, as she shut her own door with a click.

Far into the night sat Phoebe, looking out of the window on the world which she loved, but could not enjoy any more. The storm of rage and shame and hatred passed, and left her weak and miserable and lonely. At last she put her head down on the window-sill and cried out softly: "Oh, mother, mother, mother! If you were only here tonight! You would take me away where I would never see his hateful face again."

The symphony of the night wailed on about her, as if echoing her cry in sobbing, throbbing chords, growing fainter as the moon arose, with now and then a hint of a theme of comfort, until there came a sudden hush. Then softly, tenderly, the music changed into the night's lullaby. All the world slept, and Phoebe slept, too.

Chapter 2

Phoebe was late coming downstairs the next morning. Emmeline was already in the kitchen rattling the pots and pans significantly. Emmeline always did that when Phoebe was late, as her room was directly over the kitchen, and the degree of her displeasure could be plainly heard.

She looked up sharply as Phoebe entered, and eyed the girl keenly. There were dark circles under Phoebe's eyes, but otherwise her spirits had arisen with the morning light, and she almost wondered at the fear that had possessed her the night before. She felt only scorn now for Hiram Green, and was ready to protect herself. She went straight at her work without a word. Emmeline had long ago expressed herself with regard to the "Good-morning" with which the child Phoebe used to greet her when she came down in the morning. Emmeline said it was "a foolish waste of time, and only stuck-up folks use it. It was all of a piece with dressing up at home with no one to see you, and curling your hair"—this with a meaning look at Phoebe's bright waves. Emmeline's light, fady hair was straight as a die.

They worked in silence. The bacon was spluttering to the eggs, and Phoebe was taking up the mush when Emmeline asked:

"Didn't Hiram find you last night?" She cast one of her sideways searching looks at the girl as if she would look her through and through.

Phoebe started and dropped the spoon back into the mush where it sank with a sigh and a mutter. There was something enlightening in Emmeline's tone. Phoebe saw it at once. The family had been aware of Hiram's intention! Her eyes flashed one spark of anger, then she turned abruptly back to the kettle and went on with her work.

"Yes," she answered, inscrutably. Emmeline was always irritated at the difficulty with which she found out anything from Phoebe.

"Well, I didn't hear you come in," she complained, "you must have been out a long time."

Wary Emmeline. She had touched the spring that opened the secret.

"I wasn't out five minutes in all."

"You don't say!" said Emmeline, in surprise. "Why, I thought you said Hiram found you."

Phoebe put the cover on the dish of mush and set it on the table before she deigned any reply. Then she came over and stood beside Emmeline calmly and spoke in a cool, clear voice:

"Emmeline, did Hiram Green tell you what he was coming out to the orchard for last night?"

"For mercy's sake, Phoebe, don't put on heroics! I'm not blind, I hope. One couldn't very well help seeing what Hiram Green wants. Did you think you were the only member of the family with eyes?"

When Emmeline looked up from cutting the bread at the conclusion of these remarks she was startled to see Phoebe's face. It was white as marble even to the lips, and her great beautiful eyes shone like two luminous stars.

"Emmeline, did you and Albert know what Hiram Green wanted of me, and did you let him come out there to find me after you knew that?"

Her voice was very calm and low. It reminded one of some coolly flowing river, with unknown depths in its shadowed bosom. Emmeline was awed by it for a moment. She laid down the bread-knife and stood and stared. Phoebe was small and dainty, with features cut like a cameo, and a singularly sweet, childlike expression when her face was in repose. That she was rarely beautiful her family had never noticed, though sometimes Albert liked to watch her as she sat sewing. She seemed to him a pleasant thing to have around, like a bright posy-bed. Emmeline thought her too frail-looking and pale. But for the moment the delicate girl was transformed. Her face shone with a light of righteous anger, and her eyes blazed dark with feeling. Two spots of lovely rose-color glowed upon her cheeks. The morning sun had just reached the south window by the table where Emmeline had been cutting bread, and it laid its golden fingers over the bright waves of brown hair in a halo round her head, as if the sun would sanction her righteous wrath. She looked like some beautiful, injured saint, and before the intensity of the maiden's emotion her sister-in-law fairly quailed.

"Fer the land! Phoebe! Now don't!" said Emmeline, in a tone conciliatory. "What if I did know? Was that any sin? You must remember your brother and I are looking to your best interests, and Hiram is considered a real fine ketch."

Slowly Phoebe's righteous wrath sank again into her heart. The fire went out of her eyes, and in its place came ice that seemed to pierce Emmeline till she felt like shrinking away.

"You're the queerest girl I ever saw," said Emmeline, fretfully restive under Phoebe's gaze. "What's the matter with you? Didn't you ever expect to have any beaux?"

Phoebe shivered as if a north blast had struck her at that last word.

"Did you mean, then," she said, coldly, in a voice that sounded as if it came from very far away, "that you thought that I would ever be willing to marry Hiram Green? Did you and Albert talk it over and think that?"

Emmeline found it hard to answer the question, put in a tone which seemed to imply a great offence. Phoebe lived on a plane far too high for Emmeline to even try to understand without a great effort. The effort wearied her.

"Well, I should like to know why you shouldn't marry him!" declared Emmeline, impatiently. "There's plenty of girls would be glad to get him."

Emmeline glanced hurriedly out of the window and saw Albert and the hired man coming to breakfast. It was time the children were down. Alma came lagging into the kitchen, asking to have her frock buttoned, and Johnny and Bertie were heard scuffling in the rooms overhead. There was no time for further conversation. Emmeline was about to dismiss the subject, but Phoebe stepped between her and the little girl and laid her small supple hands on Emmeline's stout rounding shoulders, looking her straight in the eyes.

"Emmeline, how can you possibly be so unkind as to think such a thing for me when you know how Annie suffered?"

"Oh, fiddlesticks!" said Emmeline, shoving the girl away roughly. "Annie was a milk-and-water baby who wanted to be coddled. The right woman could wind Hiram Green around her little finger. You're a little fool if you think about that. Annie's dead and gone and you've no need to trouble with her. Come, put the things on the table while I button Alma. I'm sure there never was as silly a girl as you are in this world. Anybody'd think you were a princess in disguise instead of a poor orphan dependent on her brother, and he only a *half at* that!"

With which parting shot Emmeline slammed the kitchen door and called to the two little boys in a loud, harsh tone.

The crimson rose in Phoebe's cheeks till it covered face and neck in a sweet, shamed tide and threatened to bring the tears into her eyes. Her very soul seemed wrenched from its moorings at the cruel reminder of her dependence upon the bounty of this coarse woman and her husband. Phoebe felt as if she must leave the house at once never to return, only there was no place—no place in this wide world for her to go.

Then Albert appeared in the kitchen door with the hired man behind him, and the sense of her duty made her turn to work, that old, blessed refuge for those who are turned out of their bits of Eden for a time. She hurried to take up the breakfast, while the two men washed their faces at the pump and dried them on the long roller-towel that hung from the inside of the door.

"Hello, Phoebe," called Albert, as he turned to surrender his place at the comb and the looking-glass. "I say, Phoebe, you're looking like a rose this morning. What makes your cheeks so red? Anybody been kissing you this early?"

This pleasantry was intended as a joke. Albert had never said anything of the sort to her before. She felt instinctively that Emmeline had been putting ideas about her and Hiram into his head. It almost brought the tears to have Albert speak in this way. He was so uniformly kind to her and treated her as if she were still almost a child. She hated jokes of this sort, and it was all the worse because of the presence of Alma and the hired man. Alma grinned knowingly, and went over where she could look into Phoebe's face. Henry Williams, with the freedom born of his own social equality—he being the son of a neighboring farmer who had hired himself out for the season as there were more brothers at home than were needed—turned and stared admiringly at Phoebe.

"Say, Phoebe," put in Henry, "you do look real pretty this morning, now if I do say it. I never noticed before how handsome your eyes were. What's that you said about kissing, Albert? I wouldn't mind taking the job, if it's going. How about it, Phoebe?"

Pleasantry of this sort was common in the neighborhood, but Phoebe had never joined in it, and she had always looked upon it as unrefined, and a form of amusement that her mother would not have liked. Now when it was directed toward her, and she realized that it trifled with the most sacred and personal relations of life, it filled her with horror.

"Please don't, Albert!" she said, with trembling lips in a low voice. "Don't! I don't like it." And Alma saw with wonder, and gloated over the fact, that there were tears in Aunt Phoebe's eyes. That would be something to remember and tell. Aunt Phoebe usually kept her emotions to herself with the door shut too tight for Alma to peep in.

"No?" said Albert, perplexed. "Well, course I won't if you don't like it. I was only telling you how bright and pretty you looked and making you know how nice it was to have you around. Sit down, child, and let's have breakfast. Where's your mother, Alma?"

Emmeline entered with a flushed face, and a couple of cowed and dejected small boys held firmly by the shoulders.

Somewhat comforted by Albert's assurance, Phoebe was able to finish her work and sit down at the table; but although she busied herself industriously in putting on the baby's bib, spreading Johnny's bread, handing Alma the syrup-jug, and preventing her from emptying its entire contents over her personal breakfast, inside and out, she ate nothing herself, for every time she raised her eyes she found a battalion of other eyes staring at her.

Emmeline was looking her through, in puzzled annoyance and chagrin, taking in the fact that her well-planned match-making was not running as smoothly as had been expected. Albert was studying her in the astonishing discovery that the thin, sad little half-sister he had brought into his home, who had seemed so lifeless and colorless and unlike the bouncing pretty girls of the neighborhood, had suddenly become beautiful, and was almost a woman. Several times he opened his mouth to say this in the bosom of his family, and then the dignified poise of the lovely head, or a something in the stately set of the small shoulders, or a pleading look in the large soft eyes raised to him, held him quiet; and his own eyes tried to tell her again that he would not say it if she did not like it.

Alma was staring at her between mouthfuls of mush, and, thinking how she would tell about those tears, and how perhaps she would taunt Aunt Phoebe with them sometime when she tried to "boss," when ma was out to a sewing bee.

"Ehh! I saw you cry once, Aunt Phoebe! Ehh! Right before folks. *EHH-HH!* Cry baby! You had great big tears in your eyes, when my pa teased you. I saw um. Eh-hh-hh!" How would that sound? Alma felt the roll of the taunt now, and wished it were time to try it. She knew she could make Aunt Phoebe writhe sometime, and that was what she had always wanted to do, for Aunt Phoebe was always discovering her best laid plans and revealing them to Emmeline, and Alma longed sorely for revenge.

But the worst pair of eyes of all were those of Henry Williams, bold, and intimate, who sat directly opposite her. He seemed to feel that the way had been opened to him by Albert Deane's words, and was only waiting his opportunity to enter in. He had been admiring Phoebe ever since he came there, early in the spring, and wondering that no one seemed to think her of much account, but somehow her quiet dignity had always kept him at a distance. But now he felt he was justified in making more free with her.

"Did you hear that singing-school was going to open early this fall, Phoebe?" he asked, after many clearings of his throat.

"No," said Phoebe, without looking up. That was rather disappointing to him, for it had taken him a long time to think up that subject, and it was too much to have it disposed of so quickly, without even a glimpse of her eyes.

"Do you usually 'tend?" he asked again, after a pause filled in by Alma and the little boys in a squabble for the last scrap of mush and molasses.

"No!" said Phoebe again, her eyes still down.

"Phoebe didn't go because there wasn't anyone for her to come home with, before, Hank, but I guess there'll be plenty now," said Emmeline, with a meaningful laugh.

"Yes," said Phoebe, now looking up calmly without a flicker of the anger she was feeling. "Hester McVane and Polly said they were going this winter. If I decide to go I'm going with them. Emmeline, if you're going to dry those apples today I'd better begin them. Excuse me, please."

"You haven't eaten any breakfast, Aunt Phoebe! Ma, Aunt Phoebe never touched a bite!" announced Alma, gleefully.

"I'm not hungry this morning," said Phoebe truthfully, and went in triumph from the room, having baffled the gaze of the man and the child, and wrested the dart from her sister-in-law's arrow. It was hard on the man, for he had decided to ask Phoebe if she would go to singing-school with him. He had been a long time making up his mind as to whether he wouldn't rather ask Harriet Woodgate, but now he had decided on Phoebe he did not like to be balked in the asking. He sought her out in the wood-shed where she sat, and gave his invitaion, but she only made her white fingers fly the faster round the apple she was peeling as she answered: "Thank you, it won't be necessary for you to go with me if I decide to go." Then as she perceived by his prolonged "H'm-m-m!" that he was about to urge his case she arose hastily, exclaiming: "Emmeline, did you call me? I'm coming," and vanished into the kitchen. The hired man looked after her wistfully and wondered if he had not better ask Harriet Woodgate after all.

Phoebe was not a weeping girl. Ever since her mother died she had lived a life of self-repression, hiding her inmost feelings from the world, for her world since then had not proved to be a sympathetic one. When annoyances came she buried them in her heart and grieved over them in silence, for she quickly perceived that there was no one in this new atmosphere who would understand her sensitive nature.

Refinements and culture had been hers that these new relatives did not know nor understand. What to her had been necessities were to them foolish nonsense. She looked at Albert wistfully sometimes, for she felt if it were not for Emmeline she might perhaps in time make him understand and change a little in some ways. But Emmeline resented any suggestions she made to Albert, especially when he good-naturedly tried to please her. Emmeline resented almost everything about Phoebe. She had resented her coming in the first place. Albert was grown up and living away from home when his father married Phoebe's mother, a delicate, refined woman, far different from himself. Emmeline felt that Albert had no call to take the child in at all for her to bring up when she was not a "real relation." Besides, Emmeline had an older sister of her own who would have been glad to come and live with them and help with the work, but of course there was no room nor excuse for her with Phoebe there, and they could not afford to have them both, although Albert was ready to take in any stray chick or child that came along. It was only Emmeline's forbidding attitude that kept him from adopting all the lonely creatures, be they animal or human, that appealed to his sympathy. There were a great many nice points about Albert, and Phoebe recognized them gratefully, the more as she grew older, though he *would* come to the table in his shirt-sleeves and eat his pie with his knife.

But in spite of her nature this morning Phoebe had much ado to keep from crying. The annoyances increased as the day grew, and if it had not been for her work she would have felt desperate. As it was she kept steadily at it, conquering everything that came in her way. The apples fairly flew out of their coats into the pan, and Emmeline, glancing into the back shed, noting the set of the forbidding young shoulders, and the undaunted tilt of the head, also the fast diminishing pile of apples on the floor and the multiplying quarters in the pans, forbore to disturb her. Emmeline was far-seeing, and she was anxious to have those apples off her mind. With Phoebe in that mood she knew it would be done before she could possibly get around to help. There was time enough for remarks later; meantime perhaps it was just as well to let my lady alone until she came to her senses a little.

The old stone sun-dial by the side door shadowed the hour of eleven, and the apples were almost gone from the pile on the floor, when Emmeline came into the back shed with a knife and sat down to help. She looked at Phoebe sharply as she seated herself with a show of finishing things up in a hurry, but she intended, and Phoebe knew she did, to have it out with the girl before her.

Phoebe did not help her to begin. Her fingers flew faster than ever, though they ached with the motion, and the juicy knife against her sensitive skin made every nerve cry out to be released. With set lips she went on with her work, though she longed to fling the apple away and run out to the fields for a long, deep breath.

Emmeline had pared two whole apples before she began, in a conciliatory tone. She had eyed Phoebe furtively several times, but the girl might have been a sphinx, or some lovely mountain wrapped about with mist, for all she could read of her mood. This was what Emmeline could not stand, this distant, proud silence that would not mix with other folk. She longed to break through it by force, and reduce the pride to dust. It would do her heart good to see Phoebe humbled for once, she often told herself.

"Phoebe, I don't see what you find to dislike so in Hiram Green," she began. "He's a good man. He always attends church on Sundays."

"I would respect him more if he was a good man in his home on week-days. Anybody can be good once a week before people. A man needs to be good at home in his family."

"Well, now, he pervides well for his family. Look at his comfortable home, and his farm. There isn't a finer in this county. He has his name up all round this region for the fine stock he raises. You can't find a barn like his anywhere. It's the biggest and most expensive in this town."

"He certainly has a fine barn," said Phoebe, "but I don't suppose he expects his family to live in it. He takes better care of his stock than he does of his family. Look at the house —"

Phoebe's eyes waxed scornful, and Emmeline marvelled. She was brought up to think a barn a most important feature of one's possessions.

"His house is away back from the road out of sight," went on Phoebe, "Annie used to hunger for a sight of people going by on the road when she sat down to sew in the afternoon, but there was that great barn right out on the road, and straight in front of the house. He ought to have put the barn back of the house. And the house is a miserable affair. Low, and ugly, and with two steps between the kitchen and the shed, enough to kill one who does the work. He ought to have built Annie a pleasant home up on that lovely little knoll of maples, where she could have seen out and down the road, and have had a little company now and then. She might have been alive today if she had one-half the care and attention that Hiram gave the stock!" Phoebe's words were bitter and vehement.

"It sounds dreadful silly for a girl of your age to be talking like that. You don't know anything about Annie, and if I was you I wouldn't think about her. As for the barn, I should think a wife would be proud to have her husband's barn the nicest one in the county. Of course the barn had to have the best place. That's his business. I declare you do have the queerest notions!"

Nevertheless she set it down in her mind that she would give Hiram a hint about the house.

Phoebe did not reply. She was peeling the last apple, and as soon as it lay meekly in quarters with the rest she shoved back her chair and left the room. Emmeline felt that she had failed again to make any impression on her sister-in-law. It maddened her almost to distraction to have a girl like that around her, a girl who thought everything beneath her and who criticized the customs of the entire neighborhood. She was an annoyance and a reproach. Emmeline felt she would like to get rid of her if it could be done in a legitimate way.

At dinner, Henry Williams looked at Phoebe meaningly and asked if she made the pie. Phoebe had to own that she did.

"It tastes like you, nice and sweet," he declared, gallantly. Whereat Albert laughed, and Alma leaned forward to look into her aunt's flaming face, impudently.

"Betsy Green says she thinks her pa is going to get her a new ma," she remarked, knowingly, when the laugh had subsided. "And Betsy says she bet she knows who 'tis, too!"

"You shut up!" remarked Emmeline to her offspring, in a low tone, giving Alma a dig under the table. But Phoebe hastily drew back her chair and fled from the table.

There was a moment of uncomfortable silence after Phoebe left the room. Emmeline felt that things had gone too far. Albert asked what was the matter with Phoebe, but instead of answering him Emmeline yanked Alma from the table and out into the wood-shed, where a whispered scolding was administered as a sort of obligato solo to the accompaniment of some stinging cuts from a little switch that hung conveniently on the wall.

Alma returned to the table chastened outwardly, but inwardly vowing vengeance on her aunt, her anger in no wise softened by the disappearance of her piece of pie with Bertie. Her mother told her she deserved to lose her pie, and she determined to get even with Aunt Phoebe even if another switching happened.

Phoebe did not come downstairs again that afternoon. Emmeline hesitated about sending for her, and finally decided to wait until she came. The unwilling Alma was pressed into service to dry the dishes, and the long, yellow, sunny afternoon dragged drowsily on, while Phoebe lay upon her bed up in her kitchen chamber, and pressed her aching eyeballs hard with her cold fingers, wondering why so many tortures were coming to her all at once.

Chapter 3

Hiram Green kept his word to himself and did not go to see Phoebe for two evenings. By that time Emmeline had begun to wonder what in the world Phoebe had said to him to keep him away when he seemed so anxious to get her; and Phoebe, with the hopefulness of youth, had decided that her trouble in that direction was over. But the third evening he arrived promptly, attired with unusual care, and asked Emmeline if he might see Phoebe alone.

It happened that Phoebe had finished her work in the kitchen and gone up to rock the baby to sleep. Emmeline swept the younger children out of the sitting-room with alacrity, and called Albert sharply to help her with something in the kitchen, sending Alma up at once with a carefully worded message to Phoebe. Emmeline was relieved to see Hiram again. She knew by his face that he meant business this time, and she hoped to see Phoebe conquered at once.

"Ma says you please" — the word sounded strangely on Alma's unloving lips — "come down to the settin'-room now — to once," she added.

The baby was just dropping asleep and roused of course at Alma's boisterous tone. Phoebe nodded, and shoved the child from the room, keeping the cradle going all the time. The naughty little girl delighted to have authority behind her evil doing, and called loudly:

"Well, ma wants you RIGHT OFF, so, and I don't care!" as she thumped down stairs with her copper-toed shoes.

The baby gave a crow of glee and arose to the occasion in his cradle, but Phoebe resolutely disregarded the call below, and went on rocking until the little restless head was still on its pillow again. Then she stole softly down to the sitting-room, her eyes blinded by the darkness where she had been sitting, and explained quietly as she entered the room, "I couldn't come sooner. Alma woke the baby again."

Hiram, quite mollified by the gentle tone of explanation, arose, blandly answering: "Oh, that's all right. I'm glad to see you now you're here," and went forward with the evident intention of taking both her hands in his.

Phoebe rubbed her blinded eyes and looked up in horror! Knowing Alma stood behind the crack of the door and watched it all with wicked joy.

"I beg your pardon, Mr. Green, I thought Emmeline was in here. She sent for me. Excuse me, I must find her."

"Oh, that's all right!" said Hiram, easily, putting out his hand and shutting the door sharply in Alma's impudent face, thereby almost pinching her inquisitive nose in the crack. "She don't expect you, Emmeline don't. She sent you to see me. I asked her could I see you alone. She understands all about us,

Emmeline does. She won't come in here for a while. She knows I want to talk to you."

Cold chills crept down Phoebe's nerves and froze her heart and finger-tips. Had the horror returned upon her with redoubled vigor, and with her family behind it? Where was Albert? Would he not help her? Then she realized that she must help herself and at once, for it was evident that Hiram Green meant to press his suit energetically. He was coming towards her with his hateful, confident smile. He stood between her and the door of retreat. Besides, what good would it do to run away? She had tried that once and it did not work. She must speak to him decidedly and end the matter. She summoned all her dignity and courage and backed over to the other side of the room, where a single chair stood.

"Won't you sit down, Mr. Green?" she said, trying to get the tremble out of her voice.

"Why, yes, I will; let's sit right here together," he said, sitting down at one end of the couch and making room for her. "Come, you sit here beside me, Phoebe, and then we can talk better. It's more sociable."

Phoebe sat down on the chair opposite him.

"I would rather sit here, Mr. Green," she said.

"Well, of course, if you'd rather," he said, reluctantly, "but it seems to be kind of unsociable. And say, Phoebe, I wish you wouldn't 'mister' me any more. Can't you call me Hiram."

"I would rather not."

"Say, Phoebe, that sounds real unfriendly," blamed Hiram, in a tone which suggested he would not be trifled with much longer.

"Did you wish to speak to me, Mr. Green?" said Phoebe, her clear eyes looking at him steadily over the candle-light, with the bearing of a queen.

"Well, yes," he said, straightening up, and hitching a chair around to the side nearer to her. "I thought we better talk that matter over a little that I was mentioning to you several nights ago."

"I don't think that is necessary, Mr. Green," answered Phoebe, quickly; "I thought I made you understand that that was impossible."

"Oh, I didn't take account of what you said that night," said Hiram. "I saw you was sort of upset, not expecting me out there in the dark, so I thought I better come round again after you had plenty chance to think over what I said."

"I couldn't say anything different if I thought over it a thousand years," declared Phoebe, with characteristic emphasis. Hiram Green was not thin-skinned, and did not need saving. It was just as well to tell the truth and be done with it.

But the fellow was in no wise daunted. He rather admired Phoebe the more for her vehemence, for here was a prize that promised to be worth his winning.

For the first time as he looked at her he felt his blood stir with a sense of pleasure such as one feels in a well matched race, where one is yet sure of winning.

"Aw, git out!" scouted Hiram, pleasantly. "That ain't the way to talk. Course you're young yet, and ain't had much experience, but you certainly had time enough to consider the matter all this year I been comin' to see you."

Phoebe arose with two red spots burning on her cheeks.

"Coming to see me!" she gasped. "You didn't come to see me!"

"Aw, git out now, Phoebe. You needn't pertend you didn't know I was comin' to see you. Who did you s'pose I was comin' to see, then?"

"I supposed of course you were coming to see Albert," said Phoebe, her voice settling into that deep calm that betokened she was overwhelmed.

"Albert! You s'posed I was comin' to see Albert every night! Aw, yes, you did a whole lot! Phoebe, you're a sly one. You must of thought I was gettin' fond of Albert!"

"I did not think anything about it," said Phoebe, haughtily, "and you may be sure, Mr. Green, if I had dreamed of such a thing I would have told you it was useless."

There was something in her tone and manner that ruffled the self-assurance of Hiram Green. Up to this minute he had persuaded himself that Phoebe was but acting the part of a coy and modest maiden who wished to pretend that she never dreamed that he was courting her. Now a suspicion began to glimmer in his consciousness that perhaps, after all, she was honest, and had not suspected his attentions. Could it be possible that she did not care for them, and really wished to dismiss him? Hiram could not credit such a thought. Yet as he looked at the firm set of her lips he was bewildered.

"What on earth makes you keep sayin' that?" he asked, in an irritated tone. "What's your reason for not wantin' to marry me?"

"There are so many reasons that I wouldn't know where to begin," answered the girl, shortly.

Hiram gave his shoulders a little shake, as if to rouse himself. Had he heard her words aright?

"What reasons?" he growled, frowning. He began to feel that Phoebe was trifling with him. He would make her understand that he would not endure much of that.

Phoebe looked troubled. She wished he would not insist on further talk, but she was too honest and too angry not to tell the exact truth.

"The first and greatest reason of all is that I do not love you, and never could," she said vehemently, looking him straight in the eyes.

"Shucks!" said Hiram, laughing. "I don't mind that a mite. In fact, I think it's an advantage. Folks mostly get over it when they do feel that sentimental kind of way. It don't last but a few weeks, anyhow, and it's better to begin on a practical basis I think. That was the trouble with Annie, she was so blamed sentimental she hadn't time to get dinner. I think you an' I'd get along much better. You're practical and a good worker. We could manage things real prosperous over to the farm—"

Phoebe arose quickly and interrupted him.

"Mr. Green, you must please stop talking this way. It is horrible! I don't want to listen to any more of it."

"You set down, Phoebe," commanded Hiram. "I've got some things to tell you. It ain't worth while fer you to act foolish. I mean business. I want to get married. It's high time there was somebody to see to things at home, but I can wait a little while if you're wantin' to get ready more, only don't be long about it. As I said, I don't mind about the love part. That'll come all right. And you remember, Phoebe, if I do say so as shouldn't, there's plenty of girls around here would be glad to marry me if they got the chance."

"Then by all means, let them marry you!" said Phoebe, grandly, steadying her trembling limbs for flight. "I shall never, never marry you! Good-night, Mr. Green."

She swept him a ceremonious bit of courtesy at the door, like a flutter of wings as a bird takes affright, and was gone before he fully took it in. He reached out detaining hands towards her in protest, but it was too late. The latch clicked behind her, and he could hear the soft stir of her garments on the stairs. She had fled to her room. He heard the button on her door creak and turn. He unfolded his lank limbs from their comfortable pose around the legs of his chair, and went after her as far as the door, but the stairway was quiet and dark. He could hear Albert and Emmeline in the kitchen. He stood a moment in puzzled chagrin, going over his interview and trying to make it all out. What mistake had he made? He had failed, that was certain. It was a new experience and one that angered him, but somehow the anger was numbed by the remembrance of the look of the girl's eyes, the dainty movements of her hands, the set of her shapely head. He did not know that he was fascinated by her beauty; he only knew that a dogged determination to have her for his own in spite of everything was settling down upon him.

Albert and Emmeline were conversing in low tones in the kitchen when the door was flung open and Hiram Green stepped in, his brow dark, his eyes sullen. He felt that Emmeline owned him some explanation of Phoebe's behavior. He had come for it.

"I can't make her out!" he muttered, as he flung himself into a kitchen chair, "she's just for all the world like a wild colt. When you think you have her she gives you the slip and is off further away than when you begun. I think mebbe ef I had her where she couldn't get away I'd be able to find out the difficulty."

"Better take her out riding," suggested Albert, slyly, "and drive fast. She couldn't get out very well then."

"I ain't sure," growled Hiram, "the way she looked she might jump over a precipice. What's the matter with her anyway?" turning to Emmeline, as though she were responsible for the whole of womankind. "Is there anybody else? She ain't got in with Hank Williams, has she?"

"She won't look at him," declared Emmeline positively. "He tried to get to go to singin'-school with her just today and she shut him off short. What reason did she give you?"

"She spoke about not havin' proper affection," he answered diffidently, "but if I was dead sure that was the hull trouble I think I could fix her up. I'd like to get things settled 'fore winter comes on. I can't afford to waste time like this."

"I think I know what's the matter of her," said Emmeline, mysteriously. "She isn't such a fool as to give up a good chance in life for reasons of affection, though it is mighty high-soundin' to say so. But there's somethin' back of it all. I shouldn't wonder, Hiram, if she's tryin' you to see if you want her enough to fix things handy the way she'd like em."

"What do you mean?" asked Hiram, gruffly, showing sudden interest. "Has she spoke of anything to you?"

"Well, she did let on that your house was too far back from the street to be pleasant, and she seemed to think the barn had the best situation. She spoke about the knoll being a good place for a house."

Hiram brightened. If Phoebe had taken interest in his affairs to say all this surely she was not so indifferent after all.

"You don't say!" said Hiram, meditatively. "When did she say that?"

"Just today," Emmeline answered.

"Well, if that's the hitch why didn't she say so? She didn't seem shy."

"Mebbe she was waitin' for you to ask her what she wanted."

"Well, she didn't wait long. She lit out before I had a chance to half talk things over."

"She's young yet, you know," said Emmeline, in a soothing tone. "Young folks take queer notions. I shouldn't wonder but she hates to go to that house and live way back from the road that way. She ain't much more than a child, anyway, in some things — though she's first class to work."

"Well," said Hiram, reluctantly, "I been thinkin' the house needed fixin' up some. I don't know as I should object to buildin' all new. The old house would come in handy fer the men. Bill would like to have his ma and keep house right well. It would help me out in one way, fer Bill is gettin' uneasy, and I'd rather spare any man I've got than Bill, he works so steady and good. Say, you might mention to Phoebe, if you like, that I'm thinkin' of buildin' a new house. Say I'd thought of the knoll for a location. Think that would ease her up a little?"

"All right, I'll see what can be done," said Emmeline, importantly.

The atmosphere of the kitchen brightened cheerfully as if extra candles had been brought in. Hiram, with the air of having settled to his satisfaction a troublesome bit of business, lighted his pipe and tilted his chair back in his accustomed fashion, entering into a brisk discussion of politics while Emmeline set the sponge for bread.

Emmeline was going over the line of argument with which she intended to ply Phoebe the next day. She felt triumphant over her. Not every woman and matchmaker would have had the grit to tell Hiram just what was wanted. Emmeline felt that she had been entrusted with a commission worthy of her best efforts, and surely Phoebe would listen now.

Up in her kitchen chamber the hum of their conversation came to Phoebe, as she sat with burning cheeks looking wildly into the darkness. She did not hear the nightly symphony as it sang on all about the house. She was thinking of what she had been through, and wondering if she had finally freed herself from the hateful attentions of Hiram Green. Would he take her answer as final, or not? She thought not, judging from his nature. He was one of those men who never give up what they have set themselves to get, be it sunny pasture lot, young heifer, or pretty wife. She shuddered at the thought of many more encounters such as she had passed through tonight. It was all dreadful to her. It touched a side of life that jarred her inexpressibly. It made the world seem an intolerable place to her.

She fell to wondering what her life would have been if her mother had lived — a quiet little home, of course, plain and sweet and cosy, with plenty of hard work, but always some one to sympathize. Her frail little mother had not been able to stand the rough world and the hard work, but she had left behind her a memory of gentleness and refinement that could never be wholly crushed out of her young daughter's heart, no matter how much she came in contact with the coarse, rude world. Often the girl in her silent meditations would take her mother into her thoughts and tell her all that had passed in her life that day. But tonight she felt that were her mother here, and helpless to help her, she could not bear to tell her of this torturing experience through which she was passing. She knew instinctively that a living mother such as hers had been would shrink with horror from the thought of seeing her child united to a man like Hiram Green — would rather see her dead than married to him.

Somehow she could not get the comfort from thinking of her mother tonight that she usually could. She wanted some close, tangible help, some one all-wise and powerful; someone that could tell what life meant, and what God meant her particular life to be, and make her sure she was right in her fierce recoil from what life now seemed to be offering. She felt sure she was right, yet she wanted another to say so also, to take her part against the world that was troubling her. There were perhaps people who could do that for her if she only dared to go to them, but what would they think!

Her young pride arose and bore her up. She must tell nobody but God. And so thinking, she knelt timidly down and tried to pour out her proud, hurt spirit in a prayer. She had always prayed, but had never felt that it meant anything to her until tonight; and when she arose, not knowing what she had asked, or if indeed she had asked anything for herself, she yet felt stronger to face her life, which somehow stretched out ahead in one blank of monotonous tortures.

Meantime the man who desired to have her, and the woman who desired to have him have her, were forming their plans for a regular campaign against her.

Chapter 4

It was the first day of October, and it was Phoebe's birthday. The sun shone clear and high, the sky overhead was a dazzling blue, and the air was good to breathe. Off in the distance a blue haze lay softly over the horizon, mingling the crimsons and golds of the autumn foliage with the fading greens. It was a perfect day, and Phoebe was out in it.

She walked rapidly and with a purpose, as though it did her good to push the road back under her impatient feet. She was not walking towards the village, but out into the open country, past the farm, where presently the road turned and skirted a maple grove. But she did not pause here, though she dearly loved the crimson maple leaves that carpeted the ground alluringly. On she went, as though her only object was to get away, as though she would like to run if there were not danger she might be seen.

A farm wagon was coming. She strained her eyes ahead to see who was driving. If it should happen to be Hank, and he should stop to talk! Oh! She put her hand on her heart and hurried forward, for she would not go back. She wished she had worn her sunbonnet, for then she might hide her in its depths, but her coming away had been too sudden for that. She had merely untied her large apron, and flung it from her as she started. Even now she knew not whether it hung upon the chair where she had been sitting shelling dried beans, or whether it adorned the rosebush by the kitchen door. She had not looked back to see, and did not care.

No one knew it was her birthday, or, if they knew, they had not remembered. Perhaps that made it harder to stay and shell beans and bear Emmeline's talk.

Matters had been going on in much the way they had gone all summer — that is, outwardly; Hiram Green had spent the evenings regularly talking with Albert, while Emmeline darned stockings, and Phoebe escaped upstairs when she could, and sewed with her back to the guest when she could not. Phoebe had taken diligent care that Hiram should have no more tete-a-tetes with her, even at the expense of having to spend many evenings in her dark room when all outdooors was calling her with the tender lovely sounds of the dying summer. Grimly and silently she went through the days of work.

Emmeline, since the morning she attempted to discuss Hiram's proposed new house and found Phoebe utterly unresponsive, had held her peace. Not that she was by any means vanquished, but as she made so little headway in talking to the girl she concluded that it would be well to let her alone awhile. In fact Albert had advised that line of action in his easy, kindly way and Emmeline, partly because she did not know how else to move her sister-in-law, shut her lips and went around with an air of offended dignity. She spoke disagreeably whenever it was necessary to speak at all to Phoebe, and whenever the girl came downstairs in other than her working garments she looked her disapproval in unspeakable volumes.

Phoebe went about her daily routine without noticing, much as a bird might whose plumage was being criticised. She could not help putting herself in dainty array, even though the materials at hand might be only a hair brush and a bit of ribbon. Her hair was always waving about her lovely face, softly and smoothly, and a tiny rim of white collar outlined the throat, even in her homespun morning gown, which sat upon her like a young queen's garment.

It was all hateful to Emmeline — "impudent," she styled it, in speaking to herself. She had tried the phrase once in a confidence to Albert — for Phoebe was only a half- sister; why should Albert care? — but somehow Albert had not understood. He had almost resented it. He said he thought Phoebe always looked "real neat and pretty" and he "liked to see her round." This had fired Emmeline's jealousy, although she would not have owned it. Albert made so many remarks of this sort that Emmeline felt they would spoil his sister and make her unbearable to live with. Albert used to talk like that to her when they were first married, but she told him it was silly for married people to say such things, and he never gave her any more compliments. She had not missed them herself, but it was another thing to find him speaking that way about his sister — so foolish for a grown-up man to care about looks.

But Emmeline continued to meditate upon Phoebe's "impudent" attire, until this afternoon of her birthday the thoughts had culminated in words.

Phoebe had gone upstairs after the dinner work was done, and had come down arrayed in a gown that Emmeline had never seen. It was of soft buff merino, trimmed with narrow lines of brown velvet ribbon, and a bit of the same velvet around the white throat held a small plain gold locket that nestled in the white hollow of Phoebe's neck as if it loved to be there. The brown hair was dressed in its usual way except for a knot of brown velvet. It was a simple girlish costume, and Phoebe wore it with the same easy grace she wore her homespun, which made it doubly annoying to Emmeline, who felt that Phoebe had no right to act as if she was doing nothing unusual.

Years ago when the child Phoebe had come to live with them she had brought with her some boxes and trunks, and a few pieces of furniture for her own room. They were things of her mother's which she wished to keep. Emmeline had gone carefully over the collection with ruthless hand and critical tongue, casting out what she considered useless, laying aside what she considered unfit for present use, and freely commenting upon all she saw. Phoebe, fresh from her mother's grave, and the memory of that mother's living words, had stood by in stony silence, holding back by main force the angry tears that tried to get their way, and letting none of the storm of passion that surged through her heart be seen. But when Emmeline had reached the large hair-covered trunk and demanded the key, Phoebe had quietly dropped the string that held it round her neck inside her dress, where in lay cold against her little sorrowful heart, and answered decidedly:

"You needn't open that, Emmeline; it holds my mother's dresses that she has put away for me when I grow up."

"Nonsense!" Emmeline had answered, sharply. "I think I'm the best judge of whether it needs to be opened or not. Give me the key at once. I guess I'm not going to have things in my house that I don't know anything about. I've got to see that they are packed away from moth."

Phoebe's lips had trembled, but she continued to talk steadily:

"It is not necessary, Emmeline. My mother packed them all away carefully in lavender and rosemary for me. She did not wish them opened till I got ready to open them myself. I do not want them opened."

Emmeline had been very angry at that, and told the little girl she would not have any such talk around her, and demanded the key at once, but Phoebe said:

"I have told you it is not necessary. These are my things and I will not have any more of them opened, and I will not give you the key."

That was open rebellion and Emmeline carried her in high dudgeon to Albert. Albert had looked at the pitiful little face with its pleading eyes under which dark circles sat mournfully, and — sided with Phoebe. He said that Phoebe was right, the things were hers, and he did not see for his part why Emmeline wanted to open them. From that hour Emmeline had hard work to tolerate her little half-sister-in-law, and the enmity between them had never grown less. Little did Phoebe know, whenever she wore one of the frocks from that unopened trunk, how she roused her sister-in-law's wrath.

The trunk had been stored in the deep closet in Phoebe's room, and the key had never left its resting-place against her heart, night or day. Sometimes Phoebe had unlocked it in the still hours of the early summer mornings when no one else was stirring, and had looked long and lovingly at the garments folded within. It was there she kept the daguerreotype of the mother who was the idol of her child heart. Her father she could not remember, as he died when she was but a year old. In the depths of that trunk were laid several large packages, labeled. The mother had told her about them before she died, and with her own hand had placed the boxes in the bottom of the trunk. The upper one was labeled, "For my dear daughter Phoebe Deane on her eighteenth birthday."

For several days before her birthday Phoebe had felt an undertone of excitement. It was almost time to open the box which had been laid there over eight years ago by that beloved hand. Phoebe did not know what was in that box, but she knew it was something her mother put there for her. It contained her mother's thought for her grown-up daughter. It was like a voice from the grave. It thrilled her to think of it.

On her birthday morning she had awakened with the light, and slipping out of bed had applied the little black key to the keyhole. Her fingers trembled as she turned the lock, and opened the lid, softly lest she should wake someone. She wanted this holy gift all to herself now, this moment when her should would touch again the soul of the lost mother.

Carefully she lifted out the treasures in the trunk until she reached the box, then drew it forth, and placing the other things back closed the trunk and locked it. Then she took the box to her bed and untied it. Her heart was beating so fast she felt almost as if she had been running. She lifted the cover. There lay the buff merino in all its beauty, complete even to the brown knot for the hair, and the locket which had been her mother's at eighteen. And there on the top lay a letter in her mother's handwriting. Ah! This was what she had hoped for — a real word from her mother which should be a guide to her in this grown-up life that was so lonely and different from the life she had lived with her mother. She hugged the letter to her heart and cried over it and kissed it. She felt that she was nestling her head in her mother's lap as she cried, and it gave her aching, longing heart a rest just to think so.

But there were sounds of stirring in the house, and Phoebe knew that she would be expected in the kitchen before long, so she dried her tears and read her letter.

Before it was half done the clatter in the kitchen had begun, and Emmeline's strident voice was calling up the stairway: "Phoebe! Phoebe! Are you going to stay up there all day?"

Phoebe had cast a wistful look at the rest of her letter, patted the soft folds of her merino tenderly, swept it out of sight into her closet, and answered Emmeline pleasantly, "Yes, I'm coming!" Not even the interruption could quite dim her pleasure on this day of days. She sprang up conscience stricken. She had not meant to be so late.

It did not take long to dress, and with the letter tucked in with the key against her heart she hurried down, only to meet Emmeline's frowning words, and be ordered around like a little child. Emmeline had been very disagreeable ever since Hiram Green had proposed to Phoebe.

The morning had been crowded full of work and the letter had no chance, except to crackle lovingly against the blue homespun.

The thought of the buff merino upstairs made her thrill with pleasure, and the morning passed away happily in spite of Emmeline and hard work. Words from her mother's hastily read letter came floating to her, and calling. She longed to pull it out and read once more to be sure just how they had been phrased. But there was no time.

After dinner, however, as soon as she had finished the dishes, and while Emmeline was looking after something in the wood-shed, she slipped away upstairs, without, as usual, asking is there was anything else to be done. She had decided that she would put on her new frock, for it had been her mother's wish in the letter, and go down to the village and call on sweet-faced Mrs. Spafford. It was two years since Mrs. Spafford had invited her to spend the afternoon, and she had never plucked up the courage to go, for Emmeline always had something ready for her to do. But she felt that she had a right to a little time to herself on her birthday, and she meant to slip away without Emmeline seeing, if she could. She took her letter out, intending to read it quietly first before she dressed, but a sudden thought of Emmeline and her ability to break in upon her quietness made her decide instead to dress and start, stopping in a maple grove on the way to the village to read her letter undisturbed; so with all haste she smoothed her hair, fastened in the velvet knot, and put on the pretty frock. For just a moment she paused in front of the glass and looked at herself thrilling with the thought that this dress was planned by her dear mother, and that the loved hand had set every perfect stitch in its place. And this girl in the glass was the daughter her mother had wished her to be, at least in outward appearance. Was she also in heart life? She looked earnestly at the face in the glass, longing to ask herself many questions and unable to answer. Then with the letter safely hidden she hurried down.

But her conscience would not let her go out the front door unobserved as she had planned. It seemed a mean, sneaking thing to do on her birthday. She would be open and frank. She would step into the kitchen and tell Emmeline that she was going out for the afternoon. That would be the way her mother would desire her to do. So, though much against her own desire, she went.

And there sat Emmeline with a large basket of dried beans to be shelled and put away for the winter. Phoebe stood aghast, and hesitated.

"Well, really!" said Emmeline, looking up severely at the apparition in buff that stood in the doorway. "Are you going to play the fine lady while I shell beans? It seems to me that's rather taking a high hand for one who's dependent on her relatives for every mouthful she eats, and seems to be likely to be for the rest of her days. That's gratitude, that is. But I take notice you eat the beans — oh, yes! the beans that Albert provides, and I shell, while you gallivant round in party clo'es."

The hateful speech brought the color to Phoebe's cheeks.

"Emmeline," she broke in, "you know I didn't know you wanted those beans shelled today. I would have done them this morning between times if you had said so."

"You didn't know," sniffed Emmeline. "You knew the beans was to shell, and you knew this was the first chance to do it. Besides, there wasn't any between times this morning. You didn't get up till most noon. Everything was clear put back, and now you wash your white hands and dress up, no matter what the folks that keeps you have to do. That wasn't the way *I* was brought up, if I *didn't* have a fine lady mother like yours. *My* mother taught me *gratitude*."

Phoebe reflected on the long hard days of work she had done for Emmeline without a word of praise or thanks, work as hard, and harder than any wage-earner in the house in the same position would have been expected to do. She had earned her board and more, and she knew it. Her clothes she made altogether from the stores her mother had left for her. She had not cost Albert a cent in that way. Nevertheless, her conscience hurt her because of the late hour of her coming down that morning. With one desperate glance at the size of the bean-basket, and a rapid calculation how long it would take her to finish them, she siezed her clean apron that hung behind the door and enveloped herself in it.

"I have wanted to go for a long time, but if those beans have got to be done this afternoon I can do them first."

She said it calmly, and went at the beans with determined fingers, that fairly made the beans shiver as they hustled out of their resisting withered pods.

Emmeline sniffed.

"You're a pretty figure shellin' beans in thay rig. I s'pose that's one of your ma's contoguments, but if she had any sense at all she wouldn't want you to put it on. It ain't fit for ordinary life. It might do to have your picture took in, or go to a weddin', but you do look like a fool in it now. Besides, if it's worth anything, an' it looks like there was good stuff in it, you'll spoil it shellin' beans."

Phoebe shelled away feverishly and said not a word. Her eyes looked as though ther might be anything behind their lower lashes, from tears to fire-flashes. Emmeline surveyed her angrily. Her wrath was on the boiling point and she felt the time had come to let it boil.

A little bird, perched on the roof of the barn, piped out: "Phoe-bee! Phoebee!" The girl lifted her head toward the outside door and listened. The bird seemed to be a reminder that there were other things in the world worthwhile besides having one's own way even on one's birthday. The paper in her bosom crackled, and Emmeline eyed her suspiciously, but the swift fingers shelled on unremittingly.

"I think the time has come to have an understandin'," said Emmeline, raising her voice harshly. "If you won't talk to me, Albert'll have to tend to you, but I'm the proper one to speak, and I'm goin' to do it. I won't have this sort of thing goin' on in my house. It's a disgrace. I'd like to know what you mean, treatin' Hiram Green in this way? He's a respectable man, and you've no call to keep him danglin' after you forever. People'll talk about you, and I won't have it!"

There was an angry flash in Emmeline's eyes. She had made up her mind to have her say.

Phoebe raised astonished eyes to her sister-in-law's excited face.

"I don't know what you mean, Emmeline. I have nothing whatever to do with Hiram Green. I can't prevent him coming to my brother's house. I'm sure I wish I could, for it's most unpleasant to have him around continually."

The lofty air and cool words angered Emmeline beyond expression. She almost always lost her temper at once when she began to talk with Phoebe. Her most violent effort seemed at once so futile, and the girl was so provokingly calm, that it was out of the question to keep one's temper.

"You don't know what I mean!" mocked Emmeline. "No, of course not. You don't know who he comes here to see. You think, I suppose, that he comes to see Albert and me perhaps. Well, you're not so much of a little fool as you want to pretend. You know well enough Hiram Green is just waitin' round on your whims, and I say it's high time you stopped this nonsense, keepin' a respectable man danglin' after you forever just to show off your power over him, and when all the time he needs a housekeeper, and his children are runnin' wild. You'll get your pay, miss, when you do marry him. Those young ones will be so wild you'll never get 'em tamed. They'll lead you a life of it. It's a strange way for any decent girl to act. If it's a new house you're waiting' on I guess you can have your way at once by just sayin' so. And I think it's time for you to speak, for I tell you plainly it ain't likely another such good chance'll come your way ever, and I don't suppose you want to be a hanger-on all your life on people that can't afford to keep you."

Phoebe's fingers were still shelling beans rapidly, but her eyes were on Emmeline's angry face.

I thought I had told you," she said, and her voice was steady, "that I would never marry Hiram Green. Nothing and nobody on earth could make me marry him. I despise him. You know perfectly well that the things you are saying are wrong. It is not my fault that he comes here. I do not want him to come and he knows it. I have told him I will never marry him. I do not want him to build a house nor do anything else, for nothing that he could do would make any difference."

"You certainly are a little fool!" screamed Emmeline, "to let such a chance go. If he wasn't entirely daft about you he'd give you up at once. Well, what are you intendin' to do then? Answer me that! Are you layin' out to live on Albert the rest of your life? It's best to know what to expect and be prepared. Answer me!" she demanded again, as Phoebe dropped her eyes to hide the sudden tears that threatened to overwhelm her calm.

"I don't know." The girl tried to say it quietly, but the angry woman snatched the words from her lips and tossed them back:

"You don't know! You don't know! Well, you better know! I can tell you right now that there's going' to be a new order of things. If you stay here any longer you've got to do as I say. You're not goin' on your high and mighty way doin' as you please an hour longer. And to begin with you can march upstairs and take off that ridiculous rig of your foolish mother's — "

Phoebe shoved the kitchen chair back with a sharp noise on the bare floor, and stood up, her face white with anger.

"Emmeline," said she, and her voice was low and controlled, but reminded Emmeline somehow of the first low rumbling of a storm, and when she looked at Phoebe's white face she fancied a flash like livid lightning passed over it. "Emmeline, don't you dare to speak my mother's name in that way! I will not listen to you!"

Then in the pause of the clashing voices the little bird from the weathervane on the barn called out again: "Phoebee! Phoe-bee!"

And it was then that Phoebe cast her apron from her and went through the kitchen door, into the golden glorious October afternoon, away from the pitiless tongue, and the endless beans, — and the sorrow of her life.

The little bird on the weathervane left his perch and flew along from tree to tree, calling joyously, "Phoe-bee! Phoe-bee!" as she went down the road. He seemed as glad as though she were a comrade come to roam the woods with him. The sunlight lingered lovingly on the buff merino, as though it were a piece of itself come out to meet it, and she flitted breathlessly down the way, she knew not whither, only to get out and away.

Queer, wintry-looking worms crawled lazily to their homes across the long white road, woolly caterpillars in early fur overcoats. Large leaves floated solemnly down to their long home. Patches of rank grass rose green and pert, passionately pretending that summer was not done, scorning the deadness all about them. All the air was filled with a golden haze and Phoebe in her golden, sunlit garments, seemed a part of it.

Chapter 5

The rage and sorrow that seethed in Phoebe's soul were such as in some passionate hearts have led to deeds of desperation. And indeed she did feel desperate as she fled along the road, pursued by the thought of her sister-in-law's angry words.

To have such awful words spoken to her, and on her birthday; to feel so cornered and badgered, and to have no home where one was welcome, save that hateful alternative of going to Hiram Green's house! Oh, why was it that one had to live when life had become a torture?

She had gone a long distance before her mind cleared sufficiently to think where she was going. The sight of a distant red farm-house made her pause in her wild walk. If she went on she would be seen from the well-watched windows of that red house, and the two women who lived there were noted alike for their curiosity and for their ability to impart news.

In sudden panic Phoebe climbed a fence and struck out across the field toward Chestnut Ridge, a small hill rising to the left of the village. There she might hope to be alone a little while and think it out, and perhaps creep close to her mother once more through the letter which she pressed against her heart. She hurried over the rough stubble of the field, gathering her buff garments with the other hand to hold them from any detaining briars. She seemed like some bright golden leaf blowing across the pasture to frolic with the other leaves on the nut-crowned hillside.

Breathless at last she reached the hill and found a great log where she sat down to read her letter.

My dear little grown-up girl, it began, and as Phoebe read the previous words again the tears burst from her smarting eyes, welling up from her aching heart, and she buried her face in the letter and stained it with her tears.

It was some time before she could conquer herself and read farther.

This is your eighteenth birthday, dear child, and I have thought so much about you and how you will be when you are a young woman, that I want to be with you a little while on your birthday and let you know how much, how very much, I love you. I cannot look forward into your life and see how it will be with you. I do not know whether you will have had sad years or bright ones between the time when I said good-bye to you and now when you are reading this. I could not plan positively, dear little girl, to have them bright ones, else you surely know I would. I had to leave you in God's care, and I know you will be taken care of, whatever comes. If there have been trials, somehow, Phoebe, little girl, they must have been good for you. Sometime you will learn why, perhaps, and sometime there will be a way out. Never forget that. God has His brightness ready somewhere for you if you are true to Him and brave. Somehow I am afraid that there will have been trials, perhaps very heavy ones, for you were always such a sensitive little soul, and you are going among people who may not understand.

In thinking about your life I have been afraid for you that you would be tempted because of unhappiness to take some rash impulsive step before God is ready to show you His plan for your life. I would like to give you a little warning through the years, and tell you to be careful.

You have entered young womanhood, and will perhaps be asked to give your life into the keeping of some man. If I were going to live I would try to train you through the years for this great crisis of your life. But when it comes, remember that I have thought about you and longed for you that you may find another soul who will love you better than himself, and whom you can love better than you love anything else in the world, and who will be grand and noble in every way. Dear child, hear your mother's voice, and don't take anything less. It will not matter so much if he is poor, if only he loves you better than himself and is worthy of your love. Never marry anyone for a home, or a chance to have your own way, or freedom from good honest work. There will be no happiness in it. Trust your mother, for she knows. Do not marry anyone to whom you cannot look up and give honor next to God. Unless you can marry such a man it is better not to marry at all, believe your mother, child. I say it lovingly, for I have seen much sorrow and would protect you.

And now, my sweet child, with a face like the dawn of the morning, and eyes so untroubled, if when you read this anything has come into your life to make you unhappy, just try to lay it all down for a little while and feel your mother's love about you. See, I have made this bright sunny dress for you, every stitch set with love, and I want you to wear it on your birthday to remind you of me. It is yellow, because that is the glory color, the color of the sunshine I have always loved so much. I want you to think of me in a bright, sunny happy way, and as in a glory of happiness, waiting for you; not as dead, and lying in the grave. Think of my love for you as a joy, and not a lost one, either, for I am sure that where I am going I shall love you just the same, and more.

I am very tired and must not write any more, for there are other letters yet to write and much to do before I can feel ready to go and leave you, but as I am writing this birthday letter for you I am praying God that He will bring some brightness into your life, the beginning of some great joy, on this your eighteenth birthday, that shall be His blessing, and my birthday gift to my child. I put a kiss here where I write my name and give you with it more love than you can ever understand.

Your Mother

The tears rained down upon her hands as she held the letter, and when it was finished she put her head down on her lap and cried as she had not cried since her mother died. It seemed as if her head were once more upon that dear mother's lap and she could feel the smooth, gentle touch of her mother's hand passing over her hair and her hot temples as when she was a little child.

The sunlight sifted softly down between the yellowed chestnut leaves, sprinkling gold upon the golden hem of her gown, and glinting on her shining hair. The brown nuts dropped now and then about her, reverently, as if they would not disturb her if they could help it, and the fat gray squirrels silently regarded her, pausing in their work of gathering in the winter's store, then whisked noiselessly away. It was all quite still in the woods except for the occasional falling of a nut, or the stir of a leaf, or the skitter of a squirrel, for Phoebe did not sob aloud. Her grief was deeper than that. Her soul was crying out to one who was far away and yet who seemed so near to her that nothing else mattered for the time.

She was thinking over all her sad little life, telling it to her mother in imagination, trying to draw comfort from the letter, and to reconcile the realities with what her mother had said. Would her mother have been just as sure that it would all come out right if she had known the real facts? Would she have given the same advice? Carefully she thought it over, washing the anger away in her tears. Yes, she felt sure if her mother had known all she could not have written more truly than she had done. She would have had her say "No" to Hiram, just as she had done, and would have exhorted to patience with Emmeline, and to trust that brightness would sometime come.

She thought of her mother's prayer for her, and almost smiled through her tears to think how impossible that could be. Yet—the day was not done—perhaps there might be some little pleasant thing yet, that she might consider as a blessing and her mother's gift. She would look and wait for it and perhaps it would come. It might be Albert would be kind—he was, sometimes-or if it were not too late she might go down to the village and make her call on Mrs. Spafford. That might be a beautiful thing and the beginning of a joy—but no, that was too far away and her eyes were red with weeping. She must just take this quiet hour in the woods as her blessing and be glad over it because her mother and God had sent it to her to help her bear the rest of the days. She lifted her tear-wet face to look around on the golden autumn world, and the sun caught the tears on her lashes and turned them into flashing jewels, till the sweet, sad face looked like a tired flower with the dew upon it.

Then quite suddenly she knew she was not alone.

A young man stood in the shadow of the tallest chestnut tree, regarding her with troubled gaze. His hat was in his hand and his head slightly bowed in deference, as if in the presence of something holy.

He was tall, well-formed, and his face fine and handsome. His eyes were deep and brown, with lights in them like those on the shadowed depths of a quiet woodland stream. His heavy dark hair was tossed back from a white forehead that had not been exposed to the summer sun of the hayfield, one could see at a glance, and the hand that held the hat was white and smooth also. There was a grace about his attitude that reminded Phoebe of David Spafford, who had seemed to her the ideal of a gentleman. He was dressed in dark brown and his black silk stock set off a finely cut clean-shaven chin of unusual strength and firmness. If it had not been for the lights in eyes, and the hint of smile behind the almost tender strength of the lips, Phoebe would have been afraid of him as she lifted shy, ashamed eyes to the intruder's face.

"I beg your pardon, I did not mean to intrude," he said, apologetically, "but a party of young people are coming up the hill. They will be here in a moment, and I thought perhaps you would not care to meet them. You seem to be in trouble."

"Oh, thank you!" said Phoebe, arising in sudden panic and dropping her mother's letter at her feet. She stooped to pick it up, but the young man had reached it first and their fingers met for one brief instant over the letter of the dead. In her confusion Phoebe did not know what to say but "Thank you," and then felt like a parrot repeating the same phrase.

Voices were distinctly audible now and the girl turned to flee, but ahead and around there seemed nowhere to go for hiding except a dense growth of mountain laurel that still stood green and shining amid the autumn brown. She looked for a way around it, but the young man caught her thought, and reaching forward with a quick motion of his arms he parted the strong branches and made a way for her.

"Here, jump right in there! Nobody will see you. Hurry, they are almost here!" he whispered, kindly.

The girl sprang quickly on the log, paused just an instant to gather her golden draperies about her, and then fluttered into the green hiding-place and settled down like a drift of yellow leaves.

The laurel swung back into place, nodding quite as if it understood the secret. The young man stooped and she saw him deliberately take from his pocket a letter and put it down behind the log that lay across her hiding-place.

The letter settled softly into place and looked at her knowingly as if it, too, were in the secret and were there to help her. For even a letter has an expression if one has but eyes to see and understand.

Up the hill-side came a troop of young people. Phoebe could not see them, for the growth of laurel was very dense, but she could hear their voices.

"Oh, Janet Bristol, how fast you go! I'm all out of breath. Why do you hurry so? The nuts will keep till we get there, and we have all the afternoon before us."

"Go slow as you like, Caroline," said a sweet, imperious voice; "when I start anywhere I like to get there. I wonder where Nathaniel can be. It is fully five minutes since he went out of sight, and he promised to hail us at once and tell us the best way to go."

"Oh, Nathaniel isn't lost," said another girl's voice crossly; "he'll take care of himself likely. Don't hurry so, Janet. Maria is all out of breath."

"Hullo! Nathaniel! Nathaniel Graham, where are you!" called a chorus of male voices.

Then from a few paces in front of the laurel hiding-place came the voice that Phoebe had heard but a moment before:

"Aye, aye, sir! That way!" it called. "There are plenty of nuts up there!" He stood with his back toward her hiding-place, and pointed farther up the hill. Then, laughing, scrambling over slippery leaves and protruding logs the gay company frolicked past, and Phoebe was left, undiscovered, alone with the letter that smiled back at her in a friendly way.

She stooped a little to look at it and read the address, "Nathaniel Graham, Esq.," written in a fine commanding hand, a chirography that gave the impression of honoring the name it wrote.

The girl studied the beautiful name, till every turn of the pen was graven on her mind, the fine, even clearness of the small letters, the bold downward stroke in the capitals. It was unusual writing of an unusual name and the girl felt that it belonged to an unusual man.

Then all of a sudden, while she waited and listened to the happy jingle of voices, like bells of different tones, exclaiming over rich finds in nuts, the barren loneliness of her own life came over her and brought a rush of tears. Why was she here in hiding from those girls and boys that should have been her companions? Why did she shrink from meeting Janet Bristol, the sweetly haughty beauty of the village? Why was she never invited to their pleasant tea-drinkings, and their berry and nut gatherings? She saw them in church, and that was all. They never seemed to see her. True, she had not been brought up from childhood among them, but she had lived there long enough to have known them intimately if her life had not always been so full of care. Janet Bristol had gone away to school for several years, and was only at home in summer when Phoebe's life was full of farm work — cooking for the hands, and for the harvesters. But Maria Finch and Caroline Penfield had gone to school with Phoebe. She felt a bitterness that they were in these good times and she was not. They were not to blame, perhaps, for she had always avoided them, keeping much to herself and her studies in school, and hurrying home at Emmeline's strict command. They had never attracted her as had the tall, fair Janet, in the few summer glimpses she had had of her. Yet she would never likely know Janet Bristol or come any nearer to her than she was now, hidden behind God's screen of laurel on the hill-side, while the gay company gathered nuts a few rods away. The young man with the beautiful face and the kind ways would forget her and leave her to scramble out of her hiding-place as best she could while he helped Janet Bristol over the stile and carried her basket of nuts home for her. He would not cross her path again. Nevertheless she was glad he had met her this once, and she could know there was in the world one so kind and noble; it was a beautiful thing to have come into her life. She would stay here till they were all out of hearing, and then creep out and steal away as she had come. Her sad life and its annoyances, forgotten for the moment, settled down upon her, but with this change. They now seemed possible to bear. She could go back to Albert's house, to Emmeline where she was unwelcome, and work her way twice over. She could doff the golden garments, and take up her daily toil, even patiently perhaps, and bear Emmeline's hateful insinuations, Alma's impudence, the disagreeable attentions of Hank and the hateful presence of Hiram Green, but never again would she be troubled with the horrible thought that perhaps after all she was wrong and ought to accept the home that Hiram Green was offering her. *Never,* for now she had seen a man, who had looked at her as she felt sure God meant to a man to look at a woman, with honor, and respect, and gentle helpfulness, and deference.

All at once she knew that her mother's prayer had been answered and that something beautiful had come into her life. It would not stay and grow as her mother had hoped. This stranger could be nothing to her, but the memory of his helpfulness and the smile of sympathy that had lighted his eyes would remain with her, a beautiful joy, always. It was something that had come to save her at the moment of her utter despair.

Meantime, under the chestnut-trees but a few rods away, the baskets were being filled rapidly, for the nuts were many and the squirrels had been idle, thinking they owned them all. Nathaniel Graham helped each girl impartially, and seemed to be especially successful in finding the largest and shiniest nuts. The laughing and joking went on, but Nathaniel said little. Phoebe, from her covert could watch them, and felt that the young man would soon pilot them farther away. She could hear bits of their talk.

"What's the matter with Nathaniel?" said Caroline Penfield. "He's hardly said a word since we started. What deep subject is your massive mind engaged upon, young man?"

"Oh, Nate is thinking about Texas," said Daniel Westgate, flippantly. "He has no thoughts or words for anything but setting Texas free. We'll hear of him joining the volunteers to help them fight Mexico the next thing. I wouldn't be one bit surprised.

"Don't, Daniel," said Janet Bristol, sharply. "Nathaniel has far more sense than that."

"I should hope so!" echoed Maria Finch. "Nathaniel isn't a hot-headed fanatic."

"Don't you be too sure!" said the irrepressible Daniel. "If you'd heard the fine heroics he was getting off to David Spafford yesterday you wouldn't be surprised at anything. Speak up, Nate, and tell them whether you are going or not."

"Perhaps," said Nathaniel, lifting pleasant eyes of amusement towards the company."

"Nonsense!" said Janet, sharply. "As if he would think of such a thing! Daniel, you ought to be ashamed to spoil the lovely afternoon with talk of politics. Come, let us move on to that next clump of trees. See, it is just loaded, and the nuts are falling with every breath of wind."

"Just look at that squirrel, leaning against his tail as if it were the back of an easy chair. He is mincing away at that nut as daintily as any lady," called Caroline.

The merry company picked up baskets and began to move out of sight, but the young man Nathaniel stood still thoughtfully and felt in his pockets, until Phoebe, from her hiding-place, could see none of the others. Then she heard him call in a pleasant voice, "Janet, I have dropped a letter. It cannot be far away. Go on without me for a moment. I will be with you right away."

Then came Janet's sweet, vexed tones:

"Oh, Nathaniel! How tiresome! Can't you let it go? Was it of any consequence? Shall we come and help you find it?"

"No, Janet, thank you. I know just where I dropped it, and I will be with you again before you have missed me. Keep right on."

Then he turned, swiftly, and came back to the laurel, before the startled Phoebe, who had intended running away at once, could realize that he was coming.

She sprang up with the instinct of fleeing from him, but as if the laurel were loath to part with her, it reached out detaining fingers and caught her by the strands of her fine brown hair; and down came the soft, shining waves of hair, in shameless, lovely disorder about the flushed face, and rippling far below the waist of the buff frock. The sun caught it and kissed it into a thousand lights and shadows of brown and red and purple and gold. A strand here and there clung to the laurel as if the charm were mutual, and made a fine veil of spun gold before her face. Thus she stood abashed, with her hair unbound before the stranger, her face in a beautiful confusion.

Now this young man had gazed upon many a maiden's hair with entire indifference. In the days of his boyhood he had even dared to attach a paper kite to the yellow braids of a girl who sat in front of him in school, and laughed with the rest at recess, as after carefully following her with hidden kite and wound-up cord they had succeeded in launching the paper thing in the breeze till it lifted the astonished victim's yellow plaits high in air and she cried out angrily upon them. He had even pulled many a girl's hair. He had watched his

cousin Janet brush and plait and curl her abundant locks into the various
changing fashions, and criticized the effect freely. He had once untied a hard
knot in a bonnet-string among a mass of golden curls without a thrill. Why
therefore did he feel such awe as he approached in deep embarrassment to offer
his assistance! Why did his fingers tremble as he laid them reverently upon a
strand of hair that had tangled itself in the laurel? Why did it bring a fine ecstasy
into his being as the wind blew it across his face? Did all hair have that delicate,
indescribable perfume about it?

When he had set her free from the entangling bushes, he marvelled at the
dexterity with which she reduced the flying hair to order the imprisoned it
meekly. It seemed like magic.

Then, before she had time to spring out of her covert, he took her hands,
firmly, reverently, without undue familiarity, and helped her to the top of the
log and thence to the ground. She liked him for the way he did it, so different
from the way the other men she knew would have done it. She shuddered to
think if it had been Hank, or Hiram Green.

"Come this way, it is nearer to the road," he said, quietly, parting the
branches at his right to let her pass, and when she had gone a few steps, behold,
not two rods below lay the cross road, which met the highway by which she had
come, a quarter of a mile farther on.

"But you have forgotten your letter," she turned to say, as they came out of
the woods and began to descend the hill; "and I can get out quite well now. You
have been very kind—"

"I will get the letter presently," he said, with a smile. "Just let me help you
over the fence. I want to ask your pardon for my intrusion. I did not see you at
first, the woods were so quiet, and you looked so much like the yellow leaves
that lay all about—" and his eyes cast an admiring glance at the buff merino.

"Oh, it was not an intrusion," she exclaimed, her cheeks rosy with the
remembrance, "and I am so grateful to you for telling me they were coming. I
would not have liked to be found there—so." She looked shyly up. "I thank you
very much!" He saw that her eyes were beautiful, with ripples of laughter and
shadows of sorrow in their glance. He experienced a deep and unnecessary
satisfaction that his first impression of her face was verified, and he stood
looking down upon her as if she were something he was proud of having
discovered and rescued from an unpleasant fate.

Phoebe felt a warm glow like sunshine breaking over her in the kindness of
his look.

"Don't thank me," he said. "I felt like a criminal, intruding so upon your
trouble."

"But you must not feel so. It was only that I had been reading a letter from
my mother, and it made me feel so lonely that I cried."

"That is trouble enough," he said, with quick sympathy. "Is your mother away from home, or are you?"

"My mother is dead. She has been gone a good many years," she said, with quivering lips. "She wrote this letter long ago for me to read today, and I came away here by myself to read it. Now, you will understand."

He had helped her over the rail fence that separated the field from the road, and they were standing, she on the road side, he on the field side of the fence as they talked. Neither of them saw a farm wagon coming down the road over the brow of the hill, a mere speck against the autumn sky when they came out of the woods. The young man's face kindled as he answered:

"Thank you for telling me. Yes, now I will understand. My mother has been gone a long time, too. I wish she had written me a letter to read today."

Then, as if he knew he must not stay longer, he lifted his hat, smiled, and walked quickly up the hill, while Phoebe sped swiftly down the road, not noticing the glories of the day, not thinking so much of her own troubles, but marvelling at what had happened and living it all over once more in imagination. She knew without thinking that a wagon was rumbling nearer and nearer, but she gave it no heed.

Nathaniel Graham, when he reached the edge of the wood, turned and looked back down the road; saw the girl in her yellow draperies moving in the autumn sunshine, and watched her intently. The driver of the farm wagon, now almost opposite to him, watched glumly from behind his bags of wheat, high piled, sneered under his breath at the fine attire, half guessed who he was; then wondered who the girl was who kept tryst so far from any houses, and with a last glance at the man just vanishing into the woods he whipped up his team, resolved to find out.

Chapter 6

Nathaniel Graham went to pick up the letter he had left behind the log, but as he did so his eye caught something brown, lying on the ground among the laurel near the letter. He reached out and took it. It was a bit of a bow of brown velvet, and seemed strangely a part of the girl who had been there but a few moments before. What part had this bit of velvet played in her make-up? Had it been worn at her throat, or in her wonderful hair? He never doubted that it was hers. As he raised it wonderingly in his hand to look at it more closely he fancied he caught the same subtle fragrance that had been in her hair. His fingers closed pleasantly about the soft little thing. For a moment he pondered whether he ought to go after her and give it to her. Then farther up the hill he heard the voices calling him, and with a pleasant smile he tucked it into his inner pocket beside the letter that had played so important a part in the little affair. He rather liked to think he had that bit of velvet himself, and perhaps it was not of much value to the owner. It might at least make another opportunity of seeing her. And so he passed on up the hill with something besides the freedom of Texas to think upon.

Meantime, the load of wheat went down the road after Phoebe at a lively pace, and its driver, in no pleasant mood because he had been all the way to Albany with his wheat and had been unable to sell it, studied the graceful sunlit figure ahead of him, and wondered what there was about it so strangely familiar.

Phoebe had just reached the highroad and paused to think which way she would go, when the wagon overtook her, and turning with her face bright with pleasure, and momentary forgetfulness, she faced the lowering astonishment of Hiram Green! Her face grew deadly white with the revulsion, and she caught at the fence to steady herself. She felt as if the earth were reeling under her unprotected feet. One hand flew to her heart and her frightened eyes, with a wild thought of her late protector, sought the way by which she had come; but the hill-side lay unresponsive in the late sunshine, and not a soul was to be seen. Nathaniel Graham had just picked up his cousin Janet's basket.

"Well, I swow!" said Hiram Green, pulling his horses up sharply. "It ain't *you* tricked out that way, away off here!" Then slowly his little pig eyes traveled to the lonely hill-side, gathered up an idea, came back to the girl's guilty face, and narrowed to a hateful slit through which shone a gleam of something that might be likely to illumine outer darkness. He brought his thin, cruel lips together with satisfaction. He felt that at last he had a hold upon the girl, but he could wait and use it to his best advantage.

She, poor child, never dreamed that he had seen the young man with her, and was only frightened for the moment with instinctive dread of being alone in an unfrequented spot with him. In an instant her courage came to her aid, and she steadied her voice to reply naturally:

"Oh, is that you, Mr. Green? You almost frightened me. I was taking a walk and did not expect to see anyone I knew. This is the Albany road isn't it? Have you been to Albany?"

Her unusually friendly tones threw the man off his guard for a moment. He could not resist the charm of having her speak so pleasantly to him.

"Yes, been to Albany on business," he responded. Won't you get up and ride? 'Tain't a very pretty seat, but I guess it's clean and comfortable. Sorry I ain't got the carryall. You're a long piece from home."

"Oh, thank you, Mr. Green," she said, cordially. "I'm sure the seat would be very comfortable, and just as nice as the carryall, but I'm out taking a walk this beautiful afternoon, and I'm enjoying every minute of it. I would much rather walk. Besides, I am not going directly home. I may stop at Granny McVane's and perhaps another place before I get home. Thank you for the invitation."

Then without waiting for a reply she flew lightly in front of the horses and sped up the main highway toward the old red farm-house. It was not the direction she would have chosen, but there was no time to do anything else, and her frightened heart gave wings to her feet. She dared not look behind lest she was being pursued.

Hiram Green, thus left alone after his attempt at gallantry, looked after the flying maiden with venom in his little eyes. His mouth hardened once more into its cruel lines and he took up the reins again and said to his horses in no pleasant tones: "G'long there!" pointing his remark with a stinging cut of the whip, which made the weary beasts leap forward at a lively gait.

He did not watch Phoebe any longer, but once he turned his head and looked threateningly at the barren hill-side, and shook the fist that held his whip in a menacing way.

When Phoebe neared the old red house, where lived the two women who always saw and enlarged and told everything, she noted with relief that the shades were drawn down and there was a general air of not-at-home-ness about the place that betokened the inhabitants were away for the afternoon. With joy she went on by the house and turned down another cross road which would lead to a second road going into the village. On this road, just on the border of the town, lived Granny McVane all alone save for her silent old husband. She was a sweet old lady whom care and disappointment had not hardened, but only made more humble and patient. Phoebe had been there on occasional errands, and her kindness had won the girl's heart. From Granny McVane's it would be but a short run home across the fields, and she would thus escape meeting any more prying eyes. She was not accustomed to making calls on the neighbors without an errand, but the fancy came to her now that she would just stop and ask how Granny's rheumatism was, and wish her good-day. Perhaps, if she seemed glad to see her, she might tell her it was her birthday and this was the frock her mother had made. The girl had a longing to confide in some one.

As she walked along the country road, she began to think of home and the inevitable black looks that would be hers from Emmeline. But the day was good yet, though a chill was creeping into the air that made her cheeks tingle. The sun was dropping low now, and the rays were glowing deeper. The stubble in the cornfields that she passed was bathed in its light. The buff merino was touched with a ruddy glow and the girl, as she sped along, seemed like a living topaz in the golden setting of the day.

She reached the little double door of Granny McVane's cottage, and knocked. The old lady, in her white ruffled cap with its black band, and soft kerchief folded across her bosom, opened the upper half of the door, and on seeing Phoebe opened the lower door, too, and brought her in most cordially. She made her sit down, and looked her over with delight, her old eyes glowing with pleasure at the sweet picture the girl made sitting in the flowered calico rocking-chair. She seemed to catch the long sunbeams that slanted low across the kitchen floor, and reflect them with her gown and face till all the little room was filled with sunny brightness.

She made Phoebe tell about the frock, her birthday, her mother's letter, and her walk; and then she told her she must stay to tea with her, for the 'Squire was off to Albany on business and would not be back that night.

The old cat was winking cordially before the hearth, the pot of mush was sputtering sleepily on its crane over the fire, the kettle was singing cheerily beside it, and the old lady's face was so wistful that Phoebe put by her thought of home, and the supper that she ought to be getting this minute, and decided to stay just for once, as it was her birthday. The stiff white curtains shut the little room in cozily from the outside world, and a scarlet geranium bloomed happily on the broad window-seat. Phoebe looked around at the polished old mahogany, and the shining pewter dishes that adorned the shelf, touched the drowsy cat with gentle fingers that brought forth a purr, glanced up at the great old clock with its measured, unhurried tick-tock, tick-tock, and felt like a person who has turned her back upon life and all its duties and abandoned herself to pleasure pure and simple. Yes, for one short hour more she would have what her day offered her of joy, without a thought of trouble, and then she would go back to her duty and cherish the memory of her pleasure. Thus did Phoebe give herself over to the wild excitement of a birthday tea at Granny McVane's cottage.

Precisely at five o'clock the little round table was drawn out from the wall, and its leaves put up. A snow-white homespun cloth was laid upon it and lovely blue dishes of quaint designs in blue set upon it; a bowl, a plate, cup and saucer for each; steel knives; a great pitcher of creamy milk; a pat of Granny's delicious butter; a pitcher of "sugar-house" molasses, looking like distilled drops of amber, and delectable to the taste; a plate of shining brown rusks; a loaf of soft gingerbread, rich and dark like brown velvet. Then the tea was made in the little brown earthenware teapot, the great bowl of yellow mush taken up, and no modern debutante's dinner party, with its hand-painted dinner cards, its beribboned favors, its flowers, and its carefully-planned menu could have a lovelier color scheme, or one that better fitted the gown of the guest of honor, than was set forth for Phoebe Deane's birthday tea, all yellows and beautiful browns, with the last rays of the setting sun over all. The lazy cat got up, stretched, and yawned, and came over by the table as they sat down. The cat, by the way, was yellow, too.

It was a delicious meal, and Phoebe ate it with the appetite gained in her long walk. After it was over she bade Granny McVane good-evening, kissed her for the beautiful ending to her birthday, and hurried guiltily across the fields to the farm-house she called home, not allowing herself to think of what was before her until she reached the very door, for she would not have one moment of her precious day spoiled.

The family had just sat down to supper when Phoebe opened the door and came in. She had hoped this ceremony would be over, for the usual hour for supper was half past five, but Emmeline had waited longer than usual, thinking Phoebe would surely come back to help, and having it all to do herself had not been able to get it ready as soon as usual. Moreover, an undertone of apprehension as to what Albert might say if Phoebe should be headstrong enough to remain away after dark, kept her going to the window to look up the road for the possible sight of a girlish figure in a curious yellow frock. Emmeline had been angry, astonished, and bewildered all the afternoon. She had not been able to decide what she would do about the way her young sister-in-law had acted. She had been a little anxious, too, lest she had gone too far, and would be blamed if the truth should be known. She would have been glad, many times during the afternoon, to have seen Phoebe meekly returning, but now that she had come, after staying away till the work was done and Albert had come home and found out her absence, Emmeline's wrath was kindled anew. She stood at the hearth taking up the second pan of johnnycake when the girl came in, and when she saw Phoebe apparently as cheerful as if she had stayed at home and done her duty all the afternoon, Emmeline set her lips in cold and haughty disapproval.

Alma, with her mouth full of fried potatoes, stopped her fork midway with another supply and stared. The little boys chorused in unison: "Hullo, Aunt Phoebe! Where'd'ye get the clo'es!" Hank, who was just helping himself to a slice of bread with his fork, turned full around and after the first glimpse of the girl in her unfamiliar garments he sat in awed embarrassment. Only Albert sat in pleased surprise, his knife and fork akimbo on his plate, his chair tipped back, and a look of real welcome in his face.

"Well, now, Phoebe, I'm real glad you've got back. I was getting uneasy about you, off so long. It isn't like you to stay away from your meals. My, but you do look pretty in that rig! What took you, anyway? Where've you been?"

Not to the others would she have told for the world, but somehow Albert's pleasant tones and kindly eyes unsealed her lips and without a thought she spoke:

"I've just been for a walk in the woods this afternoon, and I stopped a few minutes to see Granny McVane. She made me stay to tea with her. I did not mean to stay so late."

"That sounds very sweet, I'm sure," broke in Emmeline's sharp voice, "but she forgets that she left me with all her work to do on top of my own."

Phoebe's cheeks flushed.

"I am sorry I did not get back in time to help get supper," she said, looking straight at Albert as if explaining to him alone, "but it was my birthday, and I thought I might take a little time to myself."

"Your birthday! To be sure you can. You don't go out half enough. Emmeline, you wouldn't want her to work all day on her birthday, of course. Sit down, child, and have some more supper. This is real good johnnycake; have a piece? You ought to have told us before that you had a birthday, and then we might have celebrated. Eh, Hank! What do you say?"

"I say yes," said Hank, chuckling in a vain endeavor to regain his usual composure. He had visions of a certain red ribbon at the village store that he might have bought her, or a green glass breastpin. He watched her furtively and wondered if it was too late yet to improve the occasion.

"Other people have birthdays too, and I don't see much fuss made over 'em either," sniffed Emmeline, flinging the tea towel up to its nail with an impatient movement. She had burned her finger, and her temper burned in sympathy.

"Thank you, Albert," said Phoebe, quietly, "I don't care for any more supper. I will go up and change my frock and be ready to wash the dishes."

She was going toward the door, but Albert detained her.

"Wait, Phoebe! You come here and sit down. I've got something to tell you. I'd clean forgot about the birthday myself, but now I remember all right. Let's see, you're eighteen today, aren't you? I thought so."

Hank lifted bold, admiring eyes to her face, and the girl, standing patiently behind her chair at the table waiting for her brother to finish, felt she would like to extinguish him for a little while till the conference was over.

"Well, now, child, I've got a surprise for you. You're eighteen, and of age, so you've got a right to know it."

"Wouldn't it be better for you to tell me by and by when the work is done?" pleaded Phoebe, casting a frightened glance about on the wide-eyed, interested audience.

"No," said Albert, genially, looking about the room. "It isn't a secret, leastways not from any that's here. You needn't look so scared, child. It's only that there's a little money coming to you, about five or six hundred dollars. It's a nice tidy little sum for a girl eighteen with good prospects. You certainly deserve it, for you've been a good girl ever since you came to live with us. Your mother wanted me to keep the money for you till you was eighteen, and then she said you would know how to use it and be more likely to need it."

"Say, Aunt Phoebe," broke in Alma, tilting her turn-up nose to its most inquisitive point, and sticking out her chin in a grown-up manner she had copied after her mother, "does Hiram Green know you got a birthday?"

"Shut up!" said Emmeline, applying the palm of her hand in a stinging slap to her offspring's cheek.

"Sister! Sister!" said Albert, in gentle reproof. "Now, Emmeline, don't be so severe with the child! She doesn't realize how impertinent she is. Sister, you mustn't talk like that to Aunt Phoebe." Then in an aside to Hank, with a wink, "It does beat all how keen children will be sometimes."

Phoebe, with scarlet cheeks, felt as if she could bear no more. "Thank you, Albert," she said, with a voice that *would* tremble despite her best efforts. "Now if you will excuse me I'll change my frock."

"Wait a minute, child; that's a mighty pretty frock you've got on. Look pretty as a peach in it. Let's have a look at you. Where'd you get it? Make it yourself?"

"Mother made it for me to wear today," said Phoebe, in a low voice, and then she vanished into the hall, leaving somehow an impression of victory behind her, and a sense of embarrassment among the family.

"There'll be no livin' with her now," snapped Emmeline over the tea-cups. "I'm sure I thought you had better sense. You never told me there was any money left for her, or I'd've advised you about it. I'm sure we've spent for her, and if there's anything left her it belongs to you. Here she's had a good home, and paid not a cent for it, and had everything just the same as us. If she had any spirit of right she wouldn't touch a cent of that money!"

"Now look here, Emmeline," said Albert, in his kind, conciliatory tone. "You don't quite understand this matter. Not having known about it before of course you couldn't judge rightly. And as it was her ma's request that I didn't tell anybody. I couldn't very well tell you. Besides, I don't see why it should affect you any. The money was hers, and we'd nothing to do with it. As for her home here, she's been very welcome, and I'm sure she's earned her way. She's a good worker, Phoebe is."

"That's so, she is," assented Hank, warmly. "I don't know a girl in the county can beat her workin'."

"I don't know as anybody asked your opinion, Hank Williams. I'm able to judge of work a little myself, and if she works well, who taught her? She'd never done a stroke when she came here, and nobody thinks of the hard time I've had breakin' her in, and puttin' up with her mistakes when she was young and her hands lily white, and soft as a baby's."

"Now, Emmeline, don't go and get excited," said Albert, anxiously. "You know we ain't letting go a mite of what you've done. Only it's fair to the girl to say she's earned her way."

"H'm!" said Emmeline, contemptuously, "that depends on who's the judge!"

"Won't Aunt Phoebe do any more work now she's got some money, ma?" broke in Alma in a panic of what might be the possibilities in store for her small selfish self.

"Haven't I told you to keep still, Alma," reproved her mother, angrily. "If you say another word I'll send you to bed without any cake."

At this dire threat Alma retired temporarily from the conversation till the cake should be passed, and a kind of family gloom settled over the room. Hank felt the constraint and made haste to bolt the last of his supper and escape.

Phoebe came down shortly afterward, attired in her everyday garb, and looking meekly sensible. Albert felt somehow a relief to see her so, though he protested weakly.

"Say, Phoebe, it's too bad for you to wash dishes your birthday night. You go back and put on your pretty things, and Alma'll help her ma wash up this time."

"No, she won't, either," broke in Emmeline. "Alma ain't a bit well, and she's not goin' to be made to work at her age unless she likes. Here, honey, you may have this piece of ma's cake, she don't want it all. It seems to me you're kind of an unnatural father, Albert Deane. I guess it won't hurt Phoebe to wash a few dishes when she's been lyin' around havin' a good time all day, while I've worked my fingers half off doin' her work. We've all had to work on our birthdays, and I guess if Phoebe's goin' to stay here she'll have to put up with what the rest of us gets, unless she's got money to pay for better."

With that Albert looked helplessly about the room and retired to his newspaper in the sitting-room, while Phoebe went swiftly about the usual evening work. Emmeline yanked the boys away from the cake plate, and marched them and Alma out of the kitchen with her head held high and her chin in the air. She did not even do the usual little duties of putting away the cake and bread and pickles and jelly, but left it all for Phoebe. Of this Phoebe was glad.

Before the dishes were quite done, the front door opened and Hiram Green sauntered into the sitting-room. Phoebe heard him, and hurried to hang up her dish towels and flee to her own room.

And thus ended the birthday, though the girl lay awake far into the night thinking over all its wonderful happenings, and not allowing her mind to dwell upon the possibilities of trouble in the future.

Chapter 7

When little Rose Spafford was born the sweet girl-mother, who had been Marcia Schuyler, found no one so helpful and reliable in the whole town as Miranda Griscom, granddaughter and household drudge of her next door neighbor, Mrs. Heath. David Spafford "borrowed" her for the first three or four weeks, and Mrs. Heath gave reluctant consent, because the Heaths and the Spaffords had always been intimate friends; but Grandma Heath realized during that time just how many steps the eccentric Miranda saved her, and she began to look forward to her return with more eagerness than she cared to show. Miranda, as she revelled in doing as she pleased in the large well-furnished kitchen of the Spafford house, using the best sprigged china to send a pretty tray upstairs to Mrs. Spafford, used often to look triumphantly over toward her grandmother's house, and wonder if she was missed. One little gleam of appreciation would have started a flame of abounding love in the queer, lonely heart of Miranda. But the grim grandmother never appreciated anything that this unloved grandchild, the daughter of an undesired son-in-law, tried to do.

As the delightful days sped by in loving service Miranda began to dread the time when she must go back to her grandmother's house again, and Marcia and David dreaded it also. They set about planning how they might keep her, and presently they had it all arranged.

David suggested it first.

It was while they both hung over the little Rose's cradle, watching her wake up, like the opening of the little bud she was. Miranda had come to the door for a direction, and stood a moment, remarking "I thought I'd find you two a-worshippin'. Just keep right on. My heart's with you. I'll see to supper. Don't you give it a thought." And then a moment later they heard her high, nasal tones voicing something about a "Sweet, sweet rose on a garden wall," and they smiled at the quaint loving soul. Then David spoke.

"Marcia, we must contrive to keep her here. She has blossomed out in the last month. It would be cruel to send her back to that dismal house over there again. They don't need her in the least with Hannah's cousin there all the time. I mean to offer her wages to stay with us. You are not strong enough to care for baby and do the housework, anyway, and I would feel safer about you if Miranda were here. Wouldn't you like her?"

Marcia's sweet laugh rang out. "Oh, David, you will spoil me! I'm sure I'm perfectly able to do the work and look after this wee flower. But of course I'd like to have Miranda here. I think it would be a good thing if she could get away from her surroundings, and she is a comfort to me in a good many ways."

"Then it is settled, dear," said David, with his most loving smile.

"Oh, but David, what will Aunt Amelia say? And Aunt Hortense! Think! They will tell me I am weak — or proud, which would be worse yet."

"What does it matter what my aunts think? We are certainly free to do as we please in our own home, and I'm sure of one thing — Aunt Clarinda will think it is all right. She'll be quite pleased. Besides, I shall explain to Aunt Hortense that I want to have you more to myself and take you with me often, and therefore it is my own selfishness, not yours, that makes me do this. She will listen to that argument, I am sure."

Marcia smiled, half doubtfully.

"And then, there is Mrs. Heath. She never will consent."

"Leave that to me, my little wife, and don't worry about it. Let us first settle it with Miranda."

"Oh, but if Mrs. Heath wouldn't hear to it, Miranda would be so disappointed," suggested Marcia.

Just then Miranda presented herself at the door.

"Your supper's spoilin' on the table. Will you two just walk down and eat it while I have my try at that baby? I haven't seen scarcely a wink of her all this blessed day."

"Miranda," said David, not looking at his wife's warning eyes, "would you be willing to stay with us altogether?"

"H'm!" said Miranda. "Jes' gimme the try and see!" and she stooped over the cradle with such a wistful longing in her gaze that the young mother's heart went out to her with a real love.

"Very well, Miranda, then we'll consider it a bargain. I'll pay you wages so that we shall feel quite comfortable about asking you to do anything, and you shall call this your home from now on."

"What!" gasped the astonished girl, straightening up. "Did you mean what you said? I never knew you to do a mean thing like tease any one, David Spafford, but you can't mean what you say. It couldn't come around so nice as that fer me. Don't go to talk about wages. I'd work from mornin' to night fer one chance at that blessed baby there in the cradle. But I know it can't be."

The supper grew quite cold while they were persuading her that it was all true and that they really wanted her; and while they talked over the possibilities of having trouble with her grandmother; but at last with her sandy eyelashes wet with tears of joy and hope Miranda went downstairs and heated the supper all over again for them, and the two upstairs, beside the little bud of life that had bloomed for them, rejoiced that a heart so faithful and true would be her watchful attendant through babyhood.

Perhaps it was with a feeling that he desired to burn his bridges behind him before his maiden aunts should hear of the new arrangement, that David went over to see old Mrs. Heath that very evening. Perhaps it was to relieve the excitement of poor Miranda, who felt that though heaven had opened before her, it could not really be for her, and was counting on being put out of her Eden at once.

No one but Marcia ever **heard** what passed between David and old Mrs. Heath, and no one else quite knows what arguments he used to finally bring the determined old woman to terms. Miranda, with her nose flattened against the window pane of the dark kitchen chamber, watching the two blurred figures in the candlelight of Grandmother Heath's "settin room," wondered, and prayed, and hoped and feared, and prayed again.

It was well that David had gone over to see Mrs. Heath that night and made all arrangements, if he cared to escape criticism from his relatives. It was the very next afternoon that Miss Amelia, on her daily visit to the shrine of her new grandniece, remarked: "Well, Marcia, has Miranda gone home yet? I should think her grandmother would need her, all this time away, poor old lady. And you're perfectly strong and able now to attend to your own work again."

Marcia's fair face flushed delicately, and she gathered her baby closer as if to protect her from the chill that would follow the words that she must speak.

"Why, Aunt Amelia," she said, brightly, "what do you think! Miranda is not going home at all. David has a foolish notion that he wants her to stay with me, and help look after the baby. Besides, he wants me to go with him as I have been doing. I told him it was not necessary, but he wanted it, so he has arranged it all, and Mrs. Heath has given her consent."

"Miranda stay here!" The words fell like long slanting icicles that seemed to pierce as they fell. They lingered in the air until their full surprise and displeasure could be distinctly felt, and then followed more.

"I am *surprised* at you, Marcia. I thought you had more self-respect than that! It is a disgrace to a young strong woman to let her husband hire a girl to do her work while she gads about the country and leaves her house and her young child. If your own mother had lived she would have taught you better than that. And then, *Miranda,* of *all people to select!* The child of a renegade! A waif dependent, utterly thankless, and irresponsible! She is scatterbrained, and untrustworthy. I you needed anyone at any time to sit with the child while you were out for a legitimate cause to pay a call, or make an occasional visit, either Hortense or I would be glad to come and relieve you. Indeed, you must not think of leaving this wild, good-for-nothing Miranda Griscom with my nephew's child. I shall speak to my sister Hortense, and we will make it our business to come down every day, one or the other of us, and do anything that you find your strength is unequal to doing. We are still strong enough, I hope, to do anything for the family honor. I should be ashamed to have it known that David Spafford's wife was such a weakling that she had to have hired help in. The young wives of our family have always been proud of their housekeeping."

Now Miranda Griscom, whatever might be said of her other virtues, had no convictions against eavesdropping; and in the case of this particular caller, she felt it most necesssary to serve her mistress in any way she could. She was keen enough to know that Miss Amelia would by no means be in favor of her advent in David Spafford's household, and she felt her beloved mistress would have to bear some persecution on her account. She therefore resolved that, come what might, she would be on hand to protect her. So, soon after the good aunt was seated in state with Marcia in the large front bedroom where the cradle was established, and which had become the centre of the little household since Rose Spafford's birth, Miranda, soft-stepping, approached the door, and applied her ear to the generous crack. She could feel the subject of herself coming on, and her ready brain had devised a plan by which she thought she could relieve the pressure if it should become unduly heavy upon Marcia at any time.

So, just as Marcia lifted her face, white with control, and tried to take the angry flash out of her eyes and think what to reply to her tormentor, Miranda, without ceremony of approach, burst into the room, exclaiming, "Oh, Miss Amelia, 'scuse me fer interruptin', but *did* your nice old gray cat mebbe foller you down here, and *could* it a' ben her out on our front porch fightin' with Bob Sykes's yellow dog?" 'Cause ef 'tis, sumpin' ought to be done right off, 'r he'll make hash out a' her. S'pose you come down an' look. I wouldn't like to make a mistake 'bout it."

Miss Amelia placed her hand upon her heart and looked helplessly at Marcia for an instant. "Oh, my dear, you don't suppose—" she began, in a trembling voice quite unlike her usual tones. Then she gathered up her shawl, which had slipped off her shoulders, and utterly unheeding that her bonnet was awry she hurried down the stairs after the sympathetic Miranda.

"Come right out here, softly," Miranda said, opening the front door cautiously. "Why, they must a' gone around the house!"

The old lady followed the girl out on the porch, and together they looked on both sides of the house, but there was no trace of dog or cat, any more than if, like the gingham dog and the calico cat of later days, they had "eaten each other up." "Where could they a' gone?" inquired Miranda, excitedly. "Mebbe I ought a' jus' called you and stayed here an' watched, but I was afraid to wake baby. You don't suppose that cat would a' run home, an' he after her? Is that them up the street? Don't you see a whirl o' dust in the road? Would you like me to go an' see? Cause I'm most afraid ef she's tried to run home; fer Bob Sykes hes trained thet dog to run races, an' he's a turrible fast runner, an' your cat is gettin' on in years. It might go hard with her." Miranda's sympathetic tone quite excited the old lady, whose old gray cat was very dear to her, being the last descendant of an ancient line of cats traditional in the family.

"No, Miranda, you just stay right here. Mrs. Spafford might need you after all this excitement. Tell her not to worry until I know the worst. I will go right home and see if anything has happened to Matthew. It really would be very distressing to me and my sister. If he has escaped from that dog he will need attention. Just tell Mrs. Spafford I will come down or send Hortense tomorrow as I promised." And the dignified old lady hurried off up the village street, for once unmindful of her dignity.

"Miranda!" called Marcia, when she had waited a reasonable time for the aunt's return and not even the girl presented herself.

Miranda appeared in a minute, with meek yet triumphant mien.

Marcia's eyes were laughing, but she tried to look grave.

"Miranda," she began, trying to suppress the merriment in her voice, "did you really see that cat out there?"

Miranda put on a dogged air and hesitated for a reply.

"Well, I heard a dog bark —" she began.

"Miranda was that quite honest!" protested Marcia who felt she ought to try to improve the moral standard of the girl thus under her charge and influence.

"I don't see anythin' wrong with that," asserted Miranda. "I didn't say a word that want true. I'm always careful 'bout that sence I see how much you think of such things. I asked her ef it might a' ben her cat, an' how do I know but 'twas? And it would be easy to a' ben Bob Sykes's dog, ef she *was* round, fer that dog never lets a cat come on his block. Anyway I heard a dog bark, and I thought it sounded like Bob's dog's voice. I'm pretty good on sounds."

"But you shouldn't frighten Aunt Amelia. She's an old lady, and it isn't good for old people to get frightened. You know she thinks a great deal of her cat."

"Well, it ain't good fer you to be badgered, and Mr. David told me to look after you, an' I'm doin' it the best way I know how. If I don't do it right I s'pose you'll send me back to Grandma's an' then who'll take care of that blessed baby!"

When Marcia told it all to David he laughed until tears came.

"Good for Miranda!" he said. "She'll do, and Aunt Amelia'll never know what happened to poor old Matthew, who was probably sitting quietly by the hearth purring out his afternoon nap. Well, little girl, I'm glad you didn't have to answer Aunt Amelia's questions. Leave her to me. I'll shoulder all the blame and exonerate you. Don't worry."

"But, David," began Marcia, in her troubled tone, "Miranda ought not to tell things that are not exactly true. How can I teach her?"

"Well, Miranda's standards are not exactly right, and we must try little by little to raise them higher, but I'll miss my guess if she doesn't manage some way to protect you, even if she does have to tell the truth."

And thus it was that Miranda Griscom because a fixture in the household of David Spafford, and did about as she pleased with her master and mistress and the baby, because she usually pleased to do pretty well.

The years had gone by and little Rose Spafford had grown into a lovely, laughing, dimpled child with charming ways that reminded one of her mother, and Miranda was her devoted slave.

On the Sunday after Phoebe Deane's birthday, David and Marcia, and Rose, and Miranda were all in church together. Little Rose, in dainty pantalettes and frock, with her rebellious curls brushed smoothly, her fat hands folded demurely in her lap, sat between her mother and Miranda, and waited for the sugared caraway seeds that she knew would be sure to be dropped occasionally into her nicely starched lap if she were good. David sat at the end of his pew, happy and devout, with Marcia, sweet and worshipful, beside him, and Miranda alert, one eye on her worship, the other on what might happen about her — or was it, quaint soul, but her way of watching for an opportunity to do good in her way?

Across the aisle the sweet face of Phoebe Deane attracted her attention. It was clouded with trouble. Miranda's keen eyes read that at once. Miranda had often noticed that about Phoebe Deane, and wondered, but there were so many other people that Miranda knew better to look after, that Phoebe Deane had heretofore not received her undivided attention.

But this particular morning Phoebe looked so pretty in her buff merino, which after much hesitation she had finally put on for church because her old church dress was so exceedingly shabby, that Miranda was all attention at once. Miranda, who had always been homely and red-haired and freckled, whose clothes had most of them been made over from Hannah Heath's cast-off wardrobe, yet loved beautiful things and beautiful people, and Phoebe, with her brown hair and deep, starry eyes, seemed like a lovely picture to her in the buff merino and with her face framed in its neat straw bonnet. The bonnet Miranda had seen for two or three summers past, but the frock was new, and a thing of beauty; therefore she studied its every detail and rejoiced that her position in the pew gave her a pretty good view of the young girl across the aisle, for something was wrong with the hinge of the door of Albert Deane's pew, and it stood wide open.

As her eyes travelled over Phoebe's frock they came finally to the face, so grave and sweet and troubled, as if already life was too filled with perplexities to have much joy left in it. Her keen gaze detected the droop to the pretty lips and the dark lines under the eyes; and then she looked at the sharp lines of Emmeline's sour face with its thin, pursed lips, and decided that Emmeline was not a pleasant woman to live with. Alma, preening herself in her Sunday clothes with her self-conscious smirk, was not a pleasant child, either, and she wondered if Phoebe could possibly take any pleasure in putting on her little garments for her, and planning surprises, and plays, the way she did for Rose. It seemed impossible. Miranda, the homely, looked down tenderly at the little Rose, and then gratefully toward David and Marcia at the end of the pew, and pitied the beautiful Phoebe, wishing for her the happiness that had come into her own barren life.

The service was about to commence when Judge Bristol, with his daughter Janet, and her cousin Nathaniel Graham, walked up the aisle to their pew, just in front of Albert Deane's.

Now there had been much debate in the heart of Phoebe Deane about coming to church that morning, for she could not keep out of her mind the thought of the stranger who had been so kind to her but a few days before, and it was impossible not to wonder if he would be there, and whether he would see her, and speak to her. It was in order to crucify this thought that she had half made up her mind not to wear the buff merino to church, and then nature triumphed and she put it on, realizing that her mother had made it for her to wear, and she had a perfect right to wear it, though Emmeline should disapprove. And Emmeline had disapproved in no uncertain tones. When she came downstairs ready for church Emmeline lifted her disagreeable eyebrows and exclaimed: "You're not going to wear that ridiculous rig to church, I hope? I should think you'd be ashamed to be decked out like that in the house of God! I'd sooner stay at home!"

And poor Phoebe would gladly have stayed at home if it had not been that Hank would have been there, and that she would have had to explain her reasons to Albert.

"I s'pose she wants people to know she's rich," piped in Alma, after a pause. This reference to her poor little pittance had been made almost hourly since Albert had told her of it, and it was growing unbearable to Phoebe. Altogether it was not with a very happy heart that she rode to church that morning, and she was half ashamed of herself for that undeniable wish to see the stranger once more. When she got out of the carryall at the church she would not look around nor even lift her eyes to see who was standing by the door. She had resolved not to think about him. If he came up the aisle, she would not know it, and her eyes should be otherwise occupied. No one should dare to say she was watching for him.

Nevertheless, as Janet and her cousin came up the aisle, Phoebe knew by the wild little beating of her heart that he was coming, and she commanded her eyes most strenuously that they should not lift from the psalm-book she had opened, albeit upside down. Yet, in spite of all resolves, when the occupants of the Bristol pew had entered it and were about to sit down, and while Nathaniel Graham stood so that his head and shoulders were just above the top of the high-back pew, those truant eyes fluttered up for one instant's glance, and in that instant were caught and held by the eyes of the young man in front in pleased recognition. 'Twas but a flash and Phoebe's eyes were back upon her book, and the young man was seated in the pew with only the top of his fine dark head showing, yet the pretty color flew into the cheek of the girl, and in the eyes of the young man there was a light of satisfaction that lasted all through the service. The glance had been too brief for any actual act of recognition like a bow or a smile, and neither would have been in place, for the whole audience could have seen them as he was faced about; moreover the service had begun. It had merely been the knowledge that each had of the other's presence in a warm glow like sunshine through the being. Not a soul had witnessed the glance, save the keen-eyed Miranda, and instantly she recognized a certain something which put her on the watch. She at once pricked up the ears of her consciousness, and if she had been living today would have said to herself, "There's 'somethin' doing' there." So Miranda, whether to her shame or her praise, sat through the whole long service, studied the faces of those two, and wove a pretty romance for herself out of the golden fabric of a glance.

Chapter 8

When the service was ended Phoebe took good care of her eyes that they should not look toward the stranger. Nathaniel Graham was kept busy for the first few moments shaking hands with old friends, and talking with the minister, who came down from the pulpit on purpose to greet him, and when he turned, as he did on the first opportunity, the pew behind him was empty, and the eyes that had met his when he came in were nowhere to be seen. He looked anxiously over the receding audience towards the open door, and caught the glimmer of the buff merino. Hastily excusing himself to Janet on the plea that he wished to speak to someone and would join her later, Nathaniel made his way down the aisle, disappointing some good old ladies who had been friends of his mother, and who were lying in wait for him at various pew doors.

Miranda, who had been awaiting the pleasure of David and Marcia, saw it all, and her eager eyes watched to see if he would catch Phoebe. The way being open just then, she pressed out into the aisle, and, for once leaving Rose to follow with her mother, hurried to the door.

Nathaniel did not overtake Phoebe until she had gone down the church steps, and was on the path in front of the churchyard that led to the shed where many of the conveyances were tied. He stepped up beside her, taking off his hat with a cheery, "Good morning," and Phoebe's pink cheeks and smiling eyes welcomed him happily.

"I wanted to be quite sure you were all right after your adventure the other day," he said, looking down into the lovely face with real pleasure; and then, before she could even answer, Hiram Green stepped up airily as if he belonged, and looked at Nathaniel questioningly as though he were intruding, saying, "Well, here you are Phoebe; I lost track of you at the church door. We better step along. The carryall is waitin'."

Nathaniel looked up annoyed, then puzzled, recognized Hiram, with astonishment, and said, "I beg your pardon, I did not know I was keeping you from your friends," to Phoebe, and, lifting his hat with a courteous "Good morning, Mr. Green," to Hiram, stepped back among the little throng coming out of the church door.

Now Miranda had been close behind, for she was determined to read every chapter of her romance that appeared in sight. She saw the whole maneuver on Hiram Green's part, and the color the flamed angrily into Phoebe's cheek when she recognized Hiram's interference. She also saw the dismay that showed in the girl's face as Nathaniel left her and Hiram Green made as if to walk beside her. Phoebe looked wildly about. There seemed no escape from him as a companion without making a deliberate scene, yet her whole soul revolted at having Nathaniel Graham see her walk off with Hiram.

Quick as a flash Miranda caught the meaning of Phoebe's look, and flew to her assistance.

She called quite clearly, "Phoebe! Phoebe Deane! Wait a minute, I want to tell you something!" She had raised her voice on purpose, for she stood directly behind Nathaniel, and, as she had hoped, he turned to see Phoebe respond. She noted the sudden light in his eyes as he saw that the girl to whom he had just been talking responded to the name, but she did not know that it was a light of satisfaction because he had found out her name without asking anyone. He stood a moment and looked after them. He saw quite plainly that Phoebe dismissed the sulky Hiram with a word and went off with Miranda. He saw that Hiram did not even raise his hat on leaving Phoebe, but slouched off angrily without a word.

"Say, Phoebe Deane," said Miranda, familiarly, "my Mrs. Spafford," —this was Miranda's common way of speaking of Marcia in the possessive— "she's ben talkin' a long time 'bout you, and wishin' you'd come to see her, an' she's ben layin' out to ask you to tea, but things hes prevented. So, could you come Tuesday? You better come early and stay all afternoon, so you can play with Rose. She's the sweetest thing!"

"Oh, I'd love to come," said Phoebe, her face aglow with pleasure. "I've always admired Mrs. Spafford so much, and little Rose is beautiful, just like a rose. Yes, tell her I will come."

Just then came the strident voice of Emmeline.

"Phoebe! Phoebe Deane! Was you intendin' to go home with us, or had you calculated to ride with Hiram Green? If you're comin' with us we can't wait all day."

With scarlet cheeks, angry heart, and trembling limbs Phoebe bade Miranda a frightened good-bye and climbed into the carriage, not daring to look behind her to see who had heard the hateful words of her sister-in-law. Oh, had the stranger hear them? How dreadful if he had! How contemptible, how unforgivable in Emmeline! How could she endure this persecution any longer? She did not even dare lift her eyes as they drove by the church, but sat with drooping lashes and burning cheeks, so missing the glance of the young man Nathaniel as he stood on the sidewalk with his cousin, waiting for another opportunity to lift his hat. Perhaps it was as well, for she would have been most unmercifully teased and cross-questioned if Emmeline and Alma had seen him speak to her.

Miranda watched the Deanes drive away, and turned with a vindictive look of triumph to stare at Hiram Green getting into his chaise alone. Then she began to reflect upon what she had done.

About four o'clock that afternoon, the dinner dishes being well out of the way, and the Sunday quiet resting upon the house, Miranda presented herself before Marcia with the most guilty look upon her face that Marcia had ever seen her wear.

"Well, I've up an' done it now, Mrs. Marcia, an' no mistake. I expect I'll have to leave you, an' the thought of it jes' breaks my heart."

"Why, Miranda!" said Marcia, sitting up very suddenly from the couch where she had been reading Bible stories to Rose. "You're not—you're surely not going to get married!"

"Not by a jugful I ain't. Do you s'pose I'd hev enny man that would take up with freckles an' a turn-up nose in a wife? I've gone and done sumpin' you'll think is a heap worse'n gittin' married. But I didn't tell no lie. I was keerful enough 'bout that. I only told her you'd been talkin' 'long back 'bout askin' her, an' you hed all right 'nough, only I oughtn't to a ast her, an' set the day an' all 'thout you knowin'. I knowed it at the time well 'nough, but I hed to do it, 'cause the circumstances wuz sech. You see thet squint-eyed Hiram Green was makin' it out that she was somewhat great to him, a paradin' down the walk there from the church, an' a driven' off that nice city cousin of Janet Bristol's with his nice, genteel manners, an' his tippin's of his hat, an' her a lookin' like she'd drop from shame, so I called her to wait, an' I runs up an' talks to her, an' course then she tels Hiram Green he needn't to trouble to wait fer her, an' we goes off together in full sight of all. My, I was glad I beat that skin-flint of a Hiram Green, but I was that excited I jes' couldn't think of 'nother thing to do 'cept to invite her."

"Who in the world are you talking about, Miranda? And what terrible thing have you done?"

Marcia's laughing eyes reassured Miranda and she went on with her story.

"Why that pretty little Phoebe Deane," she explained. "I've invited her to tea Tuesday night. I thought that would suit you better than any other time. Monday night things ain't straight from wash-day yet, and I didn't want to put it off too long, an' I can make everything myself. But if you don't like it I'll go an' tell her the hull truth on't, only she did look so mortal pleased I hate to spoil her fun."

By degrees Marcia drew the whole story from Miranda, even to a voluble description of the buff merino, and its owner's drooping expression.

"Well, I don't see why you thought I would be displeased," said Marcia. "It is only right you should invite company once in a while. I am glad you invited her, and as you do most of the work, and know our plans pretty well, you knew it would likely be convenient. I am glad you invited her."

"But I didn't invite her," said Miranda, "leastways she doesn't know I did. She thinks you done it yourself, and she sent you a whole lots of thanks, and said she 'dmired you turrible. And I didn't tell a thing but the truth either," Miranda added, doggedly.

"You blessed old Miranda. You always have a way of wiggling out. But you do manage to make things go your way in spite of truth or anything else. And it was truth after all, for I did want her, and would have asked her myself if I had known. You see you were just my messenger that time, acting in my place." And she gave Miranda one of the smiles that had so endeared her to the heart of the lonely girl. Then Miranda went back to her kitchen comforted.

Thus it came about that the buff merino had the prospect of another tea-party, and the thought of it made Phoebe forget the annoyances of her home all through the dull Sabbath afternoon, when she could not get away from the family because Emmeline had ordered her to "stay downstairs and mind the baby, and not prance off to her room like a royal lady," and through the trials of Monday with its heavy work, which did not even cease with the washing of the tea things, but continued in the form of a great basket of mending which Emmeline announced at the supper table were "all to be finished and put away that evening." Emmeline seemed to have made up her mind to be as disagreeable as possible. Phoebe sat beside the candle and sewed with weary fingers, and longed to be away from them all where she might think over quietly the pleasant things that had come into her life of late. Hiram Green came in, too, and seemed to have come with a purpose, for he was hardly seated in his usual chair with its back tilted against the wall, and the fore-legs tipped up, when he began with:

"Say, Albert, did you see that nincompoop of a nephew of Judge Bristol in the church? Does beat all how he takes on airs jest because he's been off to college. Gosh! I ken remember him goin' fishin' in his bare feet, and here he was bowin' round among the ladies like he'd always been a fine gentleman and never done a stroke of work in his life. His hands are ez white and soft ez a woman's. He strikes me very ladylike, indeed, he does. Smirkin round and takin' off his hat ez if he'd nothin' better to do. Fine feathers don't make fine birds, I say. I don't believe he could cut a swath o' hay now to save his precious little life. He makes me sick with his airs. Seems like Miss Janet better look after him ef she expects to marry him, er he'll lose his head to every girl he meets."

Something uncontrollable seemed to have stolen the blood out of Phoebe's heart for a moment, and all her strength was slipping away from her. Then a mighty anger rolled through her being, and surged to her very finger tips, yet she held those fingers steadily, as her needle pierced back and forth through the stocking she was darning with unnecessary care. She knew perfectly well that these remarks were entirely for her benefit and she resolved not to let Hiram see that she understood or cared.

"Is he going to marry his cousin Janet?" asked Albert interestedly. "I never heard that."

"You didn't? Well, where've you ben, all these years? It's ben common talk sence they was little tads. Their mothers 'lowed that was the way it was to be, and they was sent away to separate schools on that account; I s'pose they was afraid they'd take a dislike to each other ef they saw each other constant. 'Pon my word I think Janet could look higher, an' ef I was her I wouldn't be held by no promise of no dead mothers. But they do say she worships the very ground he walks on, an' she'll hold him to all right enough, so its no sort o' use fer any other girls to go anglin' after him."

"I heard he was real bright," said Albert, genially. "They say he's taken honors, a good many of 'em. He was president of the Philomathean Society in Union College, you know, and that's a great honor."

Albert read a good deal, and knew more about the world's affairs than Hiram.

"Oh, bah! That's child's play!" sneered Hiram. "Who couldn't be president of a literary society? It don't take much spunk to preside. I take it I ran the town meeting last year 'bout's well 's ef I'd ben a college president. My opinion is Nate Graham would 'v 'mounted to more ef he'd stayed t' home an' learned farmin', 'er studied law with his uncle an' worked fer his board. A feller thet's all give over to lyin' around makin' nuthin' of himself don't amount to a row o' pins."

"But they say Dr. Nott thinks he's got brains," persisted Albert. "I'm sure I'd like to see him come out on top. I heard he was studying law in New York now. He was always a pleasant-spoken boy when he was here."

"What's pleasant speakin'!" growled Hiram. "It can't sell a load o' wheat." His unsold wheat was bitterly in his thoughts.

"Well, I don't know 'bout that, Hiram." Albert felt pleasantly argumentative. "I don't know but if I was going to buy wheat I'd a little sooner buy off the man that was pleasant spoken than the man that wasn't."

Hiram sat glumly and pondered this saying for a few minutes, and Phoebe took advantage of the pause in conversation to lay down her work-basket, determinedly saying to Emmeline:

"I'll finish these stockings tomorrow, Emmeline. I feel tired and I'm going upstairs."

It was the first time that Phoebe had ever dared to take a stand against Emmeline's orders. Emmeline was too astonished to speak for a minute, but just as Phoebe reached the door she said:

"Well, really! Tired! I was down half an hour before you this mornin', and I'm not tired to speak of, but I suppose ef I was I'd have to keep right on. And who's to do your work tomorrow mornin' while you do this, I'd like to know?"

But Phoebe had escaped out of hearing, and Emmeline relapsed into vexed silence. Hiram, however, narrowed his cruel little eyes, and thought he understood why she had gone.

Chapter 9

Phoebe had pondered much on how she should announce her intended absence that afternoon, almost deciding at one time to slip away without saying a word, but her conscientious little heart would not allow that. So while the family were at breakfast she said to Emmeline:

"I wish you'd tell me what work you want done besides the rest of the ironing. I'm invited out to tea this afternoon, and I want to get everything done this morning."

"Where to?" exploded Alma, her curiosity getting the better of her superiority to her aunt for once.

"Indeed!" said Emmeline, disdainfully. "Invited out to tea! What airs we are takin' on with our money! Pretty soon you won't have any time to give at home at all. If I was you I'd go and board somewhere, you have so many social engagements. I'm sure I don't feel like askin' a young lady like you to soil her hands washin' my dishes. I'll wash 'em myself after this. Alma, you go get your apern on and help ma this mornin'. Aunt Phoebe hasn't got time. She'll have to take all mornin' to curl her hair."

"Now, Emmeline!" said Albert, gently reproachful, "don't tease the child. It's real nice for her to get invited out. She don't get much change, that's sure."

"Oh, no, two tea-parties inside of a week's nothin'. I've heard of New York ladies goin' out as often as every other day," said Emmeline, sarcastically.

Albert never could quite understand his wife's sarcasm, so he turned to Phoebe and voiced the question that the rest were just bursting with curiosity to have answered.

"Who invited you, Phoebe?"

"Mrs. Spafford," said Phoebe, trying not to show how near she was to crying over Emmeline's hateful speeches.

"Well, now, that's real nice," said Albert, in genuine earnest. "There isn't a finer man in town than David Spafford. His paper's the best edited in the whole state of New York, and he's got a fine little wife. I don't believe she's many days older than you are, Phoebe, either. She looked real young when he brought her here, and she hasn't grown a day older that I can see."

"Good reason why," sniffed Emmeline; "she's nothin' to do but lie around and be waited on. I'm sure Phoebe's welcome to such friends if they suit her; fer my part I'd ruther go to see good self-respectin' women that did a woman's work in the world, and not let their husbands make babies of them, and go ridin' round in a carriage forever lookin' like a June mornin'. I call it *lazy*, I do. It's nothing' more'n or less — and she keepin' that poor good-fer-nothin' Miranda

Griscom slavin' from mornin' to night fer her. If Phoebe was my sister I
shouldn't choose such friends fer her. Besides, she hasn't got very good manners
not to invite your wife, too, Albert Deane, but I suppose you never thought o'
that. I shouldn't think Phoebe would care to accept an invitation that was an
insult to her relations, even if they wasn't just blood relations — they're all she's
got, that's sure."

"Say, look here, Emmeline. Your speech don't hang together. You just said
you didn't care to make friends of Mrs. Spafford, and now you're fussing because
she didn't invite you, too. It looks like a case of sour grapes. Eh, Phoebe?"

Hank caught the joke and laughed uproariously, though Phoebe looked
grave, knowing how bitter it would be to Emmeline to be laughed at. Two red
spots flamed out on the wife's cheeks, and her eyes snapped.

"Seems to me things has gone pretty far, Albert Deane," she said, in a high,
excited voice, "when you — *YOU* — can insult your wife in public, and then
LAUGH! I shan't forget this of you, Albert Deane!" and with her head well up
she shoved her chair back from the table and left the room, closing the door
with loud decision behind her.

Albert's merry laugh came to an abrupt end. He looked after his wife with
startled surprise. Never in all their one-sidedly-harmonious wedded life had
Emmeline taken offence like that in the presence of others. He looked helplessly, inquiringly, from one to another.

"Well, now!" he began, aimlessly. "You don't suppose she thought I meant
that, do you?"

"'Course!" said Alma, knowingly. "You've made her dreadful mad, pa.
My! But you're goin' to get it!"

"Looks mighty like it," snickered Hank.

Albert continued to look at Phoebe for a reply.

"I'm afraid she thought you were in earnest, Albert. You better go and
explain," said Phoebe, commiseratingly.

"You better not go fer a while, pa," called out Johnny, sympathetically.
"Wait till she gets over it a little. Go hide in the barn. That's the way I do!"

But Albert was going heavily up the stairs after his offended wife and did
not hear his young hopeful's voice. Albert was tender-hearted and could not
bear to hurt any one's feelings. Besides, it never was pleasant to have Emmeline
angry. He wished if possible to explain away the offence before it struck in too
deep for healing and had to be lived down.

This state of things was rather more helpful to Phoebe than otherwise.
Hank took himself off, finding a certain embarrassment in Phoebe's dignified
silence. The children slipped away, glad to get rid of any little duties usually
required by their mother. Phoebe went at her work unhindered and it vanished
before her while her thoughts took happy flight away from the unhappy home
to the afternoon that was before her. Upstairs the conference was long and

uncertain. Phoebe could hear the low rumbling of Albert's conciliatory tones, and the angry rasp of Emmeline's tearful charges. Albert came downstairs looking sad and tired about an hour before dinnertime, and hurried out to the barn to his neglected duties. He paused in the kitchen to say to Phoebe, apologetically:

"You mustn't mind what Emmeline says, child. Her bark's a great deal worse than her bite always. And after all, she's had it pretty hard with all the children and staying in so much. I'm sure she appreciates what you do. I'm sure she does, but it isn't her way to say much about it. You just go out to tea and have a good time and don't think any more about this. It'll blow over, you know. Most things do."

Phoebe tried to smile, and felt a throb of gratitude toward the brother who was not really her brother at all.

"You're a good girl, Phoebe," he went on, patting her cheek. "You're like your mother. She was little, and pretty, and liked things nice, and had a quiet voice. I sometimes think maybe it isn't as pleasant here for you as it might be. You're made of different kind of stuff, that thinks and feels in a different way. Your mother was so. I've oftened wondered whether father understood her. Men don't understand women very well, I guess. Now, I don't really always understand Emmeline, and I guess it's pretty hard for her. Father was some rough and blunt, and maybe that was hard for your mother at times. I remember she used to look sad, though I never saw her much, come to think about it. I was off working for myself when they were married, you know. Say, Phoebe, you didn't for a minute think I meant what I said about sour grapes and Emmeline, did you? I told her you didn't, but I promised her I'd make sure about it. I knew you didn't. Well, I must go out and see if Hank's done everything."

He went out drawing a long breath as if he had accomplished an unpleasant task, and left Phoebe wondering about her own mother, and trying to get a little glimpse into her possible sorrows and joys through the words that Albert had spoken. Somehow that sentence in her birthday letter came back to her: "Unless you can marry a man to whom you can look up and honor next to God it is better not to marry at all, believe your mother, child. I say it lovingly, for I have seen much sorrow and would protect you."

Had her father been hard to live with? Phoebe put the thought from her and was half glad she could not answer it. Her own life was enough of a problem without going back and sorrowing for her mother's. But it made her heart throb with a sense of a fuller understanding of her mother's life and warnings.

Emmeline did not come downstairs until dinnertime, and her manner was freezing. Phoebe was glad that the work was all done carefully, even to the scrubbing of the back steps, and that the dinner was more than usually inviting. But Emmeline seemed not to see anything, and her manner remained as severe as when she first entered the kitchen. She poured the coffee, and drank a cup of it herself, and ate a bit of bread, but would not touch anything else on the table. She waited on the children with ostentatious care, but would not respond to the solicitations of her anxious husband, who urged this and that dainty upon her. Hank even suggested that the hot biscuits were nicer than usual. But that remark had to be lived down by Hank, for Emmeline usually made the biscuits, and Phoebe had made these. She did not condescend to even look at him in response.

Phoebe was glad when the last bit of pumpkin pie and cheese had disappeared and she could rise from her chair and go about the after-dinner work. Glad, too, that Emmeline went away again and left her to herself, for so she could more quickly finish up.

She was just hanging up her wiping towels when Emmeline came downstairs with the look of a martyr on her face, and the quilting frames in her hand. Over her shoulder was thrown her latest achievement in patchwork, a brilliant combination of reds and yellows and white known as the "rising sun" pattern. It was a large quilt, and would be quite a job to put on the frames. It was a herculean task for one person without an assistant.

Phoebe stopped with an exclamation of dismay.

"You're not going to put that on the frames today, Emmeline? I thought you were saving that for next month!"

Emmeline's grim mouth remained shut for several seconds. At last she snapped out: "I don't know that it makes any difference what you thought. This is a free country and I've surely a right to do what I please in my own house."

"But, Emmeline, I can't help you this afternoon!"

"I don't know that I've asked you!"

"But you can't do it alone!"

"Indeed! What makes you think I can't! Go right along to your tea-party and take your ease. I was brought up to work, thank fortune, and a few burdens more or less can't make much difference. I'm not a lady of leisure and means like you."

Phoebe stood a minute watching Emmeline's stubby, determined fingers as they fitted a wooden peg into its socket like a period to the conversation. It seemed dreadful to go away and leave Emmeline to put up that quilt alone, but what was she to do? There seemed to be no law in the universe that would compel her to give up her first invitation out to tea in order that Emmeline might finish that quilt this particular week. It was plain that she had brought it down on purpose to hold her at home. Indignation boiled within her. If she had slipped stealthily away this would not have happened, but she had done her duty in telling Emmeline, and she felt perfectly justified in going. It wasn't as if she had invited herself. It would not be polite, now she had accepted the invitation, not to go. So, with sudden determination Phoebe left the kitchen and went up to dress.

With swift fingers she fastened the buff merino, put her hair in order, and tied on her locket, but nowhere was the little brown velvet bow to be found that belonged to her hair. She had not missed it before, for on Sunday she had worn her bonnet, and had dressed in a hurry. In perplexity she looked over her neat boxes of scant finery, but could not find it. She had to hurry away without it. She went out the other door, for she could not bear the sight of Emmeline putting up that sunrise bedquilt all alone. The thought of it seemed to cloud the sun and spoil anticipation of her precious afternoon.

Once out in the crisp autumn air she drew a long breath of relief. It was so good to get away from the gloomy atmosphere that had been cramping her life for so many years. In a lonely place in the road between farm-houses she uttered a soft little scream under her breath. She felt as if she *must* do something to let out the agony of wrath and longing and hurt and indignity that were trying to burst her soul. Then she walked on to the town with demure dignity, and the people in the passing carryalls and farm wagons never suspected that she was aught but a happy maiden with thoughts busy with the joys of life.

The autumn days were lingering in sunny deep-blue haze, though the reds were changing into brown, and in the fields were gathering huddled groups of cornshocks like old crones, waving skeleton arms in the breeze, and whispering weird gossip. A rusty-throated cricket in the thicket by the way piped out his monotonous dirge to the summer now deceased. A flight of birds sprang into sight across the sky, calling and chattering to one another of a warmer climate. An old red cow stood in her well-grazed meadow, snuffed the short grass, and, looking at Phoebe as she passed, bawled a gentle protest at the decline of fresh vegetables. Everything spoke of autumn and the winter that was to come. But Phoebe, every step she took from home, grew lighter and lighter hearted, and could only think of the happy time she was to have.

It was not that she was thinking of the stranger, for there was no possibility of meeting him. The Bristol place, a fine old Colonial house behind a tall white fence and high privet hedge with a glimpse of a wonderful garden set off with dark borders of box through the imposing gateway, was over near the Presbyterian church. It was not near the Spaffords' house. She felt the freer and happier because there was no question of him to trouble her careful conscience.

Miranda had gone to the window that looked up the road towards the Deanes at least twenty times since the dinner dishes were washed. She was more nervous over the success of this her first tea-party than over anything she had ever done. She was beginning to be afraid that her guest would not arrive.

Everything was in train for supper. There was to be stewed chicken, with "riz biscuits" and honey, raspberry preserves, spiced peaches, fruitcake and caraway-seed cookies with delectable sugary tops. The tea was to be served in the very thinnest of the blue china cups. It was with difficulty that Marcia had suppressed a multitude of varieties of pickles and jellies and preserves and cakes, for Miranda could not understand why it wasn't "skimpin'" to have so few dishes upon the table.

"Gran'ma was never half satisfied ef you could see the tablecloth much between the dishes," she was wont to say, dubiously. But Marcia tried patiently to explain that it was not refined to load the table with too many varieties, and Miranda, half convinced, gave it up, thinking Marcia sweet, but "inexperienced."

Miranda, fidgeting from window to door and back again to the kitchen, came at last to the library where sat Marcia with her work, watching a frolic between Rose and her kitten outside the window.

"Say, Mrs. Marcia," she began, ingratiatingly, "you'll find out what troubles that poor little thing, and see ef you can't help her, won't you? She's your size an' kind, more'n she is mine, an' you ought to be able to give her some help. You needn't think you've got to tell out to me every thing you find out. I shan't ask. I can find out enough fer my own use when

I'm needed, but I think she needs you this time. When there's any use fer me I seem always to kind o' feel it in the air."

"Bless your heart, Miranda, I don't believe you care for any one unless they need helping!" exclaimed Marcia, laughing. "What makes you so sure Phoebe Deane needs helping?"

"Oh, I know," said Miranda, mysteriously, "an' so will you when you look at her real hard. There she comes now. Don't you go an' tell I said nothing 'bout her. You jes' make her tell you. She's that sweet an' so are you that you two can't help pourin' out your perfume to each other like two flowers."

"But trouble isn't perfume, Miranda."

"H'm! Flowers smells all the sweeter when you crush 'em a little, don't they? There, you set right still where you be. I'll go to the door. Don't you stir. I want her to see you lookin' that way with the sun across the top o' your pretty hair. She'll like it, I know she will."

Marcia sat quite still as she was bidden with the madonna smile upon her lips that David loved so well, smiling over Miranda's strange fancies, yet never thinking of herself as a picture against the window-panes. In a moment more Phoebe Deane stood in the doorway, with Miranda beside her, looking from one to another of the two sweet girl-faces in deep admiration, and noting with delight that Phoebe fully appreciated the loveliness of her "Mrs. Marcia."

Chapter 10

The afternoon was one of unalloyed bliss to Phoebe. She laid aside her troubles with her bonnet and mantilla, and basked in the sunlight of Marcia's smile. Here was something she had never known, the friendship of another girl not much older than herself; for Marcia, though she had grown in heart and intellect during her five years of beautiful companionship with David Spafford, had not lost the years she had skipped by her early marriage, but kept their memory fresh in her heart. Perhaps it was the girl in her that had attracted her to Phoebe Deane.

They fell into happy converse at once, Phoebe begging for a seam to sew on the frock of pale blue merino that Marcia was making for Rose, all exquisitely braided with white silk braid in a rosebud pattern.

They talked about their mothers, these two who had known so little of real mothering; and Marcia, because she had felt it herself, understood the wistfulness in Phoebe's tone when she spoke of her loneliness and her longing for her mother. Then Phoebe, with a half-apologetic flush, told of her mother's birthday letter and the buff merino, and Marcia smoothed down the soft folds of the skirt reverently, half wistfully, and told Phoebe it was beautiful, just like a present and a letter from heaven. Then she kissed her gently and made her come out where little Rose was playing. There they frolicked until the child was Phoebe's devoted slave, and then they all went back to the big stately parlor, where Miranda had a great fire of logs blazing, and there in a deep easy chair Phoebe was ensconced with Rose cuddled in her lap playing with her locket, and having it tied at will about her own dimpled neck.

While this was going on Marcia played exquisite music on her panioforte, which to the ear of the girl, who had seldom heard any music in her life save the singing in church or singing-school, seemed entrancing. She almost forgot the charming child in her lap, forgot to look about on the beautiful room so full of interesting things, forgot even to think, as she listened, and her very soul responded to the music, which seemed to be calling a great comfort across the immense distances that separated her from things she loved.

Then suddenly the music ceased and Marcia sprang up, saying in a glad voice, "Oh, there is David!" and went to the door to let him in.

Phoebe exclaimed in dismay that it was so late, and the beautiful afternoon was at an end, but she forgot her disappointment in wonder over Marcia's joy at her husband's coming. It brought back to her the subject that had been uppermost in her thoughts ever since the night when Hiram Green had dared to follow her to the orchard. Somehow she had grown up with very little halo about the institution of marriage. It had seemed to her a kind of necessary arrangement, but never anything that gave great joy. The married people whom she knew did not seem greatly to rejoice in one another's presence. Indeed, they often seemed to be a hindrance each to the other. She had never cherished many bright dreams of any such state for herself, as most girls do. Life had been too dully tinted since her little girlhood for her to indulge fancies. Therefore it was a revelation to her to see how much these two rare souls cared for one another. It was not that they displayed their affection by any act of endearment, but she saw it in the glance of each, in a sudden lighting of the eye, the involuntary cadence of the voice, the evident pleasure of yielding each to the other, aye, rather preferring one another; the constant presence of joy as a guest in that house, because of the presence of the other. One could never feel that way about Hiram Green — no one could, — it would be impossible! Wait! Had not that been the very thing possessed by his poor crushed little wife? But how could she feel it when it was not returned? She began to think over the married households she knew, but then she knew so few of them intimately. There was Granny McVane. Did the old 'Squire feel so about her? And did she spring to meet him at the door after all these years of life with its hardness? There was something about the sweet meek face in its ruffled cap that made Phoebe think it possible. And there was Albert. Of course Emmeline did not feel so, for Emmeline was not that kind of a woman, but might not a different woman have felt that for Albert? He was kind and gentle to women. Too slow and easy to gain real respect, yet — yes, she felt that it might be possible for some women to feel real joy in his presence. There lurked a possibility that he felt so toward Emmeline, in some degree; but Hiram Green, with his chair tilted back against the wall, and his hat drawn down over his narrow eyes, above his cruel mouth! Never! He was utterly incapable of so beautiful a feeling. If he only might in some way pass out of her horizon forever it would be a great relief.

David Spafford when he entered the parlor not only filled it with pleasure for his wife and little girl, but he brought an added cheer for the guest as well, and Phoebe found herself talking with this man of literature and politics and science as easily as if she had known him well all her life. Afterward she wondered at herself for it. Somehow he took it for granted that she knew as much as he did, and made her feel at her ease at once. He had ready a bright story from the newspaper office that exactly fitted someone's remark, and a joke for his little one. He asked after Albert Deane as though he were an old friend, and seemed to know more about him than Phoebe dreamed. "He has a good head," he added in response to Phoebe's timid answer about the farm and some improvements that Albert had introduced. "I had a long talk with him the other day and enjoyed it." Somehow that little remark made Phoebe more at home. She knew Albert's short-comings keenly herself, and she was not deeply attached to him, yet he was all she had, and he had been kind to her. He stood for relatives to her before the world, and it was nice to not have him at a discount, even though there were some men brighter, and Phoebe knew it.

Miranda had just called to supper, and they had reached the table, and the little preliminary flutter of getting settled in the right places, when the knocker sounded through the hall.

Phoebe looked up, startled! Living as she did in the country a guest who was not intimate enough to walk in without knocking was rare, and an occasion for the knocker to sound was wont to bring forth startled exclamations in the Deane family. But Marcia give the sign to be seated, and Miranda hastened to the door.

"It's just one of the boys from the office, I think, Marcia," said David Spafford. "I told him to bring up the mail if anything important came. The coach wasn't in when I left."

But a man's voice was heard conversing with Miranda.

"I won't keep him but a minute! I'm sorry to disturb him." A moment more and Miranda appeared with a guileless face.

"A man to see you, Mr. Spafford. I think it's that nevview of Jedge Bristol's. Shall I tell him you're eatin' supper?"

"What! Nathaniel Graham? No indeed, Miranda; just put on another plate and bring him right in. Come in, Nathaniel, and take tea with us while you tell your errand. You're just the one we need to complete our company."

Miranda, innocent and cheerful, hurried away to obey orders, while David helped the willing guest off with his overcoat, and brought him out to the table. She felt there was no need to say anything of a little conversation she had held with Judge Bristol's "nevview" about half past four that afternoon. It was while Marcia was playing the pianoforte in the parlor. Miranda had gone into the garden to pick a bunch of parsley for her chicken gravy, and as was her wont, to keep a good watch upon all outlying territory. She had sauntered up to the fence for a glance about to see if there was anything of interest happening, and Nathaniel Graham had happened. She had watched him coming, wistfully. Yet she dared not add another guest to her tea-party, though the very one she would have chosen had wandered her way.

He had tipped his hat to her and smiled. Miranda liked to have hats tipped to her even though she was freckled and red-haired. This young man had been in the highest grade of village school when she entered the lowest class, yet he remembered her enough to bow, freckled though she was, and working for her living. Her heart had swelled with pride in him, and she decided he would do for the part she wished him to play in life.

"Ah, Miss Miranda," he had paused when almost past, and stepped back a pace, "do you happen to know if Mr. Spafford will be at home this evening? I want to see him very much for a few minutes."

Now, though Miranda had dared not invite another guest, she saw no reason why she should not put him in the way of an invitation, so inclining her head thoughtfully on one side and squinting her eyes introspectively, as if she were the keeper of David Spafford's engagements, she had said, thoughtfully: "Let me see! Yes, I *think* he's at home tonight. Thur's one night this week I heerd him say he was goin' out, but I'm *pretty* sure it ain't this night. But I'll tell you what you better do ef you're real anxious to see him, you better jest stop 'long about six o'clock. He's always home then, 'thout fail, 'n' he'll tell you ef he ain't goin' to be in."

The young man's face had lighted gratefully.

"Thank you," he had said, quite as if he were speaking to a lady Miranda thought, "that will suit me very well. I need not keep him long and he can tell me if he will be in later in the evening. I shall be passing here about that time."

Then Miranda had hustled in with satisfaction to see if her biscuits were beginning to brown. If this plan worked well there was nothing further to be desired.

She had spent the remainder of the afternoon in stealthily vibrating between the kitchen and the parlor door, where, unseen, she could inspect the conversation from time to time and keep advised as to any possible developments. She had set out to see if Phoebe Deane needed any help, and she meant to leave no stone unturned to get at the facts.

So it all happened just as Miranda would have planned. Things were happening her way these days, mostly, she told herself with a chuckle and a triumphant glance over the lights in her grandmother's kitchen, as she went to get another sprigged plate for Nathaniel Graham. And when Marcia was not looking she slid another plate of quivering jelly, amber tinted to match Phoebe's frock, in between Phoebe's and Nathaniel's plates.

Meantime Phoebe's heart was in a great flutter over the introduction to her knight of the forest. The pretty color came into her cheeks, and her eyes shone like stars in the candle light as David said: "Nathaniel, let me make you acquainted with our friend Miss Phoebe Deane. I think she is a newcomer since you left us. Miss Deane, this is our friend Mr. Graham."

And then she found herself murmuring an acknowledgment as the young man took her hand and bowed low over it, saying: "Thank you, David, but I am not so far behind the times as you think. I have met Miss Deane before." That frightened her quite, so that she hardly could manage to seat herself with her chair properly drawn up to the table, and she fell to wondering if they had noticed how her cheeks burned. Ah! If they had they were keeping it to themselves, especially Miranda, who was dishing up the chicken. Wily Miranda! She had called them to supper without dishing it up, making due allowance for the digression of another guest which she had planned.

The meal moved along quite smoothly, the conversation flowing easily around until Phoebe had regained her balance and could take her small shy part in it. She found pleasure in listening to the talk of David and Nathaniel, so different from that of Albert and Hiram.

It was all about the great outside world. Politics, and the possibilities of war; money and banks and failures, and the probabilities of the future; the coming election and the part it would have in the finance of the world; the trouble with the Indians; the rumblings of trouble about slavery; the annexation of Texas; the extension of the steam railway, and its hindrances by the present state of finance.

It was all new and interesting to Phoebe, to whom had come but a stray word now and again of all these wonderful happenings. Who, for instance, was this "Santa Anna" whose name was spoken of so familiarly? Neither a saint nor a woman, apparently. And what had he or she to do with affairs so grave?

And who was this brave Indian chief, Osceola, languishing in prison because he and his people could not bear to give up the home of their fathers? Why had she never heard of it all before? O, life was very hard for everybody. She had never thought of the Indians before as anything but terrible, bloodthirsty savages, and lo! they had feelings and loves and homes like others. Her cheeks glowed and her eyes were alight with feeling, and when young Nathaniel turned to her now and again he thought how wondrously beautiful she was, and marvelled that he had not heard her praises rung from every mouth so soon as he had reached the town. He had been very little at home during his college life and years of law study.

Then the conversation came nearer home, and David and Nathaniel talked of their college days. Nathaniel spoke a great deal of Eliphalet Nott, the honored president of his college, and told many a little anecdote of his wisdom and wit.

"This chicken reminds me," he began, laughingly, as he held up a delicate wishbone toward Phoebe, "of a story that is told of Dr. Nott. It seems a number of students had planned a raid upon his chicken-house. Dr. Nott's family consists of himself and wife and his daughter Miss Sally. Well, the rumor of this plot against his chickens reached the good president's ears, and he prepared to circumvent it.

"The students had planned to go to a tree where it was known that several favorite fowls roosted, and one was to climb up while the others stood below and took the booty. They waited until it was late, and the lights in the doctor's study went out, and then they stole silently into the yard and made for the hen-roost. The man who was to catch the chickens climbed carefully, silently, into the tree so as not to disturb the sleeping birds, and the others waited in the dark below.

"The first hen made a good deal of cackling and fuss as she was caught and while this was going on the students below the tree saw some one approaching them from the house. Very silently they scattered into the dark and fled, leaving the poor man in the tree alone. Dr. Nott, well muffled about his face, came quietly up and took his stand below the tree, and in a moment the man in the tree handed down a big white rooster.

"'This is Daddy Nott,' he said, in a whisper, and the man below received the bird without a word.

"In a moment more a second fowl was handed down. 'This is Mammy Nott,' whispered the irreverent student. Again the bird was received without comment. Then a third hen was handed down with the comment: 'This is Sally Nott.' The Doctor received the third bird and disappeared into the darkness and the student in the tree came down to find his partners fled, with no knowledge of who had taken the fowls. They were much troubled about the circumstance, but hoped that it was only a joke some fellow student had played upon them. They were however extremely anxious the next day when each one concerned in the affair received an invitation to dine with Dr. Nott that evening. Not daring to refuse, nor being able to find any suitable excuse, they presented themselves dubiously at Dr. Nott's house at the appointed hour, and were received courteously as usual. They were beginning to breathe more freely when they were ushered out to dinner, and there, before the Doctor's place, lay three large platters, each containing a fine fowl cooked to a turn. They dared not look at one another, but their embarrassment came to a climax when Dr. Nott looked up pleasantly at the student on his right, who had been the man to climb the tree, and asked, 'Hastings, will you have a piece of Daddy Nott, or Mommy Nott, or Sally Nott?' pointing in order to each platter. I think if it hadn't been for the twinkle in the Doctor's eye those boys would have taken their hats and left without making any adieus, for they say Hastings looked as if you could knock him over with a feather, but that twinkle broke the horror of it, and they all broke down and laughed until they were most heartily ashamed of themselves, and every man there was cured forever of robbing chicken-roosts. But do you know, the Doctor never said another word to those fellows about that, and they were his most loyal students from that time on."

Amid the laughter over this story they rose from the table. Little Rose, who had fallen asleep at the table, was whisked off to bed by the faithful Miranda, and the others went into the parlor where Marcia played exquisite melodies as David and Nathaniel called for them, and Phoebe, entranced, listened, and did not know how her charmed day was spending itself, until suddenly she realized that it was half past eight o'clock and she was some distance from home.

Now, for a maiden to be abroad after nine o'clock in those days was little short of a crime. It would be deemed most highly improper and disreputable by every good person; therefore, as Phoebe noted the time by the great clock she started to her feet in a panic and made her adieus with haste. Marcia went after her bonnet, and tied it lovingly beneath her chin, kissing her and saying she hoped to have her come again soon. David made as if he would take her home, but Nathaniel waved him back and begged for that privilege himself, and so with happy good-nights the young man and the maiden went out into the quiet village street together and hastened along the way, where already many of the lights were out in the houses and the inhabitants gone to sleep.

Chapter 11

Phoebe's heart, as she stepped out into the moonlight with the young man, fluttered so she scarcely could speak without letting her voice shake. It seemed so wonderful that she, of all the girls in the village, should be going home with this bright, handsome, noble man. There was nothing foolish or vain in her thought about it. He was not to be anything more to her for this walk, for his life was set otherwise, and he belonged to others — notably, in all likelihood, to his cousin Janet. Nevertheless she felt highly honored that he should take the trouble to see her home, and she knew in her heart that the memory of this walk, her first alone with a young man who was not her brother, would remain long a pleasant spot in her life.

He seemed to enjoy her company as much as he had done David's, for he talked on about the things that had interested them in the evening. He told more college stories, and spoke of his literary society, so that Phoebe, remembering Albert's words, asked if it was true that he had once been president of the Philomatheans, and he modestly acknowledged it, as though the office gave him honor, not he the office. She asked him shyly of the meetings and what they did and he gave her reminiscences of his college days. Their voices rang out now and then in a merry laugh, whereat all the little cornshock ladies huddled in the moonlight seemed to wave sinister arms and shake their heads mournfully to hear mirth at so unseemly an hour. Out in the quiet country road the young man suddenly asked her:

"Tell me, Miss Deane, suppose I knew of some people who were oppressed, suffering, and wanted their freedom; suppose they needed help to set them free, what do you think I ought to do? Think of myself and my career, or go and help set them free?"

Phoebe raised her sweet eyes to his earnest face in the moonlight and tried to understand.

"I am not wise," she said, "and perhaps I would not know what you ought to do, but I think I can tell you what you *would* do. I think you would forget all about yourself and go to set those people free."

He looked down into her face, and thought what it meant to a man to have a girl like this one believe in him.

"Thank you!" he said gravely. "I am honored by your opinion of me. You have told me where duty lies. I will remember your words when the time comes."

In the quiet of her chamber a few minutes later Phoebe remembered the words of the young people that day upon the hill-side, and wondered if it were the people of Texas whom he meant needed to be set free.

He had bade her good-night with a pleasant ring in his voice, saying he was glad to know her, and hoped to see her again before he left for New York, which would be in a few days. Then the door closed behind her and he walked briskly down the frosty way. The night was cold even for October, and each startled blade of grass was furred with a tiny frost-spike.

Suddenly, out from behind a cluster of tall elder bushes that bordered the roadside stepped a man, and without warning dealt him a blow between his eyes that made him stagger and almost fall.

"Thet's to teach you to let my girl alone!" snarled Hiram Green like an angry dog, and the moonlight made his face look fairly livid with unholy wrath. "Hev yeh learned yer lesson, er d'yeh need another? 'Cause there's plenty more where that come from!"

Nathaniel's senses had almost deserted him for an instant, but he was master of the art of self-defence, and before the bully had finished his threat with a curse he found himself lying in the ditch with Nathaniel towering over him in righteous wrath.

"Coward," he said, looking down on him contemptuously, "you have made a mistake, of course, and struck the wrong man, but that makes no difference. A brave man does not strike in the dark."

"No, I haven't made no mistake, either," snarled Hiram, as he got up angrily from the ground. "I seen you myself with my own eyes, Nate Graham. I seen you trail down the hill out o' the woods after her, 'n I seen you try to get a kiss from her, an' she run away. I was an eye-witness. *I* seen yeh. Then you tried to get 'longside her after meetin' was out Sunday, tippin' yer hat so polite, as ef that was everythin' a girl wanted; an' I seen yeh takin' her home tonight after decent folks was a-bed, walkin' 'long a country road talkin' so sweet an' low butter wouldn't melt in yer mouth. No, sir! I ain't made no mistake. An' I jest want you to understand after this you're not to meddle with Phoebe Deane, for *she belongs to me!*"

By this time Nathaniel had recognized Hiram Green, and his astonishment and dismay knew no bounds. Could it be possible that a girl like that had aught to do in any way with this coarse, ignorant man? Indignation filled him. He longed to pound the insolent wretch before him and make him take back all he had said, but he realized that this might be a serious matter for the young girl, and it was necessary to proceed cautiously, therefore he drew himself up haughtily and replied:

"There has never been anything between myself and Miss Deane to which any one, no matter how close their relationship to her might be could object. I met her in the woods while nutting with a party of friends, and had the good fortune to help her out of a tangle of laurel that had caught in her hair, and to show her the short cut to the road. I merely spoke to her on Sunday as I spoke to my other acquaintances, and this evening I have been escorting her home from the house of a friend where we have both been taking tea."

"You lie!" snarled Hiram.

"What did I understand you to say, Mr. Green?"

"It don't make any matter what you understood me to say. I *said* YOU LIE, an' I'll say it again, too, ef I like. You needn't git off any more o' your fine words, fer they don't go down with me, even ef you have been to college. All I've got to say is *YOU LET MY GIRL ALONE FROM NOW ON!* D'yeh understand that? Ef yeh don't I'll take means to make ye!" And Hiram's big fist was raised threateningly again.

But somehow the next instant Hiram was sprawling in the dust, and this time Nathaniel held something gleaming and sinister in his hand as he stood above him.

"I always go armed," said Nathaniel, in a cool voice. "You will oblige me by lying still where you are until I am out of sight down the road. Then it will be quite safe for you to rise to go home and wash you face. If I see you get up before that I shall shoot. Another thing. If I hear another word of this ridiculous nonsense from you I will have you arrested and brought before my uncle on charge of assault, and blackmail, and several other things perhaps. As for speaking to the young lady in question, or showing her any courtesy whatever that is ordinarily shown between young men and women in good society, that shall be as Miss Deane says, and not in any way as you say. You are not fit to speak her name."

Nathaniel stepped back slowly a few paces, and Hiram attempted to rise, pouring forth a volley of oaths and vile language. Nathaniel halted and raised the pistol, flashing in the moonlight.

"You will keep entirely still, Mr. Green. Remember that this is loaded."

Hiram subsided and Nathaniel walked deliberately backward until the man on the ground could see but a dim speck in the gray of the distance, and a night-hawk in the trees by his home mocked him in a clamorous tone.

Now all this happened not a stone's throw from Albert Deane's front gate, and might almost have been discerned from Phoebe's window if her room had not been upon the other side of the house.

After a little Hiram crawled stiffly up from the ground, looked furtively about, shook his fist menacingly at the distance where the flash of Nathaniel's pistol had disappeared, and slunk like a shadow close to the fence till he reached his house. Presently only a bit of white paper ground down with a great heel-mark, and a few footprints in the frosty dust, told where the encounter had been. The moon spread her obliterating white light over all, and Phoebe slept smiling in her dreams and living over her happy afternoon and evening again. But Nathaniel sat up far into the night till his candle burned low and sputtered out, and even the moon grew weary and bent low. He was thinking, and his thoughts were not all of the oppressed Texans. It had occurred to him that there were other people in the world whom it might be harder to set free than the Texans.

If Hiram Green did not sleep it was because his heart was busy with evil plans for revenge. He was by no means meekly done with Nathaniel Graham. He might submit under necessity, but he was a man in whom a sense of injury dwelt long, and smoldered into a great fire that grew far beyond all proportion of the fancied offence. Hatred and revenge were the ruling passions with him.

But Phoebe slept, and dreamed not that more evil was brewing.

The lights had been out, all save a candle in Emmeline's room, when she came home, but the door was left on the latch for her. She knew Emmeline wished to reprove her for the late hour of her return, and was fully prepared for the greeting next morning, spoken frigidly:

"Oh, so you did come home last night, after all! Or was it this morning? I'm surprised. I thought you had gone for good."

At breakfast things were uncomfortable. Albert persisted in asking Phoebe questions about her tea-party, in spite of Emmeline's disagreeable sarcasms. When Emmeline complained that Phoebe had "sneaked" away without giving her a chance to send for anything to the village, and that she needed thread for her quilting that very morning, Phoebe arose from her almost untasted breakfast and offered to go for it at once.

She stepped into the crisp morning with a sigh of relief, and walked briskly down the road feeling exultantly happy that she had escaped her prison for a little hour of the early freshness. Then she stopped suddenly, for there before her lay a letter ground into the dust, and about the writing there was something strangely familiar, as if she had seen it before, yet it was not anyone's she knew. It was not folded so that the address could be seen, as the manner of letters was in those days of no envelopes, but open and rumpled with the communication uppermost, and the words that stood out clearly to her vision as she stooped to pick it up were these: *It is most important that you present this letter or it will do no good to go but BE SURE THAT NO ONE ELSE SEE IT, or great harm may come to you!*

She turned the paper over with reverent fingers, for a bit of writing was not so common then as now and was treated with far more importance. And there on the other side lay the name that had gleamed at her pleasantly but a few days before through the laurel bushes as she lay in hiding, *Nathaniel Graham, Esq.* Did it look up at her confidingly now as if it would plead to be restored to its owner? Phoebe started at the foolish fancy, and was appalled with her responsibility.

Was this letter but an old one, useless now, and of no value to its owner? Surely it must be, and he had dropped it on his way home with her last night. The wind had blown it open and a passer-by had trodden upon it. That must be the explanation, for surely if it were important he would not have laid it down behind the log so carelessly in keeping of a stranger. Yet there were the words in the letter: *It is most important that you present it when you come.* Well, perhaps he had already "come," wherever that was, and the letter had seen its usefulness and passed out of value. But then it further stated that great harm might come to the owner if any one saw it. She might make sure no one would see it by destroying it, but how was she to know but that she was really destroying an important document? And she might not read further because of that caution, *Be sure that no one else sees it.* A less conscientious soul might not have heeded it, but Phoebe would not have read another word for the world. She felt it was a secret communication to which she had no right, and she must respect it.

More and more as this reasoning became clear to her, she saw that there was only one thing to do, and that was to go at once to the owner and give it to him, telling him that she had not read another word than those she saw at first, and making him understand that not a breath of it would ever pass her lips.

Her troubled gaze saw nothing of the morning beauties. Little jewels gemmed the fringes of the grass along the road, and the dull red and brown leaves that still lingered on their native branches were coated over with silver gauze. It would have given her joy at another time, but now it was as if it was not. She passed by Hiram Green's farm just as he was coming down to his barn near the road. He was in full view, and near enough for recognition. He quickened his pace as he saw her coming in her morning tidiness and beauty. She made a trim and dainty picture. But her eyes were straight ahead and she did not turn her head to look at him. He thought she did it to escape speaking, and he had had it in mind to imitate Nathaniel and call a good-morning. It angered him anew to have her pass him by unseeing, as if he were not good enough to treat with ordinary common politeness as between neighbors at least. If he had needed anything more to justify his heart in its evil plot he had it now. With lowering brow and ugly mien he raised his voice and called unpleasantly:

"Where you goin' this early, Phoebe?" but with her face set straight ahead and eyes that were studying perplexing questions she went on her way and never even heard him. Then the devil entered into Hiram Green.

He waited until she had passed beyond the red school house that marked the boundary line between the village and the country, and then slouched out from the shelter of the barn, and with long dogged steps followed her; keeping his little eyes narrowed and intent upon the blue of her frock in the distance. He would not let her see him, but he meant to know where she was going. She had a letter in her hand as she passed, at least it was a small white article much like a letter. Was she writing his rival a letter already? The thought brought a throb of hate — hate toward the man who was better than he, toward the girl who had scorned him, and toward the whole world, even the little weak caterpillar that crawled in a sickly way across his path which he crushed with an ugly twist of his cruel boot.

Phoebe, all unsuspecting, thinking only of her duty, which was not all a pleasant one to her, went on her way. She felt she must get the letter out of her hands at once before she did anything else, so she turned down the street past the church to the stately house with its white fence and high hedge, and her heart beat fast and hard against her blue print frock. In the presence of the great house she suddenly felt that she was not dressed for such a call, yet she would not turn back, nor even hesitate, for it was something that must be done at once. She gave herself no time for thought of what would be said, but entered the great gate, which to her relief stood open. She held the letter tight in her cold trembling hand. Hiram had arrived at the church corner just in time to see her disappear within the white gates, and his jaw dropped down in astonishment. He had not dreamed she would go to his house. Yet after a moment's thought his eyes narrowed and gleamed with the satisfaction they always showed when he had thought out some theory, or seen through some possibility. The situation was one that was trying for the girl, and the fact of his being an eye-witness might some day give him power over her. He took his stand behind the trunk of a weeping willow tree in the church-yard to see what might happen.

Meantime Phoebe raised the great brass knocker held in the mouth of a lion. She felt as if all lions of the earth were come to meet her at this threshold, and her heart was beating in her throat now, so that she could scarcely speak. How hollow the sound of the knocker was as it reverberated through the great hall, not at all the cheerful thing it had been when Nathaniel knocked at Mrs. Spafford's door. A plump black woman in a large yellow turban and white apron opened the door, and was even more formidable than some of the family whom she had expected to meet might have been. She managed to ask if Mr. Graham were in.

"Missis Gra'm! Dere ain't no Missis Gra'm," ejaculated the old woman, looking her over carefully and it must be admitted rather scornfully. The young ladies who came to that house to visit did not dress as Phoebe was dressed just then, in working garb. "Dere's only jes' Mis' Brist'l. Mis' Janet, we calls her."

"Mr. Graham. Mr. Nathaniel Graham," corrected Phoebe, in trepidation. She thought she felt a rebuke in the black woman's words that she should call to see a young man. "I have a message for him," she added, bravely. "I will wait here, please. No, I'd rather not come in."

"I'll call Miss Janet," said the servant briefly, and swept away, closing the door with a bang in Phoebe's face.

She waited several minutes before it was opened again, this time by Janet Bristol.

Chapter 12

"You wished to see me?" questioned the tall, handsome girl in the doorway, scrutinizing Phoebe haughtily. There was nothing encouraging in her attitude.

"I wished to see Mr. Graham," said Phoebe, trying to look as if it were quite the natural thing for a young woman to call on a young man of a morning.

"I thought you had a message for him," said Janet sharply. She was wondering what business this very pretty girl could possibly have with her cousin.

"Yes, I have a message for him, but I must give it to him, if you please," she said with gentle emphasis. She lifted her eyes, and Janet could not help noticing the lovely face, and the beauty of the smile.

"Well, that will not be possible, for he is not here." Janet said it stiffly and Phoebe felt the disapproval in her glance.

"Oh!" said Phoebe, growing troubled. "He is not here? What shall I do? He ought to have it at once. When will he come? I might wait for him."

"He will not be at home until evening," said Janet, as if she were glad. "You will have to leave your message."

"I am sorry," said Phoebe, in troubled tone, "I cannot leave it. The one who sends it said it was private."

"That would not mean you could not tell it to his family," said Janet, in a superior tone. She was bristling with curiosity.

"I do not know," said Phoebe, turning to go.

"I can't understand how it is that you, a young girl, should be trusted with a message if it is so private that his own people are not to know." Her tone was vexed.

"I know," said Phoebe, "it is strange, and I am sorry that it happened so. But there is nothing wrong about it, really," and she looked up wistfully with her clear eyes so that Janet scarce could continue to think evil of her. "Perhaps Mr. Graham may be able to explain it to you. I would have no right." She turned and went down the steps. "I will come back this evening," she said, more as if she were making a resolve than as if it were a communication to Janet.

"Wait," said Janet sharply. "Who are you? I've seen you in church, haven't I?"

"Oh, yes," said Phoebe, glad to have something natural said. "I sit just behind you. I'm only Phoebe Deane."

"And who sends this message to my cousin."

Phoebe's face clouded over. "I do not know," she said, slowly.

"Well, that is very strange, indeed. If I were you I would not carry messages for strange people. It doesn't look well. Girls can't be too careful what they do." Janet did not mean to be hateful, but she was deeply annoyed and curious.

Phoebe's face was pained.

"I hope Mr. Graham will be able to explain," she said, sorrowfully. "I do not like you to think ill of me." Then she went away, while Janet stood perplexed and annoyed.

She tucked the letter safely in the bosom of her gown and held her hand over it as she hurried along, not looking up nor noticing any more than when she had come. She passed Miranda on the other side of the street and never saw her, and Miranda wondered where she was going and why she looked so troubled. If she had not been hurrying to the store for something that was needed at once for the day's dinner, she would have followed her to find out, and perhaps have asked her point blank. It would have been a good thing, for when one is tracked by a devil it is well to be followed also by an angel, even if it be only one with a freckled face.

Without a thought for anything but her perplexities Phoebe made her way through the village and out on the country road, and in a very short time arrived in the kitchen of her home, where Emmeline had just finished the breakfast dishes.

"Well," she said, grimly, looking up as Phoebe entered, and noticing her empty hands, "where's the thread? Didn't they have any?"

"Oh!" said Phoebe, blankly. Her hands flew to her heart in dismay as she took in her situation. "I forgot it!" She murmured, humbly; "I'll go right back!" and without waiting for a word from the amazed Emmeline she turned and sped down the road again towards the village.

"Of all things!" ejaculated Emmeline, as she went to close the door that had blown open; "she needs a nurse! I didn't suppose going out to tea and a little money in the bank could make a girl lose her head like that! She has turned into a regular scatterbrain. The idea of her forgetting to get that thread when she hadn't another earthly thing to do! I'd like to know who 'twas brung her home last night. I don't know how I could hev missed him till he was way out in the road. It didn't look 'egzactly like David Spafford, an' yet who could it 'a' ben ef 't wasn't? She must 'a' went to Mis' Spaffords again this mornin' stead o' goin' to the store, er she never would 'a' forgot. I have to find out when she gits back. It's my duty!"

Emmeline snapped her lips together over the words as if she anticipated the duty would be a pleasant one.

Phoebe in her hasty flight down the road almost ran into Hiram Green who was sulkily plodding back from his fruitless errand to his belated chores.

"Gosh!" he said, as she started back with a hasty, "Excuse me, Mr. Green. I'm in such a hurry I didn't see you." She was gone on before her sentence was quite finished, and the breeze wafted it back to him from her flying figure.

"Gosh!" he said again, looking after her, "I wonder what's up now!" Then he turned doggedly and followed her again. If this kept up, detective business was going to be lively work. He was tired already and his morning's work not half done. Two trips to the village on foot in one morning were wearisome. Yet he was determined to know what all this meant.

Phoebe did her errand swiftly this time, and was so quick in returning with her purchase that she met Hiram face to face outside the store before he had had time to conceal himself.

He was thrown off his guard, but he rallied and tired to play the gallant.

"Thought I'd come 'long and see ef I couldn't carry yer bundle fer yeh."

"Oh, thank you, Mr. Green," said Phoebe, in new dismay at this unwonted display of courtesy on his part. "But I can't wait, for Emmeline is in a great hurry for this. I shall have to run most of the way home. Besides it's very light. I couldn't think of troubling you." She had backed off as she spoke, and with the closing words she turned and flew up the street on feet as light as a thistle-down.

"Gosh!" said Hiram, under his breath, almost dazed at the rebuff. "Gosh! but she's a slippery one! But I'll catch her yet where she can't squirm out so easy. See ef I don't!" And with scowling brows he started slowly after her again. He did not intend any move on her part should go unwatched. He hated her for disliking him.

Miranda, from her watch-tower in the Spafford kitchen window, saw Phoebe's flying figure, and wondered. She did not know what it meant, but it meant something she was sure. She felt "stirrings" in her soul that usually called for some action on her part. Her alert soul was ready when the time should arrive and she felt it "arriving" fast, and sniffed the air like a trained war-horse. To be sure she sniffed nothing more dangerous than the fragrance of mince pies just out of the great brick oven, standing in a row on the shelf to cool.

The remainder of the morning was not pleasant for Phoebe. Her mind was too busy with her perplexity about how to get the letter to Nathaniel for her to spend much time in planning how to excuse her forgetfulness. She merely said: "I was thinking of something else, Emmeline, so came back without going to the store at all." Emmeline scolded, and sniffed, and scoffed to no purpose. Phoebe silently worked on, her brow thoughtful, her eyes far away, her whole manner showing she was paying little heed to what her sister-in-law said. This made Emmeline still more angry, so that she exhausted the vials of her wrath in fruitless words upon the girl. But Phoebe's lips were sealed. She answered questions when it was necessary and quietly worked on. The tasks disappeared from under her hand as if by a sort of magic. When everything else was done she seated herself at the quilt and began to set tiny stitches in a brilliant corner.

"Don't trouble yourself," said Emmeline, coldly. "You might ferget to fasten yer thread, er tie a knot in it. I wouldn't be s'prised." But Phoebe worked mechanically on and soon had got a whole block ahead of Emmeline. Her mind was busy with the problem of the evening. How should she get that letter to Nathaniel without being discovered and questioned at home?

At dinner she was unusually silent, excusing herself to go back to the quilt as soon as she had eaten a few mouthfuls. Emmeline looked scrutinizingly at her, and became silent. It seemed to her there was something strange about Phoebe. She would have given a good deal to know all about her afternoon at the Spaffords', but Phoebe's monosyllabic answers brought forth little in the way of information.

Albert looked at her in a troubled way, then glanced at Emmeline's forbidding face, and forbore to say anything.

The afternoon wore away in silence. Several times Emmeline opened her lips to ask a question, and snapped them shut again. She made up her mind that Phoebe must be thinking about Hiram Green, and if that was so she would better keep still and let her think. Nevertheless there was something serene and lofty about Phoebe's look that was hardly in keeping with a thought of Hiram Green, and there was something sphinx-like in her manner that made Emmeline feel it was useless to ask questions, though of course Emmeline had never heard of the sphinx.

Phoebe acted like one who was making up for lost time. The dishes seemed to marshal themselves into cleanly array on the shelves, and before the darkness came on she had caused a number of suns on the sunrise bedquilt to set forever behind a goodly roll of fine stitches set in most intricate patterns.

She arose like one who was wound up at five o'clock and without a word got the supper. Then, eating little or nothing herself, she cleared it rapidly away and went up to her room. Albert took his newspaper, and Emmeline went grimly at her basket of stockings. She was wondering whether the girl intended coming down to help her with them. After all it was rather profitable to have Phoebe work like that, things got done so quickly.

"Is Phoebe sick?" asked Albert, suddenly looking up from his paper.

Emmeline started and pricked her fingers with the needle.

"I should like to know what makes you think that," she snapped, frowning at the prick. "You seem to think she's made of some kind of perishable stuff that needs more'n ordinary care. You never seem to think I'm sick as I've noticed."

"Now, Emmeline!" he began pleasantly, "you know you aren't ever sick, and this is your home, and you like to stay in it, and you've got your own folks and all. But Phoebe's kind of different. She doesn't seem to quite belong, and I wouldn't want her to miss anything out of her life because she's living with us."

"Bosh!" said Emmeline. "Phoebe's made of no better stuff 'n I am. She ken do more work when the fit's on her than a yoke of oxen. The fit's ben on her today. She's got her spunk up. That's all the matter. She's tryin' to make up fer losin' yesterday afternoon, jes' to spite me fer what I said about her goin' out. I know her. She's done a hull lot on that there quilt this afternoon. At this rate we'll hev it off the frames before the week's out. She ain't et much 'cause she's mad, but she'll come out of it all right. You make me sick the way you fret about her doldrums."

Albert subsided and the darning-needle had it all its own way clicking in and out. They could hear Phoebe moving about her chamber quietly, though it was not directly over the sitting-room, and presently the sounds ceased altogether, and they thought she had gone to bed. A few minutes more and Hiram with his customary shuffle opened the sitting-room door and walked in.

"Where's Phoebe?" he asked, looking at the silent group around the candle; "she ain't out to another tea-party is she?"

"She's gone to bed," said Emmeline, shortly. "Is it cold out?"

Phoebe, upstairs by her window, arrayed in her plain brown delaine, brown shirred bonnet, and brown cape, with the letter safely pinned inside her cape, waited until the accustomed sounds downstairs told her Hiram had come and was seated. Then she softly, cautiously climbed out of her window to the roof of a shed a few feet below her window, crept out to the back edge of this and dropped like a cat to the ground. She had performed this feat many times as a child, but never since she wore long dresses. She was glad the moon was not up yet, and she hurried around the back of the house and across the side yard to the fence, which she climbed. Her feet had scarcely left the last rail ere she heard the door-latch click, and a broad beam of light was flung out across the path not far from her. To her horror she saw Hiram Green's tall form coming out and then the door slammed shut and she knew he was out in the night with her.

But she was in the road now with nothing to hinder her, and her light feet fairly flew over the ground, treading on the grassy spots at the edge so she would make no sound, and never turning her head to listen even if he were following. Somehow she felt he was coming nearer and nearer every step she took. Her heart beat wildly, and great tears started to her eyes. She tried to pray as she fled along. Added to her fear of Hiram was her dread of what he would think if he found her out there in the dark alone, and a third fear for the secret of the letter she carried, for instinctively she felt that of all people to find out a secret Hiram Green would be among the most dangerous. She put her hand upon the letter and clenched it fast as though it might be spirited away unless she held it. She was glad it was dark, and yet, if he had seen her, and were pursuing, how dreadful it would be to reach the village streets where others would be near to help, her heart would not be so frightened.

When she passed the silent, sleeping school house she turned her head as she hurried along, and felt sure she heard him coming. The sky was growing luminous. The moon would soon be up, and then she could be seen. Then quite distinctly she heard a man's heavy tread running behind her.

Her heart nearly stopped for an instant, and then, bounding up almost to bursting, she leaped ahead, her lips set, her head down, her hands clenched over the letter. A few more rods. She could not hold out to run like this much further. But at last she reached the village pavement, and could see the blessed friendly lights of the houses all about her.

She hurried on, not daring to run so fast here, for people were coming ahead, and she tried to think and to still the wild fluttering of her heart. If Hiram Green were behind and really following her it would not do for her to go to Judge Bristol's at once. She could scarcely hope to reach there and hide from him now, for her strength for running was almost spent and not for anything must he of all people know where she was going.

This thought gave new wings to her feet, and she fled past the houses, scarcely stopping to realize where she was. She could hear the man's steps on the brick pavement now and his heavy boots rang out distinctly on the frosty air. She felt as if she had been running for years with an evil fate pursuing her. Her limbs grew heavy, and her feet seemed to drag behind. She half closed her eyes to stop the surging of the blood. Her ears rang, her cheeks were burning and perspiration was standing on her lips and brow. Her breath came hard and hurt her.

And then, quite naturally, as if it had all been planned, Miranda, with a little shawl around her shoulders and over her head, stepped out from behind the lilacs in the Spafford garden by the gate, and walked along beside her, fitting her large easy gait to Phoebe's weary, flying steps.

"I heard yeh comin' an' thought I'd go a piece with yeh!" she explained, easily, as if this were a common occurrence. "D'ye hev to hurry like this, 'r was yeh doin' it fer exercise?"

"Oh, Miranda!" gasped Phoebe, slowing down her going, and putting a plaintive hand out to reach the strong red friendly one in the dark, "I am so glad you are here!"

"So'm I!" said Miranda, confidently, "but you jest wait till you git your breath. Can't you come in and set a spell 'fore you go on?"

"No, Miranda, I must hurry. I had an errand and must get right back, — but I'm almost sure some one is following me. I don't dare look behind, but I heard footsteps and — I'm — so — frightened." Her voice trailed off, trembling into another gasp for breath.

"Well, all right, we'll fix 'em. You jest keep your breath fer walkin' an' I'll boss this pilgrimage a spell. We'll go down to the village store fer a spool o' cotton Mis' Spafford ast me t' get the fust thing in the mornin' to sew some sprigged calico curtains she's been gettin' up to the spare bed, an' while we're down to the store we'll jest natcherally lose sight o' that man till he don't know where he's at, an' then we'll meander on our happy way. Don't talk 'r he'll hear you. You jest foller me."

Chapter 13

Phoebe, too much exhausted to demur, walked silently beside the self-reliant Miranda, and in a moment more they were safely in the store.

"Say, Mr. Peebles, is Mis' Peebles to home? 'Cause Phoebe Deane wants t' git a drink o' water powerful bad. Ken she jest go right in and get it whilst I get a spool o' cotton?"

"Why certainly, certainly, young ladies, walk right in," said the affable Mr. Peebles, arising from a nail keg.

Miranda had Phoebe into the back room in no time, and was calmly debating over the virtues of different spools of thread when Hiram Green entered puffing and snorting like a porpoise, and gazed about him confidently. Then suddenly a blank look spread over his face. The one he was searching for was not there? Could he have been mistaken?

Miranda, innocently paying for her thread, eyed him furtively, and began her keen putting of two and two together, figuring out her problem with a relish. "Hiram Green, to be sure—Ah! It was Hiram who had tried to walk beside Phoebe on Sunday. Hiram Green"—contemptuously—"of all men! Umph!"

These were something like her thoughts. Then with wide-eyed good nature she paid for her thread, said good-evening to Mr. Peebles, and deliberately went out the door of the store to the street. Hiram had watched her suspiciously, but she held her head high as if she were going straight home, and slipped in the dark around to the side door where she walked in on Mrs. Peebles and the astonished Phoebe without ceremony.

"Did yeh get yer drink, Phoebe? Ev'nin Mis' Peebles. Thank yeh, no I can't set down. Mis' Spafford needs this thread t' oncet. She jest ast me wouldn't I run down and git it so's she could finish up some pillar-slips she's makin'. Come on, Phoebe, ef yer ready. Ken we go right out this door, Mis' Peebles; there's so many men in the store, an' I can't bear 'em to stare at my pretty red hair, you know." And in a moment more she had whisked Phoebe out the side door into the dark yard, where they could slip through the fence to the side street.

"Now, which way?" demanded Miranda, briefly, in a low tone, as they emerged from the shadow of the store to the sidewalk.

"Oh, Miranda, you're so kind," said Phoebe, hardly knowing what to do, for she dared not tell her errand to her. "I think I can go quite well by myself now. I'm not much afraid, and I'll soon be done and go home."

"See here, Phoebe Deane, d'yeh think I'm going' t' leave a little white-faced thing like you with them two star eyes t' go buffetin' round alone in the dark where there's liable to be lopsided nimshies follerin' round? Yeh can say what yeh like, but I'm goin' to foller yeh till I see yeh safe inside yer own door."

"Oh, you dear, good Miranda!" choked Phoebe, with a teary smile, clasping her arm tight. "If you only knew how glad I was to see you."

"I knowed all right. I cud see you was scared. But come 'long quick er that hound in there'll be trackin' us again. Which way?"

"To Judge Bristol's," breathed Phoebe, in a low frightened whisper.

"That's a good place to go," said Miranda, with satisfaction. "I guess you won't need me inside with you. I'm not much on fancy things, an' I'll fit better outside with the fence-posts, but I'll be thar to take yeh home. My! but you'd orter a' seen Hiram Green's blank look when he got in the store an' seen you want there. I'm calculatin' he'll search quite a spell 'fore he makes out which way we disappeared."

Phoebe's heart beat wildly at the thought of her escape. She felt as if an evil fate were dogging her every step.

"Oh, Miranda!" she shivered. "What if you hadn't come along just then!"

"Well, there ain't no use cipherin' on that proposition. I was thar, an' I generally calculate to be thar when I'm needed. Jest you rest easy. There ain't no long-legged, good-fer-nothin' bully like Hiram Green goin' to gather you in, not while I'm able to bob 'round. Here we be. Now I'll wait in the shadder behind this bush while you go in."

Phoebe timidly approached the house, while Miranda, as usual, selected her post of observation with discernment and a view to the lighted window of the front room where the family were assembled.

Janet did not keep Phoebe waiting long this time, but swept down upon her in a frock of ruby red with a little gold locket hung from a bit of black velvet ribbon about her neck. Her dark hair was arranged in clusters of curls each side of her sparkling face, and the glow on her cheek seemed reflected from the color of her garments. Phoebe almost spoke her admiration, so beautiful did this haughty girl seem to her.

"I am afraid my cousin is too busy to see you," she said, in a kindly, condescending tone. "He is very busy preparing to leave on the early stage in the morning. He finds he must go to New York sooner than he expected."

"I will not keep him," said Phoebe, earnestly, rising, "but I must see him for just a minute. Will you kindly tell him it is Phoebe Deane, and that she says she *MUST* see him for just a moment?"

"You will find he will desire you to send the message by me," said Janet, quite confidently. "It does not do to say must to my cousin Nathaniel."

But contrary to Janet's expectation Nathaniel came down at once, with welcome in his face. Phoebe was standing with her hand upon the letter over her heart waiting for him breathlessly. The watching Miranda eyed him jealously through the front window-pane to see if his countenance would light up properly when he saw his visitor, and was fully satisfied. He hastened to meet her, and take her hand in greeting, but she, alarmed for her mission, did but hold out the letter to him.

"I found this, Mr. Graham, spread out in the road, and read the one sentence which showed it was private. I have not read any more, and I shall never breathe even that one of course. After I had read that sentence I did not dare give it into any hands but yours. I may have been wrong, but I have tried to do right. I hope you can explain it to your cousin, for I can see she thinks it very strange."

He tried to detain her, to thank her, to introduce her to his cousin, who had by this time entered and was watching them distantly, but Phoebe was in haste to leave; and Janet was haughtily irresponsive.

He followed her to the door and said in a low tone: "Miss Deane, you have done me a greater service than I can possibly repay. I have been hunting frantically for this letter all day. It is most important. I know I can trust you not to speak of it to a soul. I am deeply grateful. You may not know it, but not only my life and safety but that of others as well has been in your hands today with the keeping of that letter."

"Oh, then I am glad I have brought it safely to you. I have been frightened all day lest something would happen that I could not get it to you without its being found out. And if it has been of service I am more than glad, because then I have repaid your kindness to me in the woods that day."

Now that she was away from Janet's scrutinizing eyes Phoebe could dimple into a smile.

"Oh, what I did that day was a little, little thing beside your service," said he.

"A kindness is never a little thing," answered Phoebe, gently. "Good-night, Mr. Graham. Miranda is waiting for me," and she sped down the path without giving him opportunity for a reply. Miranda had wandered into the shaft of light down by the gate that streamed from the candle Nathaniel held, and Phoebe flew to her as if to a rock of refuge. They turned and looked back as they reached the gate. Nathaniel was still standing on the top step with the tall candle held above his head to give them light, and through the window they could dimly see Janet's slim figure standing by the mantelpiece toying with some ornaments. Phoebe gave a great sigh of relief that the errand was accomplished, and grasping Miranda's arm clung lovingly to her, and so they two walked softly through the village streets and out the country way into the road that was white with the new risen moon; while Hiram Green, perplexed and baffled, searched vainly through the village for a clue to Phoebe's whereabouts, and finally gave it up and dragged his weary limbs home. Excitement of this sort did not agree with his constitution and he was mortally tired.

Nathaniel turned back into the house again, his vision filled with the face of the girl who had just brought his letter back to him. His great relief at finding it was almost lost in his absorption in the thought of Phoebe Deane, and the sudden pang that came to him with his remembrance of Hiram Green. Could it be? Could it possibly be that she was bound in any way to that man?

Janet roused him from his thought by demanding to know what on earth the message was that made that girl so absurdly secretive.

Nathaniel smiled. "It was just a letter of mine she had found. A letter that I have searched everywhere for."

"How did she know it was your letter?" There was something offensive in Janet's tone. Nathaniel felt his color rising like a girl. He wondered what was the matter with Janet that she should be so curious.

"Why, it was addressed to me of course!"

"Then why in the world couldn't she give it to me? She was here in the morning and we had a long argument about it. She said it was a private message and the person who sent it did not wish any one but you to see it, and yet she professed not to know who the person was who sent it. I told her that was ridiculous; that of course you had no secrets from your family; but she was quite stubborn and went away. Who is she, anyway, and how does she happen to know you?"

Nathaniel could be haughty, too, when he liked, and now he drew himself to his greatest height.

"Miss Deane is quite a charming girl, Janet, and you would do well to make her acquaintance. She is a friend of Mrs. Spafford, and was visiting her last evening when I happened in on business and they made me stay to tea."

"That's no sign of where she belongs socially," said Janet, disagreeably; "Mrs. Spafford may have had to invite her just because she didn't know enough to go home before supper. Besides, Mrs. Spafford's choice in friends might not be mine at all."

"Janet, Mr. and Mrs. Spafford are unimpeachable socially and every other way. And I happen to know that Miss Deane was there by invitation. I heard her speaking of it as she bade her good-night."

"Oh, indeed!" sneered Janet, quite beside herself with jealously. " I suppose you were waiting to take her home!"

"Why, certainly," said Nathaniel, looking surprised. "What has come over you, Janet? You do not talk like your usual kind self."

His tone brought angry tears to Janet's eyes.

"I should think it was enough," she said, trying to hide the tears in her little lace handkerchief, "having you go off suddenly like this when we've scarcely had you a week, and you busy and absent-minded all the time; and then to have this upstart of a girl coming here with secrets that you will not tell me about. I want to know who wrote that letter, Nathaniel, and what it is about. I can't stand it to have that girl smirking behind me in church knowing things about my cousin that I am not told. I *must* know."

"Janet!" said Nathaniel, pained and surprised, "you must be ill. I never saw you act this way before. You know very well that I'm just as sorry as can be to have to rush off sooner than I had planned, but it can't be helped. I'm sorry if I have been absent-minded. I have been trying to decide some matters of my future and I suppose that has made me somewhat abstracted. As for the letter, I would gladly tell you about it, but it is another's secret, and I could not honorably do so. You need fear no such feeling on Miss Deane's part, I am sure. Just meet her with your own pleasant, winning way, and say to her that I have explained to you that it was all right. That ought to satisfy both you and her. She asked me to explain it to you."

"Well, you haven't done so, at all. I am sure I can't see what possible harm it could do for you to tell me about it, inasmuch as that other girl knows all about it, too. I should think you would want me to watch and be sure that she doesn't tell—-unless, indeed, the secret is between you two."

There was a hint in Janet's tone which seemed almost like an insinuation. Nathaniel grew quite stern.

"The secret is not between Miss Deane and myself," he said, "and she does not know it any more than you do. She found it open, and read only one line which told her it was absolutely private. She tells me she did not read another word."

"Very likely!" sneered Janet, coldly. "Do you think any woman would find it possible to read only one line of a secret? Your absolute faith in this stranger is quite childlike."

"Janet, would you have read further if it had fallen into your hands?"

"Well,—I—why—of course that would be different," said Janet, coloring and looking disconcerted, "but you needn't compare me—"

"Janet, you have no right to think she has a lower sense of honor than you have. I feel sure she has not read it."

But Janet, with haughty mien and flashing eyes in which tears were scarcely concealed, swept up the stairs and took refuge in her room, where a perfect storm of tears and mortification followed.

Nathaniel, confounded, dismayed, after vainly tapping at her door and begging her to come out and explain her strange conduct, went sadly to his packing, puzzling much over the strange ways of girls with one another. Here for instance were two well suited to friendship, and yet he could plainly see that they would have nothing to do with one another. He dearly loved his cousin. She had been his playmate and companion from childhood, and he could not understand why suddenly she had grown so disregardful of his wishes. He tried to put it away, deciding that he would say another little word about this charming Miss Deane to Janet in the morning before he left, but Miss Janet forestalled any such attempt by sending down word that she had a headache and would try to sleep a little longer to get rid of it. She would only call a cool little good-bye to her cousin through the closed door, as he, mildly distressed, was hurrying down to the stage waiting for him at the door.

Meantime Miranda and Phoebe had hurried out past the old red school-house into the country road white with frosty moonlight, Phoebe all the time protesting that Miranda must not go with her.

"Why not, in conscience!" said Miranda. "I'll jest enjoy the walk. I was thinkin' of goin' on a lark this very evenin', only I hadn't picked out a companion."

"But you'll have to come all the way back alone, Miranda."

"Well, what's that? You don't s'pose anybody's goin' to chase *ME*, do yeh? If they want to they're welcome. I'd jest turn round an' say: 'Boo! I'm red-haired an' freckled, an' I don't want nothin' of you, nor you of me. Git 'long with yeh!'" Miranda's inimitable manner brought a merry laugh to Phoebe's lips and helped to relieve the tension of the heavy strain she had been under. She felt like laughing and crying all at once. Miranda seemed to understand and enter into her mood and kept her in ripples of laughter till they neared her home. Then, suddenly sobering, Phoebe attempted to make Miranda go back at once, but Miranda was stubborn. Not until she saw her charge safe inside her own door would the faithful soul budge an inch.

"Well, then, Miranda, I'll have to tell you how I got out," said Phoebe, confidentially. "There was a caller—some one I didn't care to see—so I went upstairs and they thought I'd gone to bed. I just slipped out my window to the low shed roof and dropped down. I'll have to be very still, for I wouldn't care to have them know I slipped away like that. It might make them ask me questions. You see I had found a letter that I knew Mr. Graham had dropped, and it ought to go to him at once. If I had asked Albert to take it there would have been a big fuss and Emmeline would have wanted to know all about it, and maybe read it, and I didn't think it would be best—"

"I see," said Miranda, comprehensively, "so you tuk it yourself. O' course. Who wouldn't, I'd like to know? All right, we'll jest slip in through the pasture and round to your shed, an' I'll give yeh a boost up. Two's better one fer a job like that, ef one is a red-head. I take it yer caller ain't present any longer. Reckon he made out to foller yeh a piece but we run him into a hole, an' he didn't make much. Hush, now; don't go to thankin', 'taint worth while till I git through, fer I've jest begun this job, an' I intend to see it through. Here, put yer hand on my shoulder. Now let me hold this foot, don't you be 'fraid, I'm good an' strong. There yeh go! Now yer up! Is that your winder up there? Wal, hope to see yeh again soon. Happy dreams!" and she slid around the corner to watch Phoebe till she disappeared into the little dark window above. Then Miranda made for the road, looking curiously in at the side window of the Deane's sitting-room on the way, to make sure she was right about the caller being gone, and to watch if they had heard Phoebe, for she thought it might be necessary for her to invent a diversion of some sort. But she only saw Albert asleep in his chair and Emmeline working grimly at her sewing.

About half way to the red school-house Miranda met Hiram Green. He looked up, frowning. He thought it was Phoebe, and wondered if it were possible that she was going to the village for a fourth trip yet that night. If she were, she must be crazy.

"Ev'nin', Hiram," said Miranda, nonchalantly, "seen anythin' of a little white kitten with one blue eye and one green one, an' a black tip to her tail, an' a pink nose? I've been up to see if she follered Phoebe Deane home from our house las' night, but she's gone to bed with the toothache an' I wouldn't disturb her fer the world. I thought I'd mebbe find her round this way? You ain't seen her, have yeh?"

"No," growled Hiram, suspiciously, "I'd a wrung her neck ef I had."

"Oh, thank you, Mr. Green. You're very kind," said Miranda, sweetly. "I'll remember that, next little kitten I lose. I'll know jest who t' apply to fer it. Lovely night, ain't it? Don't trouble yerself 'bout the kitten. I reckon it's safe somewheres. 'Taint every one's ez blood-thirsty's you be. Good-night." And Miranda flung off down the road before Hiram could decide whether she was poking fun at him or was extremely dull. At last he roused himself from his weary pondering, uttered his accustomed ejaculation, "Gosh!" looked up the road toward the Deanes, and down toward the vanishing Miranda, brought forth the expression he reserved for the perplexing crises in his life, "Gosh Ninety!" and went home to bed. He had not been able all day to quite fathom the mystery which he was attempting to control, and this new unknown quantity was more perplexing than all that had gone before. What, for instance, had Miranda Griscom to do with Phoebe Deane? His slow brain remembered that she had been in the store where Phoebe—it must have been Phoebe; for he did not believe he could have been mistaken—had disappeared. Had Miranda spirited her away somewhere? Ah! And it was Miranda who had come up to Phoebe after church and interrupted their walk together! What had Miranda to do with it all? Hang Miranda! He would like to wring her neck, too. With such charming meditations he fell asleep.

Chapter 14

Nathaniel sat inside the coach as it rolled through the village streets and out into the country road toward Albany, and tried to think. All remembrance of Janet and her foolish pet had passed from his mind. He had before him a problem to decide. It was the harder because the advice of his nearest and dearest friends was so at variance.

He took out two letters which represented the two sides of the question and began to reread. The first was the letter which Phoebe had brought, torn, disfigured by the dust, but still legible. It bore a Texas postmark and was brief and businesslike.

Dear nephew, (it read), *if you are keen as you used to be you have been keeping yourself informed about old Texas, and know the whole state of the case better than I can put it. Ever since Austin went to ask the admission of Texas as a separate state into the Mexican Republic and was denied and thrown into prison, our people have been gathering together; and now things are coming to a crisis. Something will be done and that right soon, perhaps in a few days. The troops are gathering near Gonzales. Resistance will be made. But we need help. We want young blood, and strong arms behind which are heads and hearts with a conviction for right and freedom. No one on earth has a right to deprive us of our property, and say we shall not own slaves which we have come honestly by. We will fight and win, as the United States has fought and won its right to govern itself. Now I call upon you, Nathaniel, to rise up and bring honor to your father's name by raising a company of young men to come down here and set Texas free. I know you are busy with your law studies but they will keep and Texas will not. Texas must be set free now or never. When you were a little chap you had strong convictions about what was right, and I feel pretty sure my appeal will not come to deaf ears. Your father loved Texas and came down here to make his fortune. If he had lived he would have been here fighting. He would have been a slave-owner, and have asserted his right as a free man in a free country to protect his property. He would have taught his son to do the same. I call upon you for your father's sake to come down here in the hour of your Texas' need—for it is the place where you were born—and help us. Use your utmost influence to get other young men to come with you.*

Your uncle the Judge will perhaps help you financially. He owns a couple of slaves himself I remember, house servants, does he not? Ask him how he would like the government of the United States to order him to set them free. I feel sure he will sympathize with Texas in her need and help you do this thing which I have asked.

I am a man of few words, but I trust you, Nathaniel, and I feel sure I am not pleading in vain. I shall expect something from you at once. We need the help now or the cause may be lost. If you feel as I think you do go to the New York address given below. This letter will be sufficient identification for you as I have written to them of you, but it is important that you present this letter or it will do no good to go, but BE SURE THAT NO ONE ELSE SEES IT, or great harm may come to you! There is grave danger in being found out, but if I did not know your brave spirit I would not be writing you. Come as soon as possible!

Your uncle,
ROYAL GRAHAM.

The other letter was kept waiting a long time while the young man read and reread this one, and then let his eyes wander through the window of the coach to the brown fields and dim hills in the distance. He was going over all he could remember of his boyhood life in that far-away Southern home. He could dimly remember the form of his father, who had been to him a great hero; who had taken him with him on horseback wherever he went and never been too weary or too busy for his little son. There came a blur of sadness over the picture, the death of his beloved father, and an interval of emptiness when the gentle mother was too full of sorrow to know how the baby heart had felt the utter loneliness, and then one day his Uncle Royal, so like yet not like his father, had lifted him in his arms and said: "Good-bye, little chap. Some day you'll come back to us and do your father's work, and take his place." Then he and his mother had ridden away in an endless succession of post-chaises and coaches, until one day they had come to Judge Bristol's great white house set among the green hedges, and there Nathaniel had found a new home. There, first his mother, and then Janet's mother, had slipped away into that mysterious door of death, and he had grown up in the home of his mother's brother, with Janet as a sister. From time to time he had received letters from this shadowy uncle in Texas, and once, when he was about twelve, there had been a brief visit from him which cleared the memory and kept him fresh in Nathaniel's mind; and always there had been some hint or sentence of expectation that when Nathaniel was grown and educated he would come back to the country which had been his father's and help to make it great. This had been a hazy undertone always in his life, in spite of the fact that his other uncle, Judge Bristol, was constantly talking of his future career as a lawyer in New York City, with a possibility of a political career also. Nathaniel had gone on with his life, working out the daily plan as it came, with all the time the feeling that these two plans were contending in him for supremacy. Sometimes during leisure moments lately he had wondered if the two could ever be combined, and if not how possibly they were to both work out. Gradually it had dawned upon him that a day was coming, indeed might not be far away, when he would have to choose. And now, since these two letters had reached him, he knew the time had come. And how was he to know how to choose?

His Uncle Royal's letter had reached him the afternoon of the nutting party on the hill. Pompey, his uncle's house servant, had brought it to him on a silver salver just as they were starting. He had glanced at the familiar writing, known it for his uncle's, and put it in his pocket for reading at his leisure. He always enjoyed his uncle's letters, yet they were not of deep moment to him. He had been too long separated from him to have keen interests in common with him. Hence he had not read the letter until after his return from the hill-side, which explains how he had carelessly left it behind the log by Phoebe, as an excuse to return and help her out of the laurel.

In the quiet of his own room after Janet and the others were sleeping he had remembered the letter, and, relighting his candle, which had been extinguished, he had read it, feeling a touch of reproach that he could have so lightly put off attending to his good relative's words. How, then, was he startled to discover its contents! The talk of the afternoon floated back to him, idle talk, about his going down to set Texas free. Talk that grew out of his own keen interest in all the questions of the day, and his readiness to argue them out. But he had never had a very definite idea of going to Texas to take part in the struggle that was going on until this letter brought him face to face with a possible duty.

Perhaps he would have had no question about his decision, if, following hard upon this letter, had not come the other one, the very next day in fact, which put an entirely new phase upon some sides of the question, and made duty seem an uncertain creature with more faces than one.

The coach was half way to Albany before Nathaniel finally folded away his uncle's letter and put it in his inner pocket with great care. Then he took up the other letter with a perplexed sigh, and read:

DEAR CHUM:

I am sitting on a high point of white sand, where I can look off at the blue sea. At my right is a great hairy, prickly cactus with a few gorgeous yellow blossoms in a glory of delicate petals and fringed stamens that look as out of place amid the sand as a diamond on a plank. Just now a green lizard peered curiously out from under one of the hairy balls that pass for leaves with a cactus, and then slid back out of sight. But the next time I looked he was blue, brilliant, and palpitating as a peacock's feathers, and sunning himself, not thinking of me at all. Then just as I moved he became a dull gray-brown, hardly discernible from the sand. And thus I know he is not a lizard at all, but a chameleon. The sun is very warm and bright, and everything about seems basking in it.

As I look off to sea the Gulf Stream is distinct today, a brilliant green ribbon in the brilliant blue of the sea. It winds along so curiously and so independently in the great ocean, keeping its own individuality in spite of storm and wind and tide. I went out in a small boat across it the other day, and could look down and see it as distinctly as if there were a glass wall between it and the other water. I cannot but think that God took pleasure in making this old earth — so curious, mysterious, and beautiful.

A great lazy bird is floating high in the air, looking down to the water for prey, doubtless. I think I could almost see the bright, curious fishes of this strange clime darting in the sunny water myself, if I tried, the air is so clear and the days so bright.

There are orange groves back of me, not far away — a few miles. I fancy their perfume is wafted even here. There is a curious sweet apathy that steals over one down here, which soothes, and rests.

I am having a holiday, for my little pupils are gone away on a visit. This is a delightful land to which I have come, and a charming family with whom my lot is cast. I am having an opportunity to study the South in a most ideal manner, and many of my former ideas of it are becoming much modified. For example, there is slavery. I am by no means so sure as I used to be that it was ordained of God. I wish you were here to talk it over with me, and to study it, too. There are possibilities in the institution that make one shudder. Perhaps, after all, Texas is in the wrong. As you have opportunity drop into an Abolition meeting now and then and see what you think. I have been reading the Liberator lately. I find much in it that is strong and appeals to my sense of right. You know what a disturbance it has made in the country recently. I hear some mails have even been broken into and burned on account of it. I wonder if this question of slavery will ever be an issue in our country. If it should be I cannot help wondering what the South will do. From what I have seen I feel sure they will never stand it to have their rights interfered with.

Now, I have to confess that much as I rebelled against giving up my work and coming down here I feel that it has already benefited me. I can take long walks without the least weariness, and can even talk and sing like any one else without becoming hoarse. I do not believe my lungs have ever been affected, and I feel I am going to get well and come back to my work. With that hope in my veins I can go joyfully through these sunny days and feel the new life creeping into me with every breath of balmy air. We shall yet work shoulder to shoulder, my friend — I feel it. God bless you and keep you, and show you the right.

Yours, faithfully,
MARTIN VAN RENSSELAER.

Nathaniel folded the letter, placed it in his pocket with the other, and leaned his head back to think. It was all perplexing.

This man Van Rensselaer had been his room-mate for four years. They had grown into one another's thoughts as two who are much together and love each other will grow until each had come to depend upon the other's decision as if it were nearly his own judgment. Nathaniel could not quite tell why it was that this letter troubled him, yet he felt breathing through the whole epistle the stirring of a new principle that seemed to antagonize his sympathy with Texas.

So, through the long cold journey the question was debated back and forth. His duty to his uncle demanded that he go to the address given and investigate the matter of helping Texas, else his uncle might think him exceedingly neglectful; and when he looked at the question from his uncle's stand-point, and thought of his father, and his own natural heritage, his sympathy was with Texas. On the other hand his love for his friend and his perfect trust in him demanded that he investigate the other side also. He felt intuitively that the two things could not go together.

Martin Van Rensselaer had been preparing for the Christian ministry. His zeal and earnestness were great, too great for his strength, and before he had finished his theological studies he had broken down and been sent South, as it was feared he had serious lung trouble. This separation had been a great trial to both young men. Martin was three years older than Nathaniel, and two years ahead of him in his studies, but in mind and spirit they were as one, so that the words of the letter had great influence.

The day had grown surly as the coach rumbled on. Sullen clouds lowered in the corners of the sky as if meditating mutiny. There was a hint of snow in the biting air that whistled around the cracks of the coach windows. Nature seemed to have suddenly put on a bare, brown look—hopeless, discouraging, cold.

Nathaniel shivered and drew his cloak close about him. He wished the journey were over, or that he had some one with whom to advise. Somehow the question troubled him as if it were of immediate necessity that it be decided, and he could not dismiss it, nor put it off. He had once or twice broached the subject with Judge Bristol, but had hesitated to show him either of the letters which had been the cause of his own perplexity. He felt that his uncle's letter might arouse antagonism in Judge Bristol on account of the claim it seemed to put upon himself, as his father's son, to come and give himself.

Judge Bristol was almost jealously fond of his sister's son, and felt that he belonged to the North. Aside from that, his sympathies would probably have been with Texas. Keeping a few slaves himself as house servants, and treating them as kindly as if they had been his own children, he saw no reason to object to slavery, and deemed it a man's right to do as he pleased with his own property.

Martin Van Rensselaer's letter the Judge would have been likely to look upon as the production of a sentimental, hot-headed fanatic, whose judgment was unsound. Nathaniel was morally certain that if the Judge should read those letters he would advise against having anything to do with either cause personally; yet, dearly as he loved and honored the Judge, who had been a second father to him, Nathaniel's conscience would not let him drop the matter thus easily.

So the coach thumped on over rough roads and smooth. The coachman called to his horses, snapped his whip alluringly, and wondered why Nathaniel, who was usually so sociable, and liked to sit on the box and talk, stayed glumly inside with never a word for him. The coachman was the same one who had brought Nathaniel and his mother to the Judge's door that first time when on their last stage route from Texas. He felt aggrieved, for Nathaniel belonged to him. Had he not allowed him to drive in smooth stretches of road, even when he was a little fellow? Could it be possible that New York had spoiled him, and he was growing too proud to companion with his old friend, or was he in love? The coachman sat gloomily mile after mile, and tried to think what girl of his acquaintance was good enough for Nathaniel.

But all oblivious of his old friend's disquietude, Nathaniel sat inside with closed eyes and tried to think, and ever and anon there came a vision of a sweet-faced girl with brown hair and a golden gown sitting among the falling yellow leaves with bowed head; and somehow in his thoughts her trouble became tangled, and it seemed as if there were three instead of two who needed setting free, and he was to choose between them all.

Chapter 15

The cold weather had come suddenly and Phoebe felt like a prisoner. Emmeline's tongue became a daily torture, and the little ways in which she contrived to make Phoebe's life a burden were too numerous to count. Her paltry fortune in the bank was a source of continual trouble. Scarcely a morning passed but it was referred to in some unpleasant way. Every request was prefaced with some such phrase as: "If you're not too grand to soil your hands," or "I don't like to ask a rich lady to do such a thing," till Phoebe felt sometimes that she could bear it no longer and longed to take the few dollars and fling them into the lap of her disagreeable sister-in-law, if thereby she might but gain peace. Like the continual dropping that wears the stone, the unpleasant reference had worn upon a single nerve until the pain was acute.

But there was another source of discomfort still more trying to the girl than all that had gone before, and this was Hiram Green's new role. He had taken it upon himself to act the fine gentleman. It was somewhat surprising considering the fact that Hiram was known in the village as "near," and this new departure demanded an entirely new outfit of clothes. In his selection he aimed to emulate Nathaniel Graham. As he neither Nathaniel's taste nor his New York tailor the effect was far from perfect, except perhaps in the eyes of Hiram, who felt quite set up in his fine raiment.

On the first Sunday of his proud appearance in church thus arrayed he waited boldly at the door until the Deanes came out and then took his place beside Phoebe and walked with her to the carryall as though he belonged there. Phoebe's thoughts were on other things and for a moment she had not noticed, but suddenly becoming conscious of measured footsteps by her own, she looked up and found the reconstructed Hiram strutting by her side as consciously as a peacock. In spite of her great annoyance her first impulse was to laugh, and that laugh probably did more than any other thing to turn the venom of Hiram Green's hate upon her own innocent head. After all the effort he had made to appear well before her, and before the congregation assembled she had laughed. She had dared to laugh aloud, and the hateful Miranda Griscom, who seemed to be always around in the way whenever he tried to walk with Phoebe had laughed back. A slow ugly red rolled into his sun-burned face, and his eyes narrowed with resolve to pay back all and more than he had received of scorn.

It happened that Miranda was holding Rose by the hand, and could not without greatly attracting attention get much nearer to Phoebe that morning, so the girl could do nothing to get away from her unpleasant suitor except to hasten to the carryall. And there before the open-eyed congregation Hiram Green helped her into the carryall with a rude imitation of Nathaniel Graham's gallantry. She should see that others besides the New York college dandy could play the fine gentleman. He finished the operation with an exaggerated flourish of his hat, and just because laughter is so very near to tears, the tears sprang up in Phoebe's eyes. She could do nothing but droop her head and try as best she could to hide them. The all-seeing Alma of course discovered them, and just as they were driving by Judge Bristol and his daughter she called out: "Aunt Phoebe's cryin'. What you cryin' 'bout, Aunt Phoebe? Is it 'cause you can't ride with Hiram Green?"

Thereafter Hiram Green was in attendance upon her at every possible public place. She could not go to church without finding him at her elbow the minute the service was over, ready to walk down the very aisle beside her. She could not go to singing-school but he would step out from behind his gate as she passed and join her, or if she evaded him he would sit beside her and manage to sing out of the same book. She could not go to the village on an errand but he would appear in the way and accompany her. He seemed to have developed a strange intuition as to her every movement. He was ever vigilant, and the girl began to feel like a hunted creature. Even if she stayed at home he appeared at the door ten minutes after the family had gone, a triumphant, unpleasant smile upon his face, and sauntered into the kitchen without waiting for her to bid him, and there, tilted back in a chair in his favorite attitude, he would watch her every movement, and drawl out an occasional remark. That happened only once, however; she never dared to stay again, lest it would be repeated. She had been busy preparing something for dinner, and she turned suddenly and caught a look upon his face that reminded her of a beast of prey. It flashed upon her that he was actually enjoying her annoyance. Without waiting to think she stepped into the wood-shed, and from there fairly fled across the backyard, and the meadows between and burst into the bright little room of Granny McVane.

The dear old lady sat there rocking by the fire, with her open Bible on her knee. Phoebe was relieved to find her alone, and in answer to the gentle: "Why, dearie, what can be the matter?" she flung herself on the floor at the old lady's feet and putting her head in her lap burst into tears.

It was only for a moment that she lost her self-control, but even that moment relieved the heavy strain on her nerves, and she was able to sit up and tell the old lady all about it. She had not intended to tell anything, when in her sudden panic she had beaten a hasty retreat from the enemy, but Granny McVane's sweet face showed so much tender sympathy that all at once it seemed good to tell some one of her trouble.

She listened, watched her sympathetically, smoothed back the damp tendrils of hair that had blown about her face, and then stooped over and kissed her.

"Don't you ever marry him, Phoebe. Don't you ever do it, if you don't love him child!" she said, solemnly, like a warning. "And just you run over here, dearie, whenever he bothers you. I'll take care of you."

Phoebe, with her natural reserve, had not drawn her family into the story except to say that they favored the suit of the would-be lover. But it comforted her greatly to have someone on her side, even if it were but this quiet old lady who could not really help her much.

They watched out the back windows until they saw Hiram emerge from the Deane house and saunter off down the road. Even then Phoebe was afraid to go back until she saw the carryall far down the road. Then she flew across the fields and entered the back door before they had turned in at the great gate. When they got out and came into the house she was demurely paring potatoes, and Emmeline eyed her suspiciously.

"Seems to me you're pretty late with your potatoes," she remarked, dis-agreeably. "I suppose you had a nice easy time all morning.

But Phoebe did not explain, only she did not stay at home again when the family were all to be away. She never knew whether Emmeline was aware of Hiram's Sunday morning visit or not.

Phoebe's state of mind after this occurrence was one of constant nervous alarm. She began to hate the thought of the man who seemed to haunt her at every turn.

Heretofore one of her greatest pleasures had been to walk to the village after the daily mail, or for an errand to the store. Now such walks became a dread. One afternoon in early November she had hurried away and gone around by Granny McVane's, hoping thus to escape the vigilance of Hiram Green. She managed to get safely to the village, and get her errands done, but just as she emerged from the post-office the long, lank figure of Hiram loomed before her and slouched into his dogged gait beside her. "Did you get a letter?" he asked, looking suspiciously at the one she held in her hand. Then as she did not answer he went on: "You must have a whole lot of folks writin' you quite constant; you seem to go to the post-office so much."

Phoebe said nothing. She felt too indignant to speak. How could she get away from her tormentor unless she deliberately ran away from him? And how could she do that right here in the village where every one was watching? She glanced up furtively. Hiram wore a look of triumph as he talked on, knowing he was annoying her.

"I s'pose you get letters from New York," he said, and there was a disagree-able insinuation in his tone. Phoebe did not know what he meant, but something in his tone made the color come into her cheeks. They were nearing the Spafford house. If only Miranda would come out and speak to her! She looked up at the great bully beside her and saw he was trying to calculate just how near to the mark he had come. She stopped short on the pavement.

"I do not wish to walk with you," she said, struggling to keep her voice from trembling.

"Oh, you don't," he mocked. "How 'r ye goin' to help yourself?"

She looked up into the pitiless cruelty of his eyes and shuddered involuntarily.

"I am going in to see Mrs. Spafford," she said, with sudden inspiration, and her voice took on a girlish dignity. With that she put wings to her feet and flew to the Spafford front door, wondering if anyone would let her in before Hiram reached her.

Now Miranda was alone in the house that afternoon, and not much went on in the neighborhood that she did not keep herself informed concerning; therefore, when Phoebe, breathless, reached the front stoop the door swung open before her, and she stepped into her refuge with a gasp of relief and heard it close behind her as two strong freckled arms enclosed her and two honest lips greeted her with a resounding kiss.

"Ben waitin' quite a spell fer ye," she declared, as if it were the expected thing for Phoebe to fly into her arms unannounced in that way, "ever sence I see ye comin' down the street with that pleasant friend of yourn. Wonder you could tear yourself away. Take off yer bonnet and set a spell. Mis' Spafford's gone up t' th' aunts fer tea and took Rose. I'm all alone. You set down an' we'll have a real nice time an' then I'll take you home by 'n by."

"Oh, Miranda," gasped Phoebe, struggling hysterically between laughter and tears and trying to control the trembling that had taken possession of her body, "I'm such a miserable coward. I'm always running away when I get frightened!"

"H'm! I should hope you would!" said Miranda significantly. "Such a snake in the grass as that! Le's see ef he's gone!" and she crouched before the window and peered behind the curtain cautiously.

Hiram had watched Phoebe's sudden disappearance within the door with something like awe. It was almost uncanny having that door open and swallow her up. Besides, he had not expected that Phoebe would dare to run away from him. He stood a moment gazing after her, and then sauntered on undecidedly, calling himself a fool for having met her so near to the Spafford house. Another time he would choose his meeting-place away from her friends. He had lost this move in the game, but he by no means meant to lose the game, and the hate in his heart grew with determination to have this tempting young life in his power and crush out its resistance.

It goaded him to madness to have her dare to tell him she did not wish to walk with him. Why did she say that? Had he not always been respected, and thought well of? His farm was as good a spot of land as could be found in the whole New York state, and his barn was talked of through all the county. He was prosperous, everybody knew. Before he had married Annie any girl in the vicinity would have thought him a great catch, and he knew well, by all the indescribable signs, that many a girl as good as Phoebe would still be glad to accept his attentions. Why did this little nobody, who was after all merely a poor relation of his neighbor, presume to scorn him? He hated her for it, even while his heart was set upon having her. He wanted her at first because he admired her. Now he wanted her to conquer her and punish her for her scorn of him.

As he walked on alone his slow brain tried to form a new plan for revenge, and little by little an idea crept out of his thoughts and looked at him with its two snaky eyes until the poison of its fang had stolen into his heart. The post-office! Ah! He would watch to see if she had a letter from that fellow, for surely only the knowledge that another man was at her feet could make her scorn his attentions. If that was so he would crush the rival! He ground his teeth at the thought, and his eyes glittered with hate.

Meantime, Hiram Green's children and Alma Deane were playing together behind the big barn that had been one of the disappointments of Annie Green's married life, because it had not been a house instead of a barn. The children had dug houses in a hay-stack, and chased the few venturesome hens that had not learned to be wary when they were around; now, for the moment weary of their games, they mounted the fence to rest.

"There comes your pa," announced Alma from her perch on the top rail. The young Greens retired precipitately from the fence, and Alma was forced to follow them if she wished company. They hurried around the other side of the barn out of sight.

"Say," said Alma, after they had reached a spot of safety and ensconced themselves on the sunny exposure of a board across two logs, "my Aunt Phoebe went to the village a while ago. She'll be 'long pretty soon. Let's make up somethin' an' shout at her when she comes back. It'll make her mad as hops an' I'd just like to pay her back fer the way she acts sometimes."

"Ain't she good to you?" enquired the youngest Green, anxiously.

"Le's make up sumpin' 'bout her 'n your pa. There ain't nothin' 'll make her so mad. She's mad as mad can be when my ma says anythin' 'bout her gettin' married," went on Alma, ignoring the question.

"All right! What'll we make up?" agreed the three Greens. They were not anxious to have a step-mother who might make life's restrictions more strenuous than they were already. They were prepared to do battle valiantly if they only had a general, and Alma was thoroughly competent in their eyes to fill that position.

"It'll have to be to a song, you know," went on Alma. "Le's sing the Doxol'gy an' see how that goes." So they all stood in an enquiring row and droned out the Doxology, piping shrilly where they knew the words and filling in with home-made syllables where they did not. Alma had practiced the art of rhyming before, and was anxious to display the skill she had acquired since their last meeting.

"Now listen!" she said, and lined it out, slowly, with many haltings and corrections, until at last the doggerel was completed, and so they sang:

> "There-was-a-man-in-ow-wer-tow
> His-name-was-Hi-rum-Gre-ee-een
> And-he-did-ma-a-air-ree-a-wife
> Her-name-was-Phe-be-Dee-ee-een."

Alma was no lax general. She drilled her little company again and again until they could shout the words at the top of their voices, to saying nothing of the way they murdered Old Hundred. The young scapegraces looked at their leader with wide-eyed admiration, and fairly palpitated for the moment when their victim should arrive and they might put their drill into practice. Between rehearsals they mounted the fence by the barn and kept a watch-out down the road. At last it was announced that she was coming.

"But there's somebuddy with 'er," said a disappointed little Green. "We won't dast, will we?"

Alma held up her undaunted chin and mounted the post of observation to see who it was.

"Aw! That's all right," she presently announced. "'Taint nobody but the red-headed girl down to Spafford's. She can't do nothin'. Come on, now, le's get ready."

She marshalled her forces behind the wide board fence next to the pig-sty and there they waited for the signal to begin. Alma thought it prudent to wait until Phoebe and Miranda had almost passed before they sang. Then she raised her hand and they piped out shrilly, making the words more than plain. Phoebe started at the first line and hurried her steps, but Miranda glanced back and said: "H'm! I thought 'es much. Like father, like child!"

Maddened by such indifference the children ran along inside the fence and continued to yell at the top of their lungs, regardless of time or tune until they reached the more open fields near the Deane house, where they dared go no further. Then they retired in triumph to the shelter of the pig-sty and the hay-stack to plume themselves upon their success, and recount the numerous faces they had made, and the times they had stuck their tongues out. They did not anticipate any trouble from the incident as they were too far away from the house for Hiram to hear, and they felt sure Phoebe would never tell on them, as it involved herself too closely.

Suddenly, in the midst of the gratulations, without the slightest warning, a strong hand seized the sturdy Alma from the rear and pinioned her arms so that she could not get away. She set up a yell that could have been heard for a half mile, and began to kick and squirm, but Miranda's hands held her fast, while she took in the surroundings at a glance, moved her captive toward a convenient seat on a log, and taking her calmly over her knee administered in full measure the spanking that child deserved, Alma, meanwhile yelling like a loon, unable to believe her senses that the despised "red-haired girl from Spafford's" had displayed so much ability and thoroughness in her methods of redress.

The valiant army of little Greens had retired with haste from the scene of action, and were even then virtuously combing their hair and washing their hands and faces with a view to proving an alibi should the avenger seek further retribution. Alma was left to the mercy of Miranda and though she kicked and yelled right lustily Miranda spanked on until she was tired.

"There!" she said, at last letting her go. "That ain't half you need, but I can't spend any more time on yeh today. Ef yeh ever do that er anythin' like it again I'll come in the night when everybody's asleep and give yeh the rest, an' I ken tell you now I won't let yeh off this easy next time. Mind you behave to yer Aunt Phoebe, er I'll hant yeh! D'yeh understand? Wherever yeh go in the dark I'll be there to hant yeh. And when red-haired people hants yeh at night their hair's all on fire in the dark an' it burns yeh, so yeh better watch out!"

She shook her fist decidedly at the child, who now thoroughly frightened began to cry in earnest and ran away home as fast as her fat legs could carry her, not daring to look back lest the supernatural creature with the fiery hair and the strong hand should be upon her again. It was the first time in her brief, impertinent life that Alma had ever been thoroughly frightened.

Her first act on reaching the house was to see how the land lay. She found that her mother had gone out to get some eggs and that Phoebe was up in her room with the door buttoned. No one else was about, so Alma stole noiselessly up to Phoebe's door, righteous innocence upon her tear-stained face, her voice smoother than butter with deceit.

"Aunt Phoebe!" she called, lovingly, "I hope you don't think I sung that mean song at you. I was real 'shamed of them Green children. I run after 'em an' tried to make 'em stop, but they jest wouldn't. I think their pa ought to be told, don't you? Say, Aunt Phoebe, you didn't think 'twas me, did you?"

There was no answer from the other side of the door for Phoebe was lying on her bed shaking with suppressed sobs, and could not control her voice to reply even if she had known what to say. Her heart was filled with pain, too, that this child whom she had tended and been kind to should be so hateful.

Alma, rather nonplussed at receiving no answer, tried once or twice and then calling out sweetly: "Well, I just thought I'd let you know 'twasn't me, Aunt Phoebe," stumped off downstairs to reflect upon the way of sinners. Her main fear was that Phoebe would "tell on her" to her father, and then she knew she would receive the other half of her spanking.

But Phoebe, with a face white with suffering, and dark rings under her eyes, said not a word when she came downstairs, but went about her work not even seeming to see the naughty child, until Alma gradually grew more confident and resolved to put the "hanting" out of her mind entirely. This was easier said than done, however, for when night came she dreaded to go to bed, and she made several unsuccessful attempts to help Phoebe with the supper dishes, thereby calling upon herself much undeserved commendation from her gratified mother and father, which helped ease her conscience not a little.

Chapter 16

Hiram Green began to put his new plan into practice the very next day. He took care to be on hand when the mail coach arrived, and as soon as the mail was distributed he presented himself at the post-office corner of the store.

"Any mail fer th' Deanes?" he enquired carelessly, after he had been told there was nothing for himself. "I'm goin' up there on business an' I'll save 'em the trouble o' comin' down."

This question he put in varied forms, until it grew to be a habit with the postmaster to hand over the Deanes' mail to Hiram every day. This was rather expensive business, for Albert frequently received letters from people who did not prepay the postage, and it went much against Hiram's grain to hand out eighteen cents or more for another man's letter, even though he were sure he would receive it again. He made prompt collections from Albert, however, and by this means Phoebe became aware of Hiram's daily visits to the post-office. Not that it made any difference to her, for she did not expect a letter from any one. There was no one to write to her.

This went on for about two weeks, and during that time Hiram had been able to see very little of Phoebe, for she kept herself well out of his way, when one day a letter bearing a New York post-mark, and closed with heavy seals, arrived, addressed to Miss Phoebe Deane.

Hiram grasped it as if it had been a long sought fortune, put it hastily in his pocket, looking furtively around lest any one had seen it, and slouched off toward home. When he reached there he went straight to his own room and fastened the door. Then he took out the letter and read the address again, written in a fine large hand of a man accustomed to handling the pen. He frowned and turned it over. The seals were stamped with a crest on which was a lion, rampant, that seemed to defy him. He held the letter up to the light, but could not make out any words. Then without hesitation he took out his knife and inserted the sharpest blade under the seals one by one, prying them up carefully so that they should not be broken more than could be helped. The letter lay open before him at last and he read with rising fury:

NEW YORK, December 20th, 1835.

MY DEAR MISS DEANE:
Will you pardon my presumption in daring thus to address you without permission? My pleasant memory of our brief acquaintance has led me to wish a continuance of it, and I am writing to ask you if you are free and willing to

correspond with me occasionally. It will be a great source of pleasure to me if you can accede to my request, and I am sure I shall be profited by it also.

Night before last our city was visited by a great calamity in the shape of a terrible fire which is still burning, although they hope they now have it under control. Its course has been along Wall Street, the line of the East River, and returning to William and Wall Streets. There must be nearly thirteen acres devastated, and I have heard it estimated that there will be a loss of at least eighteen millions of dollars. I am afraid it will be the cause of much suffering and distress. I was out last evening watching the conflagration for a time, and helping to fight the fire. It was a terrible and beautiful sight.

I have just had the honor and privilege of meeting a noble and brave gentleman. His name is William Lloyd Garrison. I feel sure you would like to know about him and the work he is doing. If I am to have the pleasure of writing you again I shall be glad to tell you more of him, as I hope to meet him again, and to know him better.

Hoping that you are quite well, and that I shall soon have a favorable reply from you, I am,

Yours with esteem,
NATHANIEL GRAHAM.

Hiram Green was not a rapid reader, and in spite of Nathaniel's clear chirography it took him some time to take in all that the letter contained. The first thought that took form in his mind was that this rival of his was not out of his way yet. He had dared to write to her and ask if she was free. Ah! That showed he had taken note of what Hiram had said about her belonging to him, and he was going to find out for himself. Well, he would never find out by that letter, for Phoebe would never see it. That was easy enough. Of course it was against the law to open another person's mail, and was a state's prison offense, but who was to know that he had opened it? A letter could tell no tales when it was in ashes, and the ashes well buried. How else could they prove it? They could not. He was perfectly safe, and more and more was he getting power over these two whom he was coming to hate and to wish to crush. He congratulated himself on having been keen enough to have watched the mails. He had outwitted them, and he was pleased with himself beyond expression.

"H'm!" he ejaculated under his breath. "He's a goin' to get up a correspondence with her, is he? Like to see him! I rather think by the time she answers this letter he'll 'uv give it up. When he gets around again to give her another try — supposin' he ain't stumped at not hearin' from her this time — I reckon she'll be nicely established in my kitchen doin' my work. Yes, she's worth fightin' for, I guess, fer she ken turn off the work faster'n anybody I've seen. Wal, I guess there ain't any cause to worry 'bout this."

Then he read it over again, and yet again, noting down on an old bit of paper the date, and a few items about the fire in New York, also William Lloyd Garrison's name. After that he sent the old woman who was keeping house for him to the attic in search of a coat he knew was not there, while he carefully burned the letter on the hearth, gathering every scrap of its ashes and pulverizing them, to make sure not a trace remained to tell the tale.

As he walked away towards his barn he felt himself a man of consequence. His self-satisfaction fairly radiated from his lanky figure. For had he not outwitted a college man? And no thought of the crime had he just committed troubled his dull conscience for an instant.

That evening he took his eager way to Albert Deane's house and prepared to enjoy himself. The sunrise bedquilt was long since finished and rolled away in the chest of drawers in the spare bedroom. The spinning-wheel had taken the place of the quilting frames. And it happened that on this particular night Emmeline had demanded that Phoebe stay downstairs and spin, declaring that the yarn ought to have been ready long ago for more winter stockings.

Hiram noted this fact with satisfaction, and tilted his chair in pleasurable anticipation.

"Heard anythin' 'bout the big fire in New York?" he began, watching Phoebe's back narrowly to see if she would start. But Phoebe worked steadily on. She paid little heed to anything Hiram said, but as they talked of the fire she wondered whether Nathaniel Graham had been near it, and hoped in a maidenly way that he had been kept safe from harm.

"Why, no," said Albert, sitting up with interest, "I haven't looked at the paper yet — " unfolding it with zest. "How'd you come to know, Hiram? You say you never read the papers."

"Oh, I have better ways o' knowin' than readin' it in the papers," boasted Hiram, airily. "I had a letter from New York straight, an' the fire's goin' on yet, an' mebbe by this time it's all burnt up."

Phoebe stood so that he could see her face distinctly as he spoke about receiving a letter, but there was not a movement of a muscle to show she had heard. Hiram was disappointed. He had expected to catch some flitting expression that would show him she had interests in letters from New York. But Phoebe had no expectations of any letter from New York, so why should she start or look troubled?

"Yes," said Albert, bending over his paper, "an area of thirteen acres — six hundred and ninety-three houses burned!"

"Valued at eighteen millions!" remarked Hiram, dryly. He was enjoying the unique position of knowing more than Albert about something.

"Nonsense!" said Emmeline, sharply. "Thirteen acres! Why, that's not much bigger'n Hiram's ten-acre lot down by the old chestnut-tree. Think of gettin' that many houses on that lot! It couldn't be done. That ain't possible. It's ridiculous! They must think we're all fools to put that in the paper."

"Oh, yes, it could, Emmeline," said Albert, looking up earnestly to convince her. "Why, even so long ago as when I stayed in New York for a month they built the houses real close without much door-yard. They could easy get that many into thirteen acres built close."

"I don't believe it!" said Emmeline, flipping her spinning-wheel around skillfully, "and anyway, if 'twas so I think it was real shiftless to let 'em all burn up. Why didn't they put it out? Those New York folks were born lazy."

"Why, Emmeline, the paper says it was so cold the water froze in the hose-pipes and they couldn't put it out."

"Serves 'em right then fer dependin' on such new-fangled things as hose-pipes. It's jest some more of their laziness. Why didn't they form a line and hand buckets? A good fire line with the women an' all in it would beat all the new lazy ways invented to save folks from liftin' their fingers to even put out a fire. I'm surprised some of 'em didn't jest sit still and expect some kind of a new machine to be made in time to wheel 'em away to safety 'stead of usin' their legs and runnin' out o' harm's way. Haven't they got a river in New York?"

"'Course" said Hiram, as if he knew it all. "The fire burned the whole line of the East River." He was glad to be reminded of the rest of his newly-acquired information.

"There, that just shows it!" exclaimed Emmeline. "That's just what I said. Shiftless lot, they are. Let their houses burn up right in front of a river! Well, I'm thankful to say I don't live in New York!"

The talk hummed on about her, but Phoebe heard no more. Somehow she kept her busy wheel whirring, but her thoughts had wandered off in a sunlit wood, and she was holding sweet converse with a golden day, and a stranger hovering on the pleasant horizon. It was not until near the close of the evening that her thoughts came back to listen to what was going on. Hiram had brought the front legs of his chair down to the floor with a thud. Phoebe thought he was going home, and she was glad they would soon be rid of his hated presence.

"Oh, by the way!" said Hiram, with a sway of conceit, "Albert, have you ever heard of a man named Garrison? William Lloyd Garrison, I believe it is."

He rolled the name out fluently, having practiced in the barn during the evening milking.

"Oh, yes," said Albert, interestedly. "You know who he is, Hiram. He's a smart fellow, though I'd hate to be in his boots!"

"Why!" Hiram's voice was sharp and his eyes narrowed as they always did when he was reaching out for clue.

"Why, don't you know about Garrison? He's had a price on his head for some time back. He gets mobbed every time he turns around, too, but I guess he's pretty plucky, for he keeps right on."

"What doing?"

"Why, he's the great Abolitionist. He publishes that paper, the *Liberator,* don't you know. You remember two years ago those anti-slavery meetings that were broken up and all the trouble they had? Well, he was the man that started it all. I don't know whether he's very wise or not, but he certainly has got a lot of courage."

Hiram's eyes were narrowing to a slit now with knowledge and satisfaction.

"Oh, yes, I place him now," he drawled out. "He wouldn't be a very comfortable 'quaintance fer a man t' have, would he?"

"Well," considered Albert, thoughtfully, "I wouldn't like to have any of my relations in his place. I'd be afraid of what might happen. I think likely 'twould take a bit of courage to be friend to a man like that. But they say he has friends, a few of them."

"H'm!" said Hiram, and he rolled a thought like a sweet morsel under his tongue. "I guess I better be goin'. Night." And he shuffled away at last, casting a curious smile at Phoebe as he left.

The next morning while they were going about their work in the kitchen Emmeline remarked to Phoebe that Albert thought Hiram Green was changing for the better, he seemed to be growing real intellectual. Had Phoebe noticed how well he talked about that New York fire?

Phoebe had not noticed.

"What a queer girl you are!" exclaimed Emmeline, much vexed; "I should think you'd see he's takin' all this interest in things jest fer you. It ain't like him to care fer such things. He just thinks it will please you, and you are hard as nails not to 'preciate it."

"You are quite mistaken, Emmeline. Hiram Green never did anything to please any one but himself, I am sure," answered Phoebe, and taking her apron off went up to her room.

Phoebe was spending much more time in her room in these days than pleased Emmeline. Not that her work suffered, for Phoebe's swift fingers performed all the tasks required of her in the most approved manner, but so soon as they were done she was off. The fact that the room was cold seemed to affect her in no wise. Emmeline was in a state of chronic rage for this isolation from the rest of the family, though perhaps the only reason she liked to have her around was that she might make sarcastic remarks about her. Then, too, it seemed like an assumption of superiority on Phoebe's part. Emmeline could not bear superiority.

Phoebe's reason for hurrying to the seclusion of her own room on every possible occasion was that a new source of comfort and pleasure had been open to her through the kindness of Marcia Spafford. Miranda had reported promptly Phoebe's two escapes from Hiram Green and not only Marcia but David was greatly interested in the sweet-faced young girl. Shortly after the occasion of

Alma's unexpected punishment Miranda was sent up to the Deanes to request that Phoebe come down for the afternoon a little while, as "Mis' Spafford has a new book she thinks you'll enjoy readin' with her awhile."   Much to Emmeline's disgust, for she had planned a far different occupation for Phoebe, the girl accepted with alacrity, and was soon seated in the pleasant library poring over one of Whittier's poems which opened up a new world to her. The poem was one which David had just secured to publish in his paper, and they discussed its beauties for a few minutes, and then Marcia opened a delightful new book by Cooper.

Phoebe had naturally a bright mind, and during her days of school she had studied all that came in her way. Always she had stood at the head of her classes, sometimes getting up at the first peep of dawn to study a lesson or work over a problem, and sticking to her books until the very last minute. This had been a great source of trouble, because Emmeline objected most seriously to "taking her education so hard," as she expressed it. "Some children have measles and whooping-cough and chicken-pox and mumps real hard," she was wont to say, "but they most of 'em take learnin' easy. But Phoebe's got learnin' hard. She acts like there wasn't any use for anything else in the world but them books. Land! What good'll they do her? They won't make her spin a smoother thread, 'er quilt a straighter row, 'er sew a finer seam. She'll jest ferget everything she learnt when she's married. I'm sure I did." And no one ever disputed this convincing fact.

Nevertheless Phoebe had studied on, trying it is true to please Emmeline by doing all the work required of her, but still insisting on getting her lessons even if it deprived her of her rest, or her noon luncheon. She had acquired the habit of devouring every bit of information that came in her way, so that in spite of her environments she had a measure of true mind culture. It may have been this which so mystified and annoyed Emmeline.

So the afternoon was one of unalloyed delight to Phoebe. When she insisted that she must go home to help get supper, Miranda was sent with her, and the precious book went along to be read in odd moments. Since then Phoebe felt she had something to help her through the trying days.

These afternoons of reading with Marcia Spafford had become quite the settled thing every week or two, and always there was a book to carry home, or a new poem or article to think about.

Emmeline had grown wrathful about his constant going out, and had asked questions until she had in a measure discovered what was going on. She held her temper in for a while, for when she spoke to Albert he did not seem to sympathize with her irritation at Phoebe, but only asked the girl to let him see the book she had been reading, and became so delighted with it himself that he forgot to bring in the armful of wood Emmeline asked for until she called him the second time. After that Albert shared in the literary treasures that Phoebe brought to the house, and it became his habit to say when he came in to supper: "Been down to the village this afternoon, Phoebe? Didn't get anything new to read, did you?" This made Emmeline fairly furious, and she decided to express her mind once more freely to the girl.

She chose a morning when Phoebe was tied by a task which she could not well leave, and began:

"Now look here, Phoebe Deane, I must say you are goin' beyond all bounds. I think it's about time you stopped. I want you to understand that I think the way you're actin' is a downright sin. It isn't enough that you should scorn a good honest man that's eatin' his heart out fer yeh, an' you payin' no more 'tention to him 'n if he was the very dust o' your feet, an' him able to keep you well, too; an' you willin' to set round an' live on relations that ain't real relations at all; an' you with money in the bank a-plenty, an' never even offerin' to give so much as a little present to your little nephews and nieces that are all you've got in the world. It ain't enough that you should do all that, an' be a drug on our hands, but here you must get an' get up a 'quaintance with a woman I don't like n'er respect at all, an' let her send that poor, hard-workin', good-fer-nothin', red-headed girl after you every few days 'a takin' you away from your home, an' your good honest work that you ought to be willin' to do twice over fer all you've had. Phoebe Deane, d' you realize thet we let you go to school clear up to the top grade when other girls hed to stop an' go to work? It was all *his* doin's, I'd never hev allowed it. I think it jest spoils a girl to get so much knowledge. It's jest as I said 'twould be, too. Look at you! Spoiled. You want lily-white hands an' nothin' to do. You want to go to everlastin' tea-parties an' bring home books to read the rest o' the time. Now I stopped school when I was in the fourth reader 'n look at me. There ain't a woman round is better fixed 'n what I am. What do I need of more books? Answer that, Phoebe Deane! Answer me! Would it make me darn the children's stockin's, er cook his meals, er spin, er weave better, er would it make me any better anyway? Answer me?"

Emmeline had two bright red spots on her cheeks and she was very angry. When she was angry she always screamed her sentences at her opponent in a high key. Phoebe had the impulse to throw the wet dish-cloth at her sister-in-law, and it was hard indeed to restrain her indignation at this speech. There was the lovely Mrs. Spafford lending her books and helping her and encouraging her in every way to improve her mind by reading and study, and even Mr. Spafford seemed anxious she should have all the books to read that she desired; and here was this woman talking this way! It was beyond speech. There was nothing to say.

Emmeline stepped up close to the girl, grasped her white arm and shook it fiercely until the dish-cloth came near doing a rash deed of its own accord.

"Answer me!" she hissed in the girl's face.

"It might —" The exasperated girl hesitated. What good would it do to say it?

"Well, go on," said the woman, gripping the arm painfully. "You've got some wicked word to say, just speak it out to the one that hes been more than mother to ye, an' then I s'pose you'll feel better."

"I was only going to say, Emmeline, that more study might have made you understand others better."

"Understand! Understand!" screamed Emmeline, now thoroughly roused. "I should like to know who I don't understand! Don't I understand my husband an' my children, and my neighbors? I s'pose you mean understand you, you good-fer-nothin' hussy! Well, that ain't necessary! You're so different from everybody else on earth that an angel from heaven er a perfesser from college couldn't understand you, an' learnin' won't make you any different, no matter how much time you waste on it."

"Emmeline, listen!" said Phoebe, trying to stop this outburst; "I consider that I've worked for my board since I came here —"

"Consider! Consider! You consider! Well, really! Worked for your board, when you was scarcely more use 'n a baby when you come, an' think o' all the trouble o' raisin' ye! And you consider thet you've earned all you've got here! Well, I don't consider any such a thing, I ken tell you."

"Please let me finish, Emmeline. I was going to say that I have tried to make Albert take the money I have in the bank as payment for any expense and trouble I have been to him, but he says he promised my mother he wouldn't touch a cent of it, and he will not take it."

"Oh, yes, Albert is soft-hearted. Well, I didn't promise yer ma, by a long sight, an' I ain't bound to no such fool notions."

"Emmeline, I don't feel the money belongs to you. It was not you who brought me here, nor paid for whatever I have had. It was Albert. I cannot see why I should give you the money. You have done nothing for me but what you have had to do, and I am sure I have worked for you enough to pay for that, but I would much rather give the money to you than to have you talk in this way —"

"Oh, I wasn't askin' fer yer money. I wouldn't take it es a gift. I was only showin' yeh up to yourself, what a selfish good-fer-nothin' you are, settin' up airs to read books when there's good honest work goin' on."

It happened that Albert came in just then and the discussion dropped, but Phoebe with determined mien went on with her visits to Mrs. Spafford whenever Miranda came for her — never alone, lest she encounter Hiram Green — and so the winter dragged slowly on its way.

Chapter 17

Meanwhile Hiram Green still kept up his attention to the post-office, watching the Deanes so vigilantly that it was impossible for them to receive mail without his knowing it. This never annoyed Albert, as he was too good-natured to suspect any one of an ill turn, and he thought it exceedingly kind of Hiram to bring his mail up. As for Phoebe, it simply cut out all opportunity for her to go out, except when Miranda came for her.

"Why can't that Mirandy girl stay home an' mind her business an' let you come when you get ready?" asked Emmeline, in a loud tone one day when Miranda was waiting in the sitting-room for Phoebe to get ready to go with her. "She ac's 's if she was your nurse."

But Miranda continued her vigilance, and that without Phoebe's asking, and somehow Marcia always planned it that if Phoebe could stay to tea and she and David would walk home with her. It was all delightful for Phoebe, but everything that was done merely offended Emmeline the more.

Miranda, in these days, was enjoying herself. She lost no opportunity to observe the detestable Hiram and rejoice that she had foiled his attempts to bother Phoebe. One day, however, she happened to be in the post-office when the mail was distributed. She was buying sugar, and she loitered a moment after the package was handed her, watching Hiram Green who had slouched over to the counter and asked for his mail.

"Nothin' fer the Deanes?" she heard him ask in a low tone. "Nothin' fer Phoebe? She was 'spectin' somethin' I'm sure."

Miranda cast a sharp glance at him as she passed him. She was glad somehow that he received nothing. She wondered if Phoebe knew he was enquiring for her mail. Miranda laid it by in her mind as something that might be of use in the future, and went on her way.

That very day the old woman who kept house for Hiram, in sweeping out his room, came across a bit of red sealing-wax stamped with a part of a crest which bore a lion's head with the jaws apart. It was lying on a dark stripe in the rag carpet and had not been noticed before. She saw at once it was of no value and tossed it toward the open window, where it lodged upon the sill close up to the frame, and by and by when the window was closed it was shut in tight between sash and sill, the lion's head, erect and fierce, caught in the crack, a tiny thing and hidden, but reminding one of "truth crushed to earth."

The next day Nathaniel Graham made a flying visit to his home to have a serious conference with his uncle the Judge. His investigations concerning the two questions which had troubled him on his journey back to New York had involved him in matters that had now come to a crisis, and he found that some decision must be reached at once. He had received several more letters from his uncle in Texas, urging him persistently to come down at once and help their cause. More and more it was becoming a dangerous thing to do, as Congress had not sanctioned any such help, and in fact it might involve any one who attempted it in serious difficulties. Yet it was being done every day. People who lived near to Texas were gathering money and arms, and sending men to help, and even so far as New York there were many quietly at work. Public sentiment was strongly with Texas, save only among those who were opposed to slavery, and as yet that question was but in its infancy. Nathaniel had been put to it at last to decide definitely about Texas. He had been offered command of a company of men who were to sail soon, and he must say yes or no at once. The pressure was very strong, and sometimes he almost thought he ought to go. The time had come to speak to Judge Bristol. Nothing could be decided without his final word, for Nathaniel felt too much honor and love for the one who had been his second father to do anything without his sanction.

As was to be expected the Judge was seriously troubled at the thought of Nathaniel's going South to join in the conflict, and he argued long and seriously against any such project, telling his nephew that he had no right to even consider such questions until he had made a place for himself in the world. When Nathaniel admitted that he had been attending Abolition meetings, and was becoming intimate with some of the leaders, the Judge was roused into excited hostility.

"Nathaniel, how could you?" he exclaimed, in deep distress. "I thought your judgment was sound, but to be carried away by these wild, fanatical people is anything but evidence of sound judgment. Can you not see that this is a question that you have no business with? If your uncle in Texas chooses to keep slaves, you have no more right to meddle with his choice than if he chose to keep horses or sheep. And as for this bosh about slavery being such a terrible evil, look at Pompey and Caesar and Dianthe and the rest? Do you fancy they want to be free? Why, what would the poor things do if I didn't care for them as if they were my own children? It is all nonsense.

"Of course, there are a few bad masters, and probably will be as long as sin is in the world; but to condemn the whole system of slavery because a few men who happen to own slaves mistreat them would be like condemning marriage because a few men abused their wives. It is utmost nonsense for a few hot-headed fanatics to try to run the rest of the country into the moulds they have made and call it righteousness. Let other men alone, and they will let you go in peace is a better motto. Let every man look out to cast the beam from his own eyes before he attempts to find a mote in his brother's."

When his uncle quoted Scripture in this way Nathaniel was at a loss how to answer him.

"I wish you could hear Mr. Garrison talk, Uncle."

"I wouldn't listen to him for a moment," he answered, hotly. "He is a dangerous man! Keep away from all such gatherings, for they only breed discontent and uprisings. You will see that nothing but a lot of mobs will arise from this agitation. Slavery is a thing that cannot be overthrown, and all these meetings are mere talk to let a few men get into prominence. No man in his senses would do the things that that Garrison has done unless he wanted to get notoriety. That's what makes him so foolhardy. Keep away from him, my boy. There's a price on his head, and you'll do yourself and your prospects no good if you have anything to do with him."

They talked far into the night, Nathaniel trying to defend the man whom he had met but once or twice, but whom he had been compelled to admire. Janet pouted through the evening because Nathaniel did not come out to talk with her, and finally went to bed in a fit of the blues.

When at last Nathaniel pressed his uncle's hand at parting they both knew that he would not go to Texas. Indeed, as the young man had reflected during the night, he felt that his purpose of going there had been shaken before he came home to ask Judge Bristol's advice. However, he was not altogether sure that his uncle had considered the matter from the correct view-point either, but the talk had somehow helped to crystallize his own views. So now he felt free, nay bound, to return and complete his law course. As for the other matter, that must be left to develop in its time. He was by no means sure he was done with it yet, for his heart had been too deeply touched, and his reason stirred.

As Nathaniel climbed into the coach at the big white gate he felt that he had only put off all these questions for a time, but there was a certain relief in feeling that a decision had been reached at least for the present.

He was half a mind to ride on top with the driver, though it was a bitterly cold morning, but quite unexpectedly the driver suggested that he better sit inside this time, as the weather was so cold. Without giving it a passing thought he went inside, waving his hand and smiling at Janet, who stood at the front door with a fur-trimmed scarlet cloak about her shapely shoulders. Then the door closed and he sat down.

There was one other passenger, a girl, who sat far back in the shadows of the coach, but her eyes shone out from the heavy wrappings of cloak and bonnet and gave him welcome.

"Oh!" she said, catching her breath.

"And is it you?" he asked eagerly, reaching out to grasp her hand. Then each remembered, the girl that she was alone in the coach with this man, the man that this girl might belong to another. But in spite of it they were glad to see one another.

The coach rolled out into the main street again and as it lurched over the crossing Hiram Green, who was hurrying to his daily vigilance at the post-office, caught a good view of Nathaniel's back through the coach window. The back gave the impression of an animated conversation being carried on in which the owner of the back was deeply interested.

Hiram almost paused in his walk over the crunching snow. "Gosh Ninety!" he ejaculated in consternation, "who knowed he was here!"

Then the reflection that at least Nathaniel was about to depart calmed his perturbation and he hurried on to the office.

Hiram did not know that Phoebe was in the coach. She had managed it very carefully with a view to concealing it from him, for she felt sure that if he knew she was going that morning he would have found it possible to have accompanied her, and she would have found it impossible to get rid of his company. So when the day before Emmeline had suggested that somebody ought to go out to Miss Ann Jane Bloodgood's and get some dried saffron flowers she had promised them last fall, to dye the carpet-rags, Phoebe said nothing until after Hiram had left that night. Then as she was going upstairs with her candle she turned to Emmeline and said:

"I've been thinking Emmeline, I could go over to Bloodgood's by the morning coach if Albert could drive me down when he takes his corn to the mill. Then perhaps some of them would be coming over to the village, or I could catch a ride back, or if not I could come back by the evening coach."

Emmeline assented grimly. She wanted the dye and she did not relish the long cold ride in the coach. Ann Jane Bloodgood was too condescending to please her, anyway. So, as Albert was going to mill early, Phoebe made her simple preparations that night, and was ready bright and early. Moreover, she coaxed Albert to drive around by Granny McVane's that she might leave a bit of poetry for her which she had told her about. The poem could have waited, but Albert did not tell her that, and Phoebe did not explain to Albert that if they went around by Granny's Hiram would not know she was gone away and therefore would not try to follow her. It was a pity that Phoebe had not confided a little now and then in Albert, though he, poor soul, could do little against such odds as Emmeline and Hiram.

The ten-mile coach ride to Bloodgood's wide farm-house spun itself away into nothing in such company, and before Phoebe could believe it was half over she saw the distant roof, low-browed with overhanging snow, and the red barns glimmering warmly a little beyond. Nathaniel saw them, too, for she had told him at once where she was going and he might not think she had planned to go with him. He felt that the moments were precious.

"Do you remember what we talked of that night we walked to your home?" he asked.

"Oh, yes," she breathed, softly. "You were talking of some one who needed setting free. I have been reading some wonderful poems lately that made me think a great deal of what you said."

He looked at her keenly. How could a girl who read poems and talked so well belong to Hiram Green?

"I have been thinking much about it lately," he went on with just the breath of sign. "I may have to decide what I will do at no distant day now. I wonder if I may ask you to pray for me?"

He watched her, this girl with the drooping eyes and rosy-hued cheeks, the girl who had by her silence refused to answer his letter, and wondered if perhaps by his request he had offended her. The coach lurched up to the wide piazza and stopped, and the driver jumped heavily into the snowy road. They could hear his steps plowing through the drift by the back wheel. His hand was on the coach door. Then quickly, as if she might be too late, her eyes were lifted to his, and he saw her heart would be in those prayers, as she answered:

"Oh, I will."

Something like a flash of light went through them as they looked for that instant into one another's eyes, and lifted them above the mere petty things of earth. It was intangible. Nathaniel could not explain it to himself as he sat back alone in the empty coach and went over the facts of the case, why his heart felt light, and the day seemed brighter, just because a girl whom he knew ever so little had promised in that tone of voice to pray for him. It thrilled him anew as he thought it over, and his heart went soaring up into heavens of happiness, until he called himself a fool, and told himself nothing was changed, and that Phoebe had not even replied to his letter and politely declined the correspondence, as she would certainly have been justified in doing even if she were the promised wife of Hiram Green. Yet his heart refused to be anything but buoyant. He began to berate himself that he had not frankly spoken of his letter and heard what she had to say about the matter. Perhaps in some way it had never reached her, and yet after all that was scarcely possible. Letters clearly addressed were seldom lost. It might only have embarrassed her if he had spoken.

At the next stop he accepted the coach driver's invitation to "come up top a spell, there's a fine sun comin' up now," and he let old Michael babble on about the gossip of the town, until at last the sly old man asked him innocently enough: "And what did ye think av the other passenger, Mr. 'Than'el? An' ain't she a bonnie lassie?" And then he was treated to a list of Phoebe's virtues sounded forth by one who in reality knew very little of her save that as a child on the way home from school one day she had shyly handed him up a bunch of wayside posies as he drove by her on the road. That childish act had won his loyalty, and old Michael was not troubled with the truth. He was thoroughly capable of filling in virtues where he knew none. He went on the principle that what ought to be was. And so it was that when Nathaniel arrived in New York his heart was strangely light, and he wondered often if Phoebe Deane would remember to pray for him. It seemed as if the momentous question were now in better hands than his own.

Meantime Hiram Green, having found in the post-office a circular letter for Albert concerning a new kind of plow that was being put upon the market, plodded up to the Deanes. He knew that Albert was gone to mill that morning and would not be home yet, but he thought the letter would be an excuse to see Phoebe. He wanted to judge whether Phoebe knew of this visit of Nathaniel's. He thought he could tell by her face whether she had had a secret meeting with him or not. Yet it puzzled him to know when it could have been, for Phoebe had been quietly sewing carpet-rags all evening before, and he was sure she had not gone by with Miranda in the afternoon to the Spaffords. Had she gone to the woods again in the winter, or did she not know he was here? Perhaps his own skilful manipulating of the mail had nipped this miniature courtship in the bud, as it were, and there would be no further need of his vigilance.

But when Hiram reached the Deanes and looked about for Phoebe she was not there.

"Where's Phoebe?" he demanded, frowning.

"She's gone up to Ann Jane Bloodgood's t' get some saffron flowers," said Emmeline. "Won't you come in, Hiram? She'll be mighty sorry to know she missed you." Emmeline thought it was as well to keep up appearances for Phoebe.

"Yes, I'm sure," drawled Hiram. "How'd she go?" he asked her after an ominous silence in which Emmeline was meditating on what it would be best to say.

"She went in the coach, an' I reckon she'll come back that way by night ef there don't no one come over from Bloodgood's this way. You might meet the coach ef you was goin' in to the village again. I don't know's Albert'll feel he hes time after losin' so much o' the day t' mill."

Hiram said nothing, but Emmeline saw he was angry.

"I'd a sent you word she was goin' an' given you the chance to go 'long with her, only she didn't say a word till after you was gone home last night—" she began apologetically, but Hiram did not seem to heed her. He got up after a minute, his brows still lowering. He was thinking that Phoebe had planned to go with Nathaniel Graham.

"I'll be over t' th' village," he said, as he went out. "Albert needn't go." Emmeline looked after him meditatively.

"I shouldn't be a bit s'prised ef he give er up, the way she goes on. It's wonderful how he holds on to her. She's a fool, that's what she is, an' I've no pity on to her. I wish to goodness she was well married an' out o' the way. She does try me beyond all, with her books, an' her visitin's, an' her locked doors, an' notions."

Meantime, Phoebe, all unconscious of the plot that was thickening round her, accepted an invitation to remain over night and the next day with Ann Jane Bloodgood, and drive in to town in the afternoon when she went to missionary meeting. Ann Jane was interested in Christian missions and fascinated Phoebe with her tales of Eliot, Brainerd, Carey, Whiteman, and Robert Moffat. Phoebe, as she looked over Ann Jane's pile of missionary papers, began to wonder how many people of one sort and another there were in the world who needed setting free from something. It all seemed to be a part of the one great thing for which she was praying, the thing that Nathaniel Graham was trying to decide, and he was another just like those wonderful men who were giving their lives to save others. Phoebe was glad she had come, though perhaps she might not have been if she could have seen the thought that was working in Hiram Green's heart.

After some reflection Hiram harnessed his horses and took the long ride over to Bloodgood's that afternoon, arriving at the house just after Phoebe and Ann Jane were safely established in Ann Jane's second cousin's best room, a mile away, for a visit. Ann Jane's second cousin was an invalid and liked company, so Phoebe's bright face cheered what would otherwise have been a lonely afternoon, and she escaped the unpleasant encounter with Hiram.

Hiram, his suspicions confirmed, met the evening coach, but no Phoebe appeared. He stepped up to Albert Deane's in the evening long enough to make sure that she had not returned by any private conveyance, and the next day he drove over again, but again found the low farm-house closed and deserted, for Ann Jane had driven with Phoebe by another road to the village missionary meeting.

His temper not much improved with his two fruitless rides, Hiram returned, watched every passenger from the evening coach alight, and then betook himself to the Deanes again, where he was really surprised to find Phoebe had returned.

That evening when the saffron flowers were being discussed he remarked that there were mighty nice saffron flowers for sale in Albany, and he watched Phoebe narrowly, but the round cheek did not flush nor the long lashes flutter in any suspicious way. Nevertheless, Hiram's mind never let go an evil thought that once lodged there. He felt he had a new power over Phoebe that he might use if occasion demanded. He could bide his time.

Chapter 18

Spring was coming on at last, and Hiram Green, who had been biding his time and letting his wrath smoulder, began to think it was time to do something. All winter Phoebe had been able to keep comparatively free from him, save for his company with the family in the evening. Hiram took every opportunity possible to make it apparent that he was "keeping company" with Phoebe, through the medium of his nightly visit, and Phoebe made it plain upon every occasion that she did not consider his visit was for her. She got out of the way when she could, but Emmeline contrived to keep her unusually busy every evening, and her own room was so cold that escape was impossible.

Hiram had made several unsuccessful efforts to establish himself beside Phoebe in public, and he was getting desperate. Every Sunday when he tried to walk down the aisle with her he would find Miranda and Rose one on either side of her, Mrs. Spafford herself, sometimes all three, and all serenely unconscious of his presence. They attended her down to the carryall. She never went to the village any more that he could discover, unless Miranda came for her, or Albert took her back and forth, though once he had seen her flying across the fields from Granny McVane's house with a bundle that looked as if it came from the store. He complained to Emmeline at last and she agreed to help him. Albert was not taken into the scheme. For some reason it was deemed best not to tell Albert about it at all. He was apt to ask kindly, searching questions, and he always took it for granted that one did everything with the best motives. Besides, he was not quick at evasion and might let the cat out of the bag.

There was to be a barn raising about ten miles the other side of the village, and the whole country round about were invited. It happened that the Woodburys, whose barn was to be raised, were distant relatives of Emmeline, and of course the Deanes were going.

Emmeline had shown plainly that she would be offended if Phoebe did not go, though the girl would have much preferred remaining at home with the new book Mrs. Spafford had sent up the day before. It was a matter of selfishness with Emmeline. She wanted Phoebe to help with the big dinner and relieve her so that she could visit with the other women.

It was a part of the scheme that Albert should go in the chaise with Alma, and should start while Phoebe was still dressing. Emmeline had managed Albert very adroitly, telling him that Hiram wanted a change to "set in the front seat with Phoebe" in the carryall. Albert, always willing to do a good turn, acceded readily, though Alma was a somewhat reluctant passenger.

When Phoebe came downstairs she found Emmeline already seated in the back seat of the carryall with the other children. She gladly got into the front seat, as it was much pleasanter to be there than beside Emmeline, and she seldom had the opportunity of riding beside her brother, who was more congenial than the others. But in a moment Hiram Green appeared from around the corner of the house. He got quickly into the vacant seat beside Phoebe and whipped up the horses.

"Why, where is Albert?" asked Phoebe in dismay, wishing she could get out.

"He had to go on," explained Emmeline, blandly. "Drive fast, Hiram, we'll be late." This last because she fancied she saw a frightened sideways glance from Phoebe as if she might be going to get out.

Phoebe turned her head to the road-side and tried to watch for the chance wild flowers, and forget the talk of crops and gossip that was kept up between Emmeline and Hiram, but the whole pleasant day was clouded for her, and her annoyance was double when they passed through the village and Janet Bristol in dainty pink dimity stared at them with haughty sweetness from under her white shirred bonnet and pink-lined sunshade. Janet was not going to the barn-raising evidently. She had many interests outside of the village where she was born, and did not mingle freely with her fellow-townsmen. There were only a favored few who were her friends and had the privileges of the beautiful old house.

Her passing called forth unfavorable comment from Emmeline and Hiram, and Phoebe writhed at her sister-in-law's tone, loud enough for Janet to hear easily, if she had a mind.

"The idea of wearing such fancy things of a mornin'!" she exclaimed. "I didn't think the Judge was such a fool as to let his daughter come up like that, fixed up fit fer a party this early, an' a sunshade, too! What's she think it's for, I wonder! Her complexion's so dark a little more of this weak sunshine couldn't make much difference. Mebbe she thinks she looks fine, but she's much mistaken. A lazy girl all decked out never looks pretty to me."

"That's 'bout right," declared Hiram, as if he knew all about it. "Give me a good worker ev'ry time, I sez, in preference to one with ringlets an' a nosegay on her frock. But you couldn't expec' much of that one. She's goin' to marry that highfolutin' Nate Graham, an' they'll have money 'nough betwixt 'em to keep her in prettys all the rest of her life. Say, did you hear Nate Graham'd turned Abolitionist? Well, it's so; I heard it from a r'liable source. Hev a friend in Noo York writes me once in a while an' I know what I'm talkin' 'bout. Hed it from headquarters like, you know. Er it's so he may git into trouble enny time now. There's prices on them Abolitionists' heads!"

Hiram turned to look straight into Phoebe's startled face, with an ugly leer of a laugh. The girl's cheeks grew pink, and she turned quickly away; Hiram felt he had scored one against her. It made him good-natured all day. But Phoebe found herself trembling with a single thought. Did it mean life or death, this that Nathaniel had asked her to pray about; and had perhaps her prayers helped to put him in the way of danger? Ah! But if it were true, how grand in him to be willing to brave danger for what he thought was right. Phoebe knew very little about the real question at issue, though she had read a number of Whittier's poems which had stirred her heart deeply. The great thought in her mind was that a man should be brave enough and good enough to stand against the whole world, if need be, to help a weak brother.

The day was one of noise and bustle and, for Phoebe, hard work. By instinct the women put tasks upon her young shoulders which they wished to shirk, knowing they would be well done. It was written large on Phoebe's face that she could be trusted. So they trusted her, and the fun and frolic and feasting went on, while she toiled in the kitchen, gladly taking extra burdens upon herself, only so it kept her out of any possibility of being troubled by Hiram.

She was washing dishes and meditating on how she could manage not to sit next to Hiram on the return trip when a little Woodbury entered the kitchen.

"Say, Phoebe Deane," she called out, "your brother says you're to go in the chaise with him this time, an' when you get ready you come out to the barn an' get in. He says you needn't hurry, fer he's busy yet a while."

The child was gone back to her play before Phoebe could thank her, and with lightened heart she went on washing the dishes. Perhaps Albert had surmised her dislike to riding with Hiram and had planned this for her sake. She made up her mind to confide in Albert during this ride and see if he could not help her to get rid of her obnoxious lover once and for all. Albert was usually slow and undecided, but when once in a great while he put his foot down about something things usually went as he said.

She wiped the last dish, washed her hands, and ran upstairs for her bonnet and mantilla. Everybody else was gone. The long, slant rays of the setting sun were streaming in at the window and touching the great four-poster bed where lay her wraps alone. She put them on quickly, glad that every one else was out of the way and she would not have to wait for a lot of good-byes. The day had been a weariness to her, and she was thankful to have it over.

Mr. and Mrs. Woodbury stood together by the great stepping-stone in front of the house. They had said good-bye to Albert and Emmeline an hour before, and had just been seeing off the last wagon-load of guests. They turned eagerly to thank Phoebe for her assistance. Indeed, the girl had many warm friends among older people who knew her kindly heart and willing hands.

"What! Your folks all gone and left you, Phoebe!" exclaimed Mrs. Woodbury in dismay! "Why, they must a' forgot you."

"No, they're not all gone, Mrs. Woodbury. Our chaise is out in the barn waiting for me. Albert sent word to me by your Martha that I needn't hurry, so I stopped to finish the dishes."

"Oh! Now that's so good of you, Phoebe Deane," said the tired farmer's wife, who expected she would have plenty of cleaning to do after the departure of her large company of guests. "You shouldn't ov done that. I could a' cleaned up. I'm 'fraid you're real tired. Wouldn't you like to stay over night and get rested?"

But Phoebe shook hands happily with them and hurried down to the chaise. Now the Woodbury barn was out near the road, and the chaise stood facing the road, the horse not tied, but waiting with turned head as if his master was not far away. Phoebe jumped in with a spring, calling "Come on, Albert. I'm here at last. Did I keep you waiting long?"

Then before she had time to look around or know what was happening Hiram Green stepped out from the barn door, sprang into the seat beside her, and with unwonted swiftness caught up the whip and gave the horse such a cut that it started off at a brisk trot down the road. It was he who had sent the message by little Martha Woodbury, just as it had been given. Emmeline had managed the rest.

"Oh!" gasped Phoebe. "Why, Mr. Green, Albert is here waiting for me somewhere. Please stop the horse and let me find him. He sent word he would wait for me."

"That's all right," said Hiram, nonchalantly. "Albert decided to go in the carryall. Your sister-in-law was in a great stew to get back fer milkin' time an' made him come, so I offered to bring ye back home."

Phoebe's heart froze within her. She looked wildly about her and knew not what to do. The horse was going very fast, and to jump would be dangerous. She had no idea that Hiram would stop and let her out if she should ask him. His talk the last time they had an encounter had shown her that she must not let him see he had her in his power. Besides, what excuse could she give for stopping save that she did not wish to go with him? And how otherwise could she get home that night? How she wished that she had accepted Mrs. Woodbury's kind invitation. Could she not, perhaps, manage it yet?

"That's very kind of you," she faltered, with white lips, as she tried to marshal her wits and contrive some way out of this predicament. Then she made a feint of looking about her in the seat.

"I wonder if I remembered to bring my apron," she said faintly. "Would you mind, Mr. Green, just driving me back to see?"

"Oh, I reckon you'll find it," Hiram said, easily. "Ef you don't you got a few more, ain't you? Here, ain't this it?" and he fished out a damp roll from under the seat.

Phoebe had hoped for one wild little moment that she had really dropped it when she got into the chaise, for it did not seem to be about anywhere, but the sight of the damp blue roll dashed all her confidence. There was nothing for it but to accept the situation as bravely as possible and make the best of it. Her impulse was to turn angrily and tell Hiram Green that he had deceived her, but she knew that would do no good, and the safest thing was to act as if it were all right and try to keep the conversation upon every-day topics. If he would only keep on driving at this pace the journey would not be so intolerably long, after all, and they might hope to reach home a trifle before dark perhaps. She summoned all her courage and tried to talk pleasantly, although the countenance of the man beside her as she stole a swift glance at his profile, frightened her. There was both triumph and revenge upon it. "They had a pleasant day for the raising, Mr. Green," she began.

And then to her horror he slowed the horse to a walk and sat back close to her as if he intended to enjoy the tete a tete to its full.

It was an awful strain. Phoebe's cheeks blazed out in two red spots, and her eyes were bright with excitement. They dragged their slow way through a woods where the lights and shadows played in all the sweetness of spring odors. Phoebe sat up very straight, very much to her side of the chaise, and laughed and talked as if she were wound up.

Hiram did not say much. He sat watching her, almost devouring the changefulness of her face, fully understanding her horror of him and this ride, yet determined to make her suffer every minute of the time. It made his anger all the greater as he saw her bravely try to keep up a semblance of respect toward him and knew she did not feel it. Why could she not give it freely, and not against her will? What was there about him she disliked? Never mind, she should pay for her dislike. She should see that she would have to treat him as she would treat those she liked, whether she wished or no.

She suggested that they better drive faster, as it was getting late and would be dark. He said that did not matter, that Emmeline had said they were not to hurry. She told him she would be needed, but he told her it was right she should have a little rest once in a while, and he smiled grimly as he said it, knowing the present ride was anything but rest to the poor tired soul beside him. He seemed to delight in torturing her. The farther she edged away from him the nearer he came to her, until when they emerged from the woods and met a carryall with some people they both knew, he was sitting quite over on her side, and she was almost out of her seat, her face a piteous picture of rage and helplessness.

Emboldened by the expression on the faces of their acquaintances, Hiram threw his arm across the back of the chaise, until it quite encircled Phoebe's back, or would have if she had not sat upon the extreme front edge of the seat.

They had reached a settlement of three houses, where a toll-gate, spreading its white pole out across the way, and a little store and school-house, went by the name of The Crossroads. Hiram flung a bit of money out to the toll-man and drove on without stopping. Phoebe's heart was beating wildly. She could not sit thus on the edge of her seat another instant. Something must be done.

"Mr. Green, would you mind moving over just a little, I haven't quite enough room," she gasped.

"Oh, that's all right," said Hiram, as heartily as if he really did not understand the situation. "Just sit clos'ter. Don't be shy." His circling arm came round her waist and by brute strength drew her up to him, so that it looked from behind as if they were a pair of lovers. The top of the chaise was thrown back so that they could easily be seen.

They had just passed the last house. It was the home of old Mrs. Duzenberry and her elderly daughter Suzanna. Living so far from the village they made it a point not to miss anything that went by their door, and at this hour in the afternoon, when their simple tea was brewing, they both sat by the front window, ready to bob to the door the minute there was anything of interest. It is needless to say that they both bobbed on this occasion, the daughter with folded arms and alert beak like some old bird of prey, the mother just behind with quizzical exclamatory interrogations written in every curve of her cap-strings.

Phoebe, glancing back wildly, as she felt herself drawn beyond her power to stop it, saw them gaping at her in amaze, and her cheeks grew crimson with shame.

"Stop!" she cried, putting out her hands and pushing against him.

She might as well have tried to push off a mountain that was in her path. Hiram only laughed and drew her closer, till his ugly, grizzled face was near to her own. She could feel his breath upon her cheek, and the horse was going faster now. She did not know just how it happened, whether Hiram had touched him with the whip, or spoken a low word. They were down the road out of sight of the Duzenberrys' before she could wrench herself away from the scoundrel. Even then it was but that he might settle himself a little closer and more comfortably that he let go of her for a moment and then the strong, cruel arm came back as if it had a right around her waist, and Hiram's face came cheek to cheek with her own.

She uttered one terrible scream, and looked around, but there was no one in sight. The sun, which had been slowly sinking like a ball of burning opal, suddenly dropped behind a hill and left the world dull and leaden with a heavy sky of gray. Dark blue clouds seemed all around, which until now had not been noticed, and a quick uncertain wind was springing up; a low rumble behind them seemed to wrap them in a new dread. But the strong man's grasp held her fast, and her screams brought no help.

In the horror of the moment a thought of her mother came, and she wondered if that mother were where she could see her child, and whether it did not give her deep anguish even in the bliss of heaven to know she was in such straits. Then as the sharp stubble of Hiram's upper lip brushed the softness of her cheek fear gave her strength, and with a sudden mighty effort she broke from his grasp.

Reaching out to the only member of the party who seemed at all likely to render any aid, Phoebe caught the reins and pulled back upon them with all her might, while her heart was lifted in a swift prayer for help. Then quick, as if in instant answer, while the gray plow-horse reared back upon his haunches, and plunged wildly in the air, came a brilliant flash of jagged lightning, as if the sky was cloven in wrath, and the light of heaven let through; and this was followed on the instant by a terrible crash of thunder.

With an oath of mingled rage and awe, Hiram pushed Phoebe from him and reached for the reins to try and soothe the frightened horse, who was plunging and snorting and trembling in fear.

The chaise was on the edge of a deep ditch half filled with muddy water. One wheel was almost over the edge. Hiram saw the danger, and reached for his whip. He cut the horse a frantic lash which brought his fore-feet to the ground again and caused him to start off down the road on a terrific gallop. But in that instant, while the chaise poised on the edge of the ditch, Phoebe's resolve had crystallized into action. She gave a wild spring, just as the cut from the whip sent the horse tearing headlong down the road. Her dress caught in the arm of the chaise, and for one instant she poised over the ditch. Then the fabric gave way and she fell heavily, striking her head against the fence, and lay huddled in the muddy depths. Down the hard road echoed the heavy hoof-beats of the horse in frenzied gallop with no abatement, and over all the majestic thunder rolled.

Chapter 19

Her senses swam off into the relief of unconsciousness for a moment, but the cold water creeping up through her clothing chilled her back to life again, and in a moment more she had opened her eyes in wonder that she was lying there alone, free from her tormentor. She fancied she could hear the echo of the horse's feet yet, or was it the thunder? Then came the awful thought, what would happen if he returned and found her lying here? He would be terribly angry at her for having frightened the horse and jumped out of the chaise. He would visit it upon her in some way she felt sure, and she would be utterly defenseless against him.

There was not a soul in sight and it was growing suddenly dark. She must be at least six or seven miles away from home. She did not come that way often enough to be sure of distances. With new fear she sat up, and crept out of the water. The mud was deep and it was difficult to step, but she managed to get away from the oozy soil, and into the road again. Then in a panic she sprang across the ditch and crept under the fence. She must fly from here. When Hiram succeeded in stopping the horse he would undoubtedly come back for her, and she must get away before he found her.

Which way should she go? She looked back upon the road, but feared to go that way, lest he would go to those houses and search for her. There was no telling what he would say. She had no faith in him. He might say she had given him the right to put his arms around her. She must get away from here at once where he could not find her. Out to the right, across the road, it was all open country. There was nowhere she could take refuge near by. But across this field and another there was a growth of trees and bushes. Perhaps she could reach there and hide and so make her way home after he had gone.

She fled across the spring-sodden field as fast as her soaked shoes and her trembling limbs could carry her; slipping now and then and almost falling, but catching at the fence and going on, wildly, blindly, till she reached the fence. Once she thought she heard the distant bellowing of a bull, but she crept to the other side of the fence and kept on her way, breathless. And now the storm broke into wild splashes of rain, pelting on her face and hair, for her bonnet had fallen back and was hanging around her neck by its ribbons. The net had come off from her hair, and the long locks blew about her face and lashed her in the eyes as she ran. It was dark as night and Phoebe could see but dimly where she was going. Yet this was a comfort to her rather than a source of fear. She felt it would the better cover her hiding. Her worst dread was to come under the power of Hiram Green again.

So she worked her way through the fields, groping for the fences, and at last she reached an open road, and stood almost afraid to try it, lest somewhere she should see Hiram lurking. The lightning blazed and shivered all about her, trailing across the heavens in awful and wonderful display; the thunder shuddered above her until the earth itself seemed to answer and she felt herself in a rocking abyss of horror; and yet the most awful thing in it all was the fact of Hiram Green.

She had heard all her life that the most dangerous place in a thunderstorm was under tall trees, yet so little did she think of it that she made straight for the shelter of the wood; and though the shocks crashed about her, and seemed to be cleaving the giants of the forest, there she stayed until the storm had abated, and the genuine darkness had succeeded.

She was wet to the skin, and trembling like a leaf. Her strongest impulse was to sink to the earth and weep herself into nothingness, but her commonsense would not let her even sit down to rest. She knew she must start at once if she would hope to reach home. Yet by this time she had very little idea of where she was and how to get home. With another prayer for guidance she started out, keeping sharp lookout along the road with ears and eyes, that there might be no possibility of Hiram's coming upon her unaware. Twice she heard vehicles in the distance, and crept into the shelter of some trees until they passed. She heard pleasant voices talking of the storm and longed to cry out to them for help, yet dared not. What would they think of her, a young girl out alone at that time of night, and in a such condition? Besides, they were all strangers. She dared not speak. And neither to friends would she have spoken, for they would have been all the more astonished to find her so. She thought longingly of Mrs. Spafford, and Miranda, yet dreaded lest even Mrs. Spafford might think she had done wrong to allow herself to ride even a couple of miles with such a man as Hiram Green after all the experience she had had with him. Yet as she plodded along she wondered how she could have done differently, unless indeed she had dared to pull up the horse and jump out at once; yet very likely she would not have been able to make her escape from her tormentor as easily earlier in the afternoon as at the time when she had taken her unpremeditated leap into the ditch.

As she looked back upon the experience it seemed as though the storm had been sent by Providence to provide her a shield and a way of escape. If it had not been for the storm the horse would not have been easily frightened into running, and Hiram would soon have found her and compelled her to get into the chaise again. What could she have done against his strength! She shuddered, partly with cold and partly with horror.

A slender thread of pale moon had come up, but it gave a sickly light, and soon slipped out of sight again, leaving only the kindly stars whose lights looked brilliant but so far away tonight. Everywhere was a soft dripping sound, and the seething of the earth drinking in a good draught.

Once when it seemed as if she had been going for hours she sat down on the wet bank to rest, and a horse and rider galloped out of the blackness past her. She hid her white face in her lap and he may have thought her but a stump beside the fence. She was thankful he did not stop to see, but as yet nothing had given her a clue to her whereabouts, and she was cold, so terribly cold.

At last she passed a house she did not know, and then another, and another. Finally she made out that she was in a little settlement, about three miles from the Deanes' farm. She could not tell how she had wandered, nor how she came to be yet so far away when she must have walked at least twenty miles. But the knowledge of where she was brought her new courage.

There was a road leading from this settlement straight to Granny McVane's, and she would not need to go back by the road where Hiram would search for her, if indeed he had not already given up the search and gone home. The lights were out everywhere in this village, save in one small house at the farthest end, and she stole past that as if she had been a wraith. Then she breathed more freely as she came into the open country road again, and knew there were but two or three houses now between herself and home.

It occurred to her to wonder in a dull way if the horse had thrown Hiram out and maybe he was hurt, and whether she might not after all have to send a search party after him. She wondered what he would do when he could not find her, supposing he was not hurt. Perhaps he had been too angry to go back for her and her dread of him had been unnecessary. But she thought she knew him well enough to know he would not easily give her up.

She wondered if he would tell Albert, and whether Albert would be worried — she was sure he would be, good, kind Albert — and what would Emmeline say? Emmeline, who had been at the bottom of all this she was sure — and then her thoughts would trail on ahead of her in the wet, and her feet would lag behind and she would feel that she could not catch up. If only a kindly coach would appear! Yet she kept on, holding up her heavy head, and gripping her wet mantle close with her cold, cold hands, shivering as she went.

Once she caught herself murmuring: "Oh, mother, mother!" and then wondered what it meant. So stumbling on, slower and more slowly, she came at last to the little house of Granny McVane, all dark and quiet, but so kindly-looking in the night. She longed to crawl to the doorstep and lie down to die, but duty kept her on. No one must know of this if she could help it. That seemed to be the main thought she could grasp with her weary brain.

The fields behind Granny McVane's were very miry. Three times she fell, and the last time almost lay still, but some stirring of brain and conscience helped her up and on again, across the last hillock, over the last fence, through the garden and up to the back door of her home.

There was a light inside, but she was too far gone to think about it now. She tried to open the door but the latch was heavy and would not lift. She fumbled and almost gave it up, but then it was opened sharply by Emmeline with her hair in a hard knot, and old lines under her eyes. She wore a wrapper over her night robe, and a blanket around her shoulders. Her feet were thrust into an old pair of Albert's carpet slippers. She held a candle high above her head, and looked out shrewdly into the night. It was plain she was just awake and fretted at the unusual disturbance.

"Fer pity's sake, Phoebe! Is that you? Where on earth hev you ben? You've hed us all upside down huntin' fer yeh, an' Albert ain't got home yet. I tol' him 'twas no use, you'd mos' likely gone in somewheres out o' the storm, an' you'd be home all right in the mornin', but it's just like your crazy ways to come home in the middle o' th' night. Fer goodness sake, what a sight yeh are! You ain't comin' in the house like that! Why, there'll be mud to clean fer a week. Stop there till I get some water an' a broom."

But Phoebe, with deathly white face, and eyes that saw not, stumbled past her without a word, the water and mud oozing out of her shoes at every step, and dripping from her garments; her sodden bonnet dejectedly upon her shoulders, her hair once long drenched mantle of darkness. Emmeline, half awed by the sight, stood still in the doorway and watched her go upstairs, realizing that the girl did not know what she was doing. Then she shut the door sharply as she had opened it, and followed Phoebe upstairs.

Phoebe held out until she reached her own door, and opened it. Then she sank without a sound upon the floor and lay there as if dead. All breath and consciousness had fluttered out, it seemed, with that last effort.

Emmeline set the candle down with a sudden, startled exclamation and went to her. She felt her hands so cold, like ice, and her face like wet marble, and hard as she was, she was frightened. Her conscience, so long enjoying a vacation, leaped into a new life and became active. What part had she born in this that seemed as if it might yet be a tragedy?

She unlaced the clodded shoes, untied the soaked bonnet, pulled off the wet garments one by one and wrapped the girl in thick warm blankets, dragging her light weight to the bed; but still no sign of consciousness had come. She felt her heart and listened for a breath, but she could not tell yet if she were alive or not. Then she went downstairs with hurried steps, flapping over the kitchen floor in the large carpet slippers, and stirred up the fire that had been banked down, putting the kettle over it to heat. In a little while she had plenty of hot water, and various remedies applied, but life seem scarcely yet to have crept back to her, only a flutter of the eyelids now and then or a fleeting breath like a sigh. The dawn was coming on and Albert's voice in low strained tones could be heard outside:

"No, I'm not going to stop for anything to eat, Hiram, you may if you like, but I shall not stop till I find her. It's been a real bad night, an' to think of that little girl out in it, I can't bear it!" There seemed to be something like a sob in Albert's last words.

"Well, suit yerself," answered Hiram, gruffly. "I'm pretty well played out. I'll go home an' get a bite, an' then I'll come on an' meet yeh. You'll likely find her back at Woodbury's I reckon. She wanted to go back, I mind now. We'd ought to 'a' gone there in the first place."

The voices were under her window. Phoebe slowly opened her eyes and shuddering grasped Emmeline's hands so tightly that it hurt her.

"Oh, don't let him come; don't let him come!" she pleaded, and sank away into unconsciousness again.

It was a long time before they could rouse her, and when she finally opened her eyes she did not know them. A fierce and terrible fever had flamed up in her veins till her face was brilliant with color, and her long dark hair was scorched dry again in its fires.

Granny McVane came quietly over the next day and offered to nurse her. Then the long blank days of fever stretched themselves out for the unconscious girl, and a fight between life and death began.

Now, it happened that on that very afternoon of the barn raising, Mistress Janet Bristol, in all the bravery of her pink and white frills and furbelows, with a bunch of pink moss-roses at her breast, and her haughtiest air, drove over to the Deanes to call upon Phoebe, in long-delayed response to her cousin Nathaniel's most cousinly letter requesting her to do so. She had parleyed long with herself whether she would go or not, but at last curiosity to see what there was in this country girl to attract her handsome, brilliant cousin, led her to go.

One can scarcely conjecture what Emmeline would have said and thought if she had seen the grand carriage drive up before her door, with its colored coachman and footman in livery. But no one was at home to tell the tale save the white lilacs on the great bush near the front gate, who waved a welcome rich with fragrance. Perhaps they sent the essence of the welcome Phoebe would have gladly given to this favored girl whom she admired.

So half petulant at this reception when she had condescended to come, she scanned the house for some trace of the life of this unknown girl, and drove away with the memory of lilac fragrance floating about a dull and commonplace house. She drove away half determined she would tell her cousin she had done her best, and would not go again. There was no sign left behind to tell this other girl of the lost call. It is doubtful, if Janet had been able to carry out her purpose that afternoon and make her call upon Phoebe, whether either of the two would have been able to find and understand the other at that time.

Janet drove back to her own world again, and the door between the two closed. That very evening's mail brought a brief letter from Nathaniel, saying his dear friend and chum, Martin Van Rensselaer, would be coming North now in a few days, and he desired Janet to invite him to spend a little time in the old home. He would try and arrange to get away from his work and run up for a few days, and they would all have a good time together. So while this other girl, whose unsheltered life had been so full of sorrow, was plodding her way through the darkness and rain alone in the night with fear, Janet Bristol sat in her stately parlor, where a bright hearth-fire cast rosy lights over her white frock, and planned pretty wiles for the beguiling of the young theologue.

Chapter 20

Miranda was out in the flower-bed by the side gate. She had gathered her hands full of spicy gray-green Southern wood and was standing by the fence looking wistfully down the street. The afternoon coach was in and she was idly watching to see who came in, but not with her usual vim. The spectre of the shadow of death was hovering too near to Phoebe for Miranda to take much interest in things in general.

Three days after Phoebe's midnight walk Miranda had gone out to see her and bring her down to take tea with Mrs. Spafford. What was her dismay to find that she was refused admittance, and that too very shortly.

"Phoebe's sick abed!" snapped Emmeline. She had been tried beyond measure over all the extra work that was thrown on her hands by Phoebe's illness, and she had no time for buttered words. "No, she can't see you today nor next day. She's got a fever an' she don't know nobody. The doctor says she mus' be kep' quiet. No, I can't tell yeh how she got it. The land only knows it! Ef she ever gits well mebbe she ken tell herself, but I doubt it. She'll uv forgot by that time. What she does know she fergets mostly. No, you can't go an' take care of her. She's got folks 'nough to do that now, more'n she needs. There ain't a livin' thing to do but let her alone till she comes out of it. You don't suppose *you* c'd take care o' her, do yeh? *H'm!* Wal, I ain't got time to talk," and the door was shut in her face.

Miranda, however, was not to be turned aside thus easily. With real concern in her face she marched around the wood-shed to the place under the little window of the kitchen chamber that she knew was Phoebe's room.

"Phoebe!" she called, softly; "Phoe-bee!"

And the sick girl tossing on her bed of fever called wildly, "Don't you hear that Phoebe-bird calling, mother! Oh, mother! It's calling me from the top of the barn. It says, 'Phoebe, I'm here! Don't be afraid!'" and the voice trailed off into incoherence again.

Granny McVane hobbled to the window, perplexed, for she too had heard the soft sound.

"Oh, is that you, Granny?" whispered Miranda. "Say, what's the matter with Phoebe? Is she bad?"

"Yes, real bad," whispered back Granny. "She don't know a soul, poor little thing. She thinks her mother's here with her. I don't know much about how it happened. There was an accident and the horse ran away. She was out in that awful storm the other night. She's calling and I must go back to her."

In much dismay Miranda had hurried back to the village. She besieged the doctor's house until he came home, and could get only gravity and shakings of the head. "She may pull through, she may—" the old doctor would say, doubtfully. "She's young and strong, and it might be—but there's been a great shock to the system, and she doesn't respond to my medicines. I can't tell."

Every day the story was the same, though David and Marcia had gone themselves; and though Miranda travelled the mile-and-a-half every afternoon after her work was done, out to the Deane farm, there had been no change. The fever raged on, nor stayed one whit in its course. The faithful heart of Miranda was as near to discouragement as it had ever come in its dauntless life.

And now this afternoon she had just returned from a particularly fruitless journey to the farm. She had been unable to get sight or sound of anyone but Emmeline, who slammed the door in her face as usual after telling her she wished she would mind her own business and let folks alone that weren't troubling her, and Miranda felt as she trudged back to the village with tears in her homely eyes, as if she must cry out or do something. She had never quite come to a place before where her wits could not plan out some help for those she loved. Death was different. One could not outwit death.

Then, like a slowly dawning hope, she saw Nathaniel Graham coming up the street with his carpet-bag in his hand.

Nathaniel had come up for a day to tell his uncle and cousin all about this dear friend of his whom he so much desired to have made welcome for a week or two for his sake. He had been made junior partner in a law firm, the senior partner being an old friend of Judge Bristol's, and his work would be strenuous, else he would probably have planned to be at the old home all summer himself. As it was, he could hope for but a few days now and then when he could be spared.

Nathaniel came to a halt with his pleasant smile as he recognized Miranda.

"How do you do, Miss Miranda? Are all your folks well? Are Mr. and Mrs. Spafford at home? I must try to run over and see them before I go back. I'm only here on a brief visit, must return tomorrow. How is the place getting on? All the old friends just the same? Do you ever see Miss Deane? She's well, I hope."

Nathaniel was running through these sentences pleasantly, as one will who has been away from a town for a time, and he did not note the replies carefully, as he thought he knew pretty well what they would be, having heard from home but a day or two before. He was just going on when something deep and different in Miranda's tone and clouded eyes made him pause and listen:

"No, she ain't well, Phoebe Deane ain't. She's way down sick, an' they don't nobody think she's goin' to get well, I'm sure o' that!" Then the unexpected happened. Two big tears welled up and rolled down the two dauntless, freckled cheeks. Nobody had ever seen Miranda Griscom cry before.

A sudden nameless fear gripped Nathaniel's heart. Phoebe Deane sick! Near to death! All at once the day seemed to have clouded over for him.

"Tell me, Miranda," he said, gently, "she is my friend, too, I think. I did not know—I had not heard. Has she been ill long? What was the cause?"

"'Bout two weeks," said Miranda, mopping her face with the corner of her clean apron, "an' I can't find out what made her sick, but it's my 'pinion she's bein' tormented to death by that long-legged blatherskite of a Hiram Green. He ain't nothin' but a big bully, fer he's really a coward at heart, an' what's more, folks 'll find it out some day ef I don't miss my guess. But he ken git up the low-downdest, pin-prickenist, soul-shakenest tormentin's that ever a saint hed to bear. An' ef Phoebe Deane ain't a saint I don't know who is 'cept my Mis' Spafford. Them tow's ez much alike's two pease—sweet-pease, I mean, pink an' white ones in blow."

Nathaniel warmed to Miranda's eloquence and kindled to her poetry. He felt that here was something that must be investigated.

"I believe that man is a scoundrel!" said Nathaniel, earnestly. "Do you say he really dares to annoy Miss Deane?"

"Well, I rather guess you'd think so! She can't stir without he's at her side, tendin' like he b'longs there. She can't bar the sight o' him, an' he struts up to her at the church door like he owned her, an' ef 'twant fer me an Rose an' Mis' Spafford she couldn't get red of 'im. She can't go to the post-office any more 'thout he hants the very road, though she's told him up 'n down she won't hev a thing to do 'ith him. I hev to go after her an' take her home when she comes to see us, fear he'll dog her steps, an' he's scared her most to death twice now, chasin' after her, once at night when she was comin' down to your house to bring some letter she'd found."

Nathaniel's face grew suddenly conscious, and a warm glow of indignation rolled over it. He set down his carpet-bag and came close to the fence to listen.

"Why, w'd you b'lieve it, thet feller found she liked to go to th' post-office fer a walk, and he jest follered her every time, an' when she quit goin' he hunted up other ways to trouble her. They tell a tale 'bout th' horse runnin' away an' her bein' out in a big storm the night she took sick, but I b'lieve in my soul he's t' th' bottom of it, an' I'd like to see him get his come-uppance right now."

"Miranda, do you happen to know—I don't suppose you ever heard Miss Deane speak of receiving a letter from me."

Miranda's alert eyes were on his face.

"Long 'bout when?" she demanded, keenly.

"Why last December, I think it was. I wrote her a note and I never received any reply. I wondered if it might have got lost, or whether she did not like my writing it, as I am almost a stranger."

"No, sir-ree, she never got that letter! I know fer sure, 'cause I happened to speak to her 'bout hearin' Hiram Green askin' pertick'ler fer her mail in the post-office one day; and I found out he gets the Deane's mail quite often an' carries it out to 'em' an' I tole her I thought she wouldn't like him meddlin' with her mail, an' she jest laughed an' said he couldn't do her any harm thet way, cause she never got a letter in her life 'cept one her mother wrote her 'fore she died. Thet was only a little while back, 'bout a month 'er so, 'way after January, fer the snow was most gone the day I tol' her. She can't uv got your letter no how. I'd be willin' to bet a good fat doughnut thet thet rascally Hiram Green knows what come o' thet letter. My, but I'd like to prove it on him!"

"Oh, Miranda, he would scarcely dare to tamper with another person's mail. He's a well-informed man, and must know that's a crime. He could be put into prison for that. It must have got lost if you are sure she never received it."

"Could he?" said Miranda, eagerly; "could he be put in prison? My! but I'd like to help get him lodged there fer a spell 'til he learned a little bit o' politeness toward th' angels thet walks the airth in mortal form. Dast! Hiram Green dast? He's got cheek enough to dast ennythin'. You don't know him. He wouldn't think enny one would find out! But say, I'll tell you what you ken do. You jest write that letter over again, ef you ken rem'mber 'bout what you wanted to say b'fore, an' I'll agree to git it to her first hand this time."

Nathaniel's face was alight with the eagerness of a boy. Somehow Miranda's childish proposal was pleasant to him. Her homely, honest face beamed at him expectantly, and he replied with earnestness:

"I'll do it, Miranda, I'll do it this very day, and trust it to your kindness to get it to her safely. Thank you for suggesting it."

Then suddenly a cloud came over the freckled face, and the gray eyes filled with tears again.

"But I mightin't ever git it to 'er, after all, yeh know. They say she's jest hangin' 'tween life 'n death today, an' t'night's the crisis.

A cloud seemed suddenly to have passed before the sun again, a chill almost imperceptible came in the air. What was that icy something gripping Nathaniel's heart? Why did all the forces of life and nature seem to hang upon the well-being of this young girl? He caught his breath.

"We must pray for her, Miranda, you and I," he said, gravely; "she once promised to pray for me."

"Did she?" said Miranda, looking up with solemn awe through her tears. "I'm real glad you tole me that. I'll try, but I ain't much on things like that. I could wallup Hiram Green a grea' deal better'n I could pray; but I s'pose that wouldn't do no good, so I'll do my best at the prayin'. Ef it's kind of botched up mebbe yours'll make up fer it. But say you better write that letter right off. I've heard tell there's things like thet'll help when crisises comes. I'm goin' t' make it a pint t' git up there t'night, spite o' that ole Mis' Deane, an' ef I see a chance I'll give it to her. I kind of think it might please her to have a letter t'git well fer."

"I'll do it, Miranda, I'll do it at once, and bring it around to you before dark. But you must be careful not to trouble her with it till she is able. You know it might make her worse to be bothered with any excitement like a letter from a stranger."

"I'll use my bes' jedgment," said Miranda, with happy pride. "I aint' runnin' no resks, so you needn't worry."

With a new interest in his face Nathaniel grasped his carpet-bag and hurried to his uncle's house. He found Janet ready with a joyful welcome, but he showed more anxiety to get to his room than to talk with her.

"I suppose it was dusty on the road today," she conceded, unwillingly, "but hurry back. I've a great deal to ask you, and to tell; and I want you all to myself before your friend comes."

But once in his room he forgot dust and sat down immediately to the great mahogany desk where paper and pens were just as he had left them when he went away. Janet had to call twice before he made his appearance, for he was deep in writing a letter.

My dear Miss Deane, he wrote. *They tell me you are lying very ill and I feel as if I must write a few words to tell you how anxious and sad I am about you. I want you to know that I am praying that you may get well.*

I wrote you sometime ago asking if you were willing to correspond with me, but I have reason now to think you never received my letter, so I have ventured to write again. I know it may be sometime before you are able even to read this, but I am sending it by a trusty messenger and I am sure you will let me know my answer when you are better. It will be a great source of pleasure and profit to me if you will write to me sometimes.

Yours faithfully,
NATHANIEL GRAHAM.

He folded and addressed it, sealing it with his crest, and then Janet called for the second time:

"Yes, Janet, I'm coming now, really. I had to write a letter. I am sorry, but it couldn't wait."

"Oh, how poky! Always business, business!" cried Janet. "It is well your friend is coming tonight for it is plain to be seen we shall have no good of you. How is it that you have grown old and grave so soon, Nathaniel? I thought you would stay a boy a long time."

"Just wait until I send my letter, Janet, and I will be as young as you please for two whole days."

"Let Caesar take it for you, then. There is no need for you to go."

"I would rather take it myself, cousin," he said, and she knew by his look that he would have his way.

"Well, then, I will go with you," she pouted, and taking her sunshade from the hall table unfurled its rosy whiteness.

He was somewhat dismayed at this, but making the best of it smiled good-humoredly and together they went out into the summer street and walked beneath the long arch of maples newly dressed in green.

"But this is not the way to the post-office," she cried, when they had walked some distance.

"But this is the way for my letter," he said, pleasantly. "Now, Janet, what have you to ask me so insistently?"

"About this Martin friend of yours. Is he nice? That is, will I like him? It isn't enough that you like him, for you like some very stupid people sometimes. I want to know if I will like him."

"And how should I be able to tell that, Janet? Of one thing I am sure, he will have to like you," and he surveyed his handsome cousin admiringly. "That's a very pretty sunshade you have. May I carry it for you?"

"Well, after that pleasant speech perhaps you may," she said, surrendering it. "About this young man, is it really true, Nathaniel, that he is a minister, and that he is to preach for Dr. MacFarlane while the doctor goes to visit his daughter? Father thought you had arranged for that. You see it is very important that I like him, because if I don't I simply cannot go to church and hear him preach. In fact I'm not sure but I shall stay away anyway. I should be so afraid he'd break down if I liked him, and if I didn't I should want to laugh. It will be so funny to see a minister at home every day, and know all his faults and his little peculiarities, and then see him get up and try to preach. I'm *sure* I should laugh."

"I am sure you would dare do nothing of the kind when Martin preaches."

"Oh, is he then so terribly grave and solemn? I shall not like him in the least."

"Wait until he comes, Janet. The evening coach will soon be in."

They had reached the Spafford house now, and Nathaniel's anxiety about delivering his letter was relieved by seeing Miranda hurry out to the flower-bed again with a manner as if the demand for fresh flowers had suddenly become greater than the supply. She was quite close to the fence as they came up, but she remained unconscious of their presence until Nathaniel spoke.

"Is that you, Miss Miranda?" he said, lifting his hat as though he had not seen her before that afternoon. "Will you kindly deliver this letter for me?"

He handed her the letter directly from his pocket, and Janet could not see the address. Miranda took it serenely.

"Yes, sir," she said, scrutinizing the address at a safe angle from Janet's vision, "I'll deliver it safe an' sure. Afternoon, Mis' Janet. Like a bunch o' pink columbine to stick in yer frock? Jes' matches them posies on the muslin delaine." And she snapped off a fine whirl of delicate pink columbine. Janet accepted it graciously and the two turned back home again.

"Now I can't see why Caesar couldn't have done that," grumbled Janet. "He's just as trustworthy as that funny red-haired girl."

"You would not have got your columbine," smiled Nathaniel, "and I'm sure it was just what you needed to complete the picture."

"Now for that pretty speech I'll say no more about it," granted Mistress Janet, well pleased.

And so they walked along the shaded street, where the sunlight was beginning to lie in long slant rays on the pavement and play strange yellow fancies with the smart new leaves of the maples. Nathaniel talked as he knew his cousin liked to have him do, and all the time she never knew that his heart had gone with the letter he had given to Miranda. Perhaps it was her interest in the stranger who was coming that kept her from missing something. Perhaps it was his light-hearted manner, so free from the perplexing problems that had filled his face with gravity on his recent visits. Perhaps it was just Janet's own happy heart, glad with the gladness of life and the summer weather, and the holiday guests.

Yet underneath Nathaniel's gay manner there ran two thoughts side by side — one, the fact that Miranda had said Phoebe had repulsed Hiram Green; the other, that she was lying at death's door; and all the time his strong heart was going out in a wild, hopeful pleading that her young life might yet be spared to joy. He felt that this mute pleading was her due, for had she not lifted her clear eyes and said, "Oh, I will," when he had asked her to pray for him? He must return it in full measure.

The evening coach was late, but it rolled in at last, bringing the eagerly-watched-for guest, bronzed from his months in the South. The dinner was served around a joyous board, the Judge beaming his pleasure upon the little company. The evening was prolonged far beyond the usual retiring hour, while laughter and talk floated on around him, and all the time Nathaniel was conscious of that other house but two miles away, where life and death were battling for a victim.

He went upstairs with Martin for another talk after the house was quiet, but at last they separated; and Nathaniel was free to sit by the window in his dark room looking out into the night now grown brilliant with the late rising moon, and keep tryst with one who was hovering on the brink of the other world.

Chapter 21

"I'm a notion to go up an' stay there t'night!" announced Miranda, as she cleared off the tea things. "This's the crisis, an' they might need me fer sumthin'. Any how I'm a 'goin' ef you don't mind."

"Will they let you in?" asked Marcia.

"I shan't ask 'em," said Miranda, loftily. "There's more ways 'n one o' gettin' in, an' ef I make up my mind to git there you'll see I'll do it."

Marcia laughed.

"I suppose you will, Miranda. Well, go on. You may be needed. Poor Phoebe! I wish there was something I could do for her."

"Wal, thur is," said Miranda, with unexpected vim. "I've took a contrac' thet I don't seem to make much headway on. I'd like to hev you take a little try at it, an' see ef you can't do better. I 'greed t' pray fer Phoebe Deane, but t' save my life I can't think uv any more ways uv sayin' it thun jest to ast, an' after I've done it oncet it don't seem quite p'lite to keep at it, z' if I didn't b'lieve "twas heard. The minister preached awhile back 'about the 'fectual fervent prayer uv a righteous man 'vailin' much, but he didn't say nothin' 'bout a red-headed woman. I reckon I ain't much good at prayin', fer I'm all wore out with it, but ef you'd jest spell me a while, an' lemme go see ef thur ain't sumpthin' to do, I think it would be a sight more 'availin' than fer me to set still an' jest pray; 'sides, ef you ain't better 'n most any righteous man I ever see, I'll miss my guess."

Thus the responsibility was divided, and Marcia with a smile upon her lips and a tear in her eye went away to pray, while Miranda tied on her bonnet, tucked the letter safely in her pocket after examining its seals and address most minutely, and went her way into the night.

She did not go to the front door, but stole around to the wood-shed where with the help of a milking-stool which stood there she mounted to the low roof. Strong of limb and courageous she found the climb nothing. She crept softly along the roof till she reached Phoebe's window, and crouched to listen. The window was open but a little way, though the night was warm and dry.

"Granny, Granny McVane," she called, softly, and Granny, startled from her evening drowsiness, stole over to the window wondering. A candle was burning behind the water pitcher and shed a weird and sickly light through the room. Granny looked old and tired as she came to the window, and it struck Miranda she had been crying.

"Fer the land sake! Is that you Mirandy?" she exclaimed, in horror. "Mercy! How'd you get there? Look out! You'll fall."

"Open the winder till I come in," whispered Miranda.

Granny opened the window cautiously.

"Be quick," she said, "I mustn't let the air get to the bed."

"I should think air was jes' what she'd want this night," whispered Miranda, as she emerged into the room and straightened her garments. "How's she seem? Any change?"

"I think she's failing, I surely do," moaned the old lady, softly, the tears running down her cheeks in slow uneven rivulets between the wrinkles. "I don't see how she can hold out till morning anyhow. She's jest burnt up with fever, and sometimes she seems to be gasping for breath. But how'd you get up there? Weren't you scairt?"

"I jes' couldn't keep away a minute longer. The doctor said this was the crisis an' I had to come. My Mrs. Spafford's home prayin' an' I come to see ef I couldn't help answer them prayers. You might need help tonight, an' I'm goin' to stay. Will any of her folks be in again tonight?"

"No, I reckon not. Emmeline's worn out. The baby's teething and hasn't given her a minute's let-up for two nights. She had his gums lanced today and she hopes to get a wink of sleep, for there's likely to be plenty doing tomorrow."

Miranda set her lips hard at this and turned to the bed, where Phoebe lay under heavy blankets and comfortables, a low moan, almost a gasp, escaping her parched lips now and then.

The fever seemed to have burnt a place for itself in the whiteness of her cheeks. Her beautiful hair had been cut short by Emmeline the second day because she could not be bothered combing it. It was as well, for it would not have withstood the fever, but to Miranda it seemed like a ruthless tampering with the sacred. Her wrath burned hot within her, even while she was considering what was to be done.

"My goodness alive," was her first word, "I should think she would hev a fever. It's hotter'n mustard in here. Why don't you open them winders wide? I should think you'd roast alive yerself. And land sakes! Look at the covers she's got piled on! Poor little thing!" Miranda reached out a swift hand and swept several layers off to the floor. A sigh of relief followed from Phoebe.

Miranda placed a firm cool hand on the burning forehead, and the sufferer seemed to take note of the touch eagerly.

"Oh, mercy me! Miranda, you mustn't take the covers off. She must be kept warm to try and break the fever. The doctor's orders were very strict. I wouldn't like to disobey him. It might be her death."

"Does he think she's any better?" questioned Miranda, fiercely. "No." The old lady shook her head sadly, "he said this morning there wasn't a thread of hope, poor little thing. Her fever hasn't let up a mite."

"Well, ef he said that, then I'm goin' to hev my try. She can't do more 'n die, an' ef I was goin' to die I'd like to hev a cool comf'table place to do it in, wouldn't you, Granny, an' not a furnace? Let's give her a few minutes' peace 'fore she dies, any way. Come, you open them winders. Ef anythin' happens I won't tell, an' ef she's goin' to die any way I think it's wicked to make her suffer any longer."

"I don't know what they'll say to me," murmured the old lady, yielding to the dominant Miranda. "I don't think mebbe I ought to do it."

"Well, never mind what you think now, it's my try. Ef you didn't open 'em I would, fer I b'lieve in my heart she wants fresh air, an' I'm goin' to give it to her ef I hev to fight every livin' soul in this hoouse, an' smash all the winder lights, so there! Now, that's better. It'll be somethin' like in here pretty soon. Where's a towel? Is this fresh water? Say, Granny, couldn't you slip down to the spring without wakin' anyone an' bring us a good cold drink? I'm dyin' fer a dipper o' water, I come up here so fast, and it'll taste good to Phoebe, I know."

"Oh, she mustn't have a drop o' water," exclaimed the old lady, in horror. "Fever patients don't get a mite of water."

"Fever fiddlesticks! You git that water, please, an' then you kin lay down on that couch over there an' take a nap while I set by her."

After much whispered persuasion and bullying Miranda succeeded in getting the old lady to slip downstairs and go for the water, though the spring-house was almost as far as the barn and Granny was not used to prowling around alone at night. While she was gone Miranda boldly dipped a towel in the water pitcher and washed the fevered brow and face. The parched lips crept to the wetness eagerly, and Miranda began to feel assurance to the tips of her fingers. She calmly bathed the girl's hot face and hands, until the low moans became sounds of relief and content. Then quite unconscious that she was anticipating science she prepared to give her patient a sponge bath. In the midst of the performance she looked up to see Granny standing over her in horror.

"What are you doing, Mirandy Griscom? You'll kill her. The doctor said she mustn't have a drop of water touch her."

"I'm takin' the fever out uv her. Jes' feel her an' see," said Miranda, triumphantly. "Put yer lips on her forrid, thet's the way to tell. Ain't she coolin' off nice?"

"You're killing her, Miranda," said Granny, in a terrified tone, "and I've cared fer her so carefully all these weeks, and now to have her go like this! It's death coming that makes her cold."

"Death fiddlesticks!" said Miranda, wrathfully. "Well, ef 'tis, she'll die happy. Here, give me that water!" and she took the cup from the trembling hand of Granny and held it to Phoebe's dry lips. Eagerly the lips opened, and drank in the water as Miranda raised her head on her strong young arm. Then the sick girl lay back with a long sigh of content, and fell asleep.

It was the first natural sleep she had had since the awful beginning of the fever. She did not toss nor moan, and Granny hovered doubtingly above her, watching and listening to see if she still breathed, wondering at the fading of the crimson flames upon the white cheeks, dismayed at the cooling of the brow, even troubled at the quiet sleep.

"I fear she'll slip away in this," she said at last, in a sepulchral whisper. "That was an awful daresome thin you did. I wouldn't like them to find it out on you. They might say you caused her death."

"But she ain't dead yet," said Miranda, triumphantly, "an' ef she slips away in this it's a sight pleasanter 'n the way she was when I crep' in. Say now, Granny, don't you think so, honest?"

"Oh, I don't know," signed Granny, turning away sadly. "Mebbe I oughtn't to have let you."

"You couldn't a he'ped yerself, fer I'd come to do it, an' anyway, ef you'd made a fuss I'd hed to put you out on the roof er somethin' till I got done. Now, Granny, you're all tired out. You jes' go over an' lie down on thet couch an' I'll set by an' watch her a spell."

The conversation was carried on in close proximity to Granny's ear, for both nurses were anxious lest some of the sleeping household should hear. Granny knew she would be blamed for Miranda's presence in the sick room, and Miranda knew she would be ousted if discovery were made.

Granny settled down at last, with many protests, owned she was "jest the least mite tuckered out," and lay down for what she called a "cat-nap." Miranda, meantime, wide-eyed and sleepless, sat beside Phoebe and watched her every breath, for she felt more anxiety about what she had done than she cared to own to Granny. She had never had much experience in nursing, except in waiting upon Marcia, but her common sense told her that people were not so likely to get well as long as they were uncomfortable, therefore without much consideration she did for Phoebe what she would like to have had done for herself if she were ill. It seemed the right thing, and it seemed to be working, but supposing Granny were right, after all!

Then Miranda remembered the two who were praying.

"H'm" she said to herself, as she sat watching the still face on the pillow. "I reckon that's their part. Mine's to do the best I know. Ef the prayers is good fer anything they ought to piece out whar' I fail. An' I guess they will, too, with them two at it."

After that she got the wet towel and went to work again, bathing the brow and hands whenever the heat seemed to be growing in them again. She was bound to bring that fever down. Now and then the sleeper would draw a long sigh as of contentment, and comfort, and Miranda felt that she had received her thanks. It was enough to know that she had given her friend a little comfort, if nothing else.

The hours throbbed on. The moon went down; the candle began to sputter, and Miranda lighted another. Granny slept and actually snored, weary with her long vigil. Miranda had to touch her occasionally to stop the loud noise lest some one should hear and come to see what it was. But the rest of the household were weary, too, for it was in the height of the summer's work now, and all slept soundly.

When the early dawn crept into the sky Miranda felt Phoebe's hands and head and found them cool and natural. She stooped and listened and her breathing came regularly like a tired child's. For just one instant she touched her lips to the white forehead and was rejoiced that the parched burning feeling was gone. There remained yet the awful weakness to fight, but at least the fever was gone. What had done it she did not care, but it was done.

She went gently to Granny and wakened her. The old lady started up with a frightened look, guilty that she had slept so long, but Miranda reassured her. "It's all right. I'm glad you slep', fer you wan't needed, an' I guess you'll feel all the better fer it today. She's slep' real quiet all night long, ain't moaned once, an' jes' feel her. Ain't she feelin' all right? I b'lieve the fever's gone."

Granny went over and touched her face and hands wonderingly. "She does feel better," she admitted, "but I don't know. It mayn't last. I've seen 'em rally toward the end," dubiously; "she'll be so powerful weak now, it'll be all we can do to hold her to earth."

"What's she ben eatin'?" enquired Miranda.

"She hasn't eaten anything of any account for some time back."

"Well, she can't live on jest air an' water ferever. Say, Granny, I've got to be goin' soon, er I'll hev to hide in the closet all day fer sure, but 'spose you slip out to the barn now while I wait an' get a few drops o' new milk. Hank's out there milkin'. I heard him go down an' git his milk pails an' stool 'fore I woke you up. We'll give her a spoonful o' warm milk. Mebbe that'll hearten her up."

"It might," said Granny, doubtfully. She took the cup and hurried away, Miranda taking the precaution to button the door after her the lest Emmeline whom she could hear moving around in her room should take a notion to look in.

When Granny got back Miranda took the cup and putting a few drops of the sweet warm fluid in a spoon she touched it to Phoebe's lips. A slow sigh followed, and then Phoebe's eyes opened and she looked straight at Miranda and seemed to know her, for a flicker of a smile shone in her face.

"There, Phoebe, take this spoonful. You've ben sick, but it'll make you well," crooned Miranda, softly.

Phoebe obediently swallowed the few drops and Miranda dipped up a few more.

"It's all right, dear," she said softly. "I'll take care o' you. Jes' you drink this, an' get well, fer I've got somethin' real nice in my pocket fer you when ye' take yer milk an' go to sleep."

Thus Miranda fed her two or three spoonfuls, then the white lids closed over the trusting eyes, and in a moment more she was sleeping again.

Miranda watched her a few minutes, and then cautiously stole away from the bed, to the astonished Granny who had been watching with a new respect for the domineering young nurse that had usurped her place.

"I guess she'll sleep most o' the day," Miranda whispered. "Ef she wakes up you jes' give her a spoonful o' fresh milk, er a sup o' water, an' tell her I'll be back bime-by. She'll understan' an' that'll keep her quiet. Tell her I said she mus' lie still an' get well. Don't you dast keep them winders shet up all day again, an' don't pile on the clo'es. She may need a light blanket ef she feels cool, but don't fer mercy's sake get her all het up again, er we might not be able to stop it off so easy next time. I'll be back's soon es it's dark. Bye-bye. I mus' go. I may get ketched es 'tis."

Miranda slid out the window and down the sloping roof, dropping over the eaves just in time to escape being seen by Emmeline, who opened the back door with a sharp click and came out to get a broom she had forgotten the night before. The morning was almost come now, and the long grass was dripping with dew as Miranda swept through it.

"Reckon they'll think there's ben a fox er somethin' prowlin' round the house ef they see my tracks," she said to herself, as she hurried through the dewy fields and out to the road.

Victory was written upon her countenance as she sped along, victory tempered with hope. Perhaps she was not judge enough of illness, and it might be that her hopes were vain ones, and apparent signs deceitful, but come what might she would always be glad she had done what she had. That look in Phoebe's eyes before she fell asleep again was reward enough. It made her heart swell with triumph to think of it.

Two hours later she brought a platter of delicately poached eggs on toast to the breakfast table just as Marcia entered the room.

"Good-morning, Miranda. How did it go last night? You evidently got in and found something to do."

Miranda set down the platter and stood with hands on her hips and face shining with morning welcome.

"I tell you, Mrs. Marcia, them prayers was all right. They worked fine. When I got mixed and didn't know what was right to do I just remembered them an' cast off all 'sponsibility. Anyhow, she's sleepin' an' the fever's gone."

Marcia smiled.

"I shouldn't wonder if your part was really prayer, too," she said, dreamily. "We are not all heard for our much speaking."

It was a glorious day. The sun shown in a perfect heaven without a cloud to blur it. A soft south breeze kept the air from being too warm. Miranda sang all the morning as she went about her belated work.

After dinner Marcia insisted she should go and take a nap. She obediently lay down for half an hour straight and stiff on her bright neat patchwork quilt, scarcely relaxing a muscle lest she rumple the bed. She did not close her eyes, however, but lay joyously smiling at the bland white ceiling, and resting herself by gently crackling the letter in her pocket, and smiling to think how Phoebe would look when she showed it to her.

In exactly half an hour she arose, combed her hair neatly, donned her afternoon frock and her little black silk apron that was her pride on ordinary occasions, and descended to her usual post of observation with her knitting. Naps were not in her line and she was glad hers was over.

A little later the doctor's chaise drove up to the door, and Miranda went out to see what was wanted, a great fear clutching her heart. But she was reassured by the smile on his face, and the good will in the expressions of his wife and her sister, who were riding with him.

"Say, Mirandy, I don't know but I'll take you into partnership. Where'd you learn nursing? You did what I wouldn't have dared do, but it seemed to hit the mark. I'd given her up. I've seen her slipping away for a week past, but she's taken a turn for the better now, and I believe in my soul she's going to get well. If she does it'll be you that'll get the honor."

Miranda's eyes shone with happy tears.

"You don't say, doctor," she said. "Why, I was real scared when Granny told me you said she wasn't to hev a sup o' water, but it seemed like she must be so turrible hot —"

"Well, I wouldn't have dared try it myself, but I believe it did the business," said the doctor, heartily.

"Yes, you deserve great credit, Miranda," said the doctor's wife. "You do, indeed," echoed her sister, pleasantly.

"Granny ain't tole Mis' Deane I was there hes she?" asked Miranda, to cover her embarrassment. She was not used to praise except from her own household.

"No, she hasn't told her yet, but I think I shall tell her myself by tomorrow if all goes well. Can you find time to run over tonight again? Granny might not stay wide awake all the time. She's fagged out, and I think it's a critical time."

"Oh, I'll be there!" said Miranda, gleefully. "You couldn't keep me away."

"How'll you get in? Same way you did last night?" asked the doctor, laughing. "Say, that's a good joke! I've laughed and laughed ever since Granny told me, at the thought of you climbing in the window and the family all sleeping calmly. Good for you, Miranda. You're made of the right stuff. Well, good-bye. I'll fix it up with Mrs. Deane tomorrow so you can go in by the door."

The doctor drove on, laughing, and his wife and sister bowing and smiling. Miranda, with high head of pride and heart full of joy, went in to get supper.

Supper was just cleared away when Nathaniel came over. He talked with David in the dusk of the front stoop a few minutes and then asked diffidently if Miranda was going up to see how Miss Deane was again soon.

David, because of his love for Marcia, half understood, and calling Miranda left the two together for a moment while he went to call Marcia, who was putting Rose to bed.

"She's better," said Miranda, entering without preamble into the subject nearest their hearts, "the doctor told me so this afternoon. But don't you stop prayin' yet, fer we don't want no half-way job, an' she's powerful weak. I kinder rely on them prayers to do a lot. I got Mrs. Spafford to spell me at mine while I went up to help nurse. She opened her eyes oncet last night when I was given' her some milk, an' I tole her I had somethin' nice fer her if she'd lie still an' go to sleep an' hurry up an' git well. She kinder seemed to understand, I most think. I've got the letter all safe, an' jest ez soon ez she gits the least mite better, able to talk, I'll give it to her."

"Thank you, Miss Miranda," said Nathaniel, "and won't you take this to her? It will be better than letters for her for a while until she gets well. You needn't bother her telling anything about it now. Just give it to her. It may help her a little. Then later, if you think best, you may tell her I sent it."

He held out a single tea-rose, half blown, with delicate petals of pale saffron.

Miranda took it with awe. It was not like anything that grew in the gardens she knew.

"It looks like her," she said, reverently.

"It makes me think of her as I first saw her," he answered, in a low voice. "She wore a frock like that."

"I know," said Miranda, understandingly, "I'll give it to her, and tell her all about it when she's better."

"Thank you," said Nathaniel. Then Marcia and David entered, and Miranda went away to wonder over the rose, and prepare for her night's vigil.

Chapter 22

Granny greeted Miranda with a smile as she crept in at the window that night. Phoebe, too, opened her eyes in welcome, though she made no other sign that she was awake. Her face was like sunken marble now that the fever was gone from it, and her two great eyes shone from it like lights of another world. it startled Miranda as she came and looked at her. Then at once she perceived that Phoebe's eyes had sought the rose, and a smile was hovering about her lips.

"It was sent to you," she answered the questioning eyes, putting the rose close down to the white cheek. Phoebe really smiled then faintly.

"She better have some milk now," said Granny, anxiously. "She's been asleep so long an' I didn't disturb her."

"Yes, take some milk," whispered Miranda, gently, "an' I'll tell you all 'bout the rose when you're better."

The night crept on in quiet exultation on Miranda's part. While Phoebe slept Miranda and the rose kept vigil, and Granny sank into the first restful sleep she had had since she came to nurse Phoebe. The house was quiet. There was nothing for the watcher to do much of the time but to watch. Now and then she drew the coverlet up a little higher when a fresh breeze came through the window; or again gave a drink of water, or a spoonful of milk. The candle was shaded by the water pitcher, and the frail sweet rose looked spectral in the weird light. Miranda looked at the flower, and it looked back at her. As the hours slowly passed Miranda found her lips murmuring:

"Thanks be! Thanks be!"

Suddenly she drew herself up with a new thought.

"Land sakes! That's sounds like prayin'. Wonder ef 'tis. Anyhow it's thanks-givin', an' that's what I feel. Guess it's my turn to give thanks."

The next day the doctor had a talk with Albert Deane. He told him how Miranda had crept in at the window and cared for Phoebe; and how he believed it had been Phoebe's salvation. Albert was deeply affected. He readily agreed that it would be a fine thing for Phoebe if Miranda could be got to come and help Granny care for her, now that she seemed to be on the fair road to recovery.

It was all arranged in a few minutes and Emmeline was not told until just before Miranda arrived.

"It's very queer," she said, with her nose in the air, "that I wasn't consulted. I'm sure it's my business more'n yours to look after such things, Albert Deane. An' I wouldn't uv had that sassy creature in the house fer a good deal. Hank's sister would 'a' ben a sight better, an' could a' helped me between times with Phoebe's extry work. I'm sure it's bad enough havin' sickness this way in the midst o' hayin' season, an' me with all them men to feed, an' not havin' Phoebe to help. I could 'a' sent fer my own sister, when it comes to that, an' 'twould 'a' ben a sight pleasanter."

But before there was time for a protest or apology from Albert there came a knock at the door, and without waiting for ceremony Miranda walked in.

"Ev'nin', Miss Deane," she said, unconcernedly. "Everything goin' well? I'll go right up, shall I?" Her smiling insolence struck Emmeline dumb for the moment.

"Well, I vow!" declared Emmeline. "Will yeh listen to the impedence. 'Will I go right up?' es ef she was the Queen o' Sheby er the doctor himself."

But Miranda was marching serenely upstairs and if she heard she paid no heed.

"She doesn't mean any harm, Emmeline!" pleaded Albert. "She's jest Phoebe's friend, so don't you mind. It'll relieve you a lot, and if you want Hank's sister to come over too I guess we can manage it."

Thus was Miranda domiciled in Phoebe's room for a short space, much to the comfort of Phoebe and the satisfaction of Miranda.

Emmeline was only half mollified when she came upstairs to look around and "give that Griscom girl a settin' down," as she expressed it. But she who attempted to "sit" on Miranda usually arose unexpectedly.

"Where'd that come from?" was Emmeline's first question, as she pointed at the unoffending rose.

"Mirandy brought it," said Granny, proud of her colleague. "H'm!" said Emmeline, with a sniff. "It ain't healthy to hev plants round in a bedroom I've heard. D' you raise that kind down to Spaffords?"

"We ain't got just to say a-plenty yet," said Miranda, cheerfully, "but we might hev sometime. Would yeh like a slip?"

"No, thank yeh," said Emmeline, dryly, "I never had time to waste good daylight fussin' over weeds. I s'pose Mis' Spafford don't do much else."

"Oh, 'casionally!" answered Miranda, undisturbed. "This spring she put up a hundred glasses o' blueberry jelly, made peach preserves, spiced pears, an' crab-apple jam, crocheted a white bed-spread fer the spare bed, an' three antimacassars fer her Aunt Hortense's best parlor chairs, did up the second story curtains, tucked a muslin slip fer Rose, sewed carpet-rags enough fer a whole strip in Shorty Briscutt's new rag carpet, made a set o' shirts fer Mr. Spafford, knit nine pair o' stocking', spun the winter's yarn, cut out an' made Rose's flannel petticoats, an' went to missionary meetin', but o' course that ain't much, nothin' to what you'd do."

(Oh Miranda, Miranda! of the short prayers and the long tongue! telling all that off with a straight face to the sour-faced woman, Emmeline!)

"She must be a smart woman!" said Granny, much impressed.

"She is," said Miranda, glibly, "but here all the time I was fergettin' we'd ought not to talk. We'll bring that fever up. Is there anything special yeh wanted me to look after t'night, Mis' Deane? 'Cause ef there is jest don' hesitate to say so. I'm here to work an' not to play."

And before she knew it, Emmeline found herself disarmed and walking meekly downstairs without having said any of the things she had meant to say.

From that time forth Phoebe grew steadily better, though she came near to having a serious set-back the day Miranda went down to the village on an errand and Emmeline attempted to "clean up" in her absence, finishing the operation by pitching out the tea-rose into the yard below the window.

"I never seen such a fuss," complained Emmeline to Miranda, who stood over Phoebe and felt her fluttering pulse, "all about a dead weed. I declare I can't understand folks gettin' 'tached to trash."

Emmeline was somewhat anxious at the upset state of the patient, who was yet too weak to talk much, but who had roused herself to protest vigorously as the rose was hurled through the window, and then could not keep back the disappointed tears.

But Miranda, mindful of the weak state of her patient, and wishing to mollify Emmeline as much as possible, tried to pour oil on the troubled waters.

"Never mind, Mis' Deane, no harm done. Phoebe jest wanted to keep them leaves fer her han'kerchers, they smell real nice. I'll pick 'em up, Phoebe. They won't be hurt a mite. They're right on the green grass."

Miranda stole down and picked up the leaves tenderly, washing them at the spring, and brought them back to Phoebe. Emmeline had gone off sniffing with her chin in the air.

"I was silly to cry," murmured Phoebe, trying feebly to dry her tears, "but I loved that sweet rose. I wanted to keep it just as it was in a box. You haven't told me about it yet, Miranda, how did she come to send it?"

"It ain't hurt a mite, Phoebe, only jest three leaves come off. I'll lay it together in a box fer yeh. Now lemme put my bonnet off, an' you lay quiet an' shet your eyes while I tell you 'bout that rose. First, though, you must take your milk.

"It wan't her at all that sent you that rose, Phoebe Deane. You s'picioned 'twas Mrs. Marcia, didn't you? But 'twan't 't all. It was a man—"

"Oh, Miranda!" The words came in a moan of pain from the bed, "Not—not—Miranda, you would never have brought it if Hiram Green—"

"Land sake, child, what's took yeh? 'Course not. Why ef that nimshi'd undertake to send yeh so much ez a blade o' grass I'd fling it in his mean little face. Don't you worry, dearie, you jest listen. 'Twas Nathaniel Graham sent you that rose. He said I wan't to say nothin' 'bout it till you got better, an' then I could say 'twas from him ef I wanted to. I didn't say anythin' yet 'cause I hed more to tell, but I ain't sure you are strong 'nough to hear any more now. Better take a nap first."

"No, Miranda; do tell me now."

"Wal, I reckon I better. I've most busted wantin' to tell yeh sev'ral times. Say, did you ever get a letter from Nathaniel Graham, Phoebe?"

"Why no, of course not, Miranda. Why would I get a letter from him?"

"Wal, he said he wrote yeh one oncet, an' he ast me did I know ef you'd got it, and' I said No, I was sure you didn't, cause you said oncet you hadn't ever got a letter 'cept from your mother, an' so he said he'd write it over again fer yeh, an' I've hed it in my pocket fer a long time waitin' till I dared give it to yeh. So her 'tis, but I won't give it to yeh 'thout you promise to go right to sleep 'fore you read it fer you've hed more goin's on now than 's good fer yeh."

Phoebe protested that she must read the letter first, but Miranda was inexorable, and would not even show it to her until she promised. So meekly Phoebe promised, and went to sleep with the precious missive clasped in her hands, the wonder of it helping her to get quiet.

She slept a long time, for the excitement about the rose had taken her strength. When she awoke, before she opened her eyes she felt the letter, pressing the seals with her fingers, to make sure she had not been dreaming. She almost feared to open her eyes lest it should not be true. A letter for her all her own! Somehow she almost dreaded to break the seal and have the first wonder of it over. She had not thought what it might contain.

Miranda had brought a little pail of chicken broth that Marcia had made for Phoebe, and she had some steaming in a china bowl when Phoebe at last opened her eyes. She made her eat it before she opened the letter, and Phoebe smiled and acquiesced.

She lay smiling and quiet a long time after reading the letter, trying to get used to the thought that Nathaniel had remembered her, and cared to write to her; cared to have her write to him, too; it was not merely passing kindness toward a stranger. He wanted to be friends, real friends. It was good to feel that one had friends.

Phoebe looked over at the alert figure of Miranda, sitting bolt upright, watching her charge with anxiety to see if the letter was all that it should be, and then she laughed a soft little ripple that sounded like a shadow of her former self.

"Oh, you dear, good Miranda! You don't know how nice it all is to have friends, and a real letter."

"Is it a good letter?" asked Miranda, wistfullly.

"Read it," said Phoebe, handing it to her, smiling. "You certainly have a right to read it after all you have done to get it here."

Miranda took it shyly, and went over by the window where the setting sun made it a little less embarrassing. She read it slowly and carefully and the look on her face when she returned it showed she was satisfied.

"I seen him the mornin' he went back to New York," she admitted, after a minute. "He said he'd look fer that answer soon ez you got better. You're goin' to write, ain't you?" anxiously. "'Cause he seemed real set up about it."

"How soon may I answer it?" she answered.

"We'll see," said Miranda, briskly. "The first business is to get strong."

They spent happy days together, those two girls, with nothing to worry them; and as Phoebe began to get strong and could be propped up with pillows for a little while each day Miranda at length allowed her to write a few lines in reply to her letter, and this was the message that in a few days thereafter travelled to New York.

My Dear Mr. Graham:

It was very pleasant to receive your letter and to know that you thought of me and prayed that I might get well. I think your prayers are being answered.

It will be good to have a friend to write to me, and I shall be glad to correspond with you. I want to thank you for the beautiful rose. It helped me to get well. Its leaves are sweet yet.

I have been a long time writing this, for I am very weak and tired yet, and Miranda will not let me write any more now, but you will understand and excuse me, will you not?

Your friend
Phoebe Deane.

Miranda had to go home soon after that, for it was plain Emmeline was wanting to get rid of her, and Marcia was to have guests for a couple of weeks. 'Squire Schuyler and his wife were coming to visit for the first time since little Rose's birth, for it was a long journey for an old man to take, and the 'Squire did not like to go away from home. Miranda felt that she must go, much as she hated to leave Phoebe, and so she bade her good-bye, and Phoebe began to take care of herself.

She was able to walk around her room, and soon to go downstairs, but somehow when she got down into the old atmosphere something seemed to choke her, she felt weary and wanted to creep back to bed again. So, much to Emmeline's disgust, she did not progress as rapidly as she ought to have done.

"You need to git some ambition," said Emmeline, in disgust, the first morning Phoebe came down to breakfast, and sat back after one or two mouthfuls. There was fried ham and eggs, and fried potatoes. Anybody ought to be glad to get that, Emmeline thought.

But somehow they did not appeal to Phoebe, and she left her plate almost untasted.

"I think ef you'd get some work and do somethin' mebbe you'd get your strength again. I never see anybody hang back like you do. There ain't any sense in it. What's the matter with yeh, anyway?"

"I don't know," said Phoebe, with an effort at cheerfulness. "I try, but somehow I feel so heavy and tired all the time."

"She isn't strong yet, Emmeline," pleaded Albert, kindly.

"Wal, don't I know that?" snapped Emmeline. "But how's she ever goin' to get strong ef she don't work it up?"

Such little pin-pricks were hard to bear when Phoebe felt well, and now that her strength was but a breath she seemed not to be able to bear them at all, and after a short effort would creep back to her room and lie down.

Miranda discovered her all huddled in a little heap on her bed late one afternoon when she came up to bring Phoebe her second letter, for Nathaniel had arranged that for the present he would send his correspondence to Phoebe through Miranda. Neither of them said aloud that it was because Hiram Green brought up the Deanes's mail so often, but both understood.

Miranda and the letter succeeded in cheering up Phoebe, but the ex-nurse felt that things were not going with her charge as prosperously as they should, and she took her trouble back to Marcia.

"Let's bring her down here, Miranda," proposed Marcia. "Father and mother are going home on Monday and it will be quiet and nice here. I think she might spend a month with us and get strong before she goes back and tries to work."

Miranda was delighted and took the first opportunity to convey the invitation to Phoebe, whose cheeks grew pink and eyes bright with anticipation. A whole month with Mrs. Spafford and Miranda! It was too good to be true.

It was Monday morning when they came for her with the big old chaise. Emmeline and Hank's sister were out hanging up clothes. Emmeline's mouth was full of clothespins, and her brow was dark, for Hank's sister talked much and worked slowly. Moreover, she made lumpy starch and could not be depended upon to keep the potatoes from burning if one went out to feed the chickens. It was hard to have trained up a good worker and then have her trail off in a thunder-storm and get sick and leave the work all on one's hands without ambition enough to get well. Emmeline was very ungracious to Marcia. She told Albert that she didn't see what business Mrs. Spafford had coming round to run their house. She thought Phoebe was better off at home, but Albert felt that Mrs. Spafford had been exceedingly kind.

So it was with little regret that Phoebe was carried away from her childhood's home, and into a sweet new world of loving kindness and joy, where the round cheeks and happiness of health might be coaxed back. Yet to Phoebe it was not an unalloyed bliss, for always there was the thought with her that by and by she must go back to the old life again, and she shuddered at the very thought of it, and could not bear to face it. It was like going to heaven for a little time and having to return to earth's trials again.

The spring had changed into the summer during Phoebe's illness and it was almost the middle of July when she began her beautiful visit at the Spaffords.

Chapter 23

Hiram Green had been exceedingly quiet since the night of the runaway.

The old plow-horse had kicked something loose about the chaise in his final lurch before he started to run, and it goaded his every step. He thought Hiram was striking him with a club. He thought the thunder was pursuing him; he thought the lightning was reaching for him as it darted through the livid sky; and down the road he flew, mile after mile, not slowing up for curves or excrescences in the road, but taking a short cut at the turns, rearing and shying at every flash of lightning. The chaise came lurching after, like one tied to a whirlwind, and Hiram, clinging, cursing, lashing out madly with his whip, was finally forced to spend his time in holding on, thinking every minute would be his last.

As the horse saw his own gate at last, however, he gave a final leap into the air, and bounded across the ditch, regardless of what was behind him, perhaps hoping to rid himself of it. The chaise lurched into the air and Hiram was tossed lightly over the fence and landed in the cow pasture. Something snapped, and the horse entered his own dooryard free at last from the thing which had been pursuing him.

The rain had begun to come down in driving sheets, now, and brought Hiram to his feet in spite of his dazed condition. He looked about him in the alternate dimness and vivid brightness, and perceived that he was close to the Deanes'. A moment's reflection made it plain that he must get up some kind of story, so he put on the best face that he could and went in.

"We've hed an axident," he explained, limping into the kitchen, where Emmeline was trying to get supper and keep the fretful baby quiet. "The blamed horse got scared at th' lightnin'. I seen what was goin' to happen an' I held him on his haunches fer a second while Phoebe jumped. She's back there a piece now, I reck'n, fer that blamed critter never stopped till he landed to home, an' he placed me in a awkword persition in the cow pasture, with the chaise all broke up. I guess Phoebe's all right, fer I looked back an' thought I saw her tryin' to wave her hand to me, but I 'spect we better go hunt her up soon 's this here storm lets up. She'll likely go in somewheres. We'd just got past old Mis' Duzenberry's."

That was all the explanation the Deanes had ever had of the adventure. Phoebe had been too ill to speak of it at first, and after she got well enough to come downstairs and Albert had questioned her at the table about it she had shuddered, and turned so white saying: "Please, don't, Albert, I can't bear to think of it," that he had never asked her again.

During her illness Hiram had been politely concerned about her welfare, taking the precaution to visit the post-office every day and inquire solicitously for any mail for her in a voice loud enough to be heard all over the room, and always being ready to tell just how she was when any one inquired. It never entered Albert's head that Hiram was not as anxious as he was during those days and nights when the fever held sway over the sweet young life. As for Emmeline, she made up her mind that where ignorance was bliss 'twas folly to be wise, and she kept her lips sealed, accepting Hiram's explanation, though all the time secretly she thought there might be some deeper reason for Phoebe's terrible appearance than just a runaway. She was relieved that Phoebe said nothing about it, if there had been trouble, and hoped it was forgotten.

The day after Phoebe went to the Spaffords to visit Hiram came up to see Emmeline in the afternoon when he knew Albert was out in the hayfield.

"Say, do you still favor livin' down to the village?" he asked, seating himself without waiting for an invitation.

Emmeline looked up keenly, and wondered what was in the air. "I hev said so," she remarked, tentatively, not willing to commit herself without further knowledge.

"Wal, you know that lot o' mine down there opposite the Seceder church? It has a big weepin' willer same 's in the church yard, an a couple o' plum-trees in bearin'. How'd you like to live on thet lot?"

"H'm!" said Emmeline, stolidly. "Much good 'twould do me to like it. Albert'll never buy that lot, Hiram Green, there ain't no use askin' him. You wasn't thinkin' of buildin' there yerself, was yeh?" Emmeline looked up sharply as this new thought entered her mind. Perhaps he wanted her to hold out the bait of a house in the village to Phoebe.

"Naw, I ain't goin' to build in no village at present, Mis' Deane," he remarked, dryly. "Too fur from work fer me, thank you. But I was thinkin' I'd heard you say you wanted to live in the village, an' I thought I'd make a bargain with you. Say, Emmeline, 'taint no use mincin' matters. I'm a' goin' to marry Phoebe Deane, an' I want you should help me to it. I'll make you this offer. It's a real generous one, too. The day I marry Phoebe Deane I'll give you a deed to that lot in the village. Now, what d'yeh say? Is't a bargain?"

"What to do?" questioned Emmeline. She would be caught in no trap. "I've done all I know now. I'd like my sister Mandy to come here to live, an' there ain't room fer her while Phoebe stays; but I don't see what I kin do, more'n what I've done a'ready. Wouldn't she make up to yeh none the day you come home from the barn raisin'?"

"Wal, I was gettin' on pretty well 'til that blamed horse took an' run," said Hiram, shifting his eyes from her piercing ones.

"Wal, I can't compel her to marry you," snapped Emmeline.

"You don't hev to," said Hiram. "I've got my plans laid, an' all you got to do is stand by me when the time comes. I ain't tellin' my plans jest yet, but you'll see what they be, an' all is, you remember my offer. Ef you want that village lot jest remember to stand by me."

He unfolded his length from the kitchen chair and went out. Emmeline said nothing. When he reached the door he turned back and said:

"I broke ground this mornin' fer a new house on the knoll. Me an' Phoebe'll be livin' there by this time next year."

"Well, I hope to goodness yeh will," responded Emmeline, heartily, "fer I've hed trouble 'nough a'ready with this business. I'll do what I ken, o' course, but do fer goodness' sake hurry up!"

The house on the knoll steadily progressed. Hiram came little to the Deane house during Phoebe's absence, but spent his time at the new building when his farm work did not demand his presence. He also came often to the village and hung around the post-office. He was determined that nothing should escape his vigilance in that direction. Seeing him there one day when the mail was being distributed Miranda took her place in the front ranks and asked in a clear cool voice:

"Anythin' fer Phoebe Deane? She's stayin t' our house fer a spell now an' I'll take her mail to her."

Miranda well knew that the only mail Phoebe was likely to receive came addressed to herself, so she was more than surprised when the postmaster with his spectacles on the end of his nose held up a letter whose address he carefully studied, and handed it to her rather reluctantly. He would have liked a chance to study that letter more closely.

But nothing fazed Miranda. She took the letter as composedly as if there ought to be two or three more forthcoming, and marched off. Hiram Green, however, got down scowling from his seat on the counter and stalked over to the postmaster.

"I sh'd think you'd hev to be keerful who you give letters to," he remarked, in a low tone. "Phoebe Deane might not like that harum-scarum girl bringin' her letters. Did you take notice ef that letter was from New York? She was expectin' quite a important letter from there."

The postmaster looked over his spectacles at Hiram patronizingly.

"I sh'd hope I know who to trust," he remarked, with dignity. "No, I didn't take notice. I hev too much to do to notice post-marks."

Hiram, however, was greatly shaken up by the sight of that letter in Miranda's triumphant hands, and betook himself to the hayloft to meditate. If he had known that the letter merely contained a clipping about the progress of missions in South Africa, which Ann Jane Bloodgood had sent thinking it might help Phoebe to recover from her illness, as she heard she was feeling "poorly" yet, and "hoped she would soon hear she was better!"

But Hiram had no thought but that the letter was from Nathaniel, therefore his reflections were bitter.

Two days afterward Hiram was one of a group about a New York agent who had come down to sell goods. He was telling the story of a mob, and his swaggering air and flashy clothes attracted Hiram greatly. He thought them far superior to any of Nathaniel Graham's, and determined to model himself after this pattern in future.

"Oh, we do things in great shape down in New York," he was saying. "When folks don't please, we *mob* 'em. If their opinions ain't what we like, we *mob* 'em. If they don't pay us what we ask, we *mob* 'em. Heard 'bout the mob down in Chatham Street last summer — er it might have been two years ago. A lot of niggers met to hear a darkey preacher in a little chapel down there. We got wind of it, an' we ordered 'em to leave, but they wouldn't budge 'cause they'd paid their rent, so we just *put* 'em out. There was a man named Tappan who lived down in Rose Street, an' he was there. He was an Abolitionist, an' we didn't like him. He'd had somethin' to do with this meetin', so we follered him home with hoots and threats, and give his house a good stoning. Did him good. Oh, we do things up in great shape in New York. Next night we went down to the Bowery Theatre. Manager there's English, you know, and he'd said some imperlite things about America, we thought, something about our right to own slaves, so we give him a dose. Oh, we're not afraid of anything down in New York."

Hiram was greatly fascinated by this representative New Yorker, and after the crowd had begun to disperse he went to the stranger and buttonholed him.

"Say, look a'here!" he began, holding a five-dollar bill invitingly near to the New Yorker's hand. "I know a feller you ought to mob. I could give yeh his name an' address real easy. He's prominent down there, an' I reckon 'twould be worth somethin' to you folks to know his name. Fact is, I've an' interest in the matter myself, an' I'd like to see him come to justice, an' I'm willin' to subscribe this here bill to the cause ef you see your way clear to lookin' the matter up fer me."

"Why, certainly, certainly," said the stranger, grasping the bill affably, "I'll do anything I can for you. I'll hand this over to the treasurer of our side. In fact I'm the treasurer myself, and I thank you very much for your interest. Anything I can do I'm sure I'll be glad to. Can you tell me any more about this?"

Hiram toled him off to a quiet corner and before the interview was ended he had entered into a secret plot against Nathaniel Graham, and had pledged himself to give the stranger not only one but four more five-dollar bills when the work should be complete, and Nathaniel Graham stand revealed to the world an Abolitionist, a man who should be suppressed. It was all arranged before the stranger left on the evening stage-coach that he would write Hiram what day a move would be made in the matter, and just how far he felt they could go.

Hiram went home chuckling and felt that revenge was sweet. He would get the better of Nathaniel Graham now, and Nathaniel would never know who struck the blow.

A few days afterward there came a letter from the stranger saying that all things were prospering, but it would be impossible to get up a thoroughly organized mob and do the work without a little more money, for their funds were low; and would it be possible for Hiram to forward the twenty dollars now instead of waiting?

After a sleepless night Hiram doled out the twenty dollars. The stranger wrote that the time had been arranged, and he would let him know all about it soon. They thought they had their man pinned down tight. The night Hiram received that letter he slept soundly.

Meantime the world had been moving in an orbit of beauty for Phoebe. She was tended and guarded like a little child. They made her feel that her presence was a joy to them all. Every member of the family down to Rose made it a point to brighten her stay with them. Rose brought her flowers from the garden, David brought the latest books and poems for her to read, Marcia was her constant loving companion, and Miranda cooked the daintiest dishes known to the culinary art for her tempting. The letters went back and forth to New York every day or two, for as Phoebe was growing better she was able to write longer epistles, and Nathaniel seemed always to have something to say that needed an immediate answer. Phoebe was growing less shy of him, and more and more opened her heart to his friendship like a flower turning to a newly risen sun.

Janet Bristol had been away on a visit during Phoebe's illness, but while she was still with the Spaffords Janet returned, and one afternoon came to return Mrs. Spafford's call.

Phoebe wore a thin white frock whose dainty frills showed modestly her white throat and arms now taking on something of their old roundness. She was sitting in the cool parlor with Marcia when the caller arrived. Her mother's locket was tied about her throat with a bit of velvet ribbon, and her hair, now coming out in soft curls, made a lovely fluffy halo of brown all about her face.

Janet watched her while she talked with Marcia, and wondered at the sweet grace of form and feature. Somehow her former prejudice against this girl melted strangely as Phoebe raised her beautiful eyes and smiled at her. Janet felt drawn to her against her will, yet she could not tell why she held back, only that Nathaniel had been so strangely stubborn about that letter. To be sure that was long past, and her mind was fully occupied just now with Nathaniel's theological friend, Martin Van Renssaeler. She was attempting to teach him the ways of the world, and draw him out of his gravity. He seemed to be a willing subject, if one might judge from the number of visits he made to the Bristol home during the summer.

Then, one bright, beautiful day, just a week before Phoebe's visit was to close, Nathaniel came up from New York.

He reached the village on the afternoon coach, and as it happened Hiram Green stood across the road from the tavern where the coach usually stopped, lounging outside the post-office and waiting for the mail to be brought. He did not intend that any Miranda Griscom should stand in his way. Moreover, this night was the one that had been set for Nathaniel Graham's undoing, and there might be a letter for himself from his agent in New York. It filled Hiram with a kind of intoxication to be getting letters from New York.

He stood leaning against a post watching the coach as it rolled down the village street drawn by the four great horses, enveloped in a cloud of dust, and drew up at the tavern with a flourish. Then suddenly he noticed that there were passengers, two of them, and that one was Nathaniel himself.

Hiram felt weak in the knees. If a ghost had suddenly descended from the coach he could not have been more dismayed. Here he had just put twenty-five good dollars into Nathaniel's discomfiture, only to have him appear in his own town smiling and serene as if nothing had been about to happen. It made Hiram just sick. He watched him and the other young man who had been his fellow passenger, as they walked down the street toward the Bristol house. He had sat down when the coach stopped, feeling inadequate to the work of holding himself upright in the midst of his unusual emotions. Now he got slowly up and went away toward his home, walking heavily, as if he had been stricken. With head bent down he studied the ground as he walked. He forgot the mail, forgot everything, save that he had put twenty-five dollars into a fruitless enterprise.

Midway between the post-office and his home he stopped and wheeled around with an exclamation of dismay:

"Gosh Ninety!"

Then after a pause he let forth a series of oaths. It was plain Hiram was stirred to the depths of his evil nature. He had just remembered that Phoebe was down in the village at the Spaffords and would be likely to see Nathaniel. His ugly face contracted in a spasm of anger, that gradually died into a settled expression of vengeance. The time had come, and he would wait no longer. If he had been more impulsive and less of a coward he would have shot his victim then and there, but such was not Hiram's way. Stealthily, with deadly surety he laid his plans; with the patience and the fatality that could only come from the father of liars himself.

Three whole days did Nathaniel stay in the village, and much of that time he spent at the Spafford house, walking and talking, and reading with Phoebe. Three whole days did Hiram spy upon him at every turn, with evil countenance and indifferent mien, lounging by the house, or happening in the way. He had written an angry letter to the man in New York, who later excused himself for not having performed his mission on account of Nathaniel's absence, but promising it should yet be done, and demanding more money.

Janet and Martin Van Rensselaer came down to the Spafford house the last evening, and made a merry party. Hiram hid himself among the lilac bushes at the side of the house, like the serpent of old, and watched the affiar all the evening, his heart filled with all the evil that his nature could conceive.

Phoebe, in her simple white frock, with her lovely head crowned with the short curling hair, and her exquisite face agleam with the light and mirth that belong to youth, and which she was tasting for almost the first time, made a beautiful picture. So Miranda thought as she brought in the sugary seed-cakes, and great frosted pitcher of cool drink, made from raspberry and currant jelly, mixed with water from the spring. If Miranda could have known of the watcher outside, the evening might have ended in comedy, for she would certainly have emptied a panful of dishwater from the upper window straight into the lilac bushes. But Miranda's time had not yet come, and neither had Hiram's.

So Nathaniel and Phoebe sat by the open window and said a few last pleasant words, and looked a good-by into one another's eyes, the depth and meaning of which neither had as yet fathomed. They did not know that not two feet away was the evil face of the man who hated them both. He was so near that his viperous breath could almost have touched their cheeks, and his wicked heart, burning with the passionate fires of jealousy and hatred, gathered and devoured their glances as a raging fire will devour fuel. He watched them, and he gloated over them, as a monster will gloat over the victims he intends to destroy.

Chapter 24

The next morning on the early coach Nathaniel and Martin went away. Hiram was there to see that they were really gone, and to send word at once to New York.

That afternoon Phoebe went back to her brother's house, the light of health and happiness beginning to glow in her face. It was hard to go back, but Phoebe was happy in the thought that these friends were ture, who would continue even in the midst of daily trials.

Everybody had urged her to stay longer, but Phoebe felt that she had already stayed longer than she should have done, and insisted that she must begin life again, that it was not right to lie idle.

The truth was, Phoebe had in mind a little plan which she wanted to think about and talk over with Albert. This stay with the Spaffords had brought to a climax a great longing she had had in her heart to go to school somewhere for a little while. She had a great thirst for knowledge, and she began to think that perhaps it might be possible to gratify it, for there was that money of hers lying idle in the bank. She might take some of it and go away for a year to a good school if Albert thought so, and she almost believed he would if only he could be persuaded before Emmeline heard of it.

Phoebe had felt her own deficiencies more and more by reason of her delightful correspondence with Nathaniel Graham. She wished to make herself more his equal, that she might really be able to write letters worthy of his perusal. She little dreamed of the trouble that was swiftly descending.

In modern war we sow our harbors and coasts thick with hidden mines ready to explode should the enemy venture within our borders. In much the same fashion that morning Hiram Green started out to lay his mines in readiness for the sweet young life that was unwarily drifting his way.

He had dressed himself soberly, as befitted the part he was to play. He harnessed his horse and chaise, and taking a wide berth of country in his circuit for the day, he drove first to the home of an old aunt of his to whom he had never been bound by many loving ties, yet who served his purpose, for she had a tongue that wagged well, and reached far.

After the greetings had been exchanged Hiram sat down with a funereal air in the big chair his relative had brought out of the parlor in honor of his coming, and prepared to bring forth his errand.

"Aunt Keziah," he began, in a voice which indicated momentous things to come. "I'm in deep trouble!"

"You don't say, Hiram! What's up now? Any of the children dead or sick?"

"No I ain't afflicted in that manner this time," said Hiram. It's somethin' deeper than that, deeper than sickness er death. It's fear o' disgrace."

"What! Hiram! You ain't ben stealin' er forgin' anybody's name, surely?" The old lady sat up as if she had been shot and fixed her eyes—little eyes like Hiram's with the glitter of steel beads—on her downcast nephew's face.

"No, Aunt, I'm thankful to say I've been kep' from pussonel disgrace," murmured Hiram, piously, with a roll of his eyes indicating that his trust was in a power beyond his own.

"Well, what is it, then? Speak up quick. I'm too old to be kep' in hot water." The aunt spoke snappishly. Hiram perceived that he had made his impression.

"Well, you see it's this way, Aunt. You must uv heard I was takin' notice again."

"That was to be expected, Hiram, you so young an' with children to look after. I hope you picked out a good worker."

"Yes," admitted Hiram, with satisfaction, "she's a right smart worker, an' I thought she was 'bout as near perfect all through as you could find 'em, an' I kinder got my heart sot on her. I've done everythin' she wanted that I knowed, even to buildin' a new house down on the knoll fer her, which wan't necessary ' all, bein' as the old house is much better'n the one she's ben brung up in. Yet I done it fer her, an' I ben courtin' her fer quite a spell back now; ben to see her every night reg'lar, an' home from meetin' an' singin'-school whenver she took notion she wanted to go."

Hiram drew a long sigh, got out a big red and white cotton handkerchief and blew his nose resoundingly. The old lady eyed him suspiciously to gauge his emotion with exactness.

"Long 'but six or eight weeks ago" — Hiram's voice grew husky now — "she took sick. 'Twas this 'ere way. We was comin' home from a barn raisin' over to Woodbury's, an' it was gettin' near dark, an' she took a notion she wanted to pick some vi'lets long the roads. I seen a storm was comin' up, an' I argued with her agin it, but she would hev her way, an' so I let her out an' tole her to hurry up. She got out an' run back o' the kerridge a piece an' begun pickin' an' in a minute all on a suddent somethin' hit the horse's hind leg. I can't tell what it was, mebbe a stone er it might 'a' ben a stick, but I never took no thought at the time. I grabbed fer them reins, an' jest as the horse started to run there come a big clap o' thunder that scared the horse worse'n ever. I hung on to them reins, an' lookin back I seen her standin' kind o' scared like an' white in the road a lookin' after me, an' I hollered back, 'You go to the Widder Duzenberry's till I come back fer yeh. It's goin' to rain.' Then I hed to tend to that horse, fer he was runnin' like the very old scratch. Well, 'course I got him stopped and turned him round an' went back, but there wasn't a sign of her anywhere to be seen. The Widder Duzenberry said she hedn't seen her sence we druv by fust. I went back fer her brother, an' we searched everywhere, but we couldn't find her no place, an' will you 'blieve it, we couldn't find a sign of her all night. But the next mornin' she come sailin' in lookin' white an' scared and fainted away, an' went right to bed real sick. We couldn't make it all out, an' I never said much 'bout it, 'cause I didn't 'spicion nothin' at the time, but it all looked kinder queer afterward. An' what I'd like to know is, who threw that ar stone thet hit the horse? You see, it's all come out now thet she's been cuttin' round the country with a strange young man from New York, she's met him off in the woods an' round. They say they used 'ter meet not far from here — right down on the timber lot back o' your barn was one place they used to meet. There's a holler tree where they'd hide their letters. You 'member that big tree taller than the rest, a big white oak, 't is, that has a squirrel harbour in it? Well, that's the one. They used to meet there. And once she started off on some errand fer her sister-in-law in the coach, an' he es bold es life went 'long. Nobody knows whar they went, some sez Albany, some sez Schenectady, but anyhow she never come back till late the next day, an' no countin' fer where she'd been.

"Her sister-in-law is a nice respectable woman, and they all come of a good famlly. They'll feel turrible 'bout this, fer they've never 'spicioned her any more'n I done. She's got a sweet purty face like she was a saint — "

"Them is always the very kind that goes to the dogs," quoth Aunt Keziah, shaking her head and laying down her knitting.

"Well, Aunt Keziah," said Hiram, getting out his handkerchief again, "I come to ask your advice in this matter. What be I to do?"

"Do?" snapped Aunt Keziah. "Do, Hiram Green? Why be thankful you found out 'fore you got married. It's hard on you, 'course, but 'tain't near so hard es 'twould 'a' ben ef you'd 'a' found out after you was tied to 'er. An' you just havin' had such a hard time an' all with a sickly wife dyin'. I declare, Hiram Green, you suttin'ly hev been preserved!"

"But don't you think, mebbe, Aunt Keziah, I ought to stick to her? She's such a purty little thing, an' everybody's down on her now, an' she's begged me so hard not to give her up when she's in disgrace. She's promised she'll never hev nothin' more to do with these other fellers — "

There were actually some hypocritical tears being squeezed out of Hiram's little pig-eyes and rolling down in stinted quantities upon the ample kerchief. It would not do to wipe them away when they were so hard to manufacture, so Hiram waited till they were almost evaporated and then mopped his eyes vigorously.

"Well, Hiram Green, are you that soft-hearted! I declare to goodness, but you do need advice! Don't you trust in no sech promises. They ain't wuth the breath they're spoken in. Jest you hev nothin' more to do with the hussy. Thank goodness there's plenty more good workers in the world — healthy ones, too that won't up 'n die on ye jest in harvest"

"Well, Aunt Keziah!"—Hiram arose and cleared his throat as if a funeral ceremony had just been concluded—"I thank yeh fer yer good advice. I may see my way clear to foller it. Jest now I'm in doubt. I wanted to know what you thought, an' then I'll consider the matter. It ain't as though I hedn't been goin' with her pretty steady fer a year back. Yeh see what I'll do'll likely tell on how it goes with her from now on."

"Well, don't you go to be sentimental like, Hiram. That wouldn't set on you at your time o' life. Jest you stand by your rights an' be rid of her. It's what your ma would 'a' said ef she was alive. Now you remember what I say. Don't you be soft-hearted."

"I'll remember, Aunt," said Hiram, dutifully, and went out to his chaise.

He took his slow and doleful way winding up the road, and as soon as he was out of sight beyond the turn the alert old lady put on her sunbonnet and slipped up to her cousin's house half a mile away. She was out of breath with the tremendous news she had to tell, and marvelling all the way that Hiram had forgotten to tell her not to speak of it. Of course he intended to do so, but then of course he wouldn't object to having Lucy Drake know. Lucy was his own cousin once removed, and it was a family affair in a way.

Hiram's next visit was at the Widow Duzenberry's.

Now the Widow Duxenberry had often thought that her good daughter would made a wise choice for Hiram Green, and could rule well over the wild little Greens and be an ornament to the house and farm of Green. Therefore it seemed a special dispensation of Providence that Susanna had that afternoon donned her best sprigged chintz and done her hair up with her grandmother's high-backed comb. She looked proudly over at her daughter as Hiram sat down in the chair that Susanna had primly placed for him near her mother.

When the few preliminary remarks were concluded, and the atmosphere had become somewhat breathless with the excitement of wondering what he had come for, Hiram cleared his throat ominously and began:

"Mrs. Duzenberry," he said, and his countenance took on a deep sadness, "I called today on a very sad errand." The audience was attentive in the extreme. "I want to ask, did you take notice of me an' Phoebe Deane a ridin' by, the day of Woodbury's barn raisin'?"

"Wal, yes," admitted old Mrs. Duzenberry, reluctantly. "Now 't you mention it, I b'lieve I did see you drivin' by, fer there was black clouds comin' up an' I says to Susanna, says I, 'Susanna, we mebbe ought to bring in that web o' cloth that's out to bleach. It mebbe might blow away.'"

"Well, I thought p'raps you did, Mis' Duzenberry, an' I want to ask, did you take notice of how we was sittin' clost to one 'nother, she with her head restin' on my shoulder like? I hate to speak of it, but Mis' Duzenberry, wouldn't you 'a' thought Phoebe Deane was real fond o' me!"

Mother Duzenberry's face darkened. What had the man come for?

"I certain should," she answered, severely; "I don't approve of sech doin's in open road."

"Well, Mis' Duzenberry, mebbe 'twas a little too sightly a place, but what I wanted to know from you, Mis' Duzenberry, was this. You saw what you saw. Now, won't you tell me when a man has gone that fur, in your 'pinion is there anything that would justify him in turnin' back?"

"There might be," said the old lady, somewhat mollified.

"Well, what, fur instance?"

"Wal, he might 'a' found he thought more o' someone else," and her eyes wandered toward her daughter, who was modestly looking out the window.

"Anything else?" Hiram's voice had the husky note now as if he were deeply affected.

"Wal, I might think of somethin' else, gimme time."

"What ef he found out she wan't all he thought she was?"

Mother Duzenberry's face brightened.

"'Course that might 'fect him some," she admitted.

"I see you don't understand me," sighed Hiram. "I take it you ain't heard the bad news 'bout Phoebe Deane."

"She ain't dead, is she? I heard she was better," said Susanna, turning her sharp thin profile toward Hiram.

"No, my good friend," sighed Hiram, "it's worse'n death. It certainly is fer that poor girl. She's to be greatly pitied, however much she may have aired."

The two women were leaning froward now, eager for the news.

"I came to you in my trouble," said Hiram, mopping his face vigorously, "hopin' you would sympathize with me in my extremity, an' help me to jedge what to do. I wouldn't like to do the girl no wrong, but still, considerin' all that's come out the last two days—Say, Mis' Duzenberry, you didn't see no man hangin' round here that day little before we druv by, did you? No stranger, ner nuthin'."

"Why, yes, ma," said Susanna, excitedly. "There was a wagon come by a goin' toward the village, and there was two men, an' one of 'em jumped out an' took somethin' from the other, looked like a bundle er sumthin', an' he walked off towards the woods. He had butternut-colored trousers."

"That's him," said Hiram, frowning, "they say he always wore them trousers when anybody's seen him with her. You know the day they went off in the stage to Albany he was dressed that 'a' way!"

"Did they go off in the stage together in broad daylight? That's scandalous!" exclaimed the mother.

"You know most o' their goin's on happened over near Fundy Road. Aunt Keziah knows all 'bout it. Poor ole lady. She's all broke up. She always set a good store by me, her only livin' nephew. She'll be wantin' me to give up havin' anythin' more to do with Phoebe now, since all this is come out 'bout her goin's on, but I can't rightly make up my mind whether it's right fer me to desert her er not in her time o'trouble."

"I should think you was fully justified," said Mrs. Duzenberry, heartily. "There's other deservin' girls, an' it's puttin' a premium on badness to 'ncourage it that way."

"Good afternoon, Mis' Duzenberry." Hiram rose sadly. "I'm much 'bliged to yeh fer yer advice. I ain't sure yet what I shall do. 'Course I'll be 'bliged to yeh ef you'll jest keep people from talkin' much as yeh ken. I knowed you knowed the fac's an' I thought 'twould be best to come straight to you. Good afternoon, Miss Susanna. Perhaps we may meet again under pleasanter circumstances."

"Land alive!" exclaimed Susanna, as they watched him drive sadly away. "Don't he look broke up! Poor feller!"

"Serves him right fer makin' up to a little pink-cheeked critter like that," said the mother. "Say, Susanna, I ain't sure but you better put on yer bonnet an' run up to Keziah Dart's house an' find out 'bout this. We've got to be real keerful not to get mixed up in it, nohow, but I should like to know jest what she's done. Ef Keziah ain't home run on to Page's. They'll mebbe know. He said they'd ben seen round there. But speak real cautious. It won't do to tell everything you know. I'll mebbe jest step over to the toll-gate. They'll be wantin' to know what Hiram Green was here for. It won't be no harm to mention he was callin' on you. It might take their 'tention off'n him, so's they wouldn't speak 'bout him goin' so much with Phoebe. My! Ain't it a pity! But that's what comes o'havin' good looks. You know I allus told you so, Susanna."

Susanna tossed her head, drew her sunbonnet down over her plain face and went off, while her mother fastened the door and went up to the toll-gate.

Hiram's method as he pursued his course the rest of the afternoon was to call ostensibly on some other business, and then speak of the gossip as a matter of which every one knew, and refer to those on whom he had called before as being able to give more information concerning the facts than he could. He did not ask any more advice, but in one case where he was asked what he was going to do about it he shook his head dubiously and went away without replying.

Most of his calls were in the country, but before he went home he stopped at the home of the village dressmaker. His excuse for going there was that his oldest girl needed a frock for Sunday, and he thought the old woman who kept house for him had enough to do without making it. He asked when she could come, and said he would let her know if that day would be convenient. Just as he was leaving he told her that as she was going everywhere to other people's houses he supposed she would soon hear the terrible stories that were going round about Phoebe Deane, but he wished that if she heard anything about his breaking off with Phoebe she would just say that he intended not to do anything rashly, but would think it over and do what was right.

The keen-eyed newsmonger asked enough questions to have the facts well in hand, and looked after Hiram's tall, lanky form with admiration. "I tell you," she said to herself, "it ain't every man would hev the courage to say that! He's a good man! Poor little Phoebe Deane. What a pity! Now her life's ruined, fer of course he'll never marry her."

Then Hiram Green, having wisely scattered his calumnies against the innocent, betook himself virtuously to his home, and left his thistle seed to take root and spring up.

Phoebe Deane, meantime, settled down in her own little kitchen chamber beside her candle and prepared to write a letter to Nathaniel Graham, as she had promised him she would do that very night, and in it she told him her plans of going away to school.

Chapter 25

The tongues which Hiram had set wagging were all experts and before many days had passed the fields of gossip were green with springing slander and disgrace for the fair name of Phoebe Deane. All unconsciously she moved above it, making happy plans, and singing her sweet song of hope. She did not mind work, for it was pleasant to feel strong again. She even hummed a sweet tune that she heard Marcia play. Emmeline was puzzled to understand it all.

But the thing that puzzled Emmeline most of all was that Hiram Green had not been near the house since the day he had the talk with her about the village lot, and had boasted that he was going to marry Phoebe before another year.

Steadily every day Hiram's new house was growing. Emmeline could see it from her window, and she wondered if perhaps he was preparing to break his promise and court another girl instead of Phoebe, or was this a part of his plan to stay away until the house was done? It troubled Emmeline every day. Neither could she understand how Phoebe could be happy and settle down so cheerfully, having driven her one suitable lover away.

Phoebe had ventured to discuss the plan of her going away with Albert, who seemed rather disappointed to have her go, but was nevertheless willing, and said that he thought such a plan would have pleased her mother. He broached the subject to Emmeline, and thereupon brought down upon the family a storm of rage. Emmeline scoffed at the idea. She said that Phoebe was already spoiled for anything in life, and that if she used up her money getting more spoiling she couldn't see how in the world she expected to support herself; for *she* wouldn't be a party to Phoebe's living any longer on them if she spent her money on more schooling. Then Emmeline put on her bonnet and ran across the field to Hiram's farm, where she found him at the knoll superintending the putting up of a great stone chimney.

"Say, look-a-here, Hiram Green," she began, excitedly, getting him off a little way from the workmen, "what do you mean by sech actions? Hev you give up Phoebe Deane, er haven't yeh? 'Cause ef yeh ain't yeh better be tendin' to business. She's got it int' her fool head now to go off to school, an' she'll do it, too. I ken see Albert's jest soft enough to let 'er."

Hiram smiled a peculiar smile.

"Don't you worry, Emmeline. I know what I'm 'bout, an' you'll git your corner lot yit. Phoebe Deane won't go off to no boardin'-school, not yet awhile, 'er I'll miss my guess. Jest you leave it to me!"

"Oh, very well!" said Emmeline, going off in a huff. She returned by a roundabout route to her home, where she proceeded to make life miserable for Phoebe and Albert in spite of all that they could do.

Then one morning, lo! the little town was agog with the gossip about Phoebe Deane, and it had grown into enormous proportions, for as it travelled from the circle of country round about into the town it condensed into more tangible form, and the number of people who had seen Phoebe Deane with strange young men at the edge of dark, or in lonely places, grew with each repetition. Everybody seemed to know it, and be talking about it except Phoebe herself and her own family and friends. Somehow no one had quite dared to mention it before any of them yet, it was too new and startling.

Sunday morning the Deanes went to church, and there were strange turnings away from them, and much whispering, nodding, and nudging as they passed. It had not been expected that Phoebe would appear in church. It was considered brazen in her to do so. It was evidently all and more true.

Hiram Green came to church but he did not look toward the Deanes' pew. He sat at the back with pious manner and drooping countenance, and after church made his melancholy way out without stopping to talk, or attempting to get near Phoebe. This was observed significantly; also the fact that Mrs. Spafford walked down the aisle in friendly converse with Phoebe Deane as if nothing had happened. Evidently she had not heard yet. Somebody ought to tell her. They discussed the matter in groups on the way home.

Old Mrs. Baldwin and her daughter Belinda were much worried about it. They went so far as to call to the doctor and his wife who were passing their house that afternoon on the way to see a sick patient.

"Doctor," said Mrs. Baldwin, coming out to the sidewalk as the doctor drew up to speak with her, "I ain't a going to bother you a minute but I just wanted to ask if you knew much about this tory that's been going round about Phoebe Deane. It seems as though someone ought to tell Mrs. Spafford. She's been real kind to the girl, and she don't seem to have heard it. I don't know her so well, or I would, but somebody ought to do it. I didn't know but you or your wife would undertake to do it. They walked down the aisle together after church this morning and it seemed too bad. David Spafford wouldn't like to have his wife so conspicuous, I know. Belinda says he was out of town yesterday, so I s'pose he hasn't heard about it yet, but I think something ought to be done."

"Yes, it's a very sad story," chirped the doctor's wife. "I just heard it myself this morning. The doctor didn't want to believe it, but I tell him it comes very straight."

"Oh, yes, it's straight," said Mrs. Baldwin, with an ominous shake of her head and a righteous roll of her eyes. "It's all too straight. I had it from a friend who had it from Hiram Green's aunt's cousin. She said Hiram was just bowed with grief over it, and they were going to have a real hard time to keep him from marrying her in spite of it."

The doctor frowned. He was fond of Phoebe. He felt that they all had better mind their own business and let Phoebe alone.

"I would be quite willing to speak to Miss Hortense or Miss Amelia Spafford," said the doctor's wife. "I'm intimate with them, you know, and they could do as they thought best about telling their niece."

"That's a good idea," said Mrs. Baldwin. "That quite relieves my mind. I was real worried over that sweet little Mrs. Spafford, and she with that pretty little Rose to bring up. They wouldn't of course want a scandal to come anywhere near them. They better look out for that Griscom girl. She comes from poor stock. I said long ago she'd never be any good, and she's been with that Phoebe Deane off an' on a good bit."

"Oh, I think that was all kindness," said the doctor's wife. "Mrs. Spafford was very kind during Phoebe Deane's illness. The doctor knew all about that."

"Yes, I s'spose the doctor knows all 'bout things. That's the reason I called you, and on Sunday too; but I thought it was a work of necessity and mercy. Well, good-afternoon, Doctor, I won't keep you any longer."

"There's that pretty Miss Bristol ought to be told, too, ma," reminded Belinda.

"That's so, Belinda," said the doctor's wife. "I'll take it upon myself to warn her, too. So sad, isn't it? Well, good-bye," and the doctor's chaise drove on. The doctor was inclined to prevent his wife from taking part in the scandal business, but his wife had her own plans which she did not reveal. She shut her thin lips and generally did as she pleased.

The very next day she took her way down the shaded street and called upon the aunts of the house of Spafford, and before she left she had drooped her eyes and told in sepulchral whispers of the disgrace that had befallen the young protegee of their niece, Mrs. David Spafford.

Aunt Amelia and Aunt Hortense lifted their hands in righteous horror and thanked the doctor's wife for the information, saying they were sure Marcia knew nothing of it, and of course they would tell her at once and she would henceforth have nothing further to do with the Deanes.

Then the doctor's wife went on her mission to Janet Bristol.

Janet Bristol was properly scandalized, and charmingly grateful to the doctor's wife. She said of course Phoebe was nothing to her, but she had thought her rather pretty, and interesting. She was obviously bored with the rest of the good woman's call, and when it was over she betook herself to her writing desk where she scribbled off a letter to her cousin Nathaniel concerning a party she wished to give and for which she wanted him and his friend Martin Van Rensselaer to come up. At the close she added a hasty postscript.

"The doctor's wife has just called. She tells me I must beware of your paragon, Miss Deane, as there is a terribly scandalous story going around about her and a young man. I didn't pay much attention to the horrid details of it, I never like to get my mind filled with such things, but it is bad enough, and of course I shall have nothing further to do with her. I wonder Mrs. Spafford did not have the discernment to see she was not all right. I suspected it from the first you know, and you see I was right. My intuitions are usually right. I am glad I have not had much to do with her."

Now it happened that Rose was not well that Sunday and Miranda had stayed at home with her, else she would surely have discovered the state of things, and revealed it to Marcia. And it happened also that Marcia started off with David on a long ride early Monday morning, therefore when Aunt Hortense came down on her direful errand Marcia was not there, and Miranda, seeing her coming, escaped with Rose through the back door for a walk in the woods. So another day passed without the scandal reaching either Miranda or Marcia

It was on Monday morning that the storm broke upon poor Phoebe's defenseless head.

A neighbor had come over from the next farm a quarter of a mile away to borrow a cup of hop yeast. It was a queer time to borrow yeast, at an hour in the week when every well-regulated family was doing its washing, but that was the neighbor's professed errand. She lingered a moment by the door with the yeast cup in her hand and talked to Emmeline.

Phoebe was in the yard hanging up clothes, and singing. The little bird was sitting on the weathervane and calling merrily: "Phoe-bee! Phoe-bee!"

"Are yeh goin' to let her stay here now?" the visitor asked in a whisper fraught with meaning, and nodded her head toward the girl in the yard.

"Stay?" said Emmeline, looking up aggressively. "Why shouldn't she? Ain't she been here ever since her mother died? I s'pose she'll stay till she gets married."

Emmeline was not fond of this neighbor, and therefore did not care to reveal her family secrets to her. She lived in a red house with windows both ways and knew all that went on for miles about.

"Guess she won't run much chance of that now," said the neighbor, with a disagreeable laugh. She was prepared to be sociable if Emmeline opened her heart, but she knew how to scratch back when she was slapped.

"Well, I sh'd like to know what you mean, Mis' Prinn. I'm sure I don't know why our Phoebe shouldn't marry es likely es any other girl, an' more so'n some what ain't got good looks."

(Mrs. Prinn's daughter was not spoken of generally as a beauty.)

"Good looks don't count fer much when they ain't got good morals."

"Indeed! Mis' Prinn. You do talk kind of mysterious. Did you mean to insinuate that our Phoebe didn't have good morals?"

"I didn't mean to insinuate anything, Mis' Deane. It's all over town the way she's been goin' on, an' I don't see how you can pertend to hide it any longer. Everybody knows it, an' b'lieves it."

"I'd certainly like to know what you mean," demanded Emmeline, facing the woman angrily. "I brung that girl up, an' I guess I know what good morals is. Phoebe may have her weak points, but she's all right morally."

"Fac's is fac's, Mis' Deane," said the neighbor, with a relish.

"I deny that there is any fac's to the contrary," screamed Emmeline, now thoroughly excited into championing the girl whom she hated. The family honor was at stake. The Deanes had never done anything dishonorable or disgraceful.

"I s'pose you don't deny that she spent the night out all night the time o' the storm, do yeh? How d' ye explain that?"

"I should like to know what that hes to do with morals."

The neighbor proceeded to explain with a story so plausible that Emmeline grew livid with rage.

"Well, 'pon my word, you've got a lot to do runnin' round with sech lies as them. Wher'd you get all that, I'd like to know?"

"It all come straight enough, an' everybody knows it, ef you are stone blind. Folks has seen her round in lonely places with a strange feller. They do say he kissed her right in plain sight of the road near the woods one day. An' you know yerself she went off and stayed all night. She was seen in the stage-coach 'long with a strange man. There's witnesses! You can't deny it. What I want to know, is what are you goin' to do 'bout it? 'Cause ef you keep her here after that I can't let my dotter come here anymore. When girls is talked about like that decent girls can't hev nothin' to do with 'em. You think you know a hull lot 'bout that girl out there, singin' songs in this brazen way with the hull town talkin' 'bout her, but she's deceived you, that's what she's done; an' I thought I'd be good enough neighbor to tell you, ef you didn't know a'ready. But es you don't seem to take it as 'twas meant, in kindness, I'd best be goin.'"

"You'd best had," screamed Emmeline, "an' besure you keep your precious dotter to hum. Hum's the place fer delikit little creatures like that. You might find *she* was deceivin' *you* ef you looked sharp enough."

Then Emmeline turned and faced the wondering Phoebe, who had heard the loud voices and slipped in through the wood-shed to escape being drawn into the altercation. She had no idea what it all was about. She had been engaged with her own happy thoughts. "I'd like to know what all this scandal's about, Phoebe Deane. Jest set down there and explain. What kind of goin's on hev you hed, that all the town's talkin' 'bout you? Mis' Prinn comes an' says she can't let her dotter come over here any more ef you stay here. I don't know that it's much loss, fer she never come to 'mount to much, but I can't hev folks talkin' that way. No decent girl ought to have her name kicked around in that style. I may not hev hed a great ejjacation like you think you've got to have, but I knowed enough to keep my name off folks' tongues, an' it seems you don't. Now I'd like to know what young man or men you've been kitin' round with. Answer me that? They say you've been seen in the woods alone, and walkin' at night with a strange man, an' goin' off in the stage-coach. Now what in the world does it all mean?"

Phoebe, turning deathly white, with a sudden return of her recent weakness, sank upon a kitchen chair, her arms full of dried clothes, and essayed to understand the angry woman who stormed back and forth across her kitchen, livid with rage, pouring out a perfect torrent of wrath and incriminations.

When there came a moment's interval Phoebe would try to answer her, but Emmeline, roused beyond control, would not listen. She stormed and raged at Phoebe, calling her names, and telling her what a trial she had always been, until suddenly Phoebe's new found strength gave away entirely and she dropped back in a faint against the wall, and would have fallen if Albert had not come in just then unperceived, and caught her. He carried her upstairs tenderly and laid her on her bed. In a moment she opened her sad eyes again and looked up at him.

"What's the matter, Phoebe?" he asked, tenderly. "Been working too hard?" But Phoebe could only answer by a rush of tears.

Albert, troubled as a man always is by woman's tears, stumbled downstairs to Emmeline to find out, and was met by an overwhelming story.

"Who says all that 'bout my sister?" he demanded, in a cool voice, and rising with a dignity that sat strangely upon his kindly figure. "She ain't your sister," hissed Emmeline. "She ain't any but a half relation to you, an' it's time you told her so an' turned her out of the house. She'll be a disgrace to you an' your decent wife an' children. I can't have my Alma brought up in a house with a girl that's disgraced herself like that."

"You keep still, Emmeline," said Albert, gravely. "You don't rightly know what you're saying. You've got excited. I'll attend to this matter. What I want to know is, Who said this about my sister? I'll go get Hiram Green to help me, and we'll face the scoundrel, whoever it is, and make him take it back before the whole town."

"What ef it's true!" mocked Emmeline.

"It isn't true. It couldn't be true. You know it couldn't, Emmeline."

"I'm not so sure o' that," raged his wife. "Wait till you hear all," and she proceeded to recount what Mrs. Prinn had told her.

"I am ashamed of you, Emmeline, that you'll think of such a thing for a minute, no matter who told you. Don't say another word about it. I'm going out to find Hiram."

"Ain't you noticed that Hiram ain't ben comin' here lately?" Emmeline's voice was anything but pleasant. Albert looked at her in astonishment.

"Well, what o' that? He's a good man, and he's fond o' Phoebe. He'll be sure to go with me and defend her."

Albert went out and she saw him hurrying down the road toward Hiram's.

Hiram, like an old spider, was waiting for him in the barn. He had been expecting him for two days, not thinking it would take so long for the news to spread into the home of the victim. he looked gloomy and non-committal as Albert came up, and greeted him with half-averted eyes.

"I've come to get your help," said Albert, with expectant good will. "Hiram, hev you heard all this fool talk about Phoebe? I can't really believe folks would say that about her, but Emmeline's got it in her head everybody knows it."

"Yes, I heard it," admitted Hiram, reaching out for a straw to chew. "I spent one hull day last week goin' round tryin' to stop it, but 'twant no use. I couldn't even find out who started it. You never ken, them things. But the wust of it is, it's all true."

"What!"

"Yes," said Hiram, dismally, "'tis. I'm sorry to' say it to you, what's ben my friend, 'bout her I hoped to marry some day, but I seen some things myself. I seen thet day they talk 'bout in the edge o' the woods, an' I seen her cut an' run when she heard my wagon comin', an' when she looked up an' see it was me she was deadly pale. That was the fust I knowed she wan't true to me."

Hiram closed his lying lips and looked off sorrowfully at the hills in the distance.

"Hiram, you must be mistaken. There is some explanation."

"All right, Albert, glad you ken think so. Wish't I could. It mos' breaks my heart thinkin' 'bout her. I'm all bound up in havin' her. I'd take her now with all her disgrace an' run the resk o' keepin' her straight ef she'd promise to behave herself. She's might young, an' it does seem too bad. But yeh see, Albert, I seen her myself with my own eyes in the stage-coach along with the same man what kissed her in the woods, an' yeh know yerself she didn't come back till next night."

With a groan Albert sank down on a box near by and covered his face with his hands. He had been well brought up and disgrace like this was something he had never dreamed of. His agony amazed the ice-hearted Hiram, and he almost quailed before the sight of such sorrow in a man, sorrow that he himself had made. It embarrassed him. He turned away to hide his contempt.

"It comes mighty hard on me to see you suffer thet way, Albert, an' not be able to help you," he whined after a minute. "I'll tell you what I'll do. I'll marry her anyway. I'll marry her an' save her reputation. Nobody'll dast say anthing' 'bout my wife, an' ef I marry her that'll be es much es to say all this ain't so, an' mebbe it'll die down."

Albert looked up with manly tears in his eyes.

"That's real good of you, Hiram. I'll take it as mighty kind of you if you think there isn't any other way to stop it. It seems hard on you, though."

"I ain't thinkin' o' myself," swelled Hiram. "I'm thinking' o' the girl, an' I don't see no other way. When things is true, you know, there ain't no way o' denyin' them, 'specially when folks hes seen so many things. But just oncet get her good an' respectably married an' it'll all blow over an' be forgot."

They talked a long time, and Hiram embellished the stories that had been told by many a new incident out of his fertile brain, until Albert was thoroughly convinced that the only way to save Phoebe's reputation was for her to be married at once to Hiram.

Albert went home at last, and entered the kitchen with a chastened air. Emmeline eyed him keenly. Phoebe had not come downstairs and his wife had all the work to do again. She was not enjoying the state of things.

Albert sat down and looked at the floor.

"Hiram has been very kind," he said, slowly, "most kind. He has offered to marry Phoebe at once and stop all this talk."

A light of understanding began to dawn in Emmeline's eyes.

"H'm!" she said. Then, after a thoughtful pause. "But I guess Miss Phoebe Deane'll hev a word to say 'bout that. She don't like him a bit."

"Poor child!" moaned Albert. "She'll have to take him, whether she likes him or not. Poor little girl. I blame myself I didn't look after her better. Her mother was a real lady and so good to me when I was home. I promised her I'd keep Phoebe safe. She was such a good woman, it would break her heart to have Phoebe go like this."

"H'm! I don't reckon she was no better than other folks, only she set up to be!" sniffed Emmeline. "Anyhow this is just what might 'a' ben expected from the headstrong way that girl went on. I see now why she was set on goin' off to school. She knowed this was a' comin' an' she wanted to slip an' run 'fore it got out. But she got caught. Sinners generally does." Emmeline wrung out her dishcloth with satisfaction.

"I'll go up now and talk with Phoebe," said Albert, rising sadly as if he had not heard his wife.

"I'm sure I wish you joy of your errand. Ef she ac's to you es she does to me you'll come flyin' down faster'n you went up."

But Albert was tapping at Phoebe's door before Emmeline had finished her sentence.

Chapter 26

"Phoebe," said Albert, gently sitting down beside the bed where she lay wide-eyed, in white-faced misery, trying to comprehend what this new calamity might mean, "I'm mighty sorry for you, little girl. I wish you had come to me with things more. I might 'a' helped you better if I hadn't been so stupid. But I've found a way out of it all for you. I've found a good man that's willing to marry you and give you the protection of his name and home, and we'll just have you married right away quietly here at home, and that'll stop all the talk."

Phoebe turned a look of mingled horror and helplessness on her brother. He did not comprehend it, and thought she was grasping for a thread of hope.

"Yes, Phoebe, Hiram Green is willing to marry you right off in spite of everything, and we've fixed it up to have the wedding right away, tomorrow. That'll give you time to straighten out your things, and Hiram to get the minister—"

But Albert stopped suddenly as Phoebe uttered a piercing scream of fear and started up as if she would fly from the room.

Albert caught her and tried to soothe her.

"What's the matter now, little girl? Don't look like that. It'll all come out right. Is it because you don't like Hiram enough? But child, you'll get to like him more as you know him better. Then you'll be so grateful to think what he saved you from. And besides, Phoebe, there isn't any other way. We couldn't stand the disgrace. What would you mother think? She was always so particular about how you should be brought up. And to have you turn out disgraced would break her heart. Phoebe, don't you see there isn't any other way?"

"Albert, I would rather die than marry that wicked man. He is a bad man. I *know* he is bad. He has been trying to make me marry him for a long time, and now he is just taking advantage of this terrible story. Albert, you know these stories are not ture. You don't believe them, Albert, do you?"

She looked at him with piteous pleading in her beautiful eyes, and he had to turn his own eyes away to hide their wavering. He could not see how this sweet girl could have gone wrong, and yet—there was the evidence!

"You do," said Phoebe. "Albert, you do! You believe all this awful story about me! I never thought you would believe it. But Albert, listen! I will never marry Hiram Green! You may kill me or send me away, or anything you like, but you cannot make me marry him!"

Albert turned his eyes away from the pitiful figure of the pleading girl and set his lips firmly.

"I'm sorry Phoebe, but it's got to be done," he said, sorrowfully. "I can't have this talk go on. I'll give you a little more time to get used to it, but you can't have much, for this story has got to be stopped. We'll say a week. One week from today you'll have to marry Hiram Green, or I'll be forced to turn you out of my hosue. And you know what that means. I couldn't allow any respectable person to harbor you. You've disgraced us all. But if you marry Hiram it'll be all right presently. Marriage covers up gossip. Why, Phoebe, think of my little girl Alma. If this goes on everybody'll point their fingers at her and say her auntie was a bad girl and brought dishonor on the family, and Alma'll grow up without any friends. I've got to look out for my little girl as well as you, Phoebe, and you must believe me, I'm doing the very best for you I know." Phoebe sat down weakly on the edge of her bed and stared wildly at him. She could not believe that Albert would talk to her so. She could not think of anything to say in answer. She could only stare blankly at him as if he were a terrible apparition.

Albert thought she was quieting down and going to be reasonable, and with a few kind words he backed out of the room. Phoebe droped back upon her pillow in a frenzy of horror and grief. Wild plans of running away rushed through her brain, which was after all utterly futile, because her limbs seemed suddenly to have grown too feeble to carry her. Her brain refused to think, or to take in any facts except the great horror of scandal that had risen about her and was threatening to overwhelm her.

Emmeline declined to take any dinner up to her. She said if Phoebe wanted anything to eat she might come down and get it, she wasn't going to wait on a girl like that any longer. Albert fixed a nice plate of dinner and carried it up, but Phoebe lay motionless with open eyes turned toward the wall and refused to speak. He put the plate on a chair beside her and went sadly down again. Phoebe wondered how long it would take one to die, and why God had not let her die when she had the fever. What had there been to live for, anyway? One short bright month of happiness!

The memory of it gripped her heart anew with shame and horror. What would they say, all those kind friends? Mrs. Spafford and her husband, Miranda, and Nathaniel Graham? Would they believe it, too? Of course they would, if her own household turned against her. She was defenseless in a desolate world. She would never more have friends and smiles and comfort. She could not go away to school now, for what good would an education be to her with such a disgrace clinging to her name and following her wherever she went? It would be of no use to run away. She might better stay here and die. They could not marry her to Hiram Green if she were dead. Could one die in a week by just lying still?

So the horror in her brain raged over and over, each time bringing some new phase of grief. And now it was a question if her friends would desert her; and now it was the haughty expression on Janet Bristol's face that day she carried the letter to Nathaniel; and now it was the leer on Hiram's face as he put his arm about her on that terrible drive; and now it was the thought that she would have no more of Nathaniel's long, delightful letters.

All day long she lay in this state, and when the darkness fell a half delirious sleep came upon her, which carried the fears and thoughts of the day into its unresting slumber. The morning broke into the sorrow of yesterday, and Phoebe, weak and sick, arose with one thought in her mind; that she must write at once to Nathaniel Graham and tell him all. She must not be a disgrace to him.

With trembling hands, and eyes filled with tears, she wrote:

Dear Mr. Graham:

I am writing to you for the last time. A terrible thing has happened. Someone has been telling awful stories about me and I am in disgrace. I want you to know that these things are not true. I do not even know how they started, for there has never been any foundation for them. But everybody believes them, and I will not disgrace you by writing to you any more. You will probably be told the worst that is said, and perhaps you will believe them as others do. I shall not blame you if you do, for it seems as if even God believed them. I do not know how to prove my innocence, nor what the end of this is to be. I only know that it is not right to keep you in ignorance of my shame, and to let you write any longer to one whose name is held in dishonor. I thank you for all the beautiful times you have put into my life, and I must say good-bye forever.

Gratefully,
Phoebe Deane.

The letter was blistered with tears before it was finished. She addressed it and hid it in her frock, for she began to wonder how it would get to the mail. Probably Miranda would never come near her again, and she could not be seen in the village. She dared not ask any one else to mail the letter lest it would never reach its destination.

She spent the rest of the day in quietly putting to rights her little belongings, unpacking and gathering together things she would like to have destroyed if anything should happen to her. She felt weak and dizzy, and the food that Albert continued to bring to her seemed nauseous. She could not bring herself to taste a mouthful. It was so useless to eat. One only ate to live, and living had been finished for her, it appeared. It was not that she had resolved to make away with herself by starvation. She was too right-minded for that. She was simply stunned by the calamity that had befallen her, and was waiting for the outcome.

Sometimes as she stood at the window looking out across the fields which had been familiar to her since her childhood she had a feeling that she was going away from them all soon. She wondered if her mother felt so before she died.

Then she wondered why she did not run away; but always when she thought that, something seemed holding her back, for how could she run far when she could not keep up about her room but a few minutes at a time for dizziness and faintness! And how could she run fast enough to run away from shame? It could not be done. Whenever in her dreams she started to run away she always stumbled and fell and then seemed suddenly struck blind and unable to move further; and all the village came crowding about her and mocking her like a great company of cawing crows met around a poor dead thing.

Late Tuesday afternoon Miranda came out to see her. Emmeline opened the door and her countenance grew black when she recognized the visitor.

"Now, you ken just turn right around and march home," she commanded. "We don't want no folks around. Phoebe Deane's in turrible disgrace, an' you've hed your part in it ef I don't miss my guess. No, you ain't goin' to see her. She's up in her room, and ben shut up there ever since she heard how folks hes found out 'bout her capers. You an' yer Mis' Spafford can keep yer pryin' meddlin' fingers out o' this an' let Phoebe Deane alone from now on. We don't want to see yeh any more. Yer spoilin' an pettin' has only hastened the disgrace."

The door slammed in Miranda's indignant face and Emmeline went back to her work.

"She needs a good shakin'," remarked Miranda, indignantly to herself, "but it might tire me, an' besides I've got other fish to fry."

Undaunted she marched to the back shed and mounted to Phoebe's window, entering as if it had been always the common mode of ingress.

"Wal, fer the land, Phoebe Deane, what's ben a happenin' now?" she asked, mildly, surveying Phoebe, who lay white and weak upon her bed, with her untasted dinner beside her.

"Oh, don't you know all about it, Miranda?" Phoebe began to sob.

"No, I don't know a thing. I ben shut up in the house cookin' for two men Mr. David brung home last night, an they et an' et till I thought there wouldn't be nothin' left fer the family. They was railroad men er somthin'. No, I guess 'twas bankin' men. I fergit what. But they could eat if they did wear their best clothes every day. But say, ef I was you, I wouldn't talk very loud fer the lady downstairs wasn't real glad to see me this time, an' she might invite me to leave rather suddint ef she 'spicioned I was up here."

But Phoebe did not laugh as Miranda had hoped. She only looked at her guest with hungry, hopeless eyes, and it was a long time before Miranda could find out the whole miserable story.

"And Miranda, I've written Mr. Graham a note telling him about it. Of course I couldn't disgrace him by continuing to write any longer, so I've said good-bye to him. Will you do me one last kindness? Will you mail it for me?" Phoebe's whisper was tragic. It brought tears to Miranda's well-fortified eyes.

"'Course I'll mail it fer yeh, child, ef yeh want me to, but 'tain't the last kindness I'll do fer yeh by a long run. Shucks! D'you think I'm goin' to give in this easy an' see you sucked under? Not by a jugful. Now look-a-here, child; ef the hull fool world goes against yeh, I ain't a goin', ner my Mrs. Marcia ain't, neither, I'm plumb sure o' that. Bet *ef* she did I'd stick *anyhow*, so there! Cross my heart ef I don't! *Now*. D'yeh b'lieve me? An' I'll find a way out o' this, somehow. I ain't thought it out yet, but don't you worry. You set up 'n' eat that there piece o' bread an' butter. Never mind ef yeh don't feel like it, you eat it fer me. I can't do nothin' ef yeh don't keep yer strength up. Now you do your part an' we'll get out o' this pickle es good es we did out o' the other one. I ain't goin' to hev all my nursin' wasted. Will yeh be good?"

Phoebe promised meekly. She could not smile. She could only press Miranda's hand, while great tears welled through the long lashes on her cheeks.

"So that old serpent thinks he's got you fast, does he? Well, he'll find hisself mistaken yet, ef I don't miss my guess. The game ain't all played out by a long shot. Marry you next week, will he? Well, we'll see! I may dance at your weddin' yet, but there won't be no Hiram Green as bridegroom. I'd marry him myself 'fore I'd let him hev you, you poor little white dove." And Miranda pressed a great impulsive kiss upon Phoebe's white lips and stole out of the window.

As she hurried along down the road the waving grain in the fields on either side reminded her of whispered gossip. She seemed to see a harvest of scandal ripening all about the poor stricken girl whom she loved, and in her ignorant and original phraseology she murmured to herself the thought of the words of old, "Lo, an enemy hath done this." Miranda felt that she knew pretty well who the enemy was.

Chapter 27

"I hev a notion I'd like to go to New York," said Miranda, bouncing in on Marcia.

"Well," said Marcia, "I think you would enjoy the trip sometime. We might keep a lookout for somebody going who would be company. Or perhaps Mr. Spafford will be going again soon and he would have time to look after you."

"'Fraid I can't wait that long," said Miranda. "I've took a great notion I'd like to have a balzarine frock, an' ef I'm goin' to hev it I'd best get it straight off an' git more good out of it. I look at it this way. I ain't goin' to be young but once, an' time's gettin' on. Ef you don't get balzarine frocks when you're young you most likely won't git 'em 't all, 'cause you'll think 'tain't wuth while. I've got a good bit of money laid by, an' ef you've no 'bjections, an' think you ken spare me fer a couple o' days I think I'd like to go down to New York an' git it. I don't need no lookin' after, so you needn't worry 'bout that. Nobody steals me, an' es long es I got a tongue I ken ast my way 'round New York es well es I can 'round Fundy er any other place."

"Why, of course I can spare you, Miranda, and I suppose you'd be perfectly safe, only I thought you'd enjoy it more if you had good company. When did you think you'd like to go?"

"Well, I've been plannin' it all out comin' up the street. I've baked, an' washed, an' the sweepin' ain't much to do. Ef you don't mind I think I'll go tomorrer mornin'."

"What in the world makes you want to go in such a hurry?"

"Oh, I've just took the notion," said Miranda, smiling. "Mebbe I'll tell yeh when I get back. I shan't be gone more'n a year."

Marcia was a little worried at this sudden turn of affairs. It was not like Miranda to hide things from her. Yet she had such confidence in her that she finally settled down to the thought that it was only a whim and perhaps a good night's sleep would overcome it. But the next morning she found the table fully set for breakfast, and the meal prepared and keeping warm. Beside her plate a scrawled note lay:

Mrs. Marcia, deer. I'll liklie be bak tomorer nite er next, but donte worrie. I got biznes to tend to an I'll tel you bout it wen i get home.

yours til deth, respectfuly,
Miranda Griscom.

P.S. you mite praye ef your a mind. Tak keer uf Feby ef I dont git bak.

Before Marcia could get time to run up and see Phoebe, for she somehow felt that Miranda's sudden departure to New York had to do with her visit to Phoebe the day before, Miss Hortense arrived, with her most commandatory air.

"Marcia, I came on a very special errand," she began, primly. "I was down on Monday, but you were away." There was reproach in the tone.

"Yes, I went with David," responded Marcia, brightly, but Miss Hortense would brook no interruption.

"It's of no consequence now. I would have come yesterday, but we had company all day, the Pattersons from above Schenectady. I couldn't leave very well. But I hurried down this morning. It's about the Deane girl, Marcia. I suppose you haven't heard the dreadful reports that are going around. It really is disgraceful in a decent town. I'm only glad she got out of your house before it became town talk. It all shows what ingratitude there is in human nature, to think she should repay you kindness by allowing herself to be talked about in this shameful way."

Marcia exclaimed in dismay, but Miss Hortense went straight on to the precise and bitter end, giving every detail in the scandal that had come to her ears, details at which even Hiram Green would have opened his eyes wide in surprise, and would never have believed that they grew out of his own story.

Marcia listened in rising indignation.

"I am sorry that any such dreadful story is abroad, Aunt Hortense," she answered, earnestly, "but really, if you knew the girl, you would understand how impossible it is for this to be true. She is as sweet and pure innocent as my little Rose."

"I should be sorry to have David's child compared to that miserable girl, Marcia," said Miss Hortense, severely, rising as she spoke, "and I am sure that after my warning if you do not shut that wretched creature forever out of your acquaintance I shall feel it my duty to appeal to David, and tell him the whole story, though I should dislike to have to mention anything so indelicate before him. David is very particular about the character of women. He was brought up to be; and Amelia and I both agree that he must be told."

"I shall tell him myself, of course, and he will see if anything can be done to stop this ridiculous gossip," said Marcia, indignantly. "David is as fond of Phoebe as I am."

"You will find David will look on it in a very different way, my dear. You are young and a woman. You do not know the evil world. David is a man. Men know. Good-bye, my dear. I have warned you!" And Aunt Hortense went pensively down the street, having done her duty.

Marcia put her bonnet on, took little Rose, and walked straight out to Albert Deane's house, but when she reached there was denied admission. Alma opened the door, but did not ask the caller in. In a moment she came back from consulting her mother and said: "Ma says Aunt Phoebe's up in her room an' don't wish to see no one."

The door was shut unceremoniously by the stolid little girl, who was embarrassed before the beautiful, smiling Rose in her dainty attire. Marcia turned away, dismayed, hurt, at the reception she had received and walked slowly homeward.

"Wasn't that a funny little girl," said Rose. "She wasn't very polite, was she, mother?"

Then Marcia went home to wait until she could consult with David.

When Nathaniel received his Cousin Janet's letter his anger rose to white heat. Every throb of his heart told him that the stories about Phoebe were false. Like Miranda, he felt at once that an enemy had done this, and he felt like searching out the enemy at once and throttling him into repentance. He read the postscript through twice and then sat for a few minutes in deep thought, his face shaded by his hand. The office work went on about him, but his thoughts were far away in a sunlit autumn wood. After a little he got up suddenly and going into the inner office where he could be alone, sat down quickly, and wrote:

My Dear Phoebe: (He had never called her that before, it was always "Miss Deane.") *I have loved you for a long time, ever since that afternoon that I found you among the autumn leaves in the woods. I have been trying to wait to tell you until I could be sure you loved me, but now I can wait no longer. I am lonely without you. I want you to be here with me. I love you, darling, and will love you forever, and guard you tenderly, if you will give me the right. Will you forgive this abrupt letter, and write immediately, giving me the right to come up and tell you all the rest?*

> *Yours in faithful love,*
> *Nathaniel Graham.*

After he had sent it off enclosed to Miranda, he scribbled another, to Janet.

Dear Janet, it read, *wherever did you get those ridiculous stories about Phoebe Deane? They are as false as they are foolish. Everybody that knows her at all knows they could not be true. I insist that you deny them whenever you have the opportunity, and for my sake that you go and call upon her. I may as well tell you that I am going to marry her if she will have me, and I want you, Janet, to be like a sister to her, as you have always been to me. Any breath against her name I shall consider as against mine also, so please, Janet, stand up for her for my sake.*

> *Your loving cousin,*
> *Nathaniel.*

After these two letters had been despatched Nathaniel put in the best day's work he had ever done.

Miranda had reached Albany in time to catch the evening boat down the Hudson. She was more tired than she had ever been in all the years of her hard-working life. The bouncing of the stage-coach, the constant change of scenery and fellow passengers, the breathlessness of going into a strange region, had worn upon her nerves. She had not let a single thing pass unnoticed and the result was that even her iron nerves had reached their limit at last. Besides, she was more worried about Phoebe Deane than she had ever been about anything in her life. The ethereal look of the girl as she bade her good-bye the night before had gone to her heart. She half feared Phoebe might fall asleep and never waken while she was gone on her desperate errand of mercy.

"Land sake alive," she murmured to herself, as she crept into her bunk in the tiny stateroom and lay down without putting off any of her garments save her bonnet and cape. "Land sake alive! I feel as ef I'd ben threshin'. No, I feel as ef I'd ben *threshed*!" she corrected. "I didn't know I hed so many bones."

Nevertheless she slept little, having too much to attend to. She wakened at every stop in the night, and she heard all the bells and calls of the crew. Half the time she thought the boat was sinking and wondered if she would be able to swim when she struck the water. Anyhow she meant to try. She had heard it "came natural" to some people.

When morning broke over the heights above the river she watched them grow into splendor and majesty, and long before the city was in sight she was on deck sniffing the air like a veteran war-horse. Her eyes were dilated with excitement, and she made a curious and noticeable figure as she gripped her small bag of modest belongings, and sat strained up and ready for her first experience of city life. She felt a passing regret that she could not pause to take in more of this wonderful trip, but she promised herself to come that way again some day, and hurried over the gang-plank with the others when the boat finally landed. Tucked safely away in her pocket was Phoebe's letter to Nathaniel and safe in her memory was its address. Every passenger with whom she had talked upon the voyage — and she had entered into conversation with all except a man who reminded her of Hiram Green — had given her detailed directions how to get to that address, and the directions had all been different. Some had told her to walk one way and take a cab, some another way. Some had suggested that she take a cab at the wharf. She did none of these things. She gripped her bag firmly and marched past all the officials, through the buildings out into the street. There she stood a moment bewildered by the noise and confusion, a marked figure even in that hurrying throng of busy people. Small boys and drivers immediately beset her. She looked each over carefully and then calmly walked straight ahead. So far New York did not look very promising to her, but she meant to get into a quieter place before she made any inquiries.

At last after she had walked several blocks and was beginning to feel that there was no quiet place, and no end to the confusion, she met a benevolent old gentleman walking with a sweet-faced girl who looked as she imagined little Rose would look in a few years. These she hailed and demanded directions, and ended by being put into a Broadway coach under the care of the driver, who was to put her out at her destination.

Nathaniel was in the inner office attending to some special business when the office boy tapped at the door.

"There's a queer client out here," he whispered. "We told her you were busy and could not be bothered, but she says she has come a long distance and must see you at once. Shall I tell her to come again?"

Nathaniel glanced through the door, and there, close behind the careful office boy, stood the wily Miranda. She had run no risks of not seeing Nathaniel. She had followed the boy, strictly against orders.

Her homely face was aglow with the light of her mission, but in spite of freckles and red hair, and the dishevelled state of her appearance, Nathaniel put out an eager hand to welcome her. His first thought was that she had brought an answer to his letter to Phoebe, and his heart leaped up in sudden eagerness. Then at once he knew that it was too soon for that, for he had only sent his own letter in the evening mail.

"Come right in, Miranda," he said, eagerly, "I'm glad to see you. Are you all alone?" Then something in her face caused a twinge of apprehension.

"Is every one all well?"

Miranda sat down and waited until the door was shut. Then she broke forth.

"No, everythin' ain't all well. Everythin' 's all wrong. Phoebe Deane's in turrible trouble, an' she's wrote a letter sayin' good-bye to you, an' ast me to mail it. I said I would, an' I brung it along. I reckon it didn't make no diff'rence whether it travelled in my pocket er in the mailbag, so it got here."

She held out the letter, and Nathaniel's hand shook as he took it. Miranda noticed that he looked pale.

"What has happened, Miranda?" he asked, as he tore open the letter, hardly knowing what he feared.

"Oh, it's that ole snake-in-th'-grass," said Miranda; "I'd be willin' to stake my life on that. No knowin' how he done it, but it's done. There's plenty to help in a business like gossip, when it comes to that. There's ben awful lies told about her, and she's bein' crushed by it. Wal, I hed to come down to New York to get me a new balzarine frock an' I jest thought I'd drop in an' tell yeh the news. Yeh don't know of a good store where I won't get cheated, do yeh?" she asked, making a pretense of rising.

"Sit down, Miranda," commanded Nathaniel. "You're not going away to leave me like this. You must tell me all about it. Miranda, you know, don't you, that Phoebe is my dear friend. You know that I must hear all about it."

"Well, ain't she told you in the letter? I reckon you'll go back on her like her own folks hev done, won't you? An' let that scoundrel git her next week like he's planned."

"What do you mean, Miranda? Tell me at once all about it. You know Phoebe Deane is very dear to me."

Miranda's eyes shone, but she meant to have things in black and white.

"How dear?" she asked, looking up in a business-like way. "Be you goin' to b'lieve what they all say 'bout her, an' let them folks go on talkin', 'til she's all wilted down an' dead? 'Cause ef you be, you don't git a single word out o' me. No, sir!"

"Listen, Miranda. Yesterday I wrote to Phoebe asking her to marry me!"

Satisfaction began to dawn upon the face of the self-appointed envoy extraordinary.

"Well, that ain't no sign you'd do it again today," said Miranda, dryly. "You didn't know nothin' 'bout her bein' in trouble then."

"Yesterday morning, Miranda, I received a letter from my cousin telling me all about it, and I sat down at once and asked Phoebe to marry me."

"You sure you didn't do it out o' pity?" asked Miranda, lifting sharp eyes to search his face. "I shouldn't want to hev nobody marry her out o' pity, the way Hiram Green's going to do, the old nimshi!"

"Miranda, I love her with all my heart, and I will never believe a word against her. I shall make it the object of my life to protect her and make her happy if she will give me the precious treasure of her love in return. Now are you satisfied, you cruel girl, and will you tell me the whole story? For the little I heard from my cousin has only filled me with apprehension."

Then the freckles beamed out and were lost in smiles as Miranda reached a strong hand and grasped Nathaniel's firm white one with a hearty shake.

"You're the right stuff. I knowed you was. That's why I come. I didn't darst tell Mis' Spafford what was up, 'cause she wouldn't 'a' let me come, an' she'd 'a' tried to work it out in some other way. But I hed it all figgered out, an' there wasn't time for any fiddlin' business. It hed to be done t' woncet ef 'twas to be didn't all, so I told her I wanted a pleasure trip an' a new balzarine, an' I come. Now I'm goin' to tell you all 'bout it, an' then ef there's time fer the balzarine 'fore the evenin' boat starts I'll get it, otherwise it'll hev to git the go-by this time, fer I've got to git right back to Phoebe Deane. She looked jest awful 'fore I left, an' there's no tellin' what they'll do to her while I'm gone."

Nathaniel, with loving apprehension in his eyes, listened to the story, told in Miranda's inimitable style, his face darkening with anger over the mention of Hiram's part.

"The scoundrel!" he murmured, clenching his fingers as if he could hardly refrain from going after him and giving him what he deserved.

"He's all that," said Miranda, "an' a heap more. He's made that poor stupid Albert Deane think all these things is true, an' he's come whinin' 'round with his 'sorry this' an' 'sorry that,' an' offered to marry Phoebe Deane to save her reputation. Es ef he was fit fer that angel to wipe her feet on! Oh, I'd like to see him strung up, I would. There's only one man I ever heard tell of that was so mean, and he lived here in New York. His name was Temple, Harry Temple. Ef you ever come acrost him just give him a dig fer my sake. He an' Hiram Green ought to be tied up in a bag together an' sent off the earth to stay. One o' them big, hot-lookin' stars would be a fine place, I often think at night. Albert, he's awful taken back by disgrace, an' he's told Phoebe she hez to git married in jest a week, er he'll hev to turn her out o' the house. Monday mornin' 's the time set fer the marriage, an' Albert 'lows he won't wait 'nother day. He's promised his wife he'll keep to that."

Nathaniel's face grew stern as he listened, and asked questions. At last he said:

"Miranda, do you think Phoebe Deane cares for me? Will she be willing to marry me?"

"Wal, I sh'd think, ef I know anythin' 't all 'bout Phoebe Deane, she'd give her two eyes to, but she'll be turrible set 'gainst marryin' you with her in disgrace. She'll think it'll bring shame on you."

"Bless her dear heart," murmured Nathaniel, "I suppose she will," and he touched her letter tenderly as if it had been a living thing. Miranda's eyes glistened with jubilation, but she said nothing.

"But we will persuade her out of that," added Nathaniel, with a light of joy in his eyes.

"If you are quite sure it will make her happy," he added, looking at Miranda keenly. "I wouldn't want to have her marry me just to get out of trouble. There might be other ways of helping her, though this way is best."

"Well, I guess you needn't worry 'bout love. She'll love you all right, er my name ain't M'randy!"

"Well, then, we will just have a substitute bridegroom. I wonder if we'll have trouble with Hiram. I suppose very likely we will, but I guess we can manage that. Let me see. This is Thursday. I can arrange my business by tommorrow night so that I can leave it for a few days. If you can stay over till then I will take you to my landlady, who is very kind and will make your stay pleasant. Then we can go back together and plan the arrangements. You'll have to help me, you know, for your are the only medium of communication."

"No, I can't stay a minute longer 'n t'night," said Miranda, rising in a panic and glancing out the window at the sun as if she feared it were already too late to catch the boat; "I've got to get back to Phoebe Deane. She won't eat, an' she's just fadin' away. There might not be any bride by time you got there. 'Sides, she can't git your letter till I get back no how. I'll hev to go home on the boat tonight, an' you come tomorrow. You see, ef there's goin' to be a weddin' I'd like real well to git my balzarine made 'n time to wear to it. That'll give me plenty time, with Mis' Spafford to he'p cut 't out. Do you s'pose there's time fer me to go to the store? It took a long time to git up here from the river."

Nathaniel arose.

"You have plenty of time, and if you'll wait ten minutes I will go with you. We can get some dinner, and go to the store, and we can arrange things on the way."

Miranda settled down in the great office chair and watched Nathaniel's white fingers as they wrote on the legal paper. When it was finished and folded he took another piece of paper and wrote:

My Darling:

I have just received your letter, and I am coming to you as quickly as I can arrange my business to get away. Miranda will bring you this and will tell you all I have said. I will be there in time for the wedding morning, and if you will have me instead of Hiram Green I shall face the whole world by your side, and tell them they are liars. Then I will bring you back with me to stay with me always. My heart is longing to see you and comfort you, but I must not write any more for I have a great deal to do before I go. Only this I must say, if you do not feel you love me, and do not want to marry me, I will help you some other way to get free from this trouble, and to have it all explained before the world. There is just one thing I am resolved upon, and that is that you shall be guarded and loved by me, whether you will marry me or not. You are too precious to suffer.

Yours with more love than you can ever fathom,
Nathaniel.

He sealed, addressed it, and handed it to Miranda, who took it with a gleam of satisfaction in her honest eyes. She was almost willing to run home without her balzarine now that she had that letter. She did not know what he had written, of course, but she knew it was the right thing and would bring the light of hope again to Phoebe's eyes.

Then they went out into the bustling, strange streets of the city.

Miranda was too excited to eat much, though Nathaniel took her to his own boarding-place and tried to make her feel at home. She kept asking if it wasn't almost time for the boat to leave, until he had to explain to her just how much time there was, and how quickly they could get to the wharf.

They went to a store, and Miranda did not take long to pick out her frock. It seemed as if the very one she had always longed for most lay draped upon the counter, and with quick decision she bought it. It had great stripes of soft colors in palm-leaf pattern, blended into harmony in oriental manner, in the exquisite fabric. It seemed to her almost too fine to go with red hair, but she bought it with joyous abandon. The touch of rich blue and orange and crimson with the darker greens and browns stood out against the delicate whiteness of the background and delighted her eye. She bought a dainty ruffled muslin shoulder cape to wear with it, and a great shovel bonnet with a white veil tossed hilariously back from its cumbersome shirred depths. Then Nathaniel added a parasol with a pearl handle that would unhinge and fold up, and Miranda climbed into the coach and rode off to the evening boat feeling that she had had the greatest day of her life. She looked about her on the interesting sights of the city, with a kind of pity that they had to stay there and not go with her to the wedding.

Chapter 28

Miranda reached home on the afternoon coach and bounced into the house with a face full of importance.

"Wal, I'm glad to git back. Did you find the blueberry pies? I put 'em out the pantry winder to cool, an' fergot 'em. I thought of 'em when I was on the boat, but 'twas mos' too late to come back then, so I kep' on.

"Here's my balzarine. Do yeh like it?" and she tossed the bundle into Marcia's lap. "I'm going right at it when I git the work done in the mornin' fer I want to hev it t' wear at Phoebe Deane's weddin'. Did yeh know she was goin' to marry Nathaniel Graham? Say, where's that Rose? I'm most starved for a sight o' her little sweet face. Yer lookin' real good yerself. All's well?"

Marcia listened smilingly to Miranda's torrent of words, and gradually drew the whole story from her handmaid, laughing heartily over the various episodes of Miranda's journey and gravely tender over what Nathaniel had said. Then Miranda heard about Marcia's call on Phoebe, and how she had written Phoebe a letter asking what she could do to help her, and inviting her to come at once to them, but had received no answer.

"An' yeh won't, neither," said Miranda, decidedly. "She'll never git no letter, I'm sure o' that. Ef that old' skunk of a Hiram Green don't git it fust, Mis' Deane'll ferret it out an' keep it from her. She's the meanest thing in the shape of a woman I've seen yit, an' I've hed some experience."

Then Miranda rapidly sketched her plan of procedure, and Marcia added some suggestions. Together they prepared the supper, with the single object of getting Miranda off to Phoebe as soon as the darkness should come.

It was quite dark and Phoebe was lying in a still white heap upon her bed when Miranda stole softly in. By her side lay a long white package she had taken from her little trunk in the closet, and on it was pinned a note. "Dear Miranda, if I die, please take this, from Phoebe."

She had not lighted her candle, and she had not eaten a mouthful all day. The terrible faintness and weakness were becoming constant now. She could only lie on her bed and wait. She could not even think any more. The enemies all about her with their terrible darts had pierced her soul, and her life seemed ebbing away. She felt it going, and did not have the desire to stop it. It was good to be at rest.

Miranda stole in softly, and began to move quietly about the room, finding the candle and softly striking the flint and tinder. Phoebe became gradually conscious of her presence, as out of the midst of a misty dream. Then Miranda came and looked down tenderly into her face.

"Raise yer head up, you poor little thing, an' drink this," whispered Miranda, putting a bottle of strong cordial to her lips, that she had taken the precaution to bring with her. "I've got two o' the nicest letters fer yeh that ever was writ, an' another one from my Mrs. Marcia, an' ef yeh don't git some color into them cheeks, an' some brightness into them eyes now, my name ain't Mirandy."

Miranda handed out the letters one at a time, in their order.

She brought the candle, and Phoebe with her trembling hands opened the first, recognizing the handwriting, and then sat up and read with bated breath.

"Oh, Miranda," she said, looking up with a faint color in her cheeks, "he has asked me to marry him. Wouldn't it be beautiful! But he didn't know when he wrote it —" and the brown head went down as if it were stricken like a lily before a fierce blast.

"Shucks!" said Miranda, dabbing away the mistiness from her eyes. "Yes, he did know, too. His cousin wrote him. Here, you read the other one."

Again Phoebe sat up and read, while Miranda held her candle and tried not to seem to look over her shoulder at the words she could feel in her soul if she could not see with her eyes.

"Oh, it can't be true!" said Phoebe, with face aglow with something that almost seemed the light of another world. "And I mustn't let him, of course. It wouldn't be right for him to have a wife like this —"

"Shucks!" said Miranda again. "Yes, 'tis true, too, and right an' all the rest, an' you've got to set up and get spry, fer there's a sight to do, an' I can't stay much longer. That weddin' 's commin' off on Monday morning — time set fer it. "Tain't good luch to put off weddin's an' this one 's goin' to go through all right.

"Mr. Nathaniel, he's goin' to bring his cousin an' the Jedge, an' my Mr. David an' Mrs. Marcia's comin' wether they're ast er not, 'cause they knew 'twant no use fer um to wait fer an invite from that sister-in-law of yourn, so they're comin' anyway. Mr. Nathaniel said as how you weren't to worry. He'll git here Saturday night sure, an' ef there was any other 'rangement you'd like to make he was ready, an' you could send your word by me, but he 'greed with me 'twould make less talk ef the weddin' come off at your home where 'twas to be in the fust place, an' then you could go right away from here an' never come back no more. Say, hev ye got anythin' thet's fit to wear? 'Cause ef yeh ain't I'll let yeh have my new balzarine to wear. I'll hev it all done by Sat'day night. Mrs. Marcia's goin' to help me."

Between tears and smiles Phoebe came to herself. Miranda fed her with some strong broth which she had brought along and which she managed to heat after laboriously holding the pail over the candle flame. Then together in the dim candle-light the two girls opened the great white box that lay on the floor beside the bed.

"It's my wedding dress, Miranda. Mother made it for me long ago, before she died, and put it in my trunk to keep for me. It was marked, 'For my little girl when she is going to be married.'

"I opened it and found the letter on the top, for I thought I was going to die, and I wanted to read mother's last letter, but I did not take the frock out because I thought I would never wear it, and it made me feel so bad that I left it in its wrappings. I thought if I died I would like to have you have it, because it is the most precious thing I have and you have done more for me than anybody else ever did, but mother."

Miranda gulped a sudden unexpected sob at this tribute, and it was some time before she could recover her equanimity, though she said "Shucks!" several times.

They took the white bridal garment out of its wrappings and Phoebe tried it on, there in the dimness of the room. It was thin white book-muslin, all daintily embroidered about the neck and sleeves by the dead mother's hand. It fell in soft sheer folds about the white-faced girl, and made her look as if she were just going to take her flight to another world.

In another paper was the veil of fine thread lace, simple and beautiful, and a pair of white gloves which had been the mother's, both yellow with age, and breathing a perfume of lavender. A pair of dainty little white slippers lay in the bottom of the box, wrapped in tissue paper also. Miranda's eyes shone.

"Now you look like the right kind of a bride," she said, standing back and surveying her charge. "That's better 'n all the balzarines in New York."

"You shall wear the balzarine and stand up with me, Miranda," whispered Phoebe, smiling.

"No, sir! We ain't goin't to hev this here weddin' spoiled by no red hair an' freckles, even if 't has got a balzarine. Janet Bristol's got to stan' up. She'll make a picter fer folks to talk 'bout. Mr. Nathaniel said he'd manage his cousin all right, an' 'twould quiet the talk down ef his folks took sides along of you. No, sir, I ain't goin' to do no standin' in this show. I'm goin' to set, an' take it all in. Come now, you get into bed, an' I'll blow out the light an' go home. I reckon I'll be back tomorrer night to take any messages you want took. They'll be plenty o' chance fer you to rest 'fore Monday. Don't say nothin' to yer folks. Let 'em go on with their plans, an' then kinder s'prise 'em."

The next morning Phoebe arose and feeling much refreshed dressed herself carefully and went downstairs. She had a quiet, grave look upon her face, but in her eyes there was a strange light which she could not keep back. Emmeline looked up in surprise when Phoebe came and took hold with the work. She began to say something slighting, but the look in Phoebe's face somehow stopped her. It was a look of joyful exaltation; and Emmeline, firmly believing that the girl was justly talked about, could not understand, and thought it hypocrisy.

Albert came in in a few minutes, and looked relieved.

"Well, Phoebe, I'm glad you've made up your mind to act sensibly, and come downstairs. It wasn't right to fight against what had to be and every one of us knew was for the best," he said.

Phoebe did not answer. In spite of the help that was coming to her it hurt her that Albert believed the slander against her, and the tears came into her eyes as he spoke. Emmeline saw them and spoke up in a sermonizing tone:

"It's right she should feel her shame and repent, Albert. Don't go an' soft-soap it over es ef she hadn't done nothin' to feel sorry fer."

Then Phoebe spoke.

"I have done nothing to feel sorry for, Emmeline. I have not sinned. I am only sorry that you have been willing to believe all this against me."

Then she went quietly on with her work, and said no more, though Emmeline's speech was unsealed and she gave Phoebe much good advice during the course of the day.

The next morning near church time Emmeline told Phoebe that Hiram was coming over to see her that morning, and she might open the front parlor to receive him.

"I don't wish to see Hiram, Emmeline," she answered, calmly. "I have nothing whatever to say to him."

"Well, upon my word, Phoebe Deane," said Emmeline, getting red in the face with indignation of the girl. "Goin' to git married tomorrow mornin' an' not wantin' to see Hiram Green! I should think you'd want to talk over 'rangements."

"Yes, I am going to be married tomorrow morning," said Phoebe, with a triumphant ring to her voice, "but I do not want to see Hiram Green. I have no arrangements to talk over with him. My arrangements are all made."

Phoebe went away to her room and remained there the rest of the day.

Nathaniel had arrived. She knew that by special messenger coming and going over the wood-shed roof. There had been sweet messages of cheer, and he had promised to come for her in the morning. Everything was arranged. She could possess her soul in peace and quietness and wait. Her enemies would soon be put to flight. Nathaniel had promised her that, and although she could not see in the least how, she trusted him perfectly.

She had sent her love to him, and the locket with her mother's picture. It was all she had to give her lover, and he understood. It was the one she had worn the first time he ever saw her.

The balzarine frock was finished. The last hook was set in place before supper Saturday night, and Marcia had pronounced it very becoming. It was finished in spite of the fact that Miranda had made several secret excursions into the region of Hiram Green's house and farm. She had made discoveries which she told to no one, but over which she chuckled when quite alone in the kitchen at work. On her first trip she had seen him go out to his milking, and had passed close to the house, where his window was open. She had glanced in, and there on the sill her sharp eyes had discovered the bit of red seal with the lion's head upon it. She had carried too many letters with that seal not to know it at once, and she gleefully seized it and carried it to Nathaniel. She had evidence at last which would give her power over the enemy.

She also discovered that Hiram Green attended to his milking himself, and that he had a habit — if one might judge from two mornings as samples — of going to the spring house himself with the milk and placing the pans on the great stone shelf. This she had seen by judicious hiding behind shrubbery, and trees, and spring-house itself, and spying upon him. Birds and squirrels tell no tales, and the dewey grass soon dried off and left no trace of her footsteps. During one of these excursions she had examined the fastening of the spring-house most carefully, and knew the posibilities of button, hasp, staple, and peg.

The Spaffords and Miranda went to church as usual, and so did the Bristols. The advent of Nathaniel and his friend Mr. Van Rensselaer in the Bristol pew diverted attention from the empty seat behind them, for this morning the Deanes were conspicuous by their absence.

The day passed quietly. Miranda made her usual visit in the early evening. Phoebe had asked her to stay with her, but Miranda said she had some things to do, and departed sooner than usual. The night settled into stillness and Phoebe slept in joyous assurance that it was her last night in the room where she had seen so much sorrow.

In the morning she went down to breakfast as usual. She did not eat much, to be sure, but drank some milk, and then washed the breakfast dishes as calmly as if she expected to keep on washing them all the rest of her life in this same kitchen.

"Hiram'll be over 'bout half past nine, I reckon," said Albert. He had been instructed by Emmeline to say this. "The minister won't come till ten. If you need to talk to Hiram you'll have plenty of time between. You better be all ready."

"I shall not need to talk to Hiram," said Phoebe, as she hung up the dish towels. There was that in her voice as she said it that made Albert look after her wonderingly.

"She's the queerest girl I ever see!" grumbled Emmeline. "One would think by her looks that she expected a chariot of fire to come down an' take her straight up to heaven like 'Lijah. It's kind of dreadful the way she ac's! 'F I was Hiram I'd be 'fraid to marry her."

Miranda arrived over the shed roof soon after Phoebe went upstairs. She wore her old calico, and if one who knew had observed closely, he would have said it was a calico that Miranda never used any more, for it was very old. Her hair was combed with precision and on her head was an elaborate New York bonnet with a white barege veil, but her balzarine was in a bundle under her arm. It was not calculated for roof travel. It was well for their plans that the shed roof was back and well hidden from the kitchen door, else Miranda might have been discovered.

"There! Emmeline can hev that fer a floor cloth," said Miranda, as she flung her old calico in the corner. "I don't calculate to return fer it." She fastened her balzarine with satisfaction, adjusted her muslin shoulder cape, her bonnet, and mantilla, the latter a gift from Mrs. Spafford, laid her new sunshade on a chair, and pronounced herself ready.

"Has Hiram Green come yet?" asked Phoebe, anxiously. She was dreading a scene with Hiram.

"Wal, no, not 'zactly," said Miranda. "An what's more, I don't think he will. Fact is I've got him fixed fer a spell, but I ain't goin to say nothin' more 'bout it at present, 'cept that he's detained by bus'ness elsewhar. It's best you shouldn't know nothin' 'bout it ef there's questions ast, but you don't need to worry. 'Less sompin' quite unusual happens he ain't likely to turn up till after the ceremoney. Now, what's to do to you yet? Them hooks all fastened? My, but you do look han'some!"

"Oh, Miranda, you haven't done anything dreadful, have you?"

"No, I ain't," laughed Miranda. "You'd jest split your sides laughin' ef you could see him 'bout now. But there! Don't say 'nother word. I hear voices. The Bristols hev come, an' the minister, too. I reckon your sister-in-law'll hev her hands full slammin' the door in all them faces."

Phoebe, aghast, pulled the curtain aside and peered out.

There in the yard were several carriages, and more driving in the gate. She could hear a great many voices all at once. She saw Mrs. Duzenberry and Susanna getting out of their chaise, and Lemuel Skinner and his wife Hannah, and she thought she heard the village dressmaker's voice high above all, sharp and rasping, the way it always was when she said: "That seam needs pressin'. It does hike up a mite, but it'll be all right when it's pressed."

Phoebe retreated in dismay from the window.

"Oh, Miranda! How did all those people get down there! Emmeline will be so angry. She is in her room dressing yet. It doesn't seem as if I dared go down."

"Fer the land sake, how should I know? I s'pose Providence sent 'em, fer they can't say a single word after the ceremony's over. Their mouths'll be all nicely stopped. Don't you worry."

Miranda answered innocently, but for one instant as she looked at Phoebe's frightened face her guilty heart misgave her. Perhaps she had gone a step too far. For it was Miranda who had slipped here and there after church on Sunday and whispered a brief invitation to those who had gossiped the hardest, wording it in such a way that they all thought it was a personal invitation from Phoebe.

In every case she had added, "Don't say nothin' till after it's over," and each thinking himself especially favored had arrived in conscious pride, and as they passed Hiram Green's new house they had remarked to themselves what a fine man he was for sticking to Phoebe in spite of all the talk.

But Miranda never told her part in this, and Emmeline never got done wondering who invited all those people.

Miranda's momentary confusion was covered by a gentle tap on the door, and Phoebe in a flutter rushed to hide her friend:

"I'm afraid it's Emmeline," she whispered. "She may not let you go down."

"Like to see her keep me up," said Miranda, boldly. "My folks hes come. I ain't 'fraid now," and she boldly swept the trembling bride out of the way and threw the door open.

Janet Bristol in a silken gown of palest pink entered and walked straight up to Phoebe.

"You dear little thing!" she exclaimed. "How sweet you look. That frock is beautiful and the veil makes you perfect. Nathaniel asked me to bring you this and make you wear it. It was his mother's."

She fastened a rope of pearls around Phoebe's neck and kissed her as a sister might have done.

Miranda stood back and gazed with satisfaction on the scene. All was as it should be. She saw nothing further to be desired. Her compunctions were gone.

"Nathaniel is waiting for you at the foot of the stairs," whispered Janet. "He has his mother's ring for you. He wanted me to tell you. Come, they are ready. You must go ahead."

Down the stairs went the trembling bride, followed by her bridesmaid. Miranda grasped her precious parasol and tiptoed on behind.

Nathaniel stood at the foot of the stairs, waiting for her. Emmeline, with a red and angry face, was waiting on her most unexpected guests and had not time to notice what was going on about her. The original wedding guests, consisting of a row of little Greens and the old housekeeper, were submerged in the Sunday gowns of the new arrivals.

"Where's Hiram," whispered Albert, in Emmeline's ear, just as she was giving Hiram's Aunt Keziah Dart a seat at the best end of the room.

"Goodness! Ain't he come yet? I s'posed he was upstairs talkin' to Phoebe. I heard voices."

She wheeled around and there stood the wedding party.

Nathaniel, tall and handsome, with his shy, pale bride upon his arm; Janet, sparkling in her pink gown and enjoying the discomfiture of guests and hostess alike, and smiling over at Martin Van Rensselaer, who stood supporting the bridegroom on the other side; it bewildered Emmeline.

The little assemblage reached out into the front door yard, and peeped curiously in at the doors and windows as if loth to lose the choice scene that was passing. The old minister was talking now and a hush fell over the company.

Anger and amazement held Emmeline still as the ceremony progressed.

"Dearly beloved, we are gathered together —" said the minister, and Emmeline looked around for Hiram. Surely the ceremony was not beginning without him! And who was that girl in white under the veil! Not Phoebe! It could not be Phoebe Deane, who but a few short minutes before had been hanging up her dish towels. Where did she get that veil and frock? What had happened? How did all these people get here? Had Phoebe invited them? And why did not somebody stop it?

"Let him speak now, or forever after hold his peace," came the words, and Emmeline gave a great gasp and thought of the corner lot opposite the Seceder church.

It was then that Emmeline became conscious of Miranda in her balzarine and New York bonnet, the very impersonation of mischief, standing in the doorway just behind the bride and watching the scene with a face of triumph.

An impulse came to her to charge across the room upon the offending girl and put her out. Here surely was one who had no right in her house and knew it, too. Then all at once she caught the eye of Judge Bristol fixed sternly upon her face, and she became aware of her own countenance and restrained her feelings. For after all it was no mean thing to be allied to the house of Bristol, and to know that the cloud of dishonor which had threatened them was lifted forever. She looked at Judge Bristol's fine face and heavy white hair, and began to swell with conscious pride.

The last "I will" was spoken, the benediction was pronounced, and the hush that followed was broken by Nathaniel's voice.

"I want to say a few words," he said, "about a terrible mistake that has been made by the people of this village regarding my wife's character. I have made a most thorough investigation of the matter during the last two days and I find that the whole thing originated in an infamous lie told with intention to harm one who is entirely innocent. I simply wish to say that whoever has spoken against my wife will have to answer to me for his words in a court of justice, and if any of you who are my friends wish to question any of her past actions be kind enough to come directly to me and they will be fully explained, for there is not a thing in her past that will not bear the searching light of purity and truth."

As soon as he had ceased speaking David and Marcia stepped up with congratulations.

There was a little stir among the guests; the guilty ones melted away faster than they had gathered, each one anxious to get out without being noticed.

The Bristol coach, drawn by two white horses, with coachman and footman in livery, drew up before the door, Nathaniel handed Phoebe in and they were driven away in triumph, the guests that they passed shrinking out of sight into their vehicles as far as possible.

Albert and Emmeline looked into each other's dazed faces; then turned to the old housekeeper, and the row of little Greens, their faces abnormally shining from unusual contact with soap and water, and asked in concert:

"But where is Hiram?"

Miranda, as she rode guilelessly in the carryall with Mrs. Spafford, answered the same question from that lady, with:

"Whar d' you s'pose? I shet him in the spring-house airly this mornin'!"

Then David Spafford laid down upon his knee the reins of the old gray horse, and laughed, loud and long; could not stop laughing; and all day long it kept breaking out, as he remembered Miranda's innocent look and thought of Hiram Green, wrathful and helpless, shut in his own spring-house while his wedding went on without him.

There was a wedding breakfast elaborate and gay at Judge Bristol's, presided over by Janet, who seemed as happy as though she had planned the match herself, and whose smiling wishes were carried out immediately by Martin Van Rensselaer.

There was one more duty for Nathaniel to perform before he took his bride away to a happier home. He must find and face Hiram Green.

So, leaving Phoebe in the care of Mrs. Spafford and his cousin Janet, and himself accompanied by his uncle, Martin Van Rensselaer, and Lemuel Skinner in the capacity of village constable, he got into the family carryall and drove out to Hiram's farm.

Now Nathaniel had not been idle during the Sabbath which intervened between his coming back to the village and his marriage. Aside from the time he spent at the morning church service, he had been doing a Sabbath day's work which he felt would stand well to his account.

He had carefully questioned several of the best known gossips in the village with regard to the story about Phoebe. He had asked keen questions that gave him a plain clue to the whole diabolical plot.

His first act had been to mount his fast horse, and ride out to Ann Jane Bloodgood's, where he had a full account of Phoebe's visit together with a number of missionary items which would have met with more of his attention at another time. Possessed of several valuable facts he had gone pretty straight to most of the houses which Hiram had visited on the first afternoon when he scattered the seed of scandal, and facing the embarrassed scandal-mongers, Nathaniel had made them tell just who had been the first to speak to them of this. In every case after a careful sifting down each owned that Hiram himself had told them the first word. If Nathaniel had not been a lawyer, and keen at his calling, he might not have been able so well and so quickly to have followed the story to its source, as he did. Possibly his former encounter with Hiram Green, and his knowledge of many of his acts, helped in unravelling the mystery.

The old housekeeper and the little Greens had not been at home long when the carryall drew up in front of the door, and the four men got out.

"I ben everywhar but to the spring-house," said the housekeeper, shaking her head dolefully, "an' I can't find trace of him nowhar. 'Tain't likely he'd be in the spring-house, fer the door is shet an' fastened. I ken see the button from the buttery winder. It's the way I allus tell when he's comin' in to breakfast. It's my 'pinion he's clared out 'cause he don't want to marry that gal, that's what I think."

"When did you last see Mr. Green?" questioned the Judge, sternly.

"Why, I seen him take the milk pails an' go down towards the barn to milk, an' I aint' seen him sence. I thought 'twar queer he didn't come eat his breakfast, but he's kinder oncertain thet way, so I hurried up an' got off to he'p Mis' Deane."

"Have the cows been milked?" The Judge's voice ignored the old woman's elaborate explanations.

"The hired man, he says so. I ain't ben down to look myself."

"Where are the milk pails?"

"Well, now, I ain't thought to look."

"What does he usually do with the milk? He surely has not taken that with him. Did he bring it in? That ought to give us a clue."

"He most gen'rally takes it straight to the spring-house—" began the old woman.

"Let us go to the spring-house," said Nathaniel.

"I don't see what business 'tis o' yourn," complained the old woman, but they were already on the way, so after a moment's hesitation she threw her apron around her shoulders and went after them. The row of little Greens followed, a curious and perplexed little procession, ready for any scene of interest that might be about to open before them, even though it involved their unloving father.

It was Lemuel Skinner, with his cherry lips pursed importantly, who stepped forward by virtue of his office, turned the wooden button, drew out the peg, pulled off the hasp, and threw the heavy door open.

Out stumbled Hiram Green, half blinded by the light, and rubbing his eyes.

"Mr. Green, we have called to see you on a matter of importance," began Lemuel apologetically, quite as if it were the custom to meet householders on the threshold of their spring house. "Sorry I can't wait to hear it," swaggered Hiram, blinking, and trying to make out who these men were. "I got 'n engagement. Fact is, I'm goin' to be married, an' I'm late a'ready. I'll hev to be excused, Lem!"

"It's quite unnecessary, Mr. Green," said Lemuel, putting out a detaining hand excitedly; "quite unnecessary, I assure you. The wedding is all over. You're not expected any more."

Hiram stood back and surveyed Lemuel with contempt.

"Gosh Ninety!" he sneered. "How could that be when I wan't thar? I guess you didn't know I was goin' to marry Phoebe Deane. I'm right sure there wouldn't no one else marry her."

Nathaniel stepped forward, his face white with indignation.

"You are speaking of my wife, Mr. Green," he said, and his voice was enought to arrest the attention of even the self-complacency of a Hiram Green. "Let me never hear you speak of her in that way again. She did not at any moment in her life intend to marry you. You know that well, though you have tried to weave a web of falsehood about her that would put her in your power. The whole thing is known to me from beginning to end, and I do not intend to let it pass lightly. My wife's good name is everything to me; though it seems you were willing to marry one whom you had yourself defamed.

"I have come here this morning, Mr. Green, to give you your choice between going to jail or going with me at once and taking back all the falsehoods you have told about my wife."

Hiram, in sudden comprehension and fear, glanced around the group, took in the fact of the presence of Judge Bristol; remembered Nathaniel's threat of the year before about bringing him up before his uncle, remembered that Lemuel Skinner was constable; and was filled with consternation.

With the instinct of a coward and a bully he made a sudden lunge forward towards Nathaniel, his fists clenched, and his whole face expressing the fury of a wild animal brought to bay.

"You lie!" he hissed.

But the next instant he lay sprawling at Nathaniel's feet, with Lemuel bustling over him like an excited old hen.

It was Martin Van Rensselaer who had tripped him up just in time.

"Now, gentlemen, gentlemen, don't let's get excited," cackled Lemuel, laying an ineffective hand on the prostrate Hiram.

"Step aside, Mr. Skinner," said Nathaniel, towering over Hiram; "let me settle this matter first. Now, sir you may take you choice. Will you go to jail and await your trial for slander or will you come with us to the people before whom you scattered this outrageous scandal, and take it all back?"

"You've made a big mistake," blustered Hiram. "I never told no stories 'bout Phoebe Deane. It's somebody else 's done it 'ef 'tain't true—I was goin' to marry her to save her reputation."

"How did you think that would save her reputation?" questioned Judge Bristol, and somehow his voice made cold chills creep down Hiram's spine.

"Why, I—I was goin' to deny everythin' after we was married."

"Your stories don't hang very well together," remarked the Judge, dryly.

"You will be obliged to deny them now," said Nathaniel, wrathfully. "Take your choice at once. I'm not sure after all but the best way would be to house you in jail without further delay. It is almost a crime to let such a low-lived scoundrel as you walk at large. No one's reputation will be safe in the hands of a villain like you. Take your choice at once. I will give you two minutes to decide."

Nathaniel took out his watch.

There was silence over the meadow behind the spring-house, but a little bird from the tree up the road called:

"Phoe-bee! Phoe-be!" insistently, and strange tender light came into Nathaniel's eyes.

"The time is up," said Nathaniel.

"What do you want me to do?" asked the captive, sullenly.

"I want you to go with me to every house that you visited the day you started this mischief and take it all back. Tell them it was untrue, and that you got it up out of whole cloth for your own evil purposes."

"But I can't tell a lie," said Hiram, piously.

"Can't you? Well, it will not be necessary. Come, which will you choose? Do you prefer to go to jail?"

"Gentlemen, I'm in your hands," whined the coward. "Remember I have little children."

"You should have remembered that yourself, and not brought shame upon them and other innocent beings." It was the Judge who spoke these words, like a sentence in court.

"Where hev I got to go?"

Nathaniel named over the places.

Hiram looked black, and swallowed his mortification.

"Well, I s'pose I've got to go. I'm sure I don't want to lose my good name by goin' to jail."

They set him upon his feet, and the little posse moved slowly up the slope to the house and thence to the carryall.

After they were seated in the carryall, Hiram in the back seat with Lemuel and Martin on either side of him, Nathaniel turned to Hiram.

"Now, Mr. Green, we are going first to your aunt's house, and then around to the other places in order. You are to make the following statement and nothing else. You are to say: 'I have come to take back the lies which I told about Miss Phoebe Deane, and to tell you that they are none of them true. I originated them for my own purposes.'"

Hiram's face darkened. He looked as if he would like to kill Nathaniel. He reached out a long arm again as if he would strike him but Lemuel clutched him convulsively, while Martin threw his whole weight upon the other side and he subsided.

"You can have from now until we reach the jail to think about it, Mr. Green. If you prefer to go to jail instead you will not be hindered. Mr. Skinner is here to arrest you on my charge if you will not comply with these conditions."

Sullen and silent sat Hiram. He did not raise his eyes to see the curious passers-by as he rode through town.

They looked at Nathaniel and the Judge, driving with solemn mien as if on some portentous errand; they noted the stranger and the constable on either side of the lowering Hiram; and they drew their own conclusions, for the news of the wedding had spread like wild-fire through the village. Then they stood and watched the carryall out of sight, and even followed it to see if it stopped at the jail.

As they drew near the jail Nathaniel turned around once more to Hiram:

"Shall we stop and let you out here, or are you willing to comply with the conditions?"

Hiram raised his eyelashes and gave a sideways glance at the locality, then lowered them quickly as he encountered the impudent gaze of a small boy and muttered:

"Drive on."

Hiram went through the distasteful ordeal sullenly. He repeated the words which Nathaniel insisted upon, after one or two vain attempts to modify them in his own favor, which only made it worse for him in the eyes of his listeners.

"'Pon my word," said Aunt Keziah Dart in a mortified tone. "'F I'd uv told fibs like that I'd 'a' stuck to 'em, an' never giv in, no matter what. I'm 'shamed to own I'm kin to sech a sneak, Hiram Green. Wan't there gals 'nough 'round the country 'thout all that to do?"

At the Duzenberrys' Susanna rendered Hiram the sympathy of silently weeping in the background, while the Widow Duzenberry stood coldly in the foreground acting as if the whole performance were a personal affront. She closed the interview by calling after Hiram from her front door.

"I'm sorry to see yeh in trouble, Mister Green. Remember you'll always find a friend here," and Hiram brightened up some. Nevertheless, there was very little of his old conceit left when he had gone over the whole ground and was finally set free to go his way to his own home.

Then Nathaniel and Phoebe hastened away in the family coach towards Albany to begin their long life journey together.

Late that afternoon Hank Williams coming up from the village brought with him a letter for Hiram Green which he stopped to leave, hoping to find out from Hiram what had happened during the afternoon. The old housekeeper took the letter saying, "Hiram wan't well," and Hank went onward crestfallen.

A few minutes later Hiram tore open his letter. It read:

Mistur Grene,
You hev ben fond out. We want no mor lyres an crimnles in our toun. We hev fond the seels off'n Phebe Denes leter in yor poseshun an we hev uther good evedens thet you open unitd stats male we will giv yo 1 wek to sel ot an lev toun EF yo ever sho yer hed agin hear or in Noo York yo wil be tard an fethured an punisht cordin to law.

yors fer reveng
A Feller Tounsman.

That night while his household slept Hiram Green went forth from his home to parts unknown, leaving his little children to the tender mercies of Aunt Keziah Dart or whoever might be touched with a feeling of pity for them.

And Miranda, who, without the counsel or knowledge of anyone, had written the remarkable epistle which sent him out, lay down serenely and slept the sleep of the just.

And that same night the moon shone brightly over the Hudson River, like a path of silver for the two who sat long on deck, talking of how they loved Miranda, with laughter that was nigh to tears.